BASIC MANUAL
FOR THE LAWYER'S ASSISTANT
Ninth Edition

Prepared by

NALS®...*the association for legal professionals*

Edited by
Text Development Committee

Comprised of

Karen Kuhn, Certified PP, PLS, Chairman, Gulfport, MS
Linda K. Adair, PLS, Little Rock, AR
Jessica Baber, Corpus Christi, TX
Donna D. Barfield, Augusta, GA
Anita Campbell, Certified PP, PLS, Jackson, MS
Jane R. Cramer, Columbus, OH
Nancy M. Gates, Certified PP, PLS, CLAS, Vancleave, MS
Glenda R. Hanson, Certified PP, PLS, Seattle, WA
Patricia E. Infanti, Certified PP, PLS, Philadelphia, PA
Dawn Miller–Lawrence, PLS, Phoenix, AZ
Janice R. Miller, Certified PP, PLS, CPS, Lonoke, AR
Tammy Shatwell Mullins, Tulsa, OK
Diana Price, Tulsa, OK
Jeannie M. Shaw, Certified PP, PLS, Gulfport, MS
Joani A. Yingling, Certified PP, PLS, CLAS, CNSA, Tucson, AZ

THOMSON
WEST

Mat #40495782

ISBN 978-0-31496-645-2

ACKNOWLEDGMENTS

The NALS® Text Development Committee is comprised of NALS members from across the nation who believe that if you wish to effect change, you must participate in order to make it happen. Without the combined efforts of the attorneys and other professionals listed below and the commitment of the committee members, this textbook would not have been possible. NALS acknowledges the following members and individuals for their outstanding contributions to this edition:

Karen Kuhn, Certified PP, PLS, Chairman, Gulfport, Mississippi

Linda K. Adair, PLS, Little Rock, Arkansas

Jessica Baber, Corpus Christi, Texas

Donna D. Barfield, Augusta, Georgia

Anita Campbell, Certified PP, PLS, Jackson, Mississippi

Jane R. Cramer, Columbus, Ohio

Nancy M. Gates, Certified PP, PLS, CLAS, Vancleave, Mississippi

Glenda R. Hanson, Certified PP, PLS, Seattle, Washington

Patricia E. Infanti, Certified PP, PLS, Philadelphia, Pennsylvania

Dawn Miller–Lawrence, PLS, Phoenix, Arizona

Janice R. Miller, Certified PP, PLS, CPS, Lonoke, Arkansas

Tammy Shatwell Mullins, Tulsa, Oklahoma

Diana Price, Tulsa, Oklahoma

Jeannie M. Shaw, Certified PP, PLS, Gulfport, Mississippi

Joani A. Yingling, Certified PP, PLS, CLAS, CNSA, Tucson, Arizona

The NALS Text Development Committee worked closely with their respective attorneys to revise and update the *Basic Manual for the Lawyer's Assistant*, Ninth Edition. On behalf of NALS . . . *the association for legal professionals*, we would like to thank the following firms for their support:

Bruce D. Brown, PLLC

Phoenix, Arizona

ACKNOWLEDGMENTS

Bricker & Ecker, LLP
Columbus, Ohio

Franke & Salloum, PLLC
Gulfport, Mississippi

Frascogna Courtney, PLLC
Jackson, Mississippi

Robert A. Fortuno, P.C.
Tucson, Arizona

Hermansen, McKibben, Woolsey & Villarreal, LLP
Corpus Christi, Texas

Kilpatrick Stockton, LLP
Augusta, Georgia

Alltel Corporation
Little Rock, Arkansas

Pulaski Technical College
North Little Rock, Arkansas

Quattlebaum, Grooms, Tull & Burrow, PLLC
Little Rock, Arkansas

This project would not have been successful without the support offered by the firms listed above. Thank you for your continued professional courtesies and generosities extended throughout the development of this edition and for your support of the committee members.

ACKNOWLEDGMENTS

Staying current in such a rapidly changing field is a challenge. As the law evolves, so do our texts and accompanying materials. NALS . . . *the association for legal professionals* would like to thank the following attorneys and individuals for their contributions to this project:

Bruce D. Brown, Phoenix, Arizona

Barton Fears, Phoenix, Arizona

Michael L. Fondren, Pascagoula, Mississippi

Timothy W. Grooms, Little Rock, Arkansas

John M. Harral, Gulfport, Mississippi

Brandt Howell, Brandon, Mississippi

Seth M. Hunter, Hattiesburg, Mississippi

Patrick W. Kirby, Gulfport, Mississippi

Holly L. Larkin, Little Rock, Arkansas

S. Hubert Mayes, Jr., Little Rock, Arkansas

Shellye V. McDonald, Gulfport, Mississippi

Woodrow W. Pringle, III, Gulfport, Mississippi

Jon C. Thornburg, Biloxi, Mississippi

Cathy Underwood, Little Rock, Arkansas

Special thanks to the proofreading team:

Nancy Gates, Certified PP, PLS, Vancleave, Mississippi

Karen Kuhn, Certified PP, PLS, Gulfport, Mississippi

Jeannie Shaw, Certified PP, PLS, Gulfport, Mississippi

The assistance of these individuals was invaluable to this project. Thank you.

PREFACE

NALS® believes that continuing education is vital to every successful career in the legal profession. This Manual, the Ninth Edition, is geared toward those persons entering or returning to the legal field.

We believe this text will provide a useful tool for all legal support personnel, regardless of title, job description, or experience. Even as we remind you that the *Basic Manual for the Lawyer's Assistant* remains a general reference and not a specific map for your firm's practice, we encourage you to rely on this manual for basic knowledge and guidance.

HOW TO USE THIS TEXTBOOK

The *Basic Manual for the Lawyer's Assistant* is presented by NALS® as part of a training course for legal support personnel. It is also the official text for the NALS Legal Training Course and Independent Course of Study.

It is intended for use as a training aid for people who are entering or have recently entered the legal field. It does not attempt to teach the law.

Because of its nature, the text is broad, but the accompanying *Student Study Guide and Instructor's Manual* offer suggestions on the application of general subject matter. NALS believes that diligent attention to this text is a good basis for increasing knowledge and career advancement.

This text is not intended as a legal authority and should not be used in that manner. The intent is purely informational. The examples in the text are illustrative in nature and should be used in an office only at the direction of the lawyer. Legal procedures change daily, and legal support personnel, as well as lawyers, should maintain a knowledge of current procedures in their area.

This text emphasizes professionalism, growth through education, and empowerment.

SUMMARY OF CONTENTS

TABLE OF CONTENTS

TABLE OF CONTENTS

TABLE OF CONTENTS

Sec.

TABLE OF CONTENTS

TABLE OF CONTENTS

Sec.

CHAPTER 5. ACCOUNTING

CHAPTER 6. ORAL AND WRITTEN COMMUNICATIONS

TABLE OF CONTENTS

TABLE OF CONTENTS

TABLE OF CONTENTS

CHAPTER 8. THE LAW LIBRARY

TABLE OF CONTENTS

TABLE OF CONTENTS

TABLE OF CONTENTS

TABLE OF CONTENTS

CHAPTER 12. CONTRACTS

TABLE OF CONTENTS

CHAPTER 13. TORTS

CHAPTER 14. CRIMINAL LAW AND PROCEDURE

TABLE OF CONTENTS

CHAPTER 16. BUSINESS ORGANIZATIONS

TABLE OF CONTENTS

TABLE OF CONTENTS

CHAPTER 18. ESTATE PLANNING

CHAPTER 19. ESTATES AND GUARDIANSHIPS

TABLE OF CONTENTS

CHAPTER 20. BANKRUPTCY

CHAPTER 1

THE LAWYER'S ASSISTANT

Table of Sections

---

§ 1.1 A Professional Career

"A legal assistant/paralegal is a person, qualified by education, training or work experience who is employed or retained by a lawyer, law office, corporation, governmental agency or other entity and who performs specifically delegated substantive legal work for which a lawyer is responsible." This is the definition adopted by the American Bar Association (the ABA) and by most (if not all) of the professional associations of and for legal support professionals.

Persons in the legal field, support personnel attorneys, and others, use many different terms by which to describe the staff that assists a lawyer, including assistant, lawyer's assistant, legal assistant, legal secretary, paralegal, and secretary, to name a few. Certifications vary, as well, and include ALA, ALS, CLA, PLS®, RP and PP®. The certification varies by the certifying organization, just as the job description and the title of the position vary with the employer. There are many things that will never change in this profession, and many that are constantly changing. Regardless of the title, job description, or employer, however, the role of the legal support professional remains the same: to assist one or more lawyer or lawyers. For that reason, the term "lawyer's assistant" or "assistant" will be used throughout this text.

The legal support profession has evolved over the decades, much as the language to describe the position of the lawyer's assistant. In what may be its most basic, possibly original form, one can look to the Latin root of the word "secretary." Its etymology is from the Medieval Latin word *secretarius* meaning "confidant." Webster takes this further; one definition of the word *secretary* is: "One employed to handle correspondence and manage routine and detail work. . . ."

The legal profession is set apart in requiring skills and support of the highest quality in order for the lawyer to render the finest, most expedient service possible to clients. As everyone knows, secretaries and assistants are employed in most fields, and governments and businesses of the world would not function well, if at all, without them. It follows that the lawyer's support staff has always been the very heart of the law office. As time has passed, and the legal field has grown increasingly complex, the responsibilities of the assistant have also evolved, encompassing more and more duties.

Lawyers are unique professionals, and each is different in personality and work capability. Every lawyer, however, has certain things in common with every other lawyer. The formal education required in order to become a lawyer is extensive, and is the beginning of an education that continues with each case and each client. The lawyer is dedicated to the public and the service of justice. This often is reflected in personal activities; community service, charity and *pro bono* work—all outlets that allow a lawyer to donate time and services to the benefit and improvement of the public. The lawyer believes in the right of representation of all people in spite of frailties, gross misjudgments, even flagrant violations of the law.

A lawyer is held to the strictest standards of moral and ethical conduct, in both professional and personal life. Every lawyer is bound to the standards of conduct found in the Rules of Professional Conduct adopted by the state(s) in which they practice. The American Bar Association ("ABA") adopted the Model Rules in 1983, and most states have followed suit, adopting Rules of Professional Conduct of their own. The Rules provide statements of the professional conduct expected of lawyers, objectives toward which all lawyers should strive, and mandatory disciplinary rules. The Rules define misconduct, and provide for disciplinary procedures by which they are enforced.

NALS . . . *the association for legal professionals* has adopted a Code of Ethics and Professional Responsibility. This Code serves that same function for the lawyer's assistant as the Model Rules for the lawyer. Strict adherence to the Code of Ethics and Professional Responsibility of NALS is essential to the character, behavior, performance, and image of the professional lawyer's assistant. It is also important that you are aware of the Model Rules that govern lawyers in your state.

A lawyer's assistant contributes significantly to the image and perception of the lawyer. You must be aware of your actions, and always convey an impression of respect for the lawyer and for the law. In dealing with the lawyer's assistant, clients and members of the legal community can sense an assistant's respect for the lawyer, and for the work product. Professionalism must be maintained at all times. For example, in many offices, personnel address lawyers on a first-name basis. However, this practice may portray a more casual or unprofessional image or atmosphere, and the lawyer's assistant should avoid addressing the lawyer or clients by their first names unless instructed otherwise.

As emphasized in the NALS Code of Ethics and Professional Responsibility and in the Code of Responsibility of the American Bar Association, confidentiality is essential.

A lawyer's assistant should neither criticize nor condone criticism of the lawyer or the firm by which they are employed. In spite of interest in the quality of work and familiarity with the facts at issue, the lawyer's assistant does not have the advantage of the extensive legal training of a lawyer, and may not always understand why certain decisions are made or positions are taken. As the lawyer's assistant dealing directly with clients, you enjoy a very weighty responsibility: to the clients, you are an extension of the lawyer. The clients must understand, however, that the lawyer's assistant is prohibited from offering legal advice. Regardless of training or experience, the lawyer's assistant is not a lawyer, and cannot, under any circumstances, practice law. This is one of the most important, and oftentimes one of the most difficult, tests of the integrity of the lawyer's assistant.

In order for you as a lawyer's assistant, or one aspiring to that position, to convey professionalism to the lawyer, the firm, and the clients they serve, there is an essential first step without which you cannot progress beyond the mechanical. You must believe in yourself and in your ability to accomplish the goal.

There are many steps to take between leaving the classroom and feeling accomplished as a lawyer's assistant and these stages of progression vary according to the individual. Occasional discouragement is natural; difficulty makes one proud of an accomplishment.

The primary requirement of a successful lawyer's assistant, which underlies your work and your image on an hourly, daily, and continuing basis, is your *attitude* toward yourself and toward your career. Your attitude is reflected in each and every contact you have with others and in your completion of work assignments, often under troublesome and pressure-filled conditions. The valued lawyer's assistant has learned to remain consistently composed and efficient under the most trying circumstances, knowing that conflicts and deadlines are inevitable. Remember that your work is your career, not just a job, and each experience is a positive contribution to an investment in yourself.

The second basic ingredient in the development of the lawyer's assistant and a byproduct of the proper attitude is *initiative.* You can make an appreciable difference in the firm's productivity and in your career development if you request additional assignments after thoroughly completing delegated work. You should let the lawyer know that you are serious about your career and eager to expand your contribution to the lawyer's productivity by asking relevant questions, by inquiring about appropriate reading material, and by requesting periodic evaluations of your work. There are excellent training courses and educational materials available through national, state, and local legal professional associations, as well as from vocational schools and universities, that will help enhance the knowledge and skills of the lawyer's assistant. Continuing education is a secure investment that produces earned dividends in proportion to its application.

Development of the proper attitude and strong initiative to accomplish and excel will result in the *self-confidence* that is the third vital factor in the makeup of the professional lawyer's assistant. Real confidence is not automatic—it is developed over a period of time through a variety of experiences. You will become self-confident by satisfactorily accomplishing tasks that at the outset seem too difficult to complete. Each time you succeed at something new, your self-confidence will grow. Knowledge of requisite skills will contribute significantly to your comfort with your work responsibilities. Excellence in these skills is a definite must if you are to achieve the ultimate in performance and recognition in your field. You will know that you have acquired self-confidence when you allow someone else to be given credit for your idea or work product; when you accept sound, constructive criticism graciously and gratefully; and when you admit your mistakes honestly without an attempt to search for an excuse.

Confidence is required for honest self-evaluation. When appraising yourself as candidly and objectively as possible, ask yourself if you fulfill the assistant's key responsibilities; a professional image, and genuine support for your lawyer.

§ 1.2 Beginning Your Career

You may have just finished school and are ready to embark on a career as a lawyer's assistant, or perhaps you are changing positions or careers to become a lawyer's assistant. No matter which situation pertains to you, many of your experiences as a new lawyer's assistant will be the same.

The image of the professional lawyer's assistant is composed of many facets and often begins with the visual one. Your attitude and imagination, and your enthusiasm for the career you have chosen, should shine through. It should be obvious to everyone you meet that you like what you do, and take pride in doing it well. It is true that first impressions are lasting, and a negative impact is very difficult to reverse.

Many law offices maintain policies concerning appropriate attire. There are certain simple, basic guidelines the lawyer's assistant should follow to achieve the appearance that the position requires. The underlying goal should be to create a picture of professionalism that will encourage the client's confidence in the assistant's serious attitude toward the work and the lawyers. Avoid clothing that is too casual; look for basic styles that can be worn interchangeably, which will lend versatility to a wardrobe if careful planning is used in purchase.

Jewelry, makeup, hair styles, and neat and trimmed beards and mustaches in a law office can be in good fashion and tasteful. Take care to avoid extremes, with understatement being preferable to overstatement. Every firm has different requirements and dress codes; always remember that you are a professional and dress and act accordingly.

§ 1.2.1 The Interview

The first active step in becoming a lawyer's assistant is the interview. No matter how much practice you have gone through for this interview, you will still be nervous. You can, however, ease the situation by a calm demeanor. Do not try to "oversell" yourself. Approach the interview with a professional attitude. A courteous, dignified, pleasant, and professional manner is essential to a successful lawyer's assistant.

Be yourself. You are not being fair to either yourself or your prospective employer if you try to be something or somebody you are not. Be tidy in your appearance; be sure that your dress, hair style, and makeup at the initial interview, and at each interview that may follow, are appropriate for the position that you are seeking.

Be candid. Ask questions. Find out as much as possible about the position for which you are applying; know what will be expected of you, and what you can expect from your employer. Be honest in your responses; clarify matters that you do not understand fully. Remember, your interest—or lack of interest—is on display. It is very possible you might discover you are not compatible with the position being offered. Do not expect the interviewer to indicate immediately to you whether or not the position will be offered to you. The interviewer may have to consult with others or may have other interviews scheduled. Many firms interview prospective employees more than once. It is appropriate to inquire as to when you might expect to hear from the firm. If you do not hear at the appointed time, you may call and inquire as to whether or not you are still being considered.

Know when the interview is over, then leave. Do not linger. Be as dignified in your exit as in your entrance. Final impressions are equally as important as first impressions. Be sure to send a letter to the interviewer thanking them for taking the time to meet with you and express your interest in the position. Be polite and to the point in your letter.

§ 1.2.2 The First Day

You may have some doubts and fears as you approach your first day in your new position. Those doubts and fears can be eased or eliminated if you arrive at work well rested and ready to go. Start out organized from the minute you wake up and carry through to the end of the day. Have a notebook handy and be ready to use it. Never trust *anything* to memory. Take notes. Learn where the supplies are stored (draw a map if you have to), what type filing system is used, who is in charge of what, and where the form books are kept.

Ideally, you should have your notebook divided into classifications and take your notes down in proper sections. Organize your notes and file them in a procedures manual in the same manner—by classification. Then, every time something new comes along, you can add it to your notebook. You never know who might have to take your place in an emergency. Even if your new office has a procedures manual, it may not cover enough to get you through the first few days or weeks. Take your notes home and review them. Do this day after day, until you feel at home in the office and have a comprehensive manual of your duties.

§ 1.2.3 On With the Job

For a while, you may not understand certain methods used by your employer. The best way to learn is by asking and taking notes on the answers for future reference. Let your employer know that your job will be easier and your performance better if you understand what you are doing. The old adage, "If you are afraid to ask, you are afraid to learn," is just as true in the office as it is in the classroom.

Perhaps one of the most terrifying experiences you can have is the client who calls or comes into the office to ask about their case. Occasionally, you will get a call or visit from a client who is upset or even irate about their pending matter. The client may expect you to be able to give them up-to-date information and detailed answers to any questions. You probably have never heard of the client, much less what their case is about; however, the client will expect you to know both. Do not stammer and act foolish. Let the client know you are competent. Be calm; be truthful; be confident. Turn on your public relations; for example:

"I have just begun working here and am not familiar with your case. May I have your name? I will see if someone else may be able to assist you."

Now, follow through. Be sure someone does help the client. Remember that no matter how insignificant a case or problem may seem to you, it is very important to the client. Always strive for good public relations. Do not, however, give out information of which you are not sure. The client will probably have more respect for you if you are truthful and explain your limitations. The manner in which the lawyer's assistant deals with clients should always be gracious and professional. Treat each client as a special person with an individual problem or situation. Such an attitude is further evidence that the lawyer also regards the client and the client's circumstances as special and deserving of attention.

Remember, no matter how long you have been on the job, the lawyer's assistant cannot and should not give any information that could in any way be considered legal advice.

Take everything one step at a time. During those first few weeks, keep your notebook handy and build your office manual. Ask questions and get to know office procedures and why and how they are used. Learn the office equipment. Learn the office postal system and use it to the best advantage possible. Learn how the bookkeeping systems work and use them. Fully understand the filing system immediately. Trying to locate one misplaced file or misfiled document can cause hours of lost time.

Perhaps one of the most important things to remember is that each system in the office has been developed to make your job more efficient. Use these systems and make them work for you and with you.

Be pleasant to everyone. Remember that you may need their help some day. Good manners are a necessary part of civilized living, and we all appreciate those who consistently display them. Application of The Golden Rule is certainly appropriate in relationships with other team members. Promote mutual respect with other staff members by refusing to participate in office politics or gossip.

§ 1.2.4 The Lawyer's Assistant in the Small Firm

Looking for a challenge? That is what you will get if you are a lawyer's assistant in a small law office—one or two lawyers and you as the lawyer's assistant. The lawyer's assistant in the small office probably receives a more rounded education on the job than any other assistant and must be everything to everybody, an expert in all areas of office relations and office work.

As a lawyer's assistant in a small office, you deal with the public. You are usually the first person with whom the client or prospective client speaks, either personally or on the telephone. You set the mood. Therefore, you need all of the abilities of a good receptionist, an arbitrator, and a psychologist. You must be interesting and interested.

You get the mail and distribute it, wrap parcels, and post the mail. You also take care of postage expenses, collect return receipts, and perform a myriad of other postal duties. You must know the postal system thoroughly and how to make it work for you.

You keep the books, write checks, deposit receipts, send out bills (and rebillings), and know banking procedures as well. You handle trust and estate accounts and can verify everything you have done. You keep your records in a manner that will expedite your employer's tax preparations. You are competent at accounting and accounting procedures.

You order supplies and take care of the office equipment and repairs. You know where to get what you want at the best price available. You know what equipment and supplies provide the performance required at an economically feasible rate. You have a place for everything and everything is well marked for the convenience of everyone in the office.

You take care of the law library by keeping it up to date and orderly. You keep subscriptions current. You file new supplements, checking each old one before discarding it to determine whether pertinent information has been noted and transferred to the new supplements if necessary. You have a reference file for articles in law publications and can retrieve information based on the information in this file. You identify all library materials with your employer's name and address.

Since you prepare everything that leaves the office, you know the proper forms for communications, pleadings, and all other documents that are drafted. You proofread everything at least once, and make all corrections carefully and neatly. You know proper copying requirements for each matter. You take pride in a job well done and in a document free from error.

Because you compose a great deal of correspondence for your employer's signature, you know how your employer likes to express thoughts and ideas and can prepare correspondence accordingly. You know the components of a successful business letter, have a thorough knowledge of the English language, and know how to use it to the best advantage. You know punctuation, spelling, grammar, and word division and use all four correctly.

Every document coming in or going out of the office has a place, and you make sure it is filed properly *and promptly* for later retrieval. The files are orderly, current, and organized in a system your employer can use.

You learn all you can about the mechanics of your employer's practice and relieve your employer of the work you can perform. You prepare documents and do research under your lawyer's direction to enable the lawyer to do the job more effectively. You know your limitations, and you do not offer legal advice.

You know everything that is happening, and where everything is. You know what forms to use and what progress is being made in each case. You know what procedures to follow and what comes next. Most important of all, you have this information written in the proper files or in your office manual. You have made it possible for someone to step into your position and do your job with the least disruption necessary if an emergency should arise.

Your professional abilities are challenged every minute of every working day. You are the epitome of the truly professional lawyer's assistant. Your attitude, appearance, poise, relations with the public and your employer, as well as your skills, your initiative, and your motivation are all part of this professionalism. You are indeed the well-rounded lawyer's assistant, and without being conscious of the fact, you are daily grooming yourself to obtain the designation of PLS® . . . an advanced certification for the legal professional®—a Professional Goal. (*See* § 1.3.2.)

§ 1.2.5 The Lawyer's Assistant in the Large Firm

You now have a new job at a large law firm, and you wonder what to expect.

On your first day, the office administrator will probably give you an employee handbook that explains such things as the office hours, the vacation and sick pay policy, the fringe benefits package, and the conduct expected of all office employees. You will then be given the various local, state, and federal income tax forms and other office forms which are required to place you in the personnel system.

After that, you will be given a tour of the office, and you will be introduced to the staff members who are available for introductions. Some law firms have a map of the office layout to help you find your way around. If the support personnel have nameplates and the lawyers' offices are properly identified, use these to help you learn their names.

Usually, the office administrator's assistant or one of the other lawyer's assistants in the office will be assigned to assist you in learning how to work efficiently with and within the support functions of the office. The following are some of the functions that may be explained:

Telecommunications. Most firms now have an automated system whereby all local, WATS, long distance calls, and faxes can be automatically charged to specific files and stored in a computer for automatic recall when billing a file. Most offices have special procedures for placing long distance, WATS, and other calls.

File Clerk. Large firms may have a special procedure for setting up new files and checking for conflicts. It is imperative that you learn the correct procedures for opening and closing files and for maintaining files during the active life of the files.

Accounting. Most offices have computers and it is important that you learn the best way to utilize the equipment for particular office procedures, especially with regard to maintaining accurate time records for billing clients. You must also learn how to request checks, the turnaround time required to get checks, and how to charge such office expenses as postage, copying, long distance calls, faxes, and other out-of-pocket expenses to the individual clients or files.

Word Processing. Documents such as briefs, wills, trusts, profit sharing plans, etc., may be prepared in the word processing department, freeing the lawyer's assistant to do other work for the lawyer. You may be responsible for getting the work into the proper form to be submitted to the word processing department for actual preparation, or you may be required to keyboard some of your own work.

Copying. Many firms now have staff who either do all of the copying for the office or who are available to assist with large projects. Additionally, many firms now have several types of copying machines which are utilized for different purposes. If each lawyer's assistant is responsible for doing their own copying, you will have to learn which type of equipment to utilize for various projects and who the key operators are for the various machines, and whom to turn to if a machine malfunctions. If records are kept of copies to be billed to clients, you need to learn this procedure.

Librarian. The law library will probably be kept up to date by a librarian or by one specific person in the office. This may also include CD Rom research programs, internet research sites, and other reference materials. It is your responsibility to learn how to use the office library.

Mail Room. Each firm generally has its own procedure for handling incoming and outgoing mail. It is important that you learn this procedure so that your mail will be handled timely.

Faxes. Facsimile receipts and transmissions are sometimes handled by a separate department, a subdepartment of the telecommunications department, a support services department, or by receptionists or other designated staff members. You need to understand the firm's procedures for sending and receiving faxes, and know how to send a fax when department personnel are not available.

Errands. Generally, errands will be handled by an in-house messenger or an outside special delivery service. Get the specifics on how to get items messengered correctly and timely. In an emergency, you may have to do the errand yourself. In addition to having someone explain these various functions to you, these procedures will probably be set out in the office procedures manual that is available to all employees.

Finally, you will be taken to your desk where you will begin to learn the intricacies of your new job. You will soon learn that every lawyer has their own special way of handling matters, and you must now learn how to put your skills to work.

You will find that most firms prefer that their correspondence and legal documents be prepared in a uniform fashion. Use your office procedures manual to learn how to set up the various documents you will be required to prepare. If there are forms for your use, learn how to customize them to suit your lawyer's preferences, and how and where to save them for repeated use.

By the end of the first day, you may feel lost, overwhelmed, and unsure of yourself. Each staff member you met on your first day seemed to know everything, and you are sure you know close to nothing. If you are new to the legal field, remember that you have been properly trained, your skills met the tests necessary to be offered the position, and you have the attitude to see you through. Remember that everyone had a first day, and at some time in the past, every single one of those "expert lawyer's assistants" was a "beginner" too.

If you are an experienced lawyer's assistant, you will have to draw on your past successful experiences. Remember that in a very short time you will wonder how you ever doubted your abilities to master the responsibilities and procedures required of your position.

§ 1.2.6 The Lawyer's Assistant in the Corporate Environment

The role of the corporate lawyer's assistant is broader in scope than most assistant roles. There are seldom any routine duties, except perhaps opening the mail.

In the corporate environment, the legal department is usually an arm of top management and, as such, reaches out into every phase of the company's operations. The primary function of the legal department is the practice of preventive law in an effort to perceive, analyze, and correct legally related problems within the organization before they result in litigation. This is, of course, a noble goal, but no large corporation is without Equal Employment Opportunity (EEO) complaints, workers' compensation claims, unemployment and Department of Labor hearings, union/labor problems, complex contract claims, and liability issues. Corporate legal issues range from small dollar problems to the defense of lawsuits involving millions of dollars. The matter is further complicated if the corporation is under primary contract to the government and thus subject to the never-ending rules and regulations that have been promulgated to enforce applicable laws and statutes. These laws have been primarily enacted to assure fairness, equal opportunity, protection of the government's interests, and to absolve the government of any appearance of conflict of interest, corruption, or wrongdoing, but the paperwork and effort required to comply are added responsibilities.

The lawyer's assistant is vital to the proper and effective operation of a corporate legal office. The lawyer's assistant must have excellent secretarial skills, a working knowledge of legal terminology, and good communications skills, both oral and written. In addition, you must have a thorough understanding of the corporate structure and the responsibilities of the lawyers in the office in order to direct requests for information to the lawyer best able to assist. You must also be sensitive to political issues within or outside the company, as good public relations are essential to the smooth operation of the legal department as well as to the corporation. Finally, the lawyer's assistant is often called upon to assist with legal research, which requires a basic knowledge of the legal resources most frequently consulted by the legal department in which you work.

The role of the corporate lawyer's assistant is both administrative and clerical. Corporate legal work is often more general than private legal work, and management-related duties often consume as much time as legal duties. A lawyer's assistant position in a corporate legal department is challenging, offering opportunities for learning, as well as variety, high visibility, and frequently a close relationship with top management.

§ 1.2.7 The Clerk/Lawyer's Assistant in the Court System

When asked to express his conception of the duties and functions of a court clerk, one judge made the following statement: "It must be borne in mind that the designation court clerk is a complete misnomer, and that the duties of court clerks, regardless of what court they may be in, go far beyond the connotation of clerk, typist, or similar position. The court clerk has great responsibility not only to the court and lawyers but also to the public generally. It is the primary responsibility of these individuals to see that the courts run smoothly and that the work is done properly and expeditiously. They are required to have a reasonable understanding of the law, rules of civil and criminal procedure, and other matters that bind the court in its daily work. This is not to say that they must be legally trained, but the clerks certainly must be able to understand statutes and case law as told to them by either the judge or the lawyer involved. Therefore, it must be kept in mind that the position of court clerk is one of more responsibility than a clerk, typist, or even a secretary."

Court records are of vital importance to the general public. It is essential that a court clerk have the training and ability to organize and maintain complete, accurate files and dockets. This can, at times, be repetitious and boring; however, the variety offered in court work more than compensates. The courts handle many kinds of cases, including criminal, juvenile, civil, adoptions, divorces, traffic, etc. The court clerk is responsible for these cases from beginning to end. The clerk assists the court by swearing in witnesses; operating an electronic recorder; taking orders and motions from the judge verbatim; and receiving, marking, and safeguarding exhibits. The clerk prepares, compiles, and files minutes of court hearings and trials; issues bench warrants under direction of the judge for persons who do not appear or who fail to pay fines imposed by the court; receives and accounts for fines imposed by the court; maintains a calendar and status file on each active case; prepares forms, legal documents, and correspondence as directed by the court; compiles and tabulates statistical data and caseload reports; and performs secretarial work for the judges.

A court clerk must have the ability to exercise judgment in the proper dissemination of information and to provide good public relations in stressful, sensitive situations. It is a job that is challenging, rewarding, and fascinating. Excellent skills are important, but above all a court clerk is required to be understanding, compassionate, and dedicated to serving the public.

§ 1.2.8 The Lawyer's Assistant in Federal Government

The duties of lawyer's assistants employed in federal service are similar to civil service secretaries with GS ratings. A federal service lawyer's assistant is normally accorded confidence in all matters relating to the office in which they are employed, and the work is closely identified with the viewpoint and responsibilities of the particular agency or department. An office manager is directly answerable to the agency head or member of Congress, and the lawyer's assistant works under the direction of the office manager.

A lawyer's assistant performs or supervises the performance of a variety of tasks including:

- Performing telephone and receptionist duties.
- Keeping calendars and scheduling appointments and conferences.
- Performing liaison duties as necessary between the office manager and other office personnel, as well as with other offices.
- Receiving and distributing incoming mail and preparing replies.
- Arranging for recording of proceedings of conferences or hearings.
- Reviewing and channeling outgoing mail.
- Maintaining records and files.
- Making travel arrangements for staff members.

- Assembling and disseminating information.
- Transmitting staff instructions.
- Performing miscellaneous clerical, stenographic, and secretarial duties.

Lawyer's assistant positions may or may not require stenographic, word processing, or dictation machine transcription skills.

There are significant differences in civil service and federal service jobs. With federal service there is no job security, and salaries may vary a great deal, according to the wishes of the employer, the amount available in the clerk/hire fund of the particular office, or ceilings of grades for certain positions. Service to constituents is the prime reason for hiring of staff in congressional offices. There is a great amount of research and contact with various governmental agencies so that problems may be resolved. Because of these contacts, a certain amount of glamour and prestige is attached to federal service jobs. Many support staff positions, however, require longer hours than regular civil service jobs or jobs in private industry. No overtime is paid, but in some cases, compensatory time off is allowed.

Most federal service assistants do not come from the civil service registry but are recruited by advertisement or word of mouth. An employment service is also provided for the use of the members of Congress. Abilities are tested and evaluated in the same manner used by private industry employment agencies. Lawyer's assistant skills are much in demand. Usually, the assistant's training has included language skills, such as obtaining information for and composing correspondence and reviewing outgoing correspondence for correct grammar, spelling, and format. The advancement of the assistant depends on many factors, including length of time in the position, improved job skills, and ability to work without direct supervision. Other traits essential to the performance of duties are:

- Effectiveness in getting along with others.
- Loyalty, integrity, and discretion.
- Capacity and willingness to accept responsibility.
- Judgment, initiative, and resourcefulness.
- Poise, personal dignity, neatness, and good grooming.

§ 1.2.9 The Lawyer's Assistant in Specialized Practice

Lawyers in general practice handle all types of cases—civil and criminal. This means that the lawyer might be involved in the defense of a criminal matter one day and in a personal injury trial the next. General practice firms do not limit their practices to trial work. On the contrary, they may also handle a large volume of nonlitigation work such as property transactions, contracts, estate planning, and tax work. The lawyer's assistant in a general practice, therefore, must be especially versatile and knowledgeable about many aspects of the law.

Some lawyers thrive on the excitement and challenge of trial work, which is divided into criminal defense and civil trial work. There are further divisions in these two major areas of trial work. For example, some criminal defense trial lawyers specialize in white collar crime defenses. Likewise, some civil trial lawyers' practices emphasize personal injury, tax matters, domestic relations, bankruptcy, and/or other types of civil actions.

Other lawyers enjoy the challenge of becoming specialists in one particular phase of the law such as estate planning, property law, probate law, tax law, corporate law, admiralty law, patent law, domestic relations law, and so on. They may rarely engage in trial work but often serve as backup specialists for the trial lawyer.

For the lawyer's assistant who works for a specialist, there is the particular challenge of learning the lawyer's specialty, and becoming a specialist yourself in that particular area of the law.

§ 1.2.10 Career Advancement

Whether you advance in your career or remain in the same position year after year while others are advanced before you depends upon many things, one of which is your own attitude. Are you willing to learn? Are you able to take instructions gracefully? Are you able to do things the way your present employer desires them to be done without such remarks as, "But I've never done it this way before," or "My last job didn't do it this way"? Are you able to take constructive criticism? Are you, as a responsible professional lawyer's assistant, able to make procedural changes to keep in step with modern trends? Keep an open mind. Do not let your attitude keep your career bogged down.

Be ready for career advancement. Perhaps you work in a one-assistant office and contemplate working in a larger firm in the future. Regardless of the size of the firm in which you work, it is critical that you maintain and increase your personal knowledge base. Attend seminars and workshops. Obtain the designation of ALS ... the basic certification for legal professionals—a Career Goal, PLS® ... the advanced certification for legal professionals—a Professional Goal and/or PP®, Certified Professional Paralegal. Keep abreast of what is happening in your firm, in the local legal community, and in the world. Read newspapers, including the business and obituary columns. Do that little bit extra, without being asked. The fact that your employer is aware that you are actively involved in and seek out continuing legal education can often make a big difference in advancement.

Some lawyer's assistants find that their employers hesitate to promote them into a different position because they feel the lawyer's assistant is indispensable. As a good lawyer's assistant, you will have your job so well organized with an office manual, a forms file, a procedures manual, and systematic training of backup personnel that your employer need not be concerned about promoting you. You can be of even more help to the lawyer in an administrative capacity than in a purely assistant one. Often you can be your own worst enemy when it comes to advancement. You may get caught in a career trap of your own making, if you jealously guard your domain and keep your systems in your head. Yes, that makes you truly reliable, but by making it a major event to train someone else to take your place, your employer may find that it is easier to keep you in your present position.

Some lawyer's assistants settle for "jobs" instead of careers. However, a large part of one's adult life is spent in the working world. Planning a career takes just that—planning. Decide on some objectives for your working life and design a plan to reach those objectives. It is up to you whether you have a career or just a job.

§ 1.3 Membership in NALS

NALS ... ***the association for legal professionals***, began in 1929 as the National Association of Legal Secretaries. A young legal secretary, Eula May Jett, in Long Beach, California, was encouraged by a court clerk to talk with other legal secretaries about correct preparation of legal documents. As a result of that challenge, NALS was formed. Today NALS is a tri-level organization with membership available in local chapters, state associations, and on the national level. In order to better reflect our diverse membership, NALS dropped the acronym and because of name recognition kept the letters NALS.

NALS encourages the personal and professional growth of its members through education and the promotion of professional standards and ethics. Members support and abide by the Code of Professional Responsibility of the American Bar Association as well as the NALS Code of Ethics and Professional Responsibility. Membership is available to all persons engaged in work of a legal nature, such as law office administrators, lawyer's assistants, legal assistants, stenographers, or employees of public and private institutions. Lawyers, judges, and educators may join NALS as associate members, and there is a special class of membership available to students.

NALS, local chapters, and state associations offer many educational materials and programs, such as:

- Texts and handbooks to provide helpful how-to information for the everyday use of lawyer's assistants in both general and specialty practices.

- Manuals to assist law offices in developing their own procedures and systems and tests for hiring qualified support staff.
- Training courses and independent study courses to provide basic and advanced instruction for lawyer's assistants, and educational institutes to assist them in preparing for the certification examinations.
- Educational conferences and seminars held throughout the nation, throughout the year.
- *@LAW* is a quarterly magazine full of educational articles on general trends and emerging issues in the legal field, as well as practical information to help achieve and maintain proficiency in the delivery of legal services, and information on seminars, programs, and other educational opportunities.
- e-Learn@NALS is an educational publication, sent to all members who provide an e-mail address. It also addresses current trends in the legal support career field.
- E–News is an electronic newsletter published every other week by the various committees of NALS and available to all members via the internet.
- Leading The Way is a publication for the NALS leadership at all levels. Local, state, and national officers use Leading The Way to assist them in reaching their goals, and as a source of information to share with their constituents.
- NALS Affinity Programs provide members with discounts on a variety of goods and services.
- NALS Online Learning Center is the perfect place to find free education that can be accessed at your convenience. Online Study Groups are offered each year as well as various continuing legal education topics.

§ 1.3.1 ALS Certification

One certification which is available through NALS is ALS ... the basic certification for the legal professional—a Career Goal. This designation is achieved after passing a half-day examination designed for the individual at the apprentice level rather than veteran members of the legal support staff.

The four-hour exam covers three areas:

1. Written Communication.
2. Office Procedures and Legal Knowledge.
3. Ethics, Human Relations, and Judgment.

§ 1.3.2 PLS® Certification

PLS® . . . the advanced certification for the legal professional—a Professional Goal, certifies a lawyer's assistant as an individual who possesses *the foundation to perform substantive legal tasks*, a mastery of office and people skills, and who demonstrates the ability to interact on a professional level with lawyers, clients, secretaries, lawyer's assistants, legal assistants, office administrators, judges, and court officials. Working under the direct supervision of a practicing lawyer or judge, the PLS certified legal professional is expected to assume responsibility, exercise initiative and judgment, and make decisions within the scope of assigned authority. The certified legal professional has a working knowledge of procedural law and the law library, and is capable of drafting correspondence, legal documents, and court documents under the direct supervision of an attorney.

The full day examination includes four areas of testing:

1. Written Communication.
2. Office Procedures and Technology.
3. Ethics and Judgment.
4. Legal Knowledge and Skills.

§ 1.3.3 Professional Paralegal Certification (PP®)

Professional Paralegal (PP®) certification is an attainable goal for paralegals who wish to be identified as exceptional in all areas of law. The certificate is received after passing a one-day, four-part comprehensive paralegal certification examination. Any person who has five years of experience performing paralegal/legal assistant duties (a candidate may receive a partial waiver of one year if he or she has a post-secondary degree, other certification, or a paralegal certificate; a candidate with a paralegal degree may receive a two-year partial waiver).

This full day examination covers four areas:

1. Written Communications.
2. Legal Knowledge and Skills.
3. Ethics and Judgment Skills.
4. Substantive Law.

§ 1.3.4 The Certification Examinations

The ALS, PLS and Professional Paralegal examinations are administered concurrently and nationwide on the first Saturday in March and the last Saturday in September. The ALS exam is also offered at special times for schools and colleges. Applications and fees must be postmarked by January 1 for the March examination and by August 1 for the

September examination. The ALS examination is a half-day exam, while the PLS and Professional Paralegal examinations take a full day.

§ 1.3.5 College Credit

The American Council on Education (ACE) has reviewed the NALS examinations and recommended that persons passing the exams be granted college credit. Acceptance of the credit is at the discretion of each institution. Hundreds of colleges throughout the country offer college credits for those achieving certification. (Professional Paralegal approval is in the process.)

§ 1.3.6 NALS Information

Anyone interested in membership or information on programs and available products is encouraged to write or call:

NALS

314 East Third Street, Suite 210

Tulsa, OK 74120–2409

918/582–5188 (Telephone)

918/582–5907 (Facsimile)

http://www.nals.org (Website)

You may also obtain information from your local or state chapter membership or education chairpersons.

CHAPTER 2

ETHICS

Table of Sections

---

§ 2.1 Definition

According to the dictionary, ethics are "the principles of conduct governing an individual or profession." In law, the ethics governing the profession also govern all individuals working in the profession. A lawyer's assistant entering the field of law, as well as lawyers' assistants already in the legal field, must understand this.

§ 2.2 ABA Code of Professional Responsibility and Canons of Judicial Ethics

In 1908 the American Bar Association (ABA) adopted the Canons of Professional Ethics to be used as a guide for lawyers. This set of guidelines, although amended many times throughout the years, left many questions unanswered, and in 1969 the ABA adopted the Code of Professional Responsibility and Code of Judicial Ethics to replace the Canons of Professional Ethics. The Code of Professional Responsibility also left many questions unanswered and had limited disciplinary application. It consisted of Canons of Ethics, Ethical Considerations interpreting the Canons and Disciplinary Rules. In August of 1983, the ABA adopted the Model Rules of Professional Conduct to replace the Code of Professional Responsibility. The Model Rules of Professional Conduct with all amendments to date can be accessed on the internet at http://

www.abanet.org/cpr/mrpc/mrpc_home.html. Most states have adopted the new Model Rules of Professional Conduct, or rules patterned after the Model Rules with revisions adopted by the state. You should consult the Rules of Professional Conduct adopted by the state in which you are employed. Links to the Rules of Professional Conduct and other ethics materials of the states are provided by the ABA's web site at http://www.abanet.org/cpr/links.html.

§ 2.3 Ethical Considerations and Disciplinary Procedures

While the old Code of Professional Responsibility and the Model Rules of Professional Conduct are similar, there are significant differences. The old Code consisted of Canons which were statements in general terms of professional conduct expected of lawyers; Ethical Considerations interpreting the Canons and representing objectives to which all lawyers should strive; and Disciplinary Rules which were mandatory in character. Under the Model Rules of Professional Conduct, all rules are now enforceable through disciplinary procedures. Misconduct is specifically defined (*See* Rule 8.4), but a violation of the rules should not provide a basis for civil liability on the part of the lawyer.

Under the Model Rules of Professional Conduct, there is greater emphasis on quality control, regulation of trust accounts, regulation of potential conflicts of interest, and a requirement for written consent and waivers of any conflicts. Disclosure of client confidences, solicitation and advertising, and fees and fee splitting are also addressed in detail. New areas covered by the Model Rules address disabled clients; lawyer as an advisor or intermediary; lawyer as an author; relatives in competing firms; successive government and private employment; imputed disqualifications; organizations as clients; supervision of associates, junior lawyers, and paralegals; and reporting misconduct. This last topic is probably the most troublesome for lawyers in that not all state bar associations have adopted the "tattletale" rule.

§ 2.4 Code of Judicial Ethics

The ABA has also adopted a Code of Judicial Ethics for United States judges to be used as a guide to the standards judges should observe.

§ 2.5 The Role of the Lawyer's Assistant

While a nonlawyer employee in a law office cannot be disciplined for violating the Rules of Professional Conduct, the lawyer/employer is responsible for the conduct of the office staff and could be disciplined for a violation by an employee. A lawyer's assistant should be familiar with the Rules of Professional Conduct and should be guided by them while employed in a law office. The Rules of Professional Conduct are divided into eight categories with specific rules under each category. The ABA has also included comments to the rules which can assist both the lawyer and the lawyer's assistant in understanding how that rule should apply to specific situations.

§ 2.6 Client–Lawyer Relationship

This category governs all aspects of the client-lawyer relationship including: lawyer competence; scope of representation by a lawyer; representation with due diligence; and regular communication with the client. Other rules provide for the reasonableness of lawyer's fees, confidentiality, direct and imputed conflicts of interest, imputed disqualification, representing an organization or a client under a disability, and the safekeeping of a client's property. Of particular import to the lawyer's assistant are the rules governing competence (Rule 1.1), confidentiality of information (Rule 1.6), and conflicts of interest (Rules 1.7–1.12). A lawyer's assistant should maintain and upgrade skills often to assist the lawyer in competently representing the client. A lawyer's assistant must always remember that information obtained about a client is confidential and must be maintained as such. Matters about which a lawyer's assistant learns in the course of employment should not be discussed outside of the office no matter how tempting it may be to discuss the "juicy case" which is currently taking up considerable time. Only under very limited situations may an assistant discuss with persons other than the lawyer/employer specific facts learned in the office. Prior to any such discussion, the lawyer's assistant should present the situation to the supervising attorney. It is always better to err on the side of non-disclosure.

Regular communication with clients is extremely important. Your responsibility as a lawyer's assistant includes being a liaison between the client and the lawyer. Be sure the lawyer returns client phone calls and prepares periodic status reports for the client. One of the most common bar complaints from clients is lack of communication with their lawyer. This dilatory conduct may result in disciplinary action against the lawyer and is preventable.

Conflicts of interest are extensively regulated and the lawyer's assistant can unknowingly cause the lawyer/employee to violate these rules by improper conduct. The lawyer's assistant can also greatly assist the lawyer in making sure that no conflicts of interest arise. If the lawyer's assistant has knowledge of a potential conflict in any fashion, the conflict should immediately be brought to the attention of the lawyer. For instance, the lawyer's assistant may have a relative working as an employee in an opposing counsel's law firm, may have conducted a business transaction with an actual or potential client, may have worked on the same matter while employed by a different lawyer, or may have worked on a different matter involving a new or potential client. Lawyers need such information to evaluate the existence of a real or perceived conflict of interest.

The lawyer's assistant can also assist the lawyer in maintaining an accurate and up-to-date list of current and former clients so the lawyer can run a conflicts check at the very outset of representation. A conflict can arise even before a lawyer is actually retained.

§ 2.7 Counselor

Rules in this category require the lawyer to exercise judgment in representing a client and also set out circumstances in which the lawyer may act as an intermediary between clients or undertake an evaluation of a matter affecting a client for the use of someone other than the client. The assistant should not offer or respond to any requests for advice from clients, as that is a province exclusively reserved to the lawyer.

§ 2.8 Advocate

Rules in this category define the responsibilities for a lawyer predominantly when pursuing matters in a judicial proceeding or before a legislative or administrative tribunal. The rules address the advancement of unmeritorious claims or the use of delaying tactics in litigation. The rules also require candor to the tribunal and fairness to opposing parties and counsel. Finally, the rules govern trial and pretrial publicity, define when a lawyer may act as a witness, and contain specific rules for prosecutors. A lawyer's assistant should be careful not to inadvertently talk with the media about a case in which the lawyer is involved and should also be polite to opposing parties and/or their counsel, regardless of any personal feelings toward those people or knowledge of the feelings of the lawyer/employer.

The latter point is important to remember because, whether you like it or not, you often become a "sounding board" for the lawyer to vent frustration with a particular person or organization, whether client, judge, or opposing counsel. Regardless of how the lawyer has described the particular person or organization, the assistant must be polite and respectful.

§ 2.9 Transactions With Persons Other Than Clients

Lawyers must be truthful in their statements to others and must not fail to disclose material facts if the disclosure is necessary to avoid a criminal or fraudulent act by a client. Lawyers must also be very careful in dealing with unrepresented persons and cannot communicate with a person if the lawyer knows that person to be represented by counsel. The lawyer must also show respect for the rights of third persons.

§ 2.10 Law Firms and Associations

This category defines the responsibilities of particular members of a law firm, both lawyer and nonlawyer. The rules regulate the independence of the lawyer and prohibit the unauthorized practice of law. This is the category of rules of professional conduct that makes the lawyer responsible for the conduct of the lawyer's assistant and all other employees in the firm or association. Therefore, the lawyer's assistant should become familiar with how the term "practice of law" is defined in the state where the assistant is employed. It varies from state to state. For instance, a lawyer's assistant may be asked by a relative to draft a simple will for the relative which leaves all worldly possessions to the relative's spouse or children. The lawyer's assistant has typed hundreds of wills, has the basic format on the computer, and only has to change the names and print it out for the relative. Regardless of whether the lawyer's assistant is compensated for the services, in some states this is the unauthorized practice of law, while in others, it may be permissible. The unauthorized practice of law can have civil liability and criminal consequences in addition to ethical implications.

§ 2.11 Public Service

The Rules of Professional Conduct place an obligation on a lawyer to render public service. Some states have modified this rule to require a lawyer to either provide *pro bono* service to the public or to accept an appointment as a criminal defense lawyer for indigent persons. The model rules themselves include no such requirement, but instead encourage such service and model various ways in which a lawyer can discharge any *pro bono* commitments, and also define the lawyer/client relationship when the lawyer is a member of a legal services organization or law reform group.

§ 2.12 Information About Legal Services

Rules in this category regulate how a lawyer may describe a particular area of practice, lawyer advertising, direct solicitation of business, communication of fields of practice, and use of firm names and letterhead. The United States Supreme Court decided many years ago that a complete ban on lawyer advertising was a violation of a lawyer's First Amendment rights. States were free to regulate the manner and extent of a lawyer's advertising and solicitation of business. A lawyer may claim to be a specialist in a particular field of law under limited circumstances which vary significantly from state to state. A lawyer can disclose to prospective clients any licensing to appear before government agencies, *e.g.,* the Patent and Trademark Office, the Federal Communications Commission, or the Internal Revenue Service.

These rules are especially important to the lawyer's assistant because friends and relatives will very often ask what area of law the lawyer practices and in what area they "specialize." The assistant should feel free to respond to questions like this, but should be careful not to be boastful of the employer's capabilities or experience and should be careful to not compare the qualifications of the employer with those of other lawyers. The assistant's opinion about either the employer or other lawyers will carry significant weight with the layperson because the assistant is "in the know." The lawyer's assistant should be familiar with all of these rules to be sure that in communications with laypersons, the rules are not inadvertently violated. The lawyer's assistant must also be sure not to violate Canon 6 of the NALS Code of Ethics and Professional Responsibility that prohibits the solicitation of legal business on behalf of a lawyer.

§ 2.13 Maintaining the Integrity of the Profession

Rules in this last category define professional misconduct and specifically prohibits lawyers from refusing to comply with requests for information from disciplinary boards. The lawyer is also prohibited from making false statements about the qualifications or integrity of a judge or candidate for election to either judicial or legal office. One of the rules under this category also requires a lawyer to report the misconduct or a possible rule violation by another lawyer to the appropriate body. This last rule causes many problems for lawyers because they do not feel it is their place to determine that another lawyer has violated the rules of professional conduct. The lawyer's assistant can assist the lawyer in this by:

a. Being familiar with the rules.

b. Advising the lawyer of any instances where misconduct may have occurred.

c. Being the "sounding board" for the employer when necessary.

Some states did not adopt the reporting requirement when they adopted the Model Rules.

This category replaces Canon One under the ABA's Code of Professional Responsibility and is meant to advance the integrity of the legal profession in the eyes of the general public. The lawyer's assistant can help in this goal by acting honestly and with integrity in both professional and personal capacities, and by avoiding disparaging comments about the legal profession and the judicial system in discussions with laypersons.

§ 2.14 NALS Code of Ethics and Professional Responsibility (With Discussion)

Members of NALS are bound by the objectives of this Association and the standards of conduct required of the legal profession.

Every member shall:

Encourage respect for the law and the administration of justice;

Observe rules governing privileged communications and confidential information;

Promote and exemplify high standards of loyalty, cooperation, and courtesy;

Perform all duties of the profession with integrity and competence; and

Pursue a high order of professional attainment.

Integrity and high standards of conduct are fundamental to the success of our professional association. This Code is promulgated by NALS and accepted by its members to accomplish these ends.

Canon 1.	***Members of this association shall maintain a high degree of competency and integrity through continuing education to better assist the legal profession in fulfilling its duty to provide quality legal services to the public.***

The purpose of continuing legal education, supported by NALS, is to expand and refine the knowledge of members of this association, both to increase the self-esteem of members and to make members of greater assistance to lawyers in the delivery of legal services. NALS encourages continuing education by offering institutes, seminars, and courses.

The association encourages every lawyer's assistant to obtain the designation of ALS® . . . a basic certification for the legal professional—a Career Goal; PLS® . . . an advanced certification for the legal professional—a Professional Goal; and/or Certified Professional Paralegal (our newest certification for paralegals/legal assistants). Certification is used as a standard of excellence that signifies above-average skills and abilities, initiative and good judgment, and dedication to the profession. Certification is a valuable form of career insurance once certification is achieved.

The growth of a profession and the attainment and maintenance of individual competence requires an ongoing incorporation of new concepts and techniques. Continuing education enables law office staff to become aware of new developments in the field of law and provides the opportunity to improve skills used in the delivery of legal services.

A member of this association recognizes the importance of maintaining an interest in the development of continuing legal education. Professional competence is each member's responsibility. The exchange of ideas and skills benefits the legal profession and the general public.

A member of this association recognizes the necessity of membership and participation in a professional association. One of the hallmarks of any profession is its professional association, founded for the purpose of determining standards and guidelines for the growth and development of the profession. Through professional association, a member is able to promote a cooperative effort with others in the legal community for the delivery of legal services.

The continued and increased contribution by members of this association to the delivery of legal services is dependent upon a further delineation of their skills, qualifications, and areas of responsibility. It is, therefore, incumbent upon each member to promote the growth of the legal profession through support of and participation in the endeavors of NALS.

For a comparison to other rules of professional responsibilities and ethics, *see*:

American Bar Association Model Rules of Professional Conduct Rule 1.1.

Canon 2. Members of this association shall maintain a high standard of ethical conduct and shall contribute to the integrity of this association and the legal profession.

The highest degree of ethical conduct and integrity is the backbone of the legal profession. Because of the close professional relationship of a lawyer and a member of this association, it is essential that the member maintain an equally high standard of both ethical conduct and integrity. The public expects and deserves such ethical conduct and integrity by the lawyer and also expects and deserves such conduct by all nonlawyer staff with whom the client comes in contact.

For a comparison to other rules of professional responsibilities and ethics, *see*:

American Bar Association Model Rules of Professional Conduct Rules 8.1, 8.2, 8.3, and 8.4.

Canon 3. Members of this association shall avoid a conflict of interest pertaining to a client matter.

Loyalty is an essential element in the lawyer's relationship to a client. An impermissible conflict of interest may exist on behalf of a member of this association before representation is undertaken. In that event, such conflict of interest must be disclosed to the lawyer because of the lawyer's requirement to avoid such a conflict, even to the extent of declining representation. In the event a conflict occurs after representation has been undertaken, the member must disclose such conflict to the lawyer.

For a comparison to other rules of professional responsibilities and ethics, *see*:

American Bar Association Model Rules of Professional Conduct Rules 1.7(b), 1.8, 1.9, and 1.10.

Canon 4. Members of this association shall preserve and protect the confidences and privileged communications of a client.

The obligation of a member of this association to preserve the confidences and secrets of a client continues after the termination of employment of the lawyer by the client and after employment of the member by the lawyer. Although it may seem extreme, these confidences are held forever.

Both the fiduciary relationship between the lawyer and the client and the proper functioning of our legal system require that the lawyer preserve confidences of the person who employs or seeks to employ the lawyer. A client must feel free to discuss anything and everything with the lawyer, and the lawyer must be equally free to ask the client questions to obtain information beyond that volunteered by the client.

The normal operation of a law office exposes confidential personal information to nonlawyer employees, particularly those having access to files. The requirement of confidentiality obligates a lawyer to exercise extreme care in selecting and training law office personnel so that the sanctity of the client's confidences and privileged communications may be preserved.

Preserving client confidences is a vital part of the relationship between the client and the law office staff in the delivery of legal services. Of all of the duties and responsibilities borne by the professional lawyer's assistant, none is more important than maintaining client confidences.

If there is any doubt about what information may be disclosed to anyone other than the responsible lawyer, the assistant should seek advice from the lawyer immediately. It is better practice to tell the inquiring person, "I'll have to check with the lawyer," before providing information to the inquiring person, whether it be a client, another attorney, or a third party. When an error is made, everyone loses. It should not be a question of who is responsible for the error. Ultimately, the lawyer is responsible for all work product, good and bad. Professional lawyer's assistants should ensure that any matter that causes concern to the assistant be discussed with the attorney to whom the assistant is directly responsible. It is always better to ask questions before an error is made.

The confidentiality of information must be respected at all times.

For a comparison to other rules of professional responsibilities and ethics, *see*:

American Bar Association Model Rules of Professional Conduct Rule 1.6.

Canon 5. Members of this association shall exercise care in using independent professional judgment and in determining the extent to which a client may be assisted without the presence of a lawyer and shall not act in matters involving professional legal judgment.

It is permissible, and indeed it often occurs, that lawyers delegate tasks to members of the law office staff. In a specific ethical opinion by the American Bar Association, it was held:

> A lawyer can employ lay secretaries, lay investigators, lay detectives, lay researchers, accountants, lay scriveners, nonlawyer draftsmen, or nonlawyer researchers. In fact, he may employ nonlawyers to do any task for him except counsel clients about law matters, engage directly in the practice of law, appear in court, or appear in formal proceedings as part of the judicial process, so long as it is he who takes the work and vouches for it to the client and becomes responsible to the client.

ABA Comm. on Professional Ethics, Formal Op. 316 (1967).

For a comparison to other rules of professional responsibilities and ethics, *see*:

American Bar Association Model Code of Professional Conduct Rule 5.5(b).

Canon 6. Members of this association shall not solicit legal business on behalf of a lawyer.

Selection of a lawyer by a layperson should be made on an informed basis. Advice and recommendation of third parties—relatives, friends, acquaintances, business associates, or other lawyers—and disclosure of relevant information about the lawyer and area of practice may be helpful. A layperson is best served if the recommendation is disinterested and informed. In order that the recommendation be disinterested, a lawyer should not seek to influence another to recommend the lawyer's employment. A lawyer should not compensate another person for recommendations, for influencing employment of a prospective client, or to encourage future recommendations.

For a comparison to other rules of professional responsibilities and ethics, *see*:

American Bar Association Model Code of Professional Conduct Rule 7.2.

Canon 7.	***Members of this association, unless permitted by law, shall not perform paralegal functions except under the direct supervision of a lawyer and shall not advertise or contract with members of the general public for the performance of paralegal functions.***

See discussions under Canons 5, 8, and 9 and the comparisons to other rules of professional responsibilities and ethics referred to in those discussions.

For a comparison to other rules of professional responsibilities and ethics, *see*:

American Bar Association Model Code of Professional Conduct Rules 5.3 and 5.5.

Canon 8.	***Members of this association shall not perform any of the duties restricted to lawyers or do things which lawyers themselves may not do and shall assist in preventing the unauthorized practice of law.***

Canon 8 is similar to Canon 9, but Canon 8 specifically states that members may not do or engage in activities "which lawyers themselves may not do."

Canon 9.	***Members of this association not licensed to practice law shall not engage in the practice of law as defined by statutes or court decisions.***

Although the rules of professional conduct of the various state bar associations may not directly govern members of this association except through a supervising lawyer, it is incumbent upon a member of NALS to know the provisions of the lawyers' rules applicable in the member's state and to avoid any action which might involve a member of this association or a lawyer in a violation of a state code or in the appearance of professional impropriety.

The practice of law includes but is not limited to accepting cases or clients, setting fees, giving legal opinions or advice, and appearing in a representative capacity in court or before an administrative or regulatory agency. The definition of the practice of law varies from state to state, as does the definition of the unauthorized practice of law ("UPL"). A member of this association should determine the appropriate definition in the member's state, and should work to ensure that neither the assistant nor the attorney acts in violation of the definitions.

A member of this association may perform tasks assigned by a lawyer so long as the lawyer maintains a direct relationship with the client, supervises the delegated work, and has complete professional responsibility for the work product. The requirement that a lawyer must maintain a direct relationship with the client does not preclude a member of the law office staff from meeting with the client when such a meeting is necessary to carry out the professional duties assigned by the lawyer. The lawyer's assistant should be sure, at the commencement of any such meeting with a client, that their status as a lawyer's assistant is known. Ideally, this will be a reminder; the lawyer may have disclosed the role of the assistant to the client at the beginning of the representation. Nevertheless, the lawyer's assistant should not assume that the client is aware of or will remember this, and should be sure to mention their status as the lawyer's assistant at the beginning of each meeting with the client at which the lawyer is not also present.

In general, a lawyer's assistant can perform any task delegated by the lawyer to whom the assistant is responsible, so long as there is no violation or prohibition by statute, court rule, decision, or other rule or regulation, including applicable rules of the state and the rules to which the attorney is subject. These tasks can include, but are not limited to: interviewing and maintaining contact with clients, once the attorney-client relationship has been established and so long as the client is aware of the status of the lawyer's assistant; locating and interviewing witnesses, so long as the witness is aware of the status of the lawyer's assistant; performing statistical and legal research for the attorney; drafting legal documents, correspondence, and pleadings for review by, and signature of, the attorney; summarizing depositions, interrogatories, testimony for review by the attorney; attending execution of wills, real estate closings, and certain other administrative or court hearings with the attorney, subject to more specific limitations imposed by the state; the lawyer's assistant may also write and sign letters, so long as the status of the assistant is clear, and the letter does not contain independent legal opinions or advice.

Various states have adopted specific requirements applicable to the practice of legal assistants. Any member of this association employed as a legal assistant or whose responsibilities include those of a legal assistant should consult the appropriate requirements in that state. Where conflict exists, the requirements of that state shall control.

This canon is intended to protect the public from receiving legal services from unqualified individuals. "The prohibition of lay intermediaries is intended to insure the loyalty of the lawyer to the client unimpaired by intervening and possibly conflicting interest." Cheatham, *Availability of Legal Services: The Responsibility of the Individual Lawyer and of the Organized Bar*, 12 UCLA L. Rev. 438, 439 (1965).

For a comparison to other rules of professional responsibilities and ethics, *see*:

American Bar Association Model Code of Professional Conduct Rule 5.5(b).

Canon 10.	***Members of this association shall do all other things incidental, necessary, or expedient to enhance professional responsibility and participation in the administration of justice and public service in cooperation with the legal profession.***

§ 2.15 Summary

If a lawyer's assistant adheres to this Code of Ethics and Professional Responsibility, the lawyer or the firm should not be subjected to disciplinary action for a violation of the ABA's Model Rules of Professional Conduct based on acts or omissions of the lawyer's assistant.

Simply stated, as a lawyer's assistant you should:

- Work continually to upgrade your skills and knowledge.
- Be honest and forthright in and out of the office; display exemplary conduct; and inspire the confidence of the public in the legal system.
- Be careful not to solicit business for the lawyer or the firm.
- Be careful not to practice law by giving advice or preparing documents without the supervision of a lawyer.
- Be careful not to discuss any client or case outside the office or discuss a client's case with the client or the opposing counsel unless authorized to do so by the lawyer.
- Be certain to advise the lawyer or firm if you know any of the parties on the opposing side of a lawsuit being handled in the office.
- Do your work competently.
- Be careful to follow instructions concerning clients' funds.

Working in an atmosphere where all employees, lawyers and support staff alike, are required to adhere to a strict code of ethics, which includes a requirement to continue the learning process and to uphold and improve the judicial system under which we live, is both challenging and rewarding.

CHAPTER 3

THE LAW OFFICE

Table of Sections

---

§ 3.1 Law Firm Structure

Law firms range in size from a single lawyer and one lawyer's assistant to hundreds of lawyers and support personnel (senior partners, junior partners, associates, paralegals, document and file clerks, secretaries, lawyer's assistants, legal assistants, accountants, word processing personnel, etc.). Law office support staff consists of all of these people, and for a law office to function smoothly, everyone must be apprised of the lines of authority and responsibility within the structure of the firm. In an office where only one lawyer and one lawyer's assistant works, this is seldom a problem, for there is a single chain of command from the lawyer, and the sole responsibility for control and delegation lies with the lawyer. However, in an office where there is more than one lawyer or more than one lawyer's assistant, it is necessary to define the chain of command and the specific areas of responsibility in planning, procedures, and delegation of work.

Areas of control, unity of command, specific assignments, and delegation of authority commensurate with responsibility are usually detailed in a law office procedures manual. A copy of this manual is given to each new employee, and it is up to that individual employee to become thoroughly familiar with the contents of the manual. Not only does it outline the hierarchy of the firm, but it also contains the duties and responsibilities expected of the employee handling the work at each specific desk in the office. In other words, the work assignment depends upon the desk. The manual also sets out firm policy regarding benefits, merit increases, sick leave, vacation, and other similar items.

Even if you are in a one lawyer-one lawyer's assistant firm, you should have a written list of your duties to guide you in your routine tasks, and if you do not, you should begin work on one your first day on the job. (*See* Chapter 1.)

§ 3.2 Law Firm Personnel

Depending upon the size of the office, the following personnel will be accomplishing various tasks to make the law office run smoothly and efficiently:

- Lawyer(s)
- Paralegal(s)
- Receptionist(s)

- Secretary(ies)/Lawyer's assistants
- Legal assistant(s)
- File clerk(s)
- Bookkeeper(s) (accountant(s))
- Law clerk(s)
- Office administrator
- Administrative secretary(ies)
- Word Processing Personnel
- Computer/Information Technology Personnel
- Human Resources/Benefits Personnel
- Marketing Personnel

This chapter is concerned chiefly with the secretary/lawyer's assistant.

§ 3.3 Skills of the Lawyer's Assistant

The basic requirements for this position are good skills in keyboarding, spelling, composition, grammar, machine transcription, proofreading, and sometimes, speedwriting (shorthand) of some type.

The lawyer's assistant should correct obvious errors in dictation, such as transposing the terms "plaintiff" and "defendant." If information or instructions are questionable, incomplete, or obviously inaccurate, you should obtain the correct data either from the file or from the lawyer. Do not make assumptions or try to guess. Asking questions will save everyone's time in the long run, and your conscientiousness will be appreciated.

When transcribing material, do so accurately. Be aware of words and phrases that sound alike but have different spellings and meanings. Proofread very carefully everything you prepare. A misplaced punctuation mark, the wrong word, or an incorrect dollar amount can be catastrophic and irreversible for the client, the lawyer, and you. When proofreading, check for keyboarding errors, content errors, and format errors.

§ 3.3.1 Professional Requirements

Perhaps the single most influential element which transforms you from being a good lawyer's assistant to a professional lawyer's assistant is the attitude of professionalism which you bring to the position. A lawyer's assistant requires not only excellent skills in the basic requirements of the job but also conscientious attention to detail, creativity, initiative, courtesy, and tact in dealing with lawyers, staff, and clients. These attributes are found in the person who sets a goal to be the best lawyer's assistant possible and keeps that goal alive, day after day. No one comes to the position with this knowledge. It must be learned and cultivated. It is a known fact that how you program your thinking is how you will present yourself to others. The human brain is the most complicated computer known and the least used to its capacity.

Take an active interest in your work. Have procedures explained to you if you do not fully understand them. In most instances the lawyer will be happy to take a few minutes to answer your questions and can usually refer you to explanatory books or articles for further clarification.

If you wish to be the best lawyer's assistant possible, pursue the education which the position requires and then go further. Continually upgrade your knowledge in all areas of the law, leaving no part of it undiscovered.

Participate in educational seminars and workshops, take evening classes, or study on your own to make yourself more knowledgeable in your profession. Do not allow yourself to wonder why; find out.

Study for and attain certification as ALS ... the basic certification for legal professionals—a career goal, and as a PLS ... the advanced certification for legal professionals—a professional goal and/or PP, Certified Paralegal Professional.

§ 3.3.2 Getting the Job Done

Much of the work in a law office is performed under tremendous pressure. Meeting deadlines is a way of life for lawyers and for their support staff. The nature of the legal business is such that emergencies are not uncommon, and times arise when there is simply too much to do.

§ 3.3.3 Establishing Priorities

You can eliminate some of these pressures by handling your routine duties in an efficient, orderly manner. Establish priorities for work to be done and do your best to have things completed before the last minute. Supplies, frequently used telephone numbers and addresses, and reference tools should be kept within easy access.

§ 3.3.4 Keeping an Organized Work Area

A good lawyer's assistant will accept responsibility for keeping the secretarial work area, as well as the lawyer's area, neat and orderly. The lawyer's assistant should check before straightening or reorganizing the attorney's desk. Some lawyers prefer that the lawyer's assistant not clean their desk while others enjoy having someone straighten it up for them. If the lawyer's assistant is also serving as the receptionist, the reception area should also be kept in order. A neat work area promotes efficient work. Files should be replaced in cabinets when they are no longer needed, and law books should be returned to the library.

§ 3.3.5 Meeting Clients

At the initial visit to see the lawyer, a client generally has not yet had the opportunity to know the lawyer personally. The client may have been referred by a friend or by a lawyer referral service or may have even selected the lawyer's name randomly from a directory. The client's first impression of what to expect from the lawyer is reflected through the lawyer's staff. Be sure your professional attitude reflects the good public image the lawyer deserves.

Give your full attention to the client and remember that the client's time is just as valuable as the lawyer's. Make every effort to see that appointments are kept as near to the scheduled time as possible. If the lawyer is going to be late for appointments, call the client or inform the client immediately upon arrival that the lawyer is running late so that the client can be doing something else until the lawyer is available. The client may choose to wait or to reschedule the appointment. When the choice is to wait, make the client feel comfortable by offering a beverage, magazine or newspaper, and, if possible, use of a telephone.

Before the lawyer is ready to see the client, be sure that you locate the file and make it available for the lawyer's use during the conference. Escort the client to the lawyer's office, introduce the client to the lawyer, and close the door as you leave. Further, you should be available during the course of the conference to provide the lawyer with any other materials needed or to perform any services requested. You should know the client's name and be familiar with the nature of the case. Knowing this information indicates that the client is important to you, the attorney, and your law firm. Never allow your personal feelings toward the client to affect your business relationship. The client deserves to be treated courteously at all times and should feel that you, as the lawyer's assistant, care about the client's case.

Avoid interrupting the lawyer and the client during the allotted appointment period; the client is paying for the lawyer's time and should not have to share it.

If it is absolutely necessary to interrupt the meeting, you may either call the attorney in the conference room or office, or you may write the message on a note, knock gently on the door, enter and hand the attorney the note. Wait briefly to see what the attorney would like you to do and leave quietly. The best practice is to talk with your attorney at the beginning of your employment to find out the attorney's preferences and when it is appropriate to interrupt.

§ 3.3.6 Confidentiality

A client demands and is entitled to complete confidentiality in all matters which are disclosed to the lawyer or with which the lawyer or staff may come in contact. There can be no compromise on this subject. It is unethical, as well as in poor taste for employees to engage in gossip regarding the affairs of clients.

§ 3.3.7 Privileged Communications

A lawyer is a fiduciary (a person who manages money and property for another), and the relationship with clients is one of trust and confidence. The attorney never discusses a client's business with outsiders. In fact, statements made between the lawyer and the client are protected from forced disclosure to other parties. The information a client gives the lawyer is considered privileged communications, and any work done on behalf of the client is protected under attorney-client privilege.

Lawyer's assistants are bound by the same code of ethics as their employer. You cannot solicit business for attorneys or law firms; you must regard everything about a client or a case as confidential. Information the lawyer's assistant receives from a client in the course of work is also a privileged communication. Serious consequences may result from discussing facts pertinent to a case, revealing information concerning a legal matter, or discussing a client's personal matters.

It is mandatory that the lawyer's assistant not discuss office or client business outside the confines of the office. If a lawyer's assistant is to be trusted—and a lawyer's assistant must be trustworthy—confidentiality must be maintained at all costs.

If your employer calls you into the office to pick up a file and then starts discussing a case with you, be sure you go over and close the door. Also, it is easy to fall into the habit of discussing client affairs when you are in a room or hallway away from the reception area, and you should remember that anyone could be standing within hearing distance. Do not talk to a client on the telephone about the details of the client's case if you are sitting in an area where other people can hear your side of the conversation.

It is also important not to state to outsiders, including family members and friends, that a certain person was in the office or is a client. From that simple statement, they could draw conclusions that would make you guilty of a breach of confidentiality.

The lawyer's assistant should never discuss the client's matter with the client while in the presence of other people. Even when alone with the client, the lawyer's assistant should not discuss the case beyond lending an attentive ear and offering some words of reassurance, unless specifically authorized otherwise to do so by the lawyer in charge of the case.

You should not give clients information regarding their cases without authorization from the lawyer. Some offices make a practice of sending copies of all letters and legal documents relating to a client's case to the client. Others send only copies of certain letters and documents. The best practice is to talk with your attorney upon employment and find out what your attorney wishes you to handle with respect to copying and sending out copies of correspondence and documents to clients. Attorneys expect their assistants to use judgment in handling routine matters and in notifying the attorney when correspondence or documentation seems to warrant special handling.

Too many assistants presume that if they do not directly and intentionally tell someone about a client's case, they have not breached the confidentiality code. The trusted lawyer's assistant must go beyond that and not indirectly or inadvertently convey information to another person about the affairs of a client. The lawyer's assistant who is completely trustworthy and who adheres to the ethical guidelines set forth by the NALS Code of Ethics and Professional Responsibility will advance in the legal profession.

§ 3.3.8 Privacy of Client Files

If you are in an area where clients and persons who do not work on your clients' matters approach your desk and have conversations with you, be sure that you do not have any open files or documents on your desk. Human nature is such that people will allow their eyes to wander to whatever is available. If you are waiting to have a document signed, keep it in a file folder. If you are working on a document when someone approaches your desk, cover the material so that it cannot be read easily by the person standing there.

The legal assistant must have the attorney's permission to show a file to a client. It is usually permissible to remove personal publicly-filed papers such as a marriage certificate or IRS tax form prepared and signed by the client and let the client review these papers in your presence. The client should not have access to documents, letters, notes, or work products of the lawyer without the lawyer's permission. The client should never remove anything from the office without prior consent of the lawyer. It is good practice to establish a policy with the lawyer concerning the dissemination of information to clients and others. When in doubt, do not allow the client to look through the file.

§ 3.3.9 Grooming and Appearance

The impression created by the appearance of the legal support staff is very important because it strongly influences how clients feel about the law firm. In the law office environment, the legal assistant's clothing should be conservative and business-like. The assistant does not need an extensive wardrobe as long as it is neat, clean, and suitable for the culture of the law firm. Conservative clothing is the key. Some assistants wear clothes which are too casual for the office. If the legal assistant looks pressed, tidy, clean, and professional, attorneys and clients will have more confidence in that employee. Good grooming is also of utmost importance. The use of scents and perfumed lotions should be minimal.

§ 3.3.10 Personal Habits

Since you are often with clients, lawyers, staff, and other members of the legal and general community, you must be careful not to allow personal habits to offend the people with whom you deal.

Two complaints that employers have about staff are related to chewing gum in an unattractive and distracting manner and smoking in the presence of clients. A good rule is to smoke only in designated smoking areas out of the view of clients. This problem is becoming eliminated since many, if not most, office buildings now prohibit smoking on the premises entirely.

Care should also be taken in the language used both in the office and in public. The language you feel free to use in your home may well be offensive to others. The use of profanity is absolutely prohibited. Also, be very careful about what jokes you tell. What may not be offensive to some, may certainly be offensive to others. When in doubt, do not tell them to anyone.

§ 3.3.11 Interoffice Relationships

The lawyer's assistant who approaches each morning's tasks with anticipation and enthusiasm will find life much more pleasant than the one who arrives ready just to "put in time" and then at 5 p.m. to wake up and start living. A large portion of the assistant's waking hours are spent in the office. More time may be spent with fellow employees and clients than with family. Relationships should be enjoyable for all involved, and it takes effort on everyone's part. A key component to good working relationships is the ability to be non-judgmental and recognize and respect others' beliefs, views and practices. The lawyer's assistant possessing this skill promotes better working relationships with co-workers, attorneys and clients.

§ 3.3.12 Loyalty

Loyalty cannot be dictated or decreed. Nevertheless, the primary function of office personnel is to further the business and prosperity of the employer, while serving the needs of the clients. The interests of the employer must come first—ahead of the interests of the personnel. The employer should always be referred to with terms of respect, and every lawyer's assistant should be a one-person publicity campaign for the office. Complete and absolute confidence in the employer's ability should be reflected in the assistant's personal conduct and in the performance of duties. If you cannot give loyalty to your employer, it is in your best interest as well as for the attorney or law firm, for you to find employment elsewhere. Do not discuss your employer's foibles, idiosyncrasies, or personal life with other people. Do not downgrade the employer or your job. Talking disparagingly about your employer or the legal profession is not suitable party conversation, and it is definitely not professional.

Every employee in a law office has a part in the firm's public relations. If people are to have faith and confidence in a law firm, they must have faith and confidence not only in the lawyers, but also in the support personnel who work there. It is at the level of day-to-day contacts with clients or prospective clients (everyone is a prospective client) that the greatest opportunities for good public relations exist. All law office personnel should bear this in mind at all times.

§ 3.3.13 Tact

A good lawyer's assistant uses tact in relationships with office personnel and clients. Tact is defined as "a quick or intuitive appreciation of what is fit, proper, or right; and a fine or ready mental discernment shown in saying or doing the proper thing, or especially in avoiding what would offend or disturb." Tact is a learned skill that becomes habit. Its elements consist of sensitivity to the feelings of others, insight into the motives of others, experience as to consequences of conduct, and subtlety of reasoning with reference to detail. Tact is a requirement in the practice of law and in the efficient operation of a law office. It cannot be overrated and is a quality that is required of all personnel.

§ 3.3.14 Sense of Humor

A sense of humor is a great asset to the lawyer's assistant. It helps in handling people and in interoffice relationships. Do not permit yourself to get emotionally involved in the cases of the office. Treat other members on the staff respectfully. Be cooperative, helpful, and thoughtful.

§ 3.3.15 Evenness of Disposition

Evenness of disposition and personality are distinct business assets and are qualities that are required in lawyer's assistants. In the office just one mood should prevail—cheerfulness. Minor irritations should be shrugged off and not be allowed to interfere with efficient work. Just as you leave all affairs of the office at the office, leave personal affairs at home.

§ 3.3.16 Pleasant Personality

Be pleasant to everyone. If your workload is light and you know someone else is getting behind, offer to help. Do not form cliques within an office. This behavior is extremely bad for morale and a detriment to the firm. If there is one person with whom you simply cannot get along, avoid that person as much as possible, but do not try to turn others against that person. As long as that person is working smoothly within the firm's structure, you must not be critical. Remember, by criticizing others, you are inviting criticism of yourself.

Sometimes you may find that other employees are not completing work assignments, talking excessively on the phone, coming into work late or leaving early, or performing low quality work. If what other employees do impacts your work, you should talk to the person about their behavior. If what they are doing does not have a direct impact on you, you should leave it to your office manager or attorneys to talk to that person. If you have discussed a problem with a coworker and the problem persists, then the next step is to tell the person that you will need to talk to the office manager or attorney about the problem if it continues. Then, and only then, should you bring the situation to the office manager's or attorney's attention. This is following the chain of command procedure and is the professional manner of handling problems of this nature.

In your relationships with other employees, maintain a friendly, helpful attitude but not to such a degree that it affects the efficient progress of your duties. Personal conversation can get out of hand and consume too much of the time which should be spent attending to the business of the firm.

No edict concerning interoffice gossip is enforceable. However, you are expected to use sound discretion and good judgment in this regard at all times. Remember, gossip and rumor cannot be reinforced if there is no one to listen to or repeat them. Interoffice problems must not extend out of the office or influence the efficient conduct of business.

You are not required to socialize with other office personnel, but you should be sociable. Courtesy takes no more energy than sullenness and is infinitely more pleasant for everyone. Do not exhibit or even have a "that's not my job" attitude.

§ 3.3.17 Punctuality

Punctuality is one of the traits lawyers look for in an assistant. Habitual tardiness is a trait that seems to flow over to other areas, and a busy law office cannot tolerate a lawyer's assistant who does not discipline time. Tardiness, long lunches, and a habit of leaving early place a tremendous burden on your employer and coworkers.

§ 3.3.18 Confidence

The lawyer's assistant should demonstrate confidence to clients, attorneys and coworkers. It is unnerving for a client to feel that the lawyer's assistant is uninformed or blundering along. The beginning lawyer's assistant should act confident, even if not feeling confident. The lawyer's assistant should not say "I don't know" or "I'm not sure." The better response, "Let me check on that" or "I'll find out for you," demonstrates a caring, confident attitude. Then the lawyer's assistant should check with whomever is appropriate and get back to the client or other person as soon as possible. When the lawyer's assistant consistently acts in this manner, others see the "can do" attitude and know that the legal assistant is trustworthy and confident.

§ 3.3.19 Handling Personal Matters

All personal telephone calls and personal business should be taken care of on the assistant's own time. If personal telephone calls or personal business of an urgent nature must be taken care of during office hours, they should be handled so as not to interfere with the smooth and efficient operation of the office. Discretion and common sense should dictate the course of the assistant's conduct in this regard. Keep foremost in mind the job, its duties, and the fact that you are in a business office, and there will be no problems with abuse of this privilege.

§ 3.3.20 Addressing the Lawyer

In all conversations with the lawyer in the presence of any third person and all times over the telephone and while outside the confines of the office, the lawyer is to be addressed as "Mr. ______ or Ms. ______." The law office is a place of business and the lawyer should be treated with respect. If it is the custom in your office to address the other personnel, including lawyers, by their first names, it is certainly permissible and proper to do so. However, this is not proper or permissible when in the presence of outside people or clients unless you have been authorized to use first names with those people. In that instance, the use of first names is on a case-by-case basis. If in doubt, do not use first names.

The lawyer's assistant should learn to adjust to the moods, actions, and reactions of the lawyers and other members of the staff. Be considerate of other people's feelings. By making allowances for their perceived imperfections, you will find that they are willing to make allowances for yours.

§ 3.4 Lawyer's Assistant as a Receptionist

The necessary qualities of the receptionist are intelligence, a professional appearance, friendliness of manner suitable to the dignity of the position, courtesy, patience, resourcefulness, and attentiveness. The legal assistant must always keep in mind the lasting effect of first impressions and realize that a client's attitude may be largely influenced by the initial contact with the receptionist.

The receptionist should receive every caller courteously, give the caller prompt attention, and continue to give the person attention until the purpose of the visit is concluded. The receptionist should be as pleasant as is consistent with the efficient transaction of business and must not waste time by unnecessary visiting.

The receptionist should promptly announce the arrival of the client to the particular lawyer's assistant (or to the lawyer if that is office practice). This is essential, since it assures the client that business is being handled. The lawyer's assistant in turn immediately notifies the lawyer; if the lawyer is in conference and unavailable, the client is informed. The receptionist should make the client comfortable by offering a beverage and something to read.

Since the receptionist will be in constant contact with the public and under its scrutiny, it is expected that the desk and work area are neat at all times. The receptionist should practice good housekeeping habits to make sure that the reception area is a pleasant and comfortable place that portrays the professional image expected of law offices.

Many people visit lawyers for personal or financial problems and are often anxious, upset, and nervous. For some, it is their first visit to a lawyer, which only intensifies their anxiety. The pleasant, helpful attitude of the receptionist can do much to relieve the situation. The receptionist may need to comfort a tearful, distraught client and should arrange to have the person taken to a private area.

The receptionist should address and announce callers by titles such as Mr., Mrs., Ms., or Dr. If clients or callers are well known in the firm and have asked that you use first names, you may do so, but this should be at the request of the client.

Be conscious of reception room behavior. Take care to act professionally at all times. Personal grooming should take place in restrooms; reading personal-interest magazines and books and chatting with other employees about something you just bought during lunch should take place in the employees' rest or cafeteria area. Avoid engaging in personal conversations either in person or on the telephone in the reception area.

When making appointments, the receptionist or lawyer's assistant must be sure to get not only the client's name but also the client's telephone number. It is a good idea to make appointments for the lawyers tentative unless they are available to confirm the appointment. If a lawyer is out of the office, there is a good possibility that the attorney is meeting with a judge or a client. Encourage your lawyer to keep you informed of any scheduled appointments or hearings. The best practice is to check the attorney's calendar frequently during the day to make sure that no appointments were scheduled without your knowledge.

Always find out when your lawyer wants appointments scheduled. Some prefer to have no appointments until after 10 a.m., so that they can spend the first hours of the morning reading the mail, dictating, and giving instructions.

Another function of the receptionist is to know how long the lawyer will be away from the office. As the attorney is leaving, the receptionist or the legal assistant should ask the attorney about a return time and also remind the attorney of any scheduled appointments for that day or early the next day. This practice demonstrates teamwork between the attorney and receptionist and legal assistant and provides the team with the information needed to work effectively with clients and others.

A good receptionist will use judgment to determine which clients the lawyer will see without appointments, which should be seen by another lawyer, and which can be taken care of by someone else in the office such as the legal assistant or office manager. When a visitor comes into the office without an appointment, the receptionist should check with the lawyer or legal assistant to see if the visitor can be seen. If the attorney will not or cannot see the visitor, ask the attorney whether an appointment should be scheduled for this visitor. Then the receptionist should explain to the visitor in a non-irritating way that the attorney is unavailable, and if the visitor wants an appointment, follow the normal office procedure for scheduling appointments. It is always difficult when someone just "drops in" to see the lawyer for "a few minutes." The receptionist should always respond courteously, and it is also important to protect the lawyer from interruption when requested to do so. Note that salesmen are usually seen by the office manager, by appointment only.

§ 3.5 Lawyer's Assistant as a Notary Public

A notary public is a person authorized by law to administer oaths, take and certify depositions, and take acknowledgments of signatures on deeds, mortgages, liens, powers of attorney, and other instruments in writing. The lawyer's assistant may be requested by the employer to become a notary public. In this capacity, the legal assistant can notarize documents for clients of the law firm and others who request notarial services.

§ 3.5.1 Legal Requirements of a Notary Public

The position of notary public is one of great responsibility and is not to be considered lightly. The requirements vary from state to state but usually require a person to be a resident of the state for a stated period of time, to be 18 years of age or older, and to have good moral character. Some states administer examinations to applicants; others require only an application and a bond.

In the performance of your duties as a notary public, you should familiarize yourself with a number of the terms and practices to which you will be exposed. Read the material published by your state on the duties and limitations of a notary public in your area.

§ 3.5.2 Administration of Oath

The notary public administers an oath which is a solemn or official declaration by a person before a duly authorized official to the effect that the statements which the person has just made or is about to make are true.

§ 3.5.3 Affirmation

Affirmation is similar to an oath in meaning and importance but for religious reasons does not include an appeal to God or any supreme being.

§ 3.5.4 Affidavit and Declaration

An affidavit is a written statement sworn to as being true before a notary public or some other officer authorized to perform this function. The affidavit contains the certification of the notary public that the statement was sworn to (or affirmed) and signed in the notary's presence by the affiant (the person who is making the affidavit).

In some states and situations, a declaration may be used in place of an affidavit. A declaration does not need to be notarized and contains the language, "I declare under penalty of perjury under the laws of the state of ______ that the following is true and correct." A declaration is signed by the declarant and should include the name of the place where the declaration was signed. (Note that the term declaration can have other legal meanings.)

§ 3.5.5 Acknowledgment

An acknowledgment is required for some documents, such as deeds and mortgages, and consists of a statement that the person who signed the document (the signer) declared to and before the notary public that it was the signer who signed the document. On another signature line, the notary public then signs the acknowledgment and dates it the same day as the appearance of the signer.

§ 3.5.6 Proper Identification of Affiant

In order to perform the duties properly, the notary public must be familiar with the person who appears and is going to sign or must be presented with adequate means of identification establishing the identity of the person. The notary public must require such identification if the individual is not personally known. If adequate identification cannot be produced, the notary should refuse to take the acknowledgment. The notary public is also restricted in the performance of duties in that the notary cannot act in an official capacity in those instances in which the notary is personally involved or interested. The notary is also not permitted to function outside designated or appointed territorial limits. (Appointments are made for a county or counties or for the state, depending upon state law.)

§ 3.5.7 Necessity of Personal Appearance of Signer

The notary public should take no acknowledgments by telephone. The person whose signature is on the document and acknowledging such signature should appear personally to make the acknowledgment and/or sign the document. Where an oath is required (as in an affidavit), the notary should administer the oath, have the person sign in the presence of the notary, and then the notary should sign and affix a seal, if applicable. Some notaries are reluctant to go through the formality of the oath, but in those instances where the document reads "sworn to before me," or similar wording, it is essential that the notary perform this function.

The notary public can be liable for damages resulting from the notary public's improper performance of duties. Therefore, upon receiving the appointment of notary public, the notary should read all information relating to the duties and responsibilities which apply to a notary serving in that state's jurisdiction carefully.

It is not unusual for an affiant to ask a notary to backdate an acknowledgment. The date on which the instrument is acknowledged is the date which must appear on the acknowledgment. To do otherwise is illegal and could result not only in loss of the notary commission but also in a malpractice action against the law firm.

§ 3.6 Answering the Telephone

Often the first impression the client gets of a law firm comes from the voice of the person answering the telephone. If that voice is pleasant and the client hears a "smile," the impression will be a positive one. Unfortunately, not all assistants understand the value of this technique. Some assistants answer the phone in a very mechanical or impatient tone of voice, which makes the caller feel unwelcome. If you have a scowl on your face, you will probably have a scowl in your voice. It is a good practice for the legal assistant to hesitate a second before picking up the phone, smile, and then answer with a patient and relaxed voice. The professional legal assistant is able to do this consistently and treats each client with full attention, courtesy, and concern. Remember that the caller cannot see that you are talking to another client on another line or that you are rushing to get out an urgent document for filing before the court closes.

§ 3.6.1 Rules to Follow

Observation of good telephone courtesy will make your day as well as the client's more pleasant. Follow these rules in answering the phone:

- Use a pleasant, positive voice.
- Do not talk too quickly or too quietly.
- Take time to get the correct spelling of names and repeat phone numbers to make sure that you have written them correctly.
- Do not bang the receiver when you lay it down on your desk to get information.
- If you must leave your desk to get some information, place the person on "hold" so that the caller does not hear background conversations.
- Always ask the caller if you can place them on hold and, if you are transferring a call, let the caller know that you are going to transfer the call and to whom.
- Do not have gum or food in your mouth when you answer the phone.
- Make an effort to help the client without giving legal advice.
- Give the client an estimated time when you expect the lawyer but avoid being exact.
- Do not tell the client where the lawyer is (except when the lawyer is in court) unless specifically instructed otherwise by the lawyer on a case-by-case basis.
- Do not quote fees or discuss the client's case unless you have been instructed to do so by the lawyer in specific situations.

- Conclude a phone call with a friendly "thank you" or "good-bye."
- Use the telephone sparingly for personal calls.
- Be attentive and listen without interrupting.
- Talk quietly and calmly to clients that are upset.
- Avoid slang in your conversations.
- Convey courtesy, sincere interest, and understanding of the other person's point of view by your voice and words.

§ 3.6.2 Incoming Calls

Procedures for handling incoming calls vary in firms where there is a central receptionist, an operator, or direct dialing. In some firms, calls coming through the receptionist or operator are placed directly to the lawyer to minimize the amount of time the client must spend on the telephone. Some people resent having to go through more than one person to get to the lawyer.

In some firms, the calls are referred to the lawyer's assistant rather than placing them directly to the lawyer. The lawyer's assistant can then get any file the lawyer might need for the call or handle the call if the lawyer is unable to take it.

Most firms now have direct dial numbers for lawyers and staff as well as a general number that is answered by a receptionist or operator. Direct-dialed calls will usually ring three times at the lawyer's phone and, if not answered, automatically switch over to ring at the assistant's phone. If there is no answer by either of them, the caller will be placed into the "voice mail" system where the caller can leave a message or opt to press zero to speak with a receptionist or an operator. This gives the caller the opportunity to speak immediately to the person being called, leave a short or lengthy message in voice mail, or speak personally to another person.

§ 3.6.3 Screening Calls

Telephone etiquette suggests that calls be answered by the person to whom they are directed, and few lawyers have all calls screened as a normal procedure. There will be circumstances, however, when it is necessary to screen calls.

The receptionist or assistant must be careful not to be rude in an effort to determine who is calling. A simple "May I tell him who is calling?" or "May I ask who is calling?" is usually sufficient to obtain the name of the caller. By knowing in advance who is calling, the lawyer can get any information or file needed to handle the call in a minimum amount of time. When a call has been screened and the lawyer does not wish to take the call, you must be tactful in explaining the attorney is not available so the caller does not get the impression that the lawyer is "too busy" or that the client is not important to the lawyer. Immediately advise the attorney if the caller appears upset by being unable to speak with the attorney.

§ 3.6.4 Taking Messages

When the lawyer is in but does not wish to be disturbed by calls, the assistant or receptionist must use tact in relaying this information to the caller. Start by taking a complete message (name, phone number, time of call, and matter called about), then assure the client that the message will be given to the lawyer. Some lawyers are very good about returning calls; others are not. The assistant should keep a record of all calls coming in and messages given to the lawyer. NCR paper or carboned message pads are very useful for this purpose. It is helpful for the legal assistant to give one copy of the message to the lawyer and to keep the other copy at the desk for ready reference of phone numbers and callers.

§ 3.6.5 When the Lawyer Is Out of the Office

If the lawyer is out of the office, the assistant should not disclose the location of the attorney unless the attorney has given specific instructions otherwise. Most people are satisfied with a standard answer such as "The lawyer is in court"; "The lawyer is out of the office"; "The lawyer is in a meeting." Do not give a specific time when you expect the lawyer to return. As a rule, deal in generalities.

§ 3.6.6 Helping the Client

The client, however, does need to feel that you care and are concerned. Instead of just replying that the lawyer is not there, you might go on to ask if there is something that you can help with. If you know the nature of the problem, you can then evaluate whether you should attempt to contact the lawyer away from the office or refer the client's problem to another member of the firm.

With experience, you will learn which clients are persistent callers, which have genuine problems, and which just want a sympathetic listener. For the latter, you provide that sympathetic ear. You listen and make comments which are reassuring such as "I know Mr. Lawyer is concerned and is working on your case." "Yes, I understand how you feel. I will relay this information to Mr. Lawyer and ask him to get back with you."

Calls from any irate client should be transferred as quickly as possible to the lawyer. In the absence of the lawyer, you should listen and give the angry client an opportunity to clear the air; however, you should not permit this to go on and on. You have work to get done. Interrupt when you can and tell the caller calmly that you know how important this call is and that you will let the attorney know that the client called as soon as the attorney returns to the office. Make sure the attorney gets this message as soon as possible.

§ 3.6.7 Answering Promptly

All calls should be answered by the second ring whenever possible. If you are talking to a client, say "Excuse me" and answer the telephone. During office hours, there must always be someone available to answer the telephone; it must never be left unattended. The exception to this rule usually applies to firms that have a voice mail system for each employee. Learn to recognize voices; call clients by name except when other clients or lawyers outside your law firm are present as this may present a breach of confidentiality.

§ 3.6.8 When the Caller Is on Hold

When the caller has been placed on "hold," check back frequently and remind the lawyer if it is taking too long in answering the call. If it appears that the attorney is going to be talking for a while, ask the caller if it is possible to take a message and have the attorney call back. If you place the person on hold for a long period of time, the telephone lines are tied up and also it can be irritating for the caller.

§ 3.6.9 Calling Long Distance

Follow your firm's procedures for identifying client-chargeable long distance calls. These calls represent a substantial cost to the firm and should be promptly and carefully recorded. Many offices have telephone systems that require the caller to input the client/matter number prior to placing the call. Other law firms use handwritten logs which include the date, the phone number called, a brief description of the call, and the appropriate client/matter number for billing purposes.

§ 3.6.10 Conference Calls

Conference calls (a telephone conversation among more than two persons at the same time) can be initiated in three ways. Some in-house phone systems allow for the caller to keep adding persons to a conference call by pushing a button on the keypad, entering the added person's phone number, and pushing the conference call button again. There is also a way to "drop" a participant from a conference call, but this phone feature varies from system to system. Some in-house conference call phone systems only allow for the caller and two additional participants; some allow for six or more.

The second way to institute a conference call is to call a commercial telephone service carrier, provide them with the names and phone numbers of the participants, the approximate length of the call, and the date and time for the call. The carrier then, at the designated time, calls each participant individually and "adds" them to the call.

The third conference call method also utilizes a commercial service that works strictly with conference calls. The service is contacted and informed that a conference call needs to be arranged. It is advised of the date and time of the call, the number of participants, the approximate length of time for the call, and the individual's and firm's name who is initiating the call. The initiating caller is given a "call-in" telephone number (and sometimes a conference call code) that needs to be provided to each conference call participant.

Conference calls are time consuming to arrange, no matter what method is used. Each potential participant needs to be contacted ahead of time to ensure his or her availability. If using the third method, the participants need to be contacted again to inform them of the call-in number (and, if necessary, the conference call code). However, conference calls, in the long run, are very efficient and cost effective.

§ 3.6.11 Checking Time Zones

Be aware of time zones and check before placing a call to another area of the United States to be sure that the office will be open. It does no good to place a call from New York to California when it is 9 a.m. in New York. People in California are usually not in the office at 6:00 a.m. Most companies have an answering service, answering machine, or voice mail, so the call will be answered, and you will be charged for the call.

§ 3.6.12 Frequently Called Numbers

The lawyer's assistant should keep an accurate, up-to-date record of names, addresses, and phone numbers of clients and those persons who are not clients but with whom the firm does business. These can be kept in a card file, in a notebook, or on the assistant's computerized rolodex or contact list. It should include numbers of the courts, process servers, court reporters, insurance adjusters and agents, tax bureaus, office supply firms, home phone numbers of office employees, etc. This would also be a good place to note the lawyer's social security number and registration number as issued by the state supreme court.

§ 3.6.13 Placing Calls to Other Offices

Telephone etiquette suggests that calls be placed by the person actually making the call. However, some lawyers prefer not to follow this practice and have their assistants place their calls for them. Although you must follow the lawyer's instructions, you can encourage the attorney to place calls whenever possible by seeing that telephone numbers are readily available at the attorney's desk. If the lawyer prefers to have you place the call, put the attorney on the line as soon as you are being connected with the person you are calling. The person initiating the call should do the waiting, and you should be sure the lawyer is aware of any adverse reactions you receive from people who have been kept waiting.

§ 3.6.14 Importance of Telephone Etiquette

The telephone is the lifeline of the law office. It is the most important method of communication. If it is not answered correctly, this can create an unfavorable impression on clients, people in the legal community, and the general public. The assistant who has a positive attitude about this important function renders an invaluable service to the firm.

§ 3.7 Copying Equipment

A copying machine is an essential piece of equipment in law offices. The lawyer's assistant keyboards only the original and makes the necessary copies. Most courts permit copies to be used for originals. With the use of bond paper, the copy looks as good as the original; however, the signatures must be original.

There are too many types of copiers to describe here, but generally, the type(s) utilized by a firm might include only a few, or possibly all, of the following features:

- Automatic stapling.
- Duplex copying (double-sided copy).
- Color copies.
- Automatic tri-folding of brochures.
- Saddle binding (stapling along the binding or center of the folded-in-half booklet).
- Collating copies.
- Reduction or enlargement of originals.
- Oversized document copying.
- Automatic lightening/darkening of originals for clearer copies.
- Automatic two-hole and three-hole punching of copies.
- Creating an electronic copy in a file that can be electronically mailed (or e-mailed).

The decision on the type of copy equipment to purchase or lease and choice of specific features is dependent upon the size of the firm and its requirements and expectations of the equipment.

§ 3.8 Transcribing Equipment

Another essential piece of equipment found in law offices is the transcriber used for transcribing machine dictation. A transcriber is used to convert messages that have been dictated into written text. Some standard features of a transcriber include a headset, speech and volume modification, easy forwarding and rewinding, and a foot control (pedal).

§ 3.8.1 Dictation Equipment

Dictation equipment permits a person to originate documents much faster than by any other method. Dictating material to an assistant, who takes it down in shorthand and then transcribes it, requires the time of two persons for the dictation. If the originator hand writes the material, it is more time-consuming for the writer and is harder for the assistant to transcribe. Handwriting can be difficult to decipher, and mistakes can occur. Using machine dictation, the attorney can dictate whenever there is an opportunity without relying upon someone else to be available. When the assistant is transcribing from machine dictation, it is possible to catch errors as they are keyboarded.

Today, dictation equipment is of high quality and can be adapted to meet the needs of any office. An office that is using old equipment which is difficult to operate or not operating properly should consider updating to obtain maximum efficiency.

§ 3.8.2 Types of Dictation Equipment

Three basic categories of dictation equipment are desktop models, portable models, and central units. In addition, two types of technology—analog equipment and digital equipment—are available.

§ 3.8.3 Desktop Models

Desktop models are usually located at both the author's desk and the transcriber's desk. The author's unit provides for dictation and is equipped with a microphone; the transcriber's unit provides for transcription and is equipped with a headset and a foot pedal. Most desktop units use discrete media cassettes because cassettes are easy to handle and offer good sound quality.

§ 3.8.4 Portable Models

Portable models are used principally by persons who dictate while they are away from the office. They can be purchased in many sizes; some are small enough to fit into a shirt or coat pocket and weigh as little as five ounces. They are particularly valuable for persons who spend a lot of time in cars, planes, or remote locations, are useful for recording seminars and speeches, and are also useful in interviewing witnesses both away from the office and in the office. To accommodate the use of various sizes of dictation equipment, many companies offer transcribers which accept conventional-size cassettes and microcassettes by utilizing an adapter placed on the machine. This is cost-effective because the adapter costs less than a second transcriber, while offering the flexibility of two forms of input.

§ 3.8.5 Central Recording Systems

A central recording system is a dictation system with the recorder located in one main area, but with dictating and transcribing units in many locations. A few of the advantages to a central system, which are not available in a desktop unit, are:

- Many dictators can be accommodated at a low cost per unit.
- Input can be through the telephone or a desk microphone.
- Secured access is available with some systems.
- By use of a telephone system, one unit can record dictation by several persons, both inside and outside of the firm, without purchasing several dictation units.

§ 3.8.6 Analog Equipment

This is the type of equipment most of us are used to seeing and using. Analog equipment is basically a tape recorder and uses cassette tapes. Analog equipment is reasonably priced and is available in many sizes, from desktop units to wallet-size models. Standard-size audio cassettes or microcassettes are used with analog equipment.

§ 3.8.7 Digital Equipment

State-of-the-art centralized digital dictation systems record sound digitally, store it directly onto a computer's hard drive, and play back the voice file. With centralized digital equipment, dictation, such as record, stop, and rewind, is controlled by use of the telephone keypad. Hand held digital equipment looks much like a micro cassette recorder. It stores information on internal memory which can be downloaded to a computer hard drive and played back in a voice file. The author may be guided through the dictation process by voice prompts. Storage capacity, demands on usage, and number of phone lines necessary for link-up to the system are a few of the major factors to be determined before purchasing, centralized digital equipment.

§ 3.8.8 Special Features of Dictation Equipment

Whether purchasing an analog or a digital system, you need to investigate what special features may be available. The following sections will give you a general idea of just some of the options available with dictation equipment. Some of the features are available only on analog equipment, some on only digital equipment, and some on both.

§ 3.8.9 Automatic Measured Review

An automatic measured review is provided on many systems. The dictator can set the machine for one to nine words (usually four); after an interruption, the dictator can activate the unit to back up the desired number of words automatically. The automatic measured review is called Backspace on some transcription equipment.

§ 3.8.10 Conference Recording

The conference recording feature allows you to pick up all the voices in the room rather than minimizing background noise.

§ 3.8.11 Indexing

Some companies offer electronic indexing, which indicates by audible sound the end of the recording or special instructions from the dictator.

§ 3.8.12 Privacy Lockout

A privacy lockout is available for central systems. This ensures that material dictated by one individual is not heard by anyone queuing into the system after the dictator has finished. The sound head automatically moves forward and locks so that no one can access into that dictated material.

§ 3.8.13 Telephone Input

By using a telephone input system, the dictator can call into the system from any distance away from the firm. Material can be dictated at any hour of the day or night to be transcribed by the assistant while the dictator is away from the office. No media needs to be delivered from the dictator to the assistant.

§ 3.8.14 Voice Activation

Systems can be equipped with voice activation. These relays stop operation of the unit when the dictator is silent and reactivate the unit at the sound of a voice. This is particularly helpful when the dictator pauses to gather thoughts or to answer a phone call. Without it, the unit continues running and uses up valuable dictation space on the media.

§ 3.8.15 Selecting Dictation Equipment

The foregoing discussion of dictation equipment is not all inclusive as to what is available. Information on the numerous types and sizes of equipment, as well as storage media and equipment features, can be found through vendors or through the Internet. In determining which dictation equipment should be purchased by the firm, the amount and type of dictation should be considered. Perhaps a combination of systems would work best for the needs of the firm. The place of origination of documents should be considered. All offices should recognize that the quality of the input directly affects the quality of the output.

§ 3.9 Selecting Law Office Equipment

A person is able to produce better work on good quality equipment than on poor, inadequate equipment. It is an investment that will pay for itself many times over in the preparation of correspondence and documents, time saved, and quality of product produced. All equipment must be purchased or leased with a view toward its productivity value, cost-effectiveness, quality, serviceability, and potential down time. Many resources are available for finding suitable equipment on the Internet and by contacting reputable vendors and manufacturers.

§ 3.10 Office Supplies

The assistant is often responsible for ordering supplies and maintaining an inventory of supplies. The legal assistant can periodically visit local dealers to learn what is new on the market that would be an improvement over what the office is using. The office files should contain a list of local dealers with phone numbers and addresses. A word of caution—beware of phone solicitors offering to sell you office supplies at a large discount because of a closeout, a refused order, a bankrupt business, or an order that was sent to your area by mistake. The reasons they give for offering such savings are numerous, but when you receive your order, you may find that the supplies are old, stale, or defective.

A reputable supplier will work with you and replace defective merchandise. Do not order in quantities that are unrealistic for your firm. Discounts for buying in quantity are available, but you must be sure of the shelf life of the material purchased before you place a bulk order. You need to be cost-conscious.

An inventory should be kept in the supply area listing the minimum amount that is to be kept on hand so that more can be ordered to maintain that amount. New supplies should be placed behind older supplies so they will be used last. A well-organized supply area can save both money and time.

Following is a list of some of the stationery supplies used by law offices:

Letterhead is used for office correspondence. Full letterhead is engraved and states the firm's name, address, telephone and fax numbers, and the names of the individual members of the firm. Short letterhead is also engraved and states the firm's name, address, general and fax numbers, individual names of lawyers, direct dial phone numbers, and e-mail addresses. A high quality bond paper is used.

Continuation sheets (sometimes called second sheets) are of the same quality paper used for the letterhead. Although they do not have the letterhead on them, they may have the firm's name engraved or printed on them. These are used for additional pages of a letter.

Envelopes to match the letterhead are used for office correspondence.

Manila stock envelopes of various sizes are used to mail bulky documents that cannot or should not be folded.

Letter-size white paper, which may or may not be ruled, 8½″ × 11″, is used in most states for legal documents. This standard is set by the individual states. Federal courts require all pleadings to be on letter-size paper.

Legal cap is white paper with a wide ruled left margin (1¼″) and a narrow ruled right margin (½″). It is used for both legal and court documents. In some states, legal cap has numbers along the left margin corresponding to the line spaces of typing. Some firms have their legal cap printed with the firm's name, address, and phone number at the top directly to the right of the left-ruled margin or the lower left margin (to the left of left-ruled paper).

Legal-size paper, 8½″ × 13″ or 8½″ × 14″, unruled, is used in some states for court and legal documents. Some states use legal cap for court documents and unruled legal-size paper for legal instruments such as real estate contracts, agreements, powers of attorney, etc.

A heavier bond paper is used for preparing wills. Some firms have LAST WILL AND TESTAMENT engraved at the top for use as first pages and blank paper of the same quality for continuation pages. Will covers, with or without the firm name engraved, are used for binding wills. They are made of very heavy paper. Will envelopes are made of heavy stock and often have LAST WILL AND TESTAMENT engraved on them as well as DATE.

Manuscript covers are made of heavy colored paper and are used to bind legal instruments; in a few states court documents are also bound in them. Most states do not require any cover or backing on court documents since this takes up unnecessary room in the court file.

Legal backs, sometimes printed with the firm name, are used for binding legal instruments and court documents. They cover only the back of the paper and occasionally have a printed panel on the back to identify the document. The use of legal backs has become a rarity.

Legal pads are tablets of lined paper with a ruled margin. The lawyer's desk, briefcase, and conference table should be equipped with these at all times. They are used for making notes and writing longhand drafts. Legal pads come in 5″ × 7″, 8½″ × 11″, and 8½″ × 14″ sizes.

Law blanks are printed forms used by some offices when the majority of the information can be standardized. Blanks are left to fill in the variable information such as names, addresses, amount of money, dates, and property descriptions. Examples of law blanks would be summonses, deeds, bills of sale, promissory notes, standard forms of leases, and mortgages. These are usually carried by office supply stores or printers. Many offices keyboard or scan such forms into the computer, thus reducing the need for law blanks. Numerous software packages can be purchased from the courts, software companies, and other sources that provide forms for court documents, tax returns, real estate documents, immigration documents, copyright filings and many other types of documents.

Many organizational tasks in the law office require the use of dividers, labels, tabs, exhibit markers, and paper fasteners. Dividers can range from inexpensive color sheets of paper to expensive multi-color, heavy duty divider pages with tabs. If you are not familiar with the various supplies available, call your local vendor and ask for samples or do some research on the Internet to learn about the various styles available.

The other supplies maintained in a law office would be the same as those for any other office. What you order would depend on the systems of the firm.

§ 3.11 Handling Incoming Mail

The following are the steps in handling incoming mail:

1. Sort the mail into stacks of expedited and certified mail, first class letters, routine mail, and advertising and/or junk mail. Begin the processing of the mail with the expedited and certified mail.

2. Be careful when opening envelopes so that you do not slit material in the envelope.

3. Empty each envelope completely; check carefully to see that everything has been removed.

4. Fasten any enclosures to the letter. If the enclosures are small, they should be attached to the front of the letter; larger enclosures are attached to the back of the letter. If any enclosures mentioned in the letter are missing, make a note of this on the front of the letter.

5. Before destroying the envelope, check for two things:

   a. Be sure the return address and name of the sender are on the letter; if not, staple the envelope to the back of the letter.

   b. If the date of the letter is more than one day earlier than the postmark on the envelope, attach the envelope to the back of the letter. If delivery was delayed for any reason, also attach the envelope. If a certificate of mailing or affidavit of mailing states a date that is at variance with the postmark, keep the envelope.

6. Mend the letter or other contents of the envelope with tape if they have been damaged in the process of opening the envelope.

7. Date-stamp the letter with the date the letter is received. Also date-stamp copies of documents received from other lawyers, but be careful not to date-stamp any original document (other than letters).

8. Read through the letter, underlining or highlighting important points, especially dates. It is advisable to highlight a working copy of the letter so that the original maintains its appearance. This method saves the lawyer time because only a review of the letter is necessary. Enter any important dates in your calendar and the lawyer's calendar. Also, inform the person responsible for the firm's docket control system of all pertinent dates.

9. Do not open mail marked "Personal and Confidential" or any other mail that is obviously personal.

§ 3.11.1 Preparing Outgoing Mail

Procedures for handling outgoing mail vary greatly. Large firms often have a central mail department. In other firms, the receptionist prepares all mail for the post office. In small firms, this is often the responsibility of the lawyer's assistant.

Each lawyer's assistant should be responsible for folding and inserting the correspondence prepared into the envelopes. Being familiar with the letter and enclosures, the legal assistant will be aware that the right material gets into the right envelope. Take the time and care not to mix up the letters, enclosures, and envelopes. Such a mix-up can be very embarrassing to the lawyer and can result in divulging confidential information.

The lawyer's assistant should be familiar with the classes of mail and the services available through United States Postal Service (USPS) and other express mail services such as FedEx, DHL, and United Parcel

Services (UPS). In the following sections are discussions of the various classes of domestic mail. In addition, USPS has a great deal of information available to the public on the Internet at www.usps.com. All classes of mail are thoroughly discussed, and an automated rate calculator is available to assist the lawyer's assistant in determining the type of service to use and the associated fees.

1. Express Mail
2. Priority Mail
3. First–Class Mail
4. Standard Mail
5. Periodicals
6. Package Services

§ 3.11.2 Express Mail

Many law offices use Express Mail Next Day Service, Express Mail International Service, Custom Designed Services, and Express Mail Drop Shipment and Reshipment Services. Express Mail provides delivery service 365 days a year. Express Mail packaging supplies (envelopes, boxes, tubes) are available for free from your local post office. Express Mail rates are based on the weight of the piece, without regard for how far the piece travels; however, there is also a flat rate envelope fee for anything mailed in the special flat rate envelope provided by the USPS, regardless of weight. A list of the cities in which these services are available and rates can be obtained from the post office. This type of service is particularly useful when you are trying to meet a deadline.

Several commercial courier services offer next day mail delivery. These couriers include, but are not limited to, United Parcel Service, FedEx, and DHL.

§ 3.11.3 First–Class and Priority Mail

First–Class Mail consists of letters, postcards, greeting cards, business reply mail, bills, and checks. In fact, certain items must be mailed by First–Class Mail. These items include handwritten or typewritten material, bills, statements of account or invoices, credit cards, personal correspondence, personalized business correspondence (a handwritten letter to your customer) and all matter sealed or otherwise closed against inspection. First–Class Mail that weighs more than 13 ounces is handled as Priority Mail.

Priority mail provides air mail service for First–Class Mail weighing over 13 ounces and under 70 pounds. For law offices, this is a valuable service. Briefs, depositions, and lengthy documents can all be sent by priority mail for faster service. The maximum length and girth combined is 108 inches. The rate is determined by the distance the letter is to travel and by the weight of the letter. It is very easy to determine the actual fee by using the Rate Calculator feature at the USPS website. Priority Mail can be insured, registered, certified, or sent COD for an additional charge.

§ 3.11.4 Standard Mail, Periodicals, and Package Services

Standard Mail (also known as Bulk Mail) is used primarily by retailers, catalogers, and other advertisers who have large mailings. The types of material that can be sent by Standard Mail are printed matter, flyers, circulars, advertising, newsletters, bulletins, and catalogs, and small parcels. Churches and other eligible nonprofit organizations can also apply to the Postal Service for the use of nonprofit rates (Nonprofit Standard Mail) for large mailings. These mail classifications require a minimum of 200 pieces or 50 pounds for each mailing, and each piece of mail must weigh less than 16 ounces. Standard Mail also includes rates that anyone can use to mail individual parcels that weigh less than one pound.

Periodicals Mail is designed for newspapers, magazines, and other periodical publications whose primary purpose is transmitting information to an established list of subscribers or requesters. There are certain constraints for using this service and a formal application must be submitted along with a fee.

Package Services includes parcel post, bound printed matter, media mail, and library mail. Parcel post is used for mailing merchandise, books, circulars, catalogs, and other printed matter. Bulk rates are available for large quantities of parcel post mail. Bound printed matter includes advertising, promotional, directory, or editorial materials (or any combination of such material).The minimum quantity is 300 pieces. Media Mail is most often used for books, film, printed music, printed test materials, sound recordings, play scripts, printed educational charts, loose-leaf pages and binders consisting of medical information, and computer-readable media. Library Mail is used by libraries, schools, zoos, and research facilities.

§ 3.11.5 Certificate of Mailing

This is a receipt issued by the Postal Service which shows evidence of mailing. It can only be purchased at the time of mailing and is used with First–Class mail, Priority Mail, Parcel Post, Bound Printed Matter, and Media Mail. Insurance coverage and proof of delivery are not provided with this certificate.

§ 3.11.6 Registered Mail

When sending money and valuable papers such as stocks, bonds, or bids, registered mail is often used. Registered mail is the most secure mail service provided by the USPS and is used with First–Class Mail or Priority Mail. Additional fees are required for return receipt and restricted delivery services. Insurance on registered mail can also be purchased. The current limits are $25,000 for domestic registered mail; $1,000 for registered mail to Canada; and $40.45 for all other foreign countries. The return receipt can only be signed for by the addressee and shows the date and address of delivery.

§ 3.11.7 Restricted Delivery

This service is provided for an additional fee. It ensures that the sender's mail is delivered only to a specific addressee or a person authorized in writing to receive the addressee's mail. However, restricted mail can be delivered to an agent without the addressee's written authorization if it is addressed to officials of government agencies, members of the legislative and judicial branches of federal and state governments, members of the diplomatic corps, minors, and individuals under guardianship. This service is available only for First–Class Mail, Priority Mail, Parcel Post, Bound Printed Matter, and Media Mail that is sent certified mail, COD, mail insured for more than $50, or registered mail.

§ 3.11.8 Certified Mail

Certified mail is used for First–Class Mail or Priority Mail for which proof of delivery is desired. No insurance is provided, but this service enables the mailer to have a receipt as evidence that the material has been mailed and, for an extra fee, receive a card (return receipt) which shows that the mail was received or picked up by either the addressee or the agent of the addressee. It is also possible to stipulate that the letter be given to only the addressee and for the return receipt to show the address of delivery. This receipt is also known as a "green card." *See* the following illustration for an envelope, receipt, and return receipt. Law offices use certified mail a great deal, and the lawyer's assistant should keep the necessary forms nearby in the desk.

COLVIN, MASON & NORMAN
Attorneys at Law
3005 East Skelly Avenue
Tulsa, OK 74106-6864

CERTIFIED

P 555 938 003

MAIL

RETURN RECEIPT REQUESTED

MRS JON WILKINSON
222 MASON AVENUE
RIGBY ID 83221-1234

This illustration shows the front of the envelope which has been prepared for certified mail, return receipt requested.

Is your RETURN ADDRESS completed on the reverse side?

SENDER:
- Complete items 1 and/or 2 for additional services.
- Complete items 3, 4a, and 4b.
- Print your name and address on the reverse of this form so that we can return this card to you.
- Attach this form to the front of the mailpiece, or on the back if space does not permit.
- Write *'Return Receipt Requested'* on the mailpiece below the article number.
- The Return Receipt will show to whom the article was delivered and the date delivered.

I also wish to receive the following services (for an extra fee):
1. ☐ Addressee's Address
2. ☐ Restricted Delivery

Consult postmaster for fee.

3. Article Addressed to:
MRS JON WILKINSON
222 MASON AVENUE
RIGBY ID 83221-1234

4a. Article Number
P 555 938 003

4b. Service Type
☐ Registered ☒ Certified
☐ Express Mail ☐ Insured
☐ Return Receipt for Merchandise ☐ COD

7. Date of Delivery

5. Received By: *(Print Name)*

6. Signature: *(Addressee or Agent)*
X

8. Addressee's Address *(Only if requested and fee is paid)*

Thank you for using Return Receipt Service.

PS Form **3811**, December 1994 Domestic Return Receipt

This illustration is the return receipt card which is attached to the back of the envelope. This card will show the signature of the person delivered to and the date of delivery.

UNITED STATES POSTAL SERVICE

First-Class Mail
Postage & Fees Paid
USPS
Permit No. G-10

• Print your name, address, and ZIP Code in this box •

COLVIN MASON & NORMAN
3005 EAST SKELLY AVENUE
TULSA OK 74105-6864

This illustration shows the reverse side of the return receipt card, which is returned to your office acknowledging proof of delivery.

P 555 938 003

US Postal Service
Receipt for Certified Mail
No Insurance Coverage Provided.
Do not use for International Mail *(See reverse)*

Sent to MRS JON WILKINSON	
Street & Number 222 MASON AVENUE	
Post Office, State, & ZIP Code RITBY ID 83221-1234	
Postage	$
Certified Fee	
Special Delivery Fee	
Restricted Delivery Fee	
Return Receipt Showing to Whom & Date Delivered	
Return Receipt Showing to Whom, Date, & Addressee's Address	
TOTAL Postage & Fees	$
Postmark or Date	

PS Form **3800**, April 1995

Stick postage stamps to article to cover First-Class postage, certified mail fee, and charges for any selected optional services *(See front)*.

1. If you want this receipt postmarked, stick the gummed stub to the right of the return address leaving the receipt attached, and present the article at a post office service window or hand it to your rural carrier *(no extra charge)*.
2. If you do not want this receipt postmarked, stick the gummed stub to the right of the return address of the article, date, detach, and retain the receipt, and mail the article.
3. If you want a return receipt, write the certified mail number and your name and address on a return receipt card, Form 3811, and attach it to the front of the article by means of the gummed ends if space permits. Otherwise, affix to back of article. Endorse front of article **RETURN RECEIPT REQUESTED** adjacent to the number.
4. If you want delivery restricted to the addressee, or to an authorized agent of the addressee, endorse **RESTRICTED DELIVERY** on the front of the article.
5. Enter fees for the services requested in the appropriate spaces on the front of this receipt. If return receipt is requested, check the applicable blocks in item 1 of Form 3811.
6. Save this receipt and present it if you make an inquiry.

PS Form **3800,** April 1995 *(Reverse)*

This is the portion of the receipt which you keep for your file.

§ 3.11.9 Insured Mail

You can purchase insurance against loss or damage up to $5,000 for First–Class, Priority, Parcel Post, Bound Printed Material, and Media Mail. For materials insured for more than $50, a delivery receipt is signed by the recipient and filed at the delivery post office. Items cannot be insured for more than their value, and Insured Mail must be presented to a retail employee at a post office or to a rural carrier.

§ 3.11.10 Additional Postal Information and Services

Additional information regarding preparation of mail and other mail services provided by the United States Postal Service can be obtained from your local post office or by writing to Consumer Advocate, U.S. Postal Service, 475 L'Enfant Plaza SW, Room 5821, Washington, DC 20260–2200. The name of the publication is "Consumer's Guide to Postal Services and Products." Information about domestic and international mail services as well as postage calculators can be found on the web at www.usps.com.

§ 3.11.11 Preparing Documents for Mailing

1. When inserting letters into envelopes, verify that the letter has been signed, that all enclosures are included, and that all items are being placed in the proper envelope. If a document accompanies the letter, make sure that the lawyer has signed the document as well as the correspondence.

2. Sort mail by class, and separate mail which requires special handling, such as certified mail.

3. Weigh letters that you feel may be overweight, and mark the correct postage in the upper right-hand corner.

4. Run the regular first-class mail through the postage meter if the office uses a meter. Reset the meter for the postage required on the overweight letters.

5. Ascertain the proper postage for letters requiring special handling, and affix the postage to the letter or run it through the meter.

6. Determine weight and postage for the other classes of mail.

7. If a piece of mail is a combination of classes, make proper notations on it and check to see that proper postage is affixed.

§ 3.11.12 Electronic Mail

Electronic mail or e-mail is possible through communications equipment instead of lengthy long distance telephone calls or slow mail delivery. Messages or documents can be sent almost instantaneously from one communications device to another, both within the office or to offices down the street or around the world. The efficient lawyer's assistant will be able to add and delete names from e-mail address lists, attach files to an e-mail, sort e-mails into folders and use the various features that are found in most e-mail software. E-mail is extremely popular for sending drafts of documents since it is fast and is not subject to postage. Your law firm will provide an electronic mail account and addresses for you.

§ 3.12 Law Office Filing

Not only is it important to file materials promptly, but it is also important to file using the correct rules. The following is a summary of filing rules.

I. ALPHABETIZING UNIT BY UNIT

File first units letter by letter (alphabetically). Consider second units only when first units are identical. Consider additional units when the first two units are identical.

EXAMPLES:

Name	Unit 1	Unit 2	Unit 3
Allison	Allison		
Barrymore	Barrymore		
Computer Data Association	Computer	Data	Association
Computer Input Association	Computer	Input	Association

II. NOTHING COMES BEFORE SOMETHING

A single letter comes before a name that begins with the same letter. A one word name comes before a name that consists of the same word plus one or more words. A two or more word name comes before a name that consists of the same two or more words plus another word.

EXAMPLE 1:

Name	Unit 1	Unit 2	Unit 3
K	K		
Kathleen	Kathleen		
Kelly	Kelly		

EXAMPLE 2:

Name	Unit 1	Unit 2	Unit 3
Diversified	Diversified		
Diversified Consultants	Diversified	Consultants	
Diversified Manufacturers	Diversified	Manufacturers	
Diversified World Consultants	Diversified	World	Consultants

III. DECIDING WHICH NAME TO USE

The Association of Records Managers and Administrators (ARMA) suggests filing "under the most commonly used name or title." For example, given the choice between American Telephone & Telegraph Co. and AT & T, most people would file under AT & T. In these situations, always make a cross-reference card for the alternative name and refer to the law firm's office manual on filing procedures for the firm's preference.

IV. PERSONAL NAMES

Each part of the name of a person should be treated as a separate unit in the order of last name, first name, and middle initial. Any punctuation following the name or within an abbreviation should be ignored.

EXAMPLES:

Name	Unit 1	Unit 2	Unit 3
Brown	Brown		
G. Brown	Brown	G	
G. Mary Brown	Brown	G	Mary
John Browning	Browning	John	
John G. Browning	Browning	John	G

Foreign names are filed the same way, if identifiable. Otherwise, they are filed as written and other possible names should be cross-referenced.

EXAMPLES:

Name	Unit 1	Unit 2	Unit 3
Kwon Joo Y	Kwon	Joo	Y
Alice K. Ng	Ng	Alice	K
Ng Keng Choan	Ng	Keng	Choan
Nguyen Truc Duc	Nguyen	Truc	Duc

In names with prefixes, ignore spacing, punctuation, and capitalization. Consider D', L', M', Mac, and Mc as spelled and ignore the apostrophes. Prefixes, such as de, De, La, Los, Saint, San, Santa, Santo, St., Ste., Van, Van di, are filed as spelled.

EXAMPLES:

Name	Unit 1	Unit 2	Unit 3
Ronald DeFosset	Defosset	Ronald	
Susan de Foxxe	deFoxxe	Susan	
Jane Mack	Mack	Jane	
James MacKay	MacKay	James	
Nancy MacKay	MacKay	Nancy	
Peter McKay	McKay	Peter	
William O'Hare	OHare	William	
Edward G. Sahaydak	Sahaydak	Edward	G
John Saint Clair	SaintClair	John	
Eddie Samuels	Samuels	Eddie	
John San Marco	SanMarco	John	
Kaye St. Clair	StClair	Kaye	
F.E. Ste. Joan	SteJoan	F	E

In names with hyphens, ignore the hyphen and consider it a single unit.

EXAMPLES:

Name	Unit 1	Unit 2	Unit 3
Jean-Luc Picard	Picard	JeanLuc	
Albert J. Smith	Smith	Albert	J
Susan Smith-Akins	SmithAkins	Susan	

In abbreviated nicknames or pseudonyms, treat the abbreviated part of a name as written out in its entirety.

When the nickname is used alone, treat it as a separate unit. If the name begins with "The," "The" is considered as the last unit.

EXAMPLES:

Name	Unit 1	Unit 2	Unit 3
Chas. J. Brown	Brown	Chas	J
Diamond Lil	Diamond	Lil	
B. J. Hunnicut	Hunnicut	B	J
The Jackson Five	Jackson	Five	The

Titles and suffixes are considered as a last unit to distinguish between persons with the same names. If the title is used with one part of the person's name, treat it as a first unit. A married woman's first name is used for filing purposes. Only consider the title if her first name is unknown and she uses her husband's name.

EXAMPLES:

Name	Unit 1	Unit 2	Unit 3
Dr. Ruth	Dr.	Ruth	
Dr. Mary Jones	Jones	Mary	Dr
Miss Mary Jones	Jones	Mary	Miss
Princess Diana	Princess	Diana	
Mrs. Jean Short	Short	Jean	Mrs
Mr. Mike Short	Short	Mike	Mr
Mr. Paul Toth	Toth	Paul	Mr
Mrs. Paul Toth	Toth	Paul	Mrs

For seniority terms, such as Jr., Sr., and degrees, the numeric precedes alphabetic; Arabic numbers precede Roman numbers; numbers are sequenced in numeric order; and endings in ordinal numbers are ignored.

EXAMPLES:

Name	Unit 1	Unit 2	Unit 3
John Smith 2d	Smith	John	2
John Smith 3d	Smith	John	3
John Smith III	Smith	John	III
John Smith IV	Smith	John	IV
John Smith Jr.	Smith	John	Jr
John Smith, M.D.	Smith	John	MD
John Smith, Mr.	Smith	John	Mr
John Smith, Ph.D.	Smith	John	PhD
John Smith, Sr.	Smith	John	Sr

V. ORGANIZATIONAL NAMES

In names of organizations, treat each word as a separate unit and in the order written. Ignore all punctuation. If the name is joined by a hyphen or a diagonal, treat it as a single unit.

EXAMPLES:

Name	Unit 1	Unit 2	Unit 3
Canadian Data Associates	Canadian	Data	Associates
Canadian Data Company	Canadian	Data	Company
Data Computer Enterprises	Data	Computer	Enterprises
Data Processing Incorporated	Data	Processing	Incorporated
Frank and Johnson	Frank	and	Johnson
Frank's Nursery	Franks	Nursery	
O'Hara's Foods	OHaras	Foods	
O'Hare Airport	OHare	Airport	
Smith–Jones Company	SmithJones	Company	
Smith/Jones Store	SmithJones	Store	

Prepositions, conjunctions, and articles are treated as separate units and are kept in the same order written. However, when "the," "a," or "an" are the first words in a name, treat the word as the last unit. (Note some file managers treat only the word "the" as the last filing unit, and the words "a" or "an" are kept in the same manner as written. Use cross-reference cards if there is any doubt about finding a file.)

EXAMPLES:

Name	Unit 1	Unit 2	Unit 3
A New Idea	New	Idea	A
Pen and Ink	Pen	and	Ink
The Trump Hotel	Trump	Hotel	The

Treat a compound expression written as one word or hyphenated as a single unit. If it is written with spaces, then treat it as a separate unit.

EXAMPLES:

Name	Unit 1	Unit 2	Unit 3
East India Company	East	India	Company
Eastwest Airlines	Eastwest	Airlines	
East–West Hotel	EastWest	Hotel	

When personal names are used in an organizational name, consider the name as written and ignore the punctuation.

EXAMPLES:

Name	Unit 1	Unit 2	Unit 3	Unit 4
Ray Bracy Company	Ray	Bracy	Company	

Name	Unit 1	Unit 2	Unit 3	Unit 4
Ray Bracy, Jr., Associates	Ray	Bracy	Jr	Associates
S. Paul Jones Company	S	Paul	Jones	Company
S.R. Stover Flowers	S	R	Stover	Flowers
Sarah Ann Caterers	Sarah	Ann	Caterers	
Sarah J. Holms Inn	Sarah	J	Holms	Inn

When a prefix is used in a personal name that is part of a business name, do not treat the prefix as a separate unit.

EXAMPLES:

Name	Unit 1	Unit 2	Unit 3	Unit 4
D. de La Vega Homes	D	deLaVega	Homes	
D. D'Ellio Store	D	DEllio	Store	
Simon Saint James Hotel	Simon	Saint	James	Hotel
Simon Sinclair Agency	Simon	Sinclair	Agency	
The Thomas John Inn	Thomas	John	Inn	The
Thomas–Mary Products	ThomasMary	Products		

Titles used in an organization's name are treated as a separate unit and as they are written. Punctuation is ignored.

EXAMPLES:

Name	Unit 1	Unit 2	Unit 3	Unit 4
Capt. Jim Tours	Capt	Jim	Tours	
Captain Tom Cruises	Captain	Tom	Cruises	
Ma Barker's Gun Shop	Ma	Barkers	Gun	Shop
Miss Tuffit's Dairy	Miss	Tuffits	Dairy	

An abbreviation is treated as a single unit exactly as it is written, and punctuation is ignored.

EXAMPLES:

Name	Unit 1	Unit 2	Unit 3	Unit 4
ABC Corp.	ABC	Corp		
Brown Hotel, Incorp.	Brown	Hotel	Incorp	
Brown Metals Inc.	Brown	Metals	Inc	
U S Condominiums, Inc.	U	S	Condominiums	Inc
U.S. Condominiums, Ltd.	US	Condominiums	Ltd	

Name	Unit 1	Unit 2	Unit 3	Unit 4
US Delivery Systems	US	Delivery	Systems	

Acronyms and call letters of radio and television stations are treated as single units.

EXAMPLES:

Name	Unit 1	Unit 2	Unit 3
ABC	ABC		
CBS	CBS		
NAACP	NAACP		
NBC	NBC		
WARM Radio Station	WARM	Radio	Station

When an ampersand (&) occurs in a name, it is treated as if it were spelled out.

EXAMPLES:

Name	Unit 1	Unit 2	Unit 3	Unit 4
A & G Company	A	and	G	Company
A&C Hardware	AANDC	Hardware		
AT&T	ATANDT			

Single letters are treated as separate units. If two or more letters in a sequence are written solid or connected by a hyphen or diagonal, the sequence is treated as a single unit.

EXAMPLES:

Name	Unit 1	Unit 2	Unit 3	Unit 4
A & C Books	A	AND	C	Books
A D T Rentals	A	D	T	Rentals
AAA	AAA			
ADW Pools	ADW	Pools		
A/P Farms	AP	Farms		
A–Z Caterers	AZ	Caterers		

Geographic names are treated as a separate unit, and hyphenated names are treated as single units. If the name begins with a prefix followed by a space or hyphen, consider the prefix and the following word as a single unit.

EXAMPLES:

Name	Unit 1	Unit 2	Unit 3	Unit 4
Grand Canyon Tours	Grand	Canyon	Tours	
Las Vegas Bank	LasVegas	Bank		
Los Angeles Realty	LosAngeles	Realty		
New Jersey Cement Co.	New	Jersey	Cement	Co
Wilkes–Barre Coal Mines	WilkesBarre	Coal	Mines	

Arabic and Roman numbers are considered separate units. Ordinal numbers are treated as if they were written 2, 4, and 9. Units that contain Arabic or Roman numbers precede units expressed in words. Units with Arabic numbers precede Roman numbers, and each sequence is arranged in numeric order.

EXAMPLES:

Name	Unit 1	Unit 2	Unit 3
20th Century Fox	20	Century	Fox
1492 Tour Company	1492	Tour	Company
IV Roman Outlets	IV	Roman	Outlets
AAA Travel Club	AAA	Travel	Club
AFL–CIO Local 124	AFLCIO	Local	124
AFL–CIO Local 130	AFLCIO	Local	130

Units that contain numbers written in words are sequenced in alphabetical order. When a hyphen is used in the number, ignore the hyphen and treat it as one unit.

EXAMPLES:

Name	Unit 1	Unit 2	Unit 3	Unit 4
Sixth Avenue Movies	Sixth	Avenue	Movies	
Twelve Fourteen Rental Co.	Twelve	Fourteen	Rental	Co
Twenty–First Century Stores	TwentyFirst	Century	Stores	
The Western 200 Club	Western	200	Club	The
The Western Hotel	Western	Hotel	The	

When the phrase consists of a number linked by a hyphen or diagonal to a letter or word, the punctuation is ignored and is treated as a single unit.

EXAMPLES:

Name	Unit 1	Unit 2	Unit 3
1–A Delivery Service	1A	Delivery	Service
1/A Pizza Shop	1A	Pizza	Shop
7–Eleven Stores	7Eleven	Stores	

When the phrase consists of a figure plus a letter or word with any space or punctuation, treat it as a single unit.

EXAMPLES:

Name	Unit 1	Unit 2	Unit 3
A–1 Notary Service	A1	Notary	Service
Alice's 15–Minute Service	Alices	15Minute	Service
Alice's One–Hour Photo	Alices	OneHour	Photo

When a symbol appears with a number, treat the two elements as a single unit only if there is no space between the symbol and the number. Consider the symbol as if it were spelled out. When a dollar sign precedes the number, consider the number and then the word dollar or dollars in that order.

EXAMPLES:

Name	Unit 1	Unit 2	Unit 3	Unit 4
The $1 Store	1Dollar	Store	The	
50% Discount Outlet	50Percent	Discount	Outlet	
The 50+ Travel Club	50Plus	Travel	Club	The
The #1 Hair Salon	Number1	Hair	Salon	The

Alphabetize according to address when two organizational names are otherwise the same by city first, then by state.

EXAMPLES:

Name	Unit 1	Unit 2	Unit 3	Unit 4
Burger King, Adams, AL	Burger	King	Adams	Alabama
Burger King, Erie, ME	Burger	King	Erie	Maine
Burger King, Erie, OR	Burger	King	Erie	Oregon

If the state and city are the same, then consider the street name. If the street name is a number, treat it exactly as written.

EXAMPLES:

Name	Unit 1	Unit 2	Unit 3	Unit 4
Domino's 15th St. Bangor, ME	Dominos	Bangor	15	Street
Domino's 21st St. Bangor, ME	Dominos	Bangor	21	Street
Domino's Third St. Bangor, ME	Dominos	Bangor	Third	Street

If the street names are the same, alphabetize by direction if it is part of the street address.

EXAMPLES:

Name	Unit 1	Unit 2	Unit 3	Unit 4	Unit 5
Domino's N. 5th St. Bangor, ME	Dominos	Bangor	N	5	Street
Domino's S. 5th St. Bangor, ME	Dominos	Bangor	S	5	Street

If the names of the streets are identical, then consider the building number in numeric order.

EXAMPLES:

Name	Unit 1	Unit 2	Unit 3	Unit 4	Unit 5
Domino's 23 Coal St. Bangor, ME	Dominos	Bangor	Coal	Street	23
Domino's 39 Coal St. Bangor, ME	Dominos	Bangor	Coal	Street	39

VI. GOVERNMENTAL NAMES

The phrase "United States Government" is considered the first three units for any department of the federal government. The name of the department is considered next by moving the words "Department of" to the end. The office or bureau within the department is considered by moving the opening phrases, such as "Office of" and "Bureau of," to the end.

EXAMPLES:

Name	Unit 4	Unit 5	Unit 6	Unit 7
Office of Consumer Affairs	Consumer	Affairs	Office	of
Federal Bureau of Investigation	Federal	Bureau	of	Investigation
Food and Drug Administration	Food	and	Drug	Administration

(Note: Remember, the phrase "United States Government" is considered the first three units.)

For state and local governments, consider the distinctive place name first (except for educational institutions); then consider the individual; then department or bureau and moving the standard phrases as was done with the federal departments and bureaus.

EXAMPLES:

Name	Unit 1	Unit 2	Unit 3	Unit 4	Unit 5
Idaho Tax Division	Idaho	Tax	Division		
Iowa State Board of Labor	Iowa	State	Labor	Board	of
Water Department, City of Miami	Miami	City	of	Water	Department
Register of Wills, Miami County	Miami	County	Wills	Register	of

With foreign government names, first consider the name of the country, then the appropriate classification, and finally consider the name of the department or bureau.

EXAMPLES:

Name	Unit 1	Unit 2	Unit 3
Commonwealth of Australia	Australia	Commonwealth	of

Name	Unit 1	Unit 2	Unit 3
Republic of Austria	Austria	Republic	of
Kingdom of Belgium	Belgium	Kingdom	of
State of Israel	Israel	State	of

§ 3.12.1 Importance of File Management Systems

File management in the law office receives perhaps the least amount of attention, although it may be the most important of all clerical functions. Client files are the inventory and the memory of the law office, and they contain all work in process—a major asset of the firm. In addition, they often contain important client documents, as well as the work product of the firm, and are not always easily replaceable.

Regardless of its importance, however, file management is not popular. Assistants tend to put off filing because most find it tedious. It is equally difficult to convince law firms that both time and personnel must be allocated for adequate file management.

It is often the assistant's responsibility to develop a filing system to control the firm's files. Because it is such an important responsibility, it is necessary for the lawyer's assistant to understand the broad scope of a file management system for the law office.

§ 3.12.2 Definition of File Management

File management is the control of each file in your office from the time it is opened to the time that it is ultimately closed or destroyed. It is a crucial area of the law practice because handling a file efficiently, generally speaking, impacts on profitability. More important, effective file management provides many of the quality control mechanisms which are essential for ensuring that work is properly handled. Many malpractice claims are caused by poor file management.

§ 3.12.3 Ingredients for Successful File Management

File management includes much more than filing correspondence and documents in a file, although that is important. It also includes checking for conflicts of interest before the file is actually opened; ensuring that work in the file progresses in an orderly fashion by using a docket control system; ensuring that all deadlines are met, whether those deadlines are imposed by law or by a promise to the client; preserving new work products for future use; ensuring that anyone in the office can find the file or any correspondence or document that belongs in the file through centralized files control; closing the file once the work has been completed; and destroying the file once it serves no further useful purpose.

§ 3.12.4 Centralized and Decentralized Systems

The major categories of filing systems are centralized and decentralized. Under a highly formalized central filing system, files are removed only to be worked on and are returned to the filing cabinets at the end of each working day, regardless of whether there is still work remaining to be done. In a centralized system, there is also controlled access—no one can remove a file from the filing system without "signing out" for it. In a completely decentralized system, work originators maintain their own filing systems, store files in their own work areas, and otherwise have total responsibility and control of the files. Barcoding is often used in large law firms to track the location of files.

§ 3.12.5 Centralized Control and Decentralized Storage

While totally centralized systems work well in many corporate offices, such a centralized system is difficult to achieve in a law office. Most lawyers like to keep their most active files in their work areas for easy retrieval rather than returning them to the central file room at the end of the working day. Few totally centralized file systems are found in law firms.

Centralized control, not necessarily centralized storage, is important. It should be noted that centralized storage makes control easier. Assuming there is sufficient space, file storage in individual lawyer work areas is not usually a problem as long as there is centralized control. This means that regardless of where files are physically kept, there is a central *control system* to achieve maximum file efficiency and to maintain control. Although control is more difficult with decentralized storage, in most law firms such a compromise is necessary. Once lawyers gain confidence in the filing system, they soon become willing to turn the majority of their files over to centralized storage.

In most law firms, a centralized system means that files which are not being used frequently are kept in the active files area, usually a file room. In other words, there is a centralized storage area as well as centralized control, but lawyers and lawyer's assistants may store their files in their own work areas at their discretion.

§ 3.12.6 Importance of Effective File Control

Regardless of whether a firm has centralized storage or decentralized storage, central file control is essential to quality control. As a firm grows, it becomes more and more difficult, if not impossible, to maintain control with a decentralized system.

Since most firms tend to procrastinate in establishing controls, it is not unusual for the file function to get completely out of hand before the problem is addressed. Therefore, a lawyer's assistant who takes the initiative to develop a controlled system often makes the difference in whether or not the firm has control. While it is important to keep documents in a safe place, the most important criterion in judging the effectiveness of a file system is "findability."

§ 3.12.7 Classification of Files

In most firms there are several classifications of files. They include:

- *Active.* These constitute the firm's "work in process." They are the files in which there is work to be done and in which there may be unbilled time.
- *Inactive.* These are usually files in which there will be no activity for some time but for which all time has been billed. Additional work is anticipated at some point in the future. In a centralized system, it might not be necessary to differentiate between active and inactive files, as all files are stored together. If this is done, however, it is critical to have a system for following up on inactive files to ascertain whether they can be "closed" or when they should be pulled for review. There should also be a follow-up system for active files, and there is no reason why the same system cannot incorporate follow-up on the inactive files.
- *Closed Files.* These are usually files where all work has been done and the file has been billed, collected, culled, and marked for destruction, if it can be destroyed, or for permanent retention if it cannot.

While at first glance this may seem relatively simple, in some firms there is more than one classification for the same type of file. Unless there are standardized classifications, it is difficult to determine where a particular file belongs. In addition to the standardized classifications, there should be detailed guidelines for determining into which classification a file falls. For example:

- In some firms, there are both "permanent" files and "inactive" files because different lawyers use different words to identify the same type of file. If no one is aware of that, the firm will find itself with both "permanent" files and "inactive" files, resulting in confusion as to which is which and another place in which to look for "lost" files.
- If a file involves a matter in which there may or may not be further action, is it an "active" file or an "inactive" file? In some states, there is automatic dismissal of a lawsuit in which there has been no activity for a specified period of time. Therefore, in many situations where a law firm represents the defendant, once a responsive pleading is filed and the services are billed, the lawyer hopes that the plaintiff will "lose" its file. At what point does that "active" file become "inactive"?

- Beyond that, when does the file in the above case go from "inactive" to "closed," and when is it scheduled for destruction?
- Is each "closed" file automatically set for destruction at the time it is closed, or is there review at a later date?
- Which files should be destroyed and which should be "permanently" retained?
- Is there automatic review of files which are "inactive"?

The questions go on and on. The point is that there must be written guidelines to prevent confusion and to save time in locating files. The firm's office policy and procedures manual should include detailed explanations of its filing system and the file management procedures which are in place. If a filing system is in place, but the procedures have not been written, the legal assistant should learn how the system works and check with the office manager to see if plans for documenting the procedures exist. If no one has been assigned the task, the legal assistant should begin to write the procedures. The legal assistant should ask for input from the office manager, attorneys and coworkers so the filing system is workable for everyone in the office. If the legal assistant is working in an office that has no filing system, it would be appropriate for the legal assistant to develop a filing system, discuss the proposed system with attorney(s) and staff, and then implement the system.

§ 3.12.8 Filing Systems

Three types of filing systems commonly used in law offices are *alphabetic*, *numeric*, and *alpha-numeric*. Although some are more effective than others, the "right one" depends upon the needs of the firm. Client files are usually filed in one of three ways:

1. ***Alphabetic.*** Under an alphabetic system, which is known as a direct filing system, files are labeled and stored in alphabetical order by name, generally the name of the client, following standard filing procedures. Although many law firms still use alphabetic filing systems, they are the least efficient for law offices because of the necessity of reshuffling files constantly to make room for additional files. Additionally, people rarely interpret filing rules the same way. Even if the firm uses a numeric system, it is not unusual for lawyers and assistants to file alphabetically in their individual work area.

   In some firms, the litigation files are filed alphabetically by the name of the plaintiff, regardless of whether the firm's client is the plaintiff, the defendant, or another party to the action. Filing under this system makes controlling and finding files more difficult.

   A few firms separate and store files by practice area. For example, all real estate files would be filed together, all litigation files would be filed together, etc. This system is another which is cumbersome and outmoded.

2. ***Numeric.*** A numeric system is an indirect method of filing, since a cross-index is required. Under such a system, files are assigned a number, are identified by that number, and are stored in numerical order. There is an alphabetic cross-index. This alleviates the problem of reshuffling files. Another big advantage to a well-thought-out numeric system is that the same numbering system can be used both for files and for computerized accounting. This is less cumbersome than having both file numbers and computer numbers. Additionally, with a well-thought-out numbering system through use of a computer, a firm can develop the types of management reports and statistics it needs for assessing profitability and cost controls, and it can store and manipulate data for long-range planning and marketing.

Consecutive and terminal digit are the two primary types of numeric numbering systems.

Under a consecutive number system, numbers are assigned in straight sequential order and are filed in straight sequence, one behind the other, so that the most recent number assigned is the last in the file drawer or on the shelf.

Example: File No. 12111
File No. 12113
File No. 13220

With terminal digit filing, numbers are broken down into groups of two digits and are filed in numerical order by the last two digits. (Numbers are read from right to left.)

For example, File No. 112233 would be read as 33 22 11 and would be filed in Drawer 33, Section 22, Folder 11. The next consecutive file number would be 112234 and the file would be stored in Drawer 34, Section 22, Folder 11. Many terminal digit filing systems are also color coded for increased ease in filing. The advantage of terminal digit filing is that material is evenly distributed through the file storage area so that each drawer or each shelf grows at the same rate. Authorities state that filing is up to 40 percent faster with the terminal digit system. Since only two numbers must be remembered to file the folder, misfiles are less frequent. This system is an indirect system and must have an alphabetic cross-index. The big disadvantage to this system is the inability to accommodate client numbers as well as matter numbers. This disadvantage can be overcome by using the file number as a unique matter number, assigning client numbers as well. Filing then would be by matter number rather than client matter number, and client files would not be filed in the same location.

3. ***Alpha-numeric system.*** An alpha-numeric system is a combination of an alphabetic filing system and a numeric system. Under this type of system, numbers assigned to files are in blocks according to the letter of the alphabet which identifies the client. The purpose of such a system is to achieve alphabetic filing. Since the number blocks are filed together, the files are also more or less in alphabetic order. In such a system, however, there is still the potential problem of having to reshuffle files constantly to provide for growth. There is also the problem of using up a number block and having to assign a number from another block as near as possible to the desired one. If this happens often enough, the principal reason for the system is defeated.

Other file identification systems include:

- ***Subject system.*** A subject system is one where files are filed alphabetically by the subject matter involved. The firm's general administrative files (accounting, personnel, equipment, insurance, and other files concerning the firm's business affairs) are usually filed by subject matter in a locked designated area of the file room. Forms files and retrieval systems are also usually filed by subject matter. Needless to say, client files would not be filed by this method.
- ***Geographic system.*** A geographic system is one where filing is done by geographic area, such as a state or a region. Geographic filing would be rare in a law office except that an office which had branch locations might file its general administrative files by location of the office (geographic location) and then by subject. In some corporate law departments that work extensively with various branch offices or subsidiaries, it is not unusual for a geographic system to be used. The geographic system may also encompass a numeric system for ease in identification, but it may be necessary to access files by city, for example.

§ 3.12.9 Using a Numeric Filing System

Although some firms continue to use alphabetic systems for filing, most firms, small and large, have converted to numeric filing systems which are easier to expand and afford more confidentiality. Also, the use of microcomputers to index the files is very common and allows law office support personal to efficiently manage files. A numeric system provides a more effective base for control—a number is considerably more specific than an alphabetic designation. The right kind of file numbering system can also be used for the accounting system.

§ 3.12.10 Client Numbers

To achieve maximum utilization of computerized, statistical information in both short- and long-range planning, a file number should consist of a client number and a matter number. Under this type of system, each client is assigned a unique client number when the firm begins to represent the client. The client retains the same client number no matter how many different matters the firm may handle for the client. These numbers are usually five digits.

§ 3.12.11 Matter Numbers

A matter number is usually assigned in one of two ways: (1) Matter numbers can be assigned sequentially following the client number, or (2) client files are assigned unique matter numbers. Matter numbers are usually three or four digits, depending upon computer capability and firm preference.

§ 3.12.12 Sequential Matter Numbers by Client

If a firm finds it useful to know how many files it has opened for a particular client, it often uses a client matter number system, assigning matters by *client.* Under this system, the client number would still be the same, but matter numbers for all clients would be identical, beginning with 001 or 0001 as the first matter number opened for each client.

EXAMPLE: If ABC Corporation has a client number of 11000, the first file opened for that client is given matter number 001, making that file number 11000–001; the second file for the same client is given matter number 002, making that file number 11000–002, and so on. (Some firms reserve 001 as a general file for a client, beginning their sequential numbering of matter numbers with 002.)

§ 3.12.13 Unique Matter Numbers

Using a five-digit client number and a three-digit matter number as an example, the file number for the firm's first client file opened would be 00001–001. Regardless of whether the second file opened is for the same client or a different client, the number would be 00001–002.

§ 3.12.14 Practice Area Designation

Many firms provide codes for practice areas, as these are useful in some management reports. Most computers have the capability to handle this additional number. Sample area of practice designations are:

- 10 General
- 20 Tax
- 30 Pension and Profit Sharing

- 40 Estate Planning
- 50 Real Estate
- 60 Domestic Relations
- 70 Litigation
- 80 Corporation
- 90 Bankruptcy

In some firms, the practice area also forms part of the file number, but that is a matter of preference. Depending upon the firm's client and matter number systems, use of the practice area also could make the number too long for computer purposes.

Variations of these systems are limited only by the imagination of the individual who creates the system.

In the final analysis, however, the firm must decide which system will work best for it. A major consideration is whether the system already in place can be adapted to an effective system without starting from scratch.

§ 3.12.15 Cross–Indexing for Numeric Filing Systems

The key to a good filing system is a good central index. With a numerical system, there must be an alphabetical index to all files, both active and closed. (Usually the active and closed indexes are maintained separately.) An important aspect of this system is that index cards or computerized client and adverse party information "files" are never removed from the master index system. Another important aspect is that such information is automatically prepared or input during the file opening process.

The key to an effective cross-index system is extensive cross-referencing. This allows location of the file number, regardless of which name in the file is used in checking the index. The master file index is also used for the conflict of interest function, discussed in more detail below.

Centralized indexing and control of files have become extremely simple and cost effective due to the myriad of file management software programs that are now available.

§ 3.13 Developing a System of Centrally Controlled Files

General file management concepts must be applicable to the law firm—does the system work on a day-to-day basis? Since this is an area that is often left to chance, the lawyer's assistant can make a valuable contribution by developing a system for the law office. Let us assume for our case study that there is a file coordinator who is responsible for all aspects of the central system. If you work in an office where there is no one person responsible for the filing function, however, you may assume that you will perform those tasks.

The system described here is not the only kind of file management system that can be effective in a law firm—quite the contrary, there are numerous ways of accomplishing centralized control of a firm's filing system. This system will provide a good basis upon which to grow; a numbering system that works well for a manual system but will easily convert to computerization; an alphabetic cross-index that will work for a manual conflict of interest system and will provide a good database for a computerized conflict of interest system; a docket control system that will ensure that work is done in the ordinary course and that all deadlines are met; central control of the firm's files; and a procedure for routine file closing and retention.

§ 3.13.1 Ingredients for Effective Central Control

The following are ingredients for effective central control:

1. Filling out a new matter report properly.
2. Running a conflict of interest check on each new file opened.
3. Maintaining a record of the location of every file in the office.
4. Maintaining a master index of all active and all closed files including appropriate cross-index entries.
5. Maintaining a record of pertinent data of any files that are destroyed.
6. Maintaining a file index for each lawyer's assistant to track the flow of the files among the lawyers in the office.
7. Conducting periodic checks of files in various lawyers' offices to verify the accuracy of the file records.
8. Preparing and distributing weekly to all lawyers a new file memorandum listing all new files opened the preceding week.
9. Maintaining a docket control system.
10. Maintaining a retrieval system.
11. Keeping written procedures current.

§ 3.13.2 Master File Index

As previously mentioned, the file opening process must provide for an alphabetic cross-index (created manually or through the use of a file management software program) for a numeric filing system. The system's master file index provides the information needed to check each new file for a potential conflict of interest. Since the master index will include a listing of all subfiles opened, more than one card or entry might be necessary for one file. This information comes from the new matter report.

In most firms, there is a procedure to ensure that an alphabetic cross-index card or entry is made for each party to an action or each name which appears in the name of the file. While this might be enough information for cross-reference purposes, it is not enough for conflicts of interest information. Therefore, most firms provide a space on the new matter report for inserting names to be entered into the conflicts system and to be checked as part of the file opening process for a new matter.

Cross-reference cards/entries should be made for each plaintiff, each defendant, and any major principals of corporate parties. In the case of corporate subsidiaries, cross-reference cards/entries should be made for the parent company, with appropriate references. These cards/entries enable the file coordinator or assistant to do a manual or computerized conflicts check as part of the file opening process.

It is also necessary to maintain a master numerical listing. This numerical list can be kept in a different section of the index card drawer or as a separate computer file. A good software program provides for the use of such a listing. It is also necessary to keep a master list of matters opened for a particular client. The master file index will show a listing of all files opened for a particular client.

In manual systems, it is helpful to use colored cards for the indexes.

EXAMPLE:

CARD	**COLOR**
Master Alphabetic	White
Continuation of Master	Yellow
Alphabetic Cross–Reference	Blue
Master Numeric	Salmon
Master Alphabetic Client Matter	Pink

§ 3.13.3 New Matter Report

When a lawyer accepts a new matter, the lawyer's assistant will be given the information needed to prepare a new matter report. Typically the new matter report provides not only pertinent information to the firm for accounting purposes but also provides a brief description of the work to be performed by the firm, perhaps the fee arrangement under which the work will be performed, and the information needed to run a conflict of interest check, as well as any critical deadlines to be entered in the docket control system.

Illustration 3–1

NEW MATTER REPORT

Prepared by: ______________________ Date: __________ File No. __________

Billing Lawyer: ____

Responsible Lawyer(s): ____________________
Case name: ____________ Client No. ________ Matter No. ________
Court: ________ Docket No.: ________
CLIENT INFORMATION ______ New client ______ Present client
Client: ____________________
Address: ____________________
Business phone: ________ Fax number: ________
Home phone: ________ E–Mail Address: ________
Person to contact: ____________________

OPPOSING OR OTHER PARTY INFORMATION
Name: ____________ Lawyer: ____________
Address: ____________ Address: ____________
Phone No.: ____________ Phone No.: ____________
Fax No.: ____________ Fax No.: ____________
E–Mail Address: ____________ E–Mail Address: ____________
INSURANCE CARRIER: ____________________
COVERAGE DISPUTE: ☐ YES ☐ NO
ADVERSE OR POTENTIALLY ADVERSE PARTIES: ____________
OTHER PERSONS OR ENTITIES THAT MIGHT BE INTERESTED, AFFECTED, OR INVOLVED: ____________
MATTER INFORMATION Case Received by: ______ Case Assigned to: ______
File Name: (Client name first) ____________________
Description of case: ____________________
Subject indexing: ____________________
STATUTE OF LIMITATIONS, ANSWER OR OTHER CRITICAL DATE TO TICKLE [*specify*]: ________ Area of Practice Code: ________

IF APPLICABLE: DATE OF LOSS: DATE OF ACCIDENT:
CLAIM NO.: POLICY NO.: COURT:
CASE TYPE:
FEES AND BILLING INFORMATION Hourly Rate of $______ per hour
☐ Contingency fee of: ______
☐ Other [*specify*]: ______
Has retainer agreement been prepared? ______ Yes ______ No
☐ Standard billing (bill fees quarterly and costs monthly)
☐ Other billing agreement [*specify*]: ____________
☐ Joint Bill ☐ Send Reminder Statement

CLIENTS TO BE CHARGED FOR:	YES	NO	RATE
Computerized Research	X		Standard
Facsimiles		X	
Photocopies	X		¢¢/page
Messenger Services	X		Standard

REMARKS (Note additional cross-references or other special instructions in this space):
____
____
____

Names to be run in Conflicts System:	Additional Names to be Cross-referenced:
Shirley Atkinson	Don's Ready Air Cond.
John Smith	
Don Atkinson	

Conflicts System run by: ______________________

Date of Conflicts System run: ______

§ 3.13.4 Definition of Conflict of Interest

A conflict of interest is being in a position, intentionally or unintentionally, where a person's own needs and desires might lead that person to violate his or her duty to another who has a right to depend on him or her (from *Law Dictionary for Nonlawyers, Second Edition,* West Publishing Company, 1985).

EXAMPLE: A judge who owns stock in XYZ Company trying a case involving the XYZ Company might have a conflict of interest.

In a law office, a conflict of interest arises generally when the law firm (or the individual lawyers in the firm) places itself in the position of representing parties in adverse positions. What is difficult about conflicts of interest is that a conflict may be created by a lawyer's representation of a client years before the current situation. This is especially true if the lawyer undertakes representation of one client that places the lawyer in the position of divulging a confidence of a former or current client. What is even more difficult is that these guidelines apply to all lawyers in the firm. It is assumed that representation by one lawyer in the firm is the same as representation by all, even if they are in different cities.

EXAMPLE: Mrs. Jane Baker sees a lawyer in the firm about filing for a divorce against her husband, David Baker. Another lawyer in the firm has already agreed to represent David Baker.

EXAMPLE: The firm is general counsel for XYZ Insurance Company; Jane Baker asks a lawyer in the firm to file a claim against XYZ Insurance Company.

EXAMPLE: The firm is general counsel for XYZ Insurance Company. Jane Baker sues XYZ Insurance Company and Todd Jones for damages she sustained in an accident in which Todd Jones was driving the car which hit Jane Baker's car. The XYZ Insurance Company is Todd Jones's insurer. XYZ Insurance Company must provide a defense for Todd Jones, but it intends to take the position that Todd Jones violated the conditions of his insurance policy, so the coverage does not apply. In other words, the interests of XYZ Insurance Company and Todd Jones are at odds.

Before undertaking representation of a client, the lawyer must make certain that the law firm does not already represent another client whose interests are at odds with those of the potential client. It is unethical for a firm to represent clients whose legal positions are conflicting. It is critical, therefore, for every firm to have an index of all clients, present and past, and to check that index before it accepts new work. Unfortunately, it is not always simple to determine whether or not a potential conflict exists, and the decision is a subjective one.

EXAMPLE: The firm handled an incorporation for XYZ Corporation. One of the firm's clients wants the firm to handle a claim against Jerry Hunt, the vice president of XYZ Corporation. Is there a conflict?

This is a simple example among many gray areas, and only the lawyer or lawyers in the firm can decide whether there is a potential conflict. Even if the firm does not have a conflict, the lawyers may decide that they do not want to accept work as a matter of business practice. From a business standpoint, there are some people against whom the firm will not want to be in an adverse position.

Conflicts of interest are a real problem in some firms. Some do not have effective systems for checking new clients for potential conflicts. There are a number of reasons why, but in most instances, the lack of a conflict of interest system results from the failure of the firm to develop such a system when it is small enough to do it easily. As the firm grows, the job becomes more overwhelming, and the result is that one day the firm finds itself in the embarrassing position either of representing clients with conflicting interests, or worse, with a malpractice claim.

It is true that a conflict of interest system is not so critical for a small firm, especially one that has not been in practice for a long time, as for a large firm, since the lawyers in the small firm can remember for whom they have done work in the past. This is a shortsighted position, however, since most firms grow, and new lawyers and staff come into the firm. It is much easier to develop a system when the firm is small. Even if there is only one lawyer, there should be a conflict of interest system.

It is not the duty of the lawyer's assistant or the file coordinator to determine whether a conflict of interest exists. It is necessary only to call to the attention of the lawyer opening the file that either a potential conflict or a situation in which the firm might not want to become involved exists. This is done as part of the new file opening process.

Information for conflict of interest purposes is critical. This is true not only for checking the new matter for any potential conflicts when the file is opened, but also for future references. If the lawyer does not provide the information, you should ask if there are names in addition to those listed in the file name which must be indexed.

EXAMPLE: If the firm is representing the estate of a decedent, the name of the personal representative as well as the names of all heirs should be indexed.

If the firm is handling a real estate transaction for a development company, the names of the principals of that company should also be indexed. If the development has a project name, that should be indexed. For example, if the developer is "The Build–it–Fast Company" and the firm is doing the legal work involved in the development of the Josey Ranch Shopping Plaza, there should be a cross-index card made for "Josey Ranch Shopping Plaza."

If the firm represents a bank, the names of the bank officers should be indexed.

If the firm is incorporating a small business, the names of each of the shareholders, directors, and officers should be indexed. (Remember that there are times when the firm may not want to be an adverse party against someone for *business* reasons rather than *ethical* ones.)

After the lawyer's assistant prepares the new matter report, it is sent to the file coordinator for processing.

§ 3.13.5 Running the Conflicts Check

The conflicts check is performed at the beginning of the file opening process. Before the file coordinator assigns a number to the file, all names appearing in the file name or on the "conflicts" line of the new matter report are checked against the alphabetic cross-index. The lawyer's assistant or the file coordinator is trained as to which situations might present potential conflicts. For example, if the firm is opening a new matter for an existing client, that client's name will appear in the index. This is not a problem since the firm is again doing work for the client. If, on the other hand, the person to be sued was a former client, the file coordinator would notify the lawyer immediately for further instruction. Determining whether or not a potential conflict exists comes from judgment acquired after a good deal of experience. The safest rule is "When in doubt, ask the lawyer." (The file coordinator initials the new matter report to indicate that the conflicts check has been run.)

§ 3.13.6 Assigning File Numbers

Once the conflict of interest check has been run, the file coordinator can assign the file number (client and matter number). In some firms, assignment is made by the accounting department, depending upon the firm's structure. Some computerized systems assign numbers automatically. There is no "best" way to do this, but there must be coordination between the file person and the accounting department.

The file coordinator checks to see whether a client number has already been assigned to the client. This is done simply by checking the client master index. If the client has a number, only a matter number need be assigned. If the client does not have a number, the next one is selected from the master index.

Once the file number (client number and matter number) has been determined, the file coordinator prepares the cross-index entries for the master cross-index. Each index entry gives the name of the file, as well as the file number. The master index card should list all subfiles which are opened and should also either list the other cross-index references or indicate how many cross-index references were made. (*See* Illustrations 3–2 and 3–3.) When you close the file, you will know how many cross-index cards/entries must be transferred to the closed file index. The file number (client and matter number) must also be entered in the numerical indexes. If the client is a new client, a "client number" card is prepared. If the client is an existing one, the client number card/index is updated to indicate the matter number being assigned. (*See* Illustration 3–4.) An entry is then made for the master file number index. (*See* Illustration 3–5.)

Once the file number is assigned, the file clerk enters the file number (client and matter number) on all copies of the new matter report, retains one for central records, forwards one to the accounting department, and forwards one to the lawyer's assistant (with the file, etc., described below).

Illustration 3–2

ATKINSON, SHIRLEY vs. John Smith Auto Accident–Personal Injury	12000–001
Correspondence	12000–001(a)
Pleadings	12000–001(b)
Evidence	12000–001(c)
Discovery	12000–001(d)
Research	12000–001(e)
Briefs and legal memoranda	12000–001(f)
Lawyer's notes	12000–001(g)
Client documents	12000–001(h)
Damages	12000–001(i)
Miscellaneous	12000–001(j)
1/1/98	

(MASTER ALPHABETIC CROSS–INDEX CARD/ENTRY)

Cross-reference entries:
Smith, John
Atkinson, Don
Don's Ready Air Conditioning
1/1/98

(CONTINUATION TO MASTER ALPHABETIC CROSS–INDEX CARD/ENTRY)

Illustration 3–3

Smith, John
SEE: ATKINSON, SHIRLEY (vs.) John Smith
File No. 12000–001

1/1/98

(ALPHABETIC CROSS–INDEX CARD/ENTRY)

Illustration 3–4

ATKINSON, SHIRLEY 12000
Numbers assigned:
12000–001
12000–002
(As new files are opened for this client, the additional file numbers are noted. The next file for Shirley Atkinson would be 12000–003.)

(MASTER CLIENT CARD/ENTRY)

Illustration 3–5

12000–001

ATKINSON, SHIRLEY v.
Smith, John

1/1/98

(NUMERIC MASTER FILE INDEX CARD/ENTRY)

§ 3.13.7 Using a Rolodex or Case Book

In addition to the master file index maintained by the file coordinator, each lawyer's assistant should keep a rolodex file or case book sheet on the desk (or a similar program on the computer) containing the same information that is shown on the master index file for each active file being handled by the lawyer. As part of the file opening process, the file clerk prepares a rolodex card or case book sheet that will be returned to the lawyer's assistant with the new file. (*See* Illustration 3–6.) In this way, the lawyer's assistant has a list of the active files being handled by the lawyer and will have the file number readily available for use on time sheets and for filing purposes.

Illustration 3–6

Client: File No. 12000–001

ATKINSON, SHIRLEY
Matter: (v. John Smith)

Auto Accident–Personal Injury
Address:

100 Main Street, Any Where, USA 00000
Phone: 000–622–1111
Responsible Atty: ABC

Assigned to: DEF

(ROLODEX CARD/CASE BOOK SHEET FOR ASSISTANT'S DESK)

§ 3.13.8 Preparing File Jackets

The file coordinator prepares the file jacket, which contains subfiles and a copy of the new matter report, and sends it to the lawyer's assistant with the rolodex card/case book sheet described above that gives all pertinent information about the file.

§ 3.13.9 Setting Up Subfiles

A common complaint in many law firms is that everyone uses a different system for subfiles, so the subfile categories do not necessarily identify the contents of the subfile. Another is that no record is kept on subfiles, so a subfile could be misplaced, and no one would ever know it had existed unless the lawyer remembered. This makes control impossible and presents a problem for lawyers and staff when they are looking for a specific document. For that reason, standardized categories for subfiles by area of practice are necessary. For example:

1. *Litigation*
    a. Correspondence
    b. Lawyer's Notes
    c. Client Documents
    d. Pleadings
    e. Discovery
    f. Evidence
    g. Damages

h. Legal Research
i. Briefs and Legal Memoranda
j. Miscellaneous

2. *General Corporate*
   a. Correspondence
   b. Lawyer's Notes
   c. Client Documents
   d. Corporate Documents (charter, bylaws, minutes, agreements, etc.)
   e. Miscellaneous
3. *Real Estate*
   a. Correspondence
   b. Lawyer's Notes
   c. Title Search and Survey
   d. Contract of Sale
   e. Closing Documents
   f. Client Documents
   g. Miscellaneous
4. *Probate*
   a. Correspondence
   b. Lawyer's Notes
   c. Client Documents
   d. Probate Pleadings and Documents
   e. Will
   f. Assets
   g. Debt and Liabilities
   h. Federal Estate Tax Return
   i. Federal Income Tax Return
   j. State Inheritance Tax Return
   k. State Income Tax Return
   l. Miscellaneous
5. *Tax and Estate Planning*
   a. Correspondence
   b. Lawyer's Notes
   c. Client Documents
   d. Will for (name of husband)
   e. Will for (name of wife)
   f. Drafts
   g. Miscellaneous

Each subfile should carry the file number and name and can also be assigned a letter or other identifying mark. The correspondence subfile for File No. 00129–700 might be 00129–700(a); the pleadings file would be 00129–700(b), etc. (*See* Illustration 3–2.) It is not necessary for the subfiles to be entered into the computer records (for accounting purposes), but they are entered in the master index. By keeping a central record of the subfiles, a lawyer or an assistant can verify whether the file is complete.

The subfiles can be requested at the time the file is opened or can be opened later. A simple form can be used to advise the file clerk of the subfile which has been opened. (*See* Illustration 3–7.) In order to keep accurate records, it is essential to have the cooperation of all lawyer's assistants and lawyers. Once they realize the value of having a central record, they are more likely to make an effort to remember. Opening subfiles at the time the file is opened has the advantage of having a record of every subfile—another important ingredient of file control.

Once the file folders are prepared, the file coordinator returns the file containing a copy of the new matter report to the lawyer's assistant to keep near the attorney's office, along with the rolodex card/case book sheet. The file coordinator also prepares an "out" card and places it where the file would ordinarily be.

Illustration 3–7

SUBFILE OPENED

Client Number ____________________
File Number ____________________
Subfile
Designation ____________________
Opened By: ____________________

§ 3.14 Checklists for Opening Files

When the file is opened, the file clerk should use a checklist to open the file to ensure that all essential steps have been followed. If none is available, the file clerk with the help of the office manager or legal assistant should create a checklist to use on a consistent basis. Using such a checklist will also be beneficial for training new staff.

Illustration 3–8

OPENING FILE CHECKLIST

Date: ______

INITIAL WHEN COMPLETED

______ File checked for conflict of interest
______ File number assigned and added to master numeric list
______ Numeric master card prepared and filed in master file
______ File folder and subfolders (if any) prepared
______ Client and cross-reference index cards/entries prepared and filed
______ Tickler established for statute of limitations, answer date, and other critical dates and filed in docket system
______ "Out" card inserted on file shelf
______ New Matter Report typed and distributed: (a) Original to master file; (b) copy to lawyer's book; (c) copy in file; (d) copy circulated
______ File returned to lawyer's desk

§ 3.14.1 New Files List

As part of the file opening process, a list of all new files should be prepared periodically (perhaps weekly or daily in large firms) and distributed to all lawyers (perhaps by e-mail). This serves as an additional conflict of interest check and also keeps lawyers informed of what is going on. This is another function that can be computerized.

§ 3.14.2 Preparing File Labels

The name on the label should be placed very close to the top of the label right below the color coding so that it will be visible when materials are placed in the file. Begin at the first or second space from the left edge of the label so that all labels will be uniform. If the label contains more than one line, indent the second and third lines three spaces so the name on the first line will stand out. It is preferable to prepare labels with only initial caps instead of solid caps because they are easier to read. Insert the file number on the label, as well as the name, leaving at least three spaces between the number and words so that the number will stand out.

§ 3.14.3 Lawyer's Approval on Filing

Incoming mail should always be reviewed by the lawyer before it is filed. Some offices require a lawyer's initials on all materials coming into the office before they are filed in the client folders. Some attorneys like to have a working copy of all correspondence and pleadings. If this is the case, the lawyer's assistant would make a copy of the incoming correspondence and pleadings and place the original in the file with a notation indicating the attorney had received a working copy.

§ 3.14.4 Organizing the Files

Keep the files neat and orderly. Establish a policy for setting up the files. Each firm can set up the files so that the contents are available for easy reference. With the exception of clients' personal documents, every piece of paper should be fastened into the file. Metal prongs are excellent for this purpose; some file folders have the prongs permanently attached to the folder. There is no excuse for a sloppy file. The time you spend fastening in correspondence and documents is more than offset by the time you save in locating materials in the file.

§ 3.14.5 Using File Numbers

Once the file has been opened and assigned a file number, that number should be shown on all correspondence, statements, and other file documentation. The lawyer's assistant should note the file number on all pleadings so that the office file clerks will have no problem identifying the document for filing. If there are subfiles, the proper subfile identification should also be included. If the document should not be defaced, the file number should be written on a separate note attached to the document (such as a post-it note). The lawyer's assistant should be actively involved in the filing process. The lawyer's assistant is in a much better position than the file coordinator to identify the open and active files. For that reason, it is the responsibility of the lawyer's assistant to see that proper file numbers are noted on all filing material. The lawyer's assistant is often in a position to do filing for the attorneys and should do so as much as possible since it is very cost-effective.

§ 3.14.6 Preparing Material for Filing

Sort documents by category (client, personal, general correspondence). Check to see if the lawyer has initialed documents for filing if this is office procedure. After documents have been sorted by category, sort within the category, placing them in either numerical or alphabetical order, whichever is appropriate for the firm's filing system. Decide where the document should be filed. (This is known as "indexing.") Mark the document with the filing notation, such as the file number in numerical filing, or underline the name on the document which indicates in which file it should be placed. (This is known as "coding.") If it goes in a subject file, write the subject in the upper right-hand corner. Carefully punch holes at the top of the document. When you place a document in a folder, be sure it is not crowded into the fold of the folder. When placing material in the folder, verify the number and name.

Daily filing means just that—daily. It cannot wait until you have time. A lawyer relies on the contents of the file to reflect the file's current status. Therefore, a missing letter or document can have serious ramifications.

Filing should be done by the lawyer's assistant most familiar with the file (or the file coordinator), not by a part-time clerk or by the newest assistant in the office. The lawyer's assistant should do the filing daily in those files stored in the nearby area or the lawyer's work area; the file coordinator should do the filing in the files located in the central file room. The lawyer's assistant is responsible, however, for giving the file coordinator sufficient, accurate information to ensure that the filing is done properly and timely.

Illustration 3–9

SAMPLE TRANSMITTAL SLIP FOR ITEMS TO BE FILED

TO: ______________________________
FROM: ______________________________
DATE: ______________________________
Attached are the following items
____
____
to be filed in the following file:
Client No. ______________________________
Matter No. ______________________________

§ 3.15 When Clients Want to See Files

If a client asks to see a file, never hand over the file without prior permission from the lawyer. Upon direction of the lawyer, you may allow the client to look at certain documents in the file in your presence. All files which are released from the office should be noted in a "Release File," stating the name of the person to whom the file is released, the date the file leaves the office, and the name of the lawyer authorizing release of the file. The person taking the file should sign a receipt for it. This protects the office in the event of future questions on the file.

§ 3.16 Assigning Files to Other Lawyers

In a firm where lawyers frequently assign work to other lawyers, it is beneficial to have a system for notifying the file room that another lawyer has the file. An easy way to do this is to have the assistant to the responsible lawyer fill out a transfer slip for the file coordinator so that the "out" card can be changed to show who actually has the file. (*See* Illustration 3–10.) Additionally, the assistant to the responsible attorney should prepare a rolodex card/case book sheet for the assistant to the assigned lawyer for that file. (*See* Illustration 3–6.)

Illustration 3–10

FILE TRANSFER NOTIFICATION

Client Number	______________________	
Matter Number	______________________	
Transferred by	______________________	Date: __________
Transferred to	______________________	Date: __________
File Room Notified	______________________	Date: __________

Assignment of files to other lawyers is one of the most difficult file functions to control. At the time of assignment, the lawyer is thinking only of the necessity of forwarding the file to whoever will do the work. This creates two problems. The first is that the central file records are inaccurate if the assignment notation is not made on the "out" card. The second problem occurs when the responsible lawyer assigns many files to different lawyers and may forget that the assigned file has not yet been handed over to another attorney or the responsible attorney forgets to whom it was assigned. This makes it impossible to find the file when it is needed.

All lawyers should be encouraged to tell you when they assign a file in order that a transfer form can be prepared and sent to the file room. Lawyer's assistants should also look for new files coming to the lawyers. They can then check with the file clerk to see if a transfer slip has been completed. It requires teamwork to manage all the details of an effective file management system.

§ 3.17 Sending Active Files to Central File Room

With centralized storage, a lawyer has the option of storing many files in the central file room. With an effective system, it makes sense to keep as few files as possible in your work area. This alleviates clutter and confusion when you are looking for a misplaced file.

No file should be sent to the central file room unless a review date has been entered into the docket control system. In some firms, the docket control date is entered on the file folder so that the file coordinator can verify that a review date has been entered. This is a good procedure to follow. If a file is sent to the central file room without a tickler date, it is returned to the lawyer. (In small firms, the same person can serve as file coordinator and docket clerk.)

§ 3.17.1 Retrieving Files From Central File Room

For a more effective system, controlled access to the central file room is critical. "Controlled access" means that only the file coordinator removes files from the file room. This means that the lawyer or legal assistant tells the file coordinator which file is needed, and the file coordinator "checks the file out" to whoever wants it. The obvious reason for this is so that an "out" card can be inserted, which indicates the name of the lawyer who has the file. Thus, the file coordinator knows where files are physically located if they are not in the file room.

Controlled access does not usually exist in small firms. Unless the assistants and lawyers work together to ensure that "out" cards are always inserted when files are pulled, the system will soon lose its effectiveness and its credibility.

Even in firms where there is controlled access, it is impossible for the file coordinator to be in the file room at all times. Some firms prohibit access to said areas at such times. In other firms, lawyers and assistants are free to help themselves to files after hours and problems arise if the "out" system is not honored.

§ 3.17.2 Occasional Inventories

At regular intervals, the file coordinator should check lawyers' offices to verify that the records are correct, *i.e.,* the files are where the file room records indicate they are.

§ 3.18 Closing Files

In many law firms, lawyers feel that it is not necessary to close files. The crunch comes when sufficient filing space is no longer available. By then, the task is often so monumental that outside help is needed. Unfortunately, closing files is rarely a priority item for lawyers. This is another area where the lawyer's assistant can be of invaluable assistance. It is the lawyer's assistant's responsibility to help the lawyer close files on a regular basis. If this is done regularly, the problem of spending months cleaning out file drawers to make room for new files will be alleviated.

Since many lawyers will not cull files, the lawyer's assistant should review the contents of the file to remove duplicate copies, legal pads, and other extraneous material (excluding any legal documents). Before closing the file, the lawyer must decide the eventual disposition of the files.

Illustration 3–11

<table>
<tr><td colspan="4" align="center">CLOSING FILE FORM</td></tr>
<tr><td>TO:</td><td>File Department</td><td></td><td>DATE: __________</td></tr>
<tr><td>FROM:</td><td>____________________
(Assistant)</td><td>for</td><td>____________________
(Attorney Initials)</td></tr>
<tr><td>SUBJECT:</td><td colspan="3">____
File Name Our File No.</td></tr>
<tr><td></td><td colspan="3">__________–__________
Client and Matter No.
This file has been closed and stripped on this date.
______ Destroy file after January 1, ______
______ Review file ______ (date)
______ Retain file permanently
______ File checked for retrieval information</td></tr>
<tr><td colspan="4">Special Instructions: ______________________________
Closed File # Assigned: ______________________________</td></tr>
<tr><td colspan="3"></td><td>____________________
File Coordinator</td></tr>
</table>

§ 3.18.1 Closing File Numbers

Some firms do not renumber files when they are closed. The only disadvantage to this is that constant reshuffling of files may be necessary to make room for files which must be inserted. Therefore, it is usually preferable to have a system under which a new number is given to the file in the file closing process. There are many numbering systems available. One which works well is to have the number relate to the year in which the file is closed. An easy way is to assign numbers in strict sequential order totally unrelated to the numbering system for active files. The file coordinator maintains a register (which can be a card index or computer file) for these file numbers. For example:

94–01

94–02

94–03

The first two digits indicate that the file was closed in 1994. The last two digits give the order in which the file was closed in that year.

The file coordinator enters the closed file number on the master index and moves it to the closed file index. The file coordinator also locates all other cross-indexes pertinent to that file and moves them to the closed file index. This index is also in alphabetical order. The file coordinator notes the file number on the file and moves the file to the closed file area.

§ 3.18.2 Destroying Files

Some law firms have never destroyed files and are still storing them in expansive (and expensive) storage areas. Some files are 50 to 100 years old. Most of these firms are now changing their philosophies about the necessity to maintain these files perpetually. Storage of files that will never be used again is expensive. From a business standpoint, some firms are taking the position that it is not a depository for clients' necessary documents—tax returns, wills, etc.—and are now putting the burden of maintaining these necessary documents on the clients themselves. What must be retained from a legal standpoint is a subjective decision which only the firm can make. Generally, firms are taking the position that it is necessary to keep only those documents which cannot be replaced, are not in a court record, or for which they are not protected under the statutes of limitations.

Most firms feel that there are some files which must be retained permanently. As part of the file destruction process, the firm must develop guidelines by which files must be retained permanently. A retention timetable should be developed by area of practice.

§ 3.18.3 Returning Files to Clients

One way to avoid storage of unnecessary documents is to purge the file of "client" documents when the file goes into inactive or closed status. The file is often composed in large part of documentation furnished by the client for a particular case or contract or as resource material in an estate plan. Once the file is ready for inactive status, there is no reason not to return these documents to the client at that time—when the client can still be contacted. Many firms also offer the file to the client when the file comes up for destruction. Here again, the lawyer's assistant must be guided by the firm's policy.

§ 3.18.4 Off–Premises Storage

Particularly in larger metropolitan areas, firms are storing closed and permanent files in commercial file storage facilities. In some instances, commercial storage is less expensive than on-premises storage.

§ 3.19 Alternative Storage Methods

Some firms first transfer selected or all contents of the file to microfilm, microfiche, CD–Rom, or tape archive before closing and/or destroying the files.

§ 3.20 Filing Supplies and Equipment

In many firms, there is an astounding lack of uniformity in filing supplies. Apparently, those lawyers who prefer particular types of file folders, clamps, subfiles, expandable folders, etc., are accommodated by the firm. Other firms have adopted file procedures which include the use of standardized filing supplies. It is easier to take advantage of volume discounts, and file folders and other supplies are uniform and consistent. This eliminates the question of what supply should be used for which lawyer in a given situation. Unfortunately, this is an area in which a lawyer's assistant often has no control. If the legal assistant is asked to help standardize firm procedures, it is helpful to know the available alternatives in order to be in a position to help.

§ 3.20.1 Color Coding

The extent to which color coding helps is totally dependent upon the individual firm. In firms where there is continuous movement of files among various lawyers, color-coded file folders can be helpful in locating missing files. If color-coded folders are used, color-coded expandable files are also helpful in locating "lost" files. According to some authorities, color coding increases accuracy, speeds up the filing function, and lessens the time spent to find missing files.

Color can be used in a law office in many ways. The following are some possibilities:

- Use a different color for different types of cases, *e.g.*, green for real estate, red for domestic relations, blue for probate, etc.
- Use a different color for the first letter of the last name. Some systems assign colors as follows: The initial letter of B when followed by "a," "b," "c," or "d," is indicated by a green colored

tab. When the initial B is followed by "e," "f," "g," or "h," the tab is orange, and so on.

- In numerical filing, a different color can be used for different digits. Generally, the color is determined by the next-to-last digit. Therefore, each group of ten folders is in one color with a second contrasting color for the next ten folders. By using more than one color on the tab of tens, hundreds, and thousands, it is possible to code up to any number.

§ 3.20.2 Filing Equipment

Although for many years there was little choice of the type of filing equipment a firm could utilize, this is certainly no longer true. Many vendors are competing to sell their space-saver equipment. As with other types of office equipment, one type is not necessarily better than another. What a firm should use depends upon its needs.

Generally, the types of equipment available include:

- Vertical file drawers. These are the traditional file cabinets which have been in law offices for years. They are the least space efficient and are cumbersome to use, particularly in view of other file equipment currently on the market.
- Lateral file drawers. These are file cabinets, but the files are arranged laterally, providing more space efficiency than vertical file cabinets. They are also more convenient for the user in terms of inserting and removing files.
- Open-shelf filing. Open-shelf filing is also lateral filing, but files are placed vertically on open shelves, which are usually seven feet high. There are no drawers. Open-shelf filing is more space efficient than either lateral file cabinets or vertical file drawers.
- Space-saving retractable shelves. This is the most efficient equipment from a space-saving standpoint. The open shelves are placed on tracks so that an aisle is not required between each row of shelves. There are numerous types available, and each firm must determine which best suits its needs. From a safety standpoint, any firm purchasing this type of equipment should make certain that it is equipped with a slip clutch. This slip clutch causes the movement of the unit to stop when it makes contact with an object. Some manufacturers also feature an optional safety bar that is installed outside the aisle and physically crosses the open aisle. The bar not only locks the equipment but also serves as a visual reminder that the equipment is in use.

Before a firm can make a final decision on conversion of present space or on selection of equipment, it must make sure that the floor load capacity of the area will accommodate any added weight.

§ 3.21 Calendaring and Docket Control Systems

A docket control system is a critical ingredient of a file management system. A "docket" (also referred to as a "tickler," a "calendar," or a "diary") is a reminder system. It provides a means of keeping track of deadlines and court dates for both litigation and non-litigation matters. It should serve not only as a reminder but also as a means of file control, scheduling, and planning. It ensures that work is done in the ordinary course of business rather than at the last minute when someone remembers the deadline. Regardless of the size of the firm, there should be only one system—a firm-wide system. This means that every single file must have an entry in the docket control system.

Missed deadlines or poor follow-through is responsible for many malpractice claims. Malpractice carriers, in an effort to reduce claims, review docket control systems carefully before issuing insurance. Since malpractice coverage rates are also escalating and coverage is more difficult to obtain, firms are paying much more attention to firm-wide docket control as an effective loss prevention technique. Insurance companies encourage lawyers to develop what they define as "loss prevention programs" to help reduce malpractice claims.

Some secretarial and lawyer's assistant texts (and some law firms) differentiate between the terms "docket," "tickler," "diary," "calendar," and "follow-up." For example, in some firms, the word "docket" is used only to identify litigation deadlines. In some instances, the word "docket" is used to refer only to the number given a case by a court. The word "docket" is also used to mean a court docket or a list of cases to be tried in a certain court term.

"Tickler" system is used to identify non-litigation matters that require attention in the ordinary course of business, whether those dates are fixed by law, by commitment to the client, or by the lawyer who simply wishes to review the file at that time. "Follow-up" system, "suspense file," or "tracer" are synonyms for "tickler" system.

The words "tickler," "calendar," "diary," and "follow-up" are also sometimes used to indicate the specific entry in the docket control system.

EXAMPLES: The tickler entry shows that a trial is scheduled for May 8, 2004.

The calendar shows that a trial is scheduled for May 8, 2004.

The diary shows that a trial is scheduled for May 8, 2004.

The follow-up entry shows that a trial is scheduled for May 8, 2004.

"Diary" is used to indicate appointments with clients, court dates (a duplication of the docket control entry), and other important matters entered in the docket control system to which the lawyer or the lawyer's assistant refers on a daily basis. The diary may also contain a record of the time a lawyer spends on a given appointment or project in order to bill the client for the time spent. This is no longer a common practice as most lawyers use time sheets or time slips on which to record time. The diary is generally an appointment book or calendar. The diary or calendar is one of the tools used in an effective docket control system.

The differentiation described above is often made with the assumption that there will be more than one system to help control the firm's workflow and the lawyers' schedules. The concept is that if one system is used for entering all appointments, deadlines, court dates, and other reminders of work to be done, the system will become too unwieldy. The disadvantage to such an approach is that it is more cumbersome to keep track of several systems when one can accomplish the same objective.

It is important for the lawyer's assistant to determine how these terms are used and to learn as quickly as possible the individual attorney's or firm's system used to keep track of important dates and critical deadlines. If the system does not provide a method for handling work on which there is no particular deadline, the lawyer's assistant should ask the lawyer how this is done.

§ 3.21.1 Controlling the Workflow

The most important responsibility of the lawyer's assistant is to see that there is a docket control entry for every file for which the lawyer is responsible. The docket control system is one to which all lawyers and assistants refer on a daily basis. It is the hub from which all work flows.

The ingredients of a good docket control system (whether manual or computerized) are:

1. Diaries or calendars for the lawyer's assistant and the lawyer.
2. A tickler file or follow-up system.
3. A central office calendar.

Although a firm-wide system is preferable, some firms still allow each lawyer to maintain an individual docket control system. If the law firm or lawyer does not have an organized system of docket control, the lawyer's assistant may want to begin one with the approval of the office manager and/or attorneys.

§ 3.21.2 Types of Docket Control or Calendar Systems

Several types of docket control systems are used in law offices, and different secretarial texts and law office management experts recommend different ones. What is important is that there is a system in writing and that the system be used and maintained routinely.

§ 3.21.3 Ingredients for a Calendaring or Docket Control System

The essential ingredients of a calendaring or docket control system are:

1. Immediate and automatic calendaring.
2. A cross-check on entries and notifications.
3. Sufficient lead time to accomplish the task.
4. Follow-up on actual performance of the task.

§ 3.21.4 Responsibility for the Calendaring or Docket Control System

Although the primary responsibility for the docket control system rests with the lawyer, the lawyer's assistant is responsible for its administrative aspects and is responsible for getting the information into the system. To the extent that there is access to the information that needs to be calendared or docketed, the lawyer's assistant is often expected to make entries into the system without specific instructions from the lawyer. Therefore, the lawyer's assistant must be resourceful in determining the important dates that should be entered into the system and demonstrate reliability by consistently and timely performing this task. It is better to have more entries than are necessary rather than risk missing an important date.

§ 3.21.5 Items to Be Calendared

Any type of future commitment belongs in the docket control system. Examples are:

- All dates related to litigation, including statutes of limitations dates; due or deadline dates for various pleadings and briefs; deadlines for notices of appeal and renewals of judgments; deposition dates; due dates for answers to interrogatories; dates by which certain discovery material must be made available; dates by which subpoenas must be issued and served; and trial and hearing dates.
- Dates by which adverse parties in litigation have agreed to provide material, data, or information.

- Dates by which service of process is expected to be made.
- Dates by which the receipt of certain documents or requested information—medical opinions, accident reports, weather reports, certified copies of documents, checks for advanced costs—is expected.
- Filing and hearing dates for various estate matters, such as federal income and estate tax returns, state inheritance tax returns, notice dates required by law, and dates of annual and final accountings.
- Follow-up dates for annual reports, minutes of meetings, etc., provided for corporate clients.
- Dates by which clients must meet the requirements of a contract provision.
- Proof of publication from newspapers on advertisements required in various types of actions.
- Follow-up dates for work in progress on all files.
- Follow-up dates for review of inactive files or review of files labeled for destruction.
- Appointments.
- Professional and personal commitments.
- Accounting and administrative deadlines, such as personnel and expense accounting, tax returns and other tax-related reports, supply ordering, lease renewals, maintenance contract renewals, insurance policy renewals, etc.

§ 3.21.6 Double Calendar Systems

Some firms employ double calendar systems. Two calendar or diary entries are made for each transaction or date which requires a reminder. One entry is made on a calendar or diary kept by the lawyer who is responsible for meeting the deadline, and the other entry is made on a central calendar kept by an assistant or docket clerk. Both the lawyer and the lawyer's assistant are responsible for checking the calendar or diary each day to be sure all deadlines and appointments are kept.

§ 3.21.7 Perpetual or Tickler Calendars

A system employed by many firms—and one which overcomes the problem of the full calendar—is a perpetual or tickler calendar system. This system employs a standard pocket or desk calendar or diary kept by the lawyer, but the central calendar maintained by the lawyer's assistant is kept on index cards and can grow with the firm—it never gets full. The lawyer's assistant should also maintain a desk calendar as a supplement to the perpetual calendar.

A perpetual calendar can be kept in a 3″ × 5″ index card file or in an 8½″ × 11″ "follow-up" file folders. Both systems use the following guide system of dividers:

1. Twelve major guides labeled January through December.
2. A set of numerical guides marked from 1 through 31 for the days of the month.
3. A set of blank index guides to provide dividers for at least five future years.
4. Tickler form cards or form documents on 8½″ × 11″ paper.

Illustration 3–12

TICKLER FORM

Date to be reminded: ______

IMPORTANT REMINDER

To Lawyer(s): ____________________

Re: ____________________

____

Message: ____________________

____

____

(May be used for follow-up request and as reminder memorandum from Docket Coordinator.)

The pertinent information is placed behind the proper day of the month (if in the current month) or behind the guide for the month in which action is to be accomplished. A tickler file does not take the place of a diary or a calendar; it supplements it. Recurring items such as rent payments can be entered on one card and moved from month to month as they are paid. Only one card needs to be prepared. These entries do not need to be made 12 times in the diary. Tickler cards are particularly useful when a follow-up date is indefinite. A good example is a file on which there are no critical deadlines but there is work to be done. A simple entry of "review file" can be moved ahead easily.

§ 3.21.8 Tickler Systems Using Follow–Up Files

Some offices prefer a follow-up file system to a tickler card system because it is easier to manage 8½″ × 11″ papers and folders. For the follow-up file system, the lawyer's assistant prepares guide dividers in the same manner as used in the index card tickler system and materials are placed in the proper file folder. Offices using this system make an extra copy of any letter requiring a follow-up (such as collection letters) and place a copy of the letter in the file folder. The office file copy still goes to the client file in case it is needed before the follow-up date. Copies of short documents are also placed in the folder. In lieu of placing the document in the folder, a form document stating the name of the client, the type of response due, and the date when it is due can be used.

When sending certified or registered mail, keep the receipt in the follow-up file until you receive the return receipt or you are notified of receipt. For matters referred to other lawyers, the form document can be made giving a follow-up date for checking on progress.

§ 3.21.9 Using Automated Calendars

Many firms have computers which have records management capabilities. Reminder dates and pertinent information are fed into the computer, recorded, and later retrieved by date, by lawyer, by file, or other sequence. At regular intervals, perhaps daily, weekly, semi-weekly, or monthly, a master or office calendar (list of reminder dates) is printed for each lawyer individually and one for the entire firm. Friday is a popular day for distributing the calendar, since it is useful to lawyers in planning their work schedules for the upcoming weeks. The calendar lists by date every future commitment of all firm lawyers. In some firms, file review items are not included on the master calendar.

§ 3.21.10 Calendaring Incoming Mail

For the system to be effective, *all* incoming mail must be opened and processed by the lawyer's assistant. Under no circumstances should any mail be removed from the assistant's desk prior to processing.

The lawyer's assistant sets up ticklers from all incoming mail which notify a lawyer of any due date, such as a hearing date, brief deadline, trial date, response date for interrogatories, and many other types of important deadlines. It is a good practice for the legal assistant to use a stamp or write a note on the paper indicating that the document has been calendared, who calendared the item and when it was calendared. This process may be essential at times to provide documentation that an item was properly and timely calendared by the legal assistant.

The lawyer is equally responsible for seeing that any items in the mail requiring ticklers or calendar notations are properly handled. Any piece of mail requiring a tickler which is not marked "calendared" or "noted" (the term used in some offices) should be returned to the lawyer's assistant with instructions to set up the proper ticklers. It is critical that the docket control entries be current. Docket control requires constant attention. It is not something you can put off until later. Make the entry as soon as you learn of the date, regardless of how you learn about it. For instance, as you are reviewing the mail, enter right then dates mentioned in letters or in notices. Calculate the return time on summonses, interrogatories, etc., and enter them in the diary. If you do not know how to calculate these dates, ask the lawyer. When you are preparing notices, interrogatories, or material requiring a response by a certain date, log these in the system. The date should be calendared in both the assistant's diary and in the lawyer's diary or calendar. Deciding how much or how little should be entered on the desk calendars is a matter of judgment which the lawyer's assistant will acquire with experience. Examples of what should be entered in the calendars or diaries include appointments, meetings, court dates, birthdays and anniversaries, etc., and any deadline dates. The firm's docket control coordinator must be advised of all pertinent dates.

§ 3.21.11 Calendaring Telephone Calls and Office Conferences

Often a hearing date or other matter requiring a tickler or calendar entry results from an office or telephone conference with another lawyer, judge, clerk, etc. It is imperative that the lawyer scheduling a hearing or other appointment tells the legal assistant about the hearing or due date so it can be tickled or calendared in a timely fashion. It is very helpful for the attorney if the legal assistant makes sure that the attorney is conveniently supplied with tickler forms or document forms.

In the event a lawyer sets a hearing date, deposition, appointment, or some other event and wishes to be reminded of it, the lawyer should note the date on the calendar and on a tickler card to give to the assistant for filing. Lawyers should also use the tickler forms for establishing recall dates for files by noting the date on a tickler form and attaching it to the file folder.

Prior to filing the tickled file in the central files, the lawyer's assistant notes the tickler date in the upper right-hand corner of the face of the file folder. Thus, if a tickled file is removed from the central files for a conference, reference, or the like, it is readily apparent that the file is tickled and can be refiled.

Prior to filing a tickler prepared by a lawyer, the lawyer's assistant should check the tickler to determine if additional lead time will be needed. For instance, any item tickled that requires a written document or a personal appearance will require several tickler slips—the last of which is always the due date.

EXAMPLES:

- Statute of Limitations

  No less than five tickler slips are set up to tickle a statute of limitations as follows:

  1. Three months prior to expiration of the statute.
  2. Two months prior to expiration.
  3. One month prior to expiration.
  4. One week prior to expiration.

5. Date of expiration.

- Answer (to complaint, interrogatories, requests to produce, etc.)

  No less than four tickler slips are set up to tickle an answer due date as follows:

  1. Fifteen days prior to answer date.
  2. Ten days prior to answer date.
  3. Five days prior to answer date.
  4. Answer due date.

- Hearing dates

  There must be at least three tickler slips as follows:

  1. One for a date sufficiently ahead of the actual due date to allow for necessary preparation (dependent upon the nature of the hearing.)
  2. One for the day before the hearing.
  3. One for the date of the hearing.

When a document being prepared necessitates keyboarding, there should be one to two full working days allowed for keyboarding of the document, depending on the anticipated size of the document. For particularly lengthy briefs, contracts, and the like, three full working days should be allowed. If a document requires outside printing, sufficient time should be allowed. These deadlines must be kept in mind when setting up tickler dates. The due date means that the lawyer's work product must be completed and the final document out of the office by that date.

§ 3.21.12 Calendaring and Docket Control Duties

Some offices entrust the docket control system to one individual (often referred to as a "docket clerk" or "docket coordinator"), who is responsible for reminding all lawyers of deadlines a minimum number of days in advance. With this system, all lawyer's assistants and lawyers are required to furnish the pertinent information to the docket coordinator. In some firms, all mail and all pleadings (whether coming into the firm or leaving the firm) are routed to the docket coordinator to ensure that all critical dates are entered into the system. The docket coordinator then sends written reminders of all deadline dates. Some firms use their own specialized in-house forms for this purpose. Lawyers responsible for the work must then notify the docket coordinator that the work has been completed. The docket coordinator should always follow-up to be sure that the work was done if not notified within a reasonable time by the attorney or legal assistant.

§ 3.21.13 Final Responsibility With Lawyer's Assistant

Always remember that the final responsibility for reminding the lawyer of deadlines rests with the legal assistant. Even if there is a central reminder system operated by one member of the staff, the legal assistant must monitor it carefully and make sure that the lawyer receives the reminder and that the work has been done.

§ 3.21.14 Daily Checking of Diaries/Calendars

The first thing you should do in the morning and the last thing you should do at night is to compare the your diary with the lawyer's. Computerized diaries are very popular and allow the lawyer's assistant to have access to the lawyer's diary at all times. They should correspond, but often you may find that the attorney has made appointments without notifying you, or you have made appointments without entering them on the attorney's diary. You should then make the two diaries correspond with each other. By checking the diaries for the next several days, you will be "on top" of things. Knowing what may come up tomorrow will make life easier today. You are in a much better position to anticipate and plan ahead.

§ 3.21.15 Calendaring Unscheduled Appointments

If a client drops in without an appointment, the lawyer's assistant should make note of it on the lawyer's calendar because it may later be necessary to verify that the client was in the lawyer's office on that particular day. If you also note this information on your calendar, you can check with the lawyer to see what work must be done for the client.

§ 3.21.16 Retention of Diaries/Calendars

After the year is completed, diaries should be retained with the accounting records. Diaries serve as a handy reference to determine who was in on what date and what business might have transpired. If the lawyer keeps a computerized diary, it should be saved on some type of media and retained. Many lawyers have had to go back to their diaries to recreate a sequence of events for a client.

The assistant's diary contains all the information that the lawyer's does. It also includes the legal assistant's personal deadlines, reminders, and appointments. This might seem like a duplication of effort, but it provides good backup for the reminder system.

§ 3.21.17 Reminder System

A formal reminder system should be established, as should a good working rapport with the lawyer. Some lawyers postpone projects until the last minute. This means that you will be putting in a lot of overtime unless you develop the knack of getting the lawyer to do the work sooner. You can leave reminders on the attorney's desk or chair, taped to the attorney's briefcase, or taped to the telephone or dictation equipment. Use bright paper so the message will be obvious. Some lawyer's assistants become very original and creative in their reminders. The important thing is to get action.

A lawyer might unconsciously play "hide-and-seek" with the assistant. The attorney leaves the office and disappears. If there are several lawyers in the firm and more than one is familiar with each case, this disappearance act is not too drastic. In a small firm, however, it is essential that the lawyer's assistant be able to reach the lawyer on matters which might arise in the attorney's absence. To provide good client service, you will need to ask where the attorney is going and when to expect the attorney back in the office. If the attorney is going out of town, obtain a copy of the itinerary, including lodging. The concerned attorney should understand that you are not checking up; you just want to be prepared for any emergency which might occur.

§ 3.21.18 Importance of Docket Control Systems

It is critical to the functioning of a docket system that the lawyer's assistant receive notice of all deadline dates, appointment dates, court appearances, etc., in order that every future commitment is automatically and immediately calendared. Input must come from each staff member.

§ 3.22 Setting Up a Brief Bank or Retrieval System

A brief bank, sometimes called a retrieval system, is designed to preserve material that might be helpful to the firm in the future. The preservation of legal research, briefs, and forms can save a tremendous amount of time on future work. Not only does it save time in preparation of a document or in doing legal research, but it also saves time the lawyer and the legal assistant might otherwise spend looking for a form "used in that Jones case two years ago." Legal work received from other law firms or legal departments may be put into the system for future reference. By gathering this type of information in one place, attorneys and legal staff easily can find particular forms and legal opinions about a particular topic.

Retrieval systems are considered an important ingredient of file management and would become more efficient if the work product were integrated into the system immediately. The tendency is to postpone development of a system "until I have more time." In the meantime, there is more material which should be integrated into the system, the task becomes overwhelming and it does not get done. If a system has not been started in your law office, you may want to designate an area in the library or word processing center to start one.

As with a filing system, the key to an effective, useful retrieval system is a good index with extensive cross-indexing. A subjective filing system (and most retrieval systems) requires extensive cross-indexing. Most such systems are indexed by major practice area categories and then by subtopics. Some are tied to the West Key Number System, but that numbering system is controlled by an extensive subject matter index.

Documents in the system are considered *masters* and are not removed from the system. Anyone who wants to work from the document makes a photocopy so the original is always in the system. In some firms, the work product is not physically maintained in a separate system, but rather there is an index which identifies the file in which the work product can be found.

One of the things most systems lack is a weeding process. Should a document be pulled and should the lawyer working on it feel that it is obsolete or is a poor work product, the lawyer should either weed the document and have it removed from the index or attach a note indicating that the document may no longer be applicable because of a change in law (or whatever the reason may be). In a small firm, the system tends to be relatively simple and flexible. All lawyers contribute items to the system, update material, and even weed. In larger firms, however, one lawyer (or the librarian, if there is one) is given the responsibility for maintenance of the system. Substantive changes cannot be made to the system without approval of the person responsible.

§ 3.23 Working As a Team

You might find when you are establishing a new client file that you do not have all of the necessary information you need, such as complete names, addresses, ages, phone numbers, and so on. This might be just an oversight. If it occurs often, you need to arrange with the lawyer to sit in on the latter part of the initial interview so that you can obtain the information. In the alternative, you might prepare a checklist or client interview sheet for the attorney to use in obtaining needed information.

The good lawyer's assistant complements the lawyer by filling in any gaps. They work as a team, and everyone benefits. The word "synergy" means making the whole equal to more than the sum of its parts. In the law office, this means that when you take one good lawyer and add one good lawyer's assistant, with both working as a team, you get a work output that is greater than the total of what each could do separately.

§ 3.24 Summary

The practice of law requires close cooperation and teamwork between the lawyer and the lawyer's assistant. It is the function of the lawyer's assistant to save the lawyer time and to fulfill all secretarial and administrative requirements. The lawyer's assistant must have technical skills as well as human relations skills to be a valued employee. The practice of law is a business, and the law office is a business office. Only through teamwork, cooperation, and strict compliance with duties can progress be made.

CHAPTER 4

COMPUTERS IN THE LAW OFFICE

Table of Sections

§ 4.1 Introduction

Computers have become the law office's primary tool for providing efficient, cost effective, and flexible services to its clients. It is well known that in the late 1970s and early 1980s, dedicated word processors, that is, computers that performed only the function of word processing, revolutionized the law office. As computers became smaller, less expensive, and easier to use, they proliferated. Today, computers perform more tasks and are used by lawyer's assistants, paralegals, lawyers, and clients to communicate, exchange, process data, and to connect to the world.

This chapter provides an overview of computer components, discusses the major features of word processing, and introduces other computer applications, such as e-mail, scheduling and docketing, spreadsheets, database management, and computer-assisted legal research that are commonly being used in the legal environment. This chapter concludes with a description of the Internet, discussion of computer security issues, and recommendations for selecting a computer system.

§ 4.2 Components of Computer Systems

Computer systems are made up of hardware (the physical components) and software (the instructions that make a computer operate). Hardware and software are linked by the operations and calculations performed electronically in the central processing unit (CPU).

Hardware includes the keyboard, mouse, monitor, printer, and the case/chassis. Inside the case there are electrical components that constitute the CPU and other electrical chips and components controlling other operations of the computer. This electrical board is sometimes referred to as the motherboard. Also housed in the case are memory storage and retrieval devices called disk or hard drives. Other types of hardware components are modems, printers, uninterruptible power supplies (UPS), and scanners. Hardware is categorized as input devices, output devices, and memory components.

Software is a set of instructions written by programmers that direct the internal electronic memory and processing components of a computer to manipulate or change data in a certain way. Operating system software contains the instructions that connect and coordinate hardware to software. Application software contains instructions that transform a computer into a practical tool, such as a word processor, accounting tool, database manager, or scheduler.

The most important element in a computer system is the actual computer user. The person using a computer reads prompts or menus on the computer screen, uses a mouse or the keyboard to position the insertion point at certain places on the screen, and then makes choices from the menus or prompts, or keys in data, which is sent to the CPU. The CPU processes that data and the data may be stored for future use, displayed on the screen, or printed depending on the set of instructions contained in the software.

§ 4.2.1 Input Devices

An input device is the means of getting information or data from the operator into the computer. Keyboards, mouse/mice, optical character readers, imaging scanners, touch screen monitors and voice recognition systems are input devices.

Keyboard. The computer keyboard looks very much like a typewriter keyboard and includes alpha/numeric/symbol keys, a Tab key, Caps Lock and Shift keys, a Backspace key, and an Enter (Return) key. The computer keyboard, unlike the typewriter keyboard, has cursor movement keys, such as left, right, up, and down arrows, Home, End, PageUp, and PageDown. Other keys found on a computer keyboard are Escape (ESC), Insert (INS), and Delete (DEL), which are used to perform editing tasks, and function keys labeled F1 through F12 on the top row of the keyboard, which are used in conjunction with the Control (CTRL), Alternate (ALT), and SHIFT keys to perform specific tasks.

Special characters not found on the keyboard, such as the section mark (§); paragraph symbol (¶); registered ®, trademark ™ or copyright © marks; degree °; etc., can be inserted into a document. Check under "special characters" in the manual index that comes with your software for specific instructions.

Mouse and Trackball. The mouse is an input device. It may be rolled across the desktop, or may be stationary with a rolling ball. Either way, the movements control a pointer called an I-beam which appears on the screen. The pointer's shape can change from an I-beam into an arrow, hourglass, or hand while a person is working with a document. The mouse also has two or three buttons on top that can be clicked or double clicked to perform certain operations, or the button can be held down to drag the I-beam across the screen to select text. Some mice now have a scroll button which allows you to move up and down a page by simply moving the button with your finger. A mouse can be adapted for use by left or right-handed people, and products are available to make the mouse and/or keyboard easier to use by people who have motion, hearing, or visual limitations. A trackball is a stationary pointing device with a ball on its top that you roll with the tips of your fingers to move the pointer on the screen. Instead of moving the mouse with your hand, the trackball allows you to move the cursor by rotating a ball with your fingers. The base of a trackball device does not move so there is less strain on your wrists and hands, and less desk space that needs to be used to control the pointer.

Scanner. A flatbed scanner, which looks like a very small copier with a lid and glass plate, is a piece of hardware that electronically scans a document much like a fax machine. It sends the image scanned to the CPU. Software converts this image into a character-based text file. Recognizing the image into characters is called OCR (Optical Character Recognition). It can then be manipulated in a word processing program just as if the text was keyed into the computer by a person. OCR software sometimes does not convert each character accurately. For example, an "e" can come across as an "@" sign; an "I" can be converted into an "l" or "!". All text that is scanned for use in word processing should be proofread carefully.

Handheld scanners are being employed while away from the office. Scanned images can then be sent to PCs or printers with infrared ports.

Bar Code Scanner. This is a small scanner that reads a bar code (similar to the UPC codes on various products). Large law firms are using this technology to label client files so that the file's location can be monitored with minimal effort.

Voice Recognition Systems. This new technology recognizes speech and translates spoken words or commands into digital sound that can be interpreted by the computer. The person using this system speaks certain words and commands into a microphone attached to the computer. The computer analyzes the sounds until the computer can recognize the speech pattern of that particular person. Some commands that the computer equipped with voice recognition software can interpret are "Back," "Delete," "Print," "Save," and so on. This technology is becoming more affordable and its use may soon be commonplace.

Webcams. Webcams are small, inexpensive cameras that function like a camcorder to send images over the Internet. Firms are employing these for video conferencing. The number of sites involved in a conference is limited by the speed of each party's Internet connection.

Digital Cameras. Digital cameras format photographs into files computer programs can use. They are most notably seen in websites, but are also seen in the discovery process. Digital cameras are available for personal use.

§ 4.2.2 Output Devices

An output device is used to get information or data out of the computer and back to the operator. The two most common output devices are the monitor and the printer. After data is input and then processed, the operator can view the data on screen or print the output on paper, which is called "printing a hard copy."

Monitor. The monitor, which resembles a television screen, is an output device because it displays user and program data that has been processed by the CPU. Older computer systems used monochrome monitors, which displayed text in white, green or amber. Color monitors are widely used and come in screen sizes of 14″, 15″, 17″, 20″, 21″, 23″ and 30″. The monitor's clarity or resolution is measured in pixels, which are the small dots that create a picture on the screen, and in dots per pitch, which is the distance between each pixel measured in millimeters. The smaller the dot pitch, the better the resolution will be on the screen. Today's monitors generally have dot pitches between 0.25 and 0.28 mm and can be flat screen or flat panel. Laptop computers use the newer liquid crystal display (LCD) or light-emitting diode (LED) type display because of their slim design and reduced energy needs. The LCD is referred to as a flat panel display because of its smaller design and has the advantage of using less desk space in an office.

Printers. Printers vary in speed, print quality, and price. They are classified as impact (dot matrix) and non-impact (laser or inkjet). Dot-matrix printers are generally the least expensive printers, and because they use pressure to create the characters on the paper, they are used to print drafts and multiple-part sheets, such as those used in accounting and billing.

Laser printers use technology similar to that of a photocopier to produce printed text and graphics. Because of their low price ($300 to $2,000), speed, and excellent print quality, they are the most widely used printers in today's law firms. Law offices that have centralized word processing departments often invest in expensive, high-speed laser printers equipped with large paper storage trays and sorters.

Color printers are becoming increasingly more affordable and have a very practical place in a law office. They can be used to produce client newsletters and in-house marketing brochures, thus eliminating the cost of outside printing services. Litigation support staff can also create attractive, effective, and inexpensive trial documents and exhibits.

Sheet feeders are attachments to printers that are outfitted with trays, or bins, which hold one to three types of paper and sometimes envelopes. The operator selects the type of paper through the software rather than manually changing the paper in the tray or feeding an envelope. Sheet feeders are very convenient, huge time savers, and well worth the extra expense.

§ 4.2.3 Communication Devices

One type of device that is considered both an input and output piece of hardware is a communication device called a "modem." Computer users exchange data from computer to computer using a modem that allows data to be transmitted through cabling, telephone lines, fiber optics, or satellite links. A link is necessary for electronic mail (e-mail), voice mail, and facsimile transmission. It also is needed to connect with on-line legal research services, such as LEXIS–NEXIS and Westlaw, and to join the Internet. High speed connections employ a router rather than a modem. These connections are always active versus a temporary dial up connection via modem. It is more common to see a dedicated connection in most offices.

In order for communication devices to work properly, each computer that is communicating must have compatible software and a formal set of rules controlling the transmission of data. These rules are called "protocols." Usually setting up this software requires the help of knowledgeable computer technicians. Westlaw and LEXIS–NEXIS both provide the necessary support for connecting with their services. Once computers are connected via modems and the software is installed correctly, modems and routers are simple to use, save time, and provide a link to outside sources of information.

§ 4.2.4 The Central Processing Unit and Internal Memory

The central processing unit (CPU) directs the flow of information, performs all calculations, and controls all the components of the computer system. While it is processing, there is a continual exchange of data between the CPU and the internal and/or external memory storage area. The internal (primary) memory area stores data and program instructions that the CPU accesses most often in electronic circuitry. The external memory area is used for long-term data storage on magnetic disks.

When the electricity to a computer is switched on, the CPU begins its work by accessing BIOS (Basic Input Output System) and/or ROM (Read–Only Memory) instructions that are permanently stored or "burned" into the circuit board (motherboard) located inside the case of the computer. The CPU processes BIOS and/or ROM instruction routines that summon the software instructions of the operating system for the computer. The operating system is software, usually installed in the computer at the time of purchase, that must be in place before other software can be operated. The operating system tells the computer how to store a file, coordinates input and output devices, and does a variety of other tasks. In an IBM or IBM clone computer the operating system is called Windows. A Macintosh computer follows a similar process, but has a totally different architecture and its operating system is called Mac OS.

Both software program instructions and user input, manifested by what is displayed on the screen, are stored in the internal memory storage area called Random Access Memory (RAM). The CPU can quickly access, process, change, and replace the data, and as this occurs, the screen changes. This type of memory is volatile, which means that all the data that it holds will be lost or erased when the electricity is turned off. In order to keep or save the contents of the screen, it must be saved to memory devices, such as floppy diskettes, hard or fixed disks, travel, thumb or flash drives, magnetic tape, or on compact disks (CD–ROM) or digital video disks (DVD–Rom).

§ 4.2.5 External Memory

Processed data can be permanently stored externally on magnetic disks called floppy disks writeable CD–ROM, writeable DVD–ROM, flash drives, or on rigid magnetic disks called hard disks. The hard disk drive is nonremovable and located in the case of the computer. The storage capacity is measured in bytes. Zip drives are small portable drives which which hold large amounts of data, and are commonly used to back up hard drives. Flash drives are another small portable drive which can hold up to 8 GB of data, which is 5,555 approximately floppy disks. Flash drives are also useful because they can be plugged into any USB port. USB ports are now standard on all IBM and Macintosh computers.

The term "byte" refers to the amount of space required to store one character of information. A one-page double-spaced document is approximately 2,000 to 3,000 bytes. Instead of referring to bytes in terms of thousands, they are grouped by thousands and called kilobytes, or by millions and called megabytes, or by billions and called gigabytes. Floppy disks are inserted into slots in the computer case and can store between 360 KB and 1.44 MB. The hard disk drive housed in the case of a computer stores between 20 MB and 80 GB, and technology continually changes so the amount of data that can be stored will undoubtedly continue to increase.

Most computers are equipped with compact disk/read-write memory (CD–ROM) drives which allow the computer to read from the compact disk, and to record onto the compact disk. A single CD–ROM can hold about 650 million characters (650 MB), which is an entire set of encyclopedias or about 1,000 books that are each 300 pages long. CD–ROMs are necessary to run or execute multimedia software, which are programs that integrate text, graphics, sound, and animation. Many newer computers have hardware which can record and erase compact disks. These compact disks are called CDRW or CD Burner. The newest technology is the use of DVD disks—the digital versatile disk. DVDs are available in read-only and recordable versions and can hold from 4.7 GB to 17 GB of data or seven to twenty-six times more than the capacity of a CD–ROM.

When using floppy diskettes, the operator should take care to handle them properly because they can be damaged easily and thus can result in loss of data. Avoid exposing floppy diskettes to smoke, water, fingerprints, magnets, and high or low heat. Place the diskettes in their protective jackets when not in use and stack them upright in a tray, not flat on a desk.

Other popular storage media include: Zip drives, flash drives, 8mm, and DLT drives. Large networks typically use 8mm or DLT for nightly backups. Other media is mostly used to copy data.

§ 4.3 Operating Systems

The operating system controls the flow of information to and from the CPU and to and from the input/output devices. It interprets commands from the user and determines where data is located and stored. It also performs housekeeping chores such as allocating time and resources to each application program. (*See* § 4.5 for definitions of "application.") Some law offices that have not upgraded their equipment in the last decade are probably still using DOS-based programs. Those that have upgraded are using a version of Windows or MAC operating systems.

§ 4.3.1 Windows

Windows, introduced in 1990, is considered an operating environment rather than an operating system. Windows uses MS–DOS to perform functions, but rather than using character-based commands, Windows provides a graphical user interface or GUI (pronounced "gooey") to display menus and choices for the user. Windows has several advantages over DOS. It is easier to learn because it uses icons, or pictures, which are considered user friendly. All the programs written for the Windows environment have similar menus and basic commands, such as saving, printing, editing, and displaying documents that are performed in the same way. Windows provides for multitasking, which means that a user can be working on a word processing document, a spreadsheet document, and a presentation document all at the same time. Information in one program can be moved or copied from one application to another using a special area called the clipboard. Data and graphics can be linked to or embedded in another Windows program or application, and if the data is updated in one program, it will automatically be updated in the other program.

Perhaps the most significant feature of Windows is that it is "WYSIWYG" or "what you see is what you get"; the screen displays exactly what will be printed. It is very easy to use graphics and various fonts to make attractive and flashy documents.

§ 4.3.2 Windows 95, Windows 98, Windows NT, Windows 2000, Windows XP, and Windows Vista

Windows 95 (1995), Windows 98 (1998), Windows NT (1993) (New Technology), Windows 2000 (2000), Windows XP (Oct. 2001) and Windows Vista (Jan. 2007) are true Windows operating systems. They are graphical user interface systems, meaning that they use icons and have a WYSIWYG screen. These systems have faster processing units. Windows NT may require additional hardware, has high memory requirements, is more stable because of its memory management capabilities, and, generally, is used in large law firms. Windows XP, has an updated user interface. The interface is more intuitive and keeps screen clutter to a minimum. Users of versions of windows may opt to use the classic style of desktop or the newer XP desktop. Windows XP includes additional support for new hardware devices, advanced security features, and a feature called Remote Desktop which allows the user to log into another computer running XP and control it from the first computer. Another new feature is Remote Assistance which allows someone to connect to your computer and lend assistance over the network, and even control your computer remotely if you choose to allow it.

§ 4.4 Computer Classifications

Generally, computers are classified into four sizes: mainframes, minicomputers, microcomputers, and portables.

Mainframe computers are large, very expensive ($350,000 or more), high-speed machines that require trained operators and special temperature environments.

Minicomputers are mid-sized, powerful computers that cost in the range of $20,000 to $350,000 each. Large law firms that have branch offices and desire to share data and programs generally use this class of computers. Individual computer workstations (which cost much less than the minicomputer) are linked or networked to the main minicomputer or "server."

Microcomputers are small-sized computers known as personal or desktop computers. They are very affordable, easy to use, and require only a small area of desk space. PCs can work individually as "stand-alones," or they can be networked, meaning that the computers are connected in some way so that data and peripherals, such as printers, modems, and scanners, can be shared. Microcomputers can be part of a local area network (LAN) or part of a wide area network (WAN). A LAN system connects computers that are located close together, *i.e.,* in the same building, and are joined by ethernet or twisted-pair cables. A WAN system connects computers that are located far apart, *i.e.*, in another city. A WAN system uses microwave, telephone, and communications-satellite linkage. For both LANs and WANs, computer technicians are required to maintain these complicated systems.

Portables include notebooks, laptops, handheld, and palm devices.

§ 4.5 Software Applications

The term "application" refers to the specific uses or jobs that a computer can do for the user. The most common application is word processing. The operator uses word processing software to produce letters, memoranda, reports, pleadings, and many other legal documents. To create more complex documents, such as newsletters, catalogs, marketing materials, and business reports, the operator can use word processing software to enter the text, a graphics program to create pictures and other visual enhancements, and then using the page layout capabilities of desktop publishing software, bring it all together to make a camera-ready document to be printed on laser printers or typesetting equipment.

Many law firms use spreadsheet software for analyzing financial and statistical data. A spreadsheet is similar to a manual worksheet or an accountant's ledger but is not limited to the size of a piece of paper. It can contain hundreds of columns and thousands of rows, and when data is changed in one place, the rest of the calculations will automatically update. Another type of software commonly used in law firms is database software that is used for storing and manipulating information. For example, databases can keep track of personnel, clients, and projects, and can be used in litigation to organize and provide quick access to discovery documents. Litigation support staff also use presentation software to assemble, organize, and create persuasive trial presentations.

§ 4.6 Word Processing Programs

No matter what type of commercial word processing program is chosen, they are all basically the same. The function and tasks available will be very similar; but the keystrokes or method of invoking the task or function will be dissimilar. For example, all programs have the capability of saving a file to disk. In one program, the keystrokes may be pressing F7 and then responding to yes or no prompts. A second program would require the operator to select File on a menu bar and then choosing the menu item Save. Once an operator has learned to do fundamental tasks in one word processing program, a second or new version of software can usually be learned quickly and without too much difficulty. In the following discussion, the lawyer's assistant is introduced to features and functions of word processors. These features and concepts are the ones that an operator should understand and be proficient in no matter what word processing program the operator uses.

§ 4.6.1 Word Processing Cycle

The four steps in the word processing cycle are: (1) creating and formatting the document; (2) saving the document to an external storage area; (3) editing and proofing the document; and (4) printing the document on paper or transmitting it electronically to another computer.

First, with a clear screen, the operator begins to enter text (or changes format settings and then begins to enter text). The text appears on the screen and has to be saved in memory (on a diskette, CD–ROM, or on the hard drive) so it can be retrieved or accessed at a later time. After saving, the operator can (1) clear the screen to begin a new document, or (2) continue working on the same document—add more text, proof and spell check, or edit. Once there are changes to the document, it has to be saved again so that the new version with all its modifications replaces the older version. The operator can print a document at any time, whether it is on the screen or saved externally.

§ 4.6.2 Word Processing Basics

Default Settings. To make word processing fast and easy, default settings are used. Standard default settings are those program settings that are used unless the operator specifies others. For example, when an operator starts with a clear screen and begins to enter text, that document automatically uses settings for a standard sheet of paper (8½″ x 11″), has one inch margins, begins in single line spacing, and has tab settings every half inch.

Screen. The screen commonly displays areas such as status line, rulers, and menu selection bars. The status line, usually at the bottom or top of the screen, displays such information as page number, the vertical and horizontal position of the cursor, and the document's filename. Sometimes a ruler is visible that shows the margin and tab settings.

In word processing, it is necessary that the operator visualizes what the document on the screen will look like when printed on a piece of paper. The operator can look at the status line at the bottom (or sometimes at the top) of the screen and relate the numerical values displayed to those on a sheet of paper. Newer versions of word processing software allow viewing or previewing the document to see how it will look when printed.

Cursor or Insertion Point Movements. The flashing square or insertion point on the screen is called the cursor and it indicates where the next character will appear or where the next editing move will take place. Operators should know how to move the cursor quickly through the document, which is called "scrolling through a document." Inexperienced operators often use the up and down, left and right arrow keys to scroll through a document. The skilled operator takes the time to learn the keystrokes needed to efficiently scroll through text. Check the Help feature (search "shortcut keys"), computer manuals, or reference books to learn more about these shortcuts.

Word Wraparound. Many new computer operators used typewriters before learning word processing. In typing, it is necessary to press the Return key at the end of each line. In word processing, as text reaches the end of the line, it automatically wraps to the next line so the operator can continue entering text without worrying about where the lines will end. This feature, "word wraparound," is one reason why word processing is so popular. Following are some guidelines that should be followed when entering text so that the features of word processing perform efficiently.

(1) Instead of pressing the Return key at the end of each line of typing, the operator lets the words "wrap" to the next line.

(2) The Enter key is used to end a short line or to create blank lines.

(3) The spacebar should not be pressed and used to push the cursor to a new line to continue typing.

(4) When indenting text, as in numbered or bulleted lists, use the computer's indent or paragraph formatting features to align the text correctly. Avoid pressing the Enter key to end the line, and then pressing the spacebar or Tab keys in an attempt to indent lines of text (the typewriter method). If this incorrect method is used, each line may have to be adjusted manually when the text is edited.

Paper Size. The page format or page setup options in word processors allows the operator to select a paper size other than the standard 8½ inches x 11 inches sheet of paper. Choices include legal (8½ x 14 inches), executive (7¼ inches x 10½ inches), envelopes, numerous label sizes, and also custom sizes, which are created by the operator. The operator may also choose the direction of the printing on the page: portrait orientation prints text down the length of the page; landscape orientation prints text across the width of the paper, or the "long way." Some less sophisticated printers do not support landscape printing.

Portrait and Landscape Orientation

Pleading Paper. There are many ways to create pleading paper. The basic style required by many state and federal courts uses the blank page format, *i.e.*, no ruled margins or numbered lines. Some courts require the use of paper with left and right ruled margins. Finally, some courts use what is known as the "California format." This format uses line numbering to place the numbers on the left margin, and uses graphics to place the vertical rule lines next to the line numbers, and footers to place the law firm information, such as name, address, and phone/fax numbers on the bottom right corner of each page. Because creating the numbered lines and ruled margins placed on pleading paper requires advanced word processing skills, the software programmers have included options to easily select the pleading format as a style or template.

Margins. The standard default top and bottom margins are one inch, and the left and right margins are either one or 1¼ inches depending on the software. Margins are easy to change and the operator can change them before or after entering text. To fit more text on a page, decrease the margins. Decreasing the bottom margin from one inch to ½ inch often allows three more lines of text on a page.

Line Spacing. The default setting for line spacing is one or single. Using a word processor, the operator can change text to any line spacing—double, triple, or any fixed increment—either before or after the text is entered. Pleadings, agreements, and other legal documents may require several line spacing changes within the same document.

Tabs. The Tab key has two functions. First, the Tab key is used to align columns of text or numbers instead of pressing the spacebar to "push" characters into columns. When the spacebar is used, the text can look aligned on the screen but may print out misaligned. Also, when Tabs are used to align text rather than inserting spaces, all the text in any one column can be readjusted simply by moving the tab set, not the individual lines of text.

Most word processors have four types of tab alignments: left, center, right, and decimal alignment. The chart below demonstrates each of these types of alignment.

Date	Provider of Service	Amount Due	Status
10/15/02	County Hospital	$12,223.00	Pending
10/15/02	Anesthesiologists	1,700.00	Paid
10/18/02	Nursing Services	3,333.04	Paid
10/21/02	Nursing Services	2,752.11	Not billed
↑	↑	↑	↑
Left	**Center**	**Decimal**	**Right**

The Tab key's second function is to move the cursor or insertion point forward through user menu choices or options that are displayed in various software programs, and to move the cursor or insertion point around in tables created in word processing and spreadsheet tables. A Shift+Tab key combination moves the cursor or insertion point backwards in menus and in tables. To override the tab's cursor movement function in a table, the operator must use a special key combination such as Home+Tab or Ctrl+Tab, or Shift+Tab (which moves the cursor backward in a table).

Indent. The indent key is sometimes called a temporary left margin. It is used to push text in from the left margin. Each time the Indent key is pressed, it moves the paragraph of text over one more tab stop, which is usually ½ inch by default. This way the operator can quickly set off subsections of a document so the document is easier to read and understand. The Indent key (or other special paragraph formatting commands) makes formatting legal documents very simple when they contain numbered paragraphs, bullets to emphasize points, and quoted material.

Another type of indent is called "hanging indent." The first line hangs out and the second and consecutive lines are spaced under the first line. This format is used to format bibliography entries, glossary terms, and in some programs bulleted and numbered lists.

Justification. This term refers to the four types of text alignment. When text aligns only on the left margin with a ragged right margin (like it appears in typewritten work), it is left justified. When text aligns evenly between the left and right margins, it is called full justification. Extra space is automatically added to the line between words by the software so that each line is the same length. When the operator selects "center," the cursor moves to the center of the screen and the text is centered between the left and right margins. When the operator selects "right," the cursor is placed on the far right margin, and as the text is entered, it lines up on the right.

Left Justification	Center Justification	Right Justification	Full Justification
Word processing systems should be fast, user friendly, and easy to learn. The first word processing systems were slow, required the use of many codes, and were difficult to learn.	Word processing systems should be fast, user friendly, and easy to learn. The first word processing systems were slow, required the use of many codes, and were difficult to learn.	Word processing systems should be fast, user friendly, and easy to learn. The first word processing systems were slow, required the use of many codes, and were difficult to learn.	Word processing systems should be fast, user friendly, and easy to learn. The first word processing systems were slow, required the use of many codes, and were difficult to learn.

The type of justification to use is dependent only by the style chosen by the law firm. Left justification tends to be easier to read, and, therefore, easier to proofread; however, newsletters and marketing materials may use full justification for a more polished look.

Fonts. The term "fonts" refers to the style or design of a collection of letters, numerals, symbols, and punctuation marks. The kind of fonts available depends on the software program and also the capabilities of the attached printer. The ability to see the actual font shape and size on the computer screen is dependent on the type of word processor. Some DOS-based programs do not show fonts on the screen. Windows-based programs display the fonts on the screen like they will print out. This is called "WYSIWYG" (what you see is what you get).

There are two kinds of fonts: serif, which have small extensions that fall below the line, and sans serif, which have no extenders below the line. Following are some examples of serif and sans serif fonts in three point sizes:

This is a sample of a serif font, CG Times, 8 pt.

This is a sample of a serif font, CG Times, 12 pt.

This is a sample of a serif font, CG Times, 16 pt.

This is a sample of a sans serif font, Univers, 8 pt.

This is a sample of a sans serif font, Univers, 12 pt.

This is a sample of a sans serif font, Univers, 16 pt.

Some guidelines for using fonts in a document:

(1) Keep the number of font types or font faces to no more than three per page; more than that may make the document appear "too busy."

(2) Headings and subheadings are usually in sans serif fonts, such as Univers. The body of the document is usually in serif fonts, such as CG Times.

(3) Point sizes for headings should be balanced and proportional to the point size of the body of the document. For example, main headings should be 2 to 4 point sizes larger than subheadings. Subheadings should be 2 to 4 point sizes larger than the body of the document.

(4) For a professional look, use bold, italics, or larger font sizes to emphasize text. Underlining is generally avoided.

(5) Use the word processor's Style feature to apply formatting. This feature, which is discussed below, allows the operator to quickly make font changes in the text.

§ 4.6.3 Word Processing Editing Tools

Selecting Text. Text can be changed or formatted before or after it is entered. Once text is entered, however, the operator must "select" or "block" it and then do whatever command is needed. When the text is selected, it appears in reverse video or in a different color. The skilled operator takes the time to learn the keystrokes needed to efficiently select text. For example, if the operator is selecting a large portion of text that goes over the page break, often it is a problem to stop and get just the right amount of text selected. Using the keystroke combination of shift key and the down arrow key can allow the operator to select exactly the amount of text needed. Computer manuals or reference books show these shortcuts.

Inserting Text. There are two modes for inserting text. Automatic insert is the normal mode. The operator places the cursor (or insertion point) at the place where text needs to be inserted and then begins to enter text. The text automatically moves to the right making space for the newly entered text. Typeover or Overtype, a second type of insert, is destructive. When the operator begins to enter text, the new letters are inserted right over the top of the old characters, thus wiping out the text that was previously entered.

Deleting Text. Deleting text is a simple operation in word processing. The operator presses Backspace to delete characters to the left of the cursor (or insertion point) and presses Delete to delete characters to the right of the cursor or insertion point. There are various keystrokes to efficiently delete words, paragraphs, and sections of text. The skilled operator takes the time to learn these keystrokes. Computer manuals or reference books show these shortcuts.

Moving and Copying Text. One of the most common word processing tasks is moving or copying text. Moving text means that the blocked or selected text is deleted from its original position and moved to a new location in the same document or to an entirely different document. Copying text means that the blocked or selected text is duplicated at another place in the document or in another document.

Windows-based word processing has a feature called "drag and drop" which simplifies the procedure and is used when the text is being moved to a close location in the same file. Using the mouse, text is selected and then while holding down a mouse key (or the Control key and the mouse key when copying), the operator "drags" the text to a new location, releases the mouse button, and "drops" the text in its new position. The text that is copied or moved is placed in a temporary memory area called the Clipboard. Once text is in the Clipboard, it can easily be moved or copied to other applications or documents. (For information on moving or copying files, *see* Document Management.)

Append and Spike. Two features that are related to move and copy are called "append" and "spike." The append feature allows the operator to gather or collect, in order, each item deleted and then insert them as a group in another location or document. Note that the Clipboard can sometimes be used to collect and paste multiple items from different programs. The spike feature allows the operator to select text and copy it to the very end of an existing document without opening or retrieving that document to the screen.

Search. The Search feature is an editing tool that allows the operator to quickly find a specific word or code in a document. Searches can be performed through some or all of the document. The term "search string" refers to the actual text or code that is being searched for and matched. If the search string is entered in upper-case letters, only upper-case letters will be matched. If the string is entered in lower-case letters, both upper-case and lower-case letters will be matched. Some programs allow you to select an option to "search string" in "mixed" or "all cases." The concept of how the search string matches upper and lower-case words is referred to as case-sensitivity and each word processor has its own guidelines. An extended search is a type of search that includes such areas as headers, footers, footnotes, endnotes, graphics, and graphic captions.

Search and Replace. Search and replace allows the operator to search for text, special symbols, and/or formatting (and related codes), and replace them with other text, codes, and/or formats. For example, if the operator spells the name "Hansen" with an "en" throughout a document and then finds out the name should be spelled with an "on," the search and replace feature can be used to quickly make the correction.

Always save the document before searching and replacing. It is easy to inadvertently make a mistake in the search and replace strings, and change the document incorrectly. For example, if the operator searched for spaces and replaced them with nothing, all words would become one continuous string.

§ 4.6.4 Word Processing Formatting Tools

Headers and Footers. This term refers to the automatic placement of text and/or graphics at the top or bottom of each page. Headers place text and/or graphics at the top of each page, and footers place text and/or graphics at the bottom of each page. Automatic page numbering codes can be inserted in headers and footers so that each page is numbered consecutively. Some programs allow the operator to insert codes in the header or footer that include information about the document's computer filename and the date and/or time the file was created and saved.

Headers can save time if used to create continuation page headings in long letters, memos, and reports, rather than manually keying in the header on each page. The header should be placed at the beginning of the document and suppressed or fixed so that it does not print on the first page. With headers, the document can be edited and the operator does not have to worry about adjusting the continuation page headings because they will automatically adjust when text is inserted or deleted from the document or when spacing is changed from single to double as may be needed for printing drafts of documents.

Footers are primarily used in pleadings to place the title and page number of the pleading on each page, in wills and other estate planning documents, and real estate documents. Footers are especially useful when comparing two documents and then marking them with redline or strikeout, and each version of the document needs to be clearly identified so confusion does not result.

Footnotes. The operator can easily create footnotes in a document by simply putting the cursor or insertion point at the end of the appropriate word, phrase, or sentence in the text where the superscripted or raised footnote number should be placed. Then the operator chooses a menu option to create the footnote, and typically, a separate screen or portion of the screen appears where the operator keys the text of the footnote. When that screen is closed, the program places a superscripted number in the main text, adds a 2½ inch line to separate the main text from the footnote text, and places the text of the footnote at the bottom of the page. When footnotes are deleted, inserted, or moved, the numbering sequence is automatically updated. The footnote text may not appear on the regular screen, and in order to see how the footnotes will look when printed, the operator may have to preview or view the document. Footnote "continuation notes" can also be inserted. These notes usually state "footnote continued" or "continuation of footnote" and indicate that a footnote is continued on the next page or that the footnote is the continuation of the last footnote on the preceding page.

Columns. Text can be formatted into columns which allows the operator to simplify the task of creating newsletters, advertising brochures, catalogs, phone lists or other multi-column lists. To create newspaper-style columns or snaking columns as they are sometimes called, the operator defines the number of columns needed and the widths of the columns, which can be either equal or unequal. As the text is keyed, it wraps within the column and when the text reaches the bottom of the page, it automatically goes to the top of the next column. The operator can start a new column before the text reaches the bottom of the page. A key combination, such as Ctrl + Enter or Shift + Ctrl + Enter will start a new column. An entire document or just a selected part of the text can be formatted in columns, and the columnar format can be applied after the text is keyed. Sometimes a vertical line or rule is placed between columns to give a professional, attractive look to the document.

Tables. The ability to make a table format with just a few keystrokes is a huge time saver. A table is made up of vertical columns and horizontal rows that intersect to form cells. Each cell has an address, such as A1, B1, C1, A2, B2, and C2. To create a table, the operator identifies the number of vertical columns and horizontal rows that are needed. Once a table is created, columns and rows can be added or deleted, the widths of the columns can be adjusted, and columns or rows can be moved or copied with just a few keystrokes.

The operator then enters the text in each cell and makes formatting decisions about the appearance of the table. For example, the text can be bold, italics, various font types and sizes, centered, left-aligned, right-aligned, or aligned on the decimal point. The table itself can be enhanced by using vertical or horizontal lines called "borders" or "cell lines."

Tables without borders can also be used to present text in a side-by-side fashion. For example, a resume is often formatted with side headings on the left margin of the paper with the descriptive text set off to the right side. This table format has two columns and as many rows as there are side headings. The left column is narrower than the right column, and no border lines are used.

Some types of legal documents that can be set up in a table format without border lines are multiparty address blocks placed in letters or in certificates of mailing, deposition and medical summaries, pleading captions, side-by-side signature blocks, notary blocks, and client/case information lists.

§ 4.6.5 Word Processing Proofing Tools

Spell Checker. Word processing owes a great deal of its popularity to the spell check feature. After saving the document, the operator gives a command to spell check. The word processing program compares each word on the screen to the words in its internal dictionary, which may contain over 100,000 words. If a match is not made, the word is highlighted so that the operator can check its spelling. The operator can choose to correct the word, ignore the word, or add the word (usually proper names, abbreviations or technical terms) to a custom dictionary.

Spell check finds not only misspelled words, but also double occurrences of words, irregular case, and words that contain both alpha and numeric characters. The pitfall of the spell checker is that it does not find all mistakes. For example, it will not find an error such as "the Untied States" or incorrect word usage, as in the case of "their," "there," or "they're."

Thesaurus. This word processing tool is used to assist in finding synonyms, which are words with similar meanings, or finding antonyms, which are words with opposite meanings.

There are two additional uses of the Thesaurus. It can be used to help determine the meaning of a word. For example, if the word "egregious" was unfamiliar, the operator can use the Thesaurus feature to list the synonyms of egregious (which are "gross," "outrageous," "flagrant") giving a clue as to the word's meaning. The Thesaurus can also be used to ascertain correct word choice and to differentiate between or among the meanings of words that sound alike. For example, checking the words "personnel" and "personal" in the Thesaurus shows that the synonyms of "personnel" include the words "staff," "officers," and "organization." And looking up the word "personal" shows the words "individual," "particular," and "special" as synonyms. With this information, it would be easy to determine which word to use. Most word processing programs include thesaurus and encyclopedias. However, certain free internet thesaurus and encyclopedia websites are more complete.

Grammar Checker. This is a relatively new feature found in word processing programs. Grammar checker looks at each sentence and determines if there are any grammatical or stylistic errors based on three levels of rules: formal writing rules, business writing rules, or casual writing rules. When the grammar check is complete, readability statistics based on formulas that measure number of words, average sentence length, and the number of multi-syllable words are displayed. These statistics give the writer a good idea of how complex the writing is and whether it is a good match for any particular audience. Sometimes the grammar check program will identify ways to improve the writing.

The operator can view these suggestions and decide whether to ignore the change or insert the change into the document.

§ 4.6.6 Automating Word Processing Tasks

Automatic Paragraph Numbering. This feature allows the operator to enter a special code (instead of an actual number) to number paragraphs of text. When the operator moves, inserts, or deletes paragraphs, the paragraphs will automatically renumber sequentially. Pleadings (such as complaints, interrogatories, and affidavits), business and commercial agreements, real estate documents, and estate planning documents commonly contain numbered paragraphs.

Styles. Using styles facilitates giving a professional look to a document. For example, in this book, all the main headings are bold and use the same font type and size, the subheadings for each topic use the identical font and paragraph numbering, and the table of contents at the beginning of each chapter look alike. The tool that is used to create this consistent appearance, as well as saving time by reducing the number of keystrokes required to add formatting codes to a document, is called Styles. The codes that will be used in each section are saved with style names, such as "Main Heading," "Subheading 1," "Subheading 2," and "Text Body." The operator selects the text to be formatted in a particular way and then chooses a style name from a menu and applies it to the selected text.

This feature also makes it effortless to experiment with different formats before deciding on the best looking one for the document. After applying a style to the document, the operator simply changes the style code (not the individually formatted parts of text) and immediately all the text that was formatted according to a particular style is automatically updated with the new formatting choices.

Another advantage of styles is that once a particular set of styles are created and saved, they are available for use in every document and by every user. Many law firms use styles because lawyers, paralegals, and assistants can all use the same formatting codes contained in styles, providing consistency and uniformity throughout an office. Styles can also save time because the users do not have to learn how to do complex formatting.

Macros. Macros (or "glossaries" as they are called in some programs) are considered one of the best word processing tools for saving time. This feature allows the operator to record keystrokes and then play them back with just a few keystrokes. For example, creating a footer may require eight keystrokes. Using the macro feature, the operator can create a macro that could access the footer screen with maybe only two keystrokes—ALT + F.

By using a macro repeatedly, the operator learns the keystrokes necessary to "run" or "invoke" the most commonly used macros quickly. However, many law offices have so many macros that they provide a list of the macros and what they do to new users and to temporary workers.

Some common tasks that are usually automated using macros are:

- Letter format and dateline.
- Memo openings.
- Letter signature blocks.
- Pleading signature blocks.
- Creating captions.
- Retrieving captions.
- Standard language used in pleadings.
- Changing directories.
- Formatting (line spacing, indenting).
- Creating and editing headers and footers.
- Paper tray selection/printing commands.

The process for creating a macro usually includes four steps: (1) giving the macro a name and description, (2) turning on the recording process, (3) recording the keystrokes, and (4) turning off the recording process. Once the macro is created, it can be used at any time. Macros can be assigned to shortcut keys, to icons, or listed in menus so they are easy to access.

Complex macros that include programming language to make menus and customized screen options are most often created by expert programmers in the office or by outside programming consultants. However, the lawyer's assistant should learn how to make simple macros. The time saved and simplification of routine tasks are well worth the cost to have macros designed for the law office.

Table of Authorities. Legal briefs, such as appellate memoranda, contain citations referring to case law, statutes, rules, and other legal authorities. Some courts require that these citations be listed or indexed, including a page number reference, in a table at the beginning of the document. Sophisticated word processors have a feature that allows the operator to mark each citation and authority, categorize it as case law, statutes, etc., and then generate a list of the authorities. When changes are made to the document, the table of authorities can be corrected and updated quickly.

Form Documents. It is a good practice to save any document that may be used again as a form. The most basic form document is a document filled with blanks that can be copied and used over again by deleting the blanks and filling in the pertinent information. More complex documents incorporate a pattern or model form called a template, which includes macro and merge features. Most lawyer's assistants maintain a form file that includes a hard copy of each form marked with its computer filename so it can be accessed efficiently.

Document Assembly. Document assembly is the process of creating several short, separate documents that can be used over and over again. The small documents, sometimes referred to as "standard paragraphs" or "boilerplate paragraphs" can be combined to make one large document.

Document Comparisons. This feature allows the user to compare two versions of a document. Additions in the new version are marked with *redline* and deletions in the new version are marked with *strikeout*, making it easy to see the changes between the original and new versions. Word processing programs are able to compare documents, but for advanced and more exact comparisons, special software is more desirable.

Merging. Merging is the process of combining data from two files to make a third document. The first file contains a form letter, an envelope, or label format. This file is called the main document or primary file. The second file contains a set of names, addresses, phone numbers, and other types of individual information. This file is called the data source or secondary file. When these two files are merged, the special codes in the first file (main document or primary file) are replaced by the actual information (names, addresses, etc.) contained in the data source or secondary file. The merge process creates a third file containing personalized letters, usually separated by page breaks, envelopes, or labels for each separate name in the data source.

The data source or secondary file includes fields and records. A field is one piece of information about a person or business. It can be a person's title (Mr., Mrs., Ms., Dr.), a person's first name and last name, a business name, address, phone number, or any other piece of information. A record is made up of all the fields relating to that one person or business. For example, one record contains the person's name and business name, address, and phone number for one company. Because the data source file or secondary file can be used over and over again with various main documents or primary files, it should contain information for current and future use. For example, a data source file or secondary file listing possible witnesses might include a field containing the witness's phone number. The phone number may never be used in a letter, but it might be used to create a call-back or follow-up list for the lawyer's assistant.

Codes that match the fields in the data source or secondary file are placed in the form letter, memorandum, table, chart, list, and envelope.

The operator then performs a sequence of commands that combines or merges the primary and secondary files. The resulting document of individual letters can be treated just as if the operator keyed in the entire text.

§ 4.6.7 Troubleshooting

Help. Most word processors have a Help feature that can be accessed to explain what a feature does and how it works. In Windows-based programs, the Help feature is very comprehensive and the user is able to print the Help topics shown on the screen.

Undo. In Windows-based word processors, there is a feature that allows the user to "undo" what was previously commanded. If the operator makes a mistake, they simply click on "undo" and the last steps are reversed.

Reveal Codes. WordPerfect users must know how to use the Reveal Codes screen to see what codes have been inserted into a document and to analyze their placement and why they are or are not working. Codes are classified as either open or paired. Open codes affect only the text to the right of the code. Some examples of open codes are line spacing, margins, tab sets, font changes, justification, and page numbering. Paired codes affect only the text that is inserted between a pair of codes, such as underline, bold, italics, and the Styles On code and Styles Off codes.

Ctrl + Alt + Delete. If a computer freezes, this combination of keystrokes allows the operator to end a task or shut down (restart) the computer if necessary. Note that some data may be lost.

Printing. Printers occasionally stop working, and there are several places to check for proper operation. First, make sure all cords are plugged in and that there is a good cable connection between the computer and printer. Second, be familiar with the error messages and lights that indicate such things as paper out, paper jam, off line, etc. Third, look at the menus relating to printing to see if the proper printer type (brand name) and location (LPT1, LPT2, COM1, and COM2) are selected and change the settings if they are not correct.

§ 4.6.8 Document Management

A well-organized and managed filing system for computer document control is essential to good law office practice. A well-defined method for naming and controlling files saves time and energy in locating particular documents, provides consistency and uniformity throughout an office, is easy to learn by new or temporary employees, and is essential for easy identification of files. Many offices have a systematic method of naming their documents and routinely place a document identification name, in a small font, on the last page or in a footer in the document making the document easy to locate on the computer.

The first part of a computer filename identifies the external storage area where the document is saved. For example, a document can be saved on "A:" meaning the first floppy drive slot, on "B:" indicating the second floppy drive slot, on "C:" meaning the hard drive, or on "F:" to "Z:" drives, indicating locations on a network.

The second part of a filename is called the path. Because the C: drive (or hard drive as it is usually called) and network drives are so massive, they are subdivided into areas called subdirectories or folders in Windows-based programs, which are created and named by the operator. A subdirectory, folder, or a combination of subdirectories or folders make up the "path" to the document name. A file can be referred to by its document name or by its full path name.

The last part of the computer filename, is the document name. Some programs only allow the name to be up to eight characters long, plus an extension of three characters, for a total of 11 characters. Other programs allow for the use of more than eight characters for a file name, or automatically assign extensions to documents as they are saved. All letters and numbers can be used, plus the following symbols:
˜! @ # $ % ˆ& ( ) _ | Œ.

However, some programs do not allow the use of the following symbols:
a space, " / \ [ ] < > + = ; : * ?.

Therefore, always consult your user manual or contact your software provider before using a symbol in the document name.

The following extensions cannot be used because they are reserved by programmers and identify certain types of files:

.COM .BAT .EXE .SYS .BAS .BAK .TMP .ARC

Using a consistent schema for the extension part of the filename is very useful. Extensions can indicate the type of document. For example, a letter sent to Mr. Smith would be called SMITH.LTR; a letter to Mr. Jones would be called JONES.LTR

Windows associates extensions with applications. For example, any document/file with a .wpd extension will be opened with WordPerfect, and any document/file with a .doc extension will be opened with Micro-Soft Word.

Some other extensions that are descriptive include:

.AFF	Affidavit	.LTR	Letter
.CMP	Complaint	.MEM	Memorandum
.DEC	Declaration	.CHT	Chart
.ORD	Order for the court	.ADD	Address
.ANS	Answer	.FAX	Facsimile

.BRF	Brief	.LST	List
.NTC	Notice	.PRI	Primary merge file
.NOT	Note (motion calendar)	.SEC	Secondary merge file
.SUB	Subpoena	.IDX	Index
.SDT	Subpoena duces tecum	.FRM	Form
.ROG	Interrogatories	.ENV	Envelope
.RFP	Request for production	.MTN	Motion
.ADM	Request for admission	.MOT	Motion
.DEP	Deposition summary	.RSP	Response memo
.CRT	Certificate	.RPY	Reply memo

Some standard ways of organizing subdirectories or folders in a law office are by:

- Client name or number and then subdividing by matters
- Lawyer (each lawyer's initials)
- Practice area (litigation, real estate, probate, family law, etc.)
- Types of documents (faxes, letters, briefs, etc.)
- Combinations of the above

To help with the naming of documents and file management, some law firms purchase programs called document management software that takes the job of naming the files away from the operator and automatically assigns filenames according to programming instructions developed by word processing consultants. Other law firms hire programmers or have skilled, in-house word processing operators who write macros that automatically place the filename somewhere in the document without the operator having to do much more than a few keystrokes.

§ 4.6.9 Converting File Formats

When a document is created and saved, it is embedded with codes that distinguish its file format, which is determined by the operating system type (such as DOS, Windows, or Macintosh), the word processing software type, and the version of the software program. As a program is improved, it is given a new version number to distinguish it from earlier versions. Special conversion steps must be taken to change the file's format into one that is compatible with the other equipment. Software conversion programs are available that can be installed to assist in the process of converting file formats. Some programs have built-in conversion software.

When different versions of the same software are used, documents created and saved in an older version of the software can be used in newer versions without any additional steps. But documents created and saved in a newer version have to be converted down to the older version using special steps. Consult your user manual to learn how to use this feature.

§ 4.6.10 Spreadsheets

A computerized spreadsheet is an electronic worksheet like an accounting ledger that gives the operator tools to store, calculate, manage, analyze, and manipulate numbers. Using spreadsheet software, data can be displayed graphically using bar graphs, line graphs, pie charts, or stacked bar graphs. In the past, spreadsheets were often only used by law office management to produce financial and accounting records and by lawyers who specialized in practice areas, such as bankruptcy, tax law, real estate, and estate planning. Because the newer Windows-based programs are easier to learn and use and can be linked with word processing documents, lawyer's assistants are quickly learning how to use this software and identifying ways it can be used to help them assist lawyers in new ways. Some legal applications include tracking case costs, calculating claims for damages, calculating child support and alimony, dividing assets in divorce cases, calculating and analyzing lost wages, and creating professional-looking trial exhibits.

§ 4.6.11 Database Management Systems

Database management system (DBMS) software is used to collect, store, and organize data. A database is made up of fields and records. A *field* is one piece of information about a person or business. It can be a person's title (Mr., Mrs., Ms., Dr.), a person's first name and last name, a business name, address, phone number, or any other piece of information. A *record* is made up of all the fields relating to that one person or business. For example, one record contains the person's name, business name, address, and phone number for one company.

Once a database is created and saved, the fields can be alphabetized or sorted. Each record can be searched or queried for key words and/or specific information. New information can be added to the database; incorrect information can be modified. The information in a database can be used to create a variety of reports. The data can also be merged with primary files or main documents in word processing programs.

Lawyer's assistants can use database software in a variety of ways. It can be used to keep track of a law firm's clients. An assistant can use the database software to index discovery documents, including when a particular document was created, who created it, why it was created, who got copies of it, and so on. Some assistants organize the information contained in medical summaries, including the name of the doctor or provider of a service, date of service, medications given, prognosis notes, etc. Law librarians can use database software to keep track of the brief bank. The fields in this database may include the name of the brief, the author, the case, or key words.

§ 4.6.12 Time and Billing

Time and billing software is used to track billable and nonbillable time, calculate charges and costs, and then create the statements and invoices that are sent to the clients. Some programs have features that enable the user to start and stop a timer so that clients are accurately charged for services. In some law firms, the lawyer's assistant needs to input the time into the computer, and the accounting department generates the bills. In small law firms, the lawyer's assistants may manage the entire billing system, which includes adding and editing client data, billing rates, special rates, etc.

Time and billing software is also capable of generating work-in-progress (WIP) reports, and billable and nonbillable reports per timekeeper.

§ 4.6.13 Calendaring/Docket Programs

One of the most critical aspects of a lawyer's assistant's job is to keep track of critical dates for the client and lawyer. (*See also*, Chapter 3.) Many law offices now use electronic calendars and docket programs to monitor activities and to schedule events. Hard copies of the master calendar can be prepared and distributed to others.

§ 4.6.14 Personal Information Management (PIM)

This software is a tool used by lawyers and their assistants to organize information and schedule time. PIM software is used in place of rolodexes and phone books and is used to record notes during meetings and for scheduling.

§ 4.6.15 Presentation Software

Presentation software provides a tool to help organize and present information to an audience. This software can be used to create slides that can be displayed on a computer screen or projected onto a large screen using an LCD (liquid crystal display) panel and overhead projector. Slides using text, charts, graphics or clipart, scanned photographs, animations, shapes, and sounds are used to make an impact on the audience. These programs include automated ways of coordinating the slides to the preparation of handouts for the audience and speaker's notes.

The trial lawyer may find presentation software extremely effective—both in cost and the ability to persuade an audience. A judge and members of a jury comprehend complex ideas more quickly when they are presented with visual aids.

§ 4.7 E-mail and Facsimile

E-mail is a system of delivering and receiving messages electronically using a modem, telephone line, and communications software. Both the sender and the receiver must have an "e-mail address" in order for the computer to acknowledge the commands. The e-mail system has become increasingly recognized inside and outside most firms, as clients and lawyers are able to send documents, messages, letters, etc., via e-mail.

Facsimile is a system of delivering and receiving documents via telephone lines and facsimile machine. The facsimile machine sends an electronic image of the document over the telephone lines to a designated phone line also connected to a facsimile machine. Some courts now allow pleadings and discovery documents to be filed by facsimile.

Faxing and e-mailing documents occur frequently in the law firm today. These systems allow lawyers and clients to review documents immediately. It should be remembered, however, that a faxed document and/or an e-mailed document should also be sent by mail to ensure the receiver has the appropriate file copy.

§ 4.8 Computer Assisted Legal Research

Computer assisted legal research is the use of the computer to look up case law, citations, and other information. Some programs are updated on a daily basis with the most recent case law available to provide lawyers and their assistants with the most up to date information. Examples of these programs are Westlaw and LEXIS–NEXIS. However, the computer assisted legal research market is growing and other sources are also available.

Westlaw and LEXIS–NEXIS require a user access number. Westlaw and/or LEXIS–NEXIS assign a user number to each user. Information can then be obtained by knowing keywords, dates, names, types of cases, etc. Using either program can be costly as it is billed by time spent in the program, so knowing as much information as possible prior to accessing the research program is of great benefit to the law firm and the client.

§ 4.9 Internet

The Internet is a system that connects computers worldwide and allows computer users to receive and/or transfer text, programs, graphics images, and sounds through this network. The Internet was launched in 1969 and, for many years, was used primarily by the government as well as the scientific and academic communities. In 1989, scientists introduced the Worldwide Web and software tools called Web browsers. These new developments provided the general public with a simple way of working with the Internet and all of its resources. The Web is made up of millions of documents that are written in a special language called HyperText Markup Language or HTML. Some documents are also augmented by other languages such as Adobe, flash, java, and PHP. Each individual document is called a Web page or Web site and ranges from one to many screens in length. The first or opening page (in essence the title page) of a Web site is called a home page. Within each of the Web pages are links (also known as hypertext, hyperlinks, hotspots, and jumps) that associate one Web page to another. By selecting or pointing and clicking the mouse on a jump term or hyperlink, the user can quickly move from one location or topic to another. Each Web site and hyperlink has an address called a Uniform Resource Locator code (URL) on the Internet.

Older systems may use a Dial-up connection over a phone line which is turned on and off whenever a user wants to connect to the internet. Other connection types are constantly in contact with the Internet service provider. These connection types include cable internet, Digital Subscriber Line (DSL), and satellite internet. Each of these connection types are digital and transfer information significantly faster than Dial-up connections.

To connect with the Internet, the computer user (or client) uses a modem to contact another computer or server through a service provider. There are many commercial Internet service providers.

Once the client is connected, a Web browser, such as Netscape Navigator, Microsoft Internet Explorer, or Mosaic, is used to access Web sites using their URL. The URL contains three parts:

1. The protocol used, which can be considered the language of interpreting the computer information. Common protocol types are HTTP (HyperText Transfer Protocol), FTP (File Transfer Protocol), and Gopher (a specialized transfer protocol).

2. The domain, which indicates the computer system that stores the information or a group of people who maintain a server. Domains are divided into categories: .com (commercial), .edu (education), .org (non-profit organizations), .gov (government), .mil (military), .net (network).

3. The actual location of an item on the server.

The Internet is becoming one of the standard tools used in a law office. Court rules, form documents, and many other sources of up-to-date information are available. As the assistant finds websites that are helpful, the bookmark feature in the Web browser can be used to add the site to a personal list.

§ 4.10 Electronic Filing and Case Management

Electronic filing (e-filing) is a system used by courts, government agencies, attorneys, and the public to reduce paperwork and electronically file documents over the Internet using a standard Web browser. Using Adobe Acrobat word processing and other types of files are converted to portable document format (.pdf) and then authorized users can transmit and access them. Case Management/Electronic Case Filing (CM/ECF) systems are being implemented in many bankruptcy, district and appellate courts and the federal court system is working to meet its goal to use e-filing in all courts. Documents filed electronically are available to judges at their bench or in chambers; attorneys and their staff have access to documents from any computer. The system allows service of pleadings and court orders; service lists can easily be updated. If an attorney is not connected to the Internet, facsimile or hard copy documents can be delivered. This new use of Internet technology will be revolutionary in the practice of law.

§ 4.11 Backup

To prevent costly loss of data in a computer, routinely make a copy or "backup" of all data stored on the computer and place that duplicate in a separate location. Small law offices using stand-alone computers or individuals who use laptop computers should purchase backup software, install it on their computer, learn how to use it, and then consistently use it to back up their system's software and the ever-changing data stored on the computer. Networked computer systems require efficient, systematic backup procedures that are usually performed by trained, responsible staff member(s) on a daily basis.

At a minimum, for individual users, the first step in backing up your system is to create a bootable floppy disk that can be used to start the computer if the hard disk fails. Second, make sure the system disk contains the CONFIG.SYS, AUTOEXEC.BAT, SYSTEM.INI, and WIN. INI files and any driver files (*i.e.*, those files that command the printer, CD–ROM, and/or tape drives.) Third, keep copies or originals of all software that is used and an updated copy of all data stored on the computer. An inventory of the software is also helpful. Then in the event your computer "crashes," you can take it and your backup disks to a computer store and have the computer repaired and the software reinstalled.

§ 4.12 Computer Security

When computers are connected to other computers via modems (e-mail, Internet, on-line services) or when a user can have call-in access to the system, security is critical. Law firms need to ensure privacy by using special software with their e-mail software that will encode messages so that they are secure electronically. This software is called encryption software. Law firms must protect the computer systems from unauthorized access by using user identification passwords and higher levels of authentication systems.

Some system operators have a policy to change passwords routinely on a specific date. Passwords should be as many digits as possible and should not be obvious. The following types of passwords are easily decoded so users should avoid using them:

- Ascending digits (e.g., 1234)
- Same digits (9999)
- Digits corresponding to employee's name (e.g., 5646 for John)
- Current year (2002)
- Same number as phone extension
- Reverse phone extensions
- Numbers that identify the owner (social security, employee identification, room number)
- Pets, children, family members
- Common words or phrases for entry such as open or enter

Another security issue is "viruses." Virus protection is critical. A virus is a computer code that can be copied into an existing computer program and make itself known by flashing an innocuous message on the screen or doing something as serious as destroying data or disabling the operating system. The first virus was detected in the early 1980s and its name was coined from its ability to replicate and "infect" other computers. Computer viruses can spread through infected diskettes, e-mail, shared computer software, through an on-line service, or through a network.

Virus scanners are available that check for viruses and remove them from the system. Be sure to select a software package that will scan e-mail attachments in addition to other files found on the hard drive. Regularly updating virus signatures to detect the most recent viruses is crucial. Because new viruses are introduced all the time, no system is totally safe from a virus.

§ 4.13 Selecting Equipment

The task of selecting equipment for a law office requires some time and energy, and if a law practice is larger than four or five lawyers or if a network is going to be installed, technical assistance from computer vendors or system consultants may be required. In small firms, the following points should be considered:

(1) Determine the current and future needs of the law office. Ask questions, such as, "What do you want the computer to do? How many people will use the machine?"

(2) Research current equipment and pricing. Get price quotes (at least three) from various vendors.

(3) Think of storage needs and the possibility of upgrading the system.

(4) Assess the costs of the peripherals and software.

(5) Watch vendor demonstrations. Talk to people who have recently purchased equipment.

(6) Check availability of warranty and after-purchase support.

§ 4.14 Ergonomics

Because of the widespread use of computers, today's workforce faces problems associated with constant keyboard work, such as muscle aches, tension, and pain in the hands, arms, neck, and back. These conditions are referred to as repetitive strain injuries or RSI. Some ways of preventing RSI, without investing hundreds of dollars in new equipment, are listed below.

(1) Look away from the screen to something in the distance every 10 to 15 minutes to refocus and rest your eyes. Also, take one to five minute screen breaks every hour—get up and stretch, walk, and move around.

(2) During the day, be conscious of rotating tasks between heavy keyboarding and walking, moving, or some other desk activity where the arms are frequently changing position.

(3) Use an adjustable chair so it can be positioned so you can sit comfortably with the spine up and straight, not curved or twisted to the right, left, or hunched forward.

(4) The desk and keyboard should be at a proper height. Sit in front of the keyboard and bend your arms at the elbow so they are parallel to the floor. The keyboard should be positioned at the same height as your bent arms.

(5) The monitor screen should be placed directly in front of the operator, and the operator's eyes should be level with the top of the screen.

(6) Use good keyboarding techniques. Touch the keyboard lightly; do not hammer the keys. Keep your wrists one-half inch above the keyboard so that the wrists do not rest on anything. Keeping the wrists in a stationary, static position is the major cause of carpal tunnel syndrome and other RSIs.

§ 4.15 Getting Additional Help

The knowledge required for using computers changes rapidly. There are several resources to help the lawyer's assistant obtain the basic skills required to produce correspondence and documents or to continue updating, refining, and learning new skills. Community colleges offer short-term, inexpensive computer classes. Some firms provide in-house training programs and others purchase reference manuals, training workbooks, and/or videos to help users in self-guided training efforts. Valuable information can be found by reading periodicals and journals dealing with computers in general or specific software applications. An excellent way to develop knowledge is to share ideas with coworkers or other computer users, formally at meetings or seminars and/or informally during lunch or breaks. And last, the most important resource is yourself—have an open, willing, and exploratory attitude about learning to use the computer.

CHAPTER 5

ACCOUNTING

Table of Sections

§ 5.1 Introduction

The practice of law, like any other type of income-earning business or profession, must be run in a businesslike manner. The law office maintains an orderly system of accounts reflecting many things the lawyer must know to continue to realize a profit. Established law firms already have a system for handling the accounting and recordkeeping. Most law firms will have a computer accounting system set up and many of the mechanical steps in the process will be performed by the system. This chapter presents some of the fundamentals of accounting to enable the lawyer's assistant to understand and maintain the system in use, including the mechanics of the double-entry bookkeeping system.

§ 5.2 Accounting in a Law Office

The principal source of revenue in any personal service enterprise is compensation for professional services rendered. Professional service enterprises, such as law firms, generally use one of two systems of accounting: cash basis or accrual basis.

§ 5.2.1 Cash Basis

The cash basis of accounting is most often used in law offices, because it is simple and it may provide for a tax deferral. Accounting for revenue on a cash basis generally means fee revenue is not recorded on the books until cash is actually received for the services performed. Some of the revenue for services rendered in one period is accounted for in another period. This eliminates the need for many complicated bookkeeping tasks. The cash basis set of books basically consists of a cash receipts and expenditures journal, general journal, general ledger, payroll record book, and sometimes a petty cash record book.

Accounting on the cash basis means that expenses as well as revenues are not generally recorded on the books until they are paid. The method is really a modified cash basis because certain accounts, such as prepaid rent or insurance are expensed over time rather than when paid; likewise, loans payable are recorded on the books when incurred.

§ 5.2.2 Accrual Basis

The accrual basis of accounting, on the other hand, records revenues in the period in which they are earned and expenses in the period in which they are incurred. Revenue is considered to be earned when, in exchange for something of value, money is received or a legal claim to money comes into existence. In a service business on the accrual method, revenue is recorded when the invoice is issued. Since the lawyer's invoice to a client is a legal claim to money and the invoice is not always paid immediately, the accounts receivable ledger is used to keep track of the amounts the client owes and pays.

Under the accrual system, an accounts payable ledger is used to show such financial obligations as payroll, taxes, rent, utilities, equipment, supplies, insurance, libraries, and amounts that are paid in installments. The accounts payable ledger shows what the firm owes at any given time.

The accrual basis is used because it shows a period-by-period matching of revenues and expenses, and therefore, the profit and/or loss for that period. The accrual method recognizes changes in many types of assets and liabilities when computing net income for a specific period, not just changes in the cash account. The firm's accountant charges off bad debts before closing the books so that the income is not overstated and taxes are not incurred on income that may never be received by the firm.

§ 5.2.3 Journals

The first formal double-entry record of a transaction is usually made in a journal. The act of recording transactions in a journal is called *journalizing*. Journalizing involves analyzing each transaction and recording the significant information concerning the transaction either (1) at the time the transaction occurs or (2) subsequently, but in the chronological order in which it and the other transactions occurred. Journals provide a chronological record of all transactions completed, showing the date of each transaction, titles of accounts to be debited or credited, and amounts of the debits and credits.

§ 5.2.4 Ledgers

While the journals provide a chronological record of all transactions, ledgers show the balance in each account at any given point in time. The general ledger includes all assets, liabilities, equity accounts, revenues, and expenses. Every journal entry affects the balance in two or more general ledger accounts.

Subsidiary ledgers contain itemized support for the information found in specific accounts in the general ledger. Typical subsidiary ledgers found in law offices are accounts receivable, accounts payable, client trust fund ledger, fixed assets, payroll records, and a petty cash ledger. For example, the accounts receivable page in the general ledger may show a total in accounts receivable of $10,000. The accounts receivable subsidiary ledger will list the individual accounts that add up to $10,000.

§ 5.3 Basic Principles

Accounting is the process of analyzing, recording, classifying, summarizing, reporting, and interpreting financial transactions and events. The five basic accounting elements are assets, liabilities, equity, revenues, and expenses. Assets and expenses are debit accounts; liabilities, equity, and revenues are credit accounts. The fundamental accounting equation is *assets* = *liabilities* + *equity*. The value of these elements is increased or decreased when the firm realizes revenue or pays expenses.

Every transaction affects two (or more) accounts. For example, the receipt of fees affects both revenue (fee income) and assets (cash); the payment of a bill affects both an expense account and cash. This is the basis of double-entry bookkeeping: every event gives rise to at least two equal and offsetting entries on the books, a debit and a credit.

§ 5.3.1 Debits and Credits

Every double entry recorded in a journal is made up of one or more debits and one or more credits. The total debits must always equal the total credits. To debit an account means to record an amount on the left or debit side of the account. To credit an account means to record an amount on the right or credit side of the account. The abbreviation for debit is Dr. and for credit, Cr. The difference between the total debits and total credits posted to an account is called the "balance." Any account may have either a debit or a credit balance.

Even though an account is classified as a debit or a credit (*e.g.*, cash is a debit account), both debit and credit entries can be posted to that account. A receipt of cash is recorded as a debit to cash, while payment of a bill is a credit to the cash account. Even a debit account may at times have a credit balance, as when the bank account is overdrawn.

Assets are shown on the left side of the balance sheet and generally have balances on the left or debit side. An asset account is increased by any of the following events:

1. Additional cash or other property is invested by the owner (debit cash or equipment, credit owner's equity).
2. A loan is obtained (debit cash, credit bank loan payable).
3. Revenues are derived from services (debit cash or accounts receivable, credit fee revenue).
4. Another asset is decreased (debit cash, credit equipment when equipment is sold).

Decreases in assets are called credits and are recorded on the right side of the account. An asset is decreased by any of the following events:

1. Cash or other property is withdrawn from the business by the owner (debit owner's equity, credit cash or equipment).
2. Liabilities of the business are paid (debit accounts payable, credit cash).
3. Expenses are incurred in operations (debit operating expenses, credit cash).
4. Another asset may be increased (debit equipment, credit cash when equipment is purchased).

Since the liabilities and owner's equity are shown on the right side of the balance sheet, consistency also suggests that increases to those accounts are recorded on the right side (Cr.) of the account and decreases are recorded on the left (Dr.) side. Liabilities are increased by any of the following events:

1. Assets increase (debit equipment, credit accounts payable when equipment is purchased on contract).
2. Expenses are incurred (debit operating expenses, credit accounts payable).
3. Other liabilities are decreased (debit accounts payable, credit notes payable when debts are consolidated).

Liabilities are decreased by either of the following events:

1. Loans are paid off (debit notes payable, credit cash).
2. Other liabilities increase (debit accounts payable, credit notes payable if debts are consolidated).

Owner's equity, on the other hand, is increased only in the following ways:

1. The owner invests additional cash or other property (assets) in the business.
2. Net profits are derived from services or from other sources.

Owner's equity is decreased in only two ways:

1. Cash or other property (assets) is withdrawn from the business by the owner.
2. Net losses are incurred in the operation.

Illustration 5–1

ASSETS		LIABILITIES AND OWNER'S EQUITY	
All Asset Accounts		All Liability Accounts	
Debit to enter increases (+)	Credit to enter decreases (−)	Debit to enter decreases (−)	Credit to enter increases (+)
		All Owner's Equity Accounts	
		Debit to enter decreases (−)	Credit to enter increases (+)
All Expense Accounts		All Revenue Accounts	
Debit to enter increases (+)	Credit to enter decreases (−)	Debit to enter decreases (−)	Credit to enter increases (+)

§ 5.3.2 Sources of Information

Before recording transactions in the journal, it is necessary to analyze each transaction to ensure that it is recorded properly. The term *source documents* covers a wide variety of forms and papers. Any document that provides information about cash received, cash disbursed, fees charged, or purchases charged can be called a source document.

Some examples of source documents include:

- Check stubs or copies of checks.
- Receipt stubs or copies of receipts, cash register tapes, copies of invoices marked "paid" by clients' checks, or any other document used by the law office to record receipts.
- Purchase invoices received from vendors.
- Lawyer's time sheets for services to be billed or invoices as billed to clients.
- Sources of interest earned on savings accounts, certificates of deposit, or other asset accounts invested for profit.
- Documents used to record funds expended on behalf of clients.

§ 5.3.3 Typical Journals

Even the most basic accounting system generally utilizes several journals: the cash disbursements journal (essentially the check register), the cash receipts journal (both cash receipts and disbursements may come from the check journal), and the general journal. A separate payroll journal may be used. Generally, each bank account requires a separate journal to record transactions.

§ 5.3.4 Helpful Rules for Journalizing

Since almost all transactions in a law office involve either bank deposits and withdrawals or charging clients and receiving payments from them, the following rules are helpful:

1. CASH RECEIVED (bank deposits) is always debited to the bank account in which it is deposited and therefore must be credited to another account, usually a revenue account (cash basis).
2. ACCOUNTS RECEIVABLE is debited when a bill for services is sent to a client, and the amount charged is credited to a revenue account (accrual basis).
3. ACCOUNTS RECEIVABLE is credited when payment is received from a client, and the payment is debited to the cash account (accrual basis).
4. CASH PAYMENTS (bank withdrawals) are always credited to the bank account on which they are drawn and therefore must be debited to another account, usually an expense account (cash basis) or accounts payable (accrual basis).
5. ACCOUNTS PAYABLE is credited when a bill for expenses is received, and the amount is debited to an expense account (accrual basis).
6. ACCOUNTS PAYABLE is debited when a check is written to pay an expense and the payment is credited to the cash account (accrual basis).

§ 5.3.5 Compound Journal Entries

A compound entry is used when it becomes necessary to show a distribution of an amount to more than one account. A compound entry is used in either debit or credit amount columns or both.

For example, a loan payment has one credit entry (cash) but two debit entries (interest expense and loans payable).

dr	Interest expense	500
dr	Loans payable	100
cr	Cash	600

§ 5.3.6 The Chart of Accounts

The bookkeeper or accountant must know which accounts the business uses to be able to analyze a transaction. The first step is to determine which accounts are required for that particular business. Regardless of the number, the accounts are segregated into the five major classes and grouped according to these classes in the ledger. Asset accounts are listed first, followed by liability accounts, owner's equity accounts, revenue, and expense accounts. It is common practice to prepare a chart of accounts in outline form in the front of the general ledger for easy reference. Each account is assigned a number, and one accepted pattern of coding is to assign "100" series numbers to asset accounts, "200" series numbers to liability accounts, "300" series numbers to owner's equity accounts, "400" series numbers to income or revenue accounts, and "500" series numbers to expense accounts. Illustration 5–2 is an example of the Chart of Accounts for L.G. Lambert, a lawyer on the accrual basis.

Illustration 5–2

L.G. LAMBERT
ATTORNEY AT LAW
Chart of Accounts

Asset Accounts

Cash in Bank	111
Trust Account–Bank	112
Savings Account	113
Petty Cash Fund	114
Office Furn. & Equip.	121
Accumulated Depr.	121D
Library	122
Accts. Receivable—Services	131
Accounts Receivable—Costs	132
Prepaid Rent	141
Prepaid Insurance	142

Liability Accounts

Accounts Payable	211
Social Security and Medicare Taxes Payable	212
Withholding Taxes Payable	213
Other Taxes Payable	214
Notes Payable	221
Trust Acct.—Client Funds	231

Owner's Equity Accounts

L.G. Lambert, Capital	311
L.G. Lambert, Drawing	321

Income Accounts

Professional Fees	411
Earned Interest	421

Expense Accounts

Rent	511
Salaries	512
Telephone	513
Books and Periodicals	514
Insurance	515
Client Costs	516
Postage	517
Travel	518
Office	519
Client Entertainment	522
Payroll Tax	523
Depreciation	524
Utilities	525

§ 5.4 The General Ledger

The process of recording (entering) information in the general ledger from the journal is known as *posting*. Each amount in the journal must be posted to the proper general ledger account at frequent intervals, usually monthly in a manual system, in order to summarize the results. A computerized system automatically posts all journal entries to the ledger when recorded.

Since the ledger accounts provide the information needed to prepare the financial statements, a posting procedure that will ensure accuracy in maintaining the accounts must be followed. Posting from the journals to the ledger involves recording the following information in the accounts:

1. The date of each transaction
2. The amount of each transaction
3. The page of the journal from which each transaction is posted

As each amount in the journal is posted to the proper account in the ledger, the number of that account should be entered in the Posting Reference column in the journal so as to provide a cross-reference between the journal and ledger and a quick-check method of ensuring proper posting to the accounts.

§ 5.4.1 Subsidiary Ledgers

In every type of business, it is necessary to keep one or more subsidiary ledgers. Each ledger contains like information so that breakdowns of totals can be seen at a glance. These ledgers may pertain to accounts receivable, payroll, petty cash, or other desired information. The total of the accounts receivable subsidiary ledger must agree with the accounts receivable balance in the general ledger.

§ 5.4.2 Closing

In order to make the accounting records useful to the owner and others, such as bankers and accountants, they must be converted into periodic financial statements. These statements may be prepared monthly, quarterly or annually. The process of converting the raw accounting data into useful statements is known as *closing*.

The steps of closing include:

1. Entering general journal entries
2. Posting transactions or totals from the journals to the general ledger
3. Preparing a trial balance (or end-of-period worksheet)
4. Determining any necessary adjusting journal entries; entering them on the trial balance
5. Preparing the financial statements
6. Journalizing and posting the closing entries

These six steps are discussed in the following paragraphs.

§ 5.4.3 General Journal Entries

Only cash transactions are entered in the cash receipts and expenditures journal. Therefore, to record non-cash transactions on the books, entries are made in the general journal.

One classic example of a non-cash entry in the general journal is the recording of depreciation expense:

dr 524	Depreciation Expense	$1000	
cr 121D	Accumulated Depreciation		$1000
	To record monthly depreciation of office furniture and equipment		

Other typical general journal entries record the amortization of prepaid rent or insurance.

§ 5.4.4 Posting to the General Ledger

When all financial transactions have been recorded in the journals, the journal entries are posted to the general ledger. Frequently used journals, such as those for cash disbursements and cash receipts, are generally totaled at the end of the month, then only one entry is made to each account in the general ledger from that journal. For example, ten payroll checks may have been written but there is only one entry from the payroll journal to the payroll expense account in the general ledger.

The general journal entries are posted individually to the proper general ledger page. The entries to the individual general ledger accounts are then added to, or subtracted from, any prior balance.

§ 5.4.5 Preparing the Trial Balance

Since the fundamental equation of accounting is that the total of the assets equals the sum of the liabilities and owner's equity, a list of all the debit and credit balances must be prepared to check equality. This list is called a trial balance. The trial balance is prepared before the income and expense accounts are closed to an equity account, and those accounts must also be on the trial balance in order for it to balance.

The trial balance should be prepared as follows:

1. The heading of the trial balance should show the name of the firm, the title of the report "Trial Balance," and the date. The date shown is the date of the last transaction that is included in the accounts, which is usually the last day of the month.
2. List the account titles in numerical order, showing titles and account number.
3. Enter the account balances, placing debit balances in the left amount column and credit balances in the right amount column.

4. Add the columns and enter the totals, placing a single line across the amount columns above the totals and a double line below the totals in the manner shown in Illustration 5–3.

Illustration 5–3

L.G. LAMBERT, ATTORNEY AT LAW

Trial Balance

As of June 30, 20__

A/C #	A/C Name	Preliminary Trial Balance		Adjusting Entries		Final Trial Balance	
		dr	cr	dr	cr	dr	cr
111	Cash in Bank	$14,812.95	$				
112	Trust Account–Client Funds	1,075.00					
121	Office Furniture and Equipment	4,820.00					
122	Library	8,600.00					
141	Prepaid Rent	650.00					
142	Prepaid Insurance	429.17					
212	Social Security and Medicare Taxes Payable		51.42				
213	Withholding Taxes Payable		64.38				
311	L.G. Lambert, Capital		30,000.00				
321	L.G. Lambert, Drawing	2,800.00					
411	Professional Fees		4,790.00				
511	Rent Expense	650.00					
512	Salaries Expense	850.00					
513	Telephone Expense	116.00					
514	Periodicals Expense	16.85					
515	Insurance Expense	85.83					
	TOTALS	$34,905.80	$34,905.80				

If the column totals of the trial balance do not agree, there is an error. Possible errors include:

- The trial balance was not totaled accurately
- A transaction was incorrectly entered in the journal
- The journal was not totaled properly
- The journal totals were not posted accurately to the general ledger
- The general ledger was not totaled accurately
- The general ledger totals were copied incorrectly on the trial balance

§ 5.4.6 Adjusting Entries

Adjusting entries (adjusting journal entries) are general journal entries that are required specifically for the purpose of adjusting account balances or correcting errors. A review of the trial balance may show utilities much higher than normal. Analysis of the cash expenditures journal reveals that a $250 insurance payment was mistakenly recorded as a utility bill. The adjusting entry would be:

dr	515	insurance expense	$250
cr	525	utility expense	$250

The adjusting entries are noted in the center columns of the trial balance, and the accounts affected are recorded in the right-most two columns as the corrected amount. All unadjusted accounts are entered again in the right-most columns, and the trial balance must again be totaled to make sure it is in balance.

The adjusting entries must also be recorded in the general journal and posted to the general ledger, so that the ledger balances and the adjusted trial balance agree.

§ 5.4.7 Financial Reports

Periodic reports must be prepared according to the needs of the lawyer or firm. These may be monthly, quarterly, or annually. The two basic types of financial statements are the income statement (profit and loss) and the balance sheet (statement of financial position). Various other statements may be prepared as well.

§ 5.4.8 The Income Statement

The income statement is an itemized statement that provides information regarding the profit and loss of the operation during a specific time period. It is a statement of the changes in owner's equity resulting from the revenue and expenses of the specific period (month, quarter, year). Only the income and expense accounts are included in the statement, and the difference between the two is the net income or net loss. Since the figures for the income statement are in the adjusted trial balance, it is not necessary to take time to look up individual accounts in the ledger. (*See* Illustration 5–4.)

Illustration 5–4

L.G. LAMBERT
ATTORNEY AT LAW
INCOME STATEMENT
For the Month Ended June 30, 20__

Income		
Professional Fees		$4,790.00
Expenses		
Rent Expense	$650.00	
Salaries Expense	850.00	
Telephone Expense	116.00	
Periodicals Expense	16.85	
Insurance Expense	85.83	
Total Expenses		1,718.68
NET INCOME		$3,071.32

§ 5.4.9 The Balance Sheet

The balance sheet is an itemized statement of the assets, liabilities, and owner's equity of a business as of a specified date. Its purpose is to provide information regarding the status of these basic accounting elements. The heading of a balance sheet contains the following:

1. The name of the firm.
2. The title of the statement.
3. The date of the statement as of the close of business on that date.

The trial balance is the source of the information needed in listing the assets and liabilities in the balance sheet. The income statement is the source of information for obtaining the net loss or net profit figures. (*See* Illustration 5–5.)

Illustration 5–5

L.G. LAMBERT
ATTORNEY AT LAW
Balance Sheet
June 30, 20__

Assets		**Liabilities**		
Cash in Bank	$14,812.95	Social Security and Medicare Taxes Payable	$51.42	
Trust Acct–Client	1,075.00	Withholding Taxes Payable	64.38	
Office Furniture and Equipment	4,820.00 4,820.00	Total Liabilities		$115.80
Library	8,600.00	**Owner's Equity**		
Prepaid Rent	650.00	L.G. Lambert Capital	$30,000.00	
Prepaid Insurance	429.17	Less Drawing	2,800.00	
			27,200.00	
		Plus Net Income	3,071.32	
		Total Owner's Equity		30,271.32
TOTAL ASSETS	$30,387.12	TOTAL LIABILITIES AND OWNER'S EQUITY		$30,387.12

In a law firm with more than one owner or partner, the net income is divided according to the agreed percentages among the owners, with each owner having their own capital and drawing accounts.

§ 5.4.10 Other Periodic Financial Statements

Other financial statements that may be prepared periodically include a cash flow statement, a statement of changes in owners' equity (particularly in an office of several lawyers), a statement of accounts receivable, a statement of accounts payable, a statement of work in progress (time charges incurred but not yet billed to the client), and a comparison of the income statement to the budget.

Some offices require regular analysis of all action on each client's account (e.g., weekly, monthly, quarterly, etc.). The lawyers want to know who owes what to whom. Some offices also break down the costs recovered from each client in the analysis.

§ 5.4.11 Closing Entries

The lawyer or the accountant decides the fiscal period for the closing entries, and a time schedule is established. This last step typically is done only at year-end, even if all the preceding steps are performed more frequently. Closing the accounts means that the revenue and expense accounts and the drawing accounts of owners will have served their purpose for that fiscal period, and the balance of each of these accounts needs to be brought back to zero in order to make the accounts ready for entries in the following period. The means of closing a ledger account under the double-entry procedure is to post the amount of the account's balance to the opposite side of the account so that the account will then have a zero balance. Each of the revenue, expense, and drawing accounts are closed this way. The net effect is then debited or credited to the owner's capital account. This result is accomplished by three entries in the general journal as follows:

1. The credit balances in Professional Fees and Other Income are closed to the Owner's Capital account. (Debit Income or Fees. Credit Capital.)
2. The debit balances of all expense accounts are closed to the Owner's Capital account. This may be done as a compound total or singularly (referred to as posting in detail). (Debit Capital with the total. Credit each expense account individually.)
3. The debit balance of the owner's drawing account is closed to the owner's capital account. (Debit Owner's Capital. Credit Owner's Drawing.)

Once the posting of the closing entries has been accomplished, it is advisable to make sure the general ledger accounts still total to zero. In other words, assets = liabilities + equity. Each revenue and expense account should have a zero balance. The year-end balances, after closing, become the beginning balances in all accounts for the next fiscal period.

§ 5.5 The Petty Cash Fund

A petty cash fund, sometimes called an imprest fund, is usually established for paying small items. Such a fund eliminates the need to write checks for relatively small amounts. The fund is usually established for $50, $100, $200, or any amount considered necessary. The check to establish or replenish the fund is made payable to "Cash." Only one person should be responsible for accounting for these funds. Payments from the fund should not be made without obtaining some sort of receipt in return. This is usually known as a "petty cash voucher" and shows the name of the payee, the purpose of the payment, the account to be charged, and the amount.

The check written to establish the petty cash fund may be entered in the journal by debiting Petty Cash Fund (an asset) and crediting Cash. When it is necessary to replenish the fund, the person responsible for the fund prepares a statement of the payments properly classified. A check is then written and cashed for the exact amount of the total payments that have been made. This check is entered in the cash disbursements journal, debiting the proper expense account(s) and crediting cash.

Illustration 5–6

Jan. 1	dr. Petty Cash Fund	$200.00	
	cr. Cash		$200.00
	To establish petty cash fund.		
Mar. 1	dr. Automobile Expense	$ 22.00	
	dr. Supplies Expense	32.00	
	dr. Postage Expense	26.00	
	dr. Miscellaneous Expense	5.25	
	cr. Cash		85.25
	To replenish petty cash fund.		

The petty cash fund is a revolving fund. The petty cash account balance does not change in amount unless the fund is increased or decreased.

A statement of petty cash disbursements, or trial balance of petty cash, is prepared for the period and kept in the front of the subsidiary ledger with copies to the owner and bookkeeper according to office practice. Vouchers for the period are filed in a dated envelope and kept in a safe place.

§ 5.6 Handling Lawyers' Fees

The principal saleable commodity in a law office is the lawyer's services. Services are generally billed to clients on an hourly basis, except for contingent fee cases where the lawyer is paid a percentage of any recovery at the end of the case. An effective, non-burdensome time reporting system must be adopted. Because law firms differ so much, there is no one system suitable to all. There are many computer-based programs that can be adapted to the particular needs of your firm. "Timekeeping pays" is a cardinal rule in any law office.

No matter who is given the responsibility for client billing, duplicates of all time and costs billed must be given to the bookkeeper. If the firm is on the accrual basis, the entries are journalized by debiting Accounts Receivable and crediting the Professional Fees Income account. On either the cash or the accrual system, the fees billed are recorded on the individual client's subsidiary ledger sheet. When a cost check is written, or the amount paid out of petty cash, the costs advanced appear as a debit to the client's Accounts Receivable–Costs and a credit to the bank account. This amount is also listed on the client's ledger sheet.

When the client pays the bill, the bookkeeper must break down the amount to determine how much of the total is for costs advanced and how much is for services, and make a journal entry as follows:

Debit Cash in Bank (amount of deposit)

Credit Accounts Receivable—Client's name—Costs

Credit Accounts Receivable—Client's name—Services (accrual method) or Professional Fees (cash method)

§ 5.7 Handling Trust Accounts

Trust funds in a law office must be handled meticulously. Rule 1.15 of the ABA Model Rules of Professional Conduct, adopted in 1983, and subsequently amended, sets out the requirements for handling these funds. Unfortunately, many lawyers have found to their dismay that poor recordkeeping or commingling of firm funds and client funds can result in serious complications with lasting effects.

The rule provides:

(a) A lawyer shall hold property of clients or third persons that is in a lawyer's possession in connection with a representation separate from the lawyer's own property. Funds shall be kept in a separate account maintained in the state where the lawyer's office is situated, or elsewhere with the consent of the client or third person. Other property shall be identified as such and appropriately safeguarded. Complete records of such account funds and other property shall be kept by the lawyer and shall be preserved for a period of five years after termination of the representation.

(b) A lawyer may deposit the lawyer's own funds in a client trust account for the sole purpose of paying bank service charges on that account, but only in an amount necessary for that purpose.

(c) Upon receiving funds or other property in which a client or third person has an interest, a lawyer shall promptly notify the client or third person. Except as stated in this rule or otherwise permitted by law or by agreement with the client, a lawyer shall promptly deliver to the client or third person any funds or other property that the client or third person is entitled to receive and, upon request by the client or third person, shall promptly render a full accounting regarding such property.

(d) When in the course of representation a lawyer is in possession of property in which two or more persons (one of whom may be the lawyer) claim interests, the property shall be kept separate by the lawyer until the dispute is resolved. The lawyer shall promptly distribute all portions of the property as to which the interests are not in dispute.

Most jurisdictions have adopted the Model Rules. However, some states have adopted them with some revisions. The person responsible for the client trust funds must be sure to comply with the rules adopted by the state in which the lawyer is practicing. The rules are generally quite similar in all states.

The main admonishment of Rule 1.15 is for the lawyer to keep all client funds paid to a lawyer or law firm, other than payment for fees earned and costs incurred, in one or more identifiable bank accounts maintained in the state in which the law office is located. No funds belonging to the lawyer or law firm are deposited in the trust account except as follows:

1. Funds reasonably sufficient to pay bank charges.
2. Funds belonging in part to a client and in part or potentially to the lawyer or law firm, but the portion belonging to the lawyer or law firm may be withdrawn when due unless the right of the lawyer or law firm to receive it is disputed by the client, in which case the disputed portion is not to be withdrawn until the dispute is finally resolved.

The requirement goes on to set out that clients must be notified immediately of receipt of funds, securities, or other property that is or may be theirs and that the lawyer must maintain complete records and render a complete accounting to the client. The lawyer must promptly pay to or deliver to the client all funds, securities, or other properties in the lawyer's possession to which the client is entitled.

There are many printed forms on the market for trust accounts, and the large firm keeps a subsidiary ledger of these accounts; the smaller firm can maintain accurate records by establishing a separate checking account, preferably in a different bank from the firm's account. Trust accounts must be maintained separately from the firm's regular account. If trust moneys cannot be kept in a different bank from the firm's account, the trust account might use different-colored checks from the firm's regular checks. It should also be designated as "Trust Account," with the firm's or lawyer's name printed above the signature line. The pages in the accounts receivable subsidiary ledger under each client's name reflect all services charged, costs advanced and repaid, payments received, and balances remitted to the client. Listings of the other negotiable instruments or properties received for or remitted to the client can also be made somewhere on the ledger page. When such items are delivered to the client, they should be placed in a fireproof safe or safety deposit box and the signed receipts can be attached to the ledger page.

It is very important to remember that when funds are received as a retainer, they are to be placed in the firm's trust account. Monthly, prepare a statement of services and costs expended by the firm to the client and show what portion of the retainer has been used. At this point, funds may be transferred from the trust account to the firm's general account to cover those fees earned and expenses advanced. Following this method will ensure that clients' funds are never commingled with firm funds, and the firm is not in violation of the Rules of Professional Conduct.

§ 5.8 Cash Systems, Checking Account, Endorsements

Most businesses make payments by checks drawn on local commercial banks. Many individuals use checking accounts drawing on funds in savings banks and/or in money market funds. A check is a written order directing the "drawee" (the bank) to make payment to the "payee" (the party indicated by the words "Pay to the order of") from the account balance of the "drawer" (the party who signs the order or check).

When a checking account is opened, each person authorized to sign checks completes a signature card. A deposit slip is used to list items to be added to the account, including checks received from others, such as fees collected from clients.

Each check deposited must be endorsed. Endorse a check in ink across the reverse left end (never across the right end) within the space indicated. Endorse it exactly as the name appears on the face, even though incorrect. If incorrect, write the correct signature immediately below. It is not necessary to write the explanation of the two signatures; this practice is understood by the bank. Do not write the correct signature first and the incorrect one below in parentheses. This violates the banking rule that the last endorser must be the person to whom the money is paid. There are several types of endorsements:

1. Endorsement in blank. This is a simple signature of the payee, which makes the check payable to bearer. It should be cashed or deposited immediately.

Donna Smith

2. Special (or Full) endorsement. This states to whom a check is to be paid, *i.e.,* "Pay to the order of . . . " above the payee's signature. This requires the designated person's endorsement but is still negotiable.

Pay to the Order of
Karl Hodges
Donna Smith

3. Restrictive endorsement. This limits the further purpose or use of the check. One type of restrictive endorsement includes only the words "Pay to (name)" above the payee's signature. The check is then nonnegotiable—it must be paid to the designated person and no one else. Another restrictive endorsement marks the check "for deposit only" with a bank account number.

Donna Smith
Pay to Karl Hodges

4. Qualified endorsement. The endorser assumes no legal responsibility for payment should the drawer have insufficient funds to honor his/her own check by using the words "Without recourse" written above the payee's signature in the endorsement. This relieves the endorser of any future liability on the check.

Without recourse
Donna Smith

The "deposit only" restrictive endorsement should be used on checks to be deposited. The blank endorsement should be used only when presenting a check for immediate payment, such as when cashing one's paycheck.

Checks for deposit by a firm preferably are endorsed with a rubber stamp that includes the account number assigned by the bank. The date is also carried on some rubber stamps.

In the absence of a rubber stamp, type "For Deposit Only" and below it the payee's name and/or account number.

All checks for deposit should be endorsed immediately to safeguard them in case they are lost before presentation to the bank.

When preparing to write a check, first be sure the stubs are completed with all information; then complete each check using pen and ink. When making deposits, be sure to enter the deposit on the check stub and carry the balance forward. The check stubs can be used to prepare the journal entries. With the proper software, it is possible to produce computer generated checks.

§ 5.8.1 Certified Check

When a check is deposited, the bank credits the account subject to collection of the check. To ensure that a check is good, you may ask the drawer to have the check certified by their bank, or you may have it certified by their bank. To certify a check, the teller stamps "Certified" and the date on the check, and the certification is then signed by an authorized bank officer. After the check is certified, the bank reduces the drawer's account by the amount of the check and holds the funds for payment. The bank then becomes responsible for the payment of the certified check.

In reconciling the bank balance, an outstanding certified check is listed separately from the other outstanding checks because it has already been charged to the account by the bank and deducted as a payment. Certified checks are recorded like ordinary checks by both drawer and payee in the cash journal.

§ 5.8.2 Cashier's Check

A check drawn by a bank on its own funds is called a cashier's check. This check may be used when a depositor, in closing out an existing checking account, requests a cashier's check so that it is not necessary to carry cash. If the depositor's credit is not established, the cashier's check will be accepted as payment where the depositor's personal check may not be. Cashier's checks are recorded as ordinary checks by both buyer and seller in the cash journals.

§ 5.8.3 Bank Draft

A bank draft is a check issued by a bank upon its funds in another bank, usually located in some other city. The bank draft is used chiefly in buying goods from out-of-town concerns with whom the buyer has no credit but from whom the buyer wishes immediate delivery. If the purchaser had sent a personal check in payment, the seller would not ship the goods until the check was honored, a procedure that could take several days. The seller will generally make immediate shipment against a bank draft because the bank is responsible for its payment.

To obtain a bank draft, the buyer draws a check to the order of the bank for the amount needed, plus the bank charge for the service. The bank then prepares a bank draft for the required amount, drawn on a bank in the city where the seller resides. The bank draft should be made payable to the buyer, who then endorses it in full to the seller. This procedure makes it easy to secure the canceled bank draft from the bank as evidence of payment.

The purchaser of the bank draft enters the check in the cash disbursement journal; accounts payable or an expense account is debited for the amount of the invoice, the bank charge expense account is debited for the amount of the bank charge, and the cash account is credited for the total. The recipient treats the bank draft as any other check from a customer and records it in the cash receipt journal.

§ 5.8.4 The Money Order

If a person does not have a checking account and wants to make a payment other than in currency, this can be done by purchasing a money order for that purpose at a United States post office, bank, and many stores. The amount for which a money order can be bought is limited. Money orders are accounted for in the same manner as ordinary checks.

§ 5.8.5 Reconciling the Bank Statement

When a bank statement is received, the bookkeeper should check it immediately with the balance record on the check stubs or the bank account in the general ledger. This procedure, known as reconciling the bank statement, is simply one of making sure the record of the bank and the record of the depositor are in agreement. The balances may not be the same for one or more of the following reasons:

- Some of the checks issued during the period may not have been presented to the bank for payment by the date the statement was prepared (outstanding checks).
- Deposits made may not have been recorded in time to appear on the bank's statement (outstanding bank deposits).
- Bank service fees charged to the depositor may not yet appear on the depositor's record. (In fact, the bank statement is usually the source paper for such charges unless a carbon copy of such debit has already been received and journalized.)
- Errors may have been made by either party.

Most bank statements contain a form on the reverse side for the depositor's use in reconciliation, and after completion, these forms are filed in a predetermined place in the depositor's office.

A suggested procedure for reconciliation of a bank statement is as follows:

1. Check the amount of each deposit on the bank statement with the check stubs, duplicate deposit tickets, or the cash receipts journal. If any outstanding deposits are found, they should be enumerated and added to the bank's total.
2. Check the amount of each canceled check and the numbers of the checks returned by the bank to be sure all checks issued have been paid and the amounts have been entered properly in the check stubs and cash disbursements journal. Any checks not paid should be enumerated as outstanding and deducted from the bank's balance shown on the statement.
3. Any bank service fees or debits to the depositor not already shown on check stubs or in the accounts must be enumerated and deducted from the depositor's record total. These items must be journalized as a debit to an expense account (usually Office Expense) and a credit to the Cash In Bank account.

After these adjustments are entered on the reconciliation form, the two balances should be in agreement. If not, the depositor's records should first be checked for errors in addition, subtraction, and posting (such as a transposition of figures). If the error still cannot be found, a check of the bank's statement may reveal an error. Bank errors must be reported to the bank at once; banks will correct errors only if reported within a specified time period. If a depositor still is unable to reconcile the bank statement, it should be reported to the bank immediately. (Note: Errors in transposition are divisible by 9. Divide the amount out of balance by 9, and if it is divisible evenly, the problem very easily could be a transposition error.)

§ 5.9 Payroll Records, Earnings, and Deductions

There is absolutely no margin for error in payroll accounting. The first step in determining the amount to be paid an employee is to calculate the total or gross earnings, including any overtime pay. The second step is to determine the deductions required either by law or agreement. The third step is to pay the employee the difference between the two, the net pay.

§ 5.9.1 Determination of Total Earnings

An employee in a law office will be paid either an hourly, weekly, biweekly, semimonthly, or monthly rate.* Wages by the hour are governed by the Fair Labor Standards Act (minimum wage laws). An employee may be entitled to overtime pay in some cases. Wage and hour cases usually involve time cards and time clocks or a computer-based timekeeping system in the larger firms. Regardless of the method the employer uses to determine pay scales and dates, the bookkeeper must maintain an accurate record of the gross amount paid, the deductions (itemized), and the net amount paid.

§ 5.9.2 Deductions From Total Earnings

With few exceptions, employers are required to withhold portions of each employee's total earnings for federal income tax, Social Security, and Medicare taxes. Many states and cities also require income or earnings tax withholding by employers. Besides these deductions, an agreement between employer and employee may call for amounts to be withheld for any one or more of the following reasons:

- To pay life, accident, or health insurance premiums for the employee.
- To pay the employee's union or other professional dues.
- To add to a pension or profit sharing plan.

* Sometimes wages are based on an annual rate which is then divided into the number of pay periods, with appropriate checks being drawn for each pay period. (*e.g.*, the employee's wages are based on $40,000 annually. The employee is to receive a pay check on the 15th and the last day of each month. This equals 24 pay periods per year, for a gross paycheck twice a month of $1,666.67.)

- To pay to some charitable organization, such as United Way.
- To repay a loan from the company or the company credit union.
- To contribute to a company Flex Pay Program.

§ 5.9.3 Social Security and Employer's Identification Numbers

Each employee is required to have a social security number for payroll accounting purposes. A Form SS–5 may be secured from the Social Security office to obtain this number.

Just as each individual must have a reporting number, so must the employer have a number with which to identify tax reports. All but the new employer will have these numbers. In the case of new employers, the bookkeeper must obtain an employer identification number by submitting an application form (SS–4) to the Internal Revenue Service (IRS). After the number is obtained, it must be used on all reports submitted to the IRS.

§ 5.9.4 Circular E—Employer's Tax Guide and Federal Employment Tax Forms

The IRS publishes a booklet for the employer's use entitled "Circular E–Employer's Tax Guide." This booklet is revised periodically and supplemented regularly as tax laws change. The bookkeeper must obtain a copy of this booklet for the files. Once a mailing is established with the IRS, the subsequent editions are automatically sent to the employer.

Circular E provides the bookkeeper with the following information and instructions for performing the following tasks and completing the following forms:

- Income tax withholding and payment to the IRS.
- Social Security and Medicare tax withholding and payment to the IRS.
- Payment of employer's share of Social Security and Medicare taxes to the IRS.
- Form W–4 (Employee's Withholding Allowance Certificate).
- Form 941 (Employer's quarterly Federal Tax Return).
- Form 940 (Employer's Annual Federal Unemployment (FUTA) Tax Return).
- Charts of amounts to be withheld for both income tax and Social Security and Medicare taxes.
- Tax withholding by the percentage method.

The lawyer's assistant-bookkeeper must be alert to the changes in these laws and should inquire of the IRS periodically as to whether there have been revisions.

Literature on Social Security and Medicare taxes are included in the booklet. The bookkeeper must be aware of the maximum amount an employee is required to pay for the year and the current percentage rate for both the employee and the employer.

Federal Unemployment Tax Act (FUTA) taxes must be sent in at the close of each year, or quarterly if required, on the form provided.

The government publishes an annual booklet entitled "Federal Employment Tax Forms" (Publication 393) which contains a supply of the routine forms needed to report taxes as well as an order blank for more forms. Instructions are included for filling out each type of form. These items are usually mailed to the employers well in advance of the due dates, but the bookkeeper must be aware of the dates and should obtain a supply from the local IRS office if they have not been received.

In addition to all the federal withholding reporting and payment requirements, the law firm is faced with a myriad of state and local taxes with periodic reporting and payment requirements. These may include: state personal income taxes, local personal income taxes, state and local business taxes, personal property taxes, real property taxes, state unemployment taxes, workers' compensation insurance taxes, business license fees, and professional license fees. The bookkeeper must be able to handle all of these, or ensure that the law firm's accountants are doing so.

§ 5.9.5 Payroll Register

There are many types of payroll registers on the market in bound, spiral, and looseleaf forms. As long as the form contains necessary information, any type is satisfactory.

§ 5.9.6 Journalizing the Payroll

Payroll Expense. This is an expense account which is debited for the total amount of the gross earnings of all employees for each pay period.

Payroll Expense	
Debit	
to enter gross earnings of employees for each pay period	

Social Security and Medicare Taxes Payable. This is a liability account which is credited for (1) the Social Security and Medicare taxes withheld from employees' earnings and (2) the Social Security and Medicare taxes imposed on the employer. The account should be debited for amounts paid to the Internal Revenue Service. When all of the Social Security and Medicare taxes have been paid, the account should have a zero balance.

Social Security and Medicare Taxes Payable	
Debit	Credit
to enter payment of Social Security and Medicare taxes previously withheld or imposed	to enter Social Security and Medicare taxes (1) withheld from employees' earnings and (2) imposed on the employer

Employees' Income Tax Payable. This is a liability account which should be credited for the total income tax withheld from employees' earnings. The account is debited for amounts paid to a bank depository for the Internal Revenue Service. When all of the income taxes withheld have been paid, the account will have a zero balance.

Employees Income Tax Payable	
Debit	Credit
to enter payment of income tax previously withheld	to enter income tax withheld from employees' earnings

Other Deductions. Pension Plan Deductions Payable is a liability account credited with amounts withheld from employees' earnings for pension plan contributions. The account is debited upon the subsequent payment of these amounts to the pension plan trustee. Accounts for health insurance premiums payable, credit union contributions payable, and charitable contributions payable are treated similarly.

Journalizing Payroll Transactions. The information needed to properly enter the payment of employee wages and salaries is contained in the payroll register.

Payroll Tax Expense. The payroll taxes imposed on an employer under the federal and state laws are an expense of the employer. For the purpose of this discussion, it is assumed that a single account entitled Payroll Taxes Expense is used to summarize these taxes. This is an expense account that is debited for all payroll taxes imposed on the employer.

Payroll Taxes Expense	
Debit	
to enter Social Security and Medicare, federal unemployment taxes, and state unemployment taxes imposed on the employer	

Social Security and Medicare Taxes Payable. This is the same liability account that was illustrated above. The account is credited to enter the Social Security and Medicare taxes imposed on the employer. The account is debited when the taxes are paid to the Internal Revenue Service. When all Social Security and Medicare taxes have been paid, the account should have a zero balance.

Social Security and Medicare Taxes Payable	
Debit	Credit
to enter payment of Social Security and Medicare taxes	to enter Social Security and Medicare taxes (1) withheld from employees' earnings and (2) imposed on the employer

Federal Unemployment Tax Payable. When entering the federal unemployment tax, it is customary to keep a separate liability account entitled FUTA Tax Payable. This is a liability account that is credited for the taxes imposed on employers under the Federal Unemployment Tax Act. The account is debited for amounts paid to apply on such taxes. When all FUTA taxes have been paid, the account should have a zero balance.

FUTA Tax Payable	
Debit	Credit
to enter payment of FUTA tax	to enter FUTA tax imposed on the employer

State Unemployment Tax Payable. In entering the tax imposed under the state unemployment compensation laws, it is necessary to keep a separate liability account. This is a liability account that is credited for the tax imposed on employers under the state unemployment compensation laws. The account is debited for the amount paid to apply on such taxes. When all of the state taxes have been paid, the account should have a zero balance.

State Unemployment Tax Payable	
Debit	Credit
to enter state unemployment tax paid	to enter state unemployment tax imposed on the employer

Journalizing Employer's Payroll Taxes. The payroll taxes imposed on employers may be entered periodically, such as monthly or quarterly. It is common to enter such taxes at the same time that wages are paid so that the employer's liability for such taxes and related expenses are entered in the same period as the wages on which the taxes are based.

The information needed to enter employer payroll taxes properly is contained in the payroll register.

Strict adherence to state and federal deadlines and amounts to be deposited at certain intervals is absolutely essential, and the penalty for not doing so can be severe. The federal penalty for nonpayment can be imposed not only on the employer, but on the individual doing the accounting as well as on the employer, if that individual had any control over the decision not to pay.

§ 5.10 Computing Interest

There are three factors that must be considered when computing interest: (1) principal, (2) interest rate, and (3) time period.

The principal is the amount of money borrowed. The amount of interest is based on this figure.

The interest rate is usually given on the face of the note. If the note is interest bearing and the interest rate is not given on the face of the note, the legal rate must be used. The legal rate varies from state to state. The interest rate shown on the face of the note is always an annual percentage rate unless stated otherwise.

The time period of the note is determined by the number of days or months from the date the note is issued until the date of maturity. Interest computations are based on this time period. When the maturity date is specified in months, the fraction of the year and months represented is used to calculate interest. For example, if a note specifies maturity in four months, interest is calculated on $4/12$ or $1/3$ of a year. If maturity is specified in days, interest is calculated based on the fraction of the year those days represent. For example, if a note matures in 60 days, interest is based on $60/365$ of a year.

If the due date is specified on a note, the exact number of days from the date of the note through the due date or maturity date must be determined. For example, if a note is issued on January 1 and is due on March 17, the time period is computed as follows:

Days in January	31
Date of note, January 1	–1
Days remaining in January	30
Days in February**	28
Days in March	17
Time period in days	75

** Do not assume February to be leap year in your computations unless you are told it is.

Notice in the above computation that the date of maturity is included but the date of the note is excluded.

After determining the proper factors, interest is calculated using the following formula:

Principal x Rate x Time Period = Amount of Interest.

EXAMPLE: The principal amount is $500; the interest rate is 8%; the time period is three months. The interest payable is $10, computed as follows:

$500 x 8% x 3/12 = $10 interest.

Assume the same facts as in the above example except that the note matures 90 days after issuance instead of three months. The interest is $9.86, computed as follows:

$500 x 8% x 90/365 = $9.86 interest.

§ 5.11 Computerized Accounting Systems

Many manual accounting processes have been made obsolete by the use of computers in virtually all offices. Many software programs are available for small business accounting, as well as some specific programs for professional service firms, and come with detailed instructions as well as technical help by telephone.

These programs, plus a good personal computer, perform the majority of the steps discussed in this chapter. Even though such a system will probably be in use wherever the lawyer's assistant works, it is helpful to understand the basic steps being performed by the system.

CHAPTER 6

ORAL AND WRITTEN COMMUNICATIONS

Table of Sections

§ 6.1 Introduction

One of the most valuable skills you will ever acquire is the proper use of English grammar. We spend over 70 percent of our day using the English language. Much of our business success is in direct proportion to the manner in which we communicate. Although both oral and written communications are important, this chapter deals mainly with written communications.

In order to be effective, you must master the basic grammar skills. The next step is to learn how to use these skills effectively in creating written communications.

This chapter is not intended to offer a complete course in grammar. It is expected that the reader has some background knowledge of grammar; this chapter provides only a cursory review. If you need additional help, consult grammar textbooks such as the *Gregg Reference Manual*, find information and exercises on the Internet or take a class in grammar. Your local college bookstore can offer many suggestions about good handbooks. Keep an updated reference handbook on English usage at your desk and consult it often.

§ 6.2 The Basics of English Grammar

The eight parts of speech (the names given to words according to their usage in the sentence) are verbs, nouns, pronouns, adverbs, adjectives, prepositions, conjunctions, and interjections. The role the word plays in the sentence determines the form of the word that should be used. For example, the word *tires* is used as a noun in "The tires on the car were new," and used as a verb in "Jesse tires of watching old movies." Each of these parts of speech is examined in this chapter.

§ 6.3 Verbs

A *verb* is a word or word group that tells what the subject does, tells what the subject is, or tells what happens to the subject. A sentence is not complete without a verb; sentences may have more than one verb. Some writers define *verbs* as action words or states of being. Action verbs show the action of a sentence. Some examples are *play*, *type*, *solves*, and *write*. Action verbs are categorized as transitive and intransitive. Verbs that do not express action will express a state of being and are called linking verbs. Some linking verbs are *feels*, *appears*, *tastes*, *is*, *are*, *was*, *were*, *seems*, and *looks*. For example, "Jessie is the chairperson."

§ 6.3.1 Transitive Verbs

A *transitive verb* is an action verb and needs a direct object to complete the meaning of the sentence. When a verb is transitive, the action passes from the doer (the subject) to a receiver of the action (the direct object). The direct object tells who or what receives the action of the verb. The direct object tells who or what receives the action of the verb.

EXAMPLES: Mary *read* the book. (*Book* is the direct object.)

The table *was repaired* by Kris. (*Table* is the subject and receives the action.)

§ 6.3.2 Intransitive Verbs

An *intransitive verb* is also an action verb but does not take a direct object. The verb does not express an action that passes over to a receiver. A verb may be transitive in one sentence and intransitive in another sentence.

EXAMPLES: Chris called on the morning of August 6. (Intransitive)

Chris called the client on the morning of August 6. (Transitive)

Chris sat on the chair. (Intransitive)

Chris set the keys on the desk. (Transitive)

§ 6.3.3 Linking Verbs

Some verbs express a state of being rather than action. These are called *linking verbs* and link the subject to a word or words which are the same as the subject or describe the subject. A noun, pronoun, or adjective complements the subject.

EXAMPLES: Gerry *is* very efficient. (*Efficient* describes *Gerry.*)

Gerry *is* president of the organization. (*Gerry* and *president* are the same person and are linked by the verb *is.*)

Depending upon the grammar book you are reading, *efficient* is a *predicate adjective* or *subject complement,* and *president* is a *predicate nominative* or *predicate complement.*

§ 6.3.4 Verb Tense

The *tense* of a verb refers to the time an action or event takes place or the time of the state of being.

The three sets of tenses are primary or simple, perfect, and progressive tenses. The primary tenses are the present, past, and future tenses. The perfect tenses express actions that are completed and progressive tenses express actions that are continuing in nature.

§ 6.3.5 Regular Verbs

A *regular verb* is one that forms its past tense and past participle by adding *d* or *ed* to the present tense of the verb.

§ 6.3.6 Irregular Verbs

Verbs that do not form their past tense and past participle in this manner are called *irregular*. Illustration 6–1 shows several of the irregular verbs in their three forms. (The past participle is used in forming the perfect tenses.)

Illustration 6–1

COMMONLY USED IRREGULAR VERBS		
Present Tense	Past Tense	Past Participle (have, has, had)
arise	arose	arisen
awake	awoke or awaked	awaked or awoke
beat	beat	beaten
become	became	become
begin	began	begun
bite	bit	bitten
blow	blew	blown
break	broke	broken
bring	brought	brought
burst	burst	burst
buy	bought	bought
choose	chose	chosen
cling	clung	clung
come	came	come
cost	cost	cost
do	did	done
drag	dragged	dragged
draw	drew	drawn
drink	drank	drunk
drive	drove	driven
eat	ate	eaten
fall	fell	fallen
fight	fought	fought
fling	flung	flung
fly	flew	flown
forget	forgot	forgotten
freeze	froze	frozen
get	got	gotten
give	gave	given
go	went	gone
grow	grew	grown

COMMONLY USED IRREGULAR VERBS		
Present Tense	Past Tense	Past Participle (have, has, had)
hang	hung	hung
hang (to execute)	hanged	hanged
hear	heard	heard
hit	hit	hit
hurt	hurt	hurt
know	knew	known
lay	laid	laid
lead	led	led
leave	left	left
let	let	let
lie (recline)	lay	lain
lie (fib)	lied	lied
lose	lost	lost
pay	paid	paid
put	put	put
read	read	read
ride	rode	ridden
ring	rang	rung
rise	rose	risen
run	ran	run
say	said	said
see	saw	seen
set	set	set
shake	shook	shaken
show	showed	showed or shown
sing	sang	sung
sink	sank or sunk	sunk
sit	sat	sat
sleep	slept	slept
speak	spoke	spoken
spring	sprang or sprung	sprung
steal	stole	stolen
swear	swore	sworn
swim	swam	swum
swing	swung	swung
take	took	taken
teach	taught	taught
tear	tore	torn
tell	told	told
think	thought	thought
throw	threw	thrown
wake	woke	woken
wear	wore	worn
wet	wet	wet
write	wrote	written

§ 6.3.7 Present Tense

Present tense refers to the present time—now.

EXAMPLES: The attorney *is* ready. (Shows state of being is now.)

The receptionist *answers* the phone. (Action is occurring now.)

In the present tense, if you wish to show that the action is continuous and moving forward (progressive), use the *ing* form of the verb and add the proper form of the *be* verb.

EXAMPLES:	I *am filing.*	We *are filing.*
	You *are filing.*	You *are filing.*
	He *is filing.*	They *are filing.*

If you want to emphasize the action taking place in the present tense, use the emphatic verb *do* as the helping verb.

EXAMPLES: I *do file.*
You *do file.*
He *does file.*

§ 6.3.8 Past Tense

Past tense shows that something took place at some time in the past or that the state of being was in the past.

EXAMPLES: He *left* at five.
He *was* there all night.

In the past tense to show action that was continuous or moving forward, use the *ing* form of the verb (progressive form) with the past tense of the *be* verb.

EXAMPLES:	I *was filing.*	We *were filing.*
	You *were filing.*	You *were filing.*
	She *was filing.*	They *were filing.*

To emphasize the action in the past tense, add the past tense of the verb *do* (*did*) to the verb.

EXAMPLES:	I *did file.*	We *did file.*
	You *did file.*	You *did file.*
	He *did file.*	They *did file.*

§ 6.3.9 Future Tense

Future tense tells that the action or state of being will occur at some future time. To express future tense, use *shall* or *will* followed by a main verb. *Shall* is used in formal writing, with the first person (I, we) and *will* is used in less formal writing, with the second and third person (you, he, she, it, they). (*See* Section 6.6.2, Person and Case.)

EXAMPLES: I *shall* be glad to answer any questions you may have.

They *will* leave tomorrow.

EXAMPLES: I *will be filing.* You *will be filing.*
He *will be filing.* They *will be filing.*

§ 6.3.10 Present Perfect Tense

Present perfect tense indicates that the action or state of being is complete (perfect) at the present time. This tense is always written with *has* or *have* preceding the past participle of the main verb.

EXAMPLES: Mary *has worked* all night.
Jon and Fred *have* already *left.*

§ 6.3.11 Past Perfect Tense

Past perfect tense shows that the action or state of being was completed at some particular time in the past. It denotes action or being begun in the past and completed at some stated past time or before some other implied time. It is always formed by using *had* with the past participle of the main verb.

EXAMPLES: Sarah *had left* by the time I arrived.
By the time of the divorce, they *had lived* in separate homes for two years.

§ 6.3.12 Future Perfect Tense

Future perfect tense shows that the action will be completed by a certain time in the future. It indicates action will be completed in the future before some other future action takes place. It is formed by using *shall have* or *will have* with the past participle of the main verb.

EXAMPLES: By the time I am 21, I *shall have* bought my own car.
By the end of next year, they *will have* completed the merger.

§ 6.3.13 Active and Passive Voice

A transitive verb is either *active* or *passive.* Voice is the form of a verb that shows whether the subject is performing the action or whether the subject is receiving the action. In the active voice, someone or something acts. In the passive voice, someone or something is acted upon.

EXAMPLES: ACTIVE: The secretary *typed* the letters very quickly.
PASSIVE: The letters *were typed* very quickly by the secretary.

In business writing, active voice is preferred to passive voice. It is direct and concise. It is more personal and conversational. It is easier for the reader to follow the sequence of thoughts when active voice is used. Passive voice is impersonal; however, it does tend to sound less blunt than active voice. Therefore, it is often used for making suggestions or recommendations.

§ 6.3.14 Verb Moods (Subjunctive Mood)

Verbs are categorized into three moods: indicative, imperative, and subjunctive. The indicative mood is used to state a fact or ask a question (Terry proofreads all documents for content and format errors. Did Terry proofread the document?). The imperative mood is used to give an order, a request, or a command. (Proofread the documents this morning.) The subjunctive mood is used to express conditions that are contrary to fact or doubtful. (If I were Terry, I would proofread the document twice.) This mood is also used in *that* clauses following verbs that express a doubt, wish, request, suggestion, demand or proposal. (The attorney demanded that all documents be proofread twice. The paralegal suggested that a three-ring binder be used.) The subjunctive mood is commonly used in parliamentary motion statements. (Terry moved that a vote be taken. It has been moved and seconded that the meeting be adjourned.)

When forming the subjunctive tense, change the verb for the third person singular (he, she, it) by dropping the –s or –es. Also change the form of the verb *to be* to the word *be* in the present tense and *were* in the past tense regardless of what the subject is.

EXAMPLES: INCORRECT: I suggest that Terry *goes* to the court.
CORRECT: I suggest that Terry *go* to the court.
INCORRECT: If Jamie *was* here, she would go to court with us.
CORRECT: If Jamie *were* here, she would go to court with us.
INCORRECT: The attorney insisted that Sheila *is* allowed to go to the seminar.
CORRECT: The attorney insisted that Sheila *be* allowed to go to the seminar.

§ 6.3.15 Agreement of the Subject and Verb

A subject must agree with the verb in person and number. A singular subject must have a singular verb. A plural subject must have a plural verb.

EXAMPLES: He *does* it. (singular)
We *do* it. (plural)

You is considered to be a plural word and always takes a plural verb even when it is understood that only one person is being referenced.

EXAMPLES: *You* are the only secretary we need. (singular)
You are the only secretaries we need. (plural)

Two or more subjects connected by *and* take a plural verb.

EXAMPLE: The director of marketing and the product managers *are reviewing* the proposal.

Two or more subjects connected by *and* which refer to the same person or thing take a singular verb.

EXAMPLE: Our secretary and treasurer *is* Mary Brown.

Two or more subjects connected by *and* which are preceded by each, every, many a, or many an take a singular verb.

EXAMPLE: Every sweater, jacket, and hat *is* on sale.
Many a paralegal and secretary *has worked* on pro bono cases.

Two or more singular subjects connected with *or* or *nor* take a singular verb.

EXAMPLE: Either Sally or Mary *plans* to meet you there.

When a singular subject and a plural subject are joined by *or* or *nor,* the plural subject should directly precede the verb and a plural verb should be used whenever this can be done without sacrificing the emphasis desired.

EXAMPLE: Either Mary or the boys *plan* to meet you there.

When the subject is made up of different grammatical persons, the verb should agree in person (I, we, you) and number (has, have) with the nearer subject.

EXAMPLE: Neither you nor she *has* the time to take the case.

Neither she nor you *have* the time to take the case.

A collective noun (*see* Section 6.4.3) requires a singular verb if the noun is considered as a single unit; a plural verb should be used if the persons or things are being considered as individuals within the unit.

EXAMPLES: The jury *delivers* its verdict to the judge. (singular)
The jury *are* hopelessly deadlocked. (plural)

When the word *number* is preceded by *the*, a singular verb is used. If *a* precedes the word *number*, a plural verb is used.

EXAMPLES: The number of entries *was* large this year. (singular)
A number of entries *were* duplicates. (plural)

A sum of money used as a subject requires a singular verb.

EXAMPLE: Fifty dollars *is* the required filing fee.

§ 6.3.16 Verbals

There are three types of verbals: *infinitives, gerunds,* and *participles*. The word *verbal* is derived from the word *verb;* it is not a verb but a form of a verb used as a noun, adjective, or adverb, or as part of a noun phrase or adjective phrase. In the sentence "Trying a case may be very expensive," "Trying" is a gerund used as a noun phrase and functioning as the subject of a sentence; "Trying" in this case is not a verb.

§ 6.3.17 Infinitives

An infinitive is created by placing the word *to* in front of the verb, as in *to go*. An infinitive may be used as a noun, an adjective, or an adverb. It may be modified by adverbs and may have subjects and objects just as a verb has. The infinitive phrase consists of the infinitive and the word or words that are closely related to the infinitive.

EXAMPLE: *To read* a book is an interesting pastime. (*Book* is the direct object of the infinitive *to read.*)

Try not to use split infinitives. This occurs when a modifier is placed between "to" and the verb. Generally, if the sentence is awkward without placing the modifier before the word it describes, revising the sentence so that the verb follows *to* will usually produce a better result.

EXAMPLES: INCORRECT: To slowly improve.
CORRECT: To improve slowly.
INCORRECT: You have the right *to not see it.*
CORRECT: You have the right not *to see it.*

However, it should be noted that while it is preferable to keep the infinitive phrase together, it is acceptable to split an infinitive for emphasis or impact.

Many split infinitives are merely verbose. Rescue the split infinitives that are smothered with unnecessary adverbs.

§ 6.3.18 Gerunds

A *gerund* is the present participle form of the verb used in the sentence as a noun, or part of a noun phrase.

EXAMPLE: *Writing* gives me great pleasure. (*Writing* is a gerund and is the subject of the sentence.)

A gerund phrase consists of the gerund and the adverbs, adjectives, and words closely associated with it. It can take an object and an indirect object.

EXAMPLE: *Writing Alice a letter* was a generous gesture. (*Writing* is the gerund; *Alice* is the indirect object; and *letter* is the direct object of the gerund. The gerund phrase, *Writing Alice a letter,* is the subject of the sentence.)

When a noun or pronoun precedes the gerund, the possessive case of the noun or pronoun is generally used.

EXAMPLES:

Incorrect: I *look forward* to him going.

Correct: I *look forward* to his going.

Incorrect: *I objected* to Mary leaving.

Correct: *I objected* to Mary's leaving.

§ 6.3.19 Participles

A *participle* is a verb form that cannot stand by itself as a verb. It must have a helping verb in order to function as a verb. The participle may also function as an adjective.

The *past participle* is the third principal part of the verb. In regular verbs the past participle ends in *ed, d,* or *t* (walk, walked, walked). In irregular verbs there is no consistency in forming the past participle. Consult the irregular verb chart (Illustration 6–1) for past participles of irregular verbs. A fourth verb form is the *present participle,* which is formed by adding "*ing*" to the present form of the verb. The *perfect participle* is formed by adding *having* or *having been* to the past participle.

A participle may function as an adjective when it is used without a helping verb.

EXAMPLES: The *tired* old woman walked slowly. (*Tired* is the past participle.)
The *dancing* bear stole the show. (*Dancing* is the present participle.)
The watch, *having been broken,* no longer worked accurately. (*Having been broken* is the perfect participle.)

A *participle phrase* consists of the participle and words closely associated with it. The phrase should be placed close to the word it modifies. When it is incorrectly placed, it distorts the meaning of the sentence and is known as a dangling participle.

EXAMPLES:

Incorrect:	*Talking loudly,* the attorney observed the witnesses. (The attorney is talking.)
Correct:	The attorney observed the witnesses *talking loudly.* (The witnesses are talking.)

§ 6.4 Nouns

A *noun* is a word that names a person (secretary), place (city), thing (desk), or idea (justice).

§ 6.4.1 Common Nouns

A *common noun* is a name given to a general class of person (witness), place (mountain), thing (computer), or idea (success).

§ 6.4.2 Proper Nouns

A *proper noun* is the name of a particular person (Susan), place (Utah), or thing (Palm Pilot). Proper nouns are always capitalized.

§ 6.4.3 Collective Nouns

A *collective noun* is one that names a group of persons or things, (such as faculty, orchestra, jury, family), and takes a singular verb. (*See* Section 6.3.15, Agreement of Subject and Verb.)

§ 6.4.4 Plurals of Nouns

When forming the plural of a noun, you may use one of the following guides or consult the dictionary. When you are in doubt, use the dictionary.

- Add *s* to most common nouns (cat/cats, boy/boys, plate/plates).
- Add *es* to nouns ending in *s, x, ch, sh,* or *z* (glass/glasses, box/boxes, crutch/crutches, wish/wishes, waltz/waltzes).
- When nouns ending in *o* have a consonant preceding the *o,* add *es* to the noun (potato/potatoes, veto/vetoes); exceptions to this rule are nouns dealing with music, such as piano/pianos, solo/solos; memo/memos is another exception.
- When nouns ending in *o* have a vowel preceding the *o,* add *s* to the noun (studio/studios, ratio/ratios).

- When nouns ending in *y* have a consonant preceding the *y,* change the *y* to *i* and add *es* (fly/flies, company/companies, secretary/secretaries).
- When nouns ending in *y* have a vowel preceding the *y,* leave the noun the same and add *s* (attorney/attorneys, key/keys, gray/grays).
- When forming the plural of abbreviations and letters, the rule is that you add an apostrophe and an *s* (*'s*) to lower case letters and abbreviations (*p's* and *q's, r.p.m.'s, c.o.d.'s*); for capital letters and abbreviations ending in capital letters, add just the *s* (M.D.s, Ph.D.s, ABCs).
- Nouns ending in *f* or *fe* are made plural by changing the *f* to *v* and adding *es* (wife/wives, life/lives); exceptions are chief/chiefs and belief/beliefs.

There are exceptions to the above rules, such as man/men, woman/women, child/children, mouse/mice, sheep/sheep, tooth/teeth, foot/feet, corps/corps. Most of these exceptions are fairly well known. If you are in doubt, consult the dictionary.

§ 6.4.5 Compound Words

When forming the plural of compound words, such as *attorney general* or *notary public,* make the most descriptive word plural. This is generally the first word. For instance, *attorney* more nearly describes the function of the attorney general, so you would use *attorneys general* for the plural. This rule is not so hard and fast as it used to be, and the dictionary now recognizes both *attorneys general* and *attorney generals* as well as *notaries public* and *notary publics.* However, the first form is probably the most widely accepted. With hyphenated compound words, such as *mother-in-law* and *brother-in-law,* you again make the plural on the most descriptive word; *mothers-in-law* and *brothers-in-law* are correct. Once again, consult the dictionary when you are in doubt.

§ 6.5 Possessive Nouns

To show ownership or possession, use an apostrophe with the noun. There are three basic rules governing the form of possessives. (*See* Illustration 6–2).

Illustration 6–2

POSSESSIVE CASE OF NOUNS		
Singular	Plural	
To all singular nouns, add *'s*	To all plural nouns ending in *s,* add '	To all plural nouns NOT ending in *s,* add *'s*

§ 6.5.1 Singular Possession

Add an apostrophe and an *s* (*'s*) to the end of a singular noun (Mary's, typist's, today's). The exception to this rule is that when a proper noun ends in *s* and the addition of *'s* would make the word hard to pronounce, only an apostrophe is added (Moses'). Since opinions vary as to what is hard to pronounce, it is difficult to know when to omit the added *s*. When in doubt, add *'s*.

EXAMPLES: The glass's rim is chipped.

Moses' sister Miriam is Rachel's heroine.

§ 6.5.2 Plural Possession

First, make the word plural; then look at the end of the word. If it ends in *s*, you should add only an apostrophe. If it does not end in *s*, you should add *'s* just as you did in the singular (boy/boys/boys', child/children/children's). It is essential that you do not omit the first step of forming the plural word. Once you have done this, decide which method to use for showing possession: by adding the apostrophe (') or by adding apostrophe s ('s).

EXAMPLES: The judges' calendars were posted on the Internet.

The women's voices were loud.

§ 6.5.3 Three Steps to Forming Possession

1. Ask yourself, "Do I really need the apostrophe? Does this word show possession?"
2. If the answer is yes, spell out the singular or plural noun first.
3. Apply the rules in the chart above.

Following are some additional rules for forming possessive nouns:

- When you have a compound word and need to show singular possession, add an apostrophe and *s* (*'s*) to the last word (brother-in-law's house).
- When you have a compound word and need to show plural possession, make the plural word first; then add apostrophe and *s* (*'s*) to the end of the compound word (mothers-in-law's birthdays).
- To show separate ownership of two or more things, add an apostrophe and *s* (*'s*) to each name (Sue's and Mary's cards).
- To show joint ownership, add the possessive only to the last owner (Fred and Robyn's house).
- On personal and company names, add the apostrophe and *s* (*'s*) at the end of the name (John Q. Smith III's, Stacy & Stacy's).

§ 6.6 Pronouns

A *pronoun* is a word that replaces a noun or a name in order to avoid awkward repetitions. Instead of writing "John answered John's phone and talked to John's client," one would write "John answered his phone and talked to his client." Pronouns can be classified as personal, possessive, reflexive, relative, indefinite, interrogative, demonstrative, and reciprocal.

§ 6.6.1 Personal Pronouns

Personal pronouns are used for the person speaking, the person spoken to, and the person spoken about.

EXAMPLE: *He* told *her* about *me*. (*He, her,* and *me* are all personal pronouns.)

§ 6.6.2 Person and Case

Pronouns are classified as first person (person or persons doing the speaking), second person (person or persons being spoken to), and third person (person or persons being spoken about).

First person pronouns are I, we, me, us, my, mine, our, ours.

Second person pronouns are you, your, yours.

Third person pronouns are he, she, it, they, him, her, them, his, hers, its, their, theirs.

There are three case forms of personal pronouns: *nominative* (also known as *subjective*), *objective,* and *possessive.* Illustration 6–3 shows the pronouns in each case. The position in which the pronoun appears in the sentence determines which case you should use. Note that in the possessive case there are two forms of pronouns. When the pronoun precedes a noun, it is known as an adjective. When it stands alone and shows possession, it is a possessive pronoun.

Illustration 6–3

CASES AND FUNCTIONS OF PRONOUNS			
Nominative	Objective	Possessive	
I, we	me, us	my	mine
		our	ours
you	you	your	yours
he, she	him, her	her, his	hers, his
it, they	it, them	its, their	its, theirs
FUNCTIONS IN THE SENTENCE			
1. Subject *She* is home. 2. Predicate nominative (subject complement) The owner is *he.*	1. Direct object Ray told *her.* 2. Indirect object Ray told *me* the news. 3. Object of preposition Give the food to *him.* 4. Object of infinitive Jay wanted to send *me* instead of Alice. 5. Subject of infinitive The teacher wanted *them* to do the acting. (Pronouns preceding and following an infinitive are in the objective case.)	1. Possessive pronoun as adjective This is *your* book. 2. Possessive pronoun Is the book *yours*?	

§ 6.6.3 Possessive Pronouns

A *possessive pronoun* does not contain an apostrophe. Do not confuse *it's* with *its. It's* is a contraction meaning "it is"; *its* is a possessive pronoun. Also note the contraction *they're* meaning "they are" and the possessive pronoun *their*.

§ 6.6.4 Reflexive Pronouns

A *reflexive pronoun* is one ending in *self* or *selves,* such as *myself, ourselves.* These are used only when they refer back to a noun in the sentence meaning the same person. It is a reflexive pronoun—it reflects back.

I gave *myself* a haircut. (*Myself* refers to I.)

Incorrect: Mary and myself went shopping.

Correct: Mary and I went shopping. (In the incorrect sentence there is no one to whom the pronoun *myself* can reflect back.)

§ 6.6.5 Relative Pronouns

A *relative pronoun* joins dependent clauses to independent clauses (a subordinate clause to a main clause). It begins the subordinate clause and is related to another word or idea in the sentence. It also serves as either the subject, direct object, or object of the preposition in the dependent clause.

EXAMPLES: The file clerk *who* types the fastest will get the job.

(*Who* is a relative pronoun and is the subject of the verb types.)

The file clerk *whom* you hired is very efficient.

(*Whom* is a relative pronoun and is the direct object of the verb hired.)

The file clerk to *whom* you refer is my sister.

(*Whom* is a relative pronoun and is the object of the preposition to.)

In each of the above examples the dependent clause is related to "the file clerk" by the relative pronoun.

Illustration 6–4 shows the relative pronouns.

Illustration 6–4

RELATIVE PRONOUNS		
Pronoun	Use in Sentence	Examples
Who	*Nominative case* Used as a subject of a clause	The girl *who* gave you the package left quickly.
Whom	*Objective case* Used as a direct object Used as an object of the preposition	The teacher *whom* I knew well quit teaching. The lady to *whom* I gave your name will call you tomorrow.
Whose	*Possessive case* Used as an adjective (NOTE: WHO, WHOM, and WHOSE refer to persons only.)	The man *whose* dog was lost lives on your street.
Which	Refers to animals or things Used for clauses that are non-essential (non-restrictive) Used as a subject Used as a direct object	The desk *which* was broken was sold. The speech *which* I heard was dull.

RELATIVE PRONOUNS		
Pronoun	Use in Sentence	Examples
	Used as an object of a preposition	The chair on *which* I stood fell.
That	Refers to persons, animals, or things Used for essential (restrictive) clauses Used as a subject Used as a direct object	 I think *that* will do for now. The movers *that* I know will do it for you.

§ 6.6.6 Indefinite Pronouns

Indefinite pronouns are those that do not stand for a particular person or thing. Some of them are always singular; others are always plural; others may be either singular or plural depending upon the noun to which they refer. (*See* Illustration 6–5.)

Illustration 6–5

INDEFINITE PRONOUNS		
Use a Singular Verb	Use a Plural Verb	Use Either a Plural or Singular Verb
another, anybody, anyone, each, everybody, everyone, either, neither, someone, somebody	both, few, many, others, several	all, any, more, none, some

§ 6.6.7 Interrogative Pronouns

Interrogative pronouns are used in asking questions. *Who, whom, whomever, which, what,* and *whose* are the most common ones. Do not confuse *whose* with *who's; who's* is a contraction of *who is* and *whose* is possessive.

EXAMPLES: Whose car is that?
What are you doing?
Who is going with me?
Whom shall I appoint?
Which of the books do you want?

§ 6.6.8 Demonstrative Pronouns

Demonstrative pronouns are used to modify a noun or take the place of a noun. They point out.

Singular	Plural	
This	These	Refer to objects near at hand.
That	Those	Refer to objects at a distance, either a slight or great distance.

§ 6.6.9 Reciprocal Pronouns

Reciprocal pronouns relate specifically to another person, *i.e.*, each other and one another.

§ 6.6.10 Agreement of Pronouns and Antecedents

The word to which a pronoun refers must be clear to the reader. Maintain a consistent viewpoint by making sure that the pronoun agrees in number whether singular or plural with the word to which it refers.

EXAMPLES:

Incorrect: *Students* learning to type must be careful to type *his* papers accurately.

Correct: *Students* learning to type must be careful to type *their* papers accurately.

Incorrect: *Alice* wants to know where *you* can buy a set of striped seatcovers.

Correct: *Alice* wants to know where *she* can buy a set of striped seatcovers.

When the pronoun refers to two words, if they are connected by *and*, use a plural pronoun, and if they are connected by *or* use a singular pronoun.

EXAMPLES: Sonia *and* Dave say *they* will attend.

Either Matt *or* Charlie could bring *his* book.

When the pronoun refers to two words, one of which is plural and one of which is singular, place the plural subject closer to its pronoun, if possible.

EXAMPLES: Neither Mr. Wilson nor his employees *have* reached their quota.

Neither the employees nor Mr. Whipple *has* reached their quota.

The biggest difficulty seems to occur when indefinite pronouns are used. *See* Illustration 6–5 to determine whether the pronoun is singular or plural. Be sure that any reference back to the indefinite pronoun is also singular or plural.

EXAMPLES:

Incorrect: *Everyone* going to the picnic should bring *their* lunch.

Correct: *Everyone* going to the picnic should bring *his (or her)* lunch.

Incorrect: All *employees* working on the night shift should be sure to bring *his* lunch.

Correct: All *employees* working on the night shift should be sure to bring *their* lunches.

(or)

Each employee working on the night shift should bring *his* lunch.

When a pronoun is needed to refer to a generic noun such as doctor, writer or secretary, "he or she," "his or hers" or "him or her" should be used instead of the previously traditional male pronouns. Some readers may find the generic use of male pronouns or the use of female pronouns for occupations which are traditionally held by women to be offensive. It may be better to reword the sentence to avoid the generic pronoun or change the wording from singular to plural. Three ways to write in gender-neutral language are (1) make the subject plural, (2) omit the pronouns and use "a" or "an", or (3) refer to both feminine and masculine forms.

EXAMPLE:

Gender-biased: An employee has *his* schedule to follow.
Incorrect pronoun agreement: An employee has *their* schedule to follow.
Corrected: (1) Employees have their schedules to follow.
(2) An employee has a schedule to follow.
(3) An employee has his or her schedule to follow.

§ 6.7 Adverbs

Adverbs are words that describe or limit a verb, an adjective, or another adverb. They also modify verbals (infinitives, gerunds, and participles). They answer the questions of:

Where?	He works downtown.
When?	Mother left today.
To what degree?	She worked considerably harder than Judith.
How?	The snow melted quickly.
Why?	She worked so she would not starve. (adverb clause)

§ 6.7.1 Comparison of Adverbs

Illustration 6–6 shows the three degrees of comparison of adverbs. The *simple* expresses no comparison.

EXAMPLE: The law student studied diligently.

The *comparative* compares two persons, places, or things.

EXAMPLE: The law student studied more diligently than his friend.

The *superlative* compares three or more persons or things.

EXAMPLE: Of the three law students, Jack studied most diligently.

Illustration 6–6

COMPARISON CHART FOR ADVERBS		
Simple	Comparative	Superlative
No comparison	Compares two persons or things. Add *er* to positive form. Use the word *more* before the positive form. Use the word *less* before the positive form.	Compares three or more persons or things. Add *est* to the positive. Use the word *most* before the positive. Use the word *least* before the positive.
	EXAMPLES	
efficiently	more efficiently	most efficiently
efficiently	less efficiently	least efficiently
soon	sooner	soonest
obvious	more obvious	most obvious
much	more	most
bad	worse	worst
slowly	more slowly	most slowly

§ 6.8 Adjectives

Adjectives are words which modify, describe, or limit nouns, pronouns, and gerunds. They answer questions such as:

Which one? The red car is mine.
How many? The two books are his.
What kind? The wooden chair is broken.

Most people are familiar with adjectives preceding nouns such as those in the examples given above. There are also adjectives that follow linking verbs (forms of verbs such as *be, appear, seem*). These are called *predicate adjectives.*

EXAMPLES: The dress is *beautiful.*
She seems *happy.*
He appears *exhilarated.*

Occasionally an adjective follows a noun.

EXAMPLES: His wife found the restaurant *dirty.* (*Dirty* modifies restaurant.)
A dress *six inches longer* would not look nice on her. (*Six inches longer* modifies dress.)

Adjectives are sometimes created from proper nouns. These are called proper adjectives.

EXAMPLES: An *English* actor is appearing in the local theater.
A *European* car was seen at the used car showroom.

Some proper adjectives are no longer capitalized because they are no longer associated with the proper names from which they were derived.

EXAMPLES: pasteurized milk (Louis Pasteur)
herculean task (Hercules)

§ 6.8.1 Compound Adjectives

Compound adjectives are those that consist of two or more words that function as a unit and express a single thought. The words in a compound adjective are hyphenated when they occur directly before the noun. When they occur elsewhere in the sentence, they may or may not be hyphenated depending on how they are used.

EXAMPLES: This is a *first-class* restaurant.
She is a *well-informed* reporter.
The *up-to-date* report was given to the manager.

When they follow the noun, they are not hyphenated.

EXAMPLES: The restaurant was *first class.*
The reporter was *well informed.*
The report was *up to date.*

Sometimes what looks like a compound adjective is in reality an adverb-adjective combination. The adverb ends in *ly.* These should never be hyphenated. The test is to see if you can omit the word immediately preceding the noun and still have a combination that sounds correct. Do not confuse adjectives ending in ly such as friendly, timely, motherly, and lovely for adverbs. Adjectives ending in ly should be hyphenated when used with a participle.

EXAMPLES: The *friendly-acting* man sold teapots. (Adjective + Participle)
The *privately owned* yacht was luxurious. (Adverb + Adjective)

If you can say *friendly man,* which you can, you need a hyphen. If you cannot, you do not need a hyphen. Because *privately yacht* does not make sense without *owned,* you do not need the hyphen. The reasoning behind this is that the *ly* ending on the adverb shows the relationship of the two words without the hyphen. But two adjectives with the force of one thought, as in *worldly-wise person,* needs the hyphen to tie the two words together. (*See also* Section 6.14.11.)

A noun followed by a gerund (*profit-taking, price-cutting*) needs a hyphen when it is used as an adjective preceding a noun.

EXAMPLES: She did her *letter writing* late at night.
He entered the *letter-writing* contest.

Most words ending in *ing, ed, d, en,* or *n,* when used in compound modifiers, are hyphenated.

EXAMPLES: Far-reaching
Old-fashioned
Soft-spoken
Half-grown

The general rule is that if the phrase is out of its normal order, it should be hyphenated.

EXAMPLES: The coat looked old.
The old-looking coat was still useful.
The statement was off the record.
The off-the-record statement upset some employees.

As with the possessive form, when using the comparative or superlative forms in a compound adjective, the hyphen is used.

EXAMPLES:	a low-priced house	a lower-priced house
	a slow-burning fire	the slowest-burning fire

§ 6.8.2 Comparison of Adjectives

Adjectives are compared in the same manner as *adverbs—positive, comparative,* and *superlative.*

Positive—pretty, graceful

Comparative—prettier, more graceful

Superlative—prettiest, most graceful

Consult the chart on adverbs for additional information. (*See* Illustration 6–6.)

Some words such as certain, perfect, correct, true, right, complete, round, unique, and dead cannot be compared logically. For example, one true story cannot be more true than another true story. To make such comparisons, use the words more nearly or most nearly. This story is more nearly true than that true story.

§ 6.8.3 Distinguishing Between Adverbs and Adjectives

Adverbs are often formed by adding *ly* to adjectives (courteous/courteously, direct/directly, real/really). Occasionally, when the adjective ends with *y* preceded by a consonant, the *y* is changed to *i* and *ly* is added (ready/readily, happy/happily).

Some adverbs and adjectives are confusing. *Good* is an adjective and *well* is an adverb, except in matters of health; then, *well* is an adjective. *Bad* is an adjective and *badly* is an adverb; when you are talking about any of the five senses, be sure that you use the correct word.

EXAMPLES: I smell *bad.* (The person has a bad odor.)
I smell *badly.* (The person does a poor job of sniffing.)
I feel *bad.* (I am not well.)
I feel *badly.* (I do a poor job of touching.)

Real is an adjective; *really* is an adverb. *Real* is not a substitute for the word *very;* neither is *really* a good substitute for *very.* It may be used, but it gives the impression of *actually* rather than *very.*

EXAMPLES:
Incorrect: I worked *real* hard.
Correct: I worked *very* hard.
Incorrect: She is a *real* happy person.
Acceptable: She is a *really* happy person.
Correct: She is a *very* happy person.

Some adjectives form their degrees in an irregular manner. The following are some of the common irregular adjectives:

Positive	**Comparative**	**Superlative**
bad, ill	worse	worst
good, well	better	best
little	littler, less, lesser	littlest, least
many, much	more	most
far	farther, further	farthest, furthest

Most adjectives which end in *ful* or *less* and all adjectives of more than two syllables form their degrees by adding *more* or *less* for the comparative and *most* or *least* for the superlative.

Farther and *further* are the comparatives for *far*. *Farthest* and *furthest* are the superlatives for *far*. *Farther* and *farthest* are preferred when referring to measurable distance; *further* and *furthest* are preferred when referring to degree or quantity, as in the sense of additional or figurative distance.

Later is used to refer to time; *latter* means near the end or the second of two items.

Less and *least* are used to describe nouns that are concerned with amount and quantity; *fewer* and *fewest* are used to emphasize number by actual count. *Fewer* refers to number and is used before plurals ("fewer books"); *less* refers to degree or amount and is used before singular words ("less noise").

§ 6.9 Prepositions

A *preposition* is a word used to show the relationship of the noun or pronoun that follows it to some other word in the sentence. The prepositional phrase consisting of the preposition and its object may be used to modify other words in a sentence. It helps connect the thoughts in a sentence and offers clearer writing. The object of a preposition is never the subject of a sentence. For example, in this sentence "*The list of exhibits was ready.*" the word "list," not "exhibits" is the subject because the object of a preposition can never be the subject of the sentence.

COMMONLY USED PREPOSITIONS

about
above
according to
after
against
along with
among
around
as well as
at
before
below
beside
between
but
by
concerning
during
except
for
from
in
in addition to
into
of
off
on
over
regarding
through
to
under
up
upon
until
with

NOTE: *But* is usually a conjunction although it may also serve as a preposition. Everyone left *but* him.

§ 6.10 Conjunctions

A *conjunction* is a word used to connect two or more words, phrases, or clauses.

§ 6.10.1 Coordinating Conjunctions

Coordinating conjunctions connect words, phrases, and clauses of equal value (two independent clauses, two subjects, two verbs, two dependent clauses). The common ones are *and, but, or,* and *nor.*

§ 6.10.2 Subordinating Conjunctions

Subordinating conjunctions join dependent clauses (subordinate clauses) to independent clauses (main clauses).

Following is a list of subordinate conjunctions:

after
although
as
as if
as though
because
before
in order to
if
since
until
when
while
where
whether
whereas
unless
than
provided
inasmuch as
so that

§ 6.10.3 Conjunctive Adverbs

Conjunctive adverbs also join clauses, words, and phrases which are grammatically equal. The following is a list of conjunctive adverbs:

however
therefore
consequently
moreover
nevertheless
likewise
thus
too
hence

§ 6.10.4 Correlative Conjunctions

Correlative conjunctions are *either/or* and *neither/nor.* They also join equal sentence elements such as two subjects, two verbs, two independent clauses, or two dependent clauses.

§ 6.11 Interjections

An interjection is a word used to express strong feeling or emotion. It does not change the basic meaning of the sentence. It is usually followed by a comma or exclamation mark.

EXAMPLE: Help! I'm being robbed! (*Help* is the interjection.)

§ 6.12 Sentence Structure

Every English teacher frequently hears the question, "Why do we need to learn parts of a sentence?" The main reason is that it is difficult, if not impossible, to use pronouns correctly if one does not know how they are used in the sentence.

If a pronoun is used as a subject or predicate nominative, the nominative case must be used (I, you, he, she, they, we).

If a pronoun is used as the direct object, indirect object, or object of the preposition, the objective case must be used (me, you, him, her, them, us).

The same is true of *who* and *whom*. *Who* is in the nominative case and is used for subjects and predicate nominatives; *whom* is in the objective case and is used for direct objects, indirect objects, and objects of prepositions.

Many people pick up poor speaking habits from their associates; although it may "sound right," it may be wrong. "It's me" or "This is her" sounds good, but it should be "It's I" or "This is she." If you truly understand the nominative and objective cases, a large percentage of your grammar errors will disappear.

In addition, learning sentence structure is important in order to be able to make correct subject-verb agreements, to punctuate correctly, to use adverbs and adjectives correctly, and to write complete sentences.

§ 6.12.1 The Sentence

A *sentence* expresses a complete thought; it contains a *subject* and a *predicate* (verb plus associated words). The *subject* is the person, place, or thing being told about or doing the action. The *verb* tells something about the person, place, or thing.

§ 6.12.2 The Simple Sentence

The *simple sentence* contains a subject and a verb.

EXAMPLE: Allen sings.
S **V**

A simple sentence may also contain a compound *subject* (more than one doer) and a *compound verb* (more than one action). It still is a simple sentence because there is just one element for the subject and one for the verb.

EXAMPLE: Fred and Agnes danced and sang in the show.
S V

(*Fred and Agnes*=subject; *danced and sang*=verb)

A simple sentence may also contain a direct object, indirect object, predicate nominative, predicate adjective, and other parts of speech.

The *direct object* is the person, place, or thing receiving the action.

EXAMPLE: Jamie pounded the table.
S V DO

The *indirect object* is the person, place, or thing receiving the direct object.

EXAMPLE: Rosalie sold Anita the necklace.
S V IO DO

A *predicate nominative* means the same thing as the subject and is connected to the subject by a linking verb. The sentence can be reversed without changing the meaning.

EXAMPLE: Mrs. Smith is the teacher.
S V PN
The teacher is Mrs. Smith.
S V PN

A *predicate adjective* describes the subject and is connected to the subject by a linking verb.

EXAMPLE: The sunflowers are yellow.
S V PA

A simple sentence does not need any other element to complete its meaning. It could be called an *independent clause.*

§ 6.12.3 The Compound Sentence

The *compound sentence* consists of two or more independent clauses connected in one of the following ways:

1. By a coordinating conjunction preceded by a comma
   EXAMPLE: Devan typed the letter, and Terry organized the notebooks.
2. By a semicolon
   EXAMPLE: Devon typed the letter; Terry organized the notebooks.
3. By a conjunctive adverb preceded by a semicolon and followed by a comma

EXAMPLE: Devon typed the letter; however, Terry organized the notebooks.

If there are more than two independent clauses and they are short, they may be joined with commas. This would make a series of clauses.

EXAMPLE: Devon typed, Nicki proofread, Jamie copied, and Terry delivered the documents. (Note the coordinating conjunction preceding the last clause.)

If a stronger break between clauses is desired, use semicolons between each clause. Place a semicolon followed by *and* between the last two independent clauses.

EXAMPLE: Devon and Nicki went to court in the morning; Jamie and Terry copied the documents; and they prepared exhibits later that evening.

When joining clauses which contain commas, use a semicolon at the joining place rather than a comma. This prevents confusion and clearly establishes the break between the clauses.

EXAMPLE: Devon, Nicki, Jamie and Terry went looking for Tammy; but they did not find her until the movie had already started.

However, if no misreading is possible, it is acceptable to use commas to separate the clauses.

NEVER join two independent clauses with only a comma. This is known as a *comma splice* and is absolutely incorrect. Use one of the three methods shown above, or put a period at the end of each clause, making two sentences.

§ 6.12.4 The Complex Sentence

The *complex sentence* consists of one independent clause and one or more dependent clauses. In order to understand this type of sentence, you must have a good understanding of dependent clauses.

The *dependent clause* contains a subject and a verb; it may also contain any or all of the other sentence parts as well. It cannot stand by itself; it needs the independent clause to complete its meaning.

EXAMPLE:	While the lawyer was in court,	Sarah did the filing.
	Dep. Cl.	Indep. Cl.

Dependent clauses can serve as nouns, adverbs, or adjectives in relation to the main clause.

A *noun clause* functions as a noun; it serves as the subject, direct object, or object of the preposition.

EXAMPLES: *Who is going to be president* is anybody's guess.
(The noun clause is the subject of the sentence.)
Jack said *that Tony would not be here today.*
(The noun clause is the direct object of the verb *said.*)
Please give the promotion to *whomever you choose.*
(The noun clause is the object of the preposition *to.*)

There is no punctuation separating the noun clause from the remainder of the sentence.

An *adverb clause* functions in the same manner as an adverb; it modifies or limits verbs, adjectives, or other adverbs. It answers the questions of Where? When? How? Why? It is connected to the main clause by a subordinating conjunction. *See* Section 6.10.2 for a list of subordinating conjunctions.

If the adverb clause precedes the independent clause, the two clauses are separated by a comma. When the subordinate clause follows the independent clause, it is not preceded by a comma unless it is not essential to the sentence. When an adverbial clause ends the sentence, check to see if it is restrictive (essential to the meaning) or nonrestrictive. If it is nonrestrictive, place a comma between it and the main clause.

EXAMPLES: Please decide if you wish to purchase the suit, *inasmuch as we have other interested buyers.*
If we cannot agree, we must submit to arbitration.
We must submit to arbitration *if we cannot agree.*
Before the painter gets here, she wants to leave.
She wants to leave *before the painter gets here.*

Adjective clauses are generally introduced with *relative pronouns* (who, whom, whose, which, and that). They modify, limit, or describe nouns and gerunds. They are directly related to a noun or gerund in the sentence.

EXAMPLE: She worked quickly because the deadline *that* she made was fast approaching. (This has two dependent clauses in it: *that she made* is part of the dependent clause beginning with *because. That she made* modifies *deadline.*)

A modifier clause can be either essential or nonessential to the meaning of the sentence. If it is essential, no commas are used to separate it from the independent clause; if it is nonessential, it is set off by commas. Some books refer to these as restrictive and nonrestrictive modifiers. If necessary for identification, commas are not used.

EXAMPLES: Her brother, *who lived in Albany,* was sent to prison. (She has only one brother; therefore, the clause is nonessential.)

Her brother *who lived in Albany* was sent to prison. (She has more than one brother; therefore, the clause is essential to identify which brother was sent to prison.)

§ 6.12.5 The Compound–Complex Sentence

A *compound-complex* sentence consists of two or more independent clauses and one or more dependent clauses.

EXAMPLE: They hired a new software technician (IC) who had excellent training, (DC) but he came in late every morning. (IC)

§ 6.12.6 Phrases

A *phrase* is a group of words. Phrases usually serve as modifiers in the sentence, but infinitive and gerund phrases can also serve as nouns. Probably the most common phrase is the prepositional phrase. It can serve as an adverb or adjective in the sentence. It consists of the preposition and its object (a noun or pronoun); it may also contain several related words which serve as modifiers in the phrase itself.

EXAMPLES:

During	the	long,	extended	trial,	she	worked	continuously.
PREP		ADJ	ADJ	OB PREP	S	V	ADV

He	gave	it	to	the	very	competent	assistant.
S	V	DO	PREP		ADV	ADJ	OB PREP

§ 6.13 Review of Sentence Structure

In determining the role of the various words in the sentence, there are some basic steps you can follow:

1. Locate the verb or verbs with tense in the sentence (eat, ate, has eaten).
2. Identify a subject for each verb (who is doing what?).
3. Find the direct object and indirect object, if any (on what is the action focused?).
4. Locate the predicate nominative or predicate adjective, if there is one (the descriptive word(s) following the verb).
5. Determine the correct case for Items 3 and 4 above (singular or plural; nouns, pronouns, or verbs).
6. Look for the prepositions and the nouns following them. (Some people prefer to locate the nouns in the sentence and check to see if they are preceded by a preposition.)

7. Then look for the adverbs, adjectives, and connecting words.
8. With sentences containing *who* or *whom,* you may need to rearrange the sentence in order to identify the case correctly.

EXAMPLES: The man (who/whom) I gave it to was very handsome.
The man to *whom* (object of preposition) I gave it was very handsome.
Who/Whom are you going to call?
You are going to call *whom?* (object of the infinitive *to call*)

It can be helpful to replace *who* or *whom* with a pronoun to decide which one to use:

EXAMPLES: Tim is the one who lives on Denver Street.
He lives on Denver Street.
With whom are you working?
I am working with him.

COMMON ERRORS TO AVOID

1. A prisoner is hanged, not hung. A picture is hung.
2. Something is unique but not very unique or most unique. The same is true for words like *certain* and *perfect.*
3. There is a difference between a house and a home. A home is not sold. A house can be sold.
4. He is a sort of radical, not sort of a radical. There is a difference.
5. Injured refers to persons; damage refers to objects.
6. A resolution is adopted. An ordinance is passed.
7. Do not say a person broke his arm unless he did so deliberately. Instead say a person's arm was broken.
8. A person does not sustain a fatal injury. Sustain means to bear up under; to support by adequate proof. Instead say a person suffered a fatal injury.
9. Webster says *all right* is all right. *Allright* and *alright* are not all right.
10. The man who got married is a bridegroom, but it is permissible to refer to the couple as bride and groom. When mentioning the man alone, he is the bridegroom unless he takes care of horses.

11. Take it for granted that a marriage is consummated, but do not discuss the matter in print. Do not say, "The marriage was consummated."

12. An event that has not been arranged or planned occurs. A wedding, a party, or a conference takes place.

13. *Afterward, forward, toward,* and similar words with the suffix *ward* take no *s.*

14. Go a short way, not a short ways.

15. *Headquarters, molasses,* and *whereabouts* all take singular verbs.

16. Mrs. Jones is the widow of John Jones, not the late John Jones. He leaves his widow; his widow survives.

17. A person died of pneumonia, not from pneumonia.

18. Make it miles an hour, not miles per hour.

19. It was proved, but it has been proven.

20. Collective nouns generally take singular verbs, but there are exceptions. The pair were married. The pair spent their honeymoon in San Francisco. The public is alert. The American people are dependable.

21. A scholar is a learned person. A child in school is a pupil. A person attending high school or college is a student.

22. Heart disease is an ailment of the heart; heart failure is what occurs whenever anyone dies.

23. Murder is a technical term denoting a degree of guilt and should be used advisedly.

24. Not all real estate brokers are realtors. A realtor is an active member of the local real estate board having membership in the National Association of Real Estate Boards.

25. Fifty persons were present, not fifty people. *The people of the United States* is correct. Some authorities no longer distinguish between *persons* and *people* and use them interchangeably.

26. Character is what one really possesses; reputation is what one is reputed to have.

27. State presidents from every state association attended the Round Table conference, not Roundtable.

28. Many well-known organizations are usually identified only by their initials: YWCA for Young Women's Christian Association. Such abbreviations are written without periods or spaces in all capitals. Certain professional designations are also written in this way. In describing PLS ... an advanced certification for the legal professional®, use the full identity initially; thereafter the abbreviated Certified PLS will not be misunderstood.

29. A turkey is red-headed, but a person is red-haired.

30. The adverb *only* has slipped its moorings and now drifts anywhere in a sentence. Why do most people say, "I only have ..." when they mean, I have only ...? Instead of the faulty, "I only have eyes for you," the songwriter could have written any of three other versions:

 "I have eyes only for you."
 "I have eyes for only you."
 "I have eyes for you only."

 Most people would understand the four versions to mean essentially the same thing; however, "only I have eyes for you" means something very different and is certainly less flattering!

31. *Compare to* refers to different things (life compared to a movie). *Compare with* refers to similar things (Congress compared with Parliament).

32. When itemizing, use first, second, and third. There is no "firstly" so use initially, secondly, and last.

33. Use regardless or irrespective. "Irregardless" is not a word.

§ 6.14 Punctuation

The purpose of punctuation is to assist the reader to understand the written material. When a person is speaking, they lower or raise their voice and pause for emphasis or clarity. Punctuation accomplishes this for the reader. There are certain accepted rules and principles for punctuation that are understood by the majority of writers and readers. Everyone should be familiar with the rules of punctuation and refer to them periodically for reinforcement.

§ 6.14.1 Period

The period indicates a full stop. It is used:

- At the end of a sentence except for questions or exclamatory sentences
- After abbreviations, except when several initials are commonly used together and do not require periods (YMCA, AAA, NALS)

- After initials in a name
- Between dollars and cents ($1.89)
- To indicate a decimal (10.9 inches)

In a web address, before the suffix (com, net, org, edu, gov) the punctuation is called a dot, not a period.

§ 6.14.2 Comma

The *comma* is a partial stop. It gives pause and helps clarify the meaning of the sentence. Commas should be used only when there is a reason for using them. Some writers insert so many commas in their writing that the readers find they cannot follow the flow of the sentence. The comma is used:

1. To separate words, phrases, or short clauses in a series of three or more. Generally, a comma is placed before the *and*; however, many firms prefer to omit the comma preceding the and. Be sure you are not causing confusion: Are whisky, vodka, gin and tonic three drinks, or four?

   EXAMPLE: A lawyer's assistant needs to be prompt, efficient, and trustworthy.

   In the names of business firms, *do not use a comma before an ampersand* (&) in a firm name.

   EXAMPLE: Jackson, Hall, Roe & Stone

2. To separate clauses connected by coordinating conjunctions unless they are short and closely related.

   EXAMPLES: The lawyer was in court all day, and the assistant had to work late.
   Kristen rowed and Robyn bailed.

3. To set off a subordinate clause that precedes the main clause.

   EXAMPLE: Since he locked his key in the car, he could not open the door.

4. After an introductory phrase that contains a verb form.

   EXAMPLE: After skiing all day, he was too tired to go to a movie.

5. To set off a nonessential (nonrestrictive) clause from the rest of the sentence. Nonessential clauses contain information which is not critical to the meaning of the sentence, as opposed to essential (restrictive) clauses, which contain information which is an essential part of the meaning of the sentence. The test is whether the clause can be removed from the sentence without significantly changing its meaning.

   EXAMPLE: Terry, who had been hired recently, chose not to go. (Nonessential, use comma)
   The secretary who had been hired recently chose not to go. (Essential, no comma)

6. To set off parenthetic and transitional words from the rest of the sentence when pauses are clearly indicated. The following is a list of some of these expressions or words.

accordingly	more or less
all in all	namely
also	needless to say
as a matter of fact	of course
by and large	otherwise
by the way	so it seems
for example	therefore
however	though
if possible	too
in brief	unfortunately
meanwhile	usually

Most of the time, a pause is indicated, and the comma is used.

7. To set off an intervening phrase or clause which breaks the continuity of the sentence.

   EXAMPLE: These men, even though they were very hungry, gave the food to the children.

8. To set off contrasting phrases or clauses.

   EXAMPLE: What we need is justice, not just trite promises.

9. To set off explanatory "or" phrases which mean the same as the preceding word.

   EXAMPLE: Indexing, or coding, of the material to be filed is necessary.

10. To separate two or more coordinating adjectives.

    EXAMPLE: The tall, lovely woman came to my table. Note that no comma is used when the cumulative adjectives are used, *e.g.,* The dark red dress was stunning.

11. To set off names that are used in a direct address.

    EXAMPLE: Do you believe, Dr. Jones, that I will live?

12. To set off phrases or words used to identify a preceding word when they are not essential to the meaning.

    EXAMPLES: My mother, Madeline, was here this evening.
    George Washington, the first president, was born on February 22, 1732.

13. To set off quotations from the rest of the sentence.

    EXAMPLE: Charlie said, "Don't count on me for more money."

14. To set off explanatory words such as *Inc., Jr.,* names of states when used with the city name, and the year when used with the month and day.

    EXAMPLES: I will be there on August 11, 2005, to see you perform.
    Mason & Jones, Inc., is open for business.

Did you go to Denver, Colorado, on your birthday?
Lee James, Jr., is not my husband.

15. To set off *etc.*, a comma is placed before and after it.

    EXAMPLE: Paper, pencils, pens, etc., will be sent tomorrow.

16. To separate a title or degree from a name.

    EXAMPLE: John Jones, Ph.D., will speak at our next luncheon.

§ 6.14.3 Semicolon

The *semicolon* is used between parts of a sentence to separate phrases, clauses, and enumerations. It is used:

1. To separate independent clauses joined by a connective when one or more of the clauses contain internal commas and a strong break between clauses is desired.

   EXAMPLE: The shipment of coats, suits, and skirts will be ready tomorrow; and they will be sent air express.

2. To separate two independent clauses when no connective is used.

   EXAMPLE: I plan to leave at nine on the plane; I will be in New York by ten.

3. To precede expressions such as *that is, namely,* or *for example* when they introduce a clause.

   EXAMPLE: I plan to quit for two reasons; namely, because the hours are long and the pay is poor.

4. To set off a phrase when words are missing but understood, a comma may also be used; but if there are other commas, a semicolon makes the meaning clearer.

   EXAMPLE: To some teachers, it was a catastrophe; to others, a minor nuisance.

5. Between independent clauses of a compound sentence that are joined by a conjunctive adverb (however, therefore, etc.).

   EXAMPLE: We had car trouble; therefore, we did not arrive on time for the depositions.

§ 6.14.4 Colon

The *colon* is used:

1. After the salutation in a business letter.

   EXAMPLE: Dear Mr. Jones:

2. In stating clock time.

   EXAMPLE: 12:10 p.m.

3. After introductory expressions preceding an enumeration, such as *the following, thus, as follows.*

   EXAMPLE: Please order the following:

4. In a web address, following *http*.

   EXAMPLE: To search for anything related to government, go to http:\\www.whitehouse.gov/

5. The colon may follow a verb, preposition, or conjunction when it introduces a tabulation, but in running text no colon is used.

   EXAMPLES: Among those present were:
   Sam Brown
   George White
   James Black
   Among those present were Sam Brown, George White, and James Black.

6. To introduce a long quotation.

   EXAMPLE: Lincoln's Gettysburg Address read: "Fourscore and seven years ago. . . ."

§ 6.14.5 Question Marks

The *question mark* is used in the following ways:

1. After a direct question.

   EXAMPLE: When are you sending my discovery requests?

A question mark should not be used if action is expected; a period is okay. If you are not sure about a request, a question mark is better and is more polite.

   EXAMPLE: Will you please send me a corrected billing.

2. After each question in a single sentence.

   EXAMPLE: How do you feel about *Time? Newsweek? Fortune? Good Housekeeping?*

§ 6.14.6 Exclamation Point

The *exclamation point* may be used internally in a sentence or at the end of a sentence. It is used after a word or group of words expressing a strong command, strong feeling or emotion, or an excited exclamation.

EXAMPLE: Help! He stole my purse!

§ 6.14.7 Dash

The *dash* consists of two hyphens with no spaces between them, and no spaces to either side. The *dash* is used:

1. To set off a single word or expression for emphasis.

   EXAMPLE: His work lacked only one thing—accuracy.

2. To set off or segregate a change of thought or side command from the rest of the sentence.

   EXAMPLE: His whole unlucky life—or so it seemed to me—was wasted on that woman.

3. To take the place of parentheses.

   EXAMPLE: The five senses—smell, touch, sight, hearing, and taste—are like gems of great value.

4. To substitute for a colon where the word *namely* has been omitted.

   EXAMPLE: There are two urgent needs—prevention of crime and a balanced economy.

5. To replace the semicolon before words such as *namely, for instance,* and the like.

   EXAMPLE: The house needed three things—namely, a roof, a porch, and a front door.

6. To set off a repetition, variation, explanation, or summary of what has gone before.

   EXAMPLES: Give money—dollars and cents—right now.
   They have acquiesced—given in—to our demands.
   I went to that movie—one I had seen before—and sat through it again.
   To give your money and your life for a cause—that is dedication.

7. For emphasis (as in sales letters).

   EXAMPLE: This is not the same offer we made last year—it is a brand new plan especially created for the consumer of today.

§ 6.14.8 Parentheses

Parentheses are a strong mark of punctuation used when it is necessary to separate certain information from the rest of the sentence. Parentheses need no additional punctuation, such as commas, to set them off. All marks of punctuation, such as the ending period, question mark, exclamation point, or semicolon, should be placed outside the parentheses; the exception to this rule is when the material contained in the parentheses requires its own internal or ending punctuation. If the sentence in the parentheses stands alone and is not a part of another sentence, a period is used within the parentheses.

1. Place only material in parentheses that could be removed from the sentence without impairing the meaning of the sentence.
2. A complete sentence in parentheses that is part of another sentence should not start with a capital letter or end with a period.

EXAMPLE: His luck was running out (he lost all the money he had), and he had to sell his car.

3. Parentheses are used when writing figures after words.

   EXAMPLE: We are enclosing a check for Twenty-five Dollars ($25).

4. Use parentheses when enumerating in running text.

   EXAMPLE: There are three kinds of ending punctuation marks: (1) period, (2) question mark, and (3) exclamation point.

5. Use parentheses around explanatory or illustrative words or phrases.

   EXAMPLES: The three assistants (Miss Jones, Mrs. Smith, and Ms. Bills) were at the meeting.
   Water (H_2O) is essential to all human beings.

§ 6.14.9 Quotation Marks

Certain punctuation marks are written inside the final quotation mark; others are written outside. The period and comma always go inside the quotation marks.

1. When a quotation mark is used with a semicolon, colon, or dash, the quotation mark comes before the punctuation.

   EXAMPLE: She was told "A stitch in time saves nine"; she did not believe it.

2. A question mark or exclamation point should be placed after the quotation mark unless the quoted material itself ends in a question mark or exclamation point.

   EXAMPLES: She asked, "Where did you buy the blouse?"
   Why didn't she ignore his "idiosyncrasies"?

3. Only one ending punctuation mark should come at the end of the sentence, either before or after the quotation mark. If the quotation ends in a period, question mark, or exclamation point and is followed by a quotation mark, no further punctuation is needed.

4. When there is a quotation within another quotation, the single quotation marks are used for the internal quote.

5. Quotation marks are used to indicate conversation.

   A new paragraph should be made each time the speaker changes.

   EXAMPLES: "I would like to see Ms. Mason," said the client.
   "She is in court today. May I make you an appointment for tomorrow?" asked the assistant.
   "No," answered the client, "because I will be in the hospital tomorrow."

6. Place quotation marks around slang or coined words if they might give a poor impression. By the use of quotation marks, the reader is made aware that the writer knows the words are poor but is using them for effect.

   EXAMPLE: Granny says things "ain't" like they used to be.

7. Words which are referred to as words may be placed in quotation marks to identify them as words and not part of the sentence; however, italics or underlining can also be used.

   EXAMPLE: Place the comma before "and" in a compound sentence.

8. Use quotation marks to indicate the title of a published article. In typewritten work there are four methods for indicating titles of books: (1) placing quotation marks around the title, (2) using solid caps for the title, (3) underlining the title, and (4) italicizing the title. Italicizing has become the preferred method in many law firms. Articles are still placed only in quotation marks.

   EXAMPLES: Have you read "The Organization Man" yet?
   Have you read THE ORGANIZATION MAN yet?
   Have you read The Organization Man yet?
   (Underlining represents italics in printing.)
   Have you read *The Organization Man* yet?

§ 6.14.10 Apostrophe

The *apostrophe* is used:

1. To form contractions of words and figures. The apostrophe is used in place of omitted letters or figures.

   EXAMPLES:

is not	isn't	wherever	where'er
cannot	can't	you have	you've
'76	'50s		

2. To form possessives. Never use an apostrophe with pronouns showing possession.

   EXAMPLES: Robyn's hair looks very nice.
   Its color is red.

3. To form plurals of lower case letters.

   EXAMPLE: Be sure to dot your i's and cross your t's.

4. To set off quoted material that appears within a larger quotation.
5. In names with the prefix O, such as: O'Brien, O'Connor.

§ 6.14.11 Hyphen

There is a great deal of disagreement over just when and where a hyphen should be used. Many words that were once hyphenated are now joined as one word or separated into two words without the hyphen. The following is a list of general usage rules. The main rule to remember is that a hyphen pulls things together into a single thought.

1. Use the hyphen for one-thought expressions (two or more words functioning as one word).

   EXAMPLE: He has the know-how to do the job.

2. Use the hyphen to join two or more words which modify a noun and act as a single thought.

   EXAMPLE: She had blue-green eyes.

3. When two or more words modify a noun and are not in their normal order, they are hyphenated. To check, place them after the noun to see if the words then have separate force. If so, then they are not hyphenated after the noun and are hyphenated before the noun.

EXAMPLES:	a well-known author	an author was well known
	an up-to-date procedure	the procedure was brought up to date

If the one-thought idea remains when it is placed after the noun, it is still hyphenated.

EXAMPLE: a never-ending job   the job was never-ending

4. Three or more words serving as a single modifier are usually hyphenated.

   EXAMPLE: change-of-address cards

5. An adverb ending in *ly* preceding an adjective is not connected to the adjective with a hyphen. To test to see if it is an adverb, try to use it with a noun alone and not the adjective. If you cannot use it with the noun, then you do not use the hyphen.

EXAMPLES:	a highly respected employee	(a highly employee)
	a friendly-looking girl	(a friendly girl)

6. Use the hyphen when verbs are composed of two or more words (not including helping verbs) and have a single thought.

   EXAMPLES: Double-space the rough draft.
   She cross-referenced the material.

7. Suspended hyphens occur when two or more words share an additional word with a hyphen. Each of the words must have a hyphen following it.

   EXAMPLES: the five- and ten-cent store
   at three-, six-, and twelve-month intervals

8. When the prefix *re* is added to a word and the resulting word means to do something *again,* you add a hyphen between the *re* and the word if the unhyphenated word would be confused with another word.

EXAMPLES: recover re-cover (cover again)
reform re-form (form again)
resign re-sign (sign again)

9. Words preceded by the prefixes *ex-*, *self-*, and *quasi-* are hyphenated.

   EXAMPLES: ex-wife, self-sacrificing, quasi-legal

10. A civil or military title which stands for a single office should not be hyphenated.

    EXAMPLES: Vice President Attorney General
    Secretary of State

11. When an office consists of two functions, it is hyphenated.

    EXAMPLE: secretary-treasurer

12. A letter meant to designate shape before a word is hyphenated to the word.

    EXAMPLES: An S-curve L-shaped T-square

13. A hyphen should be used to clarify meaning.

    EXAMPLES: fifty one-dollar bills
    one half-cooked chicken or
    one-half cooked chicken

§ 6.14.12 Ellipses

These are known as omission marks and are used to denote omission of a word or words in quoted material.

1. If the quoted material is in the middle of the sentence, three periods with intervening spaces (. . .) are used. If the quoted material ends with a period, four periods with intervening spaces (. . . .) are used.
2. When you have an unfinished sentence and wish to indicate that the sentence breaks off, use four periods.
3. In quoted material, omissions of paragraphs are indicated by inserting and indenting four periods (. . . .) on a new line.

§ 6.15 Capitalization

The following selected summarized rules for capitalization will be convenient for reference purposes.

§ 6.15.1 Common Usage

The following are examples of the most common usages of capitalization:

1. The first word of every sentence is capitalized.
2. The first word of a complete direct quotation is capitalized.

3. The first word of a salutation and all nouns used in the salutation are capitalized.
4. The first word in a complimentary close is capitalized.
5. Each item displayed in a list or outline.

§ 6.15.2 First Word After a Colon

Capitalize the first word after a colon only when the colon introduces a complete passage or sentence having an independent meaning.

EXAMPLE: In conclusion I wish to say: "The survey shows that. . . ."

If the material following a colon is dependent on the preceding clause, the first word after the colon is not capitalized.

EXAMPLE: I present the following three reasons for changing: the volume of business does not justify the expense; we are short of people; the product is decreasing in popularity.

§ 6.15.3 Capitalizing Names

1. Capitalize the names of associations, buildings, churches, hotels, streets, organizations, and clubs.

   EXAMPLES: The Business Club, Merchandise Mart, Central Christian Church, Peabody Hotel, Seventh Avenue, Administrative Management Society, Chicago Chamber of Commerce
2. All proper names should be capitalized.

   EXAMPLES: Great Britain, John G. Hammitt, Internet
3. Capitalize names that are derived from proper names.

   EXAMPLES: American, Chinese, English, Chinese noodles, English grammar, Italian spaghetti

Do not, however, capitalize words that are derived from proper nouns and that have developed a special meaning.

EXAMPLES: pasteurized milk, china dishes, morocco leather

4. Capitalize special names for regions and localities.

   EXAMPLES: North Central states, the Far East, the East Side, the Hoosier State
5. Capitalize names of government boards, agencies, bureaus, departments, and commissions.

   EXAMPLES: Civil Service Commission, Social Security Board, Bureau of Navigation
6. Capitalize names of the Deity, the Bible, holy days, and religious denominations.

EXAMPLES: God, in His kingdom, Easter, Genesis, Church of Christ

7. Capitalize the names of holidays.

   EXAMPLES: Memorial Day, Labor Day

8. Capitalize words used before numbers and numerals, with the exception of common words such as page, line, paragraph, and verse.

   EXAMPLES: He found the material on page 3, line 3, Part 3 of Chapter X.
   The reservation is Lower 6, Car 27.
   The class will meet in the Fine Arts Building, Room 114.

Do not capitalize the noun when the noun and number are separated in the sentence.

EXAMPLE: The number of the room where we will meet is 932.

9. Capitalize names of the days of the week and months; do not capitalize names of seasons unless they are personified.

   EXAMPLES: I can arrange for a showing of fall styles on Tuesday, August 28.
   Winter's bitter smile graced the fields.

§ 6.15.4 Capitalizing Titles Used in Business and Professions

The following are rules for capitalizing titles in business and professions.

1. Any title that signifies rank, honor, and respect and immediately precedes an individual's name is capitalized.

   EXAMPLES: Kelly asked President Terry G. Sanders to preside.
   Kelly accompanied Dr. Alex Richards.

2. Academic degrees are capitalized when they precede or follow an individual name.

   EXAMPLES: Mrs. Constance R. Collins, Ph.D., was invited to direct the program.
   Marion R. Benson, Master of Arts

3. Capitalize titles of high-ranking government officers when the title is used in place of the proper name in referring to a specific person.

   EXAMPLES: Our Senator invited us to visit her in Washington.
   The President will return to Camp David soon.

4. Capitalize military and naval titles signifying rank.

EXAMPLES: Captain Meyers, Lieutenant White, Lieutenant Commander Murphy

§ 6.16 Word Division

Whenever possible, avoid dividing a word at the end of a line. The printed document should flow for easy reading, and a divided word may cause the reader to become confused or have to slow down in reading. When dividing a word is unavoidable, there are certain basic rules that should be followed.

§ 6.16.1 General Principles of Word Division

1. Divide only when absolutely essential.
2. Divide between syllables only. The addition of the past tense does not necessarily add an extra syllable.

   EXAMPLE: *guessed*
3. Put enough of the word to be divided on the first line to suggest what the completed word will be.
4. It is permissible to have a right margin that is approximately five spaces shorter or five spaces longer than the desired length of a line if this avoids the necessity of dividing the word.
5. In many cases syllable division of words as found in dictionaries is to be avoided, if at all possible, because the dictionary division shows each syllable and does not show the exact or best place to divide. This is indicated in the next section.

§ 6.16.2 How to Divide Words

1. As a rule divide between a prefix and the letter following it.

   EXAMPLE: *pre-sumed*
2. Divide a word with a suffix as follows:

   A. When a root word ends with the double consonant, separate the suffix from the root word.

   EXAMPLE: *express-ing*

   B. When a consonant is doubled before a suffix, the added consonant goes with the suffix.

   EXAMPLE: *stop-ping*

   C. For a word ending in *cian, cion, gion, sion, sive,* or *tion,* divide between the stem of the word and the suffix.

   EXAMPLE: *progres-sion*
3. When a word containing three or more syllables is to be divided at a one-letter syllable, divide as follows:

   A. For most words, type the one-letter syllable on the first line.

   EXAMPLE: *sepa-rate*

B. For words to be divided at a point where two vowels that are pronounced separately come together, divide between the vowels.

EXAMPLE: *gradu-ation*

C. For a word ending in such terminations as *able, ible,* or *ical,* divide between the stem of the word and the suffix.

EXAMPLE: *remov-able*

NOTE: This rule applies only when the vowel is typed correctly as a syllable by itself and does not apply to such a word as *feasible* (feasi-ble) in which the vowel is a part of the syllable *si.*

4. Divide hyphenated words and compounds at the hyphen only.

EXAMPLE: *self-explanatory*

§ 6.16.3 When Not to Divide Words

1. Do not divide a word of one syllable.
2. Do not divide a two-syllable word of four letters.
3. Do not separate a single-letter syllable at the beginning or end of a word.

   EXAMPLES: *around, steady*
4. When typing words like *e-mail,* use a hard hyphen to ensure the word will not be divided.
5. Do not separate a two-letter syllable at the end of a word.

   EXAMPLE: *difficulty*
6. Avoid separating a two-letter syllable at the beginning of a word.

   EXAMPLE: *defended*
7. Do not separate a syllable that does not contain a vowel from the remainder of the word.
8. Do not divide contractions.
9. Do not divide abbreviations.

§ 6.16.4 Word Divisions to Avoid

1. Do not divide words at the ends of more than two consecutive lines.
2. Do not divide a word at the end of the first line of a personal or business letter if it is possible to avoid it.
3. Do not divide the last word on a page. Carry the entire word to the following page.
4. Do not divide a five- or six-letter word.
5. Do not divide a proper name if it is possible to avoid it, and do not separate titles or initials.

   EXAMPLE: Dr. John C. Crosby

6. Do not separate numbers.

   EXAMPLES: 13,000,000
   $2,419.56

7. Do not separate dates. If you cannot avoid the division, retain the numeral representing the day of the month with the whole name or a syllable division of the month.

   EXAMPLES: March 7, 2005; Sep-tem-ber 23; Janu-ary 15, 2006

§ 6.16.5 Compound Words

There are numerous compound words that are used by the legal profession. Give careful attention to their proper usage. They offer exact reference with the use of a minimum of words.

AFORESAID	Stated before or stated earlier in this document
FOREGOING	What precedes or has gone before
HEREAFTER	After this present point in time
HEREBY	By this or by this document
HEREINABOVE	Within this document; however, before this point in this document
HEREINAFTER	Within this document; however, after this point in this document
HEREOF	Of this
HERETO	To this
HERETOFORE	Before now or prior to this point
HEREUNDER	Under the conditions in this document; following this point in this document
HEREUNTO	To this
HEREWITH	With this document or enclosed with this document
NOTWITHSTANDING	Regardless or however
THENCEFORTH	Following that condition or that time
THEREAFTER	After that condition or that time
THEREFOR	For it
THEREFORE	Because
THEREFROM	From that
THEREOF	Of that
THEREON	On that or on it
THERETO	To that
UNDERSIGNED	One who signed at the end of a document (under the document)
WHATSOEVER	What or whatever
WHEREAS	Considering or when in fact
WHEREFORE	For those reasons or for that reason
WHERESOEVER	A place or where it is
WHEREWITHAL	Resources, means, or money
WHOMSOEVER	Whomever
WHOSOEVER	Whoever

Watch these common compound words and their problems:

- Inasmuch as
- Insofar as
- In fact (is not a compound word)
- A lot (is not a compound word)
- Cannot (is one word)

§ 6.17 Spelling

1. Be sure to complete your root word before you add a suffix beginning with a consonant (ly, less, ful, ment).

EXAMPLES:	EXAMPLES:	EXCEPTIONS:
additional-ly	financial-ly	true-truly
accurate-ly	grate-ful	argu-ment
agree-ment	immense-ly	acknowledg-ment
accidental-ly	immediate-ly	judg-ment
achieve-ment	incidental-ly	
adjust-ment	install-ment	
advertise-ment	misstate-ment	
allot-ment	occasional-ly	
approximate-ly	sincere-ly	
arrange-ments	undoubted-ly	
develop-ment	force-ful	
final-ly		

2. Remember, "*i* before *e* except after c, or when sounded like a, as in neighbor and weigh." This means that when the sound of the diphthong is a long *e,* as in receive, believe, etc., *c* is followed by *ei* and other letters are followed by *ie.* When the sound of the diphthong is a long *a,* as in neighbor, the spelling is *ei.*

EXAMPLES:	EXAMPLES:	EXCEPTIONS:
anxiety	cashier	either
audience	fierce	neither
believe	grief	financier
boundaries	niece	weird
convenience	pier	species
efficiently	pierce	seize
grievous	relieve	leisure
necessities		forfeit
ninetieth	EXCEPT AFTER C	ancient
siege	ceiling	foreign
sieve	conceive	height
achieve	deceit	their
apiece	deceive	
chief	receive	

3. A word ending in silent *e* generally drops the *e* before a suffix beginning with a vowel.

EXAMPLES:

admire	admiration	arrive	arriving
arrange	arranging	believe	believing
desire	desirous	reconcile	reconcilable

4. Words ending in *ce* or *ge* to which is added a suffix beginning with *a* or *o* (*able* or *ous*) retain the silent *e* in order to preserve the soft sound of the *c* or *g*.

EXAMPLES:

advantage	advantageous	notice	noticeable
change	changeable	peace	peaceable
courage	courageous	service	serviceable

5. Only the word "supersede" in our language ends in "sede". Three words end in "ceed" exceed, proceed, succeed. The rest end in "cede."

EXAMPLES:

accede	cede	concede
precede	recede	intercede

6. In words of one syllable and words accented on the last syllable ending in a single consonant preceded by a single vowel, double the final consonant before adding a suffix beginning with a vowel unless adding the suffix will change the accented syllable.

EXAMPLES:

Suffix begins with a vowel (one syllable)

cut	cutting
plan	planning
stop	stopped
quit	quitting

(Accent on last syllable)

admit	admitted	equip	equipped
begin	beginning	commit	committed
remit	remitted	occur	occurred
confer	conferring	compel	compelled

(No accent on last syllable)

prefer	preference	benefit	benefited
refer	reference	marvel	marvelous
happen	happened		

(Suffix begins with a consonant)

glad	gladness
fat	fatness
man	manhood

§ 6.17.1 Words That Are Frequently Misspelled

absorbent
accessible
accidentally
accommodate
accumulate
acknowledge
acknowledgment
announced
apparent
appearance
argument
assistance
athletic
attendance
auxiliary
bankruptcy
believable
benefited
camouflage
canceled
cannot
category
cemetery
circuit
clinically
coliseum
concede
consensus
defendant
definitely
develop
disappointed
disastrous
dissatisfaction
drastically
eligible
embarrass
exaggerate
existence
extension
extraordinary
facetious
familiar
February
forfeit
forty
fulfill
gauge
governor
grammar
grievous
guarantee
harass
hemorrhage
impugn
incidentally
indict
inoculate
innocuous
insistence
intercede
investor
jeopardize
judgment
justifiable
knowledgeable
labeled
laid
liaison
lien
license
likelihood
maintenance
manageable
mathematics
minuscule
miscellaneous
mischievous
ninety-ninth
occasionally
occurred
occurrence
ophthalmology
parallel
permissible

personal
personnel
perseverance
phenomenal
precede
prerogative
principle
privilege
procedure
proceed
protein
prominence
punitive
questionnaire
recommend
referring
relevant
rescind
rhythm
resistance
safety
salable
scissors
sergeant
seize
separate
similar
singular
soluble
superintendent
supersede
surreptitious
threshold
totaled
transferable
traveled
unforeseen
usage
vacuum
various
vicinity
weird
wholly
withhold
wrought
yacht

§ 6.17.2 Vocabulary Improvement

Whether you have had any college training or not, and whether you are young or old, it is never too late to develop your language skills:

1. Look up the meaning of any word that puzzles you, including its etymology.
2. Go over any final copy you expect others to read to make sure it is free from spelling errors. *If you have any doubt about the spelling of any word, use your dictionary.*
3. Do not mispronounce words.
4. When you encounter words that can be useful to you in speaking, use them. Learn how to use and pronounce unfamiliar words.
5. Enrich your legal vocabulary by using a specialized legal dictionary, such *as Black's Law Dictionary.*
6. Learn the vocabulary of various hobbies. Plan your recreational reading to embrace as many areas as possible.
7. Keep up to date with news events.
8. Make use of fine books available on vocabulary development.

§ 6.17.3 Confusing Words

ACCEDE — To express approval or give consent as a result of urging

EXCEED — To be greater than; to go beyond a set limit

EXAMPLES: He acceded to the demands of his public and ran for office.
His vote total exceeded that of his opponent.

ACCEPT — To receive with consent; to endure without protest; (must always be used as a verb)

EXCEPT — verb: To take or leave out from a number
preposition: with the exclusion or exception of

EXAMPLE: Except for Sam, everyone accepted the new attendance policy.

ACCESS — Permission; liberty or ability to enter

EXCESS — More than the usual or specified amount

EXAMPLE: The farmer allowed them access to his property as long as they did not use it to excess.

ADAPT — To make, fit, adjust, conform

ADOPT — To take as one's own; to take by choice into a relationship
To accept formally and put into effect

EXAMPLE: The child found it hard to adapt to the decision of his parents to adopt a second son.

ADVERSE — Harmful, hostile

AVERSE — Opposed to

ADVISE — To give information; to inform or recommend; (always used as a verb)

ADVICE — Recommendation; information given; (always used as a noun)

EXAMPLE: I advise you to take your lawyer's advice.

AFFECT — To produce an influence upon or alteration in; to act upon; (always used as a verb)

EFFECT — noun: Result of a change or influence; result, consequence, outcome
verb: To cause to come into being

EXAMPLE: The new office manager will effect a change in office procedures that will affect all secretaries. Hopefully, the effect of the change will be good.

AID	verb: To give help
AIDE	noun: Assistant
	EXAMPLE: The teacher's aide tried to aid the child in reading.
ALL READY	All prepared
ALREADY	By this time; prior to some specified or implied time
	EXAMPLE: The packages are all ready for mailing; the letters have already been mailed.
ALTOGETHER	Wholly, thoroughly, in all
ALL TOGETHER	Collectively
	EXAMPLES: They are altogether too frail. Were the school children all together?
AMONG	Used when three or more persons or things are involved
AS, AS IF	Used as a conjunction and introduces a clause with a subject and verb
	EXAMPLE: The fabric looks like suede, but it washes as if it were cotton.
BETWEEN	Used when two persons or things are involved
	EXAMPLE: The cake was divided among the four boys, and the pie was divided between the two girls.
ANTE–	A prefix that means *before* when added to the beginning of a word
ANTI–	A prefix that means *against* when added to the beginning of a word
	EXAMPLES: An antecedent is a word that is referred to by a following word. An anticoagulant is a substance that hinders (works against) the clotting of the blood.
ANYONE	Any person at all; anybody
ANY ONE	Any individual person
	EXAMPLE: The winner can be any one of the three candidates; not just anyone can win.
ANXIOUS	Worry or anxiety
EAGER	Enthusiastic or impatient
APPRAISE	To set a value on; to evaluate the worth, significance, or status
APPRISE	To give notice; to tell; to inform
	EXAMPLES: Please apprise the lawyer of the value of the estate. He is the one who will appraise the assets.
APPROXIMATE	Nearly correct or exact

PROXIMATE — Very near, close

EXAMPLE: The proximate cause of the accident was that he was traveling approximately 120 miles an hour.

EXAMPLES: She was nearly as talented as he.
The amount was not nearly so large as she said it was.

ASSISTANCE — Help that is given

ASSISTANTS — Plural of assistant; those giving help

EXAMPLE: The legal assistants offered their assistance with his problem.

BESIDE — At or to the side; by the side of; disjoined from

BESIDES — Over and above; moreover, else, in addition to

EXAMPLES: She sat beside the road, but that is beside the point. Besides that, she was hurt.

BIANNUAL — Occurring twice a year

BIENNIAL — Occurring every two years

BIMONTHLY — Occurring every two months; also occurring twice a month

EXAMPLES: The biennial meetings will be held in 2005 and 2007; however, the board meetings will be held biannually in January and July.
The bimonthly newsletter will be published in January, March, May, July, September, and November. The meetings will be bimonthly on the first and third Monday.

CAPITAL — Chief in importance or influence; related to money; seat of government; a city serving as a seat of government

CAPITOL — A building in which a legislative body meets

EXAMPLE: The legislature voted a capital appropriation of $750,000 to refurbish the Capitol Building in Olympia, the Capital of Washington.

COMPLIMENT — An expression of esteem, respect, affection, or admiration

COMPLEMENT — Something that fills in, completes, or makes perfect; one of two mutually completing parts; counterpart

EXAMPLES: The dark blue tie complemented the light blue shirt.
Everyone likes to receive a sincere compliment.

CONTINUAL	Successive or one after another
CONTINUOUS	Without interruption
COURTESY	Refers to manners
CURTESY	Interest a husband has in the property of his wife
	EXAMPLE: He had the courtesy to give up his curtesy in her property.
COUNCIL	A committee's board of directors
COUNSEL	A giver of advice; an attorney
DECENT	Fitting, worthy, honorable
DEFUSE	To make less harmful; to make less tense
DIFFUSE	Wordy; badly organized
DESCENT	A downward step, as in station or value; a derivation from an ancestor; process of descending from a higher to a lower level
DISSENT	Disagree
	EXAMPLE: There was dissent that her descent down the stairs on her hands was the decent thing to do.
DESCENDANT	One descended from another (having to do with family)
DECEDENT	A deceased person
	EXAMPLE: The descendant of the decedent was Christopher Columbus.
DEVICE	A scheme to deceive; a piece of equipment or mechanism designed to serve a special purpose or function
DEVISE	The act of giving or disposing of real property in a will; property devised by will; to plan to obtain or bring about
	EXAMPLE: A will is a device by which a person can devise his real property to his heirs.
DISCREET	Having or showing good judgment in conduct and speech; capable of preserving silence
DISCRETE	Individually distinct; constituting a separate entity
	EXAMPLES: The assistant should be very discreet when discussing clients. Magnetic cards and diskettes are discrete media.
DISBURSE	To give out, to pay out
DISPERSE	To scatter randomly
	EXAMPLE: Once the raffle prizes were disbursed, the winners dispersed.
ELUSIVE	Baffling; hard to catch
ILLUSIVE	Misleading; unreal

EMINENT	Prominent, standing out, distinguished
IMMINENT	Ready to take place; hanging threateningly over one's head
	EXAMPLE: The eminent senator believed death to be imminent.
ENVELOP	To enfold or enclose completely
ENVELOPE	A container, usually for a letter
	EXAMPLES: The fog threatened to envelop the airport. She forgot to put the letter in the envelope.
FARTHER	At or to a greater distance or more advanced point (measurable)
FURTHER	To a greater degree or extent (unmeasurable)
FORMERLY	Refers to a previous time
FORMALLY	In a formal, conventional manner
	EXAMPLE: The initiation was more formally conducted than formerly.
GUARANTEE	To assure the fulfillment of a condition; to promise performance
GUARANTY	Something given as security; a pledge to answer for the payment of a debt; an assurance of performance
WARRANTY	A binding legal covenant of assurance of facts
	EXAMPLES: Can you guarantee the merchandise and is there a guaranty in writing? You have my warranty on the property.
HEALTHFUL	Promoting health
HEALTHY	Being in good health
ILLICIT	Illegal
ELICIT	To draw forth or bring out
	EXAMPLE: Did the detective elicit any information from the man about illicit activities?
IMPLY	To involve or indicate by inference, association, or necessary consequence rather than by direct statement; to suggest
INFER	To derive as a conclusion from facts or premises
	EXAMPLE: From what you say, I infer that you mean to imply she is incapable.
INSURE	To make certain by taking necessary precautions or steps; to obtain or give insurance on
ENSURE	To make sure, certain, or safe
ASSURE	To make safe from risks; to inform positively

	EXAMPLE: I assure you that I have ensured your safety by carefully checking your parachute; however, the company has refused to insure you when you are jumping.
INTERSTATE	Between two or more states
INTESTATE	Without a will
INTRASTATE	Within one state
	EXAMPLE: He runs an interstate trucking service in the Pacific Northwest; his brother has an intrastate service in Idaho.
LATER	At a future time; more recent
LATTER	Relating to the second of two groups or things or the last of several things referred to; near the end
	EXAMPLE: Later I will serve pie and coffee; the latter will be decaffeinated.
LAST	All the rest; the only remaining; final, terminal
LATEST	Most recent; after all others; at the end; following
	EXAMPLE: The latest edition was the last one sold.
LIABLE	Obligated according to law; responsible (Do not use *liable* for *likely*)
LIBEL	A written defamation or attack of another person
	EXAMPLE: Newspapers are liable if they publish a libel of a person.
LIKE	Takes an object; can substitute *similar to* or *similarly to* for *like*
LOSE	verb: To miss from one's possession; to suffer deprivation of
LOOSE	verb: To release, untie adj: Not rigidly fastened or attached
	EXAMPLE: Do not loose the reins from the post. The horse has a loose shoe; he might lose it if he runs away.
MAY BE	This is a verb phrase
MAYBE	An adverb meaning perhaps. A noun meaning uncertainty
	EXAMPLE: Maybe the lawyer may be able to win the case.
PRECEDENTS	Something done or said that may serve as an example or rule to authorize or justify an act of similar nature. In law, those previous court decisions which influence all later cases of a similar kind
PRECEDENCE	Priority of importance

	EXAMPLE: The case that took precedence on the calendar was based on precedents established in California.
PRINCIPLE	A rule or code of conduct; a fundamental law, doctrine, or assumption; the laws or facts of nature
PRINCIPAL	A person who has controlling authority; a chief or head, man or woman; one who employs another to act for him; a capital sum placed at interest; the corpus of an estate
	EXAMPLE: The school principal invested his principal at five percent interest because he was devoted to the principles of saving money.
PROCEEDING	A form of the verb "proceed" meaning to go forward; move along a course A noun meaning events, happenings; a legal action
PRECEDING	A form of the verb "precede" meaning to be, go, or come ahead or in front of; to be earlier than
	EXAMPLE: The criminal proceeding will precede the civil trial.
PRO RATA	An adverb or adjective meaning according to a precise calculable formula
PRORATED	A verb meaning evenly distributed
REBUT	To argue in opposition
REFUTE	To prove wrong
RECENT	Refers to time not long past
RESENT	A verb meaning to feel or express annoyance or ill will at a person or event
	EXAMPLE: I resent your recent attacks on my honesty.
RESIDENCE	A dwelling place
RESIDENTS	Those who reside in a place; physicians serving residencies
	EXAMPLE: Who are the residents of that two-story residence on the corner?
RESPECTIVELY	In the order given
RESPECTFULLY	With respect or deference
	EXAMPLE: The employer respectfully requested George Brown and Erin Smith, the president and vice president respectively, to report to him in his office.
SOME TIME	A period of time
SOMETIME	At some not specified or definitely known point of time
SOMETIMES	At times; now and then

EXAMPLE: Sometimes quite some time elapses between visits, but I plan to remedy that sometime soon.

SPECIALLY	In a special manner
ESPECIALLY	Particularly; usually great or significant
	EXAMPLE: The specially prepared foods were a delight to the palate, especially since the cook had so little experience.
STATIONARY	Fixed
STATIONERY	Writing materials
THAN	A word used in making comparisons
THEN	At that time
	EXAMPLE: It was later than I thought. I decided to leave then, instead of later.
THEIR	Possessive pronoun
THERE	Indicates a place or points out
THEY'RE	A contraction of *they are.* Do not confuse with *there*; used as a subject and verb
	EXAMPLE: The lawyers left their briefcases in the car, and now they're unable to proceed with the trial being held there in the city.
THEREFOR	For it
THEREFORE	Because of that, for that reason
	EXAMPLE: The debtor was unable to pay the $1,000; therefore, the lawyer agreed to accept $750 in full payment therefor.
WHO	Subject of sentence (pronouns he, she, we, and they can be substituted)
WHOM	Object of a preposition (pronouns him, her, them, and us can be substituted)
WHOSE	A possessive pronoun
WHO'S	Contraction of *who is;* should be used as a subject and verb
	EXAMPLE: Who's going to tell me whose coat this is?
YOU'RE	A contraction of *you are;* must be used as a subject and verb
YOUR	A possessive pronoun
	EXAMPLE: Did you tell me that you're going to your office this afternoon?

§ 6.18 Abbreviations

In business writing, abbreviations are appropriate in expedient documents (such as business forms, catalogs, and routine memos and letters between business offices), where the emphasis is on communicating data in the briefest form. In other kinds of writing, where a more formal style is appropriate, use abbreviations sparingly. When in doubt, spell it out. *See The Gregg Reference Manual*, 9th ed., ¶ 502(a). In formal communications, the following are satisfactory to use.

1. The title that precedes a person's name is abbreviated.

   EXAMPLES: Ms., Mrs., Mr., Dr.

2. Titles or degrees written after names are abbreviated.

   EXAMPLES: Esq., Jr., B.A., M.D., PLS.

3. Titles before surnames are never abbreviated.

   EXAMPLES: Governor Tomlinson, Professor Garrett.

4. Titles before full names can be abbreviated.

   EXAMPLES: Gov. Guy Tomlinson, Prof. Sara Garrett.

5. Titles of respect or dignity are never abbreviated.

   EXAMPLES: The Honorable Guy Tomlinson, the Reverend Doctor Bennett.

6. Firm names are not abbreviated unless the company prefers the abbreviation and uses it in its communication.

7. Names of agencies, organizations, or associations are abbreviated using the first letter of each word in the title. These are generally written "solid" with no space or punctuation to form an initialism or acronym.

   EXAMPLES: FBI for Federal Bureau of Investigation, IRS for Internal Revenue Service.

8. Technical terms such as chemical symbols or formulas that are used many times in business communications are abbreviated with no punctuation.

9. When letters are substituted for names, punctuation is unnecessary.

   EXAMPLES: Mr. A, Exhibit D, Mister X.

10. Certain words in our vocabulary that have been shortened through usage are not followed by punctuation.

    EXAMPLES: Ad for advertisement, lab for laboratory, gym for gymnasium.

11. Always abbreviate A.D. and B.C. in dates and use the punctuation. Use a.m. and p.m. to designate afternoon and forenoon; use punctuation but no spacing. Use a numeral for the hour.

    EXAMPLES: 10 a.m.; never use 10 o'clock a.m.

12. Use No. or Nos. before a numeral except when it occurs at the beginning of the sentence; then spell "number." If the numeral is specifically identified, No. or Nos. should be omitted.

13. Fort, Point, Port—that are parts of place names—should never be abbreviated.

14. Directions written in context should never be abbreviated. N, NE, NNE can be used for real estate descriptions, however.
15. Terms of measurement should not be abbreviated except in technical writing, invoices, etc. This rule applies to weight, length, capacity, area, volume, temperature, time, etc.
16. If possible, the following words should be spelled out in full:

president	building	street
superintendent	association	boulevard
honorable	department	avenue
reverend		east
professor		west
		south
		north

    The rule is that if you are in doubt, spell out the word completely.
17. Generally, city and state names should be spelled out completely; however, in the inside address the two-letter ZIP Code abbreviation may be used so that it will correspond to the address on the envelope. You may use the two-letter ZIP Code abbreviation only when it is followed by the ZIP Code. If you do not use the ZIP Code, you must type out the state name in full.
18. When an abbreviation is followed by a period, the period should be retained even if other punctuation follows the abbreviation. If the abbreviation ends the sentence, however, only one period is necessary. The plurals of abbreviations are generally formed by adding an *s* to the abbreviation before the period. Exceptions are as follows:
    - in for inch or inches
    - mi for mile or miles
    - oz for ounce or ounces
    - pp. for pages
    - ll. for lines

    Spacings between the parts of an abbreviation are usually omitted to save space except in the instance of initials.

    EXAMPLE: E. R. Farris
19. As a rule, contractions are only used in informal writing and in tables where space is limited.
20. Abbreviations of academic degrees and religious orders require a period after each element in the abbreviation but no internal space.

A list of commonly used abbreviations follows:

@	at
ab init.	from the beginning (L. ab initio)
A.D.	in the year of the Lord (L. Anno domini)
acct., a/c, A/C	account

addl., add.	additional
ad fin.	to the end (L. ad finem)
Adm.	administration, administrative, Admiral
Admr.	Administrator; Admx.-trix
agt.	agent
a.m.	before noon
amt.	amount
anon.	anonymous
app.	appendix
approx.	approximate
appt.	appointment
Apt.	Apartment
arr.	arranged
art.	article
ASAP	as soon as possible
Assn.	Association
assoc., asso.	associate
Asst.	Assistant
Attn.	Attention
Atty.	Attorney
Atty. Gen.	Attorney General
Ave.	Avenue
avg.	average
bal.	balance
bbl.	barrel(s)
bf.	boldface
B/L, BL	bill of lading
bldg.	building
Blvd.	Boulevard
bu	bushel(s)
bus.	business
Bus. Mgr.	Business Manager
bx.	box
C.	Celsius (centigrade), hundred
c	copy
cc	carbon copy, or computer copy
cap.	capital, capacity
caps	capital letters
Capt.	Captain
cat.	catalog
C/D, CD	Certificate of Deposit
cert.	certificate, -tion, certified
cf.	compare (L. confer)
cfm, cfs	cubic feet per minute, per second
chg.	charge; change
ck.	check
cm	centimeter
c/o	in care of; carried over
Co.	Company; County
COD, c.o.d.	cash on delivery
com., comm.	committee; commission

Corp.	Corporation
C.S.T., CST	central standard time
depo	deposition
dept.	department
D.S.T., DST	Daylight Savings Time
E.	East
ea.	each
e.g.	for example (L. exempli gratia)
enc.	enclosure
EOM, e.o.m.	end of month
Esq.	Esquire
et al.	and others (L. et alia, et alii)
E.S.T., EST	eastern standard time
etc.	and so forth (L. et cetera)
Ex.	Exhibit
F., Fahr.	Fahrenheit
fax	facsimile
f.b.o., FBO	for the benefit of
fig.	figure
f.o.b., FOB	free on board
ft	foot, feet
fwd.	forward
FY	fiscal year
FYI	for your information
g	gram(s)
GAAP	Generally Accepted Accounting Principle
gal	gallon(s)
govt.	government
gr. wt.	gross weight
guar., gtd.	guarantee;-ed
HQ	headquarters
hp, HP	horsepower
hr.	hour(s)
ht.	height, heat
ibid.	in the same place (L. ibidum)
id.	the same (L. idem)
i.e.	that is (L. id est)
Ill., illus.	illustration; illustrated
in	inch(es)
Inc.	Incorporated
inv.	invoice
ital.	italics
J.D.	Doctor of Jurisprudence (L. juris doctor)
K	thousand, karat, contract
kc	kilocycle
kg	kilogram(s)
km	kilometer
kw	kilowatt
L	liter(s)
l., ll.	line, lines
lb	pound(s)

L/C	Letter of Credit
l.c., lc.	lowercase
liq.	liquid
LL.B.	Bachelor of Laws (L. legum baccalaureus)
L.L.C., LLC	Limited Liability Company
LL.D.	Doctor of Laws (L. legum doctor)
loc. cit.	in the place cited (L. loco citato)
L.S.	place of the seal (L. locus sigilli)
ltr.	letter
M	1,000
m	meter(s)
mdse.	merchandise
memo	memorandum
Messrs.	plural of Mr. (F. Messieurs)
mfg.	manufacturing
mi.	mile(s)
min.	minute(s)
misc.	miscellaneous
Mlle.	Mademoiselle
mo., mos.	month, months
M.S.T., MST	mountain standard time
Mt.	mount, mountain
mtg.	mortgage, meeting
n/30	net in 30 days
N.	North
No., Nos.	number(s) (use before figures only)
obs.	obsolete
op. cit.	in the work cited (L. opere citato)
oz	ounce(s)
p., pp.	page, pages
P.C.	Professional Corporation
pd.	paid
PBX	Private Branch Exchange (telephone)
pkg.	package
p.m.	after noon (L. post meridiem)
prox.	of the next month (L. proximo)
P.S.T., PST	pacific standard time
qt	quart(s)
recd.	received
retd.	returned
rev.	revised; revision
R.F.D.	Rural Free Delivery
rm.	ream, room
R.N.	Registered Nurse
R.S.V.P.	please reply (F. respondez s'il vous plait)
Rte., Rt.	Route
Ry.	railway
S.	South
SASE	self-addressed, stamped envelope
sec.	section
seq.	the following (L. sequens)

sic	so written, thus (L.)
sq ft	square foot (feet)
Sr.	Senior
SS.	To-wit (L. scilicet)
St.	Street, Saint, Strait, Statute(s)
Ste.	Sainte (feminine for St.), Suite
Supt.	Superintendent
Twp.	township (pl. Tps., Twps.)
TWX	teletypewriter exchange
u.c.	upper case
Univ.	University
viz.	namely (L. videlicet)
vol	volume(s)
v.	versus
whsle.	wholesale
wk., wks.	work, week, weeks
wpm	words per minute
wt.	weight
yd	yard(s)
yr, yrs	year, years

	STATE ABBREVIATIONS*	ZIP			
Alabama	Ala.	AL	Montana	Mont.	MT
Alaska	Alaska	AK	Nebraska	Nebr.	NE
Arizona	Ariz.	AZ	Nevada	Nev.	NV
Arkansas	Ark.	AR	New Hampshire	N.H.	NH
California	Calif.	CA	New Jersey	N.J.	NJ
Canal Zone	C.Z.	CZ	New Mexico	N. Mex.	NM
Colorado	Colo.	CO	New York	N.Y.	NY
Connecticut	Conn.	CT	North Carolina	N.C.	NC
Delaware	Del.	DE	North Dakota	N. Dak.	ND
District of Columbia	D.C.	DC	Ohio	Ohio	OH
Florida	Fla.	FL	Oklahoma	Okla.	OK
Georgia	Ga.	GA	Oregon	Oreg.	OR
Guam	Guam	GU	Pennsylvania	Pa.	PA
Hawaii	Hawaii	HI	Puerto Rico	P.R.	PR
Idaho	Idaho	ID	Rhode Island	R.I.	RI
Illinois	Ill.	IL	South Carolina	S.C.	SC
Indiana	Ind.	IN	South Dakota	S. Dak.	SD
Iowa	Iowa	IA	Tennessee	Tenn.	TN
Kansas	Kans.	KS	Texas	Tex.	TX
Kentucky	Ky.	KY	Utah	Utah	UT
Louisiana	La.	LA	Vermont	Vt.	VT
Maine	Maine	ME	Virgin Islands	V.I.	VI
Maryland	Md.	MD	Virginia	Va.	VA
Massachusetts	Mass.	MA	Washington	Wash.	WA
Michigan	Mich.	MI	West Virginia	W. Va.	WV
Minnesota	Minn.	MN	Wisconsin	Wis.	WI
Mississippi	Miss.	MS	Wyoming	Wyo.	WY
Missouri	Mo.	MO			

* The ZIP abbreviation MUST be used with ZIP Codes and should be used ONLY with ZIP Codes; the other abbreviations should be used whenever there is a need to save space in informal writing.

§ 6.19 Number Usage

1. Spell out a number beginning a sentence. If the number is large, it is best to rearrange the sentence. It is now considered acceptable to begin a sentence with a year.

   EXAMPLES: Two hundred members were expected to attend.
   1929 was a devastating year for many people.

2. Spell out approximate numbers if they are "rounded off" in even units.

   EXAMPLE: There were approximately five hundred persons at the wedding.

3. Numbers ten and below are spelled out; numbers above ten are written in numerals.

   EXAMPLE: I have three coats.
   John has 14 shirts.

4. When two numbers follow each other in a sentence, use numbers for the larger one and spell out the smaller number. If both numbers contain three or more numerals, use figures for both.

EXAMPLES: He ordered 12 two-piece suits from his client in New York City.
They sent us 175 500–page manuals.

5. Use figures for dimensions, measurements, distances, weights, and capacities.

EXAMPLES: 8 inches × 11 inches   4 ft. 3 in or 4′3″
2 lbs 15 oz   6 mi.

If a weight or capacity is written before a noun, it is hyphenated to the singular word. If it is after the word, the plural word is used.

EXAMPLE: a 15–gallon jug
a jug holding 15 gallons

6. Use figures for page numbers and divisions of books.
7. Use figures for temperatures, election returns, and chemical terminology.
8. When keyboarding mixed numbers, do not insert a space or a hyphen to separate the whole number from the fraction. But if the fractional unit has to be typed using a diagonal line (/), add a space.

EXAMPLES: 9⅔ or 9–2/3.

Fractions used without whole numbers are spelled out except when used in a series.

EXAMPLES: Two-thirds of a mile. Measurements of 1/48, 1/24, and 1/12.

9. Fractions ¼ and ½ should be written the same as other fractions when mixed:

EXAMPLES: ¼, ½, ⅔, ¾

10. Columns of whole numbers are aligned on the right; decimals are aligned on the decimal point; Roman numerals and ordinal numbers are aligned on the right; dates and words are aligned on the left; and mixed items are aligned on the left or centered.
11. Use figures before the word "percent" or the percent symbol (%). The symbol should be used only in tables or in technical writing. Spell out "percent" in all formal writing.

EXAMPLE: He gave me a 20 percent discount on the damaged goods.

12. Spell out numbers referring to decades and centuries.

EXAMPLE: twentieth century

13. Use figures for a series of numbers in a sentence even though some of the numbers may be below ten.

EXAMPLE: I sent 20 letters, 2 postcards, and 6 packages.

§ 6.19.1 Dates

1. When writing dates, use figures without ordinal endings (st, nd, rd, d, or th) unless the day precedes the month.

   EXAMPLES: We will send the money on January 25, 2006.
   We will send the money on the 25th of January, 2006.

2. There is a difference between the first or last of the month and the 1st and 31st of the month. The latter two are definite days; first and last apply to a general period.

3. When the name of the month is not given, spell out the date.

   EXAMPLE: He will be leaving for Europe on the tenth.

4. Never indicate the month in figures except in tabulations.

   EXAMPLES: 8/11/06
   August 11, 2006

5. Use ordinal numbers when the day precedes the month.

   EXAMPLES: The 8th of March.

6. In formal invitations, spell out the dates.

   EXAMPLE: On the twelfth day of May, two thousand and four.

§ 6.19.2 Age

1. When stating age, the general rule is that when the age is definite and given as a statistic or for quick reference, use figures; if the age is indefinite or is used in formal writing, use words.

   EXAMPLES: He is dating a woman who is about thirty years old.
   Judge John J. Bell, 56, is an authority on family law.
   She will be 39 on her next birthday.

2. When writing the age in years, months, and days, use figures and no commas. The whole phrase is considered as one unit.

   EXAMPLE: His age is 87 years 9 months and 5 days.

§ 6.19.3 Time

In stating time, the following rules apply:

1. Use figures preceding a.m. and p.m.

   EXAMPLES: 10 a.m.
   9 p.m.

2. Use words or figures preceding o'clock.

   EXAMPLE: ten o'clock or 3 o'clock

   Words are more commonly used.

3. To express noon or midnight, do not use a.m. or p.m. Instead use 12 noon or 12 midnight when the figures are used in the same sentence, or noon or midnight alone.
4. Write a.m. and p.m. in lower case letters with a period after each letter and no space between them.

   EXAMPLES: 3:10 p.m.
   8:30 a.m.
5. Do not use morning or evening and a.m. or p.m. in the same phrase.

   Incorrect: I will see you this morning at 10:30 a.m.
   Correct: I will see you this morning at 10:30.
   Correct: I will see you at 10:30 a.m.

   OR

   I will see you at 10:30 a.m.
6. Do not use a.m. or p.m. with o'clock.
7. When you are using an even hour, it is not necessary to add the colon and two zeros unless you are typing a tabulation. Use 3 a.m. or 8 p.m. rather than 3:00 a.m. or 8:00 p.m.

§ 6.19.4 Money

1. In legal documents amounts of money are often written in words and figures. Be careful that the figures in the parentheses are an exact summary of the words.

   EXAMPLES:

   Incorrect: Twenty-five Dollars ($25.00). Incorrect because the No/100 was not included before the parentheses.

   Correct: Twenty-five Dollars ($25)

   Incorrect: Twenty-five and No/100 ($25.00) Dollars. Incorrect because dollars must come before the parentheses.

   Correct: Twenty-five and No/100 Dollars ($25.00). Correct because ciphers are included in the preceding phrase.
2. In correspondence, amounts of money are written in figures, when the amounts are indefinite, *e.g.,* a few million dollars.

   EXAMPLE: The estimated fee for processing your claim is $585. The cents ciphers are unnecessary for even dollar amounts: $25, not $25.00.
3. Separate hundreds from thousands with a comma.

   EXAMPLE: His annual membership fee was reported to be $1,800.
4. Spell out an amount of money if it occurs at the beginning of a sentence.

   EXAMPLE: Sixty cents is really a trifling amount.

§ 6.19.5 Addresses

1. Spell out numbered street names from one through ten; use figures for numbered streets over ten.

   EXAMPLE: 15550 Eighth Street

   Use a hyphen between a house or building number and a numbered street to prevent misreading.

   EXAMPLE: 234–44th Street
2. Do not use #or No. in addresses. When an apartment number is needed, use the abbreviation, *Apt.,* after the address.

   EXAMPLE: 600 Lake Shore Drive, Apt. 280 or
1400–B College Drive
3. Never use commas in address numbers.

§ 6.19.6 Roman Numerals

The rules for reading Roman numerals are as follows:

1. A repeated letter multiplies the value.

   EXAMPLE: II = 2 XX = 20
2. A letter occurring *after* one of higher value is added to the preceding one.

   EXAMPLE: VI = 5 + 1 = 6 LX = 50 + 10 = 60
3. A letter occurring *before* one of higher value is subtracted from the higher letter.

   EXAMPLE: IV = 5 − 1 = 4 XL = 50 − 10 = 40

The numbers and corresponding Roman numerals are as follows:

1	I	20	XX
2	II	30	XXX
3	III	40	XL or XXXX
4	IV	50	L
5	V	60	LX
6	VI	70	LXX
7	VII	80	LXXX or XXC
8	VIII	90	XC or LXXXX
9	IX	100	C
10	X	150	CL
11	XI	200	CC
12	XII	300	CCC
13	XIII	400	CD or CCCC
14	XIV	500	D
15	XV	600	DC
16	XVI	700	DCC
17	XVII	800	DCCC
18	XVIII	900	CM or DCCCC
19	XIX		

1000	M
1500	MD
2000	MM

§ 6.20 The Creative Aspects of Written Communications

Writing, like many other forms of work, is a process. To accomplish it well, plan to complete each one of its four stages:

1. Thinking and Planning
2. Researching, Organizing, and Writing
3. Revising
4. Proofreading

§ 6.20.1 Stage One—Thinking and Planning

Always be concerned with human relations and public relations in organizing and clarifying your thoughts for written communications. Some people interpret this first process as "worrying" rather than "thinking." In either event this is a vital process. Analyze the audience and the purpose for writing. Determine the level of language to use—technical, formal, or informal. Think about how the audience will react to the message—neutrally, positively, or negatively. Use brainstorming, listing, mapping, and diagramming strategies to generate ideas. Once the thinking phase is completed and ideas are collected, start planning.

§ 6.20.2 Stage Two—Researching, Organizing, and Writing

Before beginning to write, collect data informally or formally to explain and support the ideas generated. Talk to those in the know, look in files, conduct a simple survey or conduct formal research using books, magazine, official reports, interviews, and the Internet.

Organizing consists mainly of examining all ideas, eliminating the irrelevant ones, and arranging the others in a clear, logical order. Ideas can be grouped by time sequence, by importance, by logical sequence or by other methods. Whether to write an informal outline or merely jot down ideas on a scrap of paper is up to the writer.

The writing process is self-explanatory. Concentrate on formulating sentences instead of being concerned with thinking of ideas and trying to organize them. Write quickly to get thoughts down and to write the first draft. The first two stages are the preparatory work and will take about as much time as the next stage, which is revising.

§ 6.20.3 Stage Three—Revising

Few are so talented that they can express themselves clearly and concisely in a first draft. Expert writers know that they must and will revise. Examine the writing objectively so it can be revised effectively. Be eager to find fault and look for ways to increase the writing's clarity, conciseness, coherence, and for ways to improve the content and readability. Improve the structure of sentences, rearrange the text, add headings, use bold and underline for emphasis, and find concise and correct words to use. Also, to help achieve paragraph coherence, use transitional expressions for time association (before, after, first, second, next, until), contrast (although, however, but, instead), illustration (for example, in this way), cause and effect (consequently, therefore), and to include additional ideas (furthermore, in addition, moreover). After revising the document, begin the proofreading stage.

§ 6.20.4 Stage Four—Proofreading

The final task, although not as taxing as others, is just as vital. If words are missing or repeated, letters are transposed, sentences are incoherent, or one misspelled word appears on the paper, a reader may be perturbed enough to ignore or resist your ideas or information. Carelessness in your writing antagonizes readers and raises questions in their minds about your competence. Once finished with the proofreading, it is sometimes helpful to read the message or writing aloud—often mistakes are overlooked with the eyes and are found with the voice. Proofreading will be discussed in depth further in this chapter. (*See* Section 6.22.2 Proofeading.)

§ 6.21 The Paragraph

Sentences grouped together with a controlling topic or idea make a paragraph. Each idea can be its own paragraph or ideas may be grouped in a logical combination. Following are some strategies for writing clear and coherent paragraphs.

1. Start with the topic used in the plan. Put it into sentence form. Develop the topic with another sentence or two or three, whatever it takes. Then, move on to the next topic and develop it the same way as in the first.
2. Keep your paragraphs reasonably short. Short paragraphs make the reader's job easier. Try to make the first and last paragraphs in letters and memos short—not more than three or four lines. Elsewhere, if a paragraph gets to be more than eight or nine lines (100 words), consider breaking it up. Also ignore the idea that a paragraph has to be more than one sentence.
3. Paragraphs should be developed adequately to clarify and back up points. Use explanations, facts, illustrations, and examples.
4. Make sure each paragraph is unified and coherent. Take out anything irrelevant to the subject. To be in the same paragraph,

your ideas should be closely related. The topic sentence or a summary sentence helps to keep out the irrelevant.

5. Review the paragraph in context with the surrounding paragraphs. Use transitional words to move from one paragraph to the next. Use words such as *next, moreover, besides, nevertheless, on the other hand, first, second, third.* If ideas are logical, these words will not sound phony.
6. Examine the way the paragraphs are developed and the message being given to the reader—make sure the writing makes sense.

§ 6.21.1 Correctness

Some people have a distorted concept of the correctness principle. They think it comprises only proper grammar, punctuation, and spelling. The fact is that one can be correct grammatically and mechanically in every respect and fail to use the correct level of language. There are three overlapping levels of language: formal, informal, and substandard.

The first two—formal and informal language—are both correct; but they are quite different from one another, have different uses, and should not be interchanged.

The formal level of language is used for writing a scholarly dissertation, a legal document, or other material for which formality is expected. The expressions used are often long, unconversational, and impersonal—just what the term "formal" implies.

In contrast, the informal level refers to the language of business—the language of letters, reports, and other business communications. Such language is alive and everchanging. Instead of formal words one should use short, well-known, conversational words as the following illustrate:

Formal	**Informal**
domicile	home
deem	think (believe)
edifice	building
procure	get
remunerate	pay
Will attain the age of eighteen years	Will be 18 years old

§ 6.21.2 Conciseness

Many business executives believe that conciseness is the most important writing principle because a wordy message requires more time (and money) to type and to read. Conciseness is saying what one has to say in the fewest possible words without sacrificing completeness and courtesy.

To achieve conciseness—the opposite of wordiness—observe the following suggestions:

- Omit trite expressions
- Avoid unnecessary repetition and word expressions
- Include only relevant facts

Not this	But this
Enclosed herewith please find	Enclosed is
At this time	Now
Consensus of opinion	Consensus
Pursuant to your inquiry	As you requested
Please do not hesitate to write	Please write
The undersigned (the writer)	I, me, or we
Please be advised that	(four wasted words unless advice is truly to follow)
The above subject matter	Unnecessary. The subject line is enough.
According to our records	Implies that the other person is wrong. Reword.
Acknowledge receipt of	The answer itself is an acknowledgment.
Advise	Tell or inform
As per	According to
At an early date	Vague. Use a definite time period: within the next 10 days, for example.
At the present time	Unnecessary. A verb tense says the same thing.
At your earliest convenience	This could be never. State a date or definite time period.
Attached please find; attached hereto; enclosed please find	Enclosed or attached is
By return mail	Meaningless. Say: right away or immediately
Under date of January 15	January 15
Do not hesitate to call	Please call
Due to the fact that	Because
For your information	Obviously the purpose of the communication; omit the phrase
Hoping to hear from you soon, I remain	Old-fashioned; poor grammar; do not use.
I have your letter	Naturally, or you would not be answering. Do not use.
a check in the amount of $50	A check for $50
Kindly	Say: please
Our Mr. Jones	You do not own him. Omit "our."
Recent date	Use the specific date.
We take pleasure	We are glad.

Not this	But this
We take the liberty	Do not use.
We take this opportunity	Obviously you are.
Thank you in advance	Presumptuous. We will appreciate.
Under separate cover	We are sending

Be sure to begin the letter directly with the subject. Avoid repeating what the reader has already told you.

EXAMPLE: "I have your letter of June 13 in which you informed me that Mr. John Smith called on you for the first time a few weeks ago and that he appealed to you as a capable and intelligent young man."

Conciseness contributes to emphasis. By eliminating unnecessary words, one helps make important ideas stand out.

§ 6.21.3 Clarity

Clarity involves most of the other principles of business writing—especially correctness, conciseness, completeness, consideration, and concreteness. Clarity means getting across the message so the reader will not misunderstand what one is trying to convey.

Choose short, familiar, conversational words. Avoid professional jargon. The legal assistant's professional vocabulary contains words which have been accumulating since the beginning of one's business career, and these words are quite clear to the legal assistant. Furthermore, colleagues easily understand those technical terms, so it is all right to use them when talking or writing to people who also use them. Avoid professional jargon when talking or writing to a person who is not acquainted with such words.

If it is necessary to use technical words that the reader may not understand, define them briefly and clearly.

EXAMPLES:

Technical jargon	Expressions familiar to the layperson
Easement for ingress and egress	Agreement allowing passage in and out
Escrow account	Reserve account for taxes and insurance
Conveying title	Signing and recording a deed

In summary, make all writing clear by using words that are familiar to the reader.

§ 6.22 Writing Letters, Memos, and Messages

Most writing done by the legal assistant will be in the form of letters, memos, facsimiles, and e-mail messages. These messages usually fall into the categories of requesting information, responding to a request for information, or making a claim (complaint) or responding to a claim (complaint).

Like all writings, the first step for letter, memo and message writing should begin with the thinking and planning stage. Following are some specific questions to be asked and answered on paper before beginning to write:

1. What is the purpose of your letter, memo, or message?
2. Will the reader react neutrally, positively, or negatively? Will you use a direct or indirect method of getting to the main point?
3. To whom are you writing? Will you use a formal, informal, or technical style?
4. How much are you going to tell? List each item (you may have 2 or 40). Make sure to include enough information so that the reader does not need to write or call you for further information.
5. What do you wish to accomplish by writing this letter? When should it be accomplished?

In stage two of the writing process, the legal assistant researches, organizes and writes the letter, memo or message. The answers to the questions above are the basis of a good outline. Also, it is helpful when replying to correspondence to refer to the letter while composing the response. Following are some points to keep in mind when organizing and writing the first quick draft of the letter, memo, or message:

1. Use the direct method and start your first paragraph by stating the purpose of the letter in one or two sentences. Do not keep the reader guessing, or the letter might be filed before it is read. However, if conveying a message to which the reader may react to negatively, the first paragraph may want to state a goodwill message and the message may need to be delivered indirectly.
2. If answering a letter, refer to the date; the reader can then pull that letter.
3. Write from the reader's point of view. Put the "you" into it, not "I," "me," or "we." Visualize the reader's way of life. Write conversationally.
4. Use the correct tone. Be positive—your reader will be more receptive. Be polite—it is not easy when you have a gripe. It is an art to be agreeable when disagreeing. Be natural—try to write just the way you would talk. Imagine the reader sitting in front of you and you saying, "I acknowledge receipt of your letter" or "enclosed herewith please find." The acid test is to read your letter out loud when you are finished. Do not sound like a computer—sound like a human being. Do not be cute or flippant—avoid slang and colloquialisms.

5. Distinguish opinions from facts. One may have the best opinion in the world, but opinions are not facts. The legal assistant owes it to the reader to stay within the facts and to keep opinions separate.
6. Decide on a conclusion and make sure that in the last paragraph new ideas are not introduced. Include exactly what should be done and when by using an "end date."
7. Close with something simple, like "Sincerely" or "Very truly yours."

Now the legal assistant is ready for stage three—revising and putting on the finishing touches followed by a thorough proofreading. The legal assistant should make the writing perfect or the reader will think the writer does not know better or does not care.

§ 6.22.1 First Aid for Writing Problems

A major fault with letter writing is the tendency to smother the reader with words. Do not make your reader work hard to find out what you are saying. Repeating words and phrases is not good word economy—it is redundancy.

There was a time when the language of letters was in a far different style from the spoken language. Today we make every attempt to write as we talk. When you edit your writing, weed out every trite expression that flows from you to the paper. Be careful, though, that you do not begin to ramble.

Always "accentuate the positive" in your letters. Every piece of correspondence that goes from your office can make friends or alienate clients—so stress the positive. Think of your reader, the "you" out there who is going to react to your message. Eliminate "I," "me," and "we" and address "you" consistently.

Make yourself clear by using the right words and spelling them correctly. Master the spelling errors that are most commonly made in writing. If you still have a problem after studying, then at least admit you have a spelling problem; doubt everything and use your dictionary.

Along with spelling comes vocabulary improvement. In your office something new comes across your desk every day. Know what you are doing and use the dictionary. Do not just stumble over new words; learn their meanings and use the words.

§ 6.22.2 Proofreading

Poor proofreading results from failure to realize its importance, from inadequate time, and from improper effort. Unless you are convinced that scrutinizing your final copy is important, you cannot proofread effectively. Like most things, proofreading takes time, but lack of time is seldom a legitimate excuse for doing it poorly.

To proofread well, focus on the words. Slow down your reading speed, stare hard at the black print, and search for trouble rather than a way to finish quickly.

If interruptions occur while you are proofreading, place a check in the margin where you stopped reading. When you return to the proofreading, re-read the two or three sentences preceding the checkmark; you will then pick up the flow of the words.

When proofreading numbers, difficult copy, or property descriptions, you should check carefully with the original copy. Check dates with a calendar to be sure they are correct.

Carefully proofread letters that you prepare routinely, such as form letters. There is the tendency to see what is expected to be there rather than what is actually there.

Following are several troublespots in proofreading:

1. Headings, subheadings, and inside addresses often contain errors. The proofreader assumes they are correct and spends time on the body of the material. Headings which are in all capital letters or are underlined are often skipped over. There seems to be the assumption that they are correct because they look different.
2. Errors in proofreading often occur at the beginnings and ends of lines. There is a natural tendency to read more quickly as you approach the end of a line. You may pass over the beginning of the next line before you consciously realize that you have not scrutinized the beginning of the line.
3. Missed proofreading errors occur often at the bottom of the page. If things have gone well that far, the proofreader has a tendency to rush to finish and skips over errors.
4. When proofreading, read for the sense of the sentence. The text should follow logically. If you are reading only for the spelling of the words, you may miss insertions or deletions.
5. Another proofreading problem arises in long words which are very familiar to the reader. There is a tendency to expect the word to look right. Readers have mental pictures of words and recognize words without spelling them. If the word is very familiar or is repeated often in the text, it is easy to miss the omitted letter in the word. There is a tendency to assume the word is correct because it appears so often.
6. Transposed letters are easy to skip over. Sometimes the transposed word creates another word that is correct, and it is easy to pass over it. *From* can be transposed to *form.* Since both

words are spelled correctly, the eye passes over the word even though it is not the correct word for the sentence. Spell check will not discover this error; however, a grammar check program may. Transposed vowels occur frequently and are easy to miss unless you are analyzing the syllables of each word.

7. Errors often go undetected in captions and footnotes because the proofreader has a tendency to ignore them when proofreading. Once again, there is an assumption they are correct, while the proofreader only glanced at them.

8. Always verify the spelling of proper names. Do not assume that the spelling is correct. There are several spellings for certain names, *e.g.*, Alan/Allen, Brown/Browne, and Petersen/Peterson. In proofreading, the error may go undetected unless the proofreader checks the name against the source.

9. When proofreading vertical enumerations, check the continuity of the numbers. In outlines check the continuity of the letters and numbers. It is not unusual to see a list of numbers as 1, 2, 3, 4, 4, 5. Check numbers both horizontally and vertically to find all errors.

10. Number combinations cannot be proofread without checking them with the original source. Any number can look correct when in reality the numbers may be transposed.

11. One of the most common errors in proofreading occurs with the repeated word or letter. It occurs in the middle of a line, as *and and.* It occurs at the end of one line and the beginning of the next. It can occur in the middle of words, such as *bookkeeper.* These are all difficult for the proofreader to spot.

12. Check divided words carefully. It is easy to miss a mistake when half of the word is on one line and the other half at the beginning of the next line. Make sure the second half is there. Words can be divided incorrectly; or they may have letters left out when they are divided, such as *immed* on one line and *ate* on the next. In proofreading, it is hard to recognize that the *i* is missing.

13. Words that contain double letters are common sources of errors. These are also difficult to spot in proofreading. *Bookkeeping,* with two *k*'s, is easy to pass over.

Some professional proofreaders start with the last sentence and read backward to the first. Then they read it again from beginning to end. Some enlarge the page so errors are more noticeable. Whatever technique you adopt, work painstakingly, so that a few careless errors will not spoil your efforts. If you realize the importance of proofreading, view it as one of the stages in the writing process, and labor at it conscientiously, your communication will reflect your care, concern, and competency.

§ 6.22.3 Mailability

The standard for preparation of all written communications is mailability. Mailability means that the letter or document is suitable to be sent through the mail. It is in a form that represents the high standards of the office. To judge mailability, use the following checklist:

1. *Is the content accurate?*

   It is not always necessary to follow the dictator's words verbatim, but it is essential that the exact meaning be conveyed. There will be times when you will substitute one word for another to clear up the meaning or to fill in for a word that was omitted during dictation. Be sure that you have the correct name, title, and address of the addressee. A reader is quick to notice a mistake in his name, title, or address, which creates a negative impression.
2. *Does the letter have a good appearance?*

   Is the layout of the letter attractive, or is it too high or low on the page? Are the margins even or nearly so? Are the paragraphs too long? (Break up the body of the letter into paragraphs that are easy to read.)
3. *Have all errors been corrected?*

   Check the spelling. A spellcheck program will not highlight a correctly spelled word incorrectly used. Spelling errors damage the firm's prestige and divert attention from the message.

Remember, your letter is *not* mailable if it has misspelled words or faulty punctuation.

§ 6.23 The Letter Bank

Lawyers, inevitably, are very busy. Time is at a premium, and if the legal assistant can handle routine correspondence in an effective manner the lawyer's precious time will be available for other duties.

Once you get the attorney's approval to handle some routine correspondence, you will be looking for ways to slash hours off the time you spend writing letters. You can do this with a letter bank, which is a simple collection of form letters, memos, messages, and other documents used as templates.

Break up your letter bank into categories such as appointments, collections, statements, lawyer's personal correspondence, or divisions of the areas of law in which your lawyer practices. As letters enter and leave the office, select the most useful and make a copy for the appropriate category of your letter bank. Soon, you have timesaving, ready-to-use model letters at your fingertips. As your file builds up, you increase your value to your lawyer by taking on more and more of the letter writing tasks.

If you find yourself referring to a certain form letter many times, put it through the tests of good writing rules. Work on it, and polish it. Then you will have more confidence in your skills, and it is much more likely that your reader will react favorably. Once you have created a few good letters, you will have a pattern established; and you will be surprised to see that the letters you write in the future will become effortless and of high quality.

§ 6.24 Parts of a Business Letter

Letters are formatted using open or mixed punctuation. And law firms choose from several standard business styles. This information is discussed further in the chapter.

There are nine parts to a standard business letter:

1. Letterhead or return address
2. Date
3. Inside address
4. Salutation
5. Body
6. Complimentary closing
7. Signature line
8. Official title
9. Reference initials

A letter may also contain postal and addressee notations, an attention line, a subject line (sometimes placed above the salutation and sometimes placed below the salutation), typed firm or organization name, enclosure notation, copy notation, and postscript.

§ 6.24.1 Punctuation in Letters

Two common forms of punctuation used in letters are *open* punctuation and *mixed* punctuation which is also known as *standard* punctuation.

§ 6.24.2 Open Punctuation

With open punctuation, no punctuation is used following the salutation or the complimentary closing.

§ 6.24.3 Mixed or Standard Punctuation

With mixed or standard punctuation, a colon follows the salutation and a comma follows the complimentary closing. Never use semicolons; in informal writing, commas are occasionally used in place of the colon after the salutation.

§ 6.25 Letter Styles

Law offices will chose which of the four standard letter styles they prefer. The first two styles are called Modified Block With Blocked Paragraphs and Modified Block With Indented Paragraphs. These are the two most common styles used in law offices. The third style is called Block Style and is a quick and simple style of letter. The fourth style is the Simplied and it is not commonly used.

Each of these parts is illustrated on the letter shown in Illustration 6–7. Three common styles of business letters follow Illustration 6–7. It is important to remember that your letters should match the letters generated by your firm exactly, with regard to letter style.

Illustration 6–7

COLVIN, MASON & NORMAN ①

Kay Colvin
Jerry Mason
Scott Norman

Attorneys at Law
3005 East Skelly Avenue
Tulsa, Oklahoma 74105

Telephone (918) 749-6423
Facsimile (918) 749-6422

August 3, [Year] ②

Office Supply Company ③
3399 Notation Boulevard
Tulsa, OK 74105

Attention Mr. S. E. Tedesco

Gentlemen: ④

SUBJECT: Purchase Order No. 8843

Thank you for rushing to us our order for two secretarial desks and two posture chairs. They arrived yesterday in time for the opening of our new offices.

⑤

There has been a mistake, however, in the order. We requested two posture chairs, Catalog A67D, with dark blue upholstery. The ones we received are listed as Catalog A68D; they have light blue upholstery.

These chairs will not be suitable as they do not match the color scheme of our offices. Do you have the chairs we ordered in stock? If so, would you please ship them to us immediately. We are enclosing a copy of our order form.

We appreciate your assistance in this matter. By copy of this letter, we are notifying your local sales representative of the problem.

Sincerely, ⑥

COLVIN, MASON & NORMAN

⑦

P. M. Martell ⑧
Office Manager

PMM:GD ⑨

Enclosure

c Sarah Wilkins

The chairs that we received cost $12 more than the ones we ordered. We would appreciate your revising the billing.

§ 6.25.1 Modified Block With Blocked Paragraphs

The date line, the complimentary close, and the signer's identification all begin at center. The remainder of the letter begins at the left margin. (*See* Illustration 6–8.) Some firms prefer the date to be centered under the firm name or at the right margin. The subject line may be centered for emphasis.

Illustration 6–8

COLVIN, MASON & NORMAN

Kay Colvin Jerry Mason Scott Norman	Attorneys at Law 3005 East Skelly Avenue Tulsa, OK 74105	Telephone Area Code 918 749–6423

October 9, [Year]

Mrs. Jon Wilkinson
222 Mason Avenue
Rigby, ID 83221

Dear Mrs. Wilkinson:

RE: Modified Block With Blocked Paragraphs Letter Style

This letter is written in the modified block with blocked paragraph style. The first line of each paragraph begins at the left margin. Mixed punctuation is used. Note that a colon follows the salutation, and a comma follows the complimentary close.

The date and complimentary closing, as well as the writer's name and identification, begin at the horizontal center of the page.

The subject line may be typed even with the left margin, indented five spaces, or centered.

Sincerely,
COLVIN, MASON & NORMAN

Trema Kuchenbecker
Office Manager

mm
c Kristen Saunderson

MODIFIED BLOCK WITH BLOCK PARAGRAPHS

§ 6.25.2 Modified Block With Indented Paragraphs

The *modified block with indented paragraphs* is the same as the modified block with blocked paragraphs except that the first line of each paragraph is indented five spaces. (*See* Illustration 6–9.)

Illustration 6–9

COLVIN, MASON & NORMAN

Kay Colvin Jerry Mason Scott Norman	Attorneys at Law 3005 East Skelly Avenue Tulsa, OK 74105	Telephone Area Code 918 749–6423

June 26, [Year]

Mr. Joe Kelly, President
Ace Electronics
445 Tudor Square
Boise, ID 83702

Dear Mr. Kelly:

This is a modified block style letter with indented paragraphs. It is the same format as the modified block letter with blocked paragraphs except the paragraphs are indented five spaces. The date and closing information begin at the horizontal center.

If the letter contains an enclosure, the enclosure notation is placed one space below the reference initials. The copy notation should be placed one space below the enclosure notation.

Postscripts are not common in business letters, but when they do occur, they are used for after thoughts and placed at the end of the letter following the copy notation. The letters P.S. may be omitted.

Sincerely,
COLVIN, MASON & NORMAN

Lila Smith
Secretary to Jerry Mason

mm
Enclosure
c/enc Loren Siddell

MODIFIED BLOCK WITH INDENTED PARAGRAPHS

§ 6.25.3 Block

The *block* is used in many offices because it is the easiest to format, and letters can be keyboarded efficiently. Because of its clarity, the block style has become one of the more popular letter styles. Each line begins at the left margin, including the date and signature lines. (*See* Illustration 6–10.)

Illustration 6–10

A.G. LAMBERT
Attorney at Law
741 Main Street
Tulsa, OK 74105

Telephone
(918) 749–5826

July 6, [Year]

Mr. Lee James
900 Spring Place
Rexburg, ID 83440

Dear Mr. James

RE: Block Style Letter

In this type of letter, all lines begin at the left margin. The letter can use either open or mixed punctuation. This letter uses open punctuation; there is no mark of punctuation after the salutation and complimentary close.

This form of letter saves keyboarding time because no tab stops or indentions are required for paragraphs, datelines, or closings.

Sincerely

Sally Johnson
Office Manager

mm

BLOCK

§ 6.25.4 Simplified

As with the block style, begin all lines at the left margin. In addition, the *simplified style* is distinguished by a subject line, in all capital letters, which replaces the salutation. There is no complimentary closing, the writer's identification is typed on one line, in all capital letters, and open punctuation is always used.

Illustration 6–11

March 2, 2004
Joe R. Student
1536 N. Sweetwater
Creole, Alabama —

THE SIMPLIFIED LETTER

This is what the simplified letter looks like. Its subject line is in all capital letters, and there is no salutation.

Notice also that the complimentary closing is absent and open punctuation is always used.

Finally, note that the writer's identification is also in all capital letters, and all on one line.

JANE ROBINSON

JR/lb

§ 6.26 Letters of Two or More Pages

In preparing a multipage letter, do not end a page with a divided word. Also, leave at least two lines of a paragraph at the foot of the page and carry at least two lines to the next page. A single line at the bottom of a page is called an "orphan" line, whereas a single line at the top of a page is called a "widow" line.

Use plain paper of the same color and quality as the letterhead for the second and subsequent pages of a letter. Some law firms have the firm name engraved on the continuation pages as in Illustration 6–12. Use the same margins and letter style that you used on the first page.

The second page should contain a heading giving the name of the addressee, the page number, and the date. This heading should start approximately six line spaces from the top. At least two lines should be left between the heading and the first line of the resumed letter.

There are generally two methods for heading continuation pages (although your firm's style should always be followed):

1. Each line of information begins at the left margin.
2. The addressee's name is at the left margin, the page number is centered, and the date ends at the right margin.

The page number usually precedes the date, although some firms prefer that the page number be placed last when the items are placed in three lines. The numeral is preferred to the word for the page number, although some firms feel that the spelling out of the page number looks more formal.

Illustration 6–12

William E. Kerr, Ph.D.
Page 2
April 14, [Year]

food is delicious, the fireplace is bright and warm in the evenings.

BLOCK STYLE OF SECOND-PAGE HEADING

William E. Kerr, Ph.D. 2 April 14, [Year]

food is delicious, the fireplace is bright and warm in the evenings, and the fishing stories exchanged by the guests are among the best I have heard anywhere.

HORIZONTAL STYLE OF SECOND-PAGE HEADING

§ 6.27 Appearance of the Letter

The appearance and mechanics of the letter are what the reader sees first when the letter is opened. A pleasing appearance invites the reader to investigate the contents. Here are some dos and don'ts.

1. Make your letter look appealing. To project a good image, use good quality stationery, 8½″ x 11″. Keep it neat and use paragraphing, headings, bullets, enumerations, and fonts that make the document easy to read.
2. Keep letters short, one page if possible. Keep the paragraphs short.
3. The side margins of your letter will depend on the kind of stationery you are using, style and size of font, space taken by the letterhead, and the length of your message. Many tables, formulas, and measurements for calculating margins have been

published; however, with all the instructions and guidelines you can have, there is one basic rule you must follow for a neat appearance—*your finished letter must look like it is sitting in a frame of white space.* Eye it from start to finish, and if your result does not satisfy you, redo it.

4. Plan to leave a bottom margin of at least six line spaces (or one inch). If you have a long letter continuing to a second page, the bottom margin can increase to about twelve line spaces—but watch your side margins also; you want it framed.
5. You can spread a short letter over a page by using several techniques:
   - Lower the date line
   - Allow more space between the date and inside address
   - Allow more space for the signature
   - Put the signer's name and title on separate lines
   - Lower the reference initials, *cc* notation, and enclosure notation
6. You can shorten a long letter on a page by using these techniques:
   - Raise the date line
   - Allow only two or three blank spaces between the date and inside address
   - Allow only two or three spaces for the signature
   - Raise the reference initials one or two lines
7. Ordinarily, all letters should be single-spaced. If the message is very, very short you may double space; however, this will call for paragraph indentation.
8. If you are writing as an individual without a letterhead, put your return address in the upper right-hand corner. You may begin at the center; or for the best appearance, start about nine line spaces from the top and have the longest line of your address even with your right-hand margin. If you are using full block, you will start at about line nine flush with the left-hand side.
9. The date line is never abbreviated. Avoid using 6/23/05. Military or international form—23 June 2005—is acceptable, although it is not common.
10. With a letterhead, position the date line three line spaces below the letterhead. This may vary with letter length and style of letterhead, so do not feel you must adhere to this rule of three line spaces. Remember, it must look right.
11. If you send a letter of a personal or confidential nature, key in the appropriate notation two lines above the inside address at *the left margin.* This notation should be in all capital letters.
12. The inside address in a letter being sent to an individual's home should include (1) name, (2) street address, and (3) city,

state, and ZIP. If the person lives in an apartment, the apartment number should appear after the street address on the same line. If the person lives in a small town and the address is only two lines, do not separate the city from the state to make three lines.

13. For a letter going to a company, organization, or school, use the above arrangement. If possible, address it to a particular individual and place this above the company name along with that person's title. If you do not have a specific name, address it to a title, such as *Personnel Director*.

14. When a room number or suite is given, use the same form as on the letterhead or envelope.

    EXAMPLES: 416 12th Street, Room 12
    Suite 1200
    103 Ryan Center

    Room 228, Financial Center
    890 Locust Street

15. The inside address should begin between four to eight lines below the date line; use single spacing.

16. If a letter is addressed to two people at different addresses, type each name and address either one under the other, with one blank line between, or side by side, with one address aligned at the left margin and the other at center.

    EXAMPLES: Dr. J.W. Cooper
    123 Mustard Avenue
    Greenwood, MO 45983

    Dr. Jane Melody
    432 Levon Creek, Suite 22–B
    Jefferson City, MO 45976

Dr. J.W. Cooper	Dr. Jane Melody
123 Mustard Avenue	432 Levon Creek, Suite 22–B
Greenwood, MO 45983	Jefferson City, MO 45976

    Dear Dr. Cooper and Dr. Melody:

    If a letter is addressed to two people at the same address, list each name on a separate line of the same inside address.

    EXAMPLE: Dr. J.W. Cooper
    Dr. Jane Melody
    123 Mustard Avenue
    Greenwood, MO 45983

17. Use a form of address before the name of a person (*Mr., Mrs., Ms., Miss, Dr.*). If you do not know whether the person addressed is a man or a woman, do not use a courtesy title; the salutation should read *Dear Madam* or *Sir*.

18. Consult the original correspondence for a person's preference in spelling. Do not abbreviate names or omit initials.
19. When *Jr.*, *Sr.*, or a Roman numeral, such as *III*, is part of the name, omit the comma after the surname, unless that person prefers the use of a comma.
20. Do not use a form of address before a name if *M.D.* or *Esq.* follows the name. Write it either *Dr. John Jones* or *John Jones, M.D.* and *Mr. John Jones* or *John Jones, Esq.*
21. Abbreviations of religious orders, such as *S.J.*, are typed after names and preceded by a comma. An appropriate title should precede the name even though the abbreviation follows the name:

    EXAMPLE: *Reverend Neil Cahill, S.J.*
22. If a person's title is very short, it should be placed on the same line with the name. If the title is very long, you may need to put it on a separate line and also divide it. In this case, be certain that the second line of the title is indented at least two spaces beyond the first line of the title:

    EXAMPLE: Vice President and
General Manager
23. If a letter cannot be sent to the addressee but must be directed through a third person, use *In care of* . . . or *c/o* John Doe.
24. When using the name of an organization in an inside address, follow the organization's letterhead style for spelling, punctuation, capitalization, spacing, and abbreviation. If you do not have a way to determine the official form, consult the phone book or call the library. If you are still without information:
    - Spell out the word *and*—do not use &
    - Write *Inc.* for Incorporated and *Ltd.* for Limited
    - Spell out Company or Corporation; however, if the name is extremely long, abbreviate Company (Co.) or Corporation (Corp.)
    - Do not use *The* at the beginning of the name unless you are sure it is a part of the official name
25. If an address contains a building name and a street address, type the building name on the line above the street address. *See* the examples in item 13 above.
26. The street address should always be on a line by itself on the line preceding the city, state, and ZIP.
27. Do not abbreviate directions that appear before a street name: but use abbreviations if directions represent a section of a city.

    EXAMPLES: 1668 Southeast Ninth Street
1668 Ninth Street, SE
28. Use the word *and* and not & in a street address:

    EXAMPLE: Tenth and Maple Streets.

29. Never abbreviate *Street, Avenue,* or *Boulevard* in an inside address.
30. A post office box number may be used in place of a street address. Use Post Office Box 521 or P.O. Box 521. A station name, if needed as in some larger cities, should appear after the box number on the same line and before the line for city and state.
31. If an address shows both a street address and a box number in its mailing address, whatever information appears in the line preceding the city and state is where the mail will be delivered.
32. The city, state, and ZIP must always be typed on one line:

    EXAMPLE: Des Moines, IA 50322

    Use one space between the state abbreviation and the ZIP Code.
33. Never abbreviate the name of a city or words like *Fort* and *Mount* in an address.

    EXAMPLES: Fort Dodge, Mount Vernon

    Abbreviate the word *Saint* in names of American cities.

    EXAMPLES: St. Louis, St. Paul
34. When an address is given in a sentence, insert a comma after the street address and after the city. Leave one space between the state and the ZIP Code. Insert a comma after the ZIP Code unless a stronger mark of punctuation is required.
35. When addressing mail to foreign countries, type the name of the country in all capital letters on a separate line. Do not abbreviate the name of the country.
36. An attention line can be used; however, it is better to address the letter to a particular person named in the first line of the inside address. In either case, in the absence of a notation of *personal* or *confidential,* the communication will be presumed to be company business and may be handled by others.
37. Make certain that the spelling of the name in the salutation is the same as the spelling in the inside address.
38. There are a few instances when a person's title or gender is unknown.

    EXAMPLES: To a person with name known, gender unknown:
    Dear Pat Black, Dear C.L. Blue

    To a person with name and gender unknown:
    Dear Madam or Sir

    To a woman, title unknown:
    Dear Ms. Black or Dear Mary Black

    To an organization composed of all men or all women:
    Dear Gentlemen or Dear Ladies

To an organization composed of both men and women:
Ladies and Gentlemen

39. When a subject line is used in a block or modified block letter, it is placed on the second line below the salutation. In most cases it will start at the left margin for block letters or at the left margin or centered for modified block style.
40. The term "SUBJECT" or "RE:" is keyboarded in all capital letters and is followed by a colon.
41. The message will start on the second line below the subject line or salutation, whichever precedes your message.
42. All letters except the modified block with indented paragraph style will have paragraphs flush with the left margin. The modified block style paragraphs should be indented five spaces. If your letter is double spaced, you must indent each paragraph.
43. If you need to insert a quotation or other material in a display, indent the material five spaces or the same as your paragraph, leaving a line above and below. The material should be centered in this space with even margins left and right.
44. If you have a list of numbered items appearing in the body, leave a line before beginning the items and begin either at the left margin or at the point of paragraph indentation. Follow the item number with a period, and start the item even with the paragraph indentation or five additional spaces to the right. If any item requires more than one line, indent the second line so that it begins under the first word of the line above. You may wish, in this situation, to leave a line between items.
45. Capitalize only the first word of the complimentary closing, placing a comma after the last word (except when open punctuation is used).
46. The complimentary closing you choose will express the tone of your letter. For a personal tone use "Sincerely," "Cordially yours," "Sincerely yours," or "Cordially." Your reader will feel a more formal tone if you use "Yours truly," "Yours very truly," "Very truly yours," "Very sincerely yours," "Very cordially yours," or "Respectfully yours." If you use an informal closing phrase ("Best wishes," "Warmest regards," or "See you next week"), follow it with a comma. If you use one of these phrases with a complimentary close that is more formal, insert the informal phrase at the end of the last paragraph or as a separate paragraph.
47. Watch your pattern of closings in writing to the same people. In a later letter if you resort to a more formal closing, your reader may wonder what has happened to the relationship.
48. The company or firm name may be used after the complimentary close. Its use emphasizes the fact that the letter represents the views of the company as a whole. If used, the name should

be in all capitals on the second line below the complimentary close and beginning at the same point as the complimentary close.

49. As a general rule, the writer's name is on the fourth line after the complimentary closing or company name, whichever is last, beginning at the same point as the complimentary closing.
50. Professional titles or degrees may be keyboarded after the writer's name but are not written as part of the signature.
51. If a lawyer's assistant signs a letter at the lawyer's request, the lawyer's name is in the assistant's own handwriting with initials penned underneath the last part of the lawyer's name.
52. If a letter is to be signed by two people, type each name and title either one under the other, with three blank lines between, or side by side, with one name aligned at the left margin and the other aligned at the center.

    EXAMPLES: Sincerely,

    Ann A. Pitts
Office Manager

    Joan D. Moseley
Patient Representative

    Sincerely,

Ann A. Pitts Office Manager	Joan D. Moseley Patient Representative

53. Reference initials of the person keyboarding the letter are placed at the left margin on the second line below the writer's name and title. If the writer's initials are included here, they will precede the keyboarding person's initials. If the writer's name is not typed in the signature block, use capital letters followed by a colon; when using only the keyboarding person's initials, use lowercase letters.

    When writing your own personal letter, do not include reference initials.
54. If the letter mentions that one or more items are to be included with the correspondence, indicate that fact by typing "*Enclosure,*" "*Enc.,*" "*Check enclosed,*" "*Enc. 2,*" or other appropriate identification at the left margin one space below the reference initials.
55. If the letter is to be delivered in a special way, key in the appropriate notation two lines above the inside address in all caps:[1]

1. Some authorities recommend placing these notations immediately following the date line. Therefore, usage permits the placement of these special notations in either place.

EXAMPLE: *SPECIAL DELIVERY, CERTIFIED*

56. Copy notations let the reader know that one or more other persons will receive a copy of the letter. Use the initials "*c*" or "*cc*" for "*copy*" or "*copies to.*" Place the notation at the left margin under the mailing notation, if used. If more than one person receives a copy, type *c* only once; then line the second name under the beginning of the first name. The names are placed either in order of rank or alphabetically.
57. The initial *c* is not capitalized. A colon may, but need not, be placed after the *c*. (*See* Illustrations 6–7, 6–8, and 6–9 for a sample of each.) You need not use courtesy titles when indicating copies.
58. When an addressee is not to know who received copies of the letter, insert *bc* on the copies to the individuals who need to know who received blind copies. This notation should be placed two lines below the last copy notation, or a single space below the reference line, whichever is last.
59. Postscripts are used to express an afterthought. Keyboard the postscript a double space below the last reference or notation line. Use the same style for the postscript as in the body of the letter. The letters P.S. may be omitted.
60. Never use the second page of a letter only for the closing section of a letter. You should have at least two lines of the body of the letter on the second page before the complimentary close.
61. Leave a margin of from 6 to 12 lines at the bottom of each page. Make every attempt to have uniform bottom margins on each page except the last.
62. Never divide the last word of a page.

§ 6.28 Addressing Envelopes

Single-space and block the address lines. The bottom line must include the city and state names and the ZIP Code in that sequence. Leave one space between the state name or abbreviation and the ZIP Code. (*See* Illustration 6–13.)

When the ZIP Code is known, use the two-letter abbreviation in all caps without punctuation. If the ZIP Code is unavailable, call the post office if your office does not have a ZIP Code Directory.

For a small envelope, start the address lines 2″ from the top and 2½″ from the left edge.

For a large envelope, start the address lines 2½″ from the top and 4″ from the left edge. (*See* Illustration 6–13.)

§ 6.28.1 Return Address

Start the return address on the second line from the top and three spaces from the left edge.

§ 6.28.2 Postal Notations

Postal notations (such as CERTIFIED MAIL) are in all capital letters three lines below the space required for the stamp. (*See* Illustration 6–13.)

§ 6.28.3 Addressee Notations

Notations such as HOLD FOR ARRIVAL, PERSONAL, PLEASE FORWARD, and the like, are placed a triple space below the return address and three spaces from the left edge.

Illustration 6–13

COLVIN, MASON & NORMAN
Attorneys at Law
3005 East Skelly Avenue
Tulsa, OK 74106–6864

CERTIFIED MAIL

HOLD FOR ARRIVAL

ACCOUNTS PAYABLE
XYZ CORPORATION
10 ELM AVE
ANYTOWN ST 01234–5678

§ 6.28.4 Automated Mail Processing

The United States Postal Service has an electronic scanner machine that speeds up the processing of the mail by rapidly reading and sorting the mail with an optical character reader (OCR).

Getting your mail ready for machine processing actually involves few steps beyond what you are already doing. Most necessitate just a little more attention to detail. There are only a few steps with which to become familiar:

1. ZIP Codes
   ZIP Codes must be included in addresses, return addresses, and on pre-addressed business reply mail and should be placed right after the state name. An envelope address which lacks a ZIP Code is put aside until a post office employee can look it up and add it. This can delay a letter for several days.
2. Addresses
   (a) Addresses should be in block form with a uniform left margin.

(b) Print the address in block-style type fonts, preferably in uppercase letters without punctuation. Do not use italic, artistic, script, or proportionately spaced fonts.

(c) In the last two lines of the address include only the street address or box number on the next-to-last line, and the city, state, and ZIP Code on the last line.

(d) Spell street, city, and state names correctly. Some equipment depends on finding an exact match of names with those already stored in memory.

(*See* Illustration 6–14.)

(e) Activate the "delivery point bar code" feature in your software program that generates envelopes and labels. This will automatically insert a postal bar code (similar to a UPC code) above the addressee's name. The bar code is scanned by the postal service and sorted automatically for faster delivery to the correct destination.

Illustration 6–14

ADDRESSING FOR AUTOMATION
(POST OFFICE RECOMMENDATION)

---

6. ACCOUNT NUMBERS, DATES, ATTENTION LINES, etc.
Enter these on any line of the address block above the second line from the bottom.

5. STREET ADDRESS OR BOX NUMBER
These should be placed on the line immediately above the city, state, and ZIP Code. When indicating a box number at a particular station, the box number should precede the station name.

Correct spelling of street names is essential since some machines match the

1. BASIC FORMAT
The address area should be in block form with all of the lines having a uniform left margin. It should be at least ⅝ inch up from the bottom of the envelope. No print should appear to the right or below it.

ATTN MR C P JONES
GENERAL XYZ CORP
1000 MAIN ST ROOM 4325
DETROIT MI 48217-1234

4. WINDOW ENVELOPES
Inserts and envelopes must be matched so that the ad-

2. UNIT NUMBER
Mail addressed to occupants of multiunit buildings should include the number of the apartment, room, suite, or other unit. The unit number should appear immediately after the street address on the same line; never above, below, or in front of the street address.

3. CITY, STATE, AND ZIP CODE
These should appear in that sequence on the bottom line of the address block. This is where auto-

names in the address to those like it on the machine's memory.

dress will show through the window no matter how much the insert slides around in the envelope. There should be at least ¼ inch between the address and the left, right, and bottom edges of the window whatever the position of the insert.

matic sorting equipment is instructed to look for this information.

Mail presorted by ZIP Codes bypasses many processing steps in the post office and can get to its destination quicker.

---

§ 6.29 Forms of Address

Addressee	Form of Address	Salutation
	Federal, State, and Local Government Officials	
alderman or city councilman	The Honorable John Smith	Dear Alderman Smith:
cabinet officers (as the Secretary of State and the Attorney General)	The Honorable John Smith Secretary of State	Dear Mr./Madam Secretary
	The Honorable John Smith Attorney General of the United States	Dear Mr./Ms. Smith:
chief justice, Supreme Court	The Chief Justice of the United States	Dear Mr./Madam Chief Justice:
commissioner	The Honorable John Smith	Dear Mr. Smith:
former U.S. president	The Honorable John Smith	Dear Mr. Smith:
governor	The Honorable John Smith Governor of ______	Dear Governor Smith:
judge, federal	The Honorable John Smith United States District Judge	Dear Judge Smith:
judge, state or local	The Honorable John Smith Chief Judge of the Court of Appeals	Dear Judge Smith:
lieutenant governor	The Honorable John Smith Lieutenant Governor of ______	Dear Lieutenant Governor Smith:
mayor	The Honorable John Smith Mayor of ______	Dear Mayor Smith: Dear Mr. Mayor
president, U.S.	The President	Dear Mr./Madam President:
representative, state (same format for assemblyman)	The Honorable John Smith House of Representatives State Capitol	Dear Mr. Smith: Dear Representative Smith:
representative, U.S.	The Honorable John Smith The United States House of Representatives	Dear Mr. Smith: Dear Representative Smith:
senator, state	The Honorable John Smith The State Senate State Capitol	Dear Senator Smith:
senator, U.S.	The Honorable John Smith United States Senate	Dear Senator Smith: Dear Mr. Smith: Dear Senator:
speaker, U.S. House of Representatives	The Honorable John Smith Speaker of the House of Representatives	Dear Mr. Speaker:

Addressee	Form of Address	Salutation
vice-president, U.S.	The Vice President United States Senate	Dear Mr./Madam Vice President:
	Clerical and Religious Orders	
archbishop	The Most Reverend Archbishop of ______ or The Most Reverend John Smith Archbishop of ______	Your Excellency: Dear Archbishop Smith:
bishop, Catholic	The Most Reverend John Smith Bishop of ______	Your Excellency: Dear Bishop Smith:
bishop, Protestant	The Reverend or The Right Reverend John Smith	Reverend Sir: Dear Bishop Smith:
cardinal	His Eminence John Cardinal Smith	Your Eminence: Dear Cardinal Smith
clergyman, Protestant	The Reverend John Smith	Dear Reverend Smith:
	or The Reverend Dr. John Smith (if having a doctor's degree)	Dear Sir: or Dear Dr. Smith:
pope	His Holiness Pope ______ or	Your Holiness: or Most Holy Father:
priest	The Reverend John Smith	Reverend Father: Dear Father Smith:
rabbi	Rabbi John Smith	Dear Rabbi Smith:
sisterhood, member of	Sister Mary Angelica, S.C.	Dear Sister Mary Angelica: Dear Sister:
sisterhood, superior of	The Reverend Mother Superior, S.C.	Reverend Mother: Dear Reverend Mother:
	College and University Officials	
dean of a college or university	Dean John Smith	Dear Dean Smith: Dear Dr. Smith:
president of a college or university	President John Smith	Dear President Smith: Dear Dr. Smith:
professor at a college or university	Professor John Smith	Dear Professor Smith: Dear Dr./Mr./Ms. Smith:
	Miscellaneous Professional Ranks and Titles	
attorney	John Smith, Esq. or Mr. John Smith Attorney at Law	Dear Mr. Smith:
dentist	John Smith, D.D.S. (office address) or Dr. John Smith (home address)	Dear Dr. Smith:
physician	John Smith, M.D. (office address) or Dr. John Smith	Dear Dr. Smith:

Addressee	Form of Address	Salutation
veterinarian	(home address) John Smith, D.V.M. (office address) or Dr. John Smith (home address)	Dear Dr. Smith:

§ 6.30 The Memo

Memorandums, or memoranda, are the means organizations use to communicate internally. Used within an organization, a memorandum serves the same purpose as a letter does to the outside. Remember, do not rely upon what you may tell someone, put it in writing by typing a memo.

The tone of your memo will depend upon the relationship between you and the recipient, the nature of the subject, and organization policy. In some organizations the policy is that memos be written in the third person to avoid the mixing of facts with opinions. A memo addressed to top management should be more formal than to someone of equal rank with the writer. You can gain formality by not using contractions such as "here's," "can't," "you'll." Using them sets an informal tone.

When you organize the content of your memo, keep in mind that you are conveying a message, and brevity is the rule; but do not be so brief that you come across as being curt or impolite. Memos need to be as courteous as letters. Your message is selling a point of view or explaining a situation. State your purpose in the first paragraph. Deliver your message using the same rules you do for a letter. Use separate paragraphs for each idea or point. In the last paragraph close with a request, a statement of future action or your conclusions.

Do not take for granted that your subject line will cover the purpose of your memo. Always state your reason for writing. It may be here that you need to refer to a memo received, to a meeting, or perhaps to a telephone conversation.

An excellent method for stating your message briefly and quickly is to use enumerations. Use numbered paragraphs, one for each point. If you have several topics to discuss, you may use a method of bold side headings. Use all caps for the topic or underline it for emphasis.

If you rely upon the same sentence and paragraph construction and all the other rules for writing letters, you will produce an excellent product.

§ 6.30.1 Memo Format

Some organizations have memo forms printed, carrying the company's name and the designation that it is a memorandum. Many others have a variety of memo format "templates" for use by their computer users. If your organization does not have a printed form, it is easy to format one for future use. There are four basic elements you must include in your form:

TO:

FROM:

DATE:

SUBJECT:

These words should be in all caps followed by a colon. The arrangement is optional. The elements can be divided with two positioned on the left side and two at the center, or all four can be listed at the left margin. Double spacing should set them apart to allow space for long names, titles, addresses, etc.

Write dates just as you would in a letter.

When you address your memo, use a professional title for the addressee, such as Dr., but you may omit Mr., Mrs., Ms., or Miss. If your organization is large, you may wish to add the addressee's title, room number, or other identification for faster delivery.

If all the names or addresses on the memo are to the group, at the bottom of the memo, keyboard the heading "Distribution List": and list all individual names alphabetically below.

The subject line should contain the topic of the memo. Keyboard the subject matter in either initial or all capital letters.

The body or message should start three or four lines below the subject line. Use single spacing unless your message is very, very short. In a short memo, paragraphs should be blocked, leaving one line between paragraphs.

Complimentary closings are omitted in memos. The writer can initial the document either next to the name in the heading or at the end of the memo. If the writer's signature is required, place it at the bottom of the memo. Some feel it is unnecessary to repeat the reference to the writer when the name appears at the beginning of the memo.

§ 6.31 The Informal Report

You will have many occasions where you need to "put in writing" some information that the lawyer or others have requested. The practice of writing informal reports is also a form of self-protection. If you tell lawyers something, they may forget; however, if you write a report, you memorialize the information. Informal reports also stand as visible proof of your efficiency, and your efficiency is not so much an intangible thing if your report is on paper.

There are essentially three parts to the report:

1. In the introduction state your purpose with points to support the purpose.
2. In the body refer to any background necessary for clarity; then begin a discussion of each of the major points, giving details, examples, and facts. Reports rely very heavily on descriptive data.
3. The conclusion summarizes and gives results, findings or recommendations.

First, prepare your outline. This can be very short or very detailed depending upon the assignment. A firm may need to have a report on the kind of software each of the 12 lawyer's assistants in your office is using. They are planning to purchase new software to the extent the budget will allow and need prices also. In this situation, you really have two things to investigate.

1. List types of software the secretaries are using, including the capabilities of the programs.
2. Check and report on the prices of new software from two or more suppliers.

When you have gathered all the details, place the facts in the two categories. Arrange the items in each group in the order in which you should present them. You can proceed to write at this point.

In an informal report of this type, you will set it up as a memo to the person requesting the information. Whenever you make an informal report, no matter how minor you think it is, make a copy for your files. The original could be misplaced or lost.

In choosing your words, be clear, correct, complete, and concise. Say everything which needs to be said as economically as possible, using the same rules of grammar, punctuation, spelling, etc., used for letter writing. In a report, accuracy in giving your information is more important than correctness. You need not give as much attention to the tone of your report as you do when writing a letter to a client. In a report you should be factual and straightforward.

A very effective way to present information is to tabulate, chart, or graph the information. The reader has the advantage of seeing everything at a glance without wading through words.

After all the information in your research has been included in your report, you should summarize. In this situation you may recommend keeping some of the older software and adding new software.

Occasionally, you might want to write an unsolicited report, where you take the initiative. In business, any idea that you might have for increasing efficiency and productivity or changing procedures is usually more than welcome. You will want to put your idea or ideas in writing in a complete, logical, and effective manner.

Be careful to direct your idea to the person who has the authority to put it into effect.

Your subject line should be chosen carefully to describe concisely what the report is about.

The wording in the report should be tailored to appeal to the reader's interest. You are, in effect, doing a selling job. Go about the planning as you would for an informal research report. Rely on facts and not on your judgment. Give alternatives, good and bad, and back up the strong points with criteria you have gathered. In your conclusion reemphasize the strong points you have presented.

§ 6.32 The Formal Report

Formal business reports concern themselves with more complicated problems and may require weeks of extensive research. The finished product may contain anywhere from one or two pages to over one hundred. If a company is basing a decision concerning the expenditure of a great amount of money on this report, it must be very carefully and expertly done.

Before starting the report, the purpose and scope of the project must be set out. Also, it will have more parts: introduction, summary, body, conclusions, and recommendations, plus supplementary information such as an appendix and bibliography.

As the researcher gathers information, it is important to make special notes. A formal report is made up of information from many sources. Catalog this information through the use of note cards or note sheets, using one sheet for each item of information along with its source. After collection of all information, the writer then studies the material and begins the task of organizing it into a logical sequence for presentation.

A good report writer is careful to avoid any expressions which might imply that the writer's personal opinions are the basis for the evaluations presented in the paper. A successful business report separates reasoning from facts.

§ 6.33 E–Mail, Facsimile or Fax

E-mail is a system of delivering and receiving messages electronically using a modem, telephone line, and communications software. Both the sender and the receiver must have an "e-mail address" in order for the computer to acknowledge the commands. The e-mail system has become increasingly recognized inside and outside most firms, as clients and lawyers are able to send documents, messages, letters, etc., via e-mail. E-mail can be internal to an organization or firm's computer system, or can utilize the Internet.

Facsimile or fax machines are electronic machines used to transmit reproduced images of documents or photographs over standard phone lines. The machine optically scans the document to be sent and converts the image into digitized data that is transmitted over the phone, by means of a modem, to a compatible fax machine on the receiving end which converts the data back into its original image. Plug-in circuit boards are also available for personal computers. With the speed and ease of a phone call, documents are now transmitted by fax to anywhere in the world within a few minutes rather than taking days by mail.

§ 6.34 Teleconferencing

Teleconferencing once meant more than two persons sharing a phone conversation. Today, however, it includes video conferencing with the use of computers and television cameras to transmit the video images and sound to others at remote locations. Teleconferencing methods include audio conferencing and video conferencing.

§ 6.35 Voice Mail

Voice mail is the ability to leave a message, similar to leaving a message on an answering machine. The message is digitized so that it can be stored on a disk like other computer data. This allows the receiver to hear the message later (by reconverting it to audio form) and, if desired, to add comments and forward the message to someone else who has access to the voice mail system.

§ 6.36 Conclusion

Skilled writers are highly valuable in any business. The reason is obvious. The spoken word evaporates in air; the written word stands as a permanent testimony. That is why in business where large sums of money hinge on people's understanding each other—to produce items, deliver goods, promote goodwill, or render services—the accurately written word is essential.

Writing is affected by your environment, education, and intelligence. You can learn to write competently if you desire to do so, receive proper instruction and supervision, and then continue to practice in improving the skill. You should also realize that you can limit yourself by depending upon certain skills and techniques that may be obsolete. You should be curious, interested, and flexible enough to adapt to changes in forms, formats, and the mechanics of written communications.

CHAPTER 7

PREPARATION OF LEGAL DOCUMENTS

Table of Sections

---

§ 7.1 Introduction

Competent lawyer assistants take pride in their work product. All documents created in the law office reflect on the lawyer's assistant, the lawyer, and the law firm. Documents should be neat and attractively arranged on the page; conform to the specifications of the courts for preparation of documents; have been proofread and contain no keyboarding, content, or format errors. Understanding how legal documents are prepared will enable lawyer assistants to easily detect errors in grammar and/or content and correct them or bring them to the attention of the lawyer. Competent detail-oriented lawyer assistants find discrepancies and errors and work together with the lawyer to prepare the best documents possible.

An excellent background in the mechanics of English grammar, punctuation and capitalization rules, and formatting requirements is essential. Punctuation in legal documents should be logical and conform to general standards of punctuation; however, lawyer assistants may find that the rules and procedures are not always clear-cut and straightforward. Locality, time, purpose, and preferences may influence the choice of the rule or guideline to apply. For example, in eastern states, the reference or subject line in a letter is normally placed after the salutation; in western states the reference or subject line is placed above the salutation. In formal documents, the word "Street" in an address is spelled out and in an informal document it may be abbreviated. Some lawyers have very definite ideas about the use of punctuation and dictate all commas and other marks of punctuation.

Good sources of information relating to grammar, punctuation, capitalization, number usage, and formatting can easily be found. Many offices have procedures and style manuals to use as a reference for preparing letters and court and non-court documents. Other reference books include *The Elements of Style* by William Strunk, Jr. and E. B. White; *The Chicago Manual of Style*, 15th edition; *A Course in Basic Writing* by Susanna K. Horn and Ken Pramuk; and *The Gregg Reference Manual* by William A. Sabin. Most states have a prescribed procedure for the preparation of documents, and the assistant should read these guidelines and directives carefully. Become thoroughly familiar with standardized business English and when in doubt, consult a good legal procedures book for guidance.

Because it is so important that legal documents be error-free, the legal team should work together to produce the best results possible. The lawyer's assistant should be careful not to perpetuate errors, just because an office "has always done it that way." If there is a strong basis for a correction, the correction should be made; however, before making any changes, be sure to determine if the difference is a true error and not just a difference in style. Also, the lawyer's assistant should not hesitate to point out to an attorney obvious errors in a document. For example, if a lawyer dictated "defendant" and from the context, the lawyer's assistant knew it should have been "plaintiff", either the lawyer's assistant could make the correction or more prudently bring the matter to the attention of the attorney to determine if there truly is an error.

Following are some general procedures and guidelines that can be used in preparing legal documents.

§ 7.1.1 Paper and Number of Copies

After documents are typed or keyed into a computer, they are printed in draft or final mode. Inexpensive and sometimes colored paper is used for drafts and heavier bond paper is used for the final document. Copies are prepared using a less expensive paper. The usual practice is to prepare one original, have it signed or executed, and make the required number of copies on the copying machine. Most court systems, whether local, state, or federal, now require all documents filed to be on 8½ by 11–inch paper. Determine the size of the paper required for the court where the document will be filed by looking at court rule books or calling the court clerk. Because of this court requirement, most law offices now use the 8½ by 11–inch paper for the preparation of all non-court documents also.

When preparing court documents, determine the number of copies to be made as follows: original (and appropriate number of copies) for the court, a copy for each lawyer representing a party to the action, a file copy, and a copy for the client (if this is office practice). If this is the first time a document of this type is being prepared, make a copy for the form file also.

When preparing non-court documents, prepare a copy for any party signing the documents, their attorneys (if requested), as well as a file copy. In some instances it is necessary for the parties to sign more than one copy. The original and one or more of the copies will be designated as duplicate or triplicate originals. These copies will be executed just as the original and will be treated in all respects as original copies. In some cases, copies will be made after all signatures have been obtained on one original.

When lawyers dictate material or ask an assistant to prepare a document, they will often tell the assistant how many copies to make. The lawyer may ask for "two plus four," meaning an original, a duplicate original (which is a copy of the original either made on the computer printer or a copier), and four copies. Alternatively, the request may be for one plus two; that means an original and two copies. Some offices make it a practice to keep a photocopy of all executed documents if the signed original will not be retained. Also, if a document such as a letter or pleading requires a signature, copies should generally not be made until after the document is actually signed.

§ 7.1.2 Margins

Most documents are now created on computers which have standard or default settings of one-inch top and bottom margins and one-inch or one and a quarter inch left and right side margins. When documents such as pleadings or real estate documents that will be filed at the county recorder's office require extra space at the top of the first page, simply press the Enter or Return key to add the extra space at the top of the first page of the document instead of making actual margin setting changes. Usually pressing the Enter or Return key six times will equal one inch. Also, when documents are going to be bound, hole-punched, or stapled or when ruled legal paper (legal cap) is going to be used, additional margin space may be required. These new margin settings can be made using a few simple computer keystrokes.

Temporary left and right margins can be set to make typing legal descriptions and quoted materials easy. This feature, which is sometimes called Indent, is found in most word processing software and it allows for word wrapping which makes editing a simple task.

All documents should begin on the same line space from the top and end on the same line space from the bottom. This format should be followed whenever possible. Documents look neater and there is no question about lines being inserted.

Also, the lawyer's assistant has two options for aligning text between the margins: left and full justification. Left justification is more readable, but many offices prefer full justification. Avoid excessive use of hyphenation. Do not hyphenate the last word on a page.

Check the rules for the venue receiving the document to see if the court has any specific requirements regarding font, line spacing, and margins and then make a note in the office manual for future reference.

§ 7.1.3 Tab Settings

A five-space paragraph indention is usually used on legal documents. Most computers have default tab settings at five-space or one-half inch intervals. These stops will be convenient and useful in keyboarding subheadings, bulleted and numbered lists.

§ 7.1.4 Spacing

Spacing is described as single, double or triple spacing. In single spacing there is no blank line between the lines of text; in double spacing there is one blank line between the lines of text, and in triple spacing there are two blank lines. In law offices, correspondence is generally single spaced with a double space between sections and three blank lines in the signature block. Legal documents are generally double spaced for easier readability; however, some long leases and other agreements are single spaced with double spaces between sections to conserve paper.

Court pleadings are formatted according to court rules, local style, and electronic filing requirements. After keyboarding the name of the court in which the action is filed, double space to the caption. Key the caption in single space, and after the caption, double space to the body of the court document. The body of the pleading is usually double-spaced with five-space paragraph indentions. Property descriptions, quotations, and deposition or trial transcripts references are usually indented and single spaced. The spacing in signature blocks will usually be a matter of style; however, two blank lines should be included above the line keyed for the signature. Acknowledgments or verifications at the end of documents may be single spaced depending on office preference.

§ 7.1.5 Incomplete Pages

Deciding on how much space can be left at the bottom of a document and whether text can be split at certain places follow some simple guidelines. Two or more inches of space at the bottom of a document should also be avoided if possible. In correspondence, space can be added above or below the date line to adjust spacing. In pleadings, contracts, agreements and other legal documents, a Z-line or other method of marking may be used to fill up the blank space at the bottom of the document. Another option may be to simply insert the phrase: Remainder of page intentionally left blank.

Knowing how to control pagination is an important skill for the lawyer's assistant. First, the problem of having signature lines or signature blocks splitting between two pages or occurring on a page by themselves should be corrected by positioning the signature block and two lines of the preceding text on the last page. Some documents that require a number of signatures, i.e., municipal bond contracts, corporate contracts and partnership agreements, however, may have pages consisting of only signature lines. Also note that if the document being prepared has a testimonium clause, which is the paragraph just before the signatures usually starting with the words IN WITNESS WHEREOF, it must be placed on the page with the signatures.

A paragraph that is divided at the bottom of a page should have at least two lines of the paragraph on the end of the page and at least two lines of the paragraph at the top of the next page. A three-line paragraph should not be divided. A word processing function called the Widow/Orphan feature can automatically keep the first line of a paragraph from printing as the last line of a page and the last line of a paragraph from printing as the first line of a page.

Headings that are split from the text associated with the heading should be corrected by using special word processing features that control line and page breaks. The lawyer's assistant should proofread documents and specifically look for pagination errors.

There are several ways to adjust the page or pages preceding the signatures either to get the signatures on the page or some of the body of the document onto the page with the signatures:

- Use wider top and bottom margins.
- Shorten the lines slightly, thereby creating an additional line.
- If one line has only one word on it, move that word up to the line above by lengthening the lines.
- If most of the document is in double space, change spacing to an exact measurement just short of a true double space.
- Leave less space between the signatures or between the testimonium clause and the signatures.
- Put half of the signature lines on the left side of the page and half of them on the right side of the page rather than aligning them vertically on the right side of the page.

§ 7.1.6 Signatures

The document itself indicates who will sign it. Prepare the proper number of signature lines. Usually two or three blank lines between signature lines are sufficient. One blank line is also permissible if necessary to conserve space; use whatever space allows for sufficient room for the signature, but be consistent. The length of the signature line should be approximately three inches to allow for ample space for the party's signature. The signature lines or blocks can be aligned vertically one below the other close to the left margin or more centered on the page. They can also be placed in two columns, side-by-side.

Under each line, the designation of the signing party, such as "Seller," "Lessee," or other term is usually keyed in. Some offices prefer to have the name of the party keyed in below the line, along with the designation. The name can be aligned with the beginning of the line or centered under the line.

EXAMPLE: ______________________

E.G. Smith, Lessor

This method is useful for the persons signing the document because they will be less likely to sign on the wrong line.

When a corporation is a party to an instrument, the instrument is signed in the name of the corporation. On the left hand side of the page, key in "(CORP. SEAL)" in all caps. On the same line, space or tab to the center of the page and key in the name of the corporation; space down two lines and at the left side of the page key in "ATTEST:" so that it is aligned with the "CORP. SEAL" indication. Space down two more lines and set up the signature line, aligning it with the name of the corporation at the center of the page. Space down one line; key in another signature line at the left edge of the page and the name of the officer, if known, and "President" at the center of the page, aligned with the signature line above it. Space down one more line, and key in the name of the officer, if known, and "Secretary."

EXAMPLE:

(Corp. Seal)	ABC CORPORATION
ATTEST:	
______________________	By: ______________________
Jane Jones, Secretary	Mary Smith, President

The testimonium clause is the last paragraph on a legal (non-court) document before the signatures.

EXAMPLE:

"IN WITNESS WHEREOF, the parties hereto have hereunto set their hands on the day and year first above written."

If the testimonium clause states that the parties have "set their hands and seals," you know that the document is to be sealed. In the case of a corporation, the corporate seal would be affixed.

EXAMPLE:

"IN WITNESS WHEREOF, the parties hereto have caused this instrument to be executed properly on the day and year first above written."

Not all states require corporations to have seals; therefore, if the corporation does not have a seal, only the signature of the person signing for the corporation will appear.

EXAMPLE (for individual signature lines):

______________________ L.S.
or ______________________ (SEAL)

§ 7.1.7 Date Blanks

When preparing a document, the exact date on which it will be executed is not always known. The usual procedure is to leave a space sufficient to insert a date either with or without a line. Some firms prefer to underline the blank space because a blank space is hard to recognize and may be overlooked in executing this document.

EXAMPLE: the   day of July [year]
or the ______ day of July [year]

Six spaces are left so that there would be a space before the day, four spaces for the day and ordinal ending (12th), and a space following the day. Twelve spaces are used for the month. If it is near the end of the month and the month the document will be executed is unknown, leave sufficient space for the name of the longer month.

§ 7.1.8 Typing Drafts

Drafts are printed on inexpensive paper. The word DRAFT as well as the date should be keyed in at the top of the page. Some offices prefer to put draft information in the footer and remove or change it when the final is complete. When possible, double spacing or triple spacing is used for drafts so that revisions and corrections can be made. Any material directly copied from another source, such as a citation or quotation, can, however, be single spaced because it probably will not be revised.

Speed and accuracy are more important than neatness on drafts. The lawyer expects to make changes on the draft, and also expects what has been keyed in to be accurate. Be careful about citations, numbers, names, descriptions, dates and money amounts. When another revision is made to the revised first draft, mark it SECOND DRAFT and date it so that the two can be distinguished. Word processing programs allow you to insert headers or footers that will automatically update the date and time of each draft. Remember to remove this designation before printing the final version.

§ 7.1.9 Collating Documents

Collating is the process of placing the pages of a document in proper sequence. Documents can be copied in groups or collated in sets. Most copying machines have the collating feature. If not, copy and collate manually. Many copying machines will also automatically staple the collated copies. When documents are in landscape format, they should be copied and collated with the top of the next page to the left.

§ 7.1.10 Executing Documents

Executing a document is the term used for signing a document. It includes the procedure of having the appropriate parties sign the document, affixing a seal if required, acknowledgment, and notarization. The latter two steps are described in the section on notaries public in The Law Office chapter. Proper execution by a party or a duly authorized representative of a party is one element required to make a document legally binding on that party. It is usually desirable to have the parties execute documents using blue ink to more easily distinguish the originals from copies. States vary regarding the acceptability of documents executed in blue ink so be sure to check the court rules for individual jurisdictions.

§ 7.1.11 Conforming Documents

Every copy of a document must contain all of the information that has been written, stamped, or keyed into the original after the document was prepared. This is an important responsibility of the lawyer's assistant. Key in the name as it is written on the original and precede the name with an "s" inside two diagonal marks ("/s/"). Most often the lawyer's assistant makes a copy of the executed document and uses it for the file copy. This should have "COPY" stamped on it so it will not be confused with the original executed document.

EXAMPLE: */s/ Sarah Bridger*

§ 7.1.12 Legal Backs

In some states all legal documents, including court documents, must have legal backing. This is a heavy sheet of paper, longer than the document, and often of colored stock. The extra length of the backing sheet (¾ to 1″) is folded over at the top, and the document is inserted under the fold and stapled into the backing sheet with two staples about ½ inch from the top. Often, on one-fourth of the backing sheet the name of the parties, date of execution, and the printed name and address of the law firm are filled in. Office file copies are not backed.

Sometimes a legal backing sheet is used for non-court documents, such as wills. The backing sheet offers protection for the document as well as identification when the document is folded.

§ 7.1.13 Law Blanks (Printed Forms)

The use of printed forms or law blanks varies from state to state. All states use some printed forms and variable information is filled in on the form. Law blanks are used less and less, yielding to forms that are available on software from courts and software companies. Material on printed forms is generally single spaced due to the space restrictions on the form. Be very careful when preparing printed forms. Read through the form carefully, filling in all blanks. It is easy to miss a small space after a partial word, such as ha___; either an "s" or "ve" must be filled in to make a complete verb. Also remember to punctuate the law blank just as if it were keyed in completely. Too often lawyer's assistants fill in the blank and do not place a comma or period after the entered material, although they would have done so if they had keyed in the whole document. Law blanks should be punctuated just as accurately as all other documents.

§ 7.2 Capitalization

Capitalize the same words in legal documents that are capitalized in regular documents. Proper nouns and words beginning sentences are capitalized. In addition, in legal documents other words may be capitalized. When "court" refers to the courtroom or the organization dealing with a matter, the word is not capitalized. When a specific court by title is referred to, it is capitalized. When court means the judge hearing the case, it is capitalized. For example, "The Court hereby orders" means that the judge is ordering. If the lawyer's assistant can substitute "judge" for "court" and retain the meaning, then generally capitalize "Court."

In many offices whenever a party's name is mentioned in a document or pleading, it is in solid caps. Some lawyer's assistants capitalize the first letter of "plaintiff" and "defendant" when they are used in the document without a proper name following the designation. Some lawyers prefer that the name of one document be capitalized when referred to in another document, such as "in answer to the Complaint filed herein." Other offices do not capitalize in that instance. One method is probably no more correct than the other. The principal thing to remember is that you must be consistent throughout a document.

If capitalization rules have not been established by the law firm or attorney, collect and establish standard rules and follow them in all instances. For example, "City," "County," and "State" are generally not capitalized when they precede the name, but if they follow the name, they should be capitalized. Some attorneys want to emphasize the word City, County and State and therefore disregard the standard rule and capitalize. This type of information should go in a procedures or style manual and all staff should follow the same guidelines.

In legal work, it is traditional that certain phrases and words are keyed in all caps; however, some attorneys prefer the initial cap style. Before correcting these words, check with attorneys to find out their preferences, and, again, place this information in a style book. Some examples of these words are as follows:

- IN WITNESS WHEREOF
- THIS INDENTURE
- FOR VALUE RECEIVED
- RESOLVED
- WHEREAS
- NOW, THEREFORE
- WHEREFORE
- KNOW ALL PERSONS BY THESE PRESENTS
- THIS AGREEMENT
- IT IS ORDERED

§ 7.3 Numbers and Amounts of Money

The term "words and figures" is used in dictation by lawyers when they want the assistant to key in a number or amount of money in words followed by the figures in parentheses.

EXAMPLE:

"Under the age of twenty-one (21) years."

Money is written with the initial letter of the major words being capitalized. Do not include the cents fraction if the dollar amount is even.

EXAMPLE:

Twenty-five Thousand Dollars ($25,000)

Twenty-five Thousand and no/100 Dollars ($25,000.00).

The rule to remember is that the material in the parentheses summarizes what precedes the parentheses.

Incorrect: Twenty-five Thousand Dollars ($25,000.00) (The parentheses show the cents fraction but the preceding words do not.)

Correct: Twenty-five Thousand Dollars ($25,000)

Occasionally, the following expression of money is used.

Incorrect: Twenty-five Thousand and no/100 ($25,000.00) Dollars (This is incorrect because the word "Dollars" comes after the parentheses.)

Correct: Twenty-five Thousand and no/100 Dollars ($25,000.00)

A comprehensive set of guidelines for number usage and writing money amounts are provided in the *Gregg Reference Manual* or the *Chicago Manual of Style*.

§ 7.4 Legal Citations

A citation is the written notation that refers to primary and secondary legal authorities such as constitutions, statutes, cases, treatises, and legal encyclopedias. The legal citation provides an easy and uniform method for locating and referring to the authority in written documents. A case citation includes the name of the case, the volume number, the legal authority, the page number, and the year the case was decided. Following are examples of citations by category:

Cases	*Brown v. Board of Education*, 347 U.S. 483 (1954) *Kerr v. Farrey*, 95 F.3d 472 (7th Cir. 1996) *Clark v. Clark*, 725 N.E.2d 100 (Ind. Ct. App. 2000) *Allen v. Oklahoma City*, 175 Okla. 421, 52 P.2d 1054 (Okla. 1935)
Constitutions	U.S. Const., amend. XIV, § 1

	N.D. Const. art. 8, § 147
Statutes	28 U.S.C. § 1254(1) Ariz. Rev. Stat. § 36–582 (1999)
Rules	Fed. R. Civ. P. 54(b) Rule 9.130, Fla. R. App. Proc. Cal. Rules of Court, Rule 976
Secondary Authority	17 Charles Alan Wright, Arthur R. Miller & Edward H. Cooper, *Federal Practice & Procedure* § 4036 (2d ed. 1988)
	Timothy M. Cook, *The Americans with Disabilities Act: The Move to Integration*, 64 Temp. L. Rev. 393 (1991)
	Restatement (Second) of Torts, § 218 (1965)

Many legal documents and writings contain citations. Whenever attorneys want to support a position with a legal authority, they will refer to that authority by citation. A lawyer's assistant will become most familiar with citations when preparing opinion letters in all types of practice areas and when working in a litigation practice preparing briefs.

A brief is a memorandum of the material facts, the issues, the applicable law, and an argument to show the court how the law applies to the facts supporting the client's position and the law of the case. A list of all legal authorities cited in a brief will be compiled into a table of authorities. Most often this table contains the citations in order of authority as follows: case law listed alphabetically by case name, constitutional laws, statutes, administrative laws, court rules, followed by secondary authority materials.

The contents of a brief are the responsibility of the lawyer. The lawyer's assistant is responsible for keying in the brief in an attractive and accurate manner and must be knowledgeable regarding correct citation practices, including proper abbreviations, punctuation, and capitalization.

After keying in any citation, it is important that the work is checked very carefully. Because incorrect citations are unforgivable, all citations should be verified with their actual sources. No matter how attractive a brief or legal opinion is, its effectiveness is lost if it contains an incorrect citation. Judges expect accuracy in the briefs they read and look upon incorrect citations with great disfavor. The importance of checking all citations cannot be overemphasized. The lawyer's assistant is in a position to save the lawyer embarrassment by verifying every citation that leaves the office.

The most widely accepted guide for legal citations is *The Bluebook: A Uniform System of Citation* (18th ed. 2005), compiled by the editors of the Columbia Law Review, the Harvard Law Review, the University of Pennsylvania Law Review, and The Yale Law Journal (this book is often referred to as "The Bluebook").

Some states have developed their own citation practices, which should be followed where appropriate. The important thing is to be consistent, particularly within any one brief. It should be noted, however, that the name of the case must ALWAYS be italicized (or underscored).

To acquire the background for understanding and writing citations, the lawyer's assistant should read and study the information in Chapter 8 (The Law Library) and Chapter 9 (The Courts). It is especially important to understand the use of the terms "official" and "unofficial" reporters and the structure of the National Reporter System.

§ 7.4.1 Citation Sentences and Introductory Signals

When joining citations in a sentence, which is sometimes referred to as a string citation, begin with a capital letter, separate individual citations by means of a semicolon, and end with a period.

EXAMPLE:

McClanahan v. American Gilsonite Co., 494 F. Supp. 1334 (D. Colo. 1980); *Shibuya v. Architects of Hawaii, Ltd.,* 647 P.2d 276 (Haw. 1982); *Kallas Millwork Corp. v. Square D Co.,* 225 N.W.2d 454 (Wis. 1975); *Phillips v. ABC Builders Inc.,* 611 P.2d 821 (Wyo. 1980).

In citing a case, the writer will show that a certain case supports, compares, or contradicts a proposition or gives background material, and will use introductory signals such as "*See,*" "*See also,*" "*E.g.,*" "*Accord,*" "*Cf.,*" "*Contra,*" "*But,*" "*But see,*" and "*See generally,*" before the actual citation. When no signal is given, the writer is indicating that the cited authority directly supports the proposition, is the source of quoted material, or identifies the authority referred to in the text. Note that when the word "See" is used as an actual verb and part of a sentence, it is not considered a signal and is not italicized or underlined.

§ 7.4.2 Order of Citations

When more than one authority is stated as found in a string citation, they should be grouped by signal and within each signal the most persuasive or authoritative authority should be listed first. *The Bluebook: A Uniform System of Citation* (18th ed. 2005), suggests the following order for citations:

1. Constitutions (federal, state [alphabetically by state], foreign [alphabetically by jurisdiction], and then foundational documents of the United Nations, the League of Nations, and the European Union, in that order)
2. Statutes (federal, state [alphabetically by state], and foreign [alphabetically by jurisdiction])
3. Treaties and other international agreements are cited in reverse chronological order
4. Cases—arrange within a signal according to the courts issuing the cited opinions; cases decided by the same court are arranged in reverse chronological order
   a. Federal
      i. Supreme Court
      ii. Courts of Appeals; bankruptcy appellate panels; Emergency Court of Appeals; Temporary Emergency Court of Appeals; Court of Appeals for the Federal Circuit
      iii. District Courts; district bankruptcy courts; Court of International Trade
      iv. Judicial Panel on Multidistrict Litigation; Railroad Reorganization Court
      v. Court of Federal Claims; Court of Appeals for the Armed Forces; Tax Court
      vi. Administrative agencies (alphabetically by agency)
   b. State
      i. Courts (alphabetically by state and then by rank within each state)
      ii. Agencies (alphabetically by state and then alphabetically by agency within each state)
   c. Foreign
      i. Courts (alphabetically by jurisdiction and then by rank within each jurisdiction)
      ii. Agencies (alphabetically by jurisdiction and then by agency within each jurisdiction)
   d. International (International Court of Justice, Permanent Court of International Justice, then other international tribunals and arbitral panels [alphabetically by name])
5. Legislative materials
   a. Bills and resolutions
   b. Committee hearings
   c. Reports, documents, and committee prints
   d. Floor debates
6. Administrative and executive materials
   a. Federal

i. Executive Orders
ii. Current Treasury Regulations, Proposed Treasury Regulations
iii. All others currently in force
iv. Proposed rules
v. All materials repealed

b. State (alphabetically by state) currently in force, then repealed
c. Foreign (alphabetically by jurisdiction) currently in force, then repealed

7. Resolutions, decisions, and regulations of intergovernmental organizations
8. Records, briefs, and petitions (in that order)
9. Secondary materials
   a. Model codes and restatements
   b. Books, pamphlets, and shorter works in a collection
   c. Works in journals
   d. Book reviews not written by students
   e. Student-written law review materials, including book reviews
   f. Annotations
   g. Magazine and newspaper articles
   h. Unpublished materials not forthcoming
   i. Electronic sources

§ 7.4.3 Elements of Case Citations

A full case citation contains:

1. The name of the case which is always underlined or in italics;
2. The published sources in which it may be found;
3. The page upon which the cite begins;
4. In parenthetical the date of the decision and sometimes information which identifies the court making the decision: *Wyant v. SCM Corp.,* 692 S.W.2d 814 (Ky. Ct. App. 1985).

In addition, many citations include the following information:

- A "pinpoint cite" or "page cite" (page(s) particularly referred to): *Curtiss v. Hubbard,* 703 P.2d 1154, 1155 (Alaska 1985).
- A parallel citation—official reporter first: *State v. Reed,* 237 Kan. 685, 703 P.2d 756 (1985).
- Other parenthetical information regarding the decision (in parentheses): *State v. Story,* 646 S.W.2d 68 (Mo. 1983) (en banc);

State v. Brewer, 247 N.W.2d 205 (Iowa 1976) (maximum age of 65 is reasonable limitation).

- Subsequent case history: *Daniel v. International Brotherhood of Teamsters,* 561 F.2d 1223 (7th Cir. 1977), *rev'd on other grounds,* 439 U.S. 551 (1979).
- Other related authority: *Memphis Bank & Trust Co. v. Garner,* 459 U.S. 392 (1983) (construing 31 U.S.C. § 742).

§ 7.4.4 Case Names

The full case name appears at the beginning of an opinion in the official reporter. The full case name should be modified following conventions set forth in *The Bluebook* or as directed by court rule. Citations found in the context of a sentence, both the document text or in footnotes, should be changed as explained below. Citations that are preceded by a signal or are part of a string citation require additional abbreviated forms. Note that these additional forms of abbreviations are discussed in Rule 10.2.2 of *The Bluebook.*

1. If a case is a consolidation of two or more actions, cite only the first listed parties:

EXAMPLE:

Keller v. Holiday Inns, Inc. NOT *Keller v. Holiday Inns, Inc. and Burman v. Holiday Inns, Inc.*

2. Omit all parties but the first listed on each side but do not omit the first listed relator or any portion of a partnership name:

EXAMPLE:

Fry v. Mayor of Sierra Vista, NOT *Fry v. Mayor and City Council of Sierra Vista.*

3. Omit words indicating multiple parties, such as "et al." Also omit alternative names given for the first-listed party on either side:

EXAMPLE:

Cheng v. Seinfeld NOT *Cheng, et al. v. Seinfeld d/b/a The Man, Inc.*

4. In bankruptcy and similar cases, cite the adversary name first, followed by the non-adversary name in parentheses. Include either a procedural phrase such as "*In re*" or "*ex rel.*" before the non-adversary name, followed by a descriptive or introductory phrase such as "estate of" or "interest of," if any.

EXAMPLE:

In re Dreke Burnham Lambert Group, Inc., 120 B.R. 724 (Bankr. S.D.N.Y. 1990).

5. Abbreviate "on the relation of," "for the use of," "on behalf of," etc., to "ex rel." Do not omit the first-listed relator or any part of a partnership name.

EXAMPLES:

State ex rel. Clark v. Pratt NOT *State v. Pratt* or *State ex rel. Clark, Wilson & West.*

6. Abbreviate "in the matter of," "petition of," "application of," etc. to "In re."

EXAMPLE:

In re Cooper.

7. When adversary parties are named, omit all procedural phrases except "ex rel."

EXAMPLE:

Cooper v. Harris NOT *In re Cooper v. Harris* BUT *Idaho ex rel. Evans v. Oregon.*

8. Do not abbreviate the first word of a party's name unless the full name of a party can be abbreviated by commonly known initials.

EXAMPLE:

Blackstone Co. v. NLRB NOT *Blackstone Co. v. National Labor Relations Board.*

9. Do not otherwise abbreviate words in case names except for "Ass'n," "Bros.," "Co.," "Corp.," "Inc.," "Ltd.," "No.," and "&." If any of these begin a party's name, however, do not abbreviate it.

EXAMPLE:

Philadelphia Electric Co. v. Hirsch NOT *PECO v. Hirsch.*

10. Omit given names or initials of individuals except in names of business firms or where a party's surname is abbreviated.

EXAMPLE:

Mayer v. Gordon NOT *Jennifer Cannon Mayer v. Daniel S. Gordon.*

11. Omit "The" as the first word of a party name except as part of the name of the object of an in rem action or in cases in which "The King" or "The Queen" is a party.

EXAMPLE:

The King v. Broadup.

12. Do not omit any part of a surname made up of more than one word.

EXAMPLE:

Van der Velt v. Standing Horse.

13. Given names that follow, rather than precede, a surname should be retained. Retain the full name where the name is entirely in a language in which the surname is given first. If in doubt about a foreign name, use the name under which it is indexed in the reporter.

EXAMPLE:

Chun Ming v. Kam Hee Ho.

14. Omit "City of" and like expressions unless the expression begins a party name.

EXAMPLE:

Johnson v. Mayor of Clarkston NOT *Johnson v. Mayor of City of Clarkson* BUT *Schmidt v. City of Clarkston.*

15. Omit "State of," "Commonwealth of," and "People of" except in citing decisions of the courts of that state, in which case only "State," "Commonwealth," or "People" should be retained.

EXAMPLES:

People v. Lucky (when cited in California).

California v. Lucky (when cited outside California).

16. In business firm designations omit "Inc.," "Ltd.," "L.L.C.," "N.A.," "F.S.B.," and similar terms if the name also contains a word such as "Ass'n," "Bros.," "Corp.," "Co.," and "R.R.," clearly indicating the party is a business firm.

EXAMPLE:

Land v. Twin City Insurance Co. NOT *Land v. Twin City Insurance Co., Inc.*

17. Omit such terms as "administrator," "appellee," "executor," "licensee," and "trustee," etc., that describe a party already named.

EXAMPLES:

Gold v. Sullivan NOT *Gold, Trustee v. Sullivan, Executor.*

Silkwood v. Kerr–McGee Corp. NOT *Silkwood, Administrator v. Kerr–McGee Corp.*

18. Include any introductory or descriptive phrases such as "Accounting of," "Estate of" and "Will of."

EXAMPLE:

In re Estate of Freeburn.

19. Phrases or party names that would aid in identification of the case may be appended in parentheses after the formal case name.

EXAMPLE:

ILGWU v. NLRB (Bernhard–Altmann Texas Corp.).

In a bankruptcy proceeding, there may be a non-adversary name in the case name.

EXAMPLE:

Morse v. Barnard (In re Ramsey) [bankruptcy proceeding].

20. Omit all prepositional phrases of location not following "City," etc., unless the omission would leave only one word in the name of a party or the location is part of the name of a business.

EXAMPLES:

Hall v. Department of Human Resources NOT *Hall v. Department of Human Resources of State of Oregon.*

Chavez v. Industrial Commission NOT *Chavez v. The Industrial Commission of Arizona.*

21. Include designations of national or larger geographical areas except in union names, but omit "of America" after "United States." NEVER abbreviate "United States" when it stands for "United States of America."

EXAMPLES:

Smith v. Prudential Insurance Co. of America.

United States v. Widgets of America.

22. Commissioner of the Internal Revenue Service is cited simply as "Commissioner."

23. A union name should be cited exactly as given in the official report except that only the smallest unit should be cited. All industry designations except the first full one should be omitted, and all prepositional phrases of location should be omitted. Widely recognized abbreviations (CIA, UAW, etc.) may be used.

EXAMPLE:

International Brotherhood of Teamsters v. NLRB NOT *International Brotherhood of Teamsters, Chauffeurs, Warehousemen & Helpers of America v. NLRB.*

24. Case names may be abbreviated more extensively in footnotes to save space. Acceptable abbreviations are listed in The Bluebook. Remember, NEVER abbreviate United States.

EXAMPLE:

Pennsylvania Nat'l. Mut. Casualty Co.

§ 7.4.5 Federal Court Cases

Federal court cases should be cited as follows:

- United States Supreme Court:

  Hunter v. Erickson, 303 U.S. 385, 89 S. Ct. 557, 21 L. Ed. 2d 616 (1969). A recent unreported case may be cited as *United*

States v. Leon, ___ U.S. ___ (No. 86–1771, decided July 5, 1987).

- United States Court of Appeals:

  Haley v. United States, 739 F.2d 1502 (10th Cir. 1984).

- United States District Court:

  Brady v. Hopper, 570 F. Supp. 1333 (D. Colo. 1983). A recent unreported case may be cited as *Hawks v. Ingersoll Johnson Steel Co.,* U.S. District Court, S.D. Ind., No. IP 82–793–C, Apr. 4, 1984, OR *Perry v. Rockwell Graphic Systems,* ___ F. Supp. ___ (D. Mass. 1985).

§ 7.4.6 State Court Cases

In briefs and memorandums to be filed in state courts, both federal and state cases should be cited to both the official reporter (e.g., *United States Reports, Vermont Reports, Oregon Reports*) and the unofficial reporter (e.g., *Supreme Court Reports, Lawyers' Edition, Atlantic Reporter, Pacific Reporter*).

EXAMPLE:

Quinn v. Southern Pacific Transportation Co., 76 Or. App. 617, 711 P.2d 139 (1986).

If a state does not publish opinions in an official reporter or has opted to report official opinions in the National Reporter System, the court must be identified in parentheses at the end of the citation, followed by the year of the decision.

EXAMPLE:

State v. Twoteeth, 711 P.2d 789, 794 (Mont. 1985).

When the court report identifies the state but not the court, the state abbreviation may be omitted in the parenthetical.

EXAMPLE:

Lang v. Lang, 109 Idaho 802, 711 P.2d 1322 (Ct. App. 1985).

Only the jurisdiction must appear at the end of the citation if the court of decision is the highest court thereof.

EXAMPLE:

Miller v. Ottman, 136 N.E.2d 17 (Ind. 1956).

If the jurisdiction is not the court of decision, cite as follows:

EXAMPLE:

Mathes v. Ireland, 419 N.E.2d 782 (Ind. App. 1981).

If the decision has just been filed and it does not appear in the state reporter, it may be cited in one of the following ways:

EXAMPLE:

Wing v. Martin, 688 P.2d 1172 (Idaho 1984), OR

Wing v. Martin, ___ Idaho ___, 688 P.2d 1172 (1984), OR

Wing v. Martin, 84 Idaho Supreme Court Reports [I.S.C.R. when cited in Idaho] 1117, 688 P.2d 1172 (Idaho 1984).

If the advance sheets are not yet available, cite as follows:

EXAMPLE:

Wing v. Martin, No. 14790, Idaho Supreme Court (Sept. 25, 1984), OR

Wing v. Martin, ___ Idaho ___ (1984).

§ 7.4.7 Citation of Constitutions, Statutes, Session Laws, Ordinances, Rules, and Other Legal Authorities

The following are the accepted formats of citing the various authorities:

- Constitutions
  U.S. Const. art. II, § 4, cl. 1.
  U.S. Const. amend. XIV, § 1.
  Idaho Const. art. I, § 3.
- Federal Statutes
  Official Code: 28 U.S.C. § 2105(a)(1)–(3) (1964).
  Uniform Commercial Code: U.C.C. § 4–109 (1962).
  Code of Federal Regulations: 24 C.F.R. § 202.13 (1949).
  Internal Revenue Code: I.R.C. § 12.
- State Statutes

Since the statutes are not cited the same way in all states, consult the most recent edition of *A Uniform System of Citation* for the correct way to cite state statutes. Examples of abbreviations for commonly cited state statutes should be placed in a procedures manual for future reference.

EXAMPLE:

Wyo. Stat. § 7–13–904 (1977).

- Federal Session Laws
  United States Statutes at Large: Federal Land Policy and Management Act of 1976, 90 Stat. 2769, 43 U.S.C. § 1744 (1982).
- State Session Laws

Since the state session laws are not cited the same way in all states, consult the tables in The Bluebook for the correct way to cite individual state session laws and type the correct citation in a procedures manual for future reference. Always give the name of the statute and the public law or chapter number. If there is no official or popular name, identify the act with a full date.

EXAMPLES:

Act of July 1, 1972, ch. 202, 1972 Idaho Sess. Laws 535.

Michigan Sesquicentennial Act of 1984, Pub. Act No. 266, 1984 Mich. Legis. Serv. 37 (West).

- Ordinances

Cite by name of code (including municipal unit, not abbreviated, followed by state, abbreviated), section, and year of publication of the code.

EXAMPLE:

Chicago, Ill., Municipal Code § 155–1 (1931).

- Miscellaneous Codes

Model Penal Code § 303.5 (1962).

- Restatements

Restatement (Second) of Torts § 324A.

- Federal Rules

Federal Rules of Civil Procedure: Fed. R. Civ. P. 23(b).

Federal Rules of Criminal Procedure: Fed. R. Crim. P. 12.

- State Rules

Consult individual state codes to determine the correct way to cite the civil, criminal, and appellate rules in individual states and make a note in a procedures manual.

- Jury Instructions

Citation forms are usually suggested in the volumes cited. When citing a jury instruction in a foreign jurisdiction, a more detailed citation must be given for state jury instructions.

EXAMPLES:

Ninth Circuit Court: Model Jury Instr., 9th Cir. 3.08.

California Jury Instructions: BAJI (6th ed.) No. 4.01; CALJIC (4th ed.) No. 7.07.

Illinois Jury Instructions: IPI–Criminal 3d 20.02.

- Legislative Materials

Bills

Senate Bill: S. 507, 94th Cong., 1st Sess. § 311 (1975).

House Bill: H.R. 507, 95th Cong., 1st Sess. (1977).

Resolutions

Senate Resolution: S. Res. 50, 99th Cong., 1st Sess. (1983).

House Resolution: H.R. Res. 50, 98th Cong., 1st Sess. (1983).

- Committee Hearings

Give title of hearing (underlined) and add which Congress, which session, page, date, and attribution.

EXAMPLE:

Age Discrimination in Employment: Hearings on S. 830 and S. 788 before the Subcommittee on Labor of the Senate Committee on Labor and Public Welfare, 90th Cong., 1st Sess. 23 (1967) (statement of Sen. Javits).

- Committee Reports

Senate Report: S.Rep. No. 583, 94th Cong., 1st Sess. 65 (1975).

EXAMPLE:

Criminal Code Reform Act of 1977: Report of the Committee on the Judiciary, United States Senate, to accompany S. 1437, S. Rep. No. 605, 95th Cong., 1st Sess. 911 (1977).

House Report: H.R. Rep. No. 1724, 94th Cong., 2d Sess. 62 (1976).

H.R. Rep. No. 805, 90th Cong., 1st Sess. 4 (1967), 123 Cong. Rec. 34295 (1977) (remarks of Sen. Williams).

H.R. Rep. No. 867, 97th Cong., 2d Sess. 7, *reprinted in* 1982 U.S. Code Cong. & Ad. News 3362.

- Floor Debates

124 Cong. Rec. 8218–8219 (1978) (remarks of Sen. Javits).

- Congressional Records (daily edition)

130 Cong. Rec. H1847–48 (daily ed. Mar. 21, 1984) (statement of Rep. Kindness).

- Dictionaries

Black's Law Dictionary 912 (6th ed. 1991).

Stedman's Medical Dictionary 783 (4th Unabridged Lawyers' Ed. 1976).

7 Am. Jur. Proof of Facts *Last Clear Chance* (Supp. 1990 at 45).

49 Am. Jur. 2d *Eviction* § 300 (1970).

86 C.J.S. *Torts* § 61 n. 9.

- Treatises

Cite by volume (use Arabic numerals); author (initial and last name); full title; serial number (if any); page, section, or paragraph; edition (if more than one); and year.

EXAMPLES:

R. Hunter, *Federal Trial Handbook* § 15.26 (1984).

2A A. Larson, *The Law of Workmen's Compensation* § 68.21 (1976).

- Law Review Articles

If written by a student, give a designation, such as "Note" or "Comment," instead of a student author's name.

EXAMPLE:

Note, *Employee Handbooks and Employment–at–Will Contracts,* 1985 Duke L.J. 196 (1985).

Other authors are identified by last name only.

EXAMPLE:

Strauss, *Mining Claims on Public Lands: A Study of Interior Department Procedures,* 1974 Utah L. Rev. 185, 193, 215–19.

- Services

Services (cases, administrative materials, and brief commentaries that are published periodically in looseleaf form) are cited by volume, abbreviated title, publisher, subdivision, and date.

EXAMPLES:

United States v. Leon, Search & Seizure L. Rep. (Clark Boardman) 53 (Aug. 1984).

O'Brien v. Dean Witter Reynolds, Inc., [Current Binder] Fed. Sec. L. Rep. (CCH) ¶ 91,509 (D. Ariz. 1984).

- Periodicals

Cite by author (last name only), title of article in full, volume number of periodical, name of periodical found on title page (abbreviated), page on which article begins (and page or pages specifically referred to), and year of publication.

EXAMPLE:

Rothstein, *Amendments to the Federal Rules of Criminal Procedure,* 69 A.B.A. J. 1938 (1983).

- Annotations

Give the date of the volume, not of the case.

EXAMPLES:

American Law Reports, Fourth Edition: Annot., 41 A.L.R. 4th 131 (1985).

American Law Reports, Federal: Annot., 74 A.L.R. Fed. 505 (1985).

§ 7.4.8 Citation Abbreviations, Spacing, Punctuation, Capitalization, Numbers, Quotations, Sections and Subdivisions, and Underlining

The following are rules for citation abbreviations, spacing, punctuation, capitalization, numbers, quotations, sections and subdivisions, and underlining.

- Abbreviations

  "And" is always abbreviated to " & ."

  "United States" is never abbreviated when it refers to the United States of America.

Abbreviations for states, months of the year, subdivisions, and some reporters are included at the end of this chapter. A table of frequently used American abbreviations is found in The Bluebook.

- Spacing

A space should precede and follow all abbreviations that consist of more than one letter and the ampersand; close up single capitals.

EXAMPLES:

Ariz. St. L.J. [Arizona State Law Journal].

Fla. St. U.L. Rev. [Florida State University Law Review].

An exception to the spacing rule is when an entity is abbreviated by widely recognized initials and a combination of those initials with others would be confusing.

EXAMPLE:

A.B.A. J. [American Bar Association Journal].

There must be a space between the symbols "§ "and "¶ "and a number.

- Punctuation

Periods may be omitted from widely recognized initials that are read out loud as initials (NLRB, CBS, IRS) in case names but not when they refer to reporters, codes, or courts. If initials are read as words (N.D., S.C.), the periods should not be omitted.

A comma should not precede "note," "n.," and "nn."

A comma should not precede the symbols "§ "and "¶ "unless preceded by a number.

Multiple citations in a sentence are separated by semicolons.

Commas and periods are always placed inside quotation marks. All other punctuation is placed outside unless it is part of the quoted material.

Citations should never appear within parentheses.

- Capitalization

Generally, follow the "Guide to Capitalization" in the *United States Government Printing Office Style Manual.*

"Act," "bill," "rule," "statute," etc., are capitalized only when used as part of a proper name given in full.

"Court" is capitalized only when naming a specific court, when referring to the United States Supreme Court, or when referring to a specific judge (and the judge's name could be used in its place).

"Circuit" is capitalized only when used with a circuit number.

"Constitution" is capitalized only when used in the full name of a constitution or when referring to the Constitution of the United States. Parts of a constitution, such as amendments, are not capitalized.

"Judge" and "justice" are capitalized only when giving the name of the judge or justice or when referring to the Chief Justice of the United States Supreme Court.

The abbreviation for "number" (No.) is always capitalized.

When used alone, a word which refers to people or groups is capitalized only when it is used as the shortened form of a specific group or body.

EXAMPLE:

The Free–Thinkers Consolidated Dogmatists (the "Dogmatists")

- Numbers

Spell out the numbers zero to ninety-nine in text and zero to nine in footnotes.

Spell out all numbers that begin a sentence.

Round numbers may be spelled out (three hundred).

Use numerals in a series that contain any numbers.

Use numerals for numbers that include decimal points.

Do not use periods after 1st, 2d, 3d, 4th, etc.

Pages may be cited as follows:

EXAMPLES:

Pages 416 through 433: 416–33

Pages 1476 through 1517: 1476–517

Sections must be cited as follows:

EXAMPLES:

Sections 416 through 433: 416–433

Sections 1476 through 1517: 1476–1517

- Quotations

Quotations of fifty or more words are usually indented, and quotation marks should not be used. Quotations of forty-nine or fewer words should be enclosed in quotation marks but not set off from the rest of the text. Commas and periods are always placed inside the quotation marks.

When a letter is changed from lower to upper case or from upper case to lower case, enclose it in brackets. All substituted words or letters and added material should be placed in brackets.

Do not use ellipses to begin a quotation or when a word is merely altered. An omission of language from the middle of a quoted sentence is indicated by three periods separated by spaces between them. A fourth period is used to indicate the end of a sentence. Do not indicate deleted material after a period or other final punctuation that ends the quotation.

Indicate paragraph structure by indenting the first word of a paragraph. If the quotation begins in the middle of a paragraph, do not indent the first line. Omission of one or more paragraphs is indicated by inserting and indenting four periods on a separate line. Mistakes in the original of quoted material should be followed by "[sic]."

The citation following its source should not be indented. It should appear at the left margin immediately following the quotation. Omitted footnotes, omitted citations, and change in emphasis of certain words in a quotation should be indicated in a parenthetical after the citation.

- Sections and Subdivisions

The following demonstrates the proper way to cite sections and section subdivisions in citations (do not use section symbols in text).

EXAMPLES:

Section 1414: § 1414

Section 1414 through section 1452: §§ 1414–1452

Section 1414, subsections a and 3: § 1414(a)(3)

Sections 2.15–312, 2.15–314, and 2.15–320:

§§ 2.15–312, –314, –320 [drop identical digits preceding a common punctuation mark]

Subdivision designations should be enclosed in parentheses even if printed in the source without.

EXAMPLE:

§ 145(a)(1)(iii)

- Underlining

In briefs and legal memoranda underline or italicize:

1. Case names
2. Book and treatise titles
3. Titles of articles in periodicals and newspapers
4. Congressional publications (including committee hearings)
5. When referring to a publication rather than citing to it (*Yale Law Journal, Pacific Reporter,* etc.)
6. Names of titles or topics within encyclopedias
7. Introductory signals (*e.g., See,* etc.)
8. Id. and supra
9. The letter "l" when it is used to identify a subsection so it will not be confused with the number "1"
10. Letters used to designate people in hypothetical situations (*A* filed suit against *B*)
11. Foreign words not incorporated into the English language
12. For emphasis

Extend the underscore beneath the period ending an abbreviation. Do not extend the underscore beneath the period that ends a sentence.

§ 7.4.9 Abbreviations for Reporters, States, Months of the Year, and Subdivisions

The following are rules for abbreviations for reporters, states, months of the year, and subdivisions.

REPORTS:	
American Law Reports Annotated	A.L.R.
American Law Reports Annotated, Second Series	A.L.R.2d
American Law Reports Annotated, Third Series	A.L.R.3d
Atlantic Reporter	A.
Atlantic Reporter, Second Series	A.2d
Bankruptcy Reporter	Bankr.
California Appellate Reports	Cal. App.
California Appellate Reports, Second Series	Cal. App. 2d
California Reporter	Cal. Rptr.
Commissioner of Patents, Decisions	Dec. Com. Pat.
Court of Customs Appeals Reports	Ct. Cust. App.
Federal Cases	F. Cas.
Federal Reporter	F.
Federal Reporter, Second Series	F.2d
Federal Rules Decisions	F.R.D.

Federal Supplement	F. Supp.
Lawyers' Edition, United States Supreme Court Reports	L. Ed.
Lawyers' Edition, United States Supreme Court Reports, Second Series	L. Ed. 2d
Lawyers Reports, Annotated	L.R.A.
Lawyers Reports, Annotated, New Series	L.R.A. (n.s.)
Negligence Cases (CCH)	Negl. Cas.
Negligence Cases, Second Series (CCH)	Negl. Cas. 2d
New York Criminal Reports	N.Y. Crim.
New York Supplement	N.Y.S.
New York Supplement, Second Series	N.Y.S.2d
North Eastern Reporter	N.E.
North Eastern Reporter, Second Series	N.E.2d
North Western Reporter	N.W.
North Western Reporter, Second Series	N.W.2d
Pacific Reporter	P.
Pacific Reporter, Second Series	P.2d
South Eastern Reporter	S.E.
South Eastern Reporter, Second Series	S.E.2d
South Western Reporter	S.W.
South Western Reporter, Second Series	S.W.2d
Southern Reporter	So.
Southern Reporter, Second Series	So.2d
Supreme Court Reporter [United States]	S. Ct.
United States Supreme Court Reports	U.S.
United States Tax Cases	U.S. Tax Cas. (CCH)

STATES:

Ala.	Me.
Alaska	Md.
Ariz.	Mass.
Ark.	Mich.
Cal.	Minn.
Colo.	Miss.
Conn.	Mo.
Del.	Mont.
D.C.	Neb.
Fla.	Nev.
Ga.	N.H.
Haw.	N.J.
Idaho	N.M.
Ill.	N.Y.
Ind.	N.C.
Iowa	N.D.
Kan.	Ohio
Ky.	Okla.
La.	

Or.	Utah
Pa.	Vt.
R.I.	Va.
S.C.	Wash.
S.D.	W. Va.
Tenn.	Wis.
Tex.	Wyo.

MONTHS OF THE YEAR:

Jan.	July
Feb.	Aug.
Mar.	Sept.
Apr.	Oct.
May	Nov.
June	Dec.

SUBDIVISIONS:

The following terms are always abbreviated as indicated below in full citations, but never in text—except that "section" is written § in textual footnotes when followed by the number of the section and not the first word of a sentence:

amendment(s)	amend., amends.
appendix(es)	app., apps.
article(s)	art., arts.
book(s)	bk., bks.
chapter(s)	ch., chs.
clause(s)	cl., cls.
column(s)	col., cols.
folio(s)	fol., fols.
footnote(s)	n., nn.
number(s)	No., Nos.
page(s)	p., pp. [or, at]
paragraph(s), subparagraph(s)	para., paras., ¶ , ¶ ¶
part(s)	pt., pts.
section(s), subsection(s)	§, §§ [space between § and number]
series, serial(s)	ser.
title(s)	tit., tits.
volume(s)	vol., vols.

§ 7.5 Citing Electronic Media and Other Nonprint Resources

1. Commercial Electronic Databases.

Cases are often found in Westlaw and LexisNexis. Cases found in Westlaw and LexisNexis should be cited, providing the case name, docket number, database identifier, court name, and full date of the most recent major disposition of the case. The database identifier must contain enough information for a reader to identify the database and find the case. If the database has identifying, codes or numbers that uniquely identify the case, these must be given. Screen or page numbers should be preceded by an asterisk; paragraph numbers should be preceded by a paragraph symbol.

EXAMPLE:

United States v. Carlisle, No. 90–2465SI, 1991 U.S. App. LEXIS 5863, at *3 (8th Cir. Apr. 10, 1991) (per curiam).

Clark v. Homrighous, CIV.A. 90–1380–T, 1991 WL 55402, at *3 (D. Kan. Apr. 10, 1991).

When citing a code contained in an electronic database, give parenthetically the name of the database and information regarding the currency of the database as provided by the database itself. Also give the name of the publisher, editor, or compiler unless the code is published, edited, compiled by, or under the supervision of, federal or state officials:

EXAMPLE:

CAL. BUS. & PROF. CODE § 1670 (Deering, LEXIS through 1995 Sess.).

CAL. BUS. & PROF. CODE § 1670 (West, Westlaw through 1995 portion of 1995–96 Legis. Sess.).

When citing legislative, administrative, and executive materials contained in a commercial electronic database, give the name of the database and any identifying codes or numbers that uniquely identify the material as shown in the following list:

a. federal bill (unenacted)—H.R. 3781, 104th Cong. § 2(b) (1976), WL 1996 CONG US HR 3781.

b. federal report—H.R. Rep. No. 92098 (1971), *reprinted in* 1971 U.S.C.C.A.N. 1071, 1971 WL 11312.

c. congressional debate—142 Cong. Rec. H11460 (daily ed. Sept. 27, 1996) (statement of Rep. Tanner). LEXIS 142 Cong Rec H11452p*11460.

d. federal regulation cited to *Code of Federal Regulations*—FTC Credit Practices Rule, 16 C.F.R. § 444.1 (2000), WL 16 CFR § 444.1.

e. administrative adjudication—*Reichold Chems., Inc.,* 91 F.T.C. 246 (1978), WL 91 F.T.C. 246.

f. formal advisory opinion—39 Op. Att'y Gen. 484 (1940), 1940 US AG LEXIS 16.

g. revenue ruling—Rev. Rl. 86–71, 1986–1 C.B. 102, 1986 IRB LEXIS 189.

When citing secondary materials to a database, provide a complete citation, a citation to the database, and the unique identifier or code to each document within the database. When accessing a traditional source as well as a commercial electronic database, you may use "available at" to provide increased accessibility to the citation; if using only the commercial database, no explanatory should be used.

2. Elements of Internet Citation

The citation of information to Internet sources should indicate clearly and unambiguously the source actually used or accessed by the author of the citing work. The general rules of citation and style apply to such citations, and they should be provided in the form and typeface applicable to that source, with the exception of the URL. The following elements should be included in such citations:

a. available information about the authority being cited

b. appropriate explanatory phrase to indicate which source actually used by the author

c. the provider responsible for the Internet site, where not apparent from the Uniform Resource Locator (URL)

d. the URL

e. a date parenthetical

f. any explanatory parenthetical.

If only the Internet is accessed, provide the traditional and Internet citations, such as *New York v. McArthur,* No. N4–999–501 (N.Y. Ct. App. Sept. 28, 1999), http://www.courts.state.ny.us/library/archive/ctapun/9909/501.htm.

If material is found exclusively on the Internet, use the explanatory phrase "at", such as J.T. Weiss, *Ethical Issues for the Millenium,* 6 RICH. J.L. & TECH. 5, ¶ 7 (2000), at http://www.richmond.edu/jolt/v6l1/weiss.html.

An accurate URL is necessary for citation of Internet information. The URL also may provide information that may not be available on the site itself. The URL should appear in regular roman typeface, without angled brackets. Following is a typical breakdown of a URL for an Internet source:

http protocol (Hyptertext Transfer Protocol), followed by "://" (colon, double slash).

www World Wide Web server, followed by a period.

edf the organization presenting the information (here Environmental Defense Fund), followed by a period

org designation that the provider is an organization, followed by a slash where other information is provided. Other provider designators include "com" for commercial providers, "edu" for educational institutions, and "gov" for governmental organizations.

Constitutions, statutes, legislative material, administrative and executive materials must be cited first to a traditional source or electronic database. Books, journals and magazines and other secondary sources, such as news reports, newspapers, and other non-legal publications should be cited first to a traditional source, except an Internet source may be cited where information is not available in a traditional source or electronic database.

In citing e-mail messages, include the date of the message. Archival information may be included parenthetically, but the e-mail addresses of the sender and recipient are not required, although they may be included if there is a reason for doing so.

Information found on CD–ROM usually is available in print form, and citation to the print form is preferred where available. When citing CD–ROM media, include the title of the material, the publisher of the CD–ROM, the version searched, and the date of the material or the date of the version searched.

When a document is reproduced in microform, it is not necessary to indicate this fact unless it would otherwise be difficult for a reader to identify and obtain the source. If it is necessary to cite material on microform, provide a complete citation to the original document and a citation to the microform, including a unique identifier or code if one has been assigned. Include the name of the publisher of the microform series in parentheses.

If citing films, broadcasts, and noncommercial videotapes, cite films in large and small capitals, and television or radio broadcasts in italics, by exact date, including the name of the company or network that produced or aired the film or broadcast. Cite videotapes containing images that have not been commercially displayed or broadcast by the title of the tape, the name of the person or institution that produced the video, and the year of production.

Commercial audio recordings should be cited by artist and title, providing the name of the recording company and the date of release. Noncommercial audio recordings, use ordinary roman type and indicate where a copy may be obtained.

Short form of citations should be styled as follows:

a. Commercial electronic databases—use a unique database identifier, if one has been assigned.

EXAMPLE:

Tierney v. Mace, CIV.A. 90–1830–T, 1991 WL 5530, at *1 (D. Kan. Apr. 1, 2001) BECOMES *Tierney,* 1991 WL 5530, at *1.

b. CD–ROM and microform—use the short form appropriate for the original document—it is not necessary to indicate the source once it has been given in the first full citation.

c. Internet—use the short form appropriate for the original document, including the URL or Internet address.

d. Films, broadcasts, and audio recordings—"*id.,*" and "*supra*" may be used when citing films, broadcasts, and audio recordings.

§ 7.6 Summary

This material may seem difficult to grasp at first, but with study and attention to detail, most lawyer assistants become competent and confident in typing and writing citations. Learn how to write citations by being aware of the rules and conventions; practice by copying citations that have already been created. Pay close attention to the order of material, punctuation, and abbreviations that are used. The lawyer's assistant will have opportunities for typing citations from rough draft and transcription, and over time will become competent at changing the long, complete name that is found in the official reporter to a proper citation format.

CHAPTER 8

THE LAW LIBRARY

Table of Sections

---

§ 8.1 Legal Research and the Law Library

The essential job of the lawyer is to answer the question, "How does the applicable law apply to my client's legal problem?" For example, the client may ask the lawyer, "Now that my daughter has turned 18 and no longer receives child support, can I get a court to order my ex-husband to help pay her college expenses?" Legal education and law practice equip the lawyer to find and interpret the law applicable to the question at hand. To help the client get help with her daughter's college expenses, the lawyer must find some basis in existing law for the court to award such support.

Finding the law requires access to any constitutional provisions, statutes, regulations, case law, or other legal authority that may apply. Traditionally, lawyers have relied on libraries of printed legal resources to provide access to such authorities. It is extremely expensive, however, for a lawyer to buy and maintain a comprehensive law library of all the federal and state statutes, regulations, and cases that may be needed. Accordingly, many lawyers rely heavily on public or academic law libraries for access to legal resources. Increasingly, lawyers also subscribe to commercial online services (such as LexisNexis and Westlaw), CD–ROM databases, and the Internet for access to federal, state, and local law.

§ 8.2 Authority

When a lawyer asks a court to rule in favor of the lawyer's client in a given matter, the lawyer argues on the basis of some form of "legal authority." The universe of legal authority is divided into two classes: "primary legal authority" and "secondary legal authority."

§ 8.2.1 Primary Legal Authority

Primary legal authority is the law itself, as it is given in constitutional provisions, statutes, administrative regulations, municipal and county codes, published judicial decisions, court rules, etc. Primary law can issue from any governmental body legally empowered to create rules governing the conduct of others.

Federal and state governments conduct themselves in accordance with their own written constitutions. The United States Congress and individual state legislatures enact statutes to order the affairs of the people (to the extent permitted by the applicable constitution). Federal and state administrative agencies issue regulations on matters entrusted by statute to their supervision. Counties and cities enact ordinances by which to govern themselves. All of these documents are samples of primary law.

Appellate courts create "case law" or "judge-made law," a special kind of primary law. Imagine a fictional court case: the state of Washington sues the federal government in the United States District Court for the Eastern District of Washington, claiming that, under the federal Clean Water Act, the federal government should have to pay for cleaning up groundwater contamination due to radioactive waste. The radioactive waste has migrated from the Hanford Nuclear Reservation to adjacent land owned by the state of Washington. The federal government claims that it is not subject to suit under the Clean Water Act and, accordingly, brings a motion to dismiss Washington's lawsuit. The federal district court grants the motion to dismiss and publishes a written opinion explaining its rationale. The state of Washington then appeals the case to the United States Court of Appeals for the Ninth Circuit, claiming that the district court misinterpreted the Clean Water Act. In a written opinion, the Ninth Circuit reverses the district court's order and holds that the federal government is, in fact, subject to suit under the Clean Water Act. The federal government then appeals the Ninth Circuit decision to the United States Supreme Court, which, in its own written opinion, reverses the Ninth Circuit's decision and reinstates the district court's opinion.

The written opinions prepared by each court in this example are referred to as "case law." Case law is the primary law created by courts; it is an important guide to the interpretation of other forms of primary law because courts are so often called upon to interpret constitutional provisions, statutes, and regulations.

§ 8.2.2 Mandatory Versus Persuasive Primary Legal Authority

In the context of a particular legal dispute, primary legal authority can be subdivided into two kinds: mandatory and persuasive.

Mandatory legal authority is the primary law that the court is obligated to follow. Thus, in an action for child support, a court may not award support beyond the child's 18th birthday if the applicable state statute clearly terminates the parent's support obligation when the child turns 18. That state statute is the "mandatory" legal authority applicable to the case and the court must follow it, regardless of whether every other state in the country permits "post-majority" support. In researching any legal question, the lawyer's first obligation is to identify and understand the mandatory primary law applicable to the case.

The mandatory legal authority applicable to the case, however, may be ambiguous. In such cases, a court may look to "persuasive" legal authority as a guide in interpreting the applicable law. For example, a court may consider judicial interpretations of analogous federal or state statutes from other jurisdictions. In our example, the applicable child support statute may not speak directly to the issue of post-majority support. In such a case, the court might consider whether other, similarly worded statutes from other states have been interpreted to permit child support beyond the child's 18th birthday. Generally speaking, a court is not bound by the statutes of other states but judicial opinions construing them may be "persuasive" on the question of whether the statute at issue should be interpreted to permit post-majority support.

§ 8.2.3 Secondary Legal Authority

Secondary legal authority is published legal analyses that are "about" the law. Unlike primary law, secondary legal authority does not purport to be the law itself.

For example, a lawyer may wish to help a client understand the legal effect of a clause in a contract that the client is about to sign. The lawyer may consult a treatise on contracts for a discussion of judicial decisions interpreting similar contract terms. In addition to providing a better understanding of contract law, the treatise may help the lawyer find cases supporting an interpretation favorable to the client's interests in the matter. Ideally, the lawyer will find favorable cases from the highest court of the jurisdiction in question (which will be "mandatory" authority on the issue at hand). In this fashion, lawyers use secondary legal authority to find and understand the primary law relevant to a client's question.

Secondary authorities include legal encyclopedias, treatises, practice guides, sets of "annotated" statutes, law review articles, even short articles in local bar journals, etc. Courts occasionally rule in accordance with the opinions expressed by authors of secondary legal material, especially when the author is well respected and when there seems to be no rule of primary law directly applicable to the case. Courts are not required, however, to follow the opinions expressed in secondary legal material because such authority is only persuasive rather than mandatory.

§ 8.3 The Hierarchy of Legal Authority

Under the "supremacy clause" of the United States Constitution, the Constitution is "the supreme law of the land." Neither the Congress nor a state legislature may enact laws that conflict with the Constitution. A state, for example, may not enact a law that would deprive citizens of rights of free speech guaranteed by the First Amendment to the United States Constitution.

The states enjoy authority to adopt their own constitutions, statutes, and administrative regulations, as long as those laws do not contradict federal law. As at the federal level, there is a hierarchy of authority within state law: no state legislature has the power to enact a statute that violates that state's constitution; no state administrative agency has the power to promulgate a regulation that violates a state statute.

There is a similar hierarchy of judicial authority. If, for example, a court case raises a federal constitutional question, then the court will look first to any United States Supreme Court decisions concerning the constitutional provision in question. A Supreme Court case concerning the precise constitutional question at hand is mandatory: the court will simply apply the Supreme Court's analysis and dispose of the question accordingly. Case law from lower federal courts (a United States Court of Appeals or federal district court, for example) may be "persuasive" but such opinions are not mandatory if the Supreme Court has already spoken to the issue. A parallel hierarchy exists at the state court level.

§ 8.3.1 Constitutions

You will learn in the chapter on Courts that our form of government—both federal and state—provides for three branches: executive, legislative, and judicial. The organization of the government and the rules for operation are established by constitution.

§ 8.3.2 Statutes

The legislative branches of the government—both federal and state—meet on a regular schedule. It is from the legislative branches of government that we get our statutes and codes. A member of a legislature introduces a bill which, if passed, becomes an act after it is signed by the President of the United States or a state governor. At the end of each legislative session—federal or state—the acts are published in chronological order.

After a legislative session has adjourned, the laws passed during that session are compiled in volumes called "session laws." These books contain the full text of each new law. The acts appear in the session laws in the order in which they were passed during the session. The session laws enacted by Congress are called *Statutes at Large*. The session laws enacted by a state legislature are given titles such as *Laws of Washington, 1998*.

Then, the laws published in the session law volumes are "codified" according to their subject matter. Codification places or inserts the provisions of the new law in the existing state code according to the topic(s) that the new law addresses. Thus, Title 26 of the United States Code contains the Internal Revenue Code. A new law amending some aspect of the Internal Revenue Code will be codified in the pertinent section of Title 26. Frequently, different aspects of a particular session law will amend several different areas of the law. For example, a new session law amending the Internal Revenue Code may also include criminal enforcement provisions that belong in Title 18 ("Crimes and Criminal Procedure") of the United States Code. Accordingly, individual provisions of a particular session law may be assigned to a variety of titles within the pertinent code.

Codification enables the legal researcher to find the law relevant to a given legal question because codes organize legislation in a hierarchical fashion by subject matter. In addition to their topical organization, federal and state codes have indexes and other finding tools to enable the researcher to find all of the provisions relating to a particular subject. Legal research would be next to impossible if the researcher had to find all of the law relevant to a particular subject by reading volumes of session laws.

§ 8.3.3 Ordinances

Local ordinances are similar to state statutes. In fact, they can be thought of as local statutes. Towns and cities usually come into existence with state government approval, either under a specific act dealing with each municipality or under general authority which sets out the procedure for incorporation by a municipality. When a town or city is recognized as a municipality, that recognition carries with it the right to enact certain legislation. Usually, municipalities adopt their own traffic ordinances, zoning ordinances, tax ordinances, Sunday closing laws (blue laws), and other laws of that nature. They usually develop their own election procedures and their own licensing procedures as well.

§ 8.3.4 Administrative Regulations

Federal and state administrative agencies develop and administer programs entrusted to them by statute. Thus, the Social Security Act created the Social Security Administration and authorized it to promulgate rules to carry out its statutory mandate. Legislative bodies lack the time and the expertise to enact statutes that are comprehensive enough to govern administrative agencies. So, Congress and state legislatures delegate "rule-making authority" to the agencies themselves. Administrative regulations are legally binding, despite the fact that such rules are not enacted by elected officials.

On the federal level, new administrative regulations appear in the Federal Register, which is published daily. Just as new session laws are ultimately organized by topic in the applicable code, federal regulations are then "codified" by subject matter within the Code of Federal Regulations. A parallel scheme exists on the state level: new administrative rules appear first in a "register" published by the state and then are organized by subject matter into an administrative code. To make sure that an existing regulation is current, the legal researcher must understand how to check the pertinent "register" for changes in the regulation that have occurred since publication of the most recent administrative code.

§ 8.3.5 Court Rules

Each court may adopt rules for conducting business before the court. Usually these rules deal with the mechanical processes of prosecuting and defending a legal matter.

§ 8.3.6 Judicial Decisions

Every federal and state appellate court issues judicial decisions. In general, "trial courts" at the state level (often known as "superior courts") do not publish written opinions. The federal district courts, the "trial courts" of the federal judiciary, however, do publish many of their decisions.

The decisions of a particular court are published in books called "reporters." The decisions of the United States Supreme Court, for example, are published by the federal government in a series entitled the *United States Reports*. United States Supreme Court cases are also published by private legal publishers, notably the *Supreme Court Reporter* by West Group and the *Lawyers' Edition of the United States Decisions* by LexisNexis Law Publishing. Decisions of the 13 United States Circuit Courts of Appeal are reported in the Federal Reporter (F., F.2d, and F.3d). The Federal Supplement contains many reported decisions of the United States District Courts (F.Supp. and F.Supp.2d). The Federal Appendix contains selected unreported decisions of the U.S. District Courts (F.App.) Federal district court cases dealing primarily with the construction of the federal rules are reported in Federal Rules Decisions (F.R.D.).

At one time each state published its own reports, and those reports were known as official reports. West published reports containing the same cases known as unofficial reports. However, an increasing number of states have discontinued publishing their own reports and rely solely on the National Reporter System. West does publish separately the official reports of some of the states, and about one-fourth of the states which no longer publish their own official reports have officially adopted or rely on the decisions reported in the West regional reporters.

West Group publishes all reported out-of-state appellate court decisions in the United States in an accurate and timely manner. These state appellate court decisions are published by West Group in regional reporters. At present the National Reporter System is comprised of seven regional reporters as follows:

ATLANTIC: Maine, Vermont, New Hampshire, Connecticut, Rhode Island, Pennsylvania, New Jersey, Delaware, Maryland, District of Columbia

NORTH EASTERN: Illinois, Indiana, Massachusetts, New York, Ohio

NORTH WESTERN: North Dakota, South Dakota, Nebraska, Minnesota, Iowa, Wisconsin, Michigan

PACIFIC: Washington, Oregon, California, Idaho, Nevada, Montana, Wyoming, Utah, Arizona, New Mexico, Colorado, Kansas, Oklahoma, Alaska, Hawaii

SOUTHERN: Louisiana, Mississippi, Alabama, Florida

SOUTH EASTERN: West Virginia, Virginia, North Carolina, South Carolina, Georgia

SOUTH WESTERN: Texas, Missouri, Arkansas, Kentucky, Tennessee

(*See* Illustration 8–1.)

For court opinions issued prior to the beginning of the National Reporter System in 1880, one must consult older volumes of official state reports or the set called Federal Cases for lower federal courts.

Illustration 8–1

NATIONAL REPORTER SYSTEM MAP

Showing the States included in each Reporter group

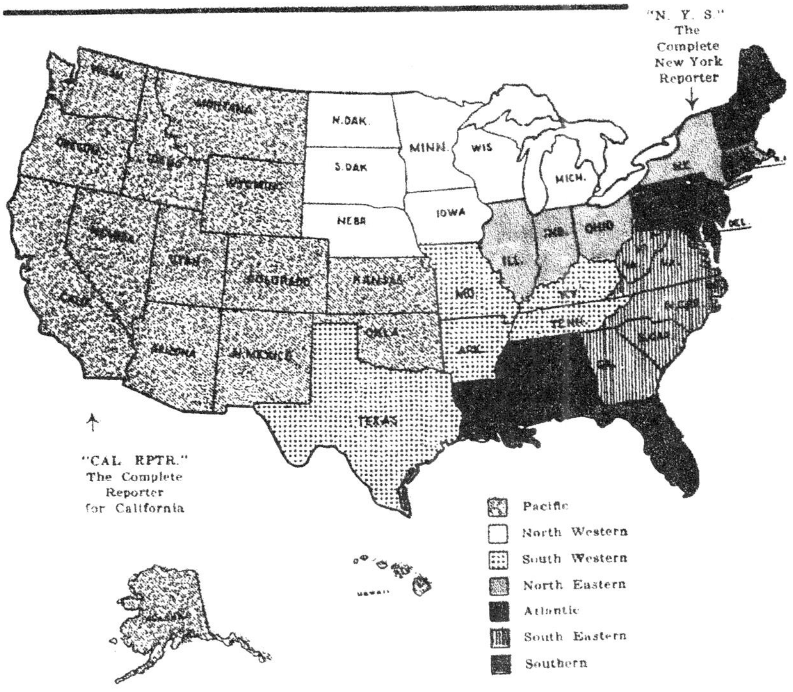

The National Reporter System also includes the Supreme Court Reporter, the Federal Reporter, the Federal Supplement, Federal Rules Decisions, West's Bankruptcy Reporter, the New York Supplement, West's California Reporter, West's Illinois Decisions, and West's Military Justice Reporter.

The reporter listed next to the states includes all appellate decisions from those states. Many states have adopted the National Reporter System as their official state reports.

§ 8.3.7 The Decision

A "decision" published in a case law reporter is the opinion of the court, written by one of the judges. It is the decision of the court, resolving legal issues properly presented to it, which constitutes primary legal authority.

Rules of citation dictate how judicial decisions should be identified. When a lawyer wants to "cite" to a judicial decision in a brief, for example, the lawyer sets forth the name of the case, the volume of the reporter in which it appears, the page on which the decision begins, and the year the opinion was issued. For example, the United States Supreme Court opinion in *Roe v. Wade* begins at page 113 of volume 410 of the United States Reports. Thus, the "citation" for the case is *Roe v. Wade*, 410 U.S. 113 (1973).

§ 8.4 The Role of Case Citators In Legal Research

Case law is dynamic. For example, the United States Supreme Court may reverse a decision by a United States Court of Appeals. With the stroke of a pen, the Supreme Court can thus invalidate a decision that had represented "good law" in the Ninth Circuit. After the Supreme Court has struck down the lower court's decision, it would be an error for a lawyer to offer that Court of Appeals' opinion as authority before any court.

Admittedly, the majority of appellate decisions are never reversed (by a higher court) or overruled (by a subsequent court with appropriate authority). The meaning of an individual case may change dramatically, however, as subsequent judicial decisions discuss, interpret, refine, and apply that case in new circumstances. Thus, for example, to fully understand the United States Supreme Court's decision in *Roe v. Wade*, the careful legal researcher considers how that decision has been subsequently construed by the Supreme Court and by any lower court whose decisions would be mandatory authority in the case at hand. Accordingly, a legal researcher must examine the subsequent history of any case they intend to cite as authority for a particular proposition.

Publications called "citators" help the lawyer with this task by listing the citations to all of the judicial decisions that have "cited" (mentioned) a given case. Citators assign "treatment codes" to the subsequent citations, so that the lawyer can tell at a glance whether the case in question "followed," "distinguished," "explained," "questioned," "criticized," or "overruled" the cited case.

§ 8.4.1 Shepardizing

The Shepard's Company is the oldest and best-known publisher of American legal citation services. Until quite recently, the Shepard's Company enjoyed a near monopoly in the publication of case citators. For this reason, generations of lawyers have referred to the process of researching the subsequent history of a case as "Shepardizing."

A Shepard's citator is published for each of the federal court reporters (Supreme Court, United States Courts of Appeals, federal district courts, etc.), for each of West's Regional Reporters, and for each of the individual state court reporters. Shepard's also offers citation services for federal and state constitutional provisions, statutes, administrative regulations, court rules, etc.; these services provide lists of cases construing such provisions.

Illustration 8–2 shows a typical page from a Shepard's case citator. Notice that the name of the reporter ("Pacific Reporter") and the pertinent reporter volume number appear at the top of the page. The numbers in bold under the pertinent volume number represent the page numbers on which individual cases begin. The entries listed underneath each page number are the citations to the judicial opinions that have cited to the case in question.

In addition to helping the legal researcher verify that a case remains "good law," case citators identify subsequent decisions that may provide additional support for the position the lawyer wants to take. All things being equal, a recent decision from the United States Supreme Court reaffirming a principle established by an earlier decision is more powerful authority than the earlier decision standing alone.

Thus, a case law citator serves two purposes: (1) it helps verify whether, in light of subsequent precedent, a case can still be cited as authority for a principle established by it, and (2) it is a "case-finding tool" that leads the researcher to other, more current cases and secondary resources concerning the cited decision.

Illustration 8–2

PACIFIC REPORTER, 2d SERIES — Vol. 440

Pa
268A2d93
321A2d882
17ALR3d146s

– 1020 –
(103Az260)
444P2d[1]450
535P2d[1]48
q390FS[4]1161
Fla
260So2d253
Va
165SE409
95ALR2d1122s

Vol. 440

– 1 –
441P2d[3]328
446P2d[4]556
463P2d[1]28
464P2d[3]534
476P2d[1]484
486P2d[1]239
549P2d[3]1171
550P2d[3]1117
j550P2d[3]1124
j550P2d[2]1126
NM
484P2d[1]342
j484P2d[1]349

– 7 –
s441P2d320
d464P2d[1]534
d464P2d[3]543
475P2d[1]549

– 15 –
(21U2d40)
458P2d[1]875
517P2d[2]1023

– 17 –
(21U2d43)
s374P2d254

– 23 –
(21U2d51)
d465P2d[4]176
504P2d37
526P2d[4]1189

– 29 –
(103Az264)
463P2d[6]111
469P2d[4]850
471P2d[6]714
471P2d[7]714
483P2d[2]557
494P2d[1]378
502P2d1334
502P2d[7]1353
506P2d[1]645
508P2d[3]339
510P2d[5]51
510P2d[7]51
511P2d[6]626
511P2d[7]695
549P2d[3]229
j549P2d[3]232
Wis
230NW903
65ALR3d1102n

– 32 –
(7AzA396)
445P2d[1]188
453P2d[1]232
459P2d[1]323
370FS[1]867
Mass
277NE118
42ALR3d31n
42ALR3d81n
42ALR3d97n
42ALR3d153n
42ALR3d157n
42ALR3d168n

– 39 –
(7AzA403)
v449P2d596

– 44 –
(7AzA408)
452P2d[9]724
j452P2d[9]726
457P2d[5]347
457P2d[8]348
459P2d[4]319
459P2d[14]320
480P2d[9]1006
485P2d[8]569
500P2d[7]1134
500P2d[9]1134
500P2d
[[12]1135
511P2d[7]183
f524P2d[3]1317
f524P2d[5]1317
f524P2d[7]1317
f524P2d[9]1318
f524P2d
[[11]1318
524P2d[5]1320
f536P2d[7]241
f536P2d[8]241
f536P2d[9]241
537P2d[1]935
537P2d[12]936
539P2d545
Okla
509P2d[1]903

– 54 –
(7AzA418)
465P2d[1]593
506P2d[1]1088

– 58 –
(7AzA422)
450P2d[8]713
451P2d[8]647
f468P2d[2]595
f468P2d[3]595
477P2d[2]751
488P2d[11]507
492P2d[6]1190
504P2d[2]957
506P2d[6]652
f512P2d
[[12]1228
q547P2d[12]479
f548P2d
[[11]1203
f548P2d
[[12]1203
j549P2d[12]232

Fla
268So2d555
Iowa
202NW76
Me
249A2d757
14ALR2d605s

– 65 –
(68C2d547)
(68CaR1)
447P2d[1]654
447P2d[5]654
d449P2d[5]211
454P2d[5]695
457P2d[9]580
458P2d[4]505
459P2d[9]259
465P2d[9]27
506P2d[3]1009
j506P2d[3]1012
j506P2d
[[11]1013
f514P2d[8]1209
f514P2d[9]1209
537P2d[1]910
537P2d[5]910
e537P2d[9]910
e537P2d[11]911
537P2d[8]917
70CaR[11]25
73CaR[1]414
73CaR[6]414
d74CaR[5]275
75CaR[5]56
77CaR[5]799
78CaR[1]129
79CaR[9]748
80CaR[4]593
81CaR[9]5
83CaR[5]129
84CaR[9]139
85CaR[11]754
90CaR[9]321
91CaR[5]793
91CaR[11]794
103CaR[3]103
103CaR[7]106
103CaR[4]681
d103CaR[6]682
106CaR[3]633
j106CaR[3]636
j106CaR[11]637
108CaR675
f110CaR[8]129
f110CaR[9]129
110CaR[1]211
114CaR864
115CaR[1]136
116CaR[9]725
121CaR56
122CaR[1]790
122CaR[5]790
e122CaR[9]791
e122CaR
[[11]791
122CaR[9]797
Alk
f526P2d[11]22
f526P2d[12]23
Ariz
468P2d[11]563

– 76 –
(50H314)
(50H452)

f517P2d[1]60
532P2d[1]398
480F2d[1]1020
402FS98
L402FS[1]99
Ore
462P2d673
Fla
294So2d78

– 95 –
(50H298)
408FS[4]51

– 100 –
(103Az267)
s463P2d65
447P2d[13]555
455P2d[13]458
464P2d[6]827
474P2d[2]865
479P2d[14]729
485P2d[7]812
490P2d[6]563
492P2d[2]1166
NM
508P2d[6]31
20ALR2d1421s

– 105 –
(103Az272)
473P2d[17]788
489P2d[17]16
493P2d[17]498
d458F2d
[[10]1267
63ALR2d1160s

– 113 –
Case 1
(7AzA429)

– 113 –
Case 2
(7AzA429)
s436P2d942
s450P2d722
8ALR2d6s

– 117 –
(21U2d60)
508P2d[2]542
Nev
472P2d[1]337

– 119 –
cc409P2d847
453P2d[5]472
d456P2d[1]454
468P2d[7]49
470P2d[1]271
488P2d[4]722
489P2d[4]459
490P2d[6]909
494P2d[5]792
494P2d[6]792
514P2d238
520P2d[5]95
520P2d[6]95
520P2d[7]95

– 122 –
(84Nev300)
f442P2d[2]913
f533F2d[1]489
f389FS[2]851

65FRD[1]636
82ALR2d1429s

– 124 –
(84Nev298)
495P2d[1]633

– 129 –
Case 2
(151Mt574)

– 129 –
Case 3
(151Mt574)

– 130 –
(79NM92)
s418P2d545
cc467P2d27
490P2d[3]464
j506P2d[2]353

– 133 –
(79NM95)
465P2d[1]286
491P2d[1]538

– 136 –
Case 1
(79NM98)

– 136 –
Case 2
(79NM98)
s439P2d567

– 136 –
Case 3
(79NM98)

– 136 –
Case 4
(79NM98)

– 137 –
(92Ida204)
442P2d[1]778
44ALR3d49n
44ALR3d65n

– 141 –
(92Ida208)
547P2d549

– 143 –
(92Ida210)
59ALR2d1299s
89ALR2d1040s

– 151 –
(165Col500)
71ALR2d284s

– 152 –
(165Col514)
458P2d[5]78
458P2d[3]79
502P2d[3]1121
511P2d[1]922
513P2d[1]1086
516P2d[1]1143

– 155 –
(165Col371)
506P2d[2]414
d533P2d[2]52

d533P2d[3]52

– 158 –
(165Col475)
498P2d[1]951
o498P2d[2]952

– 162 –
(73W582)

– 164 –
(73W608)

– 167 –
(73W634)
462P2d[20]986
466P2d[17]129
471P2d[10]136
476P2d[9]130
476P2d[10]130
544P2d[7]775
Kan
551P2d[8]833
Iowa
190NW404
Miss
301So2d863
NY
256NE174
307S2d860
338S2d801
SD
163NW546
17ALR2d146s
31ALR3d594n

– 175 –
(73W601)
472P2d[4]396
474P2d[2]108
f492P2d[2]1374
499P2d[1]876
j500P2d[2]86
510P2d[2]1121
521P2d[2]215
536P2d[2]584
549P2d[2]24

– 179 –
(73W629)
499P2d[1]236
491F2d[6]439
29ALR2d530s

– 182 –
(73W671)
444P2d[1]693
f453P2d[1]858
465P2d[1]689

– 184 –
(73W596)

– 187 –
(73W751)
95ALR2d351s

– 192 –
(73W660)
US cert den
in393US1096
cc446F2d861
444P2d[7]655
447P2d[16]608
477P2d[9]187
486P2d[1]1120

489P2d[3]170
489P2d[4]170
489P2d[6]170
489P2d[7]170
494P2d
[[11]1021
495P2d[1]678
495P2d[2]678
507P2d[1]167
507P2d[2]167
523P2d[6]1199
530P2d[1]312
538P2d[13]852
544P2d[1]777
Colo
470P2d[14]40
Nev
444P2d[18]897
Md
340A2d369
NJ
247A2d12
21ALR2d1088s
31ALR3d620n

– 199 –
(73W653)
444P2d[5]159
477P2d[7]6
479P2d[1]950
499P2d[2]904
508P2d[5]1402
518P2d[5]700
20ALR3d473s

– 204 –
v395US161
v23LE175
v89SC1647
s456P2d570
o450P2d[2]906

– 211 –
481P2d[2]187
482P2d[2]954
490P2d[1]256

– 212 –
(249Or633)

– 214 –
(250Or19)
US cert den
in393US891
479P2d[3]511

– 219 –
(250Or140)
451P2d[6]117

– 224 –
(250Or39)
440P2d867
444P2d[1]946
444P2d[2]946
445P2d[2]488
459P2d[2]995
461P2d[1]269
461P2d[2]269
461P2d[4]843
d463P2d[1]877
d463P2d[2]877
465P2d241
j465P2d242
f466P2d[1]621
470P2d[2]378

470P2d[4]380
470P2d[5]380
471P2d[4]443
471P2d[1]833
471P2d[5]836
471P2d[2]837
475P2d994
478P2d[4]650
j485P2d[2]417
j485P2d[3]417
f485P2d[4]1239
e485P2d
[[4]1240
486P2d[4]590
486P2d[5]1314
487P2d[4]109
489P2d[5]975
j491P2d[2]1001
j491P2d[5]1001
494P2d[1]468
494P2d[4]468
495P2d[5]290
500P2d[5]477
520P2d[4]469
521P2d[4]1322
527P2d[4]425
527P2d[5]425
528P2d[4]95
530P2d[5]546
550P2d[1]747
551P2d[4]493

– 229 –
(250Or54)
471P2d[3]849
527P2d[2]135
534P2d[2]192
549P2d[2]513
551P2d[2]458
Idaho
509P2d[3]1322
NJ
342A2d167
24ALR3d986s

– 231 –
(250Or196)
s417P2d1002

– 233 –
(68C2d563)
(68CaR161)
US cert den
in393US1057
s64CaR625
cc464F2d
[1293
o453P2d[4]359
464P2d[5]79
481P2d[4]242
493P2d[1]1189
j508P2d[1]1140
f70CaR[3]62
f70CaR[4]62
70CaR[4]613
72CaR[5]628
72CaR[4]749
73CaR[4]504
74CaR[4]763
75CaR865
o76CaR[4]815
77CaR[5]537
80CaR[5]206
80CaR[5]797
81CaR[5]712
Continued

963

Volume 2. Part 2. Page 963. Citing Volume 440.

§ 8.4.2 Electronic Citation Services

Shepard's

Shepardizing a case in the print volumes of Shepard's citators is a cumbersome, time-consuming task. Volumes of Shepard's citators do not cumulate. To Shepardize a case, the researcher must typically consult a bound volume of citations for the reporter in question as well as a series of supplements, each one more current than the last. To make a complete list of all cited cases, the researcher must (1) find a library that has the Shepard's reports for the case reporter in question, (2) identify and collect all of the appropriate bound volumes and supplements, (3) mark the relevant pages, and (4) take them all to the copy machine. Then, there is the task of locating and reading the cases on the Shepard's cite-list.

The process of Shepardizing cases became much easier when Shepard's created an electronic version of its library of citators. The Shepard's service is available on CD–ROM from Shepard's itself and through online legal research services such as LexisNexis.

Shepardizing a case on one of these services involves little more than simply typing its citation. Only a keystroke is required to print the entire Shepard's report for a case. The electronic version of Shepard's also allows the researcher to customize the Shepard's report, limiting it, for example, to cases of a particular jurisdiction, cases published after a certain date, cases dealing with a specific aspect of the opinion, etc. The version of Shepard's available through LexisNexis even creates "hypertext links" between the citations listed on the Shepard's report and the cases themselves, enabling the legal researcher to move easily from the Shepard's report to the text of a case listed on the report and back again. These links are a valuable service for the lawyer who lacks convenient access to a comprehensive law library. Finally, the Shepard's service available through LexisNexis, which now owns Shepard's, purports to be even more current than the print-version of Shepard's.

Shepardizing cases online is much faster, more current, and more reliable than Shepardizing cases using "the books" that most new law school graduates lack any substantial experience with Shepardizing in the traditional way (law students typically enjoy unlimited free access to LexisNexis and Westlaw). In general, this is advantageous because Shepardizing cases online is almost always more cost-effective than using the books. This lack of experience can represent a handicap, however, for new lawyers who find themselves in law offices that lack electronic access to Shepard's citation services.

Westlaw's KeyCite

In 1997, Westlaw introduced its own citator service, KeyCite. KeyCite provides the status and history of cases, statutes, patents, and federal regulations, as well as an exhaustive list of citing references. This service is designed to improve upon Shepard's by organizing cited cases according to "depth of treatment." Thus, a KeyCite report groups cases according to whether they "examine," "discuss," "cite to," or simply "mention" the cited case. Each of these categories represents a defined point along a continuum of analysis.

KeyCite's "depth of treatment" analysis can save the legal researcher substantial time by identifying those cases that have actually construed the cited case. Many cases cite to previous cases as authority for extremely well-established propositions (the standard for granting a motion for summary judgment, for example). Reading such cases by way of checking the status of the cited case is completely unnecessary. By contrast, with KeyCite, Shepard's simply lists all of the cases that have cited to the case in question. "History" and "treatment codes" assigned by the Shepard's editors do help identify cases that have analyzed the case in question but, for some, KeyCite's approach can be easier to understand.

Autocite and KeyCite

As explained earlier, Shepardizing a case enables the researcher to answer two questions: (1) Is the case still good law?, and (2) Are there other, later cases that cite to this case that might be important to me? Early in a legal research project, a lawyer uses Shepard's for both purposes.

After the lawyer has completed all the necessary research and has finished writing the brief, however, the lawyer's primary concern is whether the cases cited in the brief are still good law. At that point, the careful lawyer checks to make sure that each case can still be cited as authority for the proposition for which it is cited. For this purpose, the lawyer needs much less information than is typically supplied by Shepard's. The lawyer needs only (1) a complete "appellate history" of the cited case itself. (Has it been appealed to a higher court? Has that higher court ruled on the appeal?) and any "negative, indirect" history of the case (Has the case been overruled? Have other courts criticized its reasoning? Have other courts in the jurisdiction declined to follow the cited case?)

Both LexisNexis and Westlaw have developed online products that serve this purpose. "Autocite" (available on LexisNexis) and "KeyCite" (on Westlaw) provides a full appellate history of the cited case itself and describes any negative treatment of the case by other courts. These services are easy to use and are comparatively inexpensive.

§ 8.4.3 Digests

Digests are detailed subject indexes on points of law contained in reported cases. The American Digest System published by West Group is the master index to all cases reported in the National Reporter System. The method for compiling this index is described below in Sections 8.4.4 and 8.4.5.

Sets of digests include the comprehensive Decennial and General Digests; regional digests that correspond to some of the regional reporters (Atlantic, North Western, Pacific, South Eastern); state digests for most states (not including Delaware, Nevada, or Utah; there are combined digests for North and South Dakota and Virginia and West Virginia); and the federal digest covering all of the federal courts.

§ 8.4.4 Headnotes

When the publisher receives a decision from a court, its staff attorneys review it for the points of law decided in that case. A brief summary of each point of law is then written, and these summaries appear at the beginning of each reported case.

§ 8.4.5 Topic and Key Number System

The Topic and Key Number System is a master index of case headnotes. West Group has devised a list of over 400 general areas of law, such as Mortgages and Wills, and has further divided each of these topics into a numbered outline ("key numbers"). Every headnote composed by a West Group editor is assigned a topic and key number. The headnotes appear at the beginning of the reported case with the topic and key number designation and are then collected by topic, or subject, in the digests. Once researchers have identified the pertinent topic and key number that collects headnotes on the point of law being researched, they can consult any unit of the American Digest System to locate additional cases on point. Key Numbers provide a subject-based way to research case law, and can be used in print digests or on Westlaw.

§ 8.4.6 American Law Reports

American Law Reports (A.L.R.), originally a selective approach to court reports, is used today for the annotations or legal memoranda following the reported case. Each annotation focuses on a specialized issue of law and summarizes pertinent cases and other authority from all jurisdictions. A.L.R. annotations are located through the A.L.R. Index, American Jurisprudence, Shepard's citators, and other cross-references.

Illustration 8–3

OUTLINE OF THE LAW

Digest Topics arranged for your convenience
by Seven Main Divisions of Law
and their numerical designations

1. PERSONS
2. PROPERTY
3. CONTRACTS
4. TORTS
5. CRIMES
6. REMEDIES
7. GOVERNMENT

1. PERSONS

RELATING TO NATURAL PERSONS IN GENERAL

Civil Rights 78
Dead Bodies 116
Death 117
Domicile 135
Drugs and Narcotics 138
Food 178
Health and Environment 199
Holidays 201
Intoxicating Liquors 223
Names 269
Poisons 304
Seals 347
Signatures 355
Sunday 369
Time 378
Weapons 406

PARTICULAR CLASSES OF NATURAL PERSONS

Absentees 5
Aliens 24
Chemical Dependents 762
Children Out-of-Wedlock 76H
Citizens 77
Convicts 98
Indians 209
Infants 211
Mental Health 257A
Paupers 292
Slaves 356
Spendthrifts 359

PERSONAL RELATIONS

Adoption 17
Attorney and Client 45
Employers' Liability 148A
Executors and Administrators 162
Guardian and Ward 196
Husband and Wife 205
Labor Relations 232A
Marriage 253
Master and Servant 255
Parent and Child 285
Principal and Agent 308
Workers' Compensation 413

ASSOCIATED AND ARTIFICIAL PERSONS

Associations 41
Beneficial Associations 54
Building and Loan Associations 66
Clubs 80
Colleges and Universities 81
Corporations 101
Exchanges 160
Joint-Stock Companies and Business Trusts 225
Partnership 289
Religious Societies 332

PARTICULAR OCCUPATIONS

Accountants 11A
Agriculture 23
Auctions and Auctioneers 47
Aviation 48B
Banks and Banking 52
Bridges 64
Brokers 65
Canals 68
Carriers 70
Commerce 83
Consumer Credit 92B
Consumer Protection 92H
Credit Reporting Agencies 108A
Detectives 125
Electricity 145
Explosives 164
Factors 167
Ferries 172
Gas 190
Hawkers and Peddlers 198
Innkeepers 213
Insurance 217
Licenses 238
Manufactures 251
Monopolies 265
Physicians and Surgeons 299
Pilots 300
Railroads 320
Seamen 348
Shipping 354
Steam 362
Telecommunications 372
Theaters and Shows 376
Towage 380
Turnpikes and Toll Roads 391
Urban Railroads 396A
Warehousemen 403
Wharves 408

2. PROPERTY

NATURE, SUBJECTS, AND INCIDENTS OF OWNERSHIP IN GENERAL

Abandoned and Lost Property 1
Accession 7
Adjoining Landowners 15
Confusion of Goods 90
Improvements 206
Property 315

PARTICULAR SUBJECTS AND INCIDENTS OF OWNERSHIP

Animals 28
Annuities 29
Automobiles 48A
Boundaries 59
Cemeteries 71
Common Lands 84
Copyrights and Intellectual Property 99
Crops 111
Fences 171
Fish 176
Fixtures 177
Franchises 183
Game 187
Good Will 192
Logs and Logging 245
Mines and Minerals 260
Navigable Waters 270
Party Walls 290
Patents 291
Public Lands 317
Trade Regulation 382
Waters and Water Courses 405
Woods and Forests 411

PARTICULAR CLASSES OF ESTATES OR INTERESTS IN PROPERTY

Charities 75
Condominium 89A
Dower and Curtesy 136
Easements 141
Estates in Property 154
Joint Tenancy 226
Landlord and Tenant 233
Life Estates 240
Perpetuities 298
Powers 307
Remainders 333
Reversions 338
Tenancy in Common 373
Trusts 390

PARTICULAR MODES OF ACQUIRING OR TRANSFERRING PROPERTY

Abstracts of Title 6
Adverse Possession 20
Alteration of Instruments 25
Assignments 38
Chattel Mortgages 76
Conversion 97
Dedication 119
Deeds 120
Descent and Distribution 124
Escheat 152
Fraudulent Conveyances 186
Gifts 191
Lost Instruments 246
Mortgages 266
Pledges 303
Secured Transactions 349A
Wills 409

3. CONTRACTS

NATURE, REQUISITES, AND INCIDENTS OF AGREEMENTS IN GENERAL

Contracts 95
Customs and Usages 113
Frauds, Statute of 185
Interest 219
Usury 398

PARTICULAR CLASSES OF AGREEMENTS

Bailment 50
Bills and Notes 56
Bonds 58
Breach of Marriage Promise 61
Champerty and Maintenance 74
Compromise and Settlement 89
Covenants 108
Deposits and Escrows 122A
Exchange of Property 159
Gaming 188
Guaranty 195
Implied and Constructive Contracts 205H
Indemnity 208
Joint Adventures 224
Lotteries 247
Principal and Surety 309
Rewards 340
Sales 343
Subscriptions 367
Vendor and Purchaser 400

PARTICULAR CLASSES OF IMPLIED OR CONSTRUCTIVE CONTRACTS OR QUASI CONTRACTS

Account Stated 11
Contribution 96

PARTICULAR MODES OF DISCHARGING CONTRACTS

Novation 278
Payment 294
Release 331
Subrogation 366
Tender 374

4. TORTS

Assault and Battery 37
Collision 82
Conspiracy 91
False Imprisonment 168
Forcible Entry and Detainer 179

Fraud 184
Libel and Slander 237
Malicious Prosecution 249
Negligence 272
Nuisance 279
Products Liability 313A
Seduction 350
Torts 379
Trespass 386
Trover and Conversion 389
Waste 904

5. CRIMES

Abduction 3
Abortion and Birth Control 4
Adulteration 18
Adultery 19
Affray 22
Arson 36
Bigamy 55
Blasphemy 57
Breach of the Peace 62
Bribery 63
Burglary 67
Common Scold 86
Compounding Offenses 88
Counterfeiting 103
Criminal Law 110
Disorderly Conduct 129
Disorderly House 130
Disturbance of Public Assemblage 133
Dueling 140
Embezzlement 146
Embracery 147
Escape 151
Extortion and Threats 165
False Personation 169
False Pretenses 170
Fires 175
Forgery 181
Fornication 182
Homicide 203
Incest 207
Insurrection and Sedition 218
Kidnapping 232
Larceny 234
Lewdness 236
Malicious Mischief 248
Mayhem 256
Miscegenation 261
Neutrality Laws 273
Obscenity 281
Obstructing Justice 282
Perjury 297
Piracy 301
Prize Fighting 312
Prostitution 316
Rape 321
Receiving Stolen Goods 324
Rescue 337
Riot 341
Robbery 342
Sodomy 357
Suicide 368
Treason 384
Unlawful Assembly 396
Vagrancy 399

6. REMEDIES

REMEDIES BY ACT OR AGREEMENT OF PARTIES

Accord and Satisfaction 8
Arbitration 33
Submission of Controversy 365

REMEDIES BY POSSESSION OR NOTICE

Liens 239
Lis Pendens 242
Maritime Liens 252
Mechanics' Liens 257
Notice 277
Salvage 344

MEANS AND METHODS OF PROOF

Acknowledgment 12
Affidavits 21
Estoppel 156
Evidence 157
Oath 280
Records 326
Witnesses 410

CIVIL ACTIONS IN GENERAL

Action 13
Declaratory Judgment 118A
Election of Remedies 143
Limitation of Actions 241
Parties 287
Set-Off and Counterclaim 352
Venue 401

PARTICULAR PROCEEDINGS IN CIVIL ACTIONS

Abatement and Revival 2
Appearance 31
Costs 102
Damages 115
Execution 161
Exemptions 163
Homestead 202
Judgment 228
Jury 230
Motions 267
Pleading 302
Process 313
Reference 327
Stipulations 363
Trial 388

PARTICULAR REMEDIES INCIDENT TO CIVIL ACTIONS

Arrest 35
Assistance, Writ of 40
Attachment 44
Bail 49
Deposits in Court 123
Garnishment 189
Injunction 212
Judicial Sales 22A
Ne Exeat 271
Pretrial Procedure 307A
Receivers 323
Recognizances 325
Sequestration 351
Undertakings 392

PARTICULAR MODES OF REVIEW IN CIVIL ACTIONS

Appeal and Error 30
Audita Querela 48
Certiorari 73
Exceptions, Bill of 158
New Trial 275
Review 339

ACTIONS TO ESTABLISH OWNERSHIP OR RECOVER POSSESSION OF SPECIFIC PROPERTY

Detinue 126
Ejectment 142
Entry, Writ of 149
Interpleader 222
Possessory Warrant 305
Quieting Title 318
Real Actions 322
Replevin 335
Trespass to Try Title 387

FORMS OF ACTIONS FOR DEBTS OR DAMAGES

Account, Action on 10
Action on the Case 14
Assumpsit, Action of 42
Covenant, Action of 107
Debt, Action of 117G

ACTIONS FOR PARTICULAR FORMS OR SPECIAL RELIEF

Account 9
Cancellation of Instruments 69
Debtor and Creditor 117T
Divorce 134
Partition 288
Reformation of Instruments 328
Specific Performance 358

CIVIL PROCEEDINGS OTHER THAN ACTIONS

Habeas Corpus 197
Mandamus 250
Prohibition 314
Quo Warranto 319
Scire Facias 346
Supersedeas 370

SPECIAL CIVIL JURISDICTIONS AND PROCEDURE THEREIN

Admiralty 16
Bankruptcy 51
Equity 150
Federal Civil Procedure 170A

PROCEEDINGS PECULIAR TO CRIMINAL CASES

Extradition and Detainers 166
Fines 174
Forfeitures 180
Grand Jury 193
Indictment and Information 210
Pardon and Parole 284
Penalties 295
Searches and Seizures 349

7. GOVERNMENT

POLITICAL BODIES AND DIVISIONS

Counties 104
District of Columbia 132
Municipal Corporations 268
States 360
Territories 375
Towns 381
United States 393

SYSTEMS AND SOURCES OF LAW

Administrative Law and Procedure 15A
Common Law 85
Constitutional Law 92
International Law 221
Parliamentary Law 286
Statutes 361
Treaties 385

LEGISLATIVE AND EXECUTIVE POWERS AND FUNCTIONS

Bounties 60
Census 72
Commodity Futures Trading Regulation 83H
Customs Duties 114
Drains 137
Eminent Domain 148
Highways 200
Inspection 216
Internal Revenue 220
Levees and Flood Control 235
Pensions 296
Post Office 306
Private Roads 311
Public Contracts 316A
Public Utilities 317A
Schools 345
Securities Regulation 349B
Social Security and Public Welfare 356A
Taxation 371
Weights and Measures 407
Zoning and Planning 414

JUDICIAL POWERS AND FUNCTIONS, AND COURTS AND THEIR OFFICERS

Amicus Curiae 27
Clerks of Courts 79
Contempt 93
Court Commissioners 105
Courts 106
Federal Courts 170B
Judges 227
Justices of the Peace 231
Removal of Cases 334
Reports 336
United States Magistrates 394

CIVIL SERVICE, OFFICERS, AND INSTITUTIONS

Ambassadors and Consuls 26
Asylums 43
Attorney General 46
Coroners 100
District and Prosecuting Attorneys 131
Elections 144
Hospitals 204
Newspapers 274
Notaries 276
Officers and Public Employees 283
Prisons 310
Reformatories 329
Registers of Deeds 330
Sheriffs and Constables 353
United States Marshals 395

MILITARY AND NAVAL SERVICE AND WAR

Armed Services 34
Military Justice 258A
Militia 259
War and National Emergency 402

§ 8.5 Words and Phrases

Words and Phrases is a work that compiles, in dictionary form, judicial definitions of words and phrases. The state and federal cases from which these definitions are taken are identified. In a number of instances, this method of initiating legal research may be quite effective, as it leads researches to cases in which judges define the legal meaning of a word or phrase.

Illustration 8–4

CERTIFICATE OF STOCK

Cross References

Fund
Money
Property
Security
Share of Stock
Writing

In general

A "certificate of stock" expresses the contract between corporation and stockholders. Jay Ronald Co. v. Marshall Mortg. Corp., 40 N.Y.S.2d 391, 398, 265 App.Div. 622.

A "certificate of stock" is not the stock itself, but simply evidence of title to an interest in corporation. Lake Superior Dist. Power Co. v. Public Service Commission, 26 N.W.2d 278, 282, 250 Wis. 39.

"Certificates of stock" in a corporation are the paper representation of the incorporeal property right. Crocker v. Crocker, 257 P. 611, 617, 84 C.A. 114.

A certificate issued as part of an attempted fraudulent overissue of stock is not a "certificate of shares of stock." Smith v. Worcester & S. St. Ry. Co., 113 N.E. 462, 463, 224 Mass. 564.

In a remote sense, a "certificate of stock" is an interest in the property of the corporation, which might be in other states than either the corporation or the certificate of stock. Warner v. Brown, 121 N.E. 69, 70, 231 Mass. 333.

A "stock certificate" is merely a muniment or representative of title. The stock which it represents exists apart from the certificate, and its existence is contemplated to endure so long as the corporation continues. Zander v. New York Security & Trust Co., 70 N.E. 449, 451, 178 N.Y. 208, 102 Am.St.Rep. 492.

A certificate of stock is simply a written acknowledgment by a corporation of the interest of the holder in its property and fran-

In general—Cont'd

chises, and has no value except that derived from the company issuing it, its legal status being in the nature of a chose in action. Person v. Board of State Tax Com'rs, 115 S.E. 336, 346, 184 N.C. 499.

"Certificates of stock" take on the character of the stock in the corporation and are "choses in action" within statute providing that choses in action are not liable to be seized and sold under execution unless made so especially by statute. Tow v. Evans, 20 S.E.2d 922, 924, 194 Ga. 160.

Where debenture certificates issued by corporation, although payable out of earnings, were payable irrespective of sufficiency of earnings or surplus and there was a fixed maturity date when owner could demand payment, a finding that the certificates represented "indebtedness" rather than "stock ownership" was justified. Washmont Corp. v. Hendricksen, C.C.A.Wash., 137 F.2d 306, 308, 309.

A "certificate of stock" is a written acknowledgment by a corporation of the interest of the stockholder in its property and franchises. It has no value except that derived from the company issuing it, and its legal status is in the nature of a chose in action. The value of all the property owned by a corporation, including its franchise, is the value of all of its stock. Rhode Island Hospital Trust Co. v. Doughton, 121 S.E. 741, 747, 187 N.C. 263.

Receipt given by depositary for stockholders' committee, representing stock in bank and bank's affiliate, which was transferable on depositary's books and gave depositary power of attorney to transfer stock on corporate books, was not a "certificate of stock" within meaning of Uniform Stock Transfer Act. Commissioner of Banks v. Chase Securities Corp., Mass., 10 N.E.2d 472, 485, 298 Mass. 285.

A "certificate of stock" is, from one point of view, a mere muniment of title like a title deed. It is not the stock itself but evidence of the ownership of the stock; that is to say, it is a written acknowledgement by the corporation of the interest of the shareholder in the corporate property and franchises. It operates to transfer nothing from the corporation to the shareholders but merely affords to the latter evidence of his rights.

72

Excerpt taken from Words and Phrases Legally Defined [C4065]

§ 8.6 Legal Encyclopedias

Legal encyclopedias are books that recite principles of law supported by footnote references to pertinent cases from throughout the United States. The law topics are arranged alphabetically. The principal encyclopedias used in the United States are *Corpus Juris Secundum* (C.J.S.) and *American Jurisprudence Second* (Am. Jur. 2d). Legal encyclopedias are a good starting point for beginning legal research on a given topic. They provide a solid overview on areas of law, and are laden with footnotes directing the researcher to relevant primary and secondary legal sources.

Illustration 8–5

reasonable and ordinary care for his own safety;[82] and that it is an application of the rule, expressed in the maxim, Volenti non fit injuria, that one who invites an injury cannot make it the basis of a recovery.[83] Still another view finding favor with the courts is that the rule precluding recovery is in the nature of a penalty, established by public policy, to admonish all to use due care for their own safety.[84] In other words, the doctrine is said to be founded on the impolicy of allowing a person to recover for his own wrong, and the policy of making personal interests of men dependent on their own prudence and care.[85]

§ 117. Contributory Negligence Distinguished from Assumption of Risk and Other Doctrines

While the doctrine of assumed risk and the doctrine of contributory negligence are closely associated, and the former may be held in some cases to be a form or phase of the latter, they are nevertheless distinct doctrines of law and are not synonymous.

Library References

Negligence ⟹65.

Under certain circumstances the same acts or conduct may render one guilty of contributory negligence or give rise to the defense of assumption of risk or incurred risk.[86] Moreover, the defense of assumed or incurred risk has been held to be closely associated with contributory negligence,[87] and to be

82. La.—**Corpus Juris Secundum cited in** Normand v. Piazza, App., 145 So.2d 110, 113.
Tex.—Magnolia Petroleum Co. v. Owen, Civ.App., 101 S.W.2d 354, error dismissed.
Wash.—Hauswirth v. Pom-Arleau, 119 P.2d 674, 11 Wash.2d 354—Morris v. Chicago, M., St. P. & P. R. Co., 97 P.2d 119, 1 Wash.2d 587, opinion adhered to 100 P.2d 19, 1 Wash.2d 587—Chadwick v. Ek, 95 P.2d 398, 1 Wash.2d 117.

83. N.J.—Kimpel v. Moon, 174 A. 209, 113 N.J.Law 220—Schnackenberg v. Delaware, etc., R. Co., 93 A. 701, 86 N.J.Law 517, affirmed 98 A. 266, 89 N.J.Law 311.
N.Y.—Zurich General Accident & Liability Ins. Co. v. Childs Co., 171 N.E. 391, 253 N.Y. 324.

Relation voluntarily assumed
Maxim, Volenti non fit injuria, applies equally to any relation voluntarily assumed, contractual or otherwise.
N.Y.—Zurich General Accident & Liability Ins. Co. v. Childs Co., 171 N.E. 391, 253 N.Y. 324.

84. Wash.—Alexiou v. Nockas, 17 P.2d 911, 171 Wash. 369.
45 C.J. p 942 note 34.

85. Ariz.—MacDonald v. Eichenauer, 269 P.2d 1057, 77 Ariz. 252—Womack v. Preach, 165 P.2d 657, 64 Ariz. 61.
N.H.—Niemi v. Boston & M. R. R., 173 A. 361, 87 N.H. 1, affirmed 175 A. 245, 87 N.H. 1.
Tex.—St. Louis Southwestern R. Co. v. Arey, 179 S.W. 860, 107 Tex. 366, L.R.A.1916B 1065.

86. U.S.—Krolikowski v. Allstate Ins. Co., C.A.Wis., 283 F.2d 889.
Cal.—Vierra v. Fifth Ave. Rental Service, 383 P.2d 777, 60 C.2d 266, 32 Cal.Rptr. 193.
Hedding v. Pearson, 173 P.2d 382, 76 C.A.2d 481.
Conn.—Zullo, v. Zullo, 89 A.2d 216, 138 Conn. 712—L'Heureux v. Hurley, 168 A. 8, 117 Conn. 347.
La.—Benedetto v. Travelers Ins. Co., App., 172 So.2d 354, application denied 175 So.2d 108, 247 La. 872.
Md.—Wiggins v. State, Use of Collins, 192 A.2d 515, 232 Md. 228.
Mo.—**Corpus Juris Secundum cited in** Terry v. Boss Hotels, Inc., 376 S.W.2d 239, 247.
Neb.—Darnell v. Panhandle Co-op. Ass'n, 120 N.W.2d 278, 175 Neb. 40—**Corpus Juris Secundum cited in** Brackman v. Brackman, 100 N.W.2d 774, 780, 169 Neb. 650—Landrum v. Roddy, 12 N.W.2d 82, 143 Neb. 934, 149 A.L.R. 1041.
Ohio.—Centrello v. Basky, 128 N.E.2d 80, 164 Ohio St. 41—Morris v. Cleveland Hockey Club, 105 N.E.2d 419, 157 Ohio St. 225—Masters v. New York Cent. R. Co., 70 N.E.2d 898, 147 Ohio St. 293, certiorari denied 67 S.Ct. 1519, 331 U.S. 836, 91 L.Ed. 1848, rehearing denied 68 S.Ct. 33, 332 U.S. 786, 92 L.Ed. 369.
Straley v. Keltner, 164 N.E.2d 186, 109 Ohio App. 51.
Tenn.—**Corpus Juris quoted in** Gargaro v. Kroger Grocery & Baking Co., 118 S.W.2d 561, 564, 22 Tenn. App. 70—**Corpus Juris quoted in** Loew's Nashville & Knoxville Corporation v. Durrett, 79 S.W.2d 598, 607, 18 Tenn.App. 489—**Corpus Juris quoted in** John Bouchard & Sons Co. v. Keaton, 9 Tenn.App. 467, 481.
Vt.—Bouchard v. Sicard, 35 A.2d 439, 113 Vt. 429.
45 C.J. p 944 note 50.
Assumption of risk in law of negligence generally see infra § 174(1) et seq.

Defenses not inconsistent
"In actions based on negligence the defense of assumption of risk under the maxim 'volenti non fit injuria' is not inconsistent with the defense of contributory negligence."
Neb.—O'Brien v. Anderson, 130 N.W.2d 560, 567, 177 Neb. 635—Landrum v. Roddy, 12 N.W.2d 82, 84, 143 Neb. 934, 149 A.L.R. 1041.

Independent defenses
Doctrine of assumed risk is independent of defense of contributory negligence.
U.S.—Western Contracting Corp. v. Odle, C.A.Neb., 331 F.2d 38.
Neb.—Darnell v. Panhandle Co-op. Ass'n, 120 N.W.2d 278, 175 Neb. 40.

Conduct not mutually exclusive
Conduct which may be termed "assumption of risk" and conduct which constitutes contributory negligence are not mutually exclusive.
Wis.—Meyer v. Val-Lo-Will Farms, Inc., 111 N.W.2d 500, 14 Wis.2d 616.

87. Cal.—Hedding v. Pearson, 173 P.2d 382, 76 C.A.2d 481—Coole v. Haskins, 135 P.2d 176, 57 C.A.2d 737.
D.C.—Harris v. Plummer, App., 190 A.2d 98.
Kan.—**Corpus Juris Secundum cited in** Shufelberger v. Worden, 369 P.2d 382, 386, 189 Kan. 379—**Corpus Juris Secundum cited in** Taylor v. Hostetler, 352 P.2d 1042, 1051, 1052, 186 Kan. 788—**Corpus Juris Secundum cited in** Kleppe v. Prawl, 313 P.2d 227, 230, 181 Kan. 590, 63 A.L.R.2d 175.
Ky.—**Corpus Juris Secundum cited in** Dean v. Martz, 329 S.W.2d 371, 374—Entwistle v. Carrier Conveyor Corp., 284 S.W.2d 820—Gates v. Kuchle, 134 S.W.2d 1002, 281 Ky. 13.
Md.—Evans v. Johns Hopkins University, 167 A.2d 591, 224 Md. 234—Peoples Drug Stores v. Windham, 12 A.2d 532, 178 Md. 172—Warner v. Markoe, 189 A. 260, 171 Md. 351.
Mass.—Silver v. Cushner, 16 N.E.2d 27, 300 Mass. 583.
Mo.—**Corpus Juris Secundum cited in** Bullock v. Benjamin Moore and Company, App., 392 S.W.2d 10, 13.
Neb.—**Corpus Juris Secundum cited in** Brackman v. Brackman, 100 N.W.2d 774, 780, 169 Neb. 650.

Excerpt from 65A Corpus Juris Secundum 25

§ 8.7 Legal Texts and Treatises

Legal texts and treatises are books prepared by legal scholars and practice experts that cover specific areas of law. Legal texts usually deal with a single topic, such as contracts, torts, bankruptcy, trusts, evidence, and civil and criminal law and practice. Information about texts and treatises may be obtained through the catalog of a law library.

§ 8.8 Legal Periodicals

Articles from legal periodicals also discuss specific areas of the law and are particularly useful for prediction and analysis of trends in the law. Treatment of the subject ranges from scholarly to practical to news reporting. Information about articles can be located by subject, author, or title through legal periodical indexes, such as Index to Legal Periodicals, current Law Index, or Legaltrac.

§ 8.9 Restatements

Restatements are publications setting out and explaining, by practical examples, the law in particular fields. Restatements covering various areas of law, including agency, conflict of laws, contracts, judgments, products liability, property, restitution, security, torts, trusts, and unfair competition have been published. The purpose of the American Law Institute, the prestigious group responsible for the restatements, is to restate the common law (as reflected both by case decisions and statutory interpretation). To that end the Institute appoints committees to study and draft restatements covering assigned law topics. Eminent legal scholars are appointed to be reporters for each one of the restatements being prepared, and, as a practical matter, they principally prepare the drafts. The restatements are not adopted in whole by the highest appellate courts in the states, but they are referred to and in many instances are approved on a section-by-section basis in the written opinion. Therefore, to that extent, they do become law. Information about court opinions that have interpreted restatement provisions is contained in the appendix volumes of the restatement set.

§ 8.10 Uniform Laws Annotated

Individual lawyers, judges, and law professors are selected as commissioners to sit with the National Conference of Commissioners on Uniform State Laws. They then research and draft model legislation covering law topics dealing with specific legal problems. Their goal is to make uniform, as far as possible, many of the major areas of the law that can be codified. The state legislatures may or may not adopt the law, but the books are valuable for a comparison of case law interpretations from various states. Many of the uniform laws, for example, the Uniform Commercial Code, have been adopted by practically all of the states.

§ 8.11 Other Research Aids

Law book publishers offer additional aids to legal researchers, the most important of which are discussed and illustrated below.

§ 8.12 Annotated Statutes

An "official" statutory code is typically published by the governmental entity. Thus, the federal government publishes the United States Code. Individual states typically publish their own codes.

In addition, private legal publishers such as West Group publish "annotated codes." Annotated codes provide the text of the official code as well as other commentary helpful to understanding individual code sections, including comments on legislative history, summaries of relevant judicial decisions, citations to legal scholarship concerning the law, etc. Generally speaking, a privately published code will be more current than its official counterpart. For example, the official United States Code is published every six years. By contrast, West's United States Code Annotated ("U.S.C.A.") and United States Code Service (the "U.S.C.S.," published by LexisNexis Law Publishing) are supplemented annually to keep the practitioner up to date on recent changes in the law. Both sources are available online on Westlaw and LexisNexis.

Illustration 8–6

Ch. 9 FOOD, DRUG, AND COSMETIC ACT 21 § 355

§ 355. New drugs—Necessity of effective approval of application

(a) No person shall introduce or deliver for introduction into interstate commerce any new drug, unless an approval of an application filed pursuant to subsection (b) of this section is effective with respect to such drug.

Filing application; contents

(b) Any person may file with the Secretary an application with respect to any drug subject to the provisions of subsection (a) of this section. Such person shall submit to the Secretary as a part of the application (1) full reports of investigations which have been made to show whether or not such drug is safe for use and whether such drug is effective in use; (2) a full list of the articles used as components of such drug; (3) a full statement of the composition of such drug; (4) a full description of the methods used in, and the facilities and controls used for, the manufacture, processing, and packing of such drug; (5) such samples of such drug and of the articles used as components thereof as the Secretary may require; and (6) specimens of the labeling proposed to be used for such drug.

Official Text of the U. S. Code

Period for approval of application; period for, notice, and expedition of hearing; period for issuance of order

(c) Within one hundred and eighty days after the filing of an application under this subsection, or such additional period as may be agreed upon by the Secretary and the applicant, the Secretary shall either—

(1) approve the application if he then finds that none of the grounds for denying approval specified in subsection (d) of this section applies, or

(2) Every person required under this section to maintain records, and every person in charge or custody thereof, shall, upon request of an officer or employee designated by the Secretary, permit such officer or employee at all reasonable times to have access to and copy and verify such records.

June 25, 1938, c. 675, § 505, 52 Stat. 1052; 1940 Reorg.Plan No. IV, § 12, eff. June 30, 1940, 5 F.R. 2422, 54 Stat. 1237; June 25, 1948, c. 646, § 32(b), 62 Stat. 991; May 24, 1949, c. 139, § 127, 63 Stat. 107; 1953 Reorg.Plan No. 1, § 5, eff. Apr. 11, 1953, 18 F.R. 2053, 67 Stat.

Citations to original and amending Acts of Congress in U. S. Statutes at Large

Citation to Reorganization Plan in Federal Register

Excerpt from 21 U.S. Code Annotated § 355

[C4066]

Illustration 8–6 (CONTINUED)

Ch. 9 FOOD, DRUG, AND COSMETIC ACT 21 § 355

631; June 11, 1960, Pub.L. 86–507, § 1(18), 74 Stat. 201; Oct. 10, 1962, Pub.L. 87–781, Title I, §§ 102(b)–(d), 103(a), (b), 104(a)–(d)(2), 76 Stat. 781–783, 784, 785.

Historical Note

Notes explaining Historical Development of Act

1962 Amendment. Subsec. (a). Pub.L. 87–781, § 104(a), inserted "an approval of" preceding "an application."

Subsec. (b). Pub.L. 87–781, § 102(b), inserted "and whether such drug is effective in use" following "is safe for use."

Subsec. (c). Pub.L. 87–781, § 104(b), substituted provisions requiring the Secretary, within 180 days after filing an application, or such additional period as the Secretary and the applicant agree upon, to either approve the application, if meeting the requirements of subsec. (d) of this section, or give notice of opportunity for hearing on question of whether such application is approvable, and providing that if applicant requests hearing in writing within 30 days, the hearing shall begin within 90 days after expiration of said 30 days, unless the Secretary and applicant agree otherwise, that such hearing shall be expedited, and that the Secretary's order shall be issued within 90 days after date for filing final briefs, for provisions which had an application become effective on the sixtieth day after filing thereof unless prior thereto the Secretary postponed the date by written notice to such time, but not more than 180 days after filing, as the Secretary deemed necessary to study and investigate the application.

Subsec. (d). Pub.L. 87–781, § 102(c), inserted references to subsec. (c), added cls. (5) and (6), provided that if after notice and opportunity for hearing, the Secretary finds that cls. (1)–(6) do not apply, he shall approve the application, and defined "substantial evidence" as used in this subsection and subsec. (e) of this section.

Subsec. (e). Pub.L. 87–781, § 102(d) amended subsection generally, and among other changes, directed the Secretary to withdraw approval of an application if by tests, other scientific data or experience, or new evidence of clinical experience not contained in the application or available at the time of its approval, the drug is shown to be unsafe, or on the basis of new information, there is shown a lack of substantial evidence that the drug has the effect it is represented to have, and provided that if the Secretary, or acting Secretary, finds there is an imminent hazard to public health, he may suspend approval immediately, notify the applicant, and give him opportunity for an expedited hearing, that the Secretary may withdraw approval if the applicant fails to establish a system for maintaining required records, or has repeatedly or deliberately failed to maintain records and make reports, or has refused access to, or copying or verification of such records, or if the Secretary finds on new evidence that the methods, facilities and controls in the manufacturing, processing, and packing are inadequate to assure and preserve the drugs' identity, strength, quality and purity, and were not made adequate within a reasonable time after receipt of written notice thereof, or finds on new evidence, that the labeling is false or misleading and was not corrected within a reasonable time after receipt of written notice thereof.

Change of Name. Act June 25, 1948, eff. Sept. 1, 1948, as amended by Act May 24, 1949, substituted "United States District Court for the District of Columbia" for "District Court of the United States for the District of Columbia."

Effective Date of 1962 Amendment; Exceptions. Amendment of section by Pub.L. 87–781 effective on the first day of the seventh calendar month following Oct. 1962, see section 107 of Pub.L. 87–781, set out as a note under section 321 of this title.

Effective Date. Section effective June 25, 1938, see section 902(a) of Act June 25, 1938, set out as a note under section 392 of this title.

Legislative History. For legislative history and purpose of Act May 24, 1949, see 1949 U.S.Code Cong.Service, p. 1248. See, also, Pub.L. 86–507, 1960 U.S.Code Cong. and Adm.News, p. 2356; Pub.L. 87–781, 1962 U.S.Code Cong. and Adm. News, p. 2884, and part 2 of Senate Report No. 1744, set out as a note under section 321 of this title.

Reference to Legislative History and Purpose in U. S. Code Congressional and Administrative News

[C4067]

§ 8.13 Martindale–Hubbell Law Directory

Law directories and digests published by Martindale–Hubbell are comprised of several volumes. Martindale–Hubbell Law Directory contains names, addresses, specialties, and ratings of United States lawyers while the International Law Directory lists lawyers and law firms worldwide.

Martindale–Hubbell Law Digests summarize the statutory laws in each of the United States, the District of Columbia, Puerto Rico, the Virgin Islands, and Canada as well as over 60 other countries. The complete texts of many Uniform Acts including the Uniform Commercial Code and the Uniform Probate Code, and four Model Acts including the Revised Model Business Corporation Act are included, as are selected international conventions to which the United States is a party. Besides presenting the substantive law controlling the grant of copyright, patent, and trademark rights, the digests on these subjects provide information as to the practice to be followed in obtaining, protecting, and enforcing such rights, the fee schedules of the respective bureaus, examples of forms in use, and other practical assistance. The Law Digest also contains information on the federal judiciary and the Model Rules of Professional Conduct and the Code of Judicial Conduct of the American Bar Association.

§ 8.14 Form and Practice Books

Form books are specialized publications that provide suggested text for various legal forms, such as contracts, leases, and procedural pleadings and papers. Large sets of form books cover an encyclopedic range of forms on virtually all subjects. Smaller sets can focus on particular areas of law. Although these forms are very useful for guidance in drafting legal documents, care must be taken to verify that the suggested language is in fact applicable to the specific case.

Many other practical publications exist to assist the lawyer in procedural, evidentiary, and trial practice areas. Some examples are *AmJur Trials*, *AmJur Proof of Facts*, *Causes of Action*, and *Cyclopedia of Federal Procedure*.

§ 8.15 Keeping the Library Current

In order for a lawyer to be able to rely on the books in their library, they must be certain that they are absolutely current. There are several services provided by law book publishers which help the lawyer keep the library current.

§ 8.15.1 Pocket Parts

Most law books are equipped with pockets in the inside back covers which accommodate pamphlet inserts. All statutes and codes are kept current in this manner, and new pocket parts are issued after each legislative session. In legal research it is very important to check the pocket parts for recent changes.

In many offices it is the responsibility of the lawyer's assistant to keep the pocket parts current. Generally, these are published once a year. When new pocket parts arrive, they should immediately be placed in the pertinent volumes and the old pocket parts destroyed according to the instructions that come with each new supplement. The pocket parts are clearly labeled, so there can be no mistake as to where they belong.

§ 8.15.2 Replacement Volumes

When the pocket part becomes so bulky that the book no longer closes properly, the volume is replaced. Replacement volumes usually come with instructions on which book or books are being replaced. It is not unusual for one volume to be replaced by two. Be guided by the publisher's instructions, as they are usually very specific.

§ 8.15.3 Bound Supplements

Bound supplements may be of a temporary nature, to be used because a pocket part would be too bulky or because the particular book being updated is not equipped with a pocket part, or they may be permanent updates to the main volume. Here, again, rely on the publisher's instructions for guidance.

§ 8.15.4 Advance Sheets

The National Reporter System is crucial to legal research. The volumes are published as soon as there are a sufficient number of cases to fill a bound volume. Often, a lawyer must know about the most current cases sooner than that. To alleviate the problem, West issues advance sheets in a paperback pamphlet weekly. The advance sheets carry the correct volume numbers and page numbers of the National Reporter volume of which it will become a part. Once you receive the bound volume, you may destroy the advance sheets.

§ 8.15.5 Loose–Leaf Services

Loose–Leaf services are used extensively in administrative law areas. Changes occur at a rapid rate, and the materials must be kept current to be of any value.

These services are kept current by the publication of replacement pages or additional pages. It is a good idea to replace substitute pages as soon as they arrive, as it can be very confusing to attempt the insertion of more than one group of changes. Be very careful to follow the publisher's instructions about the replacements.

§ 8.16 Computer–Assisted Legal Research

A substantial proportion of the publications described in this chapter are located in the large computer-assisted research systems of Lexis-Nexis and Westlaw. These two databases contain the full text of federal and state case law (both current and historical), statutes and regulations, legal periodicals, treatises, forms, news, public records and other publications. Both systems utilize open-ended "keyword" search techniques, which facilitate location of pertinent materials without resorting to indexes, digests, and multiple sources for updating.

These computer systems can be a cost-effective approach to legal research. Shepardizing cases on line, for instance, is far faster and easier than using the citator volumes. Because the user is charged on a per-search or hourly basis, the lawyer must plan a search strategy to use time wisely, and should consider useful book alternatives.

Another development in computer research systems is in local and specialized Compact Disk—Read Only Memory (CD–ROM) databases. State law databases on CD–ROM can be a cost-effective alternative to LexisNexis and Westlaw because they provide unlimited access to all of the primary legal authority from that state. Drawbacks of these systems include the inability to consult legal authority from other states, accuracy of the information, and, in some cases, poorly designed search and retrieval software.

§ 8.16.1 Westlaw

Westlaw is the online legal research service provided by West Group. Through Westlaw, the legal researcher can access all published federal and state appellate cases (and numerous "unpublished" cases as well), all federal and state statutes, all federal administrative regulations, the administrative codes for most states, and a rich library of secondary research material (law review articles, practice guides, treatises, etc.).

In addition, Westlaw permits the researcher to search case law databases using West Group's proprietary "Topic" and "Key number" system. West has organized its Digest System according to a hierarchical system of Topic and Key numbers. These Topic and Key numbers appear in West reporters next to the headnotes used to summarize individual points of law discussed within the case itself. Thus, to search in Westlaw for cases involving the validity of wills executed under improper influence, for example, the researcher might include in the query the Topic and Key number that the West editors assign to cases dealing with this issue. West Topic 409 is "Wills;" Key number 154 within this topic is "undue influence." So, the researcher will create a query including the phrase "409k154" to restrict the search to cases discussing this issue.

§ 8.16.2 LexisNexis

LexisNexis is another computer-assisted legal research service. LexisNexis provides access to the vast majority of the same primary law materials available on Westlaw. Like Westlaw, LexisNexis also offers a rich collection of secondary legal resources, and has introduced a new search tool known as Key Concepts. Both services provide an assortment of nonlegal material as well (news databases, company information, public records, etc.).

LexisNexis and Westlaw, however, are not interchangeable. Each service employs a highly distinctive search interface that requires substantial training and experience to use effectively. As noted, Westlaw permits the legal researcher to employ West Group's proprietary Topic and Key numbers in constructing search queries. Westlaw also permits the researcher to restrict the search to the case "headnotes" composed by West Group editors. Both vendors offer a variety of free training options for their subscribers, including on-site training, group seminars, and web-based training.

§ 8.16.3 The World Wide Web as a Legal Research Tool

In recent years, the World Wide Web ("www") has become an increasingly important resource for the legal researcher. At the present time, official government web sites provide access to almost all of the same federal and state statutory codes and administrative regulations available on Westlaw or LexisNexis. Web sites maintained by individual federal and state courts provide convenient access to recent judicial opinions, court rules, etc.

Official government web sites offer material without charge. Thus, for certain primary law material, the web can represent a low cost alternative to using a commercial online service.

Although these government-sponsored web sites provide free access to a great deal of American primary law, they are currently no substitute for LexisNexis or Westlaw. A web site may offer the text of the law itself but it will not provide the editorial enhancements offered by these services ("headnotes" for cases, annotations for statutes, etc.). In many cases, the primary law available on the web is not as current as the same material available through a fee-based, online service. Statutory codes available on LexisNexis and Westlaw, for example, typically flag any section amended by a recent session law; no such warning appears on statutory material available via the web. The case law databases available on the web tend to have recent cases only; LexisNexis and Westlaw generally offer far more comprehensive coverage of each jurisdiction's case law. Finally, web-based search engines tend to be primitive by comparison with the search engines and robust searching capabilities employed by LexisNexis and Westlaw.

The web, however, outshines the commercial services in providing access to certain kinds of primary law. County and city municipal codes are increasingly available on the web; neither LexisNexis nor Westlaw currently offer most of these codes. There is a great deal more foreign law (in English and in the native language) on the web than is available through the commercial services. Finally, in certain cases, the web can actually be more current than the online services. Some recent judicial opinions, for example, appear at court web sites before the cases are picked up by the commercial services (the lag, however, is never more than a matter of days).

Currently, the web's most important strength as a legal resource lies in its ability to deliver timely, free access to certain secondary legal material. For example, the federal government and most state governments have created web sites for their respective legislative bodies. Through these sites, one can easily track current legislation, retrieve otherwise hard-to-locate committee reports, locate the text of recently enacted session laws, etc. Web sites maintained by federal and state administrative agencies provide excellent access to otherwise hard-to-find guidance documents published by such agencies; such documents can be crucial to the practitioner but are generally not available on LexisNexis or Westlaw because they are not "primary law." A number of academic law journals also offer online access to recent articles.

There are several useful guides to legal research on the World Wide Web. Consider, for example, G. Burgess Allison's *The Lawyer's Guide to the Internet* (American Bar Association, 1995); Diana Botluk's *The Legal List: Research on the Internet* (West Group, 1998 ed.); *Medical Legal Internet Directory, The Professional's Instant–Access Resource*, Rosie Oldham, R.N., B.S.; and Joshua D. Blackman, *The Internet Fact Finder for Lawyers: How to Find Anything on the Net* (American Bar Association, 1998).

§ 8.17 Learning the Law Library

To become an efficient researcher, you must become familiar with the books and other research tools in the law library. Knowing where the books and other research tools are and why they are there makes the lawyer's assistant much more helpful to the lawyer.

The art of effective legal research requires concentrated study and practice. As you learn your way around the library:

- Take the time to study some of the books.
- Read the table of contents, introduction, and foreword of some of the books.
- Study the indexes. Use your imagination. Try to find a key word listed for a current legal problem in the office.
- Study the topics of the Key Number System. Many legal indexes may use the same topic designations.
- Always check pocket parts or supplementary pamphlets.
- Read some of the headnotes in your state's reporter. Can you find references to the same key number anywhere else?
- Find a case in a reporter and Shepardize or KeyCite it. Pull one of the cases referred to. Can you tell whether it is on the same point of law?

- Do the same for one of your statutes.
- If your office has access to LexisNexis or Westlaw, become familiar with these databases.

§ 8.18 Law Librarians

Law Librarians are skilled information specialists working in law firm, corporate, government, public, and academic libraries. They help judges, attorneys, professors, students, legal professionals, and members of the public find information on legal issues. Many hold master's degrees in Library and Information Science, and some also hold law and other advanced degrees. Law librarians perform a variety of duties relating to the organization and distribution of legal and non-legal information, including:

- Providing specialized reference and research services.
- Executing online database searches.
- Teaching legal research and materials use.
- Training on the use of print and electronic legal information sources.
- Evaluating and collecting legal materials.
- Designing and maintaining information storage and retrieval systems.
- Preparing fiscal reports and long range plans.

Smaller firms generally do not have a designated full-time law librarian, but many mid-size and large law firms do not have one or more law librarians on staff. Many state and regional law library associations feature volunteer guest speakers who can teach group seminars on the fundamentals of legal research. Seminars on legal research basics may also be available to the public at your local, county and state law library. To determine if your state has a local chapter, and to learn more about law librarianship and law libraries, contact the American Association of Law Libraries at (312) 939–4764 or visit their web site at http://wwws.aallnet.org.

CHAPTER 9

THE COURTS

Table of Sections

---

§ 9.1 Introduction

The government of the United States is based on the concept of separation of powers. That separation of powers is accomplished by a delicate system of checks and balances in our three branches of government. Each of the three branches—the executive, the legislative, and the judicial—is independent of the other, but each is a vital part of the whole. Each branch performs its own function and when combined with the other branches, this provides us with our system of government. Under our system, however, one branch cannot dominate another.

It is the judicial branch of the government that administers individual justice. Its power to do so comes ultimately from constitutional authority. Its financial and other resources to administer justice come from the legislative branch. However, the legislative branch generally does not control the actions of the judicial branch.

§ 9.2 History of the Law

It is difficult to pinpoint when the development of our legal system began. As early as 2100 B.C., codes of conduct were written and enforced in highly developed civilizations. Religion played an important part in the history of the law after the decline of the Roman Empire when the ecclesiastical courts handled most legal matters. Hence, many ancient civilizations had relatively sophisticated written laws. Eventually all of the concepts embodied in these ancient laws evolved into the two legal systems that dominate the Western world today—Civil Law and Common Law.

§ 9.2.1 Civil Law

Civil law derives from the Roman law. Today, most of the countries in Western Europe operate under a civil law system. In the United States, Louisiana operates under a civil law system greatly influenced by France's Napoleonic Code. California and Texas law are heavily influenced by Spanish law. Some of the Spanish law influence is also evident in New Mexico and Arizona.

§ 9.2.2 Common Law

Except for a few civil law states as mentioned above, the remainder of the states operate under a common law system that is an adaptation of England's common law. Common law evolved in England after the Norman Conquest. At that time, there were no written rules to govern conduct. When disputes arose, the people involved appeared before a tribunal or a judge, and a decision was reached based upon the evidence and the facts at hand. Under that system two different courts could reach completely different conclusions in a similar fact situation because there was nothing in writing to guide the judge to a decision.

§ 9.2.3 Distinction Between Civil Law and Common Law

Civil law is based on a series of written codes or laws. These written codes are interpreted by courts if disputes arise, but it is the written law itself that is binding. Common law has evolved from earlier decisions made by courts. To solve the problem of inconsistency in decisions reached in similar fact situations, these decisions have been reduced to writing, and the courts are generally bound by them. This concept is known as the doctrine of *stare decisis* (to stand by decisions). For that reason, it is often said that common law is based on the law of "precedent." One court sets a precedent, and courts making subsequent decisions relating to similar fact circumstances are generally bound by that precedent. The primary distinction between the two systems is that civil law is based on written codes, while common law is based on judicial precedent.

§ 9.3 The American Judicial System

The distinction between civil law and common law is now primarily a historic one because our legal system today is a fusion of both systems. For example, no longer does common law in the United States rely exclusively upon case decisions. All states, whether their legal system is based on civil or common law, have written laws. The Constitution of the United States became effective in 1788 and, of course, is written law. Although the civil law states use written law, case law has become a very important part of the whole of civil law. Tort law (thoroughly discussed in the chapter on Torts) is a common law concept, but in Louisiana (a civil law state) the law of torts for the most part is applied as it is in the rest of the United States. Furthermore, most commercial laws in force in the United States today, although written in commercial codes, have found their origin in common law.

§ 9.3.1 The Law

The law establishes rules of conduct that define what is legally right and what is legally wrong. Laws are nothing more than rules of human behavior enforced by the state or federal government by means of various penalties for their violation. To a great extent laws are influenced by moral and social habits or customs. Therefore, as society changes its customs and traditions, laws change. These changes are accomplished when new laws are enacted by the legislative branch of government or when the judiciary interprets existing laws.

§ 9.3.2 Significance of the Law

Regardless of whether one is employed in the legal field, it is very important that each person understand the basic elements of our judicial system. Unfortunately, many people do not realize the extent to which laws affect their daily lives. Common events, such as a birth, a death, applying for a driver's license, buying or selling a house or a car, paying taxes, buying a bus or airplane ticket, banking, and using electricity or other utilities, are all governed by specific laws. Many lay people have the mistaken impression that laws apply only to those who commit violent crimes. That simply is not the case. The law affects everyone, and all of us should have some idea as to our legal rights so that we are in a position to know when to consult a lawyer. As a matter of fact, the law encompasses such a broad spectrum of our daily activities that even categorizing it for ready reference is difficult.

§ 9.3.3 Categorizing the Law

Generally, there are two types of legal actions—criminal and civil.

§ 9.3.4 Criminal Actions

Criminal actions are generally brought by the people through a government (either federal, state, or local) against the person or persons accused of a crime. Because society is wronged by the commission of a crime, the government prosecutes the wrongdoer on behalf of society. Therefore, in a criminal action the government is always the plaintiff.

EXAMPLES:

United States of America v. Albert Jones

State of Texas v. John Smith

County of Tulsa v. Barry Green

City of Apple Grove v. June Collins

§ 9.3.5 Civil Actions

Civil actions are generally brought by one party against another to resolve a controversy. These actions include any kind of legal action that is not a criminal action, but they typically seek one of the following remedies:

1. Money generally referred to as "damages"
2. Specific performance of some conduct
3. Restrictions on some conduct

In actions for performance or restrictions, the relief usually requested is in the form of a restraining order or an injunction.

§ 9.4 Substantive v. Procedural Law

The law is separated based upon its nature (substantive law) or how it is applied in deciding issues of substantive law (procedural law). Substantive law tells us what to do, and procedural law tells us how to apply the law and how to get relief using the judicial system.

§ 9.4.1 Substantive Law

Substantive law sets out the rights and obligations of individuals. It tells us what we can legally do or what we cannot legally do.

§ 9.4.2 Procedural Law

Procedural law defines and describes the process that must be followed to enforce the substantive law. The most common source of procedural law is court rules adopted and published by the courts to which the rules apply.

EXAMPLE:

> *A*, who owns property, has the right to enjoy it without interference from anyone else. (This right comes from substantive law.) *B* installs a fence which is partly on *A*'s property. When *B* refuses to remove the fence, *A* sees a lawyer, who files a lawsuit asking the court to force *B* to remove the fence from *A*'s property. (The lawyer knows in which court to file the suit and how to obtain a particular remedy by referring to applicable procedural law.)

§ 9.5 Source of the Law

Law is often classified on the basis of where it is found. Constitutional law is that which is set out in the Constitution of the United States and in the 50 state constitutions. Statutory law is that body of laws promulgated by the United States Congress, by the 50 state legislatures, and by local governments. However, rules and regulations promulgated by governmental agencies and commissions that are empowered by statutory law are given the force of statutory law. Case law is that body of court decisions resulting from legal controversies over interpretations of substantive and procedural law. Remember that the doctrine of *stare decisis* generally binds a court to follow a decision made previously in a similar fact situation. Although courts can overturn earlier decisions, this does not happen very often, and the doctrine of *stare decisis* adds stability to our legal system.

§ 9.5.1 United States Constitution

The Constitution of the United States carries the greatest degree of dignity of any law in this country. No other law—regardless of whether it is adopted by Congress or by a state legislature—can conflict with the United States Constitution.

§ 9.5.2 State Constitutions

Each of the 50 states has its own constitution. However, those constitutions may not contain any provision that is contrary to a provision in the United States Constitution.

§ 9.5.3 Statutory Law

Statutory law is that enacted by United States Congress, by the 50 state legislatures, and by local governments. Many local governments also have charters that control their form of government and establish their local governmental agencies.

§ 9.6 Summary of Classification of Laws

Any specific law must be considered from several different viewpoints. A law can be classified as a constitutional law, a statutory law, or case law, as a substantive law or a procedural law. (*See* Illustration 9–1.)

Illustration 9–1

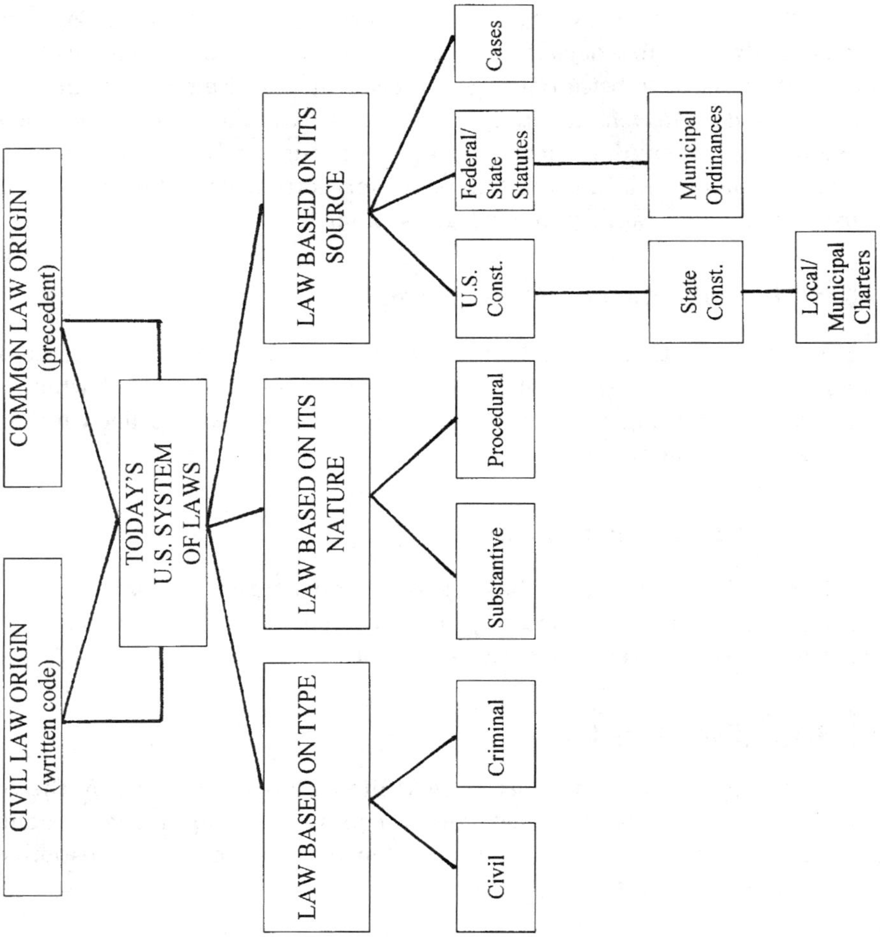

§ 9.7 Creation of Court Systems in the United States

Courts are created by constitutional authority. The Constitution of the United States is the primary source of the judicial powers of federal courts. No state constitution or legislative body can create any court or give authority to any court which conflicts with the United States Constitution. The state constitutions do create courts for their states, and the legislative bodies, both federal and state, have the power to create courts and give judicial authority to those courts subject to any restrictions set forth in the state constitutions or the United States Constitution. Regardless of whether a court is established pursuant to the United States Constitution or a state constitution, that court has authority to decide only those cases that the constitution ultimately gives it authority to decide.

The basis of the judicial authority of federal courts is found in Article III, § 2 of the United States Constitution.

Without authority granted in the state's constitution, a legislative body may not alter, abolish, or restructure a constitutional court, but it may alter, abolish, or restructure any court that it has created pursuant to constitutional authority. State courts are not under the authority and control of Congress, but Congress may authorize state courts to enforce federal laws. Both federal and state legislative bodies may increase, decrease, create, or change the number of judicial districts or circuits as long as they act under constitutional authority. They also may divide a court into divisions or departments. A court so divided remains a single court, and any decisions or judgments rendered by that division or department are considered as having been rendered by the whole court.

Courts, whether federal or state, apply the laws created by constitutions, legislative bodies, and all administrative agencies having authority to enact rules and regulations. They do this in two ways: they adjudicate or settle controversies and disputes between parties, or they decide which laws are applicable to the cases that are before them. Once their decisions are final, they are binding and the interpretation and application of the laws indicate how similar cases will be determined in the future pursuant to the doctrine of *stare decisis*.

In addition to the application and interpretation of laws, courts may adopt rules that affect procedural law within their jurisdiction. These court rules cannot conflict with the Constitution of the United States, the state's constitution, or any law enacted by Congress or state legislatures.

§ 9.8 Determining the Correct Court

To determine whether a case should be brought in federal court or in state court, the following is considered:

- If the subject matter involved is covered exclusively by state law, the case usually is brought in a state court.
- If federal law is involved or if a federal court has original jurisdiction (discussed later), the matter usually is brought in federal court.

Remember, however, that this is just a general rule to which there are many exceptions, as you will see in the discussion of jurisdiction of state and federal courts.

§ 9.8.1 Jurisdiction

Jurisdiction is the power of a court to hear and decide certain cases. There are many limitations on that power, and very often those limitations are the product of constitutional or legislative restrictions. Just as it is necessary to understand the many classifications of law, you must also understand the many facets of jurisdiction. Before a court may hear a particular case, it must have power to hear and decide the types of case involved (subject matter jurisdiction) and must have authority over the parties in the case (personal jurisdiction). These determinations are based upon several factors.

§ 9.8.2 Original Jurisdiction

Original jurisdiction is the authority granted to a court to hear and determine a matter for the first time. Actions are begun in courts of original jurisdiction. It is in the court of original jurisdiction that the lawsuit is filed and the trial is held or the matter is otherwise resolved.

§ 9.8.3 Jurisdiction Over the Subject Matter

Jurisdiction over the subject matter is the authority given to a court to render binding decisions over the matter in dispute. Lack of subject matter jurisdiction cannot be waived by the court or by the parties. In fact, if a court lacks jurisdiction over the subject matter, any judgment it renders is void.

EXAMPLE:

Patent disputes are heard exclusively by federal courts. If a patent dispute were to be filed in state court, the matter would be dismissed for lack of subject matter jurisdiction.

§ 9.8.4 Jurisdiction *in Personam* (Over the Person)

Jurisdiction *in personam* (personal jurisdiction) is the power of a court to render a judgment against a person or to subject the disputing parties to the decisions and rulings made by it. Ordinarily this means that a defendant has the right to be tried only in those states where he or she has sufficient contacts. This is only a general rule, and other types of *in personam* jurisdiction may preempt that general rule. A person may be subjected to the jurisdiction of a court by statute, by agreement, or if they do not file a formal objection to the court's personal jurisdiction. In order for the judgment to be valid in such an instance, the court must also have subject matter jurisdiction.

EXAMPLES:

A lives in Dallas, Texas, and made a contract with *B*, who lives in Oklahoma City, Oklahoma, to pay *B* $10,000 for delivery of certain merchandise. The contract was made in Texas and all negotiations took place in Texas. *A* now refuses to pay *B*. The state courts of Oklahoma have authority to hear and decide this type of case (breach of contract) because the state courts have subject matter jurisdiction to hear contract disputes. However, the state courts of Oklahoma probably do not have personal jurisdiction over *A* because he has insufficient contacts with that state. The Oklahoma courts would therefore have subject matter jurisdiction, but they would lack personal jurisdiction over *A*; and *B* therefore cannot sue *A* in Oklahoma.

Assume the same facts. *B* sues *A* in Oklahoma City, where *A* now spends a lot of time on business. *A* employs the services of an Oklahoma City lawyer to defend the suit which *B* files. When *A* makes an appearance in that matter through his lawyer and does not dispute the jurisdiction, he has subjected himself to the jurisdiction of the Oklahoma City court. Therefore, the Oklahoma court can render a valid judgment against *A*.

§ 9.8.5 Jurisdiction *in Rem* (Over the Thing)

Jurisdiction *in rem* is the authority of a court to render a judgment concerning property over which it has jurisdiction. Ordinarily, this means that the court and the property are in the same geographic location, even if the owner of the property is not subject to personal jurisdiction in that court. When a court renders an *in rem* judgment, that judgment affects only the property that is the subject of the court's jurisdiction. The judgment does not apply to the owner of the property if the court does not have personal jurisdiction over the owner. This means that any such judgment would have to be satisfied only from the property subject to the court's jurisdiction. Other personal assets and property of the owner that are located elsewhere beyond the court's jurisdiction could not be seized by a court that did not have personal jurisdiction over the owner.

EXAMPLE:

A lives in Dallas and owes *B*, who lives in Oklahoma City, $10,000, which is secured by a mortgage on property located in

Oklahoma City. *B* must sue *A* in Oklahoma City if he wishes to regain possession of the property in payment of the mortgage, since only the Oklahoma City court has jurisdiction *in rem*. However, if *B* is not interested in the property but only wants to get his money back, he may sue *A* in a Dallas court which has *in personam* jurisdiction over *A* so that, once he has a judgment, he can seize other assets owned by *A* to satisfy his judgment, if such assets are located in Texas.

§ 9.8.6 Limited Jurisdiction

A court of limited jurisdiction is one that is restricted in the type of case it can hear or in the amount of money involved in the litigation.

EXAMPLE:

A juvenile court, probate court, or a family court can hear only cases involving that particular subject matter if their jurisdiction is limited by state statute.

Many municipal courts (or other state courts) are limited by the amount of money involved in a particular lawsuit.

EXAMPLE:

A owes *B* $10,000. *B* wishes to sue *A*. If the municipal court where *A* lives does not have monetary jurisdiction of $10,000, *B* must sue *A* in the appropriate court having monetary jurisdiction of that amount.

§ 9.8.7 Exclusive Jurisdiction

Exclusive jurisdiction is the authority granted to a court to hear certain matters to the exclusion of all other courts. No other court within the same territorial limits may hear any matter for which there is a court with exclusive jurisdiction. The court also may be restricted to that type of case.

EXAMPLE:

Patent litigation or litigation under the National Labor Relations Act is exclusively vested in federal court. No state court may hear such matters.

§ 9.8.8 Territorial Jurisdiction

Territorial jurisdiction applies to the actual geographic area over which the court has authority. Both the federal and state court systems have various divisions which limit jurisdiction to specific geographic areas.

§ 9.8.9 General Jurisdiction (Sometimes Referred to as Unlimited Jurisdiction)

If a court has general jurisdiction, this usually means that the court has no limitation as to the types of cases it can hear and no limitation on its monetary jurisdiction. Since there is no limit as to subject matter or as to the amount in controversy, it is often referred to as a court of general or unlimited jurisdiction. However, courts are limited in some regard because most court systems contain courts of special, exclusive jurisdiction; courts of general jurisdiction cannot hear cases over which special courts have exclusive jurisdiction.

EXAMPLE:

> Many states have juvenile courts that handle all matters concerning juveniles. In such a jurisdiction, the courts of general or unlimited jurisdiction could not hear any matters concerning juveniles. Therefore, the courts of general jurisdiction are limited to that extent.

§ 9.8.10 Concurrent Jurisdiction

Concurrent jurisdiction refers to jurisdiction granted to different courts at the same time over the same matters and within the same territorial limit. This means that in certain situations, the plaintiff has a choice of the court in which to file suit. This is particularly true, for example, where municipal or small claims courts are established to alleviate crowding in the courts of general jurisdiction. Usually, the jurisdiction of the small claims court is concurrent with that of the court of general jurisdiction. The whole purpose of the small claims court is to give claimants a faster, more efficient, more economical court than the court of general jurisdiction in which to process claims which do not involve large sums of money.

§ 9.8.11 Monetary Jurisdiction

Monetary jurisdiction refers to the limitation on dollar amount that a court may award. Usually, courts of general jurisdiction are not limited by monetary jurisdiction, but municipal courts and small claims courts are. Federal district courts have jurisdiction in diversity of citizenship cases (which generally means that the plaintiff and defendant are from different states) only when the amount in dispute is more than $75,000.

§ 9.8.12 Appellate Jurisdiction

Appellate jurisdiction grants the authority to a court to review cases tried in lower courts. Some courts have both original jurisdiction and appellate jurisdiction.

EXAMPLES:

Very often, a judgment of a municipal or small claims court can be appealed to a court of general or unlimited jurisdiction. In that instance, therefore, the court of general jurisdiction, which is usually a trial court, becomes an appellate court.

Most states have a court of last resort (often called the supreme court). Often, these courts have a right to decide whether or not they will even hear an appeal. In addition, it is often the court of last resort that handles disbarment cases against lawyers. In that instance the court may act as a trial court of original jurisdiction, although it is usually an appellate court.

§ 9.8.13 Venue

Venue refers to the particular geographic location of a lawsuit. It is a matter of convenience and efficiency. Various factors are considered in determining the geographical location of a particular dispute and are very important in determining where lawsuits are to be filed. For example, in a state having a trial court of general jurisdiction encompassing four counties, the court has the same subject matter jurisdiction and thus can hear the same type of disputes in all four counties, but venue differs from one county to the next. Even if the four counties share one judge, each county has its own courthouse and personnel. Venue determines in which county that particular dispute is to be tried. Generally, but subject to many exceptions, venue is based on the residence of the defendant. In federal court, civil action based on diversity of citizenship is proper where the defendant resides if all defendants reside in the same state. Otherwise, venue is generally proper where the events giving rise to the claim occurred. Venue is generally determined by statute.

§ 9.9 Dual System of Courts

You now have seen several references to state courts and federal courts. Although there are many similarities in the two systems, they operate independently of each other. There are instances when the United States Supreme Court might review a judgment rendered by a state court, but those instances are rare, occurring only when there has been a final judgment or decree of the highest court of the state in which a decision involved a substantial federal question. You will find that lawsuits that are initiated in either the state or federal system will remain there and that lawsuits usually are not switched from one system to the other. There are exceptions to this rule, of course, because some state actions can be removed to federal court.

Historically, there are certain types of legal matters which are exclusively reserved to state courts in which federal courts are very hesitant to intervene.

EXAMPLES:

Matters of marriage, divorce, custody, probate proceedings, and property.

On the other hand, there are matters over which federal courts have exclusive jurisdiction.

EXAMPLES:

Criminal matters involving violation of federal laws, admiralty and maritime matters, United States copyright matters, bankruptcy proceedings, proceedings against ambassadors, consuls, and ministers.

§ 9.9.1 Concurrent Jurisdiction of State and Federal Courts

There are times when state courts and federal courts have concurrent jurisdiction. The most common instance is where there is diversity of citizenship (the parties are from different states, or one party is from a foreign country) and where the amount in dispute is more than $75,000. In such a situation, if a lawsuit is filed in the federal court, the federal court applies state substantive law. Since the federal court and the state court have concurrent jurisdiction, however, the plaintiff may file his suit in either court, but once the court is selected, the suit is usually brought to conclusion in that court.

§ 9.9.2 Federal Court System

We will discuss the judicial system starting with the highest court down through the lowest court. This is directly opposite to the way a matter moves through the courts. Most actions are started in the lowest court authorized to hear the matter. If the parties are dissatisfied with the result, they can appeal to the next higher court authorized to hear appeals, and they may be able to have their case heard by the highest appellate court. The United States Supreme Court is the highest court in the United States.

§ 9.10 The United States Supreme Court

The United States Supreme Court is the only court created by the United States Constitution. Its jurisdiction is varied and usually of an appellate nature. There are three principal ways in which a case can be heard by the United States Supreme Court:

1. In most instances the United States Supreme Court may decide whether or not it will hear a particular case. This discretion is very similar to that of state courts of last resort which are discussed below. Once there has been a decision in a trial court and in an appellate court, the losing party may petition the United States Supreme Court for a writ of *certiorari* (review). If

the Supreme Court wishes to hear the case, it grants the writ. If it does not, the writ is denied. No reasons need to be stated for the Court's decision. Once the writ is denied, the litigant generally has no more avenues to seek relief.

2. There are some cases that the Supreme Court is obligated to hear. These cases come to the Supreme Court on appeal rather than by petition for a writ of *certiorari*.
3. There are even a few instances in which the United States Supreme Court has original jurisdiction.

EXAMPLE:

Texas and Louisiana have a dispute over their common boundary along the Sabine River. Only the United States Supreme Court has jurisdiction to hear this dispute.

Since it has original jurisdiction over disputes between states, it is a trial court in this instance. Because the United States Supreme Court is the highest court in the land, there is no right to appeal from its decision.

§ 9.11 United States Courts of Appeals

United States Courts of Appeals—these courts hear appeals from various federal district courts, bankruptcy courts, and tax courts. They also review decisions of federal administrative agencies. In many cases that are appealed to a United States Court of Appeals, the losing party may petition the United States Supreme Court for a Writ of *Certiorari*. However, the Supreme Court need not hear such cases. There are 13 circuit courts of appeals, including one for Washington, D.C. (*See* Illustration 9–2.)

Illustration 9–2

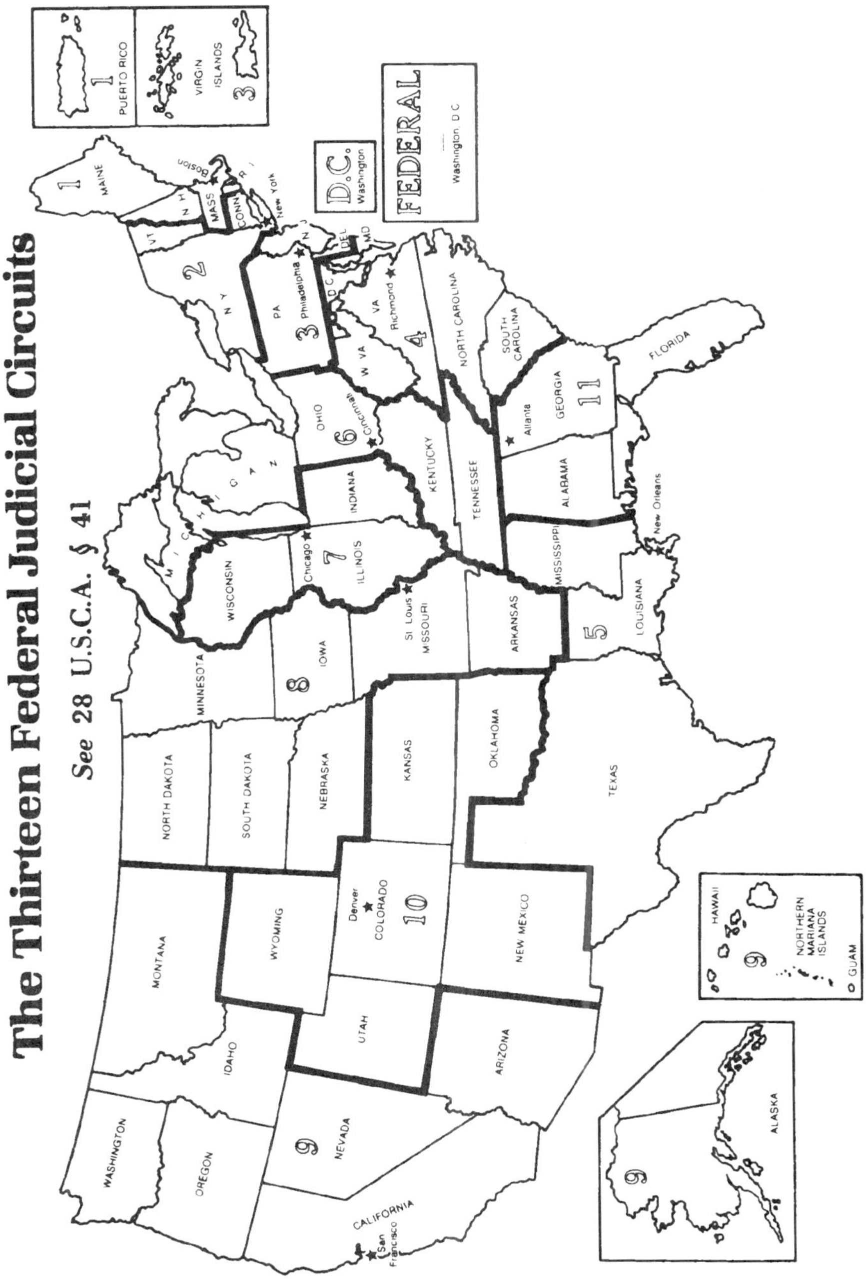

§ 9.12 United States District Courts

These federal courts have both civil and criminal subject matter jurisdiction. They have original jurisdiction in the following types of actions:

- Civil actions arising under the United States Constitution, laws, or treaties of the United States.
- Actions where the matter in controversy exceeds the sum or value of $75,000, exclusive of interest and costs, and is between citizens of different states; citizens of a state and foreign states or citizens or subjects thereof; or citizens of different states in which foreign states or citizens or subjects thereof are additional parties (diversity jurisdiction).
- All criminal offenses against the laws of the United States.
- Admiralty, maritime, and prize cases.
- Bankruptcy matters and proceedings.
- Actions of interpleader involving money or property of a value equal to or greater than the dollar amount set forth in the current rules, claimed by citizens of different states.
- Actions to enforce, enjoin, set aside, annul, or suspend, in whole or in part, any order of the Interstate Commerce Commission.
- Actions or proceedings arising under any act of Congress regulating commerce or protecting trade and commerce against restraints and monopolies.
- Any civil action arising under any act of Congress relating to the postal service.
- Actions arising under any act of Congress providing for internal revenue or revenue from imports or tonnage except matters within the jurisdiction of the Court of International Trade.
- Any civil action authorized by law to be commenced by any person dealing with civil rights, election disputes, and voting rights.
- All civil actions, suits, or proceedings commenced by the United States or by any agency or officer thereof.
- Actions for recovery of taxes levied by the Internal Revenue Service or actions not exceeding the current monetary limit set forth in the rules, founded upon the Constitution, any act of Congress, or any regulation of any executive department (Claims Court has concurrent jurisdiction in those actions).
- Actions for the partition of lands where the United States is one of the tenants in common or joint tenants.
- Actions involving banks and other corporations.

- Actions involving labor disputes by specific statute.
- Aliens' actions for torts.
- Actions and proceedings against consuls or vice consuls of foreign states.
- Actions on bonds executed under any law of the United States (state courts have concurrent jurisdiction in those actions).
- Actions involving Indian allotments and land grants from different states.
- Actions involving injuries under federal laws.
- All proceedings to condemn real estate for the use of the United States or its departments or agencies.

§ 9.13 Other Federal Courts

- United States Court of Appeals for the Federal Circuit—this court replaced the United States Court of Customs and Patent Appeals effective October 1, 1982. It hears appeals from the United States Claims Court, the United States Court of International Trade, the Merit Systems Protection Board, and appeals in cases relating to patents, copyrights and trademarks, among others. Its decisions may be reviewed by the United States Supreme Court on *certiorari*.
- United States Court of Military Appeals—this court hears appeals from court martial decisions. Its decisions may be reviewed by the Supreme Court by writ of *certiorari* in certain cases.
- United States Claims Court—this court, formerly called the United States Court of Claims, hears actions against the United States Government. These cases may be appealed to the United States Court of Appeals for the Federal Circuit.
- United States District Courts—these courts try both criminal and civil actions for which there is federal subject matter jurisdiction and sit as admiralty courts. They may also review decisions of federal administrative agencies. There is at least one United States District Court in each state. Their decisions may be appealed to the United States Courts of Appeals.
- United States Tax Court—this court, formerly called the Tax Court of the United States, hears cases concerning federal tax laws. Its decisions may be appealed to the United States Circuit Courts of Appeals (other than the Court of Appeals for the Federal Circuit).
- United States Court of International Trade—this court replaced the United States Customs Court, effective October 1, 1982. It hears cases concerning federal tariff laws. Its decisions may be

appealed to the United States Court of Appeals for the Federal Circuit.

- United States Bankruptcy Courts—these courts are units of the United States District Courts and hear bankruptcy and reorganization matters referred to bankruptcy judges by the District Courts. Their decisions may be appealed to the United States District Court and, in some cases, to the United States Circuit Courts of Appeals or a bankruptcy appellate panel, if one has been established in the particular circuit.

§ 9.14 State Court System

Because each state has the authority to create its own courts, there are more differences among state courts than federal courts.

Generally, each state has:

- A court of last resort that is the highest court in the state from which there is no appeal, except in certain instances when a decision may be reviewed by the United States Supreme Court.
- An intermediate appellate court or courts to which most appeals are brought before reaching the court of last resort.
- Courts of original jurisdiction having general unlimited jurisdiction. These courts may also have a division that has appellate jurisdiction to hear appeals from lower courts of limited power.
- On a level with these courts, there may be courts with limited jurisdiction, such as a court for family matters, a separate court to handle estate matters, and perhaps a separate criminal court. There also may be a court of claims to hear and determine claims by or against the state.
- The lowest courts in a state are typically courts with lesser monetary and territorial jurisdictions, such as small claims courts and traffic courts.

§ 9.15 Who May Sue?

Virtually anyone may sue anyone else. The important factor is whether or not the lawsuit has merit. Most lawsuits arise out of legitimate controversies where one party believes that it is entitled to some kind of relief, the other party disagrees, and they cannot come to terms through negotiation. Therefore, they must rely on the decision of a court and/or jury to determine which party has taken the correct position.

§ 9.15.1 Standing

The Litigation chapter explains the requirement of "standing" to mean that the person injured must be the one who brings suit. The word "person" here includes many legal entities, including corporations and partnerships, and is not limited to a human being. To have standing, the person must have the legal capacity to sue.

§ 9.15.2 Legal Capacity

Legal capacity refers to whether a person may sue in his or her own right and represent his or her own interests without the assistance of someone else. Each state sets the age at which a person reaches what is known as "the age of majority." Until a person reaches majority (usually 18 to 21 years of age), that person is a minor. A minor is someone under the age of majority whose legal affairs must be handled by a parent or a guardian. Therefore, minors lack the legal capacity to sue in their own right. Once that person reaches majority, that person then may handle their own legal affairs because the person then has legal capacity.

Most states have a provision that allows a minor to be emancipated before reaching the age of majority. This is most often accomplished by a petition of the parent or the minor asking that the court grant an order relieving the minor of the "legal disabilities that attach to minors." Although there is usually a minimum age at which a state will allow a minor to be emancipated, once that emancipation is granted, the minor has the legal capacity and the legal authority to handle their own legal affairs.

§ 9.15.3 Corporations and Other Business Entities

In law the word "person" has many meanings. Various business entities that are not really persons (humans) are recognized in the law as being legal persons. A corporation, for example, is a person (legal entity) that is separate and distinct from the people who run it; for purposes of "standing," it is a person, and it has legal capacity to sue.

§ 9.15.4 Incapacitated and Deceased Persons

An adult who is mentally incapacitated cannot sue except through a guardian who has been appointed by the court to handle the legal affairs of that person. A deceased person's estate has standing to be a party to a lawsuit only through a fiduciary (administrator, executor, or personal representative) appointed by a court.

§ 9.15.5 Parties

Often, the natural persons, corporations, or other legal entities involved in a lawsuit are referred to as "parties." The word "parties" is not limited only to natural persons but includes corporations, guardians of minors, estates of deceased persons, etc. A party to an action is a person by or against whom a legal suit is brought.

§ 9.15.6 Parties to an Action

The word "plaintiff" is most commonly used to refer to the party who files a lawsuit. The term "petitioner" is often used to refer to a party who files a nonlitigious legal proceeding (such as an adoption or probate matter) or the party who initiates dissolution proceedings in states having no-fault divorce laws.

The defendant is the party who is sued. In states having no-fault divorce laws, the party being sued is often called the "respondent."

After the complaint has been filed, many other pleadings (see next section) involving additional claims may ensue. The defendant may file a counterclaim against the plaintiff. In this instance, the defendant would then become the counter-plaintiff, and the plaintiff would be the counter-defendant. In addition, other parties may be joined by the defendant in the lawsuit as third-party defendants by a process known as impleader.

When a case is appealed, the party appealing is referred to as the appellant. The party against whom the appeal is filed is known as the appellee or, in some states, as the respondent.

EXAMPLES:

Alice Williams, Defendant–Appellant

v.

Sam Jones, Plaintiff–Respondent

Jack White, Plaintiff–Appellant

v.

Sandra Black, Defendant–Appellee

§ 9.16 Pleadings

Written statements called "pleadings" are made by each side of a lawsuit concerning the respective claims and defenses that will be decided in court. The term "pleading" generally denotes only those documents that contain statements or denials of fact, such as the complaint, the answer, the reply (where permitted), an answer to a crossclaim, or a third-party complaint and answer. Other papers filed in court may include petitions, orders, motions, memoranda, and affidavits. These documents, however, are generally not included within the term "pleading," which is typically defined by the rules of a particular court.

§ 9.16.1 Filing

When a pleading is stamped and placed in the court file by the clerk or deputy clerk, the pleading is considered "filed." If it is the first pleading in the case, the clerk opens a new file and issues a docket number (also sometimes known as a civil number, a case number, or an index number). The case number is to be used on all future pleadings and documents filed in that case.

Some courts charge a fee in order to file certain types of pleadings or documents. Some courts charge a fee only for commencing the action when the first pleading (complaint) is filed; others charge a fee for each additional pleading initiating action (such as counterclaims). Still other courts charge for filing certain other documents, such as jury demands. Most courts require the correct filing fee to be paid at the time the applicable document is filed. Some federal courts accept and/or require electronic filing. This is certainly where most federal courts are headed at this writing.

§ 9.16.2 Summons and Subpoena

After a complaint has been filed, the clerk in some states will sign and "issue" a summons that must be served on the defendant. In other states the summons may be issued by the plaintiff's lawyer after it is file stamped with the case number by the clerk. Service of the summons upon each defendant is generally necessary to bring that defendant within the power or jurisdiction of the court.

After a case is filed, the clerk can issue subpoenas summoning witnesses to testify at depositions or at trial. These subpoenas usually are prepared by the lawyer for issuance by the clerk. In some states, lawyers can issue subpoenas in a pending case without the approval of the clerk.

§ 9.16.3 Appearance of Counsel

After receiving the summons and complaint, most defendants hire an attorney. The first thing an attorney will generally do is file an "appearance" with the court. This tells the court and the plaintiff that the defendant is represented by counsel, and that all contact with defendant must be through his or her attorney.

§ 9.16.4 At Issue

A case is said to be "at issue" or the issues are said to be "joined" when the complaint and a responsive pleading (usually an answer) have been filed. This means that the plaintiff has pleaded his or her claims and the defendant has pleaded his or her defenses to those claims. There now exists a preliminary indication of which facts or issues are in dispute.

§ 9.16.5 Default

In some instances after a complaint is filed, the defendant enters no responsive pleading. After the time set by rule or statute has passed and the defendant has made no answer, the defendant is said to be in "default." The plaintiff, through his or her lawyer, can then apply for a default judgment against the defendant. *See* § 9.20.4.

§ 9.16.6 Service

Court rules require that each party to an action must be provided with copies of all court documents filed in the lawsuit. Except for summonses, complaints, and subpoenas, which are usually required to be served personally on the defendant (in the case of the summons and complaint) or the witness (in the case of a subpoena), this is accomplished by mailing or hand delivering copies to the attorneys of record or to the defendant if there is no attorney of record.* A certificate of service, which can be typed at the end of the document or an entirely separate document, states that the appropriate copies have been provided to the lawyers for the parties. A copy of the certificate of service is filed with the court.

EXAMPLE:

I certify that on the _______ day of _______ [year], I mailed (or hand delivered) a copy of the foregoing Answer to John Q. Jones, Esq., 999 Tudor Avenue, Salt Lake City, Utah 84111, attorney for plaintiff.

____

(name of lawyer)
Attorney for Defendant

This method of service does not apply to complaints, summonses, and subpoenas, because they must be served personally by an authorized person. In some jurisdictions service may be obtained by certified mail, return receipt requested. If personal service is not possible, upon approval of the court, service usually can be accomplished by publication of appropriate notice in a newspaper.

Service in federal court is outlined in Rule 4 of the Federal Rules of Civil Procedure.

Generally, Plaintiffs have several options for service:

(1) Waiver of service: In this method, plaintiff mails to defendant, other than an infant or incompetent person, a copy of the

* Although the term "lawyer" is used throughout this text, courts generally use the phrase "attorney of record" and "attorney for _______."

complaint (no summons is issued by the clerk) and a notice of right to waive formal service of process. If defendant returns the notice within 30 days of waiving formal service, no further service is required, and the defendant has 60 days from the date the notice was placed in the mail to formally answer the complaint.

(2) Personal service of summons (issued by the clerk of the court) and complaint: Anyone at least 18 years of age and not a party to the case can serve process.

(3) Certified mail service by the clerk of the court: In this method, plaintiff files a written request with the clerk of court for certified mail service, and prepares and submits with the request—2 summonses for each defendant and a pre-addressed, postage pre-paid envelope, along with certified mail green cards for each defendant. The service envelope(s) and certified mail card(s) must be return addressed to the clerk of the court.

There are special rules for serving governmental defendants and foreign defendants. (*See* Rule 4, Fed. R. Civ. P.).

§ 9.16.7 Leave of Court

In the course of a lawsuit, it may become necessary to obtain the permission of the court to take some action, such as permission to amend a complaint or to extend the time within which to answer. This permission is termed "leave of court." Usually applicable rules of civil procedure dictate when leave is required.

§ 9.17 The Court

Technically the word "court" means a tribunal with judicial authority to handle the administration of justice. That administration requires a meeting place, a system for meeting at particular times, and administrative personnel. Therefore, when a person is said to be "in court," that phrase usually means that person is attending a formal court hearing. However, the day-to-day usage of the word "court" also includes:

1. Reference to a hearing date or place.
   EXAMPLE:
   Court will be held on June 10; or court will recess and reconvene at 2 p.m.
2. Reference to the judge who presides at a hearing or over a particular court.
   EXAMPLE:
   The Court believes; may it please the Court; if the Court please; or with the Court's permission. (All these remarks are made by or to the presiding judge.)

3. Reference to the physical facility which houses the court (the courtroom or the courthouse).
4. Reference to a specific court.
   EXAMPLE:
   Court of Common Pleas; or Probate Court, Tulsa County.

§ 9.17.1 Term of Court

Court rules sometimes designate the period of time during which a court sits to conduct business. This is known as a "term of court." A term may be divided into different periods that are referred to as sessions. These terms are often given a name related to the time of year, such as "spring term" or "October term." Some courts use a descriptive name such as "general term" or "trial term."

§ 9.17.2 The Bar

In a courtroom, there is usually a railing separating the area where the lawyers, witnesses, court reporters, jury, and judge sit from the spectators' area. This railing is generally referred to as "the bar." When a lawyer is licensed to practice, they are permitted to go beyond the railing into that particular part of the courtroom. Hence, being licensed to practice law is known as being "admitted to the bar." The "bar" also refers to the whole body of lawyers who have been admitted to practice law in a particular state or court system. Their organization is known as the "Bar Association."

§ 9.17.3 The Bench

The raised podium at the front of a courtroom behind which the judge sits is known as "the bench." During a trial, lawyers may request permission to "approach the bench," meaning that they wish to confer privately with the judge out of the hearing of the jury.

§ 9.17.4 In Chambers

In some instances, a judge may meet with the lawyers and parties in chambers (the judge's office) rather than in the courtroom. These meetings are usually more informal than hearings in open court. Proceedings in chambers are generally not recorded unless the lawyers make a specific request to do so.

§ 9.17.5 In Open/Closed Court

Hearings conducted in the courtroom at which members of the general public may be present as spectators are said to be "open." In contrast, hearings that exclude spectators are "closed" hearings. A judge, in some instances, may exercise discretion as to whether or not to close a hearing. Generally, however, unless a closed hearing is required by law (such as juvenile hearings and adoptions), court hearings are open to members of the public.

§ 9.17.6 *Ex Parte*

Ex parte communication is communication to the court that does not involve all of the parties to the matter. *Ex parte* communication is generally prohibited and under most circumstances, is considered an ethical violation. However, there may be exceptions in some areas of law.

The prevention of injury or harm may necessitate *ex parte* communication; the party who was not included will be "informed" in due time by service of process. For example, a petition for a Temporary Restraining Order or a Personal Protection Order may be permitted *ex parte*.

If a party has not yet been served in a lawsuit, an application for an extension of time to effect service would also be an *ex parte* communication that could be permitted. Note, however, that the party is not involved in the communication because they have not yet been served.

An order granted *ex parte* generally makes provision for a date and time at which the opposing side may appear before the court to present arguments against the continuation of such order.

§ 9.17.7 Show Cause

A Petition for an Order to Show Cause requests relief and requires the opposition to appear and "show cause" why an order granting the relief sought should not be entered or continued in force. The opposition must be served with a copy of the Petition within a specific time prior to the date set for hearing. At the hearing, the requested relief can be granted, denied or modified. An order to show cause may initially be made *ex parte* but the opposing party must be served and have the opportunity to reply.

§ 9.17.8 Contempt of Court

When an individual refuses to obey either a written or an oral order of the judge, the judge may find that person "in contempt of court." The judge usually has the option of levying a fine or imposing a jail sentence (or both) upon the person who is adjudged to be in contempt of court.

§ 9.17.9 *Pro Se* (In Proper Person)

When a person decides to represent him or herself and appears without a lawyer, that person is said to be appearing *pro se* (literally "for myself") or "in proper person." The *pro se* party uses that designation when signing pleadings as well. Generally, corporations, partnerships and other legal entities cannot appear *pro se* and must use a lawyer.

§ 9.17.10 Law and Motion Day

A court generally sets aside a specific time or day to hear routine matters, such as show cause orders and argument on motions. "Motions" are essentially an application by a party made to the court for the purpose of obtaining some relief in the form of an order. Motions may pertain to purely procedural matters such as an extension of time, or exclusion of evidence, or may seek substantive relief, such as motions to dismiss an action. Hearings at which only the lawyers but not the parties need appear, or which will be of short duration by nature, are usually set on these days or times.

§ 9.18 Court Officers

Most of the people involved in the administration of justice are known as "officers of the court."

§ 9.18.1 Judge

The judge is the presiding officer of the court. Most state judges are elected, although some are appointed. All federal judges are appointed. A judge's principal duties are to preside over hearings and the trial of a case and to rule on issues raised by pleadings or issues that arise during a hearing or trial. The judge instructs the jury on matters of law in jury trials.

§ 9.18.2 Clerk of Court

The court clerk is the administrator or chief clerical officer of the court. The clerk is responsible for the clerical details of a case. In most jurisdictions the clerk of the court is the custodian of all public records filed with the court. In some jurisdictions, the clerk of court is ex-officio recorder of conveyances and of mortgages, and in this capacity, the clerk may keep records of sales and mortgages on property.

§ 9.18.3 Secretary/Deputy Clerk/Law Clerk

Most judges have at least one assistant or deputy clerk or law clerk. This person may function as a secretary, assistant, and/or researcher for the judge. The assistant or deputy clerk may attend court sessions, and may be responsible for the judge's calendar, files, and exhibits that are filed with the court. Judges in federal courts and in the higher state courts usually have at least one law clerk in addition to a secretary.

§ 9.18.4 Minute Clerk or Court Reporter

A court generally has a court reporter attend in-court sessions and record all legal proceedings verbatim with some type of recording equipment. The court may also have a courtroom deputy clerk or minute clerk to keep track of files, exhibits, and proceedings, and to administer oaths.

§ 9.18.5 Bailiff

The bailiff is the peace officer of the court and is responsible for keeping order. The bailiff is also responsible for the protection of everyone in the courtroom and for maintaining appropriate decorum during proceedings.

§ 9.18.6 Sheriff or Marshal

The Sheriff is a county officer, and the United States Marshal is the law enforcement officer for federal court. Their duties are similar. The Sheriff and Marshal may serve summonses and complaints and subpoenas. They may serve orders of court, garnishments, and executions. The Marshal is responsible for the transportation of federal prisoners and protection of federal judicial officers. The Marshal makes civil seizures to satisfy judgments, holds public auctions, and reports the results to the court regarding these matters. In a few jurisdictions, there are civil sheriffs and criminal sheriffs. In such systems, the civil sheriff handles only civil matters, and the criminal sheriff handles only criminal matters.

§ 9.18.7 Lawyers

Each lawyer is also an officer of the court and as such is obligated to uphold the dignity of the court and to abide by the rules of the court.

§ 9.19 Complaint/Petition

The pleading that is filed to initiate an action is usually called a complaint or a petition. In some jurisdictions, the term "complaint" is used in litigated matters, and the term "petition" is reserved for legal proceedings that do not involve a contest, such as petitions for adoption.

The federal courts and some state courts adhere to the doctrine of "notice pleading." This simply means that a complaint or answer to a complaint is sufficient if it puts the other party "on notice" of the claims asserted in the pleading.

§ 9.19.1 Caption

The caption of the case is the title of the case. The actual form of the caption varies from jurisdiction to jurisdiction, but it usually sets out:

1. The full name of the court in which the action is filed;
2. The full names of the parties involved, with the plaintiff's name listed first. The Federal Rules of Civil Procedure, and some state courts, REQUIRE the caption of the complaint to include the full names of all parties involved. An abbreviated style is acceptable on subsequent pleadings in which case, if there are numerous plaintiffs involved, only the name of the first plaintiff must be given, followed with the designation "et. al." to indicate that there are other plaintiffs. This abbreviation is proper on all pleadings subsequent to the initial pleading. The same procedure is generally used for cases having numerous defendants;
3. The number of the case. On initial pleadings, the court will assign a docket or case number when the action is filed; and
4. The name of the pleading.

EXAMPLE OF A COMPLETE CAPTION:

IN THE DISTRICT COURT OF THE SIXTH JUDICIAL
DISTRICT OF THE STATE OF IDAHO, IN AND
FOR BANNOCK COUNTY

JOHN DOE, FRED WHEELER,	)	
SAM SMITH, GEORGE	)	
ALCOTT, ACE LINCOLN,	)	Civil No. ______
and JOHN BRYAN,	)	
Plaintiffs,	)	COMPLAINT
vs.	)	
	)	
JANE X. BROWN,	)	
Defendant.	)	

§ 9.19.2 Opening Paragraphs

The opening paragraphs of a complaint usually provide introductory information about the name, legal capacity, and domicile of the parties, as well as the legal basis for jurisdiction of the court and venue (the geographic location of the court).

§ 9.19.3 Allegations/Claims

The opening paragraphs are followed by numbered paragraphs setting forth the background and reasons for filing the suit. These paragraphs are referred to as "allegations," which must set forth a short, concise statement of the claim(s) or cause(s) of action.

§ 9.19.4 Prayer

The complaint usually ends with a "prayer" or a request for relief that sets forth a summary of what the plaintiff or petitioner is asking the court to do.

§ 9.19.5 Verification

A complaint must be signed by the plaintiff's lawyer and it must contain the lawyer's address and state bar member number. Because it contains allegations of fact, in some jurisdictions the complaint may contain a statement by the plaintiff asserting that the allegations are true and correct to the best of his or her knowledge and belief. This is called a "verification" and is placed at the end of the complaint following the lawyer's signature. (*See* Illustration 9–3.) A verified complaint may be used as an Affidavit in later proceedings in the case.

Illustration 9–3

NO. ______

JANE DOE,	)	IN THE DISTRICT COURT
Plaintiff,	)	
v.	)	______ JUDICIAL DISTRICT
	)	
ALEX PRINCE,	)	BEXAR COUNTY, TEXAS
Defendant.	)	

COMPLAINT

Plaintiff makes the following complaint:

1. The plaintiff is a resident of the City of ______, County of ______, State of ______, and the defendant is a resident of ______ County, residing at ______ Street, ______, ______. [*If either party is a corporation, give place and where incorporated.*]

2. On or about the ______ day of ______, [year], a ______ automobile owned by plaintiff was being driven by ______ in a ______ direction on ______ Street, in the City of ______. [*Here set out facts upon which the plaintiff bases her cause of action.*]

3. The defendant was negligent in the operation of his automobile at the time of the collision in the following particulars: [*here state facts indicating negligence*].

Each of the foregoing acts of omission and of commission was negligent, and each was a proximate cause of the accident that is the basis of the suit.

4. As a result of the collision, plaintiff has been forced to spend the sum of $______ in order to repair her automobile.

5. Plaintiff's automobile prior to said collision had a reasonable market value of $______, and just after the collision it had a reasonable market value of $______. Therefore, the plaintiff has been damaged in the amount of $______.

WHEREFORE, plaintiff prays that upon final hearing, the plaintiff recover her damages as alleged above, together with all costs; and for such other, further, and general relief to which she may be entitled.

____

(name and address of lawyer)
Attorney for Plaintiff

STATE OF TEXAS)
) ss.
COUNTY OF ______)

JANE DOE, being duly sworn, deposes and states that she is the plaintiff in the above entitled action, that she has read the foregoing complaint and that every statement contained in the complaint is within her personal knowledge and is true and correct.

____

JANE DOE

Subscribed and sworn to before me the ______ day of ______, [Year].

____

Notary Public, State of Texas
My commission expires:

§ 9.19.6 Types of Relief Sought

Although most lawsuits seek awards of money, some seek other types of relief.

EXAMPLES:

Assume *A* and *B* entered into a contract in which *B* agreed to begin building a residence for *A* within 90 days after execution of the contract. *B* does not begin the work as he promised. *A* sues *B* for "specific performance," which means he wants *B* to perform the terms of the contract.

A is demolishing a building in a residential area using explosives. *B* is concerned that his building next to *A*'s also will be demolished by the explosion. *B* may seek injunctive relief asking the court to issue an injunction preventing *A* from using explosives to demolish his building.

Injunctive relief also may be sought to require that something be done rather than to stop something.

EXAMPLE:

A and the phone company are involved in a dispute over the nonpayment of a commercial account, a portion of which *A* guaranteed. *A* refuses to pay the disputed portion of the bill, so the phone company terminates *A*'s phone service at his residence. *A* seeks mandatory injunctive relief to require the phone company to restore his service.

§ 9.19.7 Alternative Relief

In suits that seek one type of relief, it is not uncommon to ask for alternative relief as well.

EXAMPLE:

Assuming the facts in the house construction contract example above, *A*'s complaint could contain a plea in the alternative that if the court decides he is not entitled to specific performance, then he should be awarded a sum of money damages for the harm he sustained in not having his residence timely built.

§ 9.19.8 Docket or Case Number

When a legal proceeding is filed with the clerk of court, it is given a docket or case number. Most courts having numbering systems assign numbers in numerical order, but sometimes the numbering systems are divided into various subject matters. Some courts use their numbering systems to keep track of the number of lawsuits filed in a particular category each year. Docket numbers may be referred to in different jurisdictions as, for example, Civil No. ______, Criminal No. ______, or Case No. ______.

§ 9.20 Conduct of the Lawsuit

The following subsections describe procedures involved in lawsuits.

§ 9.20.1 Filing Pleadings and Other Papers

With exceptions in some courts (especially federal trial courts) concerning certain discovery requests, the original of the pleadings and other papers, created by the lawyers during litigation, generally are filed with the clerk of the appropriate court. These pleadings and other papers are placed in the court record. Additional copies are sometimes required to give to the judge to whom the case is assigned. Check your state and federal court rules for the filing of discovery and disclosure requirements.

§ 9.20.2 Summons

When a lawsuit is filed in a court, the clerk generally issues a notice to the defendant that a lawsuit has been filed against them. This notice is called a "summons." In some states, the summons may be signed and issued by the plaintiff or the lawyer. The summons and a copy of the complaint, if any, may be served by the sheriff, the deputy, or by any other authorized person who is over the age of 18 and not a party to the action.

§ 9.20.3 Answer

The answer is a responsive pleading in which the defendant responds to the allegations of the complaint, paragraph by paragraph. The response to the complaint must be filed within a statutory period of time (usually 20 or 30 days from the date the defendant is served with the summons; be sure to check your rules) unless the defendant is given additional time by the plaintiff's lawyer and/or by the court. In federal court, extensions of time are obtained only with permission of the Court. In some instances, an answer may never be filed because:

- The defendant never appears in the case, or
- The case has been settled out of court.

A trial cannot be held until the answer is filed.

§ 9.20.4 Default

If the defendant does not file an answer within the time required by the court rules, the defendant is in "default." Generally, a court will set aside a default if a defendant asks the court to do so and has a reasonable explanation for failure to file an answer. However, if the default is not set aside, the plaintiff is generally entitled to have a "default judgment" entered granting the relief requested in the complaint. Usually a default judgment requires a hearing where the plaintiff offers minimal evidence to support allegations stated in the complaint. This evidence is usually the sworn testimony of the plaintiff and any documents (such as a contract or a lease) on which the claim is based.

§ 9.20.5 Motions

Often during the course of a legal proceeding, one of the parties to the proceeding must seek some type of interim order from the court. This is usually done by asking the court for some specific relief. This request is accomplished by a written motion.

EXAMPLE:

If there is a hearing set in a case on a date when one of the lawyers already has a trial scheduled, he can file a Motion for

Continuance. (The lawyer asks the court to continue the trial to another date.)

Some courts require supplementary documents supporting the request, such as an Affidavit, Memorandum of Law, or legal brief.

§ 9.20.6 Notices

Whenever a hearing is scheduled, all parties must be informed of the date, time, place, and subject matter to be heard. This is accomplished by sending a Notice of Hearing to all lawyers involved. The lawyer requesting the hearing generally prepares and sends the notice. Federal courts set the time for the motion and it notifies unrepresented parties. Local state courts often have specific and varied requirements for setting hearings. Check local rules, and, when in doubt, call the court to confirm its procedures.

§ 9.20.7 Orders

When a motion and Notice of Hearing are filed, the judge may hold a hearing and issue an order on the motion. In some instances, no hearing is held because the motion is routine, opposing counsel does not object, or the particular court does not hold hearings on motions. The order usually is prepared for the judge's signature by the lawyer who prevails on the motion, though in federal court, the judges generally prepare their own orders.

§ 9.20.8 Judgment

When a court issues a decision, it is said that the court "renders judgment."

When a plaintiff sues a defendant, that plaintiff is seeking a judgment or order of the court granting some type of relief. It may be that the defendant owes the plaintiff money, or it may be that the plaintiff wishes the defendant to do some particular thing. If the judge believes that the plaintiff is entitled to the relief sought, the judge will sign the judgment or order granting that requested relief. This generally occurs after a trial on the merits, though it could follow a motion. If the court believes the plaintiff is not entitled to any relief, a case may be dismissed by an order of the court.

If the judgment rendered is against the defendant and is for a certain sum of money, in most jurisdictions, the plaintiff can seek satisfaction of the judgment by seizing assets that belong to the defendant. The plaintiff might seize the defendant's bank account, wages, a car, or anything of value that the defendant owns. There are many variances from state to state as to what property can be seized in satisfaction of a judgment and the procedures that must be followed to accomplish the seizure.

In most states a judgment is recorded in the county where it was rendered, and becomes a lien attaching to any property owned by the defendant in that county. This means that the defendant will be unable to dispose of the property until the lien is satisfied. Once a judgment has been paid, the judgment is said to have been satisfied. Once a judgment has been satisfied, evidence of satisfaction is recorded so that the judgment can be canceled. The mechanics of recording and canceling judgments vary considerably from state to state.

§ 9.20.9 Opinion of Court

Most courts provide written reasons for the judgments entered on the merits of a case. This is a document signed by the judge that sets out the factual and legal reasons as to how the decision was reached. This document is generally known as the "Memorandum Opinion" or simple "Opinion" of the Court. Some courts will also issue detailed "Findings of Fact and Conclusions of Law" in support of the judgment.

§ 9.20.10 Appeals

Once a judgment is rendered by the court, the losing party may appeal. Except in rare instances, the losing party has the right to one automatic appeal, frequently referred to as an "Appeal of Right." If the appeal is filed within the statutory time period, the appellate court must review the law as applied to the facts of the case by the trial judge. It may also review questions of evidence or the fact-findings of a jury. The procedure in the appellate court is quite different from that in the trial court because there is not another trial. The appellate court reviews the lower court record of the entire proceeding (in some states a shortened version of the record is required). When the record has been prepared and delivered to the appellate court, it is said to have been "filed" or "lodged." The lawyers for the parties file briefs and may later appear before the appellate court for oral argument. No witnesses appear at such a hearing. After the appellate court has studied the record of the case, the briefs filed by the parties, and the oral arguments, if any, the appellate court renders its decision. The appellate court has a number of options in reviewing a case:

1. It can "affirm" the judgment of the trial court. This means that the appellate court agrees with the trial court's decision.
2. It can "amend" the judgment of the trial court. This means that the appellate court believes that all or a portion of the judgment of the trial court was in error and it therefore amends (changes) it.

3. It can "remand" the case back to the trial court. This means that the appellate court believes that the trial court failed to consider an important point, or failed to apply the law correctly, so the case is sent back to the trial court for reconsideration. This may result in a complete new trial or a partial retrial.
4. It can "reverse" the judgment of the trial court. This means that it believes that the trial court reached the wrong decision, and the appellate court completely reverses the trial court's decision (reaches the opposite decision).
5. It can affirm in part and reverse in part.

After the appeal court renders its judgment, the losing party may request a rehearing.

In states having intermediate courts of appeal, there is a court of last resort (most often called the Supreme Court) which has the right to review the lower appellate court decisions. In those instances, however, that court usually has the right to decide whether or not it will review the decisions of the intermediate courts of appeal in the first place. The party seeking the review (the losing party in the intermediate appellate court) applies to the Supreme Court for a Writ of *Certiorari* (review) or petitions for leave to appeal. The Supreme Court, on the basis of the application, decides whether or not it will grant the writ or the petition and hear the case. If it does, the entire court record of the proceedings up to that point (from the initial pleading in the lawsuit to the decision of the intermediate appellate court) is sent to the Supreme Court. The same procedure as in the intermediate appellate court then is followed. The lawyers for all parties involved file briefs. There may be oral argument before a panel of judges and after reviewing the entire record with the additional briefs and arguments, the Supreme Court reaches a decision, usually set forth in a written opinion. In some states, once the Supreme Court has reached its decision, a party may petition the court for a rehearing. Even when a court has the right to grant a rehearing, it rarely does. Rehearings are granted if the losing party can convince the Court that it made a grave error or failed to consider an important legal point.

If the court of last resort is a state court, a losing party may be able to seek review by the United States Supreme Court. Such review is limited to cases of the utmost significance, generally involving review of constitutional issues.

Once a legal matter has been heard by the court of last resort or once that court has refused a further hearing of a case, the judgment in that case is said to be *res judicata*. This means that the particular dispute has been resolved once and for all, and neither party to the suit can sue the other again regarding the same dispute.

§ 9.21 Decorum in the Courtroom

Most court proceedings are not conducted as portrayed on television. Judges and courts are entitled to be treated with respect not always accorded their TV counterparts. Generally, each time a court convenes, the bailiff enters the courtroom immediately before the judge, asks that all stand, and makes an announcement such as: "Oyez, oyez (or Hear ye, hear ye), the Honorable 19th Judicial District Court in and for the County of Tulsa, State of Oklahoma, is now in session. The Honorable Mary Ann Spencer presiding."

The judge also stands, because it is the court itself (the tribunal) that is being honored, not the judge. In most cases, spectators are allowed in the courtroom, but if the spectators are disruptive, the judge may have them removed.

§ 9.22 Contact With Courts

In performing your daily tasks, you will often find it necessary to talk with personnel in the clerk's office or the judge's office. Having an amicable relationship with these people can make your job much easier. Remember that they are the people who process most of your work. Because they are thoroughly familiar with the procedural aspects of the matters they handle, you should seek guidance from them when you are uncertain as to how to proceed. Set up a filing system of names, addresses, and telephone numbers of the people with whom you deal noting that person's expertise. It is helpful to address the clerks and their staff by name. Displaying such initiative will also demonstrate to your employer that you are interested and know how to do a good job.

§ 9.23 Court Records

Courts, both federal and state, generally must keep a record of all judicial proceedings. The record is the written history of all proceedings in a legal matter, regardless of whether the matter is tried. A court record is opened or begun when the complaint or petition is filed. All subsequent pleadings in that case, all actions taken by the court, all written material filed for discovery or evidence, and the transcript of the trial, if there is one, are filed in the record. Electronic filing in federal and state courts is becoming more prevelant. If an appeal is taken, the appeal also forms part of the record. In the event of an appeal, the entire record, or some designated portion, is sent to the appellate court. The proceedings in the appellate court also become part of the record; and when all appeals have been exhausted, the record on appeal is sent back to the trial court, where it remains. Some courts, such as justice of the peace courts, however, do not keep written records of all proceedings in a legal matter, because these are not "Courts of Record."

§ 9.24 Rules of Court

Each court, whether federal or state, has its own rules and procedures that govern the conduct of matters filed with the court. These rules have the effect of law, and are very important to the efficient preparation of pleadings or documents, as well as your interaction with the court. It is essential that you have a copy of the court rules for each court in which you will file pleadings. Copies of these rules are usually available from the clerk of court's office. If your firm subscribes to publications of West Group, your office each year receives from West a publication giving the court rules of the United States Supreme Court, the United States Courts of Appeals in which your state is situated, the federal district courts for your state, and the major state courts of your state. Look for this publication in your library and become familiar with it. Most courts also publish their rules on their respective web pages.

The rules of court provide the court's requirements as to the number of copies of pleadings which must be filed, any costs and fees for filing, information about getting orders signed by the judge, priority of some kinds of cases, how to get on the trial docket, and other useful information. It is critically important that you consult the rules whenever you are unsure how to proceed in a matter pending in court.

As well as the official Federal Rules of Court which are adopted by Congress, and the state rules that are generally adopted by the Supreme Court of a given state, local courts often adopt their own local rules that tend to fill in the gaps found in the federal and state rules. Therefore, you must have a copy of the local rules for your district as well.

§ 9.25 Summary

Although the subject of courts is very broad and sometimes difficult to comprehend, it is essential for a lawyer's assistant to have a thorough understanding of court structure and procedure. Court rules and procedures change constantly. You can keep current by reading bar association publications and by attending workshops and seminars sponsored by your local chapter of NALS and by the local and state bar associations. Often notice of changes in court rules and procedures come through the mail from law book publishers. You should study these changes after they have been routed to the lawyer, noting any important changes. It is your responsibility to be aware of current rules and procedures.

CHAPTER 10
ADMINISTRATIVE AGENCIES

Table of Sections

---

§ 10.1 Introduction

Administrative agencies are created by the legislative branch of government exclusively to administer a specific law or group of similar laws. Congress creates federal agencies, and individual state legislatures create state agencies. A lawyer's assistant must frequently interact with these agencies and should have a general knowledge of the functions performed by the agencies.

§ 10.2 Federal Agencies

The lawyer's assistant employed in a large city is often able to secure needed information from local branches of the various agencies and the public library. Local offices are listed under United States government offices in the telephone directory. However, for special kinds of information it may be necessary for the lawyer's assistant to communicate directly with the main office in the Washington, D.C. area. A useful internet site is www.FirstGov.gov.

Some of the agencies that the lawyer's assistant is most likely to encounter are:

1. Bureau of Land Management (BLM)
   www.blm.gov

The Bureau of Land Management, an agency within the U.S. Department of the Interior, administers 262 million surface acres of America's public lands, located primarily in 12 Western states. These lands are managed for multiple uses in three broad categories: commercial activities, recreation, and conservation. The BLM provides for acquisition, use, disposal, and adjustment of land resources; determines the boundaries of federal land; and maintains historic records for these ownership transactions.

2. Consumer Product Safety Commission (CPSC)
www.cpsc.gov

The purpose of this commission is to protect the public against unreasonable risks of injury from consumer products and to assist in the evaluation of the comparative safety of consumer products.

3. Department of Veterans Affairs (VA)
www.va.gov

Veterans' benefits, administered by the Department of Veterans Affairs (formerly the Veterans Administration), include cash benefits and services for veterans and their dependents and survivors. Among these benefits are education benefits; compensation for service-connected disability or death; pensions for non-service-connected disability or death, based on age and financial need; medical benefits including nursing home, domiciliary, or hospital care; burial benefits; and life insurance. Except for life insurance, these benefits do not create vested rights in the recipients and can be withdrawn by Congress or forfeited by the individual's beneficiaries.

4. Environmental Protection Agency (EPA)
www.epa.gov

The EPA works to protect and enhance our environment now and for the future by a coordinated effort with state and local governments to abate all forms of environmental pollution.

5. Equal Employment Opportunity Commission (EEOC)
www.eeoc.gov

The purpose of this commission is to eliminate employment discrimination in all areas and to promote voluntary compliance by employers.

6. Federal Aviation Administration (FAA)
www.faa.gov

The FAA is charged with regulating air commerce to foster aviation safety.

7. Federal Bureau of Investigation (FBI)
www.fbi.gov

The FBI has jurisdiction over and investigates all violations of federal laws except those specifically assigned to other federal agencies. Some of the areas in which the FBI is involved are espionage, sabotage, kidnapping, extortion, bank robbery, civil rights matters, interstate gambling violations, terrorist and foreign intelligence threats, and assault or killing of the President or a federal officer.

8. Federal Communications Commission (FCC)
www.fcc.gov

The Federal Communications Commission (FCC) is an independent United States government agency directly responsible to Congress. The FCC was established by the Communications Act of 1934 and is charged with regulating interstate and international communications by radio, television, wire, satellite, and cable. The FCC's jurisdiction covers the 50 states, the District of Columbia, and U.S. possessions.

9. Federal Deposit Insurance Corporation (FDIC)
www.fdic.gov

The FDIC preserves and promotes public confidence in the U.S. financial system by insuring deposits in banks and thrift institutions for at least $100,000; by identifying, monitoring and addressing risks to the deposit insurance funds; and by limiting the effect on the economy and the financial system when a bank or thrift institution fails. The FDIC insures deposits only. It does not insure securities, mutual funds or similar types of investments that banks and thrift institutions may offer.

10. Federal Mediation & Conciliation Service
www.fmcs.gov

This agency promotes the development of equitable and stable labor-management relationships and assists in settling disputes in the event of work stoppages or threatened work stoppages.

11. Federal Trade Commission (FTC)
www.ftc.gov

The basic objective of the FTC is to administer a wide variety of consumer protection laws, including the Telemarketing Sales Rule, the Pay–Per–Call Rule and the Equal Credit Opportunity Act, in order to maintain a free and fair competitive enterprise system within the American economic system.

12. Food and Drug Administration (FDA)
www.fda.gov

FDA activities are directed toward protecting the public against impure and unsafe drugs, food, cosmetics, and medical devices.

13. Government Printing Office (GPO)
www.gpo.gov

The GPO is the Federal Government's primary centralized resource for gathering, cataloging, producing, providing, authenticating, and preserving published information in all its forms. It is responsible for the production and distribution of information products and services for all three branches of the Federal Government. There are approximately a quarter of a million titles available to the public via the Internet on the GPO Access Web site at www.gpoaccess.gov. Through GPO's partner Web sites, an additional half a million titles are accessible to the public. Printed copies of more than 5,500 of those documents ranging from Supreme Court opinions to reports from the Bureau of Labor Statistics may also be purchased from the GPO Sales Program.

Superintendent of Documents

A free informational brochure, *Consumers Guide to Federal Publications,* designed to familiarize the public with the material is available from the GPO.

14. Internal Revenue Service (IRS)
www.irs.gov

The IRS administers all federal tax laws except those relating to alcohol, tobacco, firearms, and explosives.

15. National Labor Relations Board (NLRB)
www.nlrb.gov

The NLRB is vested with the power to safeguard employees' rights to form bargaining units and to prevent and remedy unfair labor practices.

16. Occupational Safety & Health Administration (OSHA)
www.osha.gov

OSHA develops and regulates occupational safety and health standards.

OSHA's mission is to assure the safety and health of America's workers by setting and enforcing marketplace safety and health standards; providing training, outreach, and education; establishing partnerships; and encouraging continual improvement in workplace safety and health.

17. Securities and Exchange Commission (SEC)
www.sec.gov

The SEC monitors the securities industry by providing disclosure to the investing public and protects the interests of investors against malpractice and illegal trades and sales in the securities and financial markets.

18. Small Business Administration (SBA)
www.sba.gov

The SBA seeks to maintain and strengthen the nation's economy by aiding, counseling, assisting and protecting the interests of small businesses and by helping families and businesses recover from national disasters.

19. Social Security Administration (SSA)
www.ssa.gov

This agency administers Social Security and Medicare programs.

20. United States Citizenship and Immigration Services (USCIS)
www.uscis.gov

The USCIS, within the Border and Transportation Security Directorate of the Department of Homeland Security, is responsible for the administration of immigration and naturalization adjudication functions and establishing immigration services policies and priorities. Immigration and Customs Enforcement include the enforcement and investigation components of the former INS, Customs, and the Federal Protective Services. U.S. Customs and Border Protection include the Border Patrol, as well as former INS, Customs, and Agricultural Quarantine Inspectors.

21. United States Marshals Service
www.usdoj.gov/marshals

The U.S. Marshals Service shares the responsibility for maintaining the integrity of the federal judicial process by ensuring the security of court facilities and the personal safety of judges, including around-the-clock protection when a real or apparent threat has been made because of court action. The Marshals Service has the primary responsibility for the tracking and apprehension of fugitives, assists other law enforcement agencies in apprehending fugitives, and is the principal contact for all international investigations and extraditions. This agency provides protection to witnesses whose testimony endangers their own lives or the lives of their families. It maintains custody of federal prisoners after arrest and during transport and also houses unsentenced prisoners in federal, state, and local jails throughout the nation. It is responsible for seizing, managing, and disposing of forfeited properties and assets from major drug and criminal cases. The Special Operations Group of the Marshals Service is a highly trained, self-supporting mobile (within six hours from anywhere in the United States) reaction force designated to provide federal assistance in emergency situations of national significance.

22. U. S. Patent and Trademark Office (USPTO)
    www.uspto.gov

The primary services of the USPTO include processing patent and trademark applications, issuing patents and trademarks if appropriate, and disseminating patent and trademark information.

23. United States Postal Service (USPS)
    www.usps.com

The Postal Service provides mail processing and delivery to individuals and businesses within the United States, and processes mail for delivery to areas outside of the United States.

§ 10.3 State Agencies

Each state government and many local governments have their own administrative agencies.

EXAMPLES:

Public service or public utilities commissions regulate utilities (oil, gas, water, telephone, and electricity). Workers' compensation boards or industrial commissions handle claims of workers injured on their jobs. Civil service commissions regulate the hiring of government employees.

Licensing boards regulate the issuance of licenses for any specific field designated by the acts that create these boards. (For example, the Licensing Board for Contractors would regulate licenses to contractors, and the Licensing Board for Realtors would regulate the issuance of licenses to realtors.)

Boards of health regulate matters concerning the health and well-being of the public.

Zoning commissions regulate the use of property within their respective jurisdictions.

School boards regulate matters involving the public school systems.

Banking boards regulate certain aspects of the banking business within their respective jurisdictions.

§ 10.4 Maintain an Agency Contact List

Many state and local governments publish a directory or manual that lists the various agencies and their functions. Your state website or Secretary of State should be able to provide a directory if available or tell you where you can secure such a list. Use this information to construct a contact sheet listing personal notes, the name, title, department/agency telephone and fax numbers, mailing addresses (e-mail, post office box, and street, as applicable) and notes of specific procedures for the respective department/agency.

CHAPTER 11

LITIGATION

Table of Sections

---

§ 11.1 Definition

Webster's Dictionary defines the word "litigation" as "the act or process of litigating; a suit at law." Litigation is the means of resolving a dispute between parties in a court of law. Simply stated, litigation is the handling, preparation, and trial of lawsuits.

This chapter offers a discussion of the steps in a civil lawsuit where a private party brings suit against another to resolve a dispute or a controversy.

§ 11.2 How Lawsuits Arise

The American legal system provides that any person injured by another may bring a civil suit seeking damages for that legal wrong. The reason for the lawsuit, then, arises when one party suffers an injury or damage as a result of a legal wrong committed by another. These factors are basic to any lawsuit—a wrong done by one and an injury or damage suffered by another.

§ 11.3 A Cause of Action

Generally, a person who suffers an injury from an automobile accident or a physical attack realizes a reason exists for suing to seek damages from the person who caused the injury. Even though the ordinary person may not know anything about the law, that person may realize that this cause of action is something for which to recover damages. Usually, a lawyer will be asked for advice and to handle the case.

§ 11.4 Res Judicata

Parties to a dispute have the right to have their case tried. However, under normal circumstances, it may be tried only once. This rule is known as the *res judicata* principle. As you learned from your study of courts, this rule means that once there has been a final judicial decision (usually by a court of last resort), the same matter cannot be litigated again. That matter has been set to rest forever. It is necessary to have such a rule so that the losing party will not return to court to keep asking for the case to be retried in the hope a sympathetic judge or jury will grant the requested relief. If that were to happen, the losing party would attempt retrials until the desired results were obtained.

§ 11.5 Beginning a Lawsuit—Initial Client Interview

The lawyer's first interview with the client is to determine whether there is a cause of action. In the early stages of the first interview, the lawyer must learn the names of all parties involved, if an insurance company is involved, and the names of any potential adverse parties. An initial or preliminary conflicts check should then be made before the lawyer elicits too much information from the prospective client. If not obtained during the initial telephone call, the lawyer is sometimes able to decide during the course of the interview whether to accept the case. Other times, further research may be done before deciding to handle the matter.

The lawyer will then answer the client's questions about the matter, explain how the case will be handled, the length of time it may take to resolve the matter, and the fee arrangement.

§ 11.5.1 The Fee Arrangement

Legal management experts and state ethical rules for lawyers recommend that a lawyer have a full understanding with the client of the fee arrangement. Most lawyers recognize the value of this advice and make it a point to reach an agreement on the fee and obtain it in writing during the first interview.

§ 11.5.2 Contingency Fees

When a client's case involves a personal injury for which damages may be recovered, the most common fee arrangement is a contingency fee. Under a contingency fee arrangement, the client pays a specified percentage of the total recovery as a fee. Usually, the percentage is less if the case is settled before a suit is filed. Under a contingency arrangement, if there is no recovery, there is no fee. However, the client is still responsible for costs because it is unethical for the lawyer to absorb these. Costs include all of the lawyer's expenses, such as service and filing fees, witness fees, etc.

§ 11.5.3 Fees Based on a Flat Fee or on an Hourly Basis

Depending on the kind of case involved, the fee may be an agreed amount for the work to be done. Often, the client is billed on an hourly basis, particularly in legal matters where it is difficult to assess how much time will be involved.

Regardless of the fee arrangement, the lawyer will want to have it in writing and may ask you to prepare the usual fee agreement letter while the client waits. Some offices have forms for this purpose. It is easy to tailor a form agreement to fit a particular situation.

§ 11.5.4 Authorization by Client

Depending upon the nature of the legal matter involved, there are probably several forms that the client will need to sign. It is usually more convenient for both the lawyer and the client to do this at the time of the initial client interview. Many offices use printed forms for this purpose.

§ 11.5.5 Medical Authorization

This form is necessary to secure medical reports, x-rays, and other medical data from doctors and hospitals. They do not release this information without a signed authorization by the patient. You will need to prepare a medical authorization for each doctor who treated the client and for each hospital or clinic in which the client was a patient.

§ 11.5.6 Employer Authorization

Employers need authorization to release payroll information, and it may be necessary to have this information to establish lost wages.

§ 11.5.7 Request for Copies of Income Tax Returns

Income tax returns may also be needed to establish damages or lost wages. State taxing agencies and the Internal Revenue Service have special forms for this purpose.

§ 11.5.8 Authorization for Lawyer to Settle

The client sometimes signs an authorization for the lawyer to settle the claim for a specified amount. Once the lawyer assesses the value of the claim, the client must authorize settlement for that amount.

§ 11.5.9 General Authorizations

The contents of general authorizations vary with each situation and are written to suit a particular need. The lawyer usually dictates the contents of these documents.

§ 11.5.10 Organizing the File

One of the most valuable services that you can render to the lawyer in litigation matters is to learn to organize the contents of the client's litigation file. From the information obtained during the initial interview, add the client's information to your rolodex/contact list, and prepare a billing record and ledger sheet for the client. Different offices have various systems for opening files. Familiarize yourself with the system used in your office and follow that procedure.

If there is no specific system used in your office for litigation matters, you may wish to consider the system discussed below. Ask the lawyer for permission to use it.

In organizing the file, the most important file is the pleadings file, which contains copies of all court documents and the affidavits or certificates showing that copies were sent to all other parties. Separate folders should also be prepared for different types of information. An exhibit folder, for instance, holds photographs, drawings, documents, and other materials the lawyer uses as exhibits at the trial of the case. An investigation folder holds accident reports, investigation reports, statements, and other items of that nature. Folders for depositions and statements of witnesses are also helpful and allow easy reference to those items. A folder or a notebook for all medical reports and bills may be kept up-to-date easily as the case progresses. In addition, depending on the complexity of the case, folders may be prepared for different legal research issues concerning the law applicable to the case.

If the lawyer uses a trial notebook, keep a supply of three-ring binders on hand so that the notebook can be prepared step by step as the case progresses.

Careful organization of the file will keep it in readiness for the lawyer's review at any time. Using this system, information will always be available to the lawyer at any stage of the case, and you will always be able to locate quickly any items and will be able to file any new materials in the proper place. By following this system throughout the course of the case, when trial time arrives, the file will be in excellent condition, and the lawyer will have available everything needed to present the case in an orderly fashion.

§ 11.6 Types of Litigation

The notes that the lawyer makes during the initial client interview will probably include a reference to the type of litigation involved in that particular case. The type of litigation is important because many decisions must be made to ensure that the lawsuit is properly filed and that proper proof is accumulated for the file.

§ 11.6.1 Workers' Compensation Suits

Workers' compensation suits are processed under the workers' compensation act of each individual state and are handled initially by a state administrative agency, such as an industrial accident board or industrial commission. A workers' compensation action is one which grows out of an on-the-job injury or occupational disease/illness. Most employers are required by state law to provide insurance to cover these claims unless they receive special permission to be self-insured. However, to qualify for self-insurance status, employers usually must prove that they are able to pay any workers' compensation award granted. Following the filing of notice by the employee and the compilation of various medical records, the agency conducts a hearing and enters an award. In most states, the award rendered by the board or commission is directly appealable to a state trial court and is then handled in the same manner as other lawsuits.

§ 11.6.2 Damage Suits

Damage suits cover a wide range of subject matter. A damage suit seeks an award of money. Some examples of damage suits seeking money damages are those arising from tortious acts, such as automobile accident cases; slip-and-fall cases; contract disputes; title actions (boundary disputes and other land matters); consumer actions; civil antitrust actions; and professional malpractice.

§ 11.6.3 Equity Suits

Rather than seeking monetary judgments, equity suits seek some specific action coercive in nature. Included are actions for an injunction (to prevent a party from committing some action or requiring them to perform some action) or for specific performance as, for instance, on a contract.

EXAMPLE:

> *A*, whose land borders *B*'s land, is digging postholes for a fence. *B* is sure that the holes are on his property. He seeks an injunction preventing *A* from further digging until the property can be surveyed and the property lines established.

§ 11.6.4 Role of Lawyer as a Negotiator

Regardless of the kind of litigation that might be involved if a lawsuit is filed, a lawyer may seek an amicable solution to the client's problem before filing the lawsuit. Litigation is expensive and time-consuming; and, therefore, the art of negotiation plays a vital role in trial practice. Even if a matter cannot be settled before the lawsuit is actually filed, negotiations between the lawyers usually continue throughout the course of the litigation up to the trial itself. It is not unusual for lawyers to reach a settlement the day of the trial.

If negotiations break down, the lawyer must file the suit because no purpose could be served by further negotiation. Some of the factors that must be considered in preparing the suit are discussed below.

§ 11.7 Factors to Be Considered Before Filing the Lawsuit

When a lawyer decides to file a lawsuit on behalf of a client, the lawyer must be certain that the lawsuit is properly brought. It must be filed by the correct parties in the proper court within the legal time periods. Following is a discussion of some of the factors that influence the lawyer's decision as to:

Who may sue?

Where must the suit be filed?

What is the statute of limitations involved?

§ 11.7.1 Mediation

Mediation is a nonbinding settlement discussion between the parties. A neutral, impartial third party assists with the negotiations and promotes reconciliation, settlement, or understanding among the parties. A mediator makes no decisions for the parties involved in the mediation process. The mediator must hold in confidence all information received during a mediation. Pre-suit mediation is not intended as a substitute for litigation or trial by jury, but as a method of settling a claim before filing suit. Mediation is commonly ordered by the Court. It is usually done while the case is pending and long after discovery is underway.

§ 11.7.2 Who May Sue

The injured party (or the party who has a claim) is the person best able to determine whether to seek a recovery through the legal system to rectify the alleged wrong done to them. Therefore, there is a concept in the law called standing, which means that only the party injured by another may bring a civil suit. This rule of standing is designed to control the amount of litigation that might arise from one incident or wrong by letting only the injured party sue. Anyone else would be denied the right to bring suit.

In the case of a minor child, parents may bring suit on the minor's behalf; the legal guardian of a ward of the court may sue on behalf of that ward; a fiduciary appointed by the court might sue on behalf of a deceased person's estate; and a shareholder might sue on behalf of a corporation in which the shareholder owns stock.

To summarize, the one who has standing to bring a suit is the claimant.

§ 11.7.3 Jurisdiction

The jurisdiction of the courts is set forth by Congress or by the legislatures of the various states and is the authority of a court to hear a matter. If the complaint or petition is not filed in a court having jurisdiction, then the lawsuit is worthless and any action by the court is void. Venue, often referred to as geographical jurisdiction, is the place of the lawsuit–the county or parish. Congressional statutes or the statutes of the various states govern the place where an action may be brought. Usually, it is where the incident causing the lawsuit occurred or where the parties reside. An important difference to consider between jurisdiction and venue is that the parties may waive venue, but jurisdiction may not be conferred upon a court by agreement of the parties.

Jurisdiction covers both the parties and the subject matter, as well as the amount or value in controversy and other relevant factors. As you will recall from your study of courts, courts may be said to have original jurisdiction or appellate jurisdiction. A new lawsuit may be brought only in a court of original jurisdiction. (For a more complete discussion of jurisdiction and venue, *see* the chapter on Courts.)

Often, courts have concurrent jurisdiction; that is, an action may be filed properly in any of several courts. For instance, some suits may be filed either in an appropriate state court or in a United States district court, provided the jurisdictional requirements of both courts are met.

§ 11.7.4 Statute of Limitations

Each state, as well as the federal government, has a statute of limitations, or time limit, within which a particular type of lawsuit must be filed. This does not mean that the suit cannot be filed. Anyone can file a lawsuit. It does mean that a defendant can ask to have the suit dismissed on the grounds that the statute of limitations has run. Most of the statutes of limitations do have exceptions that toll (delay) the running of the period of limitations. Such a tolling would have the effect of an extension of time in which to file the suit. However, if a defendant can show that their situation is not covered by an exception, the suit will probably be dismissed.

Note that the statute of limitations does not require that the litigation be completed within that time period; the lawsuit simply must be filed within that time period.

There are many statutes of limitations, and they vary in length of time. The statutes usually fix the time limits based on the kind of claim or lawsuit involved. These vary considerably from state to state; within states, they vary considerably among the types of claims. The statute of limitations might be one year for one kind of claim, ten years for another, etc.

§ 11.7.5 The Importance of Diarying the Statute of Limitations

Many legal malpractice claims arise out of missed statute of limitations dates. You can play a significant role in not allowing the statute of limitations to run against a client; do this by keeping an accurate tickler (reminder) system. As you open each file (or work on it for the first time), ask the lawyer to help you determine the statute of limitations date so that you can enter it on the calendar. You will find it beneficial to be thoroughly familiar with the statute of limitations in your state.

§ 11.8 Filing the Complaint or Petition

The first pleading filed in any lawsuit is the complaint or petition. This is filed with the clerk of the court having venue and jurisdiction over the parties and the subject matter. The person who files the lawsuit is known as the plaintiff, and the person sued is the defendant. The action may be by one or more plaintiffs against one or more defendants.

The complaint must follow a certain format when it is prepared. It begins with the jurisdiction of the case, *i.e.*, the name of the state and court. Next are the names of the parties involved in the suit, beginning with the plaintiff.

(Note sample complaint printed for reference in The Courts chapter.)

The court assigns a case number to every complaint that is filed. You should prepare a place for this number to be entered on your complaint. The name of the document should be spelled out; then the allegations of the plaintiff regarding the cause of action are set forth in numbered paragraphs. The complaint ends with a prayer for relief from the defendant, usually in a specific amount, and is signed by a lawyer.

Make enough copies of the complaint for each defendant, the client, and for the lawyer's file. The original is filed with the clerk of the court having jurisdiction of the case. You will also want to make a copy for your forms manual if it does not yet contain a sample of this kind of form. A filing fee is required at the time of filing the complaint.

§ 11.8.1 Verification

Since the lawyer signs the complaint and does not have firsthand knowledge of the case, it may be necessary in some jurisdictions for the plaintiff to sign a verification stating that the allegations of the complaint are true and correct. In some jurisdictions, this must be sworn to before a notary public. (*See* The Courts chapter for the form of an individual verification.)

§ 11.8.2 The Summons

A defendant must be served with the complaint and must be officially notified that suit has been filed. The official notification to the defendant that suit has been filed is called a summons. It should be noted that some jurisdictions do not use a summons. The summons also advises the defendant that there is a time limit within which an appearance in court must be made to answer the complaint or a default judgment can be taken against the defendant.

In some jurisdictions, the suit is not considered filed until the defendant has been served with the summons and complaint because it is the service upon the defendant that brings them within the jurisdiction of the court. Failure to make proper service on the defendant within a prescribed time period can cause the complaint to be dismissed. This could cause the claimant to lose the right to sue if, by that time, the statute of limitations has run.

§ 11.8.3 Preparation of the Summons

The summons is prepared by the lawyer's assistant or by the clerk of court, depending upon the rules of the court. In some jurisdictions, even if the assistant prepares the summons, the clerk must still issue it. In such cases, the clerk must sign it, seal it, and date it before it is served on the defendant.

You must prepare sufficient copies of both the complaint and the summons for service upon each defendant named in the complaint. You should prepare two copies for each defendant if the lawyer must provide an extra copy for the return of service in your jurisdiction (discussed below).

§ 11.8.4 Information for Service

Since it is vitally important that the summons and complaint be served promptly once the complaint has been filed with the court, you should be certain that you have given the process server correct information to help them locate the defendant. Some persons are very hard to locate, and any information about those persons, such as their place of employment or working hours, can be extremely helpful in arranging for prompt service. As a rule, you should make a point of providing the following information about each defendant: complete name, gender, race, home address, and place of employment including address, work hours, and telephone number. Any other information you may have about the person, such as type of car, places frequented, is helpful to the process server. If you make the extra effort to have all the above information available, the process server will stand a much better chance of making quick, effective service without incurring additional costs.

§ 11.8.5 Service on Corporations

Service on corporations is made through an agent for service, who may be an officer of the corporation, at its corporate offices within the state where the suit is instituted, or upon a separate professional agent for service, registered with the designated office of that particular state, commonly known as the "registered agent." Call the office of the corporate department or division of the secretary of state's office or the lieutenant governor's office to ask whether there is an agent for service within the state. When the defendant is a corporation, it is important to learn the name and address of the registered agent or the officers of the corporation so that the proper person may be served on behalf of the corporation.

The defendant corporation is often a foreign corporation, particularly in the case of insurance companies. A foreign corporation is a corporation that is domiciled in another state. It is important to determine whether that company has designated a registered agent to accept service of process in your state. This information is usually available from your secretary of state with whom foreign corporations must register or with the insurance commissioner for insurance companies. Most states provide for service through the secretary of state or insurance commissioner if no agent has been designated.

§ 11.8.6 Delivery to the Court Clerk

In preparing the complaint for filing with the clerk: check to see that the original complaint is signed by the lawyer and notarized, if applicable; confirm that the verification of the client is attached, if applicable; verify that you have sufficient copies for service and return of service; verify that you have the appropriate number of summonses prepared for issuance by the clerk, if appropriate; and verify that you have a check for the filing fee.

The court clerk assigns a new file number for the case, stamps the complaint to indicate the filing date, and prepares a file folder and record (docket sheet) for the new case. The clerk then puts the court seal on the summonses, signs and dates the summonses, and returns them to you to make arrangements for service on the defendants or delivers them to the sheriff if that is the procedure in your state.

§ 11.8.7 Service of Process

The method of service on defendants varies from state to state. In state courts, service is made by a sheriff, a constable, or other authorized person. Service is made by delivering a copy of the summons, together with a copy of the complaint, to each defendant. The process server then completes the return on the original of the summons or the copy you have prepared (depending upon the jurisdiction) which shows the name of the person served, the place, the date, and time of service. (*See* Illustration 11–1.) The summons showing the return of service is then filed with the clerk of the court.

In some jurisdictions, the process server prepares a separate certificate or affidavit as to the service which has been accomplished.

Illustration 11–1

RETURN OF SERVICE

STATE OF __________)
) ss.
COUNTY OF _________)

_______, being duly sworn, states that he is a person of suitable age and discretion and that on the _______ day of _______, [Year], he served the

Summons and the Complaint, a copy of which is attached hereto, upon ______________, at ______, by personally delivering same to said de-
(name of defendant)

fendant.

____

Subscribed and sworn to before me

this ______ day of ______, [Year].

____

Notary Public

My commission expires:

§ 11.8.8 Service on a Nonresident

For service of a defendant who is a nonresident, a process server in the defendant's area can be used. However, be sure to provide the process server with a copy of the rules of service for the jurisdiction in which the case is filed. Many states have a long arm statute, according to which service may be made on the office of the secretary of state, who forwards the lawsuit documents by certified mail, return receipt requested, to the out-of-state defendant at their last known address. A small fee is usually charged by the secretary of state at the time service is made. In some states, "long-arm" statute service can be made by the lawyer if sent by certified mail, return receipt requested.

§ 11.8.9 Other Types of Service

Some states also provide, under certain circumstances, for:

- Service on a third party at the residence of defendant.
- Service by posting the summons on the door of the defendant's residence or in a public place.
- Service by publication of a notice in a newspaper of general circulation for a specific period of time.

Affidavits as to the necessity of service by one of these means are sometimes required, and the court grants an order giving permission for service by one of these methods.

§ 11.9 Response or Answer to Complaint

The defendant has a specific time after being served within which to file an answer or other response to the complaint. The time varies from state to state and even from court to court within a state. In the federal courts, the time is usually 20 days if the defendant resides within the same state or unless the United States is a party defendant, in which case the answer date is extended to 60 days.

The summons usually specifies the time within which the defendant must respond to the complaint. Failure to respond within the time specified can result in a default judgment against the defendant. There are various responses or defenses that a defendant can advance. Since some responses could result in dismissal of the suit, they are filed before an answer is filed, often with a special (or limited) appearance for that purpose only. Ultimately, however, if the defendant is unsuccessful in having the suit dismissed, an answer must be filed.

The defendant's answer tells their version of the lawsuit. Often the defendant simply denies all allegations of the complaint.

EXAMPLES:

> The defendant John Good, by and through his attorney of record, for answer to the complaint filed herein, denies each and every allegation as though his denials were set out at length herein.
>
> The defendant John Good, by and through his attorney of record, for answer to the complaint filed herein, denies the allegations of paragraphs 1 through 10, inclusive, as though his denials were set out at length herein.

Sometimes the allegations contain information about which the defendant has no knowledge. However, each of the allegations must be answered. In this situation, those allegations are denied for lack of information sufficient to justify a belief as to the truth or falsity of a particular allegation in the complaint. (When the lawyer dictates such an answer to you, the dictation may simply say, "Deny number 3 for lack" and will expect you to be able to put it in the proper form.)

EXAMPLE:

> The defendant denies the allegations of paragraphs 5, 6, 7, 9, and 10 and states he does not have sufficient information or belief to answer those allegations.

Note that in federal court, and in most state courts, each specific allegation of the plaintiff's complaint must be either denied or admitted. Those allegations not specifically denied are deemed admitted unless the defense counsel can show good cause why they can neither be admitted nor denied (usually due to lack of sufficient information with which to respond). Consequently, it is good practice to include in the answer a general denial to the effect that "All allegations not specifically admitted herein are denied."

§ 11.9.1 Affirmative Defenses

There are special defenses available by law to certain types of actions. These special defenses are called affirmative defenses, and to be considered by the court, they must be asserted in the defendant's answer. If they are not included in the answer, the affirmative defenses are, in most courts, waived and may not be asserted later.

§ 11.9.2 Contributory Negligence

The defendant specifically pleads the contributory negligence of the plaintiff as an affirmative defense. Contributory negligence means that the injuries and damages complained of by the plaintiff were caused in whole, or in part, or were contributed to as a result of plaintiff's own negligence.

§ 11.9.3 Comparative Negligence

The defendant specifically pleads comparative negligence as an affirmative defense. Comparative negligence means that if an accident was caused in part by the negligence of plaintiff, any award to the plaintiff should be diminished in the proportion of their negligence.

§ 11.9.4 Assumption of Risk

The defendant specifically pleads assumption of risk as an affirmative defense. Assumption of risk means, for example, that the plaintiff was fully aware of the icy condition of the sidewalk and made a conscious decision to attempt to negotiate it.

§ 11.9.5 Statute of Limitations

The defendant specifically pleads as an affirmative defense that plaintiff's claim is barred by the applicable statute of limitations.

§ 11.10 Special Exceptions

The defendant may specially except and object to specific allegations in the plaintiff's complaint and may ask the court either to strike (eliminate) such allegations or require the plaintiff to replead more specifically. This is an objection to the form of the complaint.

§ 11.10.1 Plea to the Jurisdiction (Sometimes Called Special or Limited Appearance or Notice of Appearance)

A plea to the jurisdiction is filed, when appropriate, in lieu of an answer. It sets out that the court has no jurisdiction over the party filing it and states the reason for such lack of jurisdiction. Its purpose is to prevent the entering of a default judgment pending a decision by the court on the jurisdictional question. Usually this pleading must be sworn to and filed before any answer is filed, or the party entitled to file such an appearance may waive the right to file it.

§ 11.10.2 Plea to the Venue (Sometimes Called Plea of Privilege or Motion to Change Venue)

A plea to the venue must be filed before an answer is filed, must be sworn to, and must give reasons why the case should be transferred to another county or parish.

EXAMPLES:

The incident occurred in a different county from where the suit is filed, so this court does not have venue.

The residence of the parties is in a different county, so the court does not have venue.

The plaintiff, within a time set out by statute, may file a sworn controverting (opposing) plea, setting out any exceptions under the statutes that would allow the lawsuit to remain in the county where it was originally filed. If the plaintiff does not timely file such a plea, the court may automatically transfer the case to the county requested by the defendant (usually the county of his residence). After the time for filing such controverting plea has passed, the order of transfer is prepared by the defendant's lawyer and submitted to the court for entry. Unlike a plea to the jurisdiction, an answer to the petition or complaint must be filed in addition to the plea to venue, and such answer should always contain language to the effect that the answer is subject to the plea to venue and does not waive that issue.

§ 11.10.3 Motion to Quash Service

If service is improperly made, the wrong party is served, or the summons does not show the date of service, a motion may be made to quash service (declare the service invalid). This requires the plaintiff's lawyer to have the summons reissued and new service attempted.

§ 11.10.4 Removal to Federal Court

If the plaintiff's action was filed in a state court, jurisdiction would be valid in that district's federal court. If the defendant is from a different state and other requirements are met, the defendant may, within 30 days of service of first filing, file a petition to remove the case to the United States District Court for the particular district having jurisdiction. A defendant may also file a petition for removal if the case involves a question of federal law. If the plaintiff's lawyer desires, a motion to remand (return) the case to state court may be filed. The federal court then determines whether the case should remain in federal court or be returned to state court. If the plaintiff's lawyer does not file such a motion to remand, and the judge does not remand the case, the removal is effective and the case remains in federal court. The defense lawyer must then file an answer and a demand for jury trial if a jury trial is desired, and the case is handled as any other federal court case.

§ 11.10.5 Third–Party Complaint

During the preparation of the defense of the lawsuit, it may become evident that a party not named as a defendant may be responsible for the cause of action. The defendant (becoming the third-party plaintiff) files a third-party action against the additional party. In some jurisdictions, leave of court may be required. The defendant (now the third-party plaintiff) files the third-party complaint, and the new party (the third-party defendant) is served with a summons in the same manner that an original defendant is served. The third-party complaint must be complete in its allegations as to the third-party defendant. Within the time limit shown on the summons, the third-party defendant must file responsive pleadings. This situation occurs frequently in products liability cases.

EXAMPLE:

A buys a car from *B*, a car dealer. The car simply will not run, and *B*'s service department cannot get it to run. *A* sues *B* to rescind the sale and get his money back. When *B* answers *A*'s suit against him, he admits that he sold *A* the car but since he did not manufacture the car, he files a third-party complaint against *C*, the manufacturer of the car.

§ 11.11 Counterclaim

The defendant as a counterclaimant may file an action for damages (counterclaim) against the plaintiff, who then becomes a counter-defendant. This claim is usually a claim that would reduce the amount owed by the defendant to the plaintiff if the defendant is successful in establishing the claim.

EXAMPLE:

A hires *B* to install bathroom plumbing and agrees to pay $500. *A* pays $250 and does not pay the rest. *B* sues *A* for the $250. *A* counterclaims against *B* for $1,000, stating that the plumbing leaks and has destroyed his flooring worth $750 and he should have the $250 back.

§ 11.11.1 Cross–Claim (Also Called Cross–Complaint or Cross–Action)

Where there is more than one defendant, any defendant (who then becomes a cross-plaintiff) may file an action against any other defendant (who then becomes a cross-defendant) alleging that the cross-defendant was responsible for the matter which is the subject of the complaint. When a defendant files a cross-claim, the position taken is one that if defendant owes the plaintiff any money, then the cross-defendant owes defendant that same amount (or some portion of it). Therefore, if a cross-plaintiff is successful in presenting a cross-claim, a judgment against the cross-defendant will probably be similar to the one granted the plaintiff against defendant.

EXAMPLE:

A owns a building that he leases to *B* for $30,000 per year, payable in monthly installments. After *B* has been in the building two months, he subleases the building to *C* for the same rental. *C* pays the rent for one month and moves out of the building. *A* sues *B* and *C* for all unpaid rent under the lease. *B* files a cross-claim against *C*. *A* gets a judgment against *B* and *C*, and *B* gets a judgment against *C* on his crossclaim. *B* must pay *A* but he can collect from *C*.

§ 11.11.2 Distinction Between Cross–Claim and Counterclaim

Cross-claims are litigated by parties on the same side of the main litigation, while counterclaims are litigated between opposing parties to the principal action.

§ 11.12 Amended and Supplemental Pleadings

There are times when it is necessary to amend a pleading. Under the Federal Rules of Civil Procedure and in most state courts, any change in pleadings can be made once without court order at any time before responsive pleadings are filed. Afterward, either leave of court or consent of opposing counsel is usually needed to amend or supplement pleadings. The amendment changes the original pleading.

A supplemental pleading supplements or adds to the original pleading facts or events that have happened since the original pleading was filed.

§ 11.12.1 Distinction Between an Amended Pleading and a Supplemental Pleading

An amendment to a pleading involves the correction of the pleading. The content of the amendment was in existence at the time the original pleading was filed. On the other hand, a supplemental pleading involves events that were not known or not in existence at the time the original pleading was filed.

§ 11.12.2 Interventions

An additional party (intervenor) having an interest in the outcome of the lawsuit may attempt to intervene by filing a written petition in intervention, setting out the reasons why the intervenor has an interest and the amount the intervenor seeks.

EXAMPLES:

An insurance company, which has paid money damages to the plaintiff for injuries growing out of the same cause of action, may seek to recover its payment.

Where several parties claim injuries in the same incident and only one party has filed suit, others may petition to intervene, claiming they also were damaged and thus are entitled to recover damages.

In wrongful death cases that are usually filed by the spouse or an heir at law of the deceased, other heirs may intervene, claiming a legal interest in the estate of the decedent. This often happens in cases of prior marriages, where children of the prior marriage intervene for a portion of the recovery.

§ 11.13 Discovery

Evidence is needed by each party to a lawsuit to support its side of the case, and both attempt to gather by means of discovery all the necessary evidence for their use at trial. Discovery is the vehicle by which one party to a lawsuit is entitled to obtain certain facts, documents, and other information to help it prepare for trial. The purposes of discovery are to clarify the issues, to eliminate surprise in the courtroom, and to avoid wasting the time of the court.

Every lawyer knows that lawsuits usually are not won in the courtroom by brilliant trial tactics; rather, lawsuits are won in advance of trial by thorough preparation. Preparation may include use of any or all of the discovery procedures available under the law.

Discovery procedures include request for admissions, interrogatories, request for production of documents and other things, and depositions.

§ 11.13.1 Request for Admissions

As the name of the instrument implies, either party may request the other party to admit or deny certain facts in regard to the lawsuit, which are not in dispute. The reason for using such requests for admissions is to avoid having to prove such undisputed facts at the trial.

EXAMPLES:

1. Admit you were the owner of a blue automobile, license No. 0000, on the date of the incident that is the basis of this suit.

2. Admit you were the operator of that vehicle on the occasion in question.

OR:

1. Admit that you were a partner in the firm of Smith and Smith on August 1, 1997.

2. Admit that the firm of Smith and Smith entered into a contract (a copy of which is attached) on August 1, 1997, with the Jones Construction Company.

OR:

1. Exhibit A attached hereto is a true and correct copy of the contract entered into between A and B on March 1, 1997.

NOTE: In each of the sample requests, the admissions requested are easily established by testimony. However, to call witnesses at trial and ask them a series of questions designed to show those facts would be needlessly time-consuming and expensive. Note that the first two sample requests do not ask whether an accident took place and that the second two requests do not ask whether there was a problem concerning the contract because these likely would involve disputed facts. The requests simply resolve some basic, undisputed issues.

Requests for admissions are served on counsel for the opposing party and consist of:

1. The caption or style of the case;
2. The title of the pleading;
3. The name of the party to whom such requests are directed;
4. An opening paragraph setting out the state or federal rule under which the requests are made and the time within which to respond;
5. The requests;
6. The signature of the lawyer requesting the admissions;

7. A certificate that the request was served on the opposing lawyer and the method of service (mail or in person).

§ 11.13.2 Responses to Request for Admissions

When the lawyer receives a request for admissions on behalf of the client, you should stamp it with the date it is received and place a note in your tickler system in advance of the date the response is due. This is a very important service that you perform because failure to respond (usually within 30 days) results in a finding that the requests are admitted. There are several possible responses to such requests, but each separate request must be answered. For example, the lawyer responding may:

- Admit any statement.
- Deny any statement.
- Neither admit nor deny. (This must be done specifically and a reason given for the refusal to admit or deny must be given; this typically is due to lack of sufficient information with which to respond.)
- Omit any statement in the request. (This last method, however, must not be an oversight on the part of the lawyer's assistant or word processor, but must consciously be made by the lawyer because failure to respond to any statement in the request results in the statement being deemed admitted.)

The response may be short and need contain only the caption, title, and the responses, which may be shortened. Examples of responses might be:

1. Admitted.
2. Denied.
3. Neither admitted nor denied due to lack of information at this time with which to respond.

The response must be signed by the lawyer, and a verification (sworn statement) by the person making the response as to the truth of the responses must be attached. A certificate that the response has been served on opposing counsel is necessary.

§ 11.13.3 Interrogatories

One of the simplest and most economical discovery tools is the use of interrogatories (questions). At any time after the suit is filed, either party may propound (file) interrogatories to the opposing party and/or their lawyer. It should be noted that some jurisdictions no longer require the filing of interrogatories with the court. Instead, a certificate of service signed by the lawyer indicating service on the opposing counsel should be filed. The lawyer's assistant should check the local court rules to determine which documents need not be filed with the court. Interrogatories include:

- The caption or style of the case.
- The title of the pleading.
- The name of the party to whom the interrogatories are directed.
- An opening paragraph setting out the state or federal rule under which the interrogatories are propounded and the time within which to answer.
- The interrogatories.
- A statement that the interrogatories are ongoing and that the answering party must supply additional information as it becomes available in the future.
- The signature of the party serving the interrogatories.
- A certificate of service on the opposing lawyer and the method of service (mail, facsimile where permitted, or personal delivery).

Some states require that sufficient space be left after each question for the opposing party to fill in their answer, which may then be photocopied and returned.

Parties generally are not limited in the types of interrogatories that may be asked but the number of interrogatories (together with subparts) may be limited. Some states, however, allow only certain specific interrogatories to be asked. Some typical interrogatories, in a personal injury case, include questions about:

- Name.
- Address.
- Marital status.
- Previous marriages.
- Social security and driver's license numbers.
- Previous accidents.
- Version of the incident.
- What is claimed by the other party as the cause of the incident.
- Injuries.
- Amount of time lost from work.
- Whether the injured party has returned to work.
- Lost wages.
- Names of doctors.
- Location and custodian of records.

- Names of hospitals.
- Amount of medical expenses to date.
- The existence and limits of coverage on insurance policies.
- Names of witnesses to be called at trial.
- Names of experts consulted and their fields of expertise.

§ 11.13.4 Answers to Interrogatories

On receipt of interrogatories, the lawyer's assistant should note both the date received and the date answers are due and make a tickler notation. The client should be contacted and an appointment made for the client to come in and provide answers to the interrogatories. If the client lives in another city, a copy of the interrogatories should be forwarded immediately, requesting that the information needed to prepare the answers be provided. Provide a date by which the client must respond so that the lawyer may timely file the answers.

Answers to the interrogatories may be read at the trial of the case and must be sworn to by the person answering the interrogatories. Some states require the answers to be signed by the party, while other states permit the lawyer to respond for their client.

Some courts do not want interrogatories filed with the court. Instead, a certificate of service signed by the lawyer indicating service on the opposing counsel should be filed (this corresponds to the federal rules). The lawyer's assistant should check the local court rules to determine which documents need not be filed with the court.

§ 11.13.5 Objections to Interrogatories

In some instances, the lawyer may file objections to some of the interrogatories on various grounds. However, a good faith effort must be made to answer the remaining interrogatories within the time allowed. Occasionally, the lawyer filing the interrogatories may grant additional time in which to answer if there is a real difficulty in obtaining the information requested, but this is an agreement between the lawyers.

After the answers are completed, they are signed and sworn to, and a certificate of service is attached showing that the answers have been served.

§ 11.13.6 Continuing Interrogatories

In many states, once served, interrogatories are continuing; that is, if after answers are made initially, there is a change in the situation (for example, an additional witness is located or a new expert is employed), supplemental answers must be served upon the initiating party to reflect the changed situation.

§ 11.13.7 Request for Production of Documents and Things

While one party cannot secure privileged communications in the file of the opposing lawyer or any materials considered to be the lawyer's work product, there are numerous documents, photographs, and other materials which may be obtained through discovery. This is accomplished by filing a request for production listing each item requested. The request is then served upon opposing counsel. Such request for production does not require leave of court. Samples of discoverable documents include: photographs, contracts, corporate records, income tax records, and drawings and plans of equipment or buildings involved in the litigation. The request should be addressed to the party from whom the materials are requested, show the federal or state rule under which the request is filed, specify the time within which to respond, and list each item requested. The request, like all other pleadings, must be signed by the lawyer and must show a certificate of service on opposing counsel.

Some jurisdictions do not require the filing of requests for production but do require filing a notice that the request has been made.

§ 11.13.8 Responses to Request for Production of Documents and Things

As soon as such a request is received, the lawyer's assistant should prepare a tickler entry noting the date the response is due. A letter to the client should then be drafted for the lawyer's approval, enclosing a copy of the request, with instructions to produce the requested documents.

§ 11.13.9 Objections to Request for Production of Documents and Things

The party on whom the request is served (through their lawyer) may file objections, for example, that the requests are unduly oppressive or that the materials requested are irrelevant to any issue in the lawsuit. Upon motion, the court rules on the validity of the objections. If the objections are overruled, the materials must be produced within a specified period of time. If the objections are sustained, those particular documents need not be produced.

If a written response to a request is not received in the specified time limit, the requesting party may file a motion asking the court to compel compliance and to award costs of filing the motion.

§ 11.13.10 Subpoena Duces Tecum

The subpoena duces tecum is authorized by the Federal Rules of Civil Procedure, and most states have a similar provision. Such a rule authorizes the issuance of a subpoena to custodians of certain documents to appear at a designated time and place with certain records described in the subpoena for the purpose of producing them. Often, since these are ordinary business records of the custodian, by agreement of the parties, they are simply copied and supplied to the requesting party. Since some of the material so produced is of a technical, statistical nature, it is often time-consuming to analyze the information contained in them, and the legal secretary can play an important part in the preliminary review of the data contained in the records.

§ 11.14 Depositions

One of the most useful discovery tools is the deposition, either oral or written. Each side in a lawsuit has the right to question the parties on the other side, as well as other persons who are not parties, such as eyewitnesses, doctors, and experts employed by either side to investigate and give an opinion in the case.

Either party may take an oral deposition after the lawsuit is filed that consists of sworn testimony in the presence of counsel for all parties before a court reporter, who transcribes the testimony verbatim. The testimony is as binding as any testimony given at the actual trial of the case, and often entire depositions or portions of depositions are read into the record during the course of trial.

§ 11.14.1 Setting the Depositions

Depositions are usually set by agreement between the lawyers as to time and place. It is your responsibility as the lawyer's assistant, once depositions are set, to calendar the time and place on both on the lawyer's calendar and your own. You should draft a follow-up letter to the opposing lawyer confirming the date and time. In addition, the lawyer's assistant should inform the deponent (witness) or their lawyer of record, if represented by counsel, both by telephone and letter of the time and place of the deposition, and advise them to be present. A court reporter must also be contacted; therefore, it is necessary to verify which side will obtain the reporter to avoid duplication of effort and to ensure that a reporter will be available to take the testimony. The party requesting the deposition usually makes the arrangements for the court reporter. If the deposition is to be taken in the office, the lawyer's assistant should reserve a conference room or other suitable place for the deposition. The room should be large enough to accommodate the lawyers for each side, the person whose deposition is being taken, and the court reporter. Shortly before the scheduled time of the deposition, the lawyer's assistant should check the room where the deposition will be taken to ensure that it is ready.

§ 11.14.2 Notice of Depositions

If your state requires it, a notice to take the deposition is filed, setting out the time and place of the deposition, and any subpoenas (for the depositions of nonparties to the action) or subpoenas duces tecum (commanding the deponent to produce specified items) are issued. The notice is served on opposing counsel well in advance of the date of the deposition.

§ 11.14.3 Use of Checklists

Many lawyers use a checklist during depositions to make certain all pertinent information is obtained. This checklist should be placed in the file shortly before the deposition for the lawyer's use.

§ 11.14.4 Meeting With Client and Opposing Lawyer

Time should be allotted prior to the deposition for the lawyer to discuss the case with the deponent to explain the procedures and purpose of the deposition. To prepare the deponent properly, the lawyer should explain the manner and method of responding to questions and the necessity of answering such questions. The deponent is often nervous when appearing for the deposition, and the lawyer's assistant can help to put the deponent at ease by using tact and courtesy.

Following a deposition, lawyers sometimes discuss the possibility of settlement. Therefore, the lawyer's calendar for the date of deposition should allow sufficient time for both the deposition and for a discussion with the opposing lawyer afterward.

§ 11.14.5 Transcription of Depositions

The verbatim written transcript of the testimony is prepared by the court reporter. The original copy is sent to the lawyer for the deponent or directly to the deponent if not represented by counsel. The deponent may then be asked to read the transcription of the testimony given, make any corrections necessary, and sign it before a notary public that will notarize the deponent's signature. This right is commonly waived by deponent's attorney. It is then returned to the court reporter that, in some jurisdictions, files it with the clerk of the court and also provides copies of the transcription to the parties who requested them.

§ 11.14.6 Videotape Depositions

Use of videotape depositions is extremely valuable when it is anticipated that a witness will be unavailable to testify at the trial of the case. This is especially appropriate if the client or witness is due to leave the country or is terminally ill. Use of a videotape deposition enables the trier of fact to see the demeanor of the witness and thus evaluate their credibility. There are some jurisdictions, however, where videotape depositions are not admissible.

§ 11.14.7 Written Depositions

Written depositions may also be taken and generally are less expensive than oral depositions. Notice of taking a written deposition, together with a list of the questions to be asked by the reporter, must be sent to all opposing counsel, and sufficient time must be allowed (usually 10 to 15 days, according to the rules of the jurisdiction) for the opposing lawyer to submit cross-questions. These questions are mailed to the reporter, who sometimes obtains any necessary subpoenas or subpoenas duces tecum, contacts the witness, and makes an appointment with them. At the time of the appointment, the reporter asks the questions and obtains any records requested by the questions. The answers are sworn to by the witness and are filed by the reporter in the same manner as an oral deposition.

Written depositions are often used to obtain a doctor's testimony, employment records, income tax records, and other information, but they also may be used in the case of a witness who is in a distant city or state, thereby avoiding the expense of the lawyers for all parties traveling to the deposition.

§ 11.15 Motions Prior to Trial

After pleadings are filed and during the course of discovery, various facts may come to light which require the necessity of filing motions with the court. In some jurisdictions, a courtesy copy of the motion must be delivered to the judge. This is in addition to the original that is filed with the clerk of the court. In many jurisdictions, courts and/or judges may require the hearing date and time be placed on the motion or the motion will automatically be denied. Some common pretrial motions are discussed below.

§ 11.15.1 Motion for Continuance

This is simply a motion to postpone or continue a trial date or hearing date. The content of the motion and requirements for filing vary considerably from jurisdiction to jurisdiction.

§ 11.15.2 Motion to Compel

This motion is filed to require the opposing party to perform some act, usually to answer interrogatories or to produce documents in accordance with a request for production. The motion, if not responded to or if the action sought in the motion is not performed, may be set for hearing; and the court may impose any of numerous sanctions (relief), including an order that the act be performed. If this order is not obeyed, the noncomplying party may be held in contempt of court, or certain pleadings of the noncomplying party may be stricken or removed by the court. The court also may impose a money penalty on the noncomplying party and may require them to pay the costs of the hearing, including a reasonable lawyer's fee, to the other side.

§ 11.15.3 Motion for Protective Order

A motion for protective order is filed in response to some action by the opposing side, requesting the court to take some action. For example, such a motion can be filed regarding a notice to take a deposition if the distance involved in travel or the shortness of time of the notice makes it difficult or impossible for the deponent or the lawyer to appear at the time and place of the deposition. It also may be used when interrogatories are oppressive or when requests for production are unduly burdensome.

A protective order may also be used to specify who may see confidential documents and/or the handling of lawyer/client privileged and lawyer work product documents.

§ 11.15.4 Stipulations

A written stipulation is an agreement made and signed by the lawyers for both sides of a case regulating any matter pertaining to the proceeding or trial which is within their ability to agree. This may be used to dispose of or narrow certain issues so that trial time and proof are not required for those issues. A stipulation can be used also in an attempt to have the court vacate a trial date, reset a hearing date, or extend the time within which to respond to a pleading.

§ 11.15.5 Motion to Dismiss for Want of Jurisdiction

A defendant may file a motion to dismiss the case for want of jurisdiction because of the belief that the court does not have authority to hear or decide the case.

§ 11.15.6 Motion to Dismiss for Lack of Prosecution

A defendant's motion to dismiss a case for lack of prosecution may be made for failure to respond to discovery after a motion to compel is granted. Granting such a motion is within the discretion of the court if there is no specific length of time within which to file such a motion. Most judges, however, are reluctant to grant such motions unless the case has been inactive for a very long time.

§ 11.15.7 Motion for Nonsuit

This is a plaintiff's motion that requests the court to dismiss the case either with prejudice or without prejudice and can be presented any time before the case goes to the jury. In some states, it is called simply a voluntary dismissal. When such a motion is granted without prejudice, the plaintiff may later refile the same action. However, if the case is dismissed with prejudice, the plaintiff is prevented from again filing the same cause of action. In federal court, this motion is known as a motion for dismissal pursuant to the Federal Rules of Civil Procedure.

§ 11.15.8 Motion for Summary Judgment

If, during preparation of the case, it becomes obvious to either party that there is no real issue of fact to be decided at trial, a motion for summary judgment may be made. This motion requests the court to grant judgment, in whole or in part, in favor of the party filing the motion. It is usually accompanied by affidavits or answers to discovery stating the undisputed facts that entitle the party to a judgment in their favor. In many jurisdictions, it is difficult to obtain a summary judgment, and the party filing such a motion has the burden of proving that there is no genuine issue of fact in dispute. The opposing party has time in which to respond, and the court usually holds a hearing on the motion. If the court determines that there is no fact issue, it can grant judgment, in whole or in part, to the moving party. However, if in the court's opinion there is any factual question that is in dispute, the court may deny the motion, and the case is then tried on its merits.

§ 11.16 Pretrial Hearings

A pretrial hearing is held for the purpose of clarifying the issues that will be tried and for determining the approximate length of time that will be necessary for the trial of the case. A pretrial conference is a meeting with the trial judge at which each lawyer states the basis of the case and how the lawyer intends to prove it. The pretrial conference serves as a clearinghouse at which the lawyers discuss the discovery that must be completed and disclose exhibits or witnesses they might use for trial.

A pretrial conference helps to speed up court procedures because it establishes ground rules for the trial and helps to eliminate courtroom surprises and delays.

§ 11.16.1 Pretrial Orders

A pretrial order usually is agreed to by both sides and is presented to the court for entry, or the court prepares a pretrial summary. Such pretrial orders typically contain a basic statement of the contested and uncontested issues and facts, a stipulation of agreed facts, a list of witnesses to be called by each side, exhibits to be introduced by each side, and the date of trial.

§ 11.17 Trial Notebooks

In organizing the file for trial, the lawyer's assistant may assist in indexing the file or trial notebook for the lawyer's use during trial. The lawyer will likely include the following instruments and/or items:

- All pleadings filed in the case, with the first pleading filed being labeled "No. 1".
- All depositions clearly indexed for easy access by the lawyer, along with any summaries of the depositions which may have been prepared.
- All interrogatories and answers, request for admissions, any other discovery materials and photographs.
- Any other documents which the lawyer will present for evidence during trial.

Certain motions, which will be presented by the lawyer during the trial, may be prepared in advance so the lawyer will have them ready at the proper time.

In addition to organizing the file with the pleadings and documents, a list of witnesses and their telephone numbers should be placed in a convenient place for the lawyer's use. The witness list should enumerate the names in the order their testimony will be presented. Likewise, the documents to be presented as evidence should be placed in the order in which they will be introduced. If the court rules permit, the lawyer's assistant could mark the documents with appropriate exhibit stickers. (*See* Illustration 11–2 for a trial notebook checklist.)

Illustration 11–2

CLIENT______

Our File No.______

TRIAL NOTEBOOK CHECKLIST

______ Check pleadings for amendments.

_______ Pleadings amended.

_______ Amend prayer to: _______.

_______ Prepare subpoena for each witness.

_______ Basic information sheet prepared.

_______ All witnesses listed.

_______ List all expenses.

_______ Copies of all bills.

_______ Exhibits numbered and listed.

_______ Medical and/or other expert reports.

_______ All doctors and/or other expert witnesses alerted.

_______ Depositions read and marked.

_______ Case law, law notes inserted.

_______ Requested instructions prepared.

NOTE: This is a sample list and may be adjusted to include/delete other items applicable and pertinent to your particular case.

§ 11.18 Settlement

At any time during the course of a lawsuit, the parties may be open to settlement. If the lawyers can reach settlement, whether prior to the commencement of the suit or prior to the trial, costs may be minimized, and the plaintiff may realize more actual money than if the case is ultimately tried and appealed. Even if financial savings are minimal, in some situations, avoiding the emotional costs of trial may make settlement more desirable.

Once a lawsuit is filed, lawyers for both sides evaluate the case at various points throughout the course of the matter. Factors that enter into such evaluations, among others, are:

- Extent of injuries or damages.
- Duration of injuries or damages.
- Time lost from work, if any.
- Medical or other expenses in connection with the incident.
- Probable cost of trial.
- Liability (fault).
- Credibility (believability) of the parties or witnesses.
- Recent court decisions on similar matters.

Settlements are often reached shortly after the depositions of all parties are obtained, when the lawyers for all parties have had an opportunity to assess the credibility of the witnesses as well as other factors.

At any time during the course of a case, the settlement value may go up or down. Changes in the valuation may be brought about because, for example, the plaintiff incurs additional medical or other expenses, such as an additional operation. If the plaintiff returns to work or presents a poor impression as a witness, the lawyer may recommend acceptance of a settlement offer. Other factors that could affect settlement value could include: an extremely large verdict in a similar case, a total loss by a plaintiff in a similar case, favorable or unfavorable facts ascertained in a deposition, or new information revealed by discovery or disclosure. Each factor, while not controlling in itself, becomes part of the overall picture to the lawyers, who place evaluations on the case and make recommendations to their respective clients based on such evaluations. Occasionally, a client refuses the recommendations and insists the case be tried unless their lawyer can settle the case for an amount different than that recommended.

Settlement negotiations are usually conducted up until the time the trial begins or even during trial. It is not unheard of for a lawsuit to result in settlement after the jury retires to deliberate, but before the verdict is reached (often to the disappointment of the jury members). Settlement may also be reached after judgment is entered and during the course of an appeal.

Once a settlement has been agreed to by all parties, the documents reflecting the settlement must be prepared, usually by the lawyer for defendant. These include a release of all claims that will be signed by the plaintiff and possibly by their lawyer, and an order dismissing the lawsuit. In some matters (workers' compensation and cases involving minor plaintiffs), court approval is necessary; consequently, a hearing is held before the trial judge to approve the fairness of the settlement. These hearings are usually informal hearings; the judge hears testimony regarding the injuries, expenses, and the amount involved, and then may enter an order granting judgment. In some cases, the court allows the use of interrogatories in place of a hearing to determine the fairness of the settlement; these are filed by the defendant's lawyer and answered by the plaintiff.

The judgment in a settled case reflects who pays the costs of the case. In a judgment that is based on a jury verdict, the costs may be taxed against the losing party at the court's discretion.

After releases are executed and the court enters the judgment, the amount of the settlement is paid to the prevailing party and their lawyer. The case can then be closed. If the prevailing party is a minor, however, the award is handled through a guardian or next friend and deposited according to the order of the court for the use and benefit of the minor. The guardian or next friend of the minor may be required to post a bond with the court to ensure proper handling of the minor's funds. The court, however, retains jurisdiction over the disbursement of funds, in most cases, until the minor reaches majority.

§ 11.19 The Trial

At the trial of the case, the dispute of the parties will be settled. The plaintiff is given the opportunity in court to present their case and relevant evidence. The defendant also has that opportunity.

§ 11.19.1 Role of the Judge

The judge presides in the courtroom and ensures that only proper evidence and arguments are presented. In a jury trial, the judge instructs the jury on issues they will consider. This is called a "charge." A judgment will be entered based on the jury's verdict. In a nonjury or "bench" trial, the judge is both the trier of law and the trier of fact creating a role of judge and jury. Judgment is entered on the evidence and arguments presented to the judge.

§ 11.19.2 Role of the Jury

The jury listens to the testimony, reviews all the exhibits, considers the arguments of counsel, and the instructions from the judge. At the conclusion of the trial, and after final arguments by both sides, the jury retires to deliberate what has been presented to them and arrives at a verdict. After returning to the jury box, the juror who was chosen foreman announces the verdict to the court.

§ 11.19.3 Selection of the Jury

A jury trial begins when the first prospective juror is called for *voir dire* (examination). Both plaintiff's and defendant's lawyers have the right to examine the prospective jurors after they are sworn. This questioning is called the *voir dire* examination of the jurors. The court may disqualify a prospective juror from service in a particular case when, for any reason, doubt exists as to their competency to serve in the case. After the juror is questioned, either lawyer may accept them, challenge them for cause, or reject them by use of a peremptory challenge. In federal court, the judge conducts the *voir dire*.

§ 11.19.4 Challenge for Cause

During *voir dire*, either the plaintiff or defendant may challenge for cause when the prospective juror lacks a qualification required by law, is not impartial, is related to any of the parties, or will not accept the law as given to them by the court.

§ 11.19.5 Peremptory Challenge

During *voir dire*, each party has a given number of peremptory challenges established by law, which enable the lawyers to reject prospective jurors without cause. This decision is based on subjective considerations of the lawyer when it is thought a prospective juror would be detrimental to the client's side of the case, and is allowed until both sides have used all of their peremptory challenges or a sufficient number of jurors have been agreed upon by all lawyers. The jury is then impaneled.

§ 11.19.6 Request for Jury Trial

In most jurisdictions, the lawyer must request a jury well in advance of the trial date. Usually, a jury fee accompanies the request for a jury. *See* Illustration 11–3 for jury request. Failure to make a timely request for a jury may later prevent the parties from having a jury trial, resulting in a trial before the judge as the trier of fact. In some cases, the request for a jury trial may be contained within another document, such as a Motion to Set.

Illustration 11–3

NO. ______

JOHN W. BROWN,	)	IN THE DISTRICT COURT
Plaintiff	)	
v.	)	______ JUDICIAL DISTRICT
	)	
CHARLES M. WHITE,	)	______ COUNTY, TEXAS
Defendant	)	

DEMAND FOR JURY TRIAL

Now comes CHARLES M. WHITE, defendant in the above-referenced cause, and demands a trial by jury.

____
(Name and address of lawyer)
ATTORNEY FOR DEFENDANT,
CHARLES M. WHITE

CERTIFICATE OF SERVICE

I certify that a true and correct copy of the foregoing Demand for Jury Trial was served on the attorney for plaintiff, Mr. Jack Jones, 717 Main Street, Your town, Your State, by certified mail, return receipt requested, on this ______ day of ______, [year].

____
(Defendant's Lawyer)

§ 11.19.7 Opening Statement

After the jury is impaneled, each side may present an opening statement. The plaintiff has the burden of proving the alleged wrong doing, suffered damages from such wrong, and that the defendant caused such damages. The plaintiff is allowed to present their opening statement first. The opening statement of defendant's lawyer follows.

§ 11.19.8 Direct Examination

After the opening statements, the receipt of testimony and documents begins. The plaintiff sometimes is the first person to testify and gives their version of the incident involved, the injuries and damages, and other matters on questioning by their counsel. This is known as direct examination. The plaintiff's lawyer may present additional witnesses to support or prove their case, and the order of presentation of witnesses will be determined by the lawyer to best prove the case.

§ 11.19.9 Cross–Examination

The defense lawyer has an opportunity to cross-examine each witness after the plaintiff's lawyer has questioned them.

§ 11.19.10 Redirect Examination

The plaintiff's lawyer then has an opportunity to re-question each witness on the points covered by the defense lawyer. This re-questioning process is known as redirect examination.

§ 11.19.11 Presentation of Defense

After the plaintiff's case is presented, the defense lawyer may present witnesses on direct examination and introduce documents into evidence.

§ 11.19.12 Impeachment of Witnesses on Cross–Examination

Either party may cross-examine any witness called by opposing counsel. On cross-examination, counsel may introduce documents to impeach or discredit the testimony of a witness. If a witness testifies to one fact and a statement or document in the files contradicts that testimony, the document can then be used to question the witness as to the accuracy of their statements and/or cast doubt on the witness' credibility in general.

§ 11.19.13 Trial Memorandum or Trial Brief

This is a written explanation to the judge of the law and facts involved in the case.

§ 11.19.14 Motions During Course of Trial

Before the closing arguments and up until the time the case is sent to the jury for deliberation, certain motions may be made during the course of the trial.

§ 11.19.15 Motion in Limine

This motion is presented before jury selection. The moving party sets out certain facts, and requests the court to instruct opposing counsel and their client (or other witnesses) to refrain from mentioning such facts. Such facts might include the existence or content of any insurance policies, subsequent marriages, criminal records (if applicable), issuance of traffic citations on either the incident in question or prior or subsequent traffic citations, and other matters which are either not relevant to the particular case involved or which might influence the jury unfairly.

§ 11.19.16 Trial Amendment

A short amendment or addition to the pleadings can be filed only after a motion is made to the court for permission to file an amendment and an order is entered by the judge granting the motion.

§ 11.19.17 Motion for Instructed or Directed Verdict

This motion usually is made by the defendant's lawyer at the close of evidence presented by the plaintiff, and is based on the premise that the plaintiff has failed to prove their case. If it is granted, the court instructs the jury to render a verdict for the defendant and against the plaintiff, and the trial is concluded in the defendant's favor. If the court denies the motion, the defendant may present it again following the presentation of the evidence and again after closing arguments.

§ 11.19.18 Motion for Mistrial

Either party may petition the court to declare a mistrial at any time during the course of the trial if certain matters which are not admissible as evidence are presented by any witness either purposely or unintentionally in the presence of the jury. For example, the mentioning of any items set out in a motion in limine, if the motion previously was granted by the court, results in a mistrial. When the court grants a motion for mistrial, the jury is immediately dismissed, and the trial ends. The case must then be set for a new trial with a new jury.

§ 11.19.19 Objections

An objection is a procedure taken during trial by either lawyer by simply stating an objection to the preceding question or testimony. The purpose is to prevent the introduction of testimony or evidence that is about to be given and exclude it from the record. If the judge sustains the objection, that particular question, testimony, or evidence is excluded. If the objection is overruled, the question is asked, and the testimony or evidence is given. Often, the lawyers will approach the bench and present oral arguments for or against the objection. At this point, the judge usually sends the jury out while the arguments are heard. Rulings on objections are usually the basis for appeal. The objection must be made at the time the question, testimony, or evidence is introduced during the trial in order to preserve the right to later appeal on that point. The court reporter must also be asked to include the objection and arguments in the record. This is called "preserving the record."

§ 11.19.20 Rebuttal Testimony

After the defendant has presented their evidence, the plaintiff may be allowed to present rebuttal (response) testimony.

§ 11.19.21 Closing Arguments

Each side is given the opportunity to present closing arguments. Each party summarizes their case and presentation in a closing argument to the jury, giving the reasons why the jury should find in their favor. Time limits are set by the court for closing arguments, and each side must adhere to the time allowed. The plaintiff's lawyer presents their closing argument first and may choose to reserve some of their allotted time to use for rebuttal to the defendant's argument.

§ 11.19.22 Charge to the Jury

The presiding judge delivers the charge to the jury after both sides have completed their closing arguments. In some jurisdictions, the charge is in the form of written instructions prepared in advance by the lawyers for both sides and approved and/or modified by the court. These instructions then become the charge to the jury, setting forth the jury's responsibility to render a verdict on the facts and applicable rules of law. Some jurisdictions permit the lawyers to prepare specific questions or issues that the jury is asked to answer. The answers of the jury to such issues or questions then constitute the verdict. Otherwise, the jury would return a "general verdict," finding for the defendant or the plaintiff and awarding damages, if any, to the plaintiff.

§ 11.19.23 Mistrial

Following the court's charge, the jury retires (goes to the jury room) to deliberate the facts presented at the trial and reaches its verdict. The jury may find for the defendant or for the plaintiff, or it may be unable to reach a verdict. In this event, the court declares a mistrial, and the case must be tried again before a new jury. A jury that cannot reach a verdict is usually referred to as a *hung jury*.

§ 11.19.24 Preparation of Judgment

Following the jury's verdict, the judgment is prepared by the prevailing party and presented to the court for entry. Either side may give notice of its intention to appeal. The losing party may file post-trial motions before a judgment is entered. One such motion may include a judgment *non obstante veredicto* (notwithstanding the verdict), setting out the reasons why the court should disregard the jury verdict and render judgment for the movant. The losing party may object to the prepared judgment and present its own version of the judgment in keeping with the jury verdict. There is a time frame set by the rules within which all post-trial motions may be filed.

§ 11.19.25 Nonjury Trials

In a nonjury trial, the judgment may be prepared by the prevailing party and presented to the court in much the same manner as in a jury trial. The judgment is usually based on the findings of facts and conclusions of law reached by the court. The procedure for preparing the judgment in final form for court entry varies from state to state, and local adopted procedure should be followed.

§ 11.19.26 Costs

If the jury or the judge awarded costs to the prevailing party, it is necessary to prepare a bill or statement of costs for approval by the court. Rule or statute specifies allowable costs. Upon approval of the costs, the prevailing party is entitled to payment for those costs. If the plaintiff was the prevailing party, the plaintiff is also entitled to receive the amount of damages awarded in the judgment.

As soon as possible after the trial, the lawyer may wish to prepare a complete written report of the trial for the client, together with results and recommendations. If the prevailing party, the calendar should be marked with the final date for appeal. The final date for appeal must also be calendared by the lawyer for the losing party. If no appeal is filed by the losing side, a closing report and final bill for services is prepared. If the losing party files an appeal, the client should be notified immediately, advising them of the procedures and costs of an appeal.

At this point, negotiations for a settlement may be renewed, as both parties must determine whether or not it is advantageous to continue expending more time and money on the case.

§ 11.19.27 Motion for New Trial

In most jurisdictions, the first step to an effective appeal is the filing of a motion for new trial, setting out the grounds why a new trial should be granted. Any alleged error by the trial judge that prevented a fair trial, such as overruling objections or allowing testimony, is set out in the motion. If the motion is denied, the appealing party then files a notice of appeal, posts a bond for costs, requests the preparation of the record for appeal, and serves notice to all parties of their intent.

§ 11.20 Appeals

A party who is dissatisfied with the trial court's decision or jury verdict may appeal to a higher court on the theory that error was committed during the trial procedure.

When an appeal is filed, the party filing the appeal becomes the appellant, and the party against whom the appeal is filed is the appellee.

The function of the appellate court is to ensure that the trial court acted properly in its conduct of the trial and that proper legal principles were recognized and applied correctly.

It should be noted that appeals are not based on the facts involved in the case but on questions of law. The appellate court considers whether the trial court committed error in conducting the trial, thus adversely affecting the outcome. Its review of the record is limited to determining whether the trial court erred in admitting testimony that should not have been allowed or refusing to admit testimony that should have been allowed. The appellate court also determines whether the court's instructions to the jury correctly reflected the law, whether the court correctly sustained or overruled objections of the lawyers, and whether there was jury misconduct.

The appeal usually requires:

1. Notice of filing an appeal.
2. Bond for costs and filing fees, if required.
3. The record on appeal (transcript, statement of facts) as designated by parties.
4. Briefs.

5. Oral arguments (sometimes required).
6. Trial court decision.

Procedures for requesting the preparation of the record for the appellate court vary with different jurisdictions. However, the appealing party is responsible for initiating the requests to the proper parties. The record will consist of the statement of facts (transcription by the court reporter of the proceedings at the trial) and the transcript (requested documents from the court file prepared by the clerk of court).

The statement of facts: the appellant's lawyer will notify the court reporter at the trial to prepare a transcript of the proceedings. This is usually done by letter, along with payment for such transcript. The court reporter will forward the completed original transcript directly to the appellate court within the time allowed.

The transcript: the appellant's lawyer will notify the clerk of court by letter (or in the manner otherwise governed by local rules) of the request for the transcript. In the letter, the documents wanted will be listed and included in the transcript. Some courts have a special form that must be used for this purpose. By copy of this letter request, the opposing counsel will be advised of the documents requested and be given an opportunity to add any other documents that may be relevant. The transcript is prepared, sealed, and forwarded to the appellate court by the clerk of court.

§ 11.20.1 Communication With the Client

Effective communication between a client and the lawyer is as necessary after the trial as it is before the trial. After the trial, the prevailing party is often under the mistaken impression that what was granted in the trial, whether money, land, objects, or rights, will be received within a short period of time. While this may happen in some isolated instances, it is not usually the case. The losing party will usually appeal the decision. This will mean additional time and expenses before the decision can be final. Until the appellate court renders an opinion, the execution of the terms of the judgment is on hold. The prevailing party in the trial court may be the losing party in the appellate court if the appeal is successful. Lawyers for both parties must explain all the possible results from an appeal so that everyone understands the risks involved.

§ 11.20.2 Time Limits

The applicable rules of procedure, including local and federal rules, set out specific time limits within which each step on appeal must be taken. These rules are strictly enforced, and if a deadline is missed, the appeal may be invalid. The time limits are jurisdictional requirements, and the appellate courts do not have the power to waive them. If a deadline has passed, the appellate court can only dismiss the appeal. Thus, a tickler file is of vital importance in an appeal. The time table begins with the date the judgment was entered in the trial court. The appellate court may, when good cause is shown in a written motion filed by either lawyer, grant an extension of time to file the record or briefs. However, the request for extension of time must be filed prior to the time limit expiration and must state a specific requested time for extension.

§ 11.20.3 Briefs

Briefs are filed by both sides, with the appellant's brief due first. The appellee then responds. The appellant's brief is a written argument setting out the points of error alleged in the appeal. Relevant rules, statutes, and case law are cited and argued in the brief. The appellee's brief will respond to the appellant's points and arguments.

§ 11.20.4 Oral Argument

Once the briefs have been filed, and if the lawyers have timely filed their requests, the appellate court may set a date for oral argument. It is, however, the court's discretion whether or not to allow oral argument in the case. Both lawyers may appear before the court and present oral statements to support their case. No further testimony or witnesses are allowed. The lawyers can only address the law involved in their case. The panel of judges hearing the arguments may question either or both lawyers during the oral argument, or may simply listen. Oral arguments are limited to a specific time set by the court. When oral arguments are not presented, the case is said to be submitted on the record.

§ 11.20.5 Opinion

The opinion of the appellate court either:

1. Upholds the judgment of the trial court.
2. Reverses and remands (overturns the judgment and orders the trial court to retry the case or enter a new judgment).
3. Reverses and renders (overturns the judgment and enters a new judgment).
4. Remands in part (some of the results were correct, but other points need to be clarified).

§ 11.20.6 Collecting a Judgment

Once all the appeals have been exhausted, the outcome of the suit is final. If the defendant has prevailed, the matter ends with no monetary payment from the defendant. If the plaintiff has prevailed and was awarded a monetary sum from the defendant, the plaintiff then becomes a judgment creditor. The losing party becomes a judgment debtor.

Often, at this point, the amount of the judgment is paid by the judgment debtor, together with any interest accrued and court costs, if awarded. Upon such payment, a satisfaction of judgment or release is entered.

Sometimes a judgment debtor is said to be judgment proof, meaning there are no assets with which to satisfy the judgment. Some assets, such as a homestead, are exempt from judgment. These exemptions vary according to the jurisdiction, as do the methods of seizing property to satisfy a judgment.

Local or state rules dictate the time limit for collecting a judgment, as well as whether this time limit may be renewed and the process of renewal. The lawyer's assistant should note the tickler file with the expiration date of all judgments for clients. The lawyer should then be advised of the time limits so judgments can be renewed in a timely manner.

The court provides for writs of execution and writs of garnishment to enforce collection of a judgment. A writ of execution instructs a court official, usually the sheriff, to seize the judgment debtor's property and sell it at auction. Any money collected from the sale is given to the judgment creditor. If this is not sufficient to satisfy the judgment, that judgment remains in force for the balance due until it can be paid or collected.

A writ of garnishment enables the judgment creditor to seize property from other people who hold assets belonging to the debtor. Funds from a bank account or wages, which may be subject to garnishment, may be seized in this manner. The bank would be forced to release the funds in that account, or the employer would withhold wages of the debtor, until the judgment is satisfied.

§ 11.20.7 Billing

The method for billing a lawsuit depends upon the fee arrangement made with the client. Many plaintiffs' lawyers handle lawsuits on a contingent fee arrangement, either asking the client to pay expenses as they occur or advancing those costs for the client. When the case is either settled or tried, the lawyer is reimbursed for advanced expenses from the award or settlement funds realized. Examples of expenses would be court costs, service fees, witness or expert fees, and deposition costs. If costs have been taxed against the defendant, the plaintiff's lawyer must ensure that a bill of costs, including allowable expenses, is filed with the court. After the lawyer has recovered allowable expenses and all court costs are paid, the contingent fee is calculated from the balance of the judgment recovered, the balance is paid to the client, and the lawyer then receives payment for fees incurred. Remember, all funds must be deposited in the firm's trust account until the time for distribution.

If the plaintiff with a contingent fee agreement recovers nothing from the judgment, the plaintiff is still liable to the lawyer for expenses incurred or paid on plaintiff's behalf. The lawyer, in such instances, collects no fee.

If the fee arrangement is on an hourly basis, careful records of the time spent by the lawyer are kept and maintained by the lawyer's assistant. The client is billed according to office procedure and the agreement with the client, be it monthly, quarterly, annually, or at the conclusion of the case. The bill should include the time spent, rate charged for fees, and the expenses incurred and/or paid by the lawyer for the client.

§ 11.21 The Team Concept in Litigation

Many law firms utilize team strategy for handling cases. This concept can be very effective in litigation practice. Usually the team consists of one or more lawyers, lawyer's assistants, and legal assistants. Proper use of the lawyer's assistant and legal support staff can help keep the cost of litigation down. Each member of the team is important and contributes to the effective preparation and trial of the lawsuit.

§ 11.21.1 Duty of the Lawyer

It is the lawyer who first examines the claim and decides whether or not to accept the case. This may be based on several factors, one of which may involve a disqualification. The lawyer may be familiar with the case or have represented or talked with an opposing party about the same case. The lawyer, at various stages while the case is pending, evaluates the case and offers the client an opinion of the possible outcome based on the law involved. The recommendations to the client are based on that opinion. The lawyer is responsible for the preparation of briefs and makes all necessary court appearances and ultimately tries the lawsuit in court. The lawyer must be aware of the progress of support staff assigned to the case. Since the ultimate responsibility for the case belongs to the lawyer, all members of the trial team are under the direct supervision of the lawyer at all times. The lawyer will assign tasks, and correct work when necessary.

§ 11.21.2 Legal Assistant

The legal assistant always works under the supervision of the lawyer. Based upon this supervision and upon instructions, the legal assistant may question witnesses, prepare such discovery items as request for admissions and interrogatories, and obtain information with which to answer interrogatories. The legal assistant can gather and index documentary materials for use as evidence, do basic legal research, and write a memorandum for the lawyer as to statutes and cases pertaining to the case at hand. Additionally, the legal assistant may discuss cases with the lawyer and on the lawyer's instructions, do further research. If the lawyer uses a trial notebook, the legal assistant can gather the materials for the book, prepare indices, and have it ready for the lawyer's use at trial.

§ 11.21.3 Lawyer's Assistant

As a lawyer's assistant, you may often function as both a lawyer's assistant and a legal assistant, performing some or all of the services listed under the paragraph on legal assistants. You work closely with each member of the team to maintain files and gather such information as is necessary for use at the trial. Often the docket control and tickler system are your responsibility. You remind the lawyer and the legal assistant of deadlines and appointments well in advance of the date they are scheduled; keep time records for both the lawyer and the legal assistant; either prepare or supervise the billing; and make appointments for the lawyer for depositions with clients and witnesses. When a deposition is to be taken, you arrange for a court reporter, a place for the deposition, and travel arrangements for witnesses and lawyers. When a legal assistant is not assigned to the team, the lawyer's assistant assumes the dual role.

§ 11.22 Summary

Litigation is a particularly interesting field in the practice of law. The lawyer's assistant or support staff member involved in litigation will find a varied and interesting career in this field. A lawyer's assistant should develop an understanding of the various procedures involved in litigation in order to make a valuable contribution. An understanding of the process enables the lawyer's assistant to maintain organized files and good relationships with the lawyer, coworkers, clients, and the courts.

CHAPTER 12

CONTRACTS

Table of Sections

---

§ 12.1 In General

The law of contracts is a broad, general area upon which many other areas of law hinge. Contract law evolved from the British Statute of Frauds passed in 1676 plus common law prior to that time. Because of their importance, the Statute of Frauds required that certain contracts be in writing and further provided that such contracts could not be changed merely by an oral agreement. The Statute of Frauds, though somewhat altered, remains in place today. The types of contracts required to be in writing by the Statute of Frauds are:

1. Contracts by executors or administrators to pay an estate's debts out of their own funds.
2. Contracts to answer for the debt or default of another.
3. Contracts made in consideration of marriage.
4. Certain contracts creating an interest in land.
5. Contracts that by their terms cannot be performed within one year.
6. Certain contracts for the sale of goods of $500 or more.

§ 12.2 Definition

A contract is an enforceable agreement between two or more competent parties, which creates an obligation to do or not to do a particular thing. Generally, contracts may be oral or written. However, prudence typically calls for contracts to be in writing.

Contracts affect the daily lives of all of us, whether we think of them as contracts or not. A written agreement to purchase a car or a house is a contract. Just by turning the lights on in the morning and taking showers, we are parties to contracts with both the light and water companies. They make utilities available, and we pay for the amount we use.

Much of contract law relates to the sale of goods, either for cash or on credit. The Uniform Commercial Code (U.C.C.), which has been enacted in all states except Louisiana (although Louisiana has enacted a code which includes many comparable provisions), governs most of these transactions and specifies the rules which the parties must follow.

§ 12.3 Essential Elements

There are four elements essential to a valid contract. Unless all four are present, no contract exists.

1. Mutual assent (offer and acceptance)
2. Competent parties.
3. Lawful consideration.
4. Lawful subject matter.

§ 12.3.1 Mutual Assent

Generally, there must be a meeting of the minds concerning the contract terms. In other words both parties must agree to the aspect of the performance required of each. To meet this requirement, there must be both a valid *offer* by one party (known as the offeror) and a valid *acceptance* by the party to whom the offer was made (the offeree).

EXAMPLES:

A offers to wash *B*'s windows for $10. *B* agrees to pay $10 for that service. There is both an offer and an acceptance, so there is mutual assent.

A offers to wash *B*'s windows for $10. *B* thinks the price is too high, but his friend *C* is willing to accept *A*'s offer for the stated price. There is no mutual assent at this point, since *A* made the offer to *B*. *A* did not make the offer to *C*.

Offer. The offer must be clear and definite and it must be made in such a way that it will be taken seriously. An offer that is made in jest or is too vague may not be deemed to be an offer under the law.

EXAMPLES:

At a party one evening, *A* pulls out a very expensive ring and says, "Anyone who can guess what I actually paid for this ring can have it for $15." This would not be a serious offer.

B is very desirous of purchasing *A*'s house at any price. *A* finally tells *B*, "Okay, I'll sell you my house someday." The word someday is too vague to consider the statement an offer.

Some contracts call for the offer to remain open for a specified period of time in exchange for which the offeree pays a sum of money. This is called an options contract.

EXAMPLE:

A wants to lease a portion of *B*'s property to construct a new factory; however, *A* does not want to enter into the lease until *A* completes all of the details for financing and is assured the loan will materialize. In order to hold the property until *A* is ready, *A* agrees to pay $1,000 to *B* in exchange for *B*'s promise that *B* will not lease the property to anyone else for a period of six months and will permit *A* to execute the option and obtain a lease within that period. This is an *option* to lease.

Offers can be made specifying a time limit during which the offer must be accepted. If the offer is not accepted within that period, the offer is automatically withdrawn. Offers for sale of real estate are good examples of this.

EXAMPLE:

An offer to buy real estate is made by a prospective buyer to the owner. The offer includes a provision that if it is not accepted within three days, the offer is automatically withdrawn. (This eliminates the possibility of the offer being open indefinitely.)

Where no time limit is specified, the offer remains open until any one of these events occur:

- Acceptance of the offer by the offeree.
- Rejection of the offer by the offeree.
- Revocation or withdrawal of the offer by the offeror.
- Passage of a reasonable length of time without any of the previous three actions by the parties.

(Death or insanity of the offeror or offeree may also cause an offer to terminate automatically, especially where personal services are involved.)

EXAMPLES:

A offers to wash *B*'s windows for $10; *B* accepts. There is no longer an offer, but rather mutual assent.

A offers to wash *B*'s windows for $10 but *B* refuses. Later *B* changes his mind and wants to accept *A*'s offer. Acceptance is not valid now, since the offer terminated when *B* originally refused it.

A offers to wash *B*'s windows for $10, and *B* wants to think about it. In the meantime *A* withdraws the offer. There is no longer a valid offer, so there can be no acceptance.

A offers to wash *B*'s windows for $10, but *B* wants to think about it. One year later, *B* decides it would be a good bargain. The offer would not generally be considered valid, since a year is more time than is reasonable under the circumstances to hold the offer open.

A offers to wash *B*'s windows for $10, but before *B* has a chance to accept, *A* dies. The offer terminates, since it was based upon personal services.

Advertisements by retailers, mail circulars, auctions, and the like do not generally constitute offers. Instead they are characterized as "invitations to offer." Parties who bid on or respond to an invitation to offer are typically characterized as the offerors.

Acceptance. Typically, acceptance by an offeree must be in total agreement with the offer, point for point, or it is not an acceptance. At common law, this principle is typically referred to as the mirror image rule. If the acceptance changes any of the terms of the offer, it actually becomes an independent offer, frequently called a counteroffer.

EXAMPLE:

A offers to wash *B*'s windows for $10. *B* is willing to accept but only if *A* will also wash the screens for that amount. There is no acceptance, since *B* has changed the terms of the offer and has made a counteroffer to *A*. If *A* agrees to the new terms, it is *A* who makes the acceptance.

Silence does not generally constitute acceptance. The exception to this rule is where prior dealings of the parties have incorporated silence as part of their normal method of acceptance or if it is reasonable under the circumstances to infer that silence should constitute acceptance.

EXAMPLES:

A offers to wash *B*'s windows for $10, but *B* makes no response. *B*'s silence would not generally be considered an acceptance.

A and *B* have had a mutual understanding over the years that periodically *A* would leave a note stating that *A* would be in the neighborhood on Saturday and would wash *B*'s windows at that time, for which *B* would then pay *A* the usual $10 fee. As a part of the understanding, *B* would then contact *A* only on those occasions when *B* would not be home on the day indicated by the note. They would then set another day. Because of the prior dealings between the parties over the years, silence on the part of *B* would constitute acceptance.

Unless the offer specifies the manner in which acceptance must be made, the acceptance is generally valid if communicated in the same way as the offer.

EXAMPLE:

An offer arrives by letter, stating that acceptance must be made within 24 hours. *B* immediately writes an acceptance letter and drops it in the mail during lunch. The letter is not received by the offeror until two days later.

The acceptance would be valid as soon as it was deposited in the mail. Since this was done within the 24–hour period specified, the acceptance is valid even though it was not actually received until two days later.

§ 12.3.2 Competent Parties

Competent parties are persons having the legal capacity to enter into a contract. Attention must be given, then, to those persons who do not generally have legal capacity. They include:

- Minors
- The mentally disabled
- Intoxicated persons
- Corporations (under certain circumstances)

Claims related to incompetence may be confusing because there are many instances in which hard and fast rules have not been established by the courts. For instance, a minor may be held liable for contracts entered into to obtain necessities of life *provided* such necessities could not be obtained from a parent or guardian. Those necessities would include food, shelter, clothing, and certain education expenses. For most other contracts, the minor has the choice of disaffirming or avoiding a contract once the age of majority is reached, *provided* this is done within a reasonable length of time after the minor reaches the age of majority. If a minor marries, the minor is considered emancipated, and emancipation automatically makes the minor an adult for purposes of making a contract. A minor can be emancipated by a judicial proceeding and sometimes simply by leaving home and becoming self-supporting.

Contracts made by persons declared to be mentally disabled or by persons who are so intoxicated that they are temporarily incapacitated can be voided but only if such person wishes to do so. Such person must be legally competent at the time of disaffirming the contract. Until the claim is made, the contract is valid.

Corporations are given certain powers under state statutes. Corporations can enter into contracts but only within the limitations upon their powers set forth by state law. Some contracts of corporations that exceed the limitations of such power (*ultra vires* contracts) can be voided. However, as long as the subject matter of the contract is not illegal, such contracts will typically be deemed valid.

In summary, the concept of competency may be complicated when claimed in a contract suit. Because there are as many exceptions as there are rules, lawyers must review the facts of each case before determining what rule or rules apply.

§ 12.3.3 Lawful Consideration

Consideration is that thing which leads one party to do something they would not otherwise be obliged to do or forego doing something they would otherwise have the legal right to do. Basically, consideration represents a bargained for exchange of value, and each party must receive some form of consideration for a contract to be valid. Common items of consideration include money, property, or a promise to do or not to do some act.

Common law presumes that if the consideration is acceptable enough for the party making the contract, it is sufficient to bind that party to the contract terms.

The consideration must pass from one party to the other during the term of the contract. Past acts or promises of either party do not usually provide consideration for a new contract. If an individual makes a bad bargain, but some form of sufficient consideration exists, they generally may not claim lack of consideration to void the contract.

§ 12.3.4 Lawful Subject Matter

A contract cannot be based upon anything that is illegal or against public policy. Examples of illegal subject matter are:

- Wagers
- Usury
- Illegal drugs
- Unfair trade practices

Examples of contracts against the public policy are:

- Agreements requiring performance that violates criminal laws
- Agreements requiring performance that is a tort.

If a thing or act is illegal outside the realm of the contract, then no legal contract can be made concerning it.

§ 12.4 Types of Contracts

Once it is determined that all necessary elements are present and that a contract exists, the rights and duties of the parties are further clarified by determining the type of contract that exists. The contract can be unilateral or bilateral; executory or executed; express or implied; and valid, voidable, or void.

§ 12.4.1 Unilateral and Bilateral Contracts

A unilateral contract is one in which a person makes a promise conditioned upon the performance of another. The contract is not binding until the performance occurs because performance is what constitutes the consideration provided by such party.

EXAMPLE:

> *A* promises *B* to pay *B* a commission if *B* locates a buyer for *A*'s house. When *B* finds a willing buyer, a contract is formed and *A* must pay *B*.

A bilateral contract is one where both parties make a promise. If either party fails to keep the promise, the other may be entitled to recover damages.

EXAMPLE:

> *A* promises to pay *B* 90 cents per dozen of eggs if *B* will deliver 50 dozen eggs by tomorrow morning. *B* promises to deliver them. Under these facts, the contract is formed upon the promises made by both parties.

§ 12.4.2 Executory and Executed Contracts

Executory contracts are those that have not been fully performed.

EXAMPLE:

Same as above. *B* delivers the 50 dozen eggs on time but *A* has not yet paid. At this point the bilateral contract is also executory.

Executed contracts are those that have been fully performed by both parties. The transaction is complete and nothing remains to be done.

EXAMPLE:

Same as above. Upon delivery of the 50 dozen eggs, *B* receives $45 from *A*. At this point there is an executed bilateral contract.

§ 12.4.3 Express and Implied Contracts

An express contract is one where the terms are specifically stated and agreed to by both parties. Express contracts are generally written. An insurance policy is an express contract because it is written and specifies terms and conditions. Leases are also express contracts.

An implied contract is one created by law and imposed upon parties because of their actions or because of their relationship. The action of using electricity creates an implied contract with the power company. The relationship of husband and wife creates an implied contract of financial support.

§ 12.4.4 Formal and Informal Contracts

A formal contract is one where the format of the contract (the way it appears) must meet certain requirements established by law. Negotiable instruments, for instance, fall into the formal contract category. Note that all checks follow the same basic format, since checks are negotiable instruments and formal contracts.

An informal contract is a term used to refer to all contracts that are not formal. A contract may be written and still be an informal contract if its format is not as prescribed by law.

§ 12.4.5 Valid, Voidable, and Void Contracts

A valid contract is one that contains all the necessary elements for the making of a contract. See § 12.3.

A voidable contract is one that is potentially defective in some respect. If the defect is asserted, the contract could be voided. See the following sections on defenses to contract enforcement. In each instance, one of the parties has the option of making a claim to void or invalidate the contract. Voidable contracts are treated as valid contracts until a defect is asserted.

Void contracts are those that do not comply with the law and are unenforceable at the time of their inception. Oral contracts for the sale of land are not enforceable because the law requires those contracts to be in writing. The same is true of a negotiable instrument that does not appear in the form prescribed by law. A contract to commit murder is also void. The law (through use of courts) cannot enforce contracts that do not conform to the law.

§ 12.5 Defenses to Contract Enforcement

Though the parties have made both an offer and an acceptance, lack of mutual assent may be claimed to void the contract where any of the following factors can be proved:

- Mistake
- Fraud
- Misrepresentation
- Duress
- Undue influence

§ 12.5.1 Mistake

It is possible that mutual assent may have been given on the basis of a genuine misunderstanding. This would not include misunderstandings created because a party failed to reasonably investigate the facts or because a party was negligent in reading a document. Either of these events would certainly be a mistake, but they would not be mistakes the law will recognize. In both cases the mistake arose out of the person's failure to use reasonable care. A genuine misunderstanding occurs when, even after reasonable care, the end result of the contract is not what the parties intended.

EXAMPLES:

A wants to buy a lot on Poplar Street in Los Angeles and obtains the name of the owner from municipal authorities. *B* agrees to sell *B*'s lot to *A*, and an agreement is signed. Unknown to either party, there are two Poplar Streets in Los Angeles. *A* intended to purchase a lot on the other Poplar Street. There has been a mistake as to the subject matter, and the contract may be voided.

A has several cases of what *A* believes are apples in the warehouse. *A* sells them as apples to *B*. When the cases are opened, they are found to contain oranges. The contract may be voided because of the parties' mutual mistake.

§ 12.5.2 Fraud

To prove fraud, there must have been (1) a false statement (2) of a material fact (3) made with the intent to deceive (4) that is relied upon

(5) and is intended to be relied upon (6) which causes a loss to the victim. If all six elements can be proven, the contract may be voided because of the fraud.

EXAMPLE:

A, a jeweler, convinced *B*, a wholesale jeweler, that *A* was from St. Louis and that *A*'s credit was excellent. Relying on *A*'s intentional representation, *B* delivered to *A* $5,000 worth of jewelry. *B* later learned that *A* was actually from Kansas City and that *A* had a very poor credit rating. Once proved, this fact situation would constitute fraud by *A*.

§ 12.5.3 Misrepresentation

Misrepresentation differs from fraud in principally one way. Misrepresentation does not involve the intent to deceive. The other five elements are the same, and if they are proven, the contract may be voided. Because misrepresentation can result from an honest mistake, it is often called innocent misrepresentation.

EXAMPLE:

A sells a block of stock in a certain corporation to *B*, representing it to be worth $10,000 based upon the corporation's net worth. It is later determined that losses of the corporation had reduced its net worth substantially, even though *A* honestly believed he had given the correct information to *B*. It is possible that the contract could be voided on the basis of misrepresentation.

§ 12.5.4 Duress

Duress is the use of force or threatened force to gain consent. In either case the consent would not be the voluntary act of the person giving consent, and that person could void the contract if duress were shown to exist. The person must be reasonably convinced the threat can be implemented, thereby compelling him or her to submit. Where duress is claimed, the claim must be made reasonably soon after the force or threat of force is removed. Failure to make the claim promptly could be considered a waiver that would bar the claim entirely.

EXAMPLES:

A paid a ridiculously high freight charge in order to take possession of some goods shipped to *A*. Six months later *A* demanded a refund, claiming duress. Though duress was present, there may be some question of *A*'s right to claim it since *A* let so much time pass.

A, a city official, threatened to turn off *B*'s water unless *B* immediately paid an illegal license fee. *B* needed the water supply to operate *B*'s factory, so *B* paid the fee and immediately initiated an action to recover the money. Duress would apply, and *B* would probably recover *B*'s damages.

§ 12.5.5 Undue Influence

Undue influence is the dominance of a stronger-willed person over a weaker-willed one. Constant pressure and persuasion may impair the will of a victim so that the victim's consent is not a voluntary act but, rather, is the expression of the will of the dominant person. A contract created under these circumstances is valid until the victim takes some action to void it. As with duress whatever action the victim takes must be done within a reasonable amount of time.

Some relationships may create a presumption of undue influence because the parties are not on equal footing in the transaction. In those relationships, one party is presumed to be in a position to take advantage of the other. Guardian-ward, physician-patient, and lawyer-client relationships may give rise to this undue influence presumption.

§ 12.6 Assignment of Contracts

To assign is to transfer. Sometimes, contracts involving special skills, knowledge, or judgment cannot be assigned. For example, a musician may not be able to assign a contract for performance at a certain event to another person without the consent of the other to the contract.

Generally, contracts involving money or property may be assigned to third persons without the specific consent of the other party to the original contract. The third person is called the assignee. The person who transfers his interest in the contract to the assignee is called the assignor.

The assignee usually has responsibility for notifying the other party to the original contract that the assignment was made.

Assignment is simply a substitution of one party for another in a contractual relationship. The assignee "stands in the shoes" of the assignor having the same rights and duties as the assignor—no more and no less. If an assignee fails to perform under the contract terms, however, the responsibility falls back on the assignor to make that performance.

Assignments are not always voluntary. Bankruptcy requires that the property of the debtor be assigned to a trustee for the benefit of creditors. Probate proceedings have the effect of assigning property to the personal representative (sometimes called executor or administrator) of the deceased for distribution to heirs.

§ 12.7 Discharge of a Contract

Discharge in contract law means the cessation (termination) of the contract—the point at which the contractual duties are ended. There are many ways to discharge a contract, although only the ones used most often will be discussed.

§ 12.7.1 Performance

The most obvious method of discharge is performance of all the contractual terms by both parties. Most contracts are discharged by performance.

EXAMPLE:

A offers to wash *B*'s windows for $10. *B* accepts. *A* washes the windows, and *B* pays the $10. The contract is discharged.

§ 12.7.2 Accord and Satisfaction

Accord is accepting another thing in place of the thing promised in the original contract (substitution). Once the substituted thing has been given or the substituted act performed, it satisfies the original contract and the agreement for substitution. Accord and satisfaction occurs at that point.

EXAMPLE:

After receiving $10 to wash *A*'s windows, *B* becomes concerned about working on a ladder and offers to clean the garage instead. *A* agrees. *B* cleans the garage.

It is not correct to say accord and satisfaction occurred at any point before *B* completed cleaning the garage.

§ 12.7.3 Rescission

If both parties agree to cancel (rescind) a contract, it can be done by rescission. Rescission requires only the agreement to cancel or repeal the contract plus whatever is necessary to restore both parties to their original condition. In effect, rescission is a contract to cancel the original contract.

EXAMPLE:

A offers *B* $10 to wash *A*'s windows. *A* changes his mind and asks *B* to agree to cancel the deal. *B* agrees.

§ 12.7.4 Novation

Discharge by novation involves the two original parties to a contract and a newcomer. One of the original parties is removed from the contract, and the newcomer takes their place absolutely. All three parties must consent. This should not be confused with assignment of contract, since the two have very different consequences.

EXAMPLE:

B agrees to wash *A*'s windows for $10. *B* later realizes he doesn't want to wash windows and convinces *C* to do it. *A*, *B*, and *C* agree that *A* will pay *C* $10 to wash the windows.

In this situation, *B* is discharged from the contract by novation. The duty to *A* is ended. Because there is no legal duty, *B* cannot be held liable if *C* fails to wash the windows. Note, however, that if *B* had assigned only the duty to perform to *C*, and *C* later failed to wash the windows, *B* would have been ultimately liable to *A* for the failure to perform. Novation discharges *B*. Assignment does not.

§ 12.7.5 Account Stated

Suppose a debtor and creditor have had several transactions, and the creditor sends one statement as a summary of the transactions, with a price shown for each. If the debtor holds the bill for an unreasonable time, the creditor may use the summary statement as a basis for suit on "account stated." This has the effect of discharging the underlying transactions/contracts in favor of the "account stated." The debtor can object if done within a reasonable time. In that case the creditor would be required to justify each transaction listed.

§ 12.7.6 Release and Covenant Not to Sue

This method of discharge is typically used for contracts that are not fully performed but are too far along for rescission. In other words one party has performed all or part of their obligation, while the other has not. Yet, they both want to end the contractual relationship.

§ 12.7.7 Impossibility of Performance

If a contract has been formed and an unforeseeable event occurs which makes performance of the contract impossible, the contract will be discharged. Impossibility means that no person could legally or physically perform the contract terms.

The city passes an ordinance requiring all those who wash windows to be licensed. While this places an unforeseen burden on *B*, it is not an impossibility. However, if the ordinance stated that no person could wash the windows of another, *B* would be discharged. Washing *A*'s windows after the ordinance had passed would require them to do an illegal act.

Suppose that *A*'s house burned down after the contract was formed. It would be impossible for *B* to wash windows after the house had been destroyed, and *B* would be discharged.

Suppose that *B* died before the windows were washed. Again, *B*'s performance would no longer be possible, and *B* would be discharged.

This last situation may seem ridiculously obvious—one cannot perform an act after death—but not all legal obligations end at death. Recall the binding effect of a contract to sell land, for instance, on the estate of the deceased. Contracts for personal services, such as *B*'s window washing, are discharged at death. The legal effect of the discharge is to free *B*'s estate from performing the balance of the contract.

Discharge for impossibility of performance only means the rest of the contract does not have to be performed. It does not cancel the contract obligations for prior performance. Suppose *B* washed *A*'s windows for three months and then died. *B*'s estate would be entitled to receive payment for three months, even though the remaining nine months were discharged for impossibility.

§ 12.8 Breach and Remedy for Breach

Once a contract has been formed, both parties have a duty to fully comply with its terms. If either fails to do so, the noncomplying party is in breach of the contract. It is possible for each party to breach or break the contract terms and to have a claim against the other because of the respective breach.

The theory of contract law is simply to enforce binding promises people make to each other. If a person makes a binding promise and then fails to carry it out, the law will step in to require that person to either (1) keep the promise, or (2) pay for the damage caused by the broken promise. There are several methods of doing this, called remedies for breach of contract.

Remedies generally include:

- Specific performance
- Restitution
- Money damages
- Some combination of these

§ 12.8.1 Specific Performance

Specific performance is a legal remedy requiring the defendant to comply with the terms of an agreement. However, courts are usually reluctant to award specific performance unless money damages are adequate. Contracts for the sale of real estate are the most notable exception to the general rule, as land is regarded as being unique.

§ 12.8.2 Restitution

Restitution is the act of restoring a thing to its rightful owner. Restitution lends itself to those situations where personal property has changed hands, but payment has not been made. The wrongful possessor of the property could be ordered to return the property to the rightful owner.

§ 12.8.3 Money Damages

Money damages is the term applied to a court proceeding seeking a money judgment. Money damages represent the largest percentage of remedies awarded, simply because most breaches can be reduced to a dollar value.

In assessing money damages, the loss must generally be mitigated (reduced) by the person making the claim. By doing this, compensation is for the actual loss.

Under the ancient English case of *Hadley v. Baxendale,* damages cannot be awarded to a party merely because the result meant breach of the contract. The damages that resulted must have been foreseeable by the party breached or by a reasonable person in the same situation. In the *Hadley* case, a common carrier failed to deliver machinery that had been sent out by a factory for repair. When the carrier failed to return the machinery on time, the factory sued for lost profits. The court held that those damages were not foreseeable and therefore not recoverable.

Or suppose that before *A* was fired, the employer acted in some truly outrageous manner toward *A* (requiring *A* to work very late, harassing *A* at home about job questions, etc., to get *A* to quit so as not to have to fire *A*). If the conduct was outrageous enough, it is conceivable that *A* could be awarded pecuniary damages in addition to the actual lost wages. These could include the cost of counseling for the emotional distress the employee suffered, so long as that distress was a natural and consequential result of the outrageous conduct. Finally, extremely outrageous conduct could justify punitive damages. Generally speaking, punitive damages are more prevalent in tort cases than in contracts.

EXAMPLE:

A is employed by *B* under an employment contract for one year at $2,000 per month. After eight months *A* is fired. *A* would not generally be permitted to sit at home during the remaining four months. *A* would be expected to seek other employment. Suppose *A* found another job two months later at a salary of $1,500 a month. *A*'s actual damages would be computed:

$4,000 for two months unemployed and $1,000 ($2,000–$1,500) for two months employment at a lesser rate or a total of $5,000 actual damage for four months remaining under the contract.

Suppose *A* went to work the very next day at a greater salary. *A* sustained no actual loss; however, it is very possible that, in declaring a breach of the contract, *A* could be awarded nominal damages simply because the breach had occurred.

§ 12.9 Summary

Nothing in this material is intended to imply that the area of contracts is simple. It can be highly complex and is usually a far cry from the simple dilemma of having *B*'s windows washed. It is presented here to give the beginning legal support person a basic understanding of the concepts involved and to emphasize the importance of lawyer involvement.

CHAPTER 13

TORTS

Table of Sections

---

§ 13.1 Definition

The law of torts is a broad general area of civil law that is very difficult to define. Some legal scholars say that the law of torts cannot be defined, and the Restatement of the Law (Second), Torts[1] devotes many

1. American Law Institute, Restatement of the Law (Second), Torts. West Group, St. Paul, Minnesota, 1979.

pages to its definition. The word *tort* comes from the Latin word *tortus* meaning twisted or crooked and from the French word *tort* meaning injury or wrong. Generally, a tort is an act or omission causing an injury or wrong to someone else. A person so wronged or injured is provided a remedy or cure under the law. The law of torts, therefore, deals with injuries or wrongs for which society *permits* compensation or some kind of remedy or relief.

§ 13.2 Distinction Between Tort Law and Contract Law

Most civil actions arise out of contracts or torts. Generally, persons are free to enter into agreements or contracts with other persons. These agreements form the bases of rights and obligations of the parties to a contract. By entering into such a contract, the parties commit to perform certain acts and in return they usually acquire certain rights. Assuming the contract is valid, it has the force of law between the parties. Without a contract, the only rights and obligations that exist between persons are found in the law of torts.

§ 13.3 Distinction Between Tort Law and Criminal Law

Torts are civil wrongs against individuals or entities. Criminal wrongs are against the state. Tort law deals with conduct of individual society members with each other, and criminal law deals with conduct in relation to society as a group. An act may be both a tort and a crime, but a tort is not necessarily a crime, and a crime is not necessarily a tort.

EXAMPLE:

> An automobile driver runs a traffic light. An accident results in which the other driver is injured. Under the law of torts the injured person could bring a civil action seeking compensation for his injuries, and the state could bring a criminal action against the driver for running a red light.

If such were the case, however, the civil action filed by the injured driver would not involve the action brought by the state for the traffic violation. Different courts would probably hear them at different times, and the result in one case would not necessarily have any effect on the other.

§ 13.4 Kinds of Torts

Since the law of torts provides a remedy for any injury or wrong not covered by the law of contracts, there are a large variety of cases encompassed within the law of torts. Some kinds, of course, are more common than others, but they all arise out of one of three kinds of torts categorized according to the nature of liability involved. In other words, the tort action is classified according to the conduct causing the harm. The three categories are:

1. Intentional
2. Negligence
3. Strict liability

§ 13.4.1 Intentional Torts

Intentional torts are those resulting from the intentional interference with another's person or property. There are two broad categories of intentional torts:

1. Those interfering with the person, such as battery, assault, and false imprisonment;
2. Those interfering with property, such as trespass and conversion.

§ 13.4.2 Battery

DEFINITION:

A battery is a harmful, offensive touching of another's person.

RULE:

In our society a person may expect freedom from harmful or offensive bodily contact from another.

EXAMPLES:

A intentionally pushes *B* off a sidewalk. *A* is liable in tort if *B* proves that *A* intended for the pushing action to be offensive.

A punches *B* in the nose. *A* has committed a battery.

A taps *B* on the shoulder to get his attention. *A* has not committed a battery. Reasonable people would not be offended by this intrusion.

§ 13.4.3 Assault

DEFINITION:

An assault is an act that creates in a person the immediate fear of an attempted battery.

RULE:

A person may expect freedom from apprehension of immediate contact, whether harmful or merely offensive.

EXAMPLES:

A throws a brick at *B*. *B* sees the brick coming at him and steps aside to avoid being hit. Although *B* is not injured (only very frightened), *A* may be liable in tort.

A puts his hand in his pocket so that it appears to *B* that *A* has a gun. *A* tells *B* to give him his money or his life. *A* has committed an assault. Any reasonable person would believe the danger was real and was likely to occur immediately.

A tells *B* that if it were not a holiday, he would punch him in the nose. *A* has not committed an assault. Threats alone are not an immediate danger.

A tells *B* he is going to punch him in the nose and then draws back his fist. *A* has committed an assault. *B* is concerned and believes that *A* has the ability to carry out the threat.

§ 13.4.4 False Imprisonment

DEFINITION:

False imprisonment is holding a person against their will without legal authority.

RULE:

One is free to choose their own location. If a person is held against their will by threats, intimidation, or physical force, they are entitled to be compensated for their time, physical discomfort, and inconvenience, any resulting illness, mental anguish, or emotional distress.

EXAMPLES:

A shopper in a department store triggers an alarm as he is leaving the store. He is detained by the security guard, who searches the shopper's packages. It is discovered that the clerk failed to remove a security tag from one of the shopper's purchases. The department store may be liable to the shopper.

A, a police officer, stops *B*'s automobile, asks to see *B*'s driver's license, and tells *B* not to leave until he is cleared through telephone contact with police headquarters. This is not false imprisonment. *A* is authorized to do this to preserve society's safety.

A offers *B* a ride home, and *B* accepts. *A* then refuses to take *B* to his house or to stop the car so *B* can get out of the car. This is false imprisonment. *B* is completely confined and cannot escape a moving vehicle without risking serious injury to himself.

§ 13.4.5 Trespass to Land

DEFINITION:

Illegal entry upon the land of another is trespass.

RULE:

A landowner has the right to keep one's land intact (the surface, air space above it, and the minerals below it) so that anyone violating that right is liable in tort.

EXAMPLES:

If a person enters the land of another person without permission and cuts the timber, that person is liable to the owner for the value of the timber.

The airline flight pattern of *A* calls for its plane to travel above *B*'s land. This is not trespass.

§ 13.4.6 Conversion

DEFINITION:

Conversion is taking property that belongs to another and using it as one's own.

RULE:

Only the owner of a thing is entitled to possess it and use it.

EXAMPLE:

Some of *A*'s cattle stray into *B*'s field. *B* knows *A* owns the cattle, but instead of returning them, *B* sells them at a cattle market. *B* is liable to *A* for the fair market value of the cattle.

§ 13.4.7 Proving Damages

In intentional torts, it is not necessary for the plaintiff to prove alleged damage. In other areas of tort law, it is usually necessary for a plaintiff to prove that actual damages were suffered. Therefore, it is sometimes difficult for a layman to understand that there can be tort liability without damage. To recover for an intentional tort, the plaintiff need only prove *intent,* that is, they must convince the court that the defendant intended the act in question.

EXAMPLE:

If one person intentionally strikes another, a battery results. One can distinguish this from a person accidentally striking another by carelessly waving his arms.

As noted earlier, however, only a court and/or jury can decide what the defendant's intent was, and in making the decision, the finder of fact must apply many technical elements.

§ 13.4.8 Negligence

Those torts, which are unintentional and not controlled by the doctrine of strict liability (which are discussed later), fall under the broad category of negligence. In establishing negligence, a plaintiff must prove that the defendant owed a duty to the plaintiff. This duty falls into two categories:

1. That which a reasonable person owes to another in the particular circumstances—called "duty of due care"; and
2. A special duty or care required by a specific statute or by case law. This special duty may be in addition to or in place of the duty of due care.

The definition of *due care*, like the definition of *intent*, is very elusive. Ordinarily *due care* is that care which a reasonable, prudent person would exercise in a particular situation. What constitutes a reasonable action depends upon a balancing process. The court weighs the act's usefulness against the foreseeability and severity of any harm that might result. Society is constantly changing, and what constitutes an unreasonable act also changes. Therefore, an act that was reasonable 20 years ago may be considered unreasonable today. Although this balancing process is based upon practical considerations, in the final analysis the court must define an unreasonable act. The lawyer must look to current case law to evaluate the client's claim. Examples of some of the most common kinds of torts resulting from negligence follow.

§ 13.5 Personal Injury Cases

DEFINITION:

Personal injury is the term usually applied to describe the kind of suit filed to recover damages for a physical injury.

RULE:

If one person's negligence causes injury to another, the negligent person is said to be liable in tort.

EXAMPLE:

A driver fails to obey a traffic signal, causing an accident. Someone is injured in that accident. The driver is said to be liable in tort to the injured person. The injured person is entitled to compensation for those injuries.

§ 13.6 Defamation (Libel and Slander)

DEFINITION:

Damage to a person's reputation caused by the publication or repetition of false information is libel or slander. (The defamation is *libel* if the information is written or published and *slander* if the information is spoken.)

RULE:

A person who publishes an untruthful statement, which is defamatory of someone, is held liable for any damage to that person's reputation or business.

§ 13.7 Malpractice

Malpractice has become one of the most controversial areas of tort law. It applies to doctors, lawyers, ministers, counselors, teachers, realtors, and almost any other professionals or quasi-professionals. In general, it is an action for negligence with the standard of performance measured by what is expected of a similar professional rendering similar professional services based on their geographical area, level of alleged expertise, and what was represented to the patient/client. A tremendous rise in the cost of malpractice insurance in some professions has prompted the statutory creation in some jurisdictions of procedural prerequisites to suit, such as peer review boards, arbitration, and notice requirements.

§ 13.8 Strict Liability

Strict liability is imposed by the law to provide a remedy for injuries received as a result of certain kinds of accidents or situations regardless of the degree of care exercised by the defendant. Under the strict liability concept, neither negligence nor intent is a consideration. The plaintiff need only establish to the court that strict liability applies to their case. This theory is most often used in real estate or products liability cases.

§ 13.9 Products Liability

DEFINITION:

The term "products liability" is usually applied to cases in which a person is injured as the result of an alleged defective product.

RULE:

Manufacturers are liable for damages caused by their defectively designed or manufactured products. Liability is based on the theories of negligence or strict liability.

EXAMPLE:

An automobile accident occurs as a result of a defective steering mechanism in the car. The driver of the car is injured. The manufacturer of the car is liable in tort to the injured person, who is entitled to compensation for those injuries. It is assumed that the product was fit to be used for its intended purpose.

§ 13.10 Animal Cases

DEFINITION:

For purposes of tort law, these cases involve injuries or damages caused by animals, including livestock, domesticated wild animals, household pets, or farm animals.

RULE:

An owner is strictly liable for damage caused by their livestock, domestic animals, or any wild animals they might keep regardless of whether due care was exercised. Some states have statutes governing animal bite situations.

EXAMPLE:

A child is playing with a neighbor's pet dog when the dog bites the child. Regardless of whether the bite was playful or unexpected, the neighbor is liable for it.

§ 13.11 Extra–Hazardous Activities

DEFINITION:

An extra-hazardous activity is one that carries the likelihood of causing some type of damage even if reasonable care is exercised.

RULE:

A person who maintains a dangerous thing or engages in a dangerous activity which produces a high risk of harm to other persons or property is liable to those damaged or injured regardless of whether the person exercises due care.

EXAMPLE:

A demolition company is leveling a building by using carefully placed explosive charges. Every possible precaution is taken, but when the charges are detonated, some flying debris breaks some nearby windows. The demolition company is liable since explosives are inherently dangerous by nature.

It is important to note that some torts do not fall specifically into one of these broad categories. Recovery could be based on more than one kind of tort liability. A particular tort (for example, products liability or defamation) might sometimes be classified as falling under strict liability in one situation and as negligence in another. In those cases, the kind of tort liability depends upon the circumstances of that particular case.

It is also important to note that the examples listed above are not all-inclusive and are given simply to provide the reader with a basic understanding of the most common types of torts that the lawyer's assistant is likely to encounter. In fact, our courts continue to expand the realm of tort law by applying it to types of claims for which there is no other legal remedy.

§ 13.12 Importance of Categorization to Lawyer's Assistant

Why is the categorization of the tort important to the lawyer's assistant? Having some knowledge of the basis for lawsuits and pleadings that are prepared in the law office enhances the performance of the lawyer's assistant. If a person understands the importance of a particular task, a better job is done. The single most important reason for classifying torts is for establishing proof and determining applicable defenses. The types of defenses available to a defendant vary with the kind of tort liability. These defenses, of course, are very broad, and this discussion is limited to the most common defenses available.

§ 13.13 Defenses in Intentional Torts

The most important defenses available to a defendant charged with an intentional tort are (1) consent, (2) self-defense, (3) privilege, (4) defense of property, (5) immunity, and (6) recapture of chattels. Therefore, if a defendant were charged with an intentional tort, one of the foregoing examples of defenses might be used in an attempt to convince the court that the defendant was not legally responsible for the plaintiff's alleged damages or injuries.

§ 13.13.1 Consent

A defendant sued for battery might take the position that although the defendant did cause the plaintiff's injuries, the plaintiff agreed and consented to the fist fight which resulted in those injuries, so plaintiff's consent bars recovery.

§ 13.13.2 Self–Defense

Using the same example, the defendant could take the position that the plaintiff provoked the fight, attacked the defendant, and that the defendant injured the plaintiff in self-defense.

§ 13.13.3 Privilege

As a defense to an action for trespass, a defendant might assert privilege to enter upon the land, alleging there was a written agreement authorizing the entry.

§ 13.13.4 Defense of Property

A defendant might also allege as a defense to an injury received by a plaintiff on the defendant's property that the defendant was forced to take such action for the purpose of protecting their property.

§ 13.13.5 Immunity

A defendant sued for an injury could defend such an action if they were a police officer acting in the course and scope of employment and who used reasonable force necessary to keep the plaintiff, who had been charged with a crime, in custody.

§ 13.13.6 Recapture of Chattels

In an action by a plaintiff to recover for a personal injury, the defendant could assert that the plaintiff was injured while force was used to recapture money that the plaintiff stole from defendant a few minutes earlier.

§ 13.14 Defenses to Negligence

Two basic defenses to negligence are available—contributory negligence and assumption of risk.

Contributory negligence is a negligent act or action by a plaintiff that contributes to the cause of the accident. In some jurisdictions if a plaintiff is held to be contributorily negligent, they cannot recover from the defendant. Many jurisdictions have now modified the contributory negligence doctrine by adopting some variation of the comparative negligence doctrine. Under the comparative negligence theory, if the plaintiff is found to be contributorily negligent, the finder of fact makes a decision as to what percentage each party was negligent and awards damages accordingly.

EXAMPLE:

> In a suit involving an automobile accident where Driver *A* failed to obey a stop sign, but Driver *B* was traveling over the speed limit, the jury might decide that Driver *A* was 80 percent at fault and Driver *B* was 20 percent at fault. If the court then determines that Driver *B*'s injuries are worth $50,000, Driver *B* is awarded 80 percent of $50,000, or $40,000.

The method of awarding damages varies in some jurisdictions. Contributory negligence is a defense only to negligence.

An assumption of risk defense is employed when the defendant contends that the plaintiff was aware of the risks involved and made a conscious decision to proceed in spite of them.

EXAMPLE:

> If *A* slips and falls on *B*'s obviously icy driveway, is injured, and sues *B*, *B* can allege as a defense that *A* knew the driveway was icy but still took the risks involved.

§ 13.15 Defenses to Strict Liability Actions

Traditional defenses cannot be employed in a strict liability action. The concept of strict liability is such that liability is intended under specific circumstances. That is not to say that a defendant cannot successfully defend this kind of lawsuit. It merely means that the nature of defenses available in other tort areas (*e.g.*, subsequent modification or state of the art) are not available in the strict liability cases, and a defendant must look to other ways to rebut the plaintiff's claim.

§ 13.16 Summary

Whether or not a defendant is found liable in tort depends upon whether or not the plaintiff can prove that the defendant's act or failure to act falls within one of those three areas of liability that we have discussed. In the general practice of law, much of the litigation in an office involves torts, and the lawyer's assistant should refer to the chapter on litigation for an overview of trial procedures and a general description of duties in litigation matters.

CHAPTER 14

CRIMINAL LAW AND PROCEDURE

Table of Sections

---

§ 14.1 Introduction

An assistant employed by a lawyer who specializes in criminal law will find the job to be not only demanding and challenging but perhaps one of the most diversified, interesting, and sensitive in the legal field.

The defense of a person charged with a crime is one of the most important events in their life. If they are convicted, the punishment may include a substantial fine, a prison term, or even the death penalty. Even if acquitted, the fact that an individual has been accused of a crime will undoubtedly affect their personal and business relationships. The mere filing of a criminal charge may ruin a future business opportunity or political career. Frequently there are related civil suits and administrative proceedings that are being conducted at the same time as a criminal investigation.

§ 14.2 Definition

In the early days of England, every crime was a crime against the peace and dignity of the king since he owned everything, and it was the duty of his subjects to live in peace. To some extent, this concept remains the basis of criminal charges today, and the government brings charges because an act has been committed against the peace and dignity of the people of a political entity, such as a state.

A crime is usually defined as an act that violates the laws of a community, state, or country and for which a specific punishment is prescribed. A person convicted of a crime may be imprisoned, fined, or receive both a fine and imprisonment.

Criminal actions are prosecuted in federal cases by the United States. State case actions are brought by the state, generally in the county where the crime has occurred. The government is always the plaintiff in a criminal action.

§ 14.3 Initial Client Interview

The initial interview of the criminal client is very important. At that time, the lawyer must obtain from the client the details of the arrest to determine whether the client's rights were potentially violated or if any illegal acts may have been committed by the arresting officer.

The criminal client is frequently apprehensive, nervous, extremely distraught, and may even be irrational. Communicating with an illiterate client may be extremely difficult. That client requires special handling and understanding, regardless of the type of crime with which that client may be charged or how reprehensible the lawyer's assistant might personally find that particular offense. Although a crime with which a client is accused may be a high visibility crime with notoriety in the community, the lawyer's assistant should never discuss the matter nor divulge information regarding the case to anyone.

§ 14.4 Jurisdictional Differences

Because of the differences among the federal, state, and local governments, specific matters and procedures outlined in this chapter may relate to the requirements of only some jurisdictions. Therefore, variations among the diverse jurisdictions must always be kept in mind.

§ 14.5 Criminal Law

Crimes are those offenses, either felonies or misdemeanors, considered harmful to the community.

EXAMPLE:

A man who murders another man threatens the safety of people in general, and therefore the community punishes him for his crime.

In early society, all crimes were considered torts or civil wrongs. Even murder was a private matter and was settled by the murderer and the family of the victim, either by the family's accepting payment from the murderer or by taking revenge on the murderer. Punishment remained primarily a matter of revenge until people began to consider punishment as a deterrent to committing crimes. Later, the idea of crime as an offense against society led to the development of criminal laws. There are some acts, however, such as vehicular homicides and wrongful deaths, which may constitute both a crime and a civil tort.

EXAMPLE:

After having consumed several alcoholic drinks, *A* drives through a stop sign and hits *B*, a male pedestrian, who later dies of injuries sustained in the accident. The state charges *A* with vehicular homicide. *B*'s spouse also files a civil lawsuit against *A* seeking monetary compensation from *A* for the wrongful death of *B*.

§ 14.5.1 Scope of Criminal Law

Criminal law includes matters involving the administration of criminal justice and encompasses such aspects as substantive criminal law, criminal procedure, and special problems in administering and enforcing criminal law.

§ 14.5.2 Substantive Criminal Law

Substantive criminal law is the law that defines what conduct is criminal and prescribes the type of punishment to be imposed for such conduct.

§ 14.6 Sources of Law

The rules that are enforced by the government are found in customs, constitutions, legislation, decisions of courts, and orders of administrative agencies, which are enumerated below.

§ 14.6.1 The United States Constitution and Federal Statutes

The United States Constitution is the supreme law of the land and establishes the basic rights and liberties of the American people. The Supreme Court of the United States is the final authority in interpreting the Constitution and can set aside any law—federal, state, or local—that conflicts with any provisions of the Constitution. Congress enacts federal laws that prohibit certain conduct, *i.e.,* price fixing in violation of the federal antitrust laws, or counterfeiting United States currency, in which the federal government is deemed to have an interest.

§ 14.6.2 State Constitutions and Statutes

State constitutions and statutes enacted by state legislatures comprise state laws and are found in the various state codes. State law governs the usual "street" crimes, such as robbery, murder, burglary, etc.

§ 14.7 Common Law

Common law rules are made by courts. These rules have developed from custom and usage and, as might be expected, can vary widely from state to state because of the differences in local customs.

§ 14.8 Administrative Rulings

Administrative rules are made by bureaus of the government called administrative agencies.

EXAMPLES:

> The Federal Communications Commission is a federal agency that issues regulations and enforces certain statutes regarding use of the radio and television licenses on a nationwide basis.
>
> A local board of health may regulate standards of cleanliness in restaurants within its jurisdiction.

§ 14.9 Classes of Crime

A person accused of a crime is entitled to certain rights under the Constitution of the United States and the constitutions of the individual states, as well as under federal and state statutes. The criminal charges must be filed in the proper court before the statute of limitations has expired, and the case must be brought to trial on a reasonably speedy basis.

The two major classes of crimes are:

1. Felony: A crime which generally carries a potential jail term of greater than one year, such as murder, grand larceny, arson,

and rape. The penalty may include a fine or imprisonment, both a fine and prison term, or even the death penalty.

2. Misdemeanor: A crime which generally carries a maximum potential jail term of one year or less, such as petty larceny, drunkenness, disorderly conduct, and vagrancy. Like a felony, the penalty may include a fine, imprisonment, or both a fine and imprisonment.

§ 14.10 Commencement of Proceedings

Criminal proceedings are initiated by filing a criminal complaint, an information, or an indictment. A complaint is usually filed under oath in order to secure an arrest warrant. An information is an accusation, filed in writing by the prosecutor, charging a person with a public offense. An indictment is an accusation, filed in writing by the grand jury, charging a person with a public offense which is usually more serious than those offenses prosecuted by a complaint or information.

§ 14.10.1 The Grand Jury

A grand jury is a body of citizens assembled to investigate complaints and accusations in criminal cases, to hear evidence, to determine whether probable cause exists that a crime has been committed, and whether an indictment should be returned against a person for such a crime. If probable cause does exist, the grand jury returns a "true bill." If probable cause does not exist, the grand jury returns a "no bill." A grand jury is usually comprised of a greater number of jurors than the ordinary trial jury or "petit jury." A grand jury does not decide guilt or innocence but decides only whether there is enough evidence, (*i.e.,* probable cause), to require an individual to stand trial. A grand jury's work is done in secrecy to avoid improper influence and to avoid harm to the reputation of those it may be investigating. The grand jury is assisted or directed by a prosecuting lawyer.

§ 14.10.2 Arrest

An arrest is an actual restraint of the person for submission to custody. An arrest may be made pursuant to a warrant signed by an appropriate judicial officer, such as a judge or magistrate. The arrest warrant indicates that the judge has found that probable cause exists to believe the named individual has committed an offense. The warrant authorizes any law enforcement officer to arrest the individual to be brought before the court. Under proper circumstances, an officer may be authorized to make an arrest without a warrant. An officer may make an arrest:

1. Pursuant to an arrest warrant.
2. Without an arrest warrant:
   a. With reasonable cause to believe that a felony has been committed and that the person to be arrested has recently committed it.
   b. For a public offense, either a felony or misdemeanor, committed or attempted in their presence.

§ 14.10.3 Bail

Usually a person charged with a crime is entitled to be released on bail pending trial. Bail is security given for the release of a jailed person that guarantees attendance at all required court appearances. A person charged with an offense has a right to have bail set in all cases except where the evidence of guilt is strong that any of the following may have been committed:

- A capital offense.
- A felony while free on bail awaiting trial on a previous felony.
- A felony while on probation or parole for a felony.

Any person who is granted bail may likewise be released on their own recognizance, *i.e.,* released without posting bail at the discretion of the court. In setting bail, the following criteria are usually used:

- Financial condition of the accused.
- Address of the accused and employment history.
- Occupation, name, and address of employer.
- Family situation and history.
- Prior criminal record and pertinent facts of the particular offense.

Since the purpose of bail is to ensure the attendance of the accused at all required court appearances, if the lawyer can show that the accused resides and works in the immediate area, or perhaps owns property in that area, the likelihood of that person's being granted bail increases. At the discretion of the court, bail may be posted in cash or by a written guarantee called an undertaking or bail bond. The person who posts the bail bond is called a surety. A commercial surety is an insurance company that posts a bond for a premium. Individual sureties are persons who collectively own real or personal property within the state with a net worth of at least the amount set in the order for bail. In some jurisdictions, the net worth of the sureties must be at least twice the amount of the undertaking. Each surety must sign an affidavit that their net worth is sufficient to pay the undertaking. Each may also be examined under oath by the court or by the prosecuting lawyer in the presence of the court. The sureties who have signed the undertaking are then liable for all appearances required of the defendant up to and including the time when sentence, if any, is imposed. Upon approval of the undertaking by the court, the officer having custody of the arrested person releases them.

§ 14.10.4 Reduction of Bail

Sometimes the lawyer feels that the amount set by the court is excessive, considering the accused person's financial status, the nature of the alleged offense, and other facts. If that is the case, the lawyer files a motion to reduce bail. (*See* Illustration 14–1.) The motion is an application to the court for an order reducing the bail, stating the grounds upon which it is made. It must be filed within the time prescribed by law.

The sample forms in this chapter are only a few of many that may be used during the course of a criminal proceeding. These are included primarily to acquaint the reader with some of the basic forms and should be used for guideline purposes only.

Illustration 14–1

[*NAME OF COURT*]

______________________________,	)	
Plaintiff,	)	MOTION FOR
vs.	)	REDUCTION OF BAIL
______________________________,	)	No. ______
Defendant.	)	

Defendant hereby moves the Court for an order reducing the bail which has been set in this matter in the sum of $______ for the reason that said amount is excessive, and for the further reasons [*here the lawyer will set out the facts concerning the defendant's financial condition, ties in the community, employment history and status, and prior criminal record or lack of it*].

DATED this ______ day of ______, [year]

____

JOHN SMITH
[*address*]
Lawyer for Defendant

CERTIFICATE OF SERVICE

I hereby certify that a copy of the foregoing Motion for Reduction of Bail was mailed, postage prepaid, to [*name and address of lawyer for plaintiff*][*or was personally served on lawyer for plaintiff*], this ______ day of ______, [Year].

____

§ 14.11 Misdemeanor Cases

At the first appearance in court by both the defendant and their lawyer, a written entry of appearance may be filed. (*See* Illustration 14–2.)

Illustration 14–2

[*NAME OF COURT*]

______________________,	)	
Plaintiff,	)	
vs.	)	ENTRY OF APPEARANCE
	)	No. ______
______________________,	)	
Defendant.	)	

JOHN SMITH hereby enters his appearance as lawyer for defendant in the above-entitled matter.

DATED this ______ day of ______, [year]

____

JOHN SMITH
[*address*]
Lawyer for Defendant

CERTIFICATE OF SERVICE

[Similar to Illustration 14–1]

§ 14.11.1 Arraignment

The initial appearance in a misdemeanor case is usually the arraignment. An arraignment is conducted in open court, where the judge reads the criminal charges to the defendant or states the substance of the charge and gives the defendant a copy of the complaint or information before calling on the defendant to plead. At the arraignment, the defendant may plead not guilty or guilty. If the defendant enters a plea of guilty, the defendant is then scheduled for sentencing. If the defendant enters a plea of not guilty, a trial date is set.

§ 14.11.2 Trial

In all cases the defendant has the right to appear and defend the charges levied, in person or by counsel. Depending on the maximum potential sentence, misdemeanors in some jurisdictions may be tried without a jury unless the defendant makes a written demand for a jury within the time prescribed by law prior to trial or unless otherwise ordered by the court. (*See* Illustration 14–3.)

Illustration 14–3

[*NAME OF COURT*]

______________________________,)	
Plaintiff,)	
vs.)	DEMAND FOR JURY TRIAL
)	No. ______
______________________________,)	
Defendant.)	

Defendant hereby demands a trial by jury in the above-entitled matter.

DATED this ______ day of ______, [year]

____
JOHN SMITH
[*address*]
Lawyer for Defendant

CERTIFICATE OF SERVICE

[Similar to Illustration 14–1]

§ 14.11.3 Sentencing

Upon the entry of a plea or a verdict of guilty, the court sets a date for imposing sentence. Pending sentence, the court may commit the defendant to jail or may continue or alter the bail. At the time of sentencing, the court imposes sentence and enters judgment of conviction. There are several purposes for a sentence, including:

- Prevention
- Restraint
- Rehabilitation
- Deterrence
- Education
- Restitution

§ 14.12 Felony Cases

When a person is arrested for a felony, the procedure is more complicated because the charge is more serious. After the arrest, the accused is brought before the court, who advises the defendant of their right to a preliminary hearing or examination and sets a date for the hearing unless it is waived or relinquished voluntarily by the defendant. The preliminary hearing is a hearing by the court to ascertain whether there is probable cause to believe that a crime was committed and the defendant may have committed it. If the court believes there is probable cause, the defendant is bound over or transferred to the appropriate trial court of general jurisdiction to answer the charges. If the defendant is bound over to the trial court of general jurisdiction, the prosecuting lawyer will either file a complaint within the prescribed time or seek an indictment from the grand jury if state law requires an indictment for that particular offense.

§ 14.12.1 Arraignment in Trial Court of General Jurisdiction

Upon the filing of an information by the prosecuting lawyer or the return of an indictment by the grand jury, the defendant is arraigned in the trial court of general jurisdiction. As in a misdemeanor case, an arraignment is conducted in open court, where the charge is read to the defendant or the substance of the charge is stated. A copy of the indictment or information is given to the defendant before the plea is entered.

Upon arraignment, a defendant is usually represented by counsel, unless counsel is waived in open court. At the arraignment, or within a reasonably brief time thereafter, a defendant may enter one of the following pleas:

1. Guilty
2. Not guilty
3. No contest

If the defendant wants to plead guilty, the court should make the following findings:

1. If the defendant is not represented by counsel, that defendant has knowingly waived right to counsel and does not desire counsel.
2. The plea is made voluntarily.
3. The defendant knows the legal rights including the right against compulsory self-incrimination, their right to a jury trial, and their right to confront and cross-examine in open court the witnesses against the defendant, and that by entering the plea all of those rights are waived.
4. The defendant understands the nature and elements of the offense to which the plea is being entered; that at a trial the prosecution would have the burden of proving each of those elements beyond a reasonable doubt; and that the plea is an admission of all those elements.

5. The defendant knows the minimum and maximum sentences that may be imposed in the case for each offense to which a plea is entered, including the possibility of the imposition of consecutive sentences.
6. Whether the tendered plea is a result of a prior plea discussion and plea agreement, and if so, what agreement has been reached.

If the defendant pleads guilty, the court sets a date for sentencing.

If the defendant pleads not guilty or refuses to plead, the court enters a plea of not guilty and the case is set for trial.

§ 14.12.2 Discovery and Preparing for Trial

Even before a defendant's arraignment, the lawyer should have begun preparing for trial by interviewing witnesses and preparing witnesses to be examined and cross-examined. Exhibits may be gathered and prepared for presentation as evidence in the trial, investigations may be made, and research done concerning the various issues pertinent to the case. The government is required, by statute or rule, in most jurisdictions to provide certain basic information or discovery to the accused, *e.g.,* results of scientific tests such as drug analyses, the defendant's own statement made to the police, etc.

Only by thorough preparation can the lawyer evaluate the nature and strength of the evidence which will be produced by the prosecution, and the lawyer then will be able to prepare and to present properly the best possible defense of the client.

§ 14.12.3 Bill of Particulars

An indictment or information may contain, in addition to the formal accusation, certain details of the alleged crime. If the indictment or information does not provide these details, the defendant may file a written motion for a bill of particulars asking for details concerning the offense charged. This enables the defendant to prepare a proper defense and to avoid double jeopardy, *i.e.,* being tried more than once for the same offense. (*See* Illustration 14–4.)

Illustration 14–4

[*NAME OF COURT*]

______________________,	)	
Plaintiff,	)	MOTION FOR
vs.	)	BILL OF PARTICULARS
______________________,	)	No. ______
Defendant.	)	

Defendant hereby moves the Court to direct the State to file a bill of particulars in the above-entitled matter, particularly setting forth the following:

[*List items about which more particulars are sought, e.g., where and to whom does the State allege the defendant sold narcotics.*]

DATED this ______ day of ______, [year]

____

JOHN SMITH
[*address*]
Lawyer for Defendant

CERTIFICATE OF SERVICE

[Similar to Illustration 14–1]

§ 14.12.4 Motion to Dismiss

After the lawyer reviews the charging document, *i.e.*, the information or indictment, against the provisions of the statute alleged to have been violated, a motion to dismiss based upon failure to have a speedy trial, lack of jurisdiction, or other grounds may be filed. Motions to dismiss must be filed within a specific time after the defendant is arraigned. Failure to file such a motion on time could result in a defendant's waiver of all such grounds other than lack of jurisdiction or failure of the charge to state an offense.

Whether a charge is sufficient to state an offense is generally governed by the rule that it is not sufficient unless it contains all necessary elements of the statute. In the event the statute does not specifically define the act or acts constituting the offense created thereby, the acts must be alleged sufficiently or the charge is deficient. Defenses and objections based on defects in the indictment or information other than that it fails to establish jurisdiction in the court or to charge an offense must usually be raised prior to trial by written motion. (*See* Illustration 14–5.)

Illustration 14–5

[*NAME OF COURT*]

______________________,)	MOTION TO DISMISS THE IN-
Plaintiff,)	DICTMENT FOR FAILURE TO
vs.)	STATE AN OFFENSE
______________________,)	No. ______
Defendant.)	

Defendant hereby moves the Court for an order dismissing the indictment in the above-entitled action on the grounds it fails to state a cause of action against defendant as set forth in [*cite the relevant statute*].

DATED this ______ day of ______, [year]

____

JOHN SMITH
[*address*]
Lawyer for Defendant

CERTIFICATE OF SERVICE

[Similar to Illustration 14–1]

§ 14.12.5 Change of Venue

The lawyer may also feel that the client cannot receive a fair and impartial trial in the county where the crime was committed. In cases receiving much publicity and notoriety, the lawyer may seek a change of venue by filing a motion for such change. A change of venue is a change in the location of the trial. This motion must be in writing supported by facts as to why the defendant cannot receive a fair trial in that county. (*See* Illustration 14–6.)

Illustration 14–6

[*NAME OF COURT*]

______________________,)	
Plaintiff,)	MOTION FOR A
vs.)	CHANGE OF VENUE
______________________,)	No. ______
Defendant.)	

Defendant hereby moves the Court for an order transferring this case to a court of competent jurisdiction in any county other than the county of ______. In support of this motion, defendant sets forth the following facts showing that by reason of extensive and prejudicial publicity regarding the offense herein charged the defendant cannot receive a fair trial in the county of ______.

DATED this ______ day of ______, [year]

____

JOHN SMITH
[*address*]
Lawyer for Defendant

CERTIFICATE OF MAILING

[Similar to Illustration 14–1]

§ 14.12.6 Evidence Illegally Seized

If the lawyer feels there was not probable cause for the arrest of the defendant or that the evidence was illegally seized, a motion to suppress evidence seized illegally, such as drugs found on the defendant by the police or a statement given to the police after the defendant's arrest should be filed. (*See* Illustration 14–7.)

Illustration 14–7

[*NAME OF COURT*]

______________________,)	
Plaintiff,)	MOTION TO SUPPRESS
vs.)	EVIDENCE
______________________,)	No. ______
Defendant.)	

Defendant hereby moves the Court to suppress as evidence against the defendant in this case all items which were seized during the execution of a search warrant of the premises located at ______, executed on ______, including but not limited to the following items:

[*List items seized*]

and as a basis for this motion, defendant states the search and seizure of said evidence was illegal in the following respects:

A. The search warrant is insufficient on its face and fails to state probable cause for its issuance,

B. [*List other bases*]

Further, said search warrant is in violation of the rights of the defendant under the Fourth Amendment of the United States Constitution and a violation of [*here set forth state constitution section violated and section of the state statute violated*].

DATED this ______ day of ______, [year]

____

JOHN SMITH
[address]
Lawyer for Defendant

CERTIFICATE OF SERVICE

[Similar to Illustration 14–1]

§ 14.12.7 Plea Bargaining

Plea bargaining agreements have received much attention in the administration of law and justice in our country. While the plea agreement system may need some reform, the United States Supreme Court expressly recognized the need for this system.

A plea agreement means that if there are numerous charges filed against the defendant, several may be dismissed with the acceptance of a plea of guilty to one of the charges. If there is only one charge filed against the defendant, sometimes the charge is reduced to a lesser offense that provides for lesser punishment.

To protect the accused, the courts have held that there must be evidence in the record of the trial court that:

1. The guilty plea is entered into knowingly and intelligently.
2. The defendant is aware of the maximum penalty that may be imposed.
3. The defendant is aware that by entering the plea a number of important rights, including the right against compulsory self-incrimination, to a trial, and to confront and cross-examine witnesses in open court are waived.

Although the client must make the final decision as to whether to plead guilty or go to trial, it is the defense lawyer's duty to advise and inform the client so that the client may make the choice intelligently.

§ 14.12.8 Jury Trial

The defendant has the right to appear and defend against charges brought in person or by counsel and to be personally present during the trial.

A defendant has a right to be tried by a jury of peers. In capital cases, *i.e.*, felonies punishable by death, the jury is usually comprised of twelve persons, whereas in other felony cases the jury may consist of fewer persons. The number of jurors depends upon the jurisdiction. The prosecution and defense may proceed to trial or complete a trial then in progress with any number of jurors less than otherwise required with the consent of the accused and the approval of the court.

After the jury has been impaneled and sworn, the trial proceeds in the following order:

1. The charge is read.
2. The prosecuting lawyer makes an opening statement. The defense lawyer may make an opening statement at that time or reserve it until the prosecution has rested.
3. The prosecution offers evidence in support of the charge, and the defendant may cross-examine the state's witnesses.

4. When the prosecution has finished its case or rested, the defense may present its case through witnesses.
5. Thereafter, the parties may offer only evidence to rebut or refute the other side's case, unless the court otherwise permits.
6. At the conclusion of the evidence, the defense lawyer and the prosecuting lawyer make closing arguments.
7. When the arguments are concluded, the court instructs the jury on what law to apply in deliberating on a verdict.
8. The jury deliberates or considers the case in secret and returns a unanimous verdict of guilty or not guilty.

If a judgment of not guilty (an acquittal) is returned by the jury, the defendant is discharged.

If a guilty verdict is returned, the court may order the defendant to be taken into custody to await judgment on the verdict, *i.e.,* sentencing, or may permit the defendant to remain on bail.

Upon the entry of a verdict of guilty, the court sets a time for imposing sentence.

§ 14.12.9 Sentencing

Before imposing sentence, the court affords the defendant an opportunity to make a statement on their own behalf and to present any information in mitigation (to make less severe) of punishment or to show any legal cause why sentence should not be imposed. The prosecuting lawyer is also given an opportunity to present any information material to the imposition of sentence.

If the judgment calls for imprisonment, the sheriff of the county or other appropriate custodial officer designated by the court, upon receipt of a certified copy of the judgment, delivers the defendant to the appropriate place, *i.e.,* the state prison, for service of the sentence.

When judgment of death is rendered, a warrant signed by the judge is delivered to the sheriff of the county where the defendant is convicted. The sheriff delivers the warrant and a certified copy of the judgment to the warden of the prison at the time of delivering the defendant to the prison. The warrant states the conviction and judgment and the appointed day on which the judgment is to be executed.

In capital cases, where the sentence of death has been imposed, the case is automatically reviewed by the supreme court of the state.

§ 14.13 Post-Trial Proceedings

After a defendant has been convicted, a motion for a new trial may be filed. This motion is made in writing within a specified time and should be accompanied by affidavits or evidence of the essential facts in support of the motion. (*See* Illustration 14–8.)

Illustration 14–8

[*NAME OF COURT*]

______________________________,	)	
Plaintiff,	)	
vs.	)	MOTION FOR NEW TRIAL
	)	No. ______
______________________________,	)	
Defendant.	)	

Defendant hereby moves the Court for an order granting a new trial in the above-entitled matter, based on the grounds that [*set forth grounds*].

DATED this ______ day of ______, [year]

____
JOHN SMITH
[*address*]
Lawyer for Defendant

CERTIFICATE OF SERVICE

[Similar to Illustration 14–1.]

The court may, upon motion of a party or upon its own initiative, grant a new trial in the interest of justice if there is any error or impropriety that had a substantial adverse effect on the rights of a party.

If a new trial is granted, the defendant is in the same position as if no trial had been held, and the former verdict cannot be used or mentioned either in evidence or in argument.

§ 14.13.1 Appeals

Following imposition of sentence, the court advises the defendant of the right to appeal and the time within which any appeal must be filed.

After the court has imposed sentence, the defendant may file a motion for a correction or reduction of the sentence within the time period specified in the local rules. In considering a motion to reduce or correct the sentence, the court has virtually unlimited discretion to reduce or modify the sentence.

If the defendant takes an appeal from the conviction, the defendant must file a brief setting forth the facts and law upon which the conviction should be reversed. After the defendant has filed this brief, the state is given an opportunity to file a brief in opposition to the defendant's brief. Thereafter, the defendant may file a reply brief to the state's brief in opposition.

§ 14.13.2 Collateral Attack

After the defendant has exhausted the so-called direct appellate remedies, the defendant may still seek to attack the conditions of confinement or otherwise "collaterally attack," *i.e.*, indirectly attack, the conviction. Many states and the federal government have provisions by which inmates may seek to have their conviction set aside or conditions of confinement changed. In some cases, a defendant convicted in a state court may also file a motion in federal court seeking to have a federal court review the conviction on constitutional grounds.

§ 14.13.3 Parole

At some point during confinement, a defendant may come up for periodic review by the state or federal parole board. If the parole board determines to release the defendant upon certain conditions, the defendant will be released on parole. If the defendant commits another offense, or is even arrested for another offense during the period of parole, parole may be revoked and the defendant may be ordered back to the institution to complete the sentence. In certain cases, the defendant will also face additional incarceration resulting from parole revocation on top of the original sentence.

CHAPTER 15

FAMILY LAW

Table of Sections

§ 15.1 Definition

Family law is just what the name implies—all areas of the law pertaining to the family: abortion laws, adoption laws, child custody laws, duties to disabled persons laws, juvenile laws, civil and criminal support enforcement laws, parentage and paternity laws, and marriage and divorce laws. In many areas the term *domestic relations* is used to refer to family law.

Family law is a rapidly changing area of the law. If your office handles these types of cases, it will be necessary for you to keep current with the changes as they occur. Learn to watch for articles from bar associations and other publications to which your firm subscribes so that you can discuss any changes with your lawyer. Your local and/or state professional organization will also help to keep you informed of changes in forms, procedures, laws, and so on. If your local "divorce" court is online, checking there for changes in the rules is also a good idea to keep informed and up-to-date.

§ 15.2 Influence of Uniform Acts

Although state law controls family law, this is an area that has been greatly influenced by uniform acts. Many state legislatures use these acts as models and modify or expand them to suit their needs. There are probably as many variations as there are states, and the material in this chapter is very general. Therefore, you must refer to the pertinent statutes of your state to ascertain the applicable laws in your state. Some of the uniform acts pertinent to this chapter are the Uniform Marriage and Divorce Act, the Uniform Adoption Act, the Uniform Interstate Family Support Act (UIFSA), the Uniform Child Custody Jurisdiction Enforcement Act (UCCJEA), the Uniform Parentage Act, the Uniform Duties to Disabled Persons Act, and Parental Kidnapping Prevention Act (PKPA).

§ 15.3 Definition of Marriage

Marriage is a civil contract governed by state law. All states have laws regulating the licensing, solemnization, and registration of a marriage.

§ 15.4 Types of Marriages

Generally, there are two types of marriages:

1. The ceremonial marriage authorized by legislative action and validated according to statutes for licensing, solemnization, and registration.

2. The common law marriage which is an agreement to marry between two people, followed by their living together and representing themselves to the public as husband and wife. Common law marriages are recognized in only a few states.

§ 15.4.1 Ceremonial Marriage

Each state has its own rules and regulations concerning application for a marriage license, the license itself, and the registration of a marriage.

§ 15.4.2 Prohibited Marriages

There are marriages that are prohibited by law. Marriage by a person before the dissolution or invalidity of a previous marriage is prohibited. Marriage between persons within specific degrees of blood relationship are also prohibited. Very often, a prohibition of this type includes persons who are adopted, since in most cases they are treated as blood children of the adopting family. The exact prohibitions are set out in state statutes. The licensing clerk requires satisfactory proof that any proposed marriage is not prohibited.

§ 15.4.3 Application for License

The application for a marriage license usually requires certain biographical data of the marrying couple, such as:

- Names, ages, and sexes
- Addresses
- Birthdates and birthplaces
- Occupations
- Race
- Names and birthplaces of the respective parents
- Information on any previous marriages
- Method of termination of any previous marriages
- Whether or not the couple is related and, if so, how related
- Social Security numbers of the couple

§ 15.4.4 Blood Tests

Many states require applicants to have blood tests taken prior to applying for the license. The tests are for the purpose of assuring that neither person has a venereal disease, and for verifying immunity to rubella. Certification of these tests is supplied to the couple at the time they take the test, on a form prescribed by the appropriate state agency. This certification must be presented at the time of application for the license.

§ 15.4.5 Consent of Parents or the Court

In the event either person is a minor under the law of his or her state, that individual's parents or guardians must give their consent to the marriage. The consent of the court is also sometimes required. The minimum age at which a license may be obtained is commonly 16, but this varies from state to state. Pregnancy is not necessarily an automatic reason for obtaining a license by an underaged applicant.

§ 15.4.6 Premarital Counseling

Some states require the marrying couple to have professional counseling prior to issuance of the license if either of the couple is a minor or if required by statute. This counseling may be done by someone appointed by the court or by an ordained minister (depending upon state law). After the required counseling has been completed, the counselor then files with the court their written statement that the requirements of law have been met, together with any appropriate comments.

§ 15.4.7 The License

The clerk of court or deputy clerk usually issues the marriage license. There is a fee for the license, which must be paid before the license is issued. The amount of the fee varies among states.

§ 15.4.8 The Waiting Period

Sometimes there is a minimum waiting period after issuance of the license before the marriage can be legally solemnized. Likewise, there is also usually a maximum period during which the license may be used before it expires (usually around 6 months to a year). In some jurisdictions the court has the authority to shorten the waiting period or to waive it completely.

§ 15.4.9 Solemnization

The clerk explains at the time of issuance of the license that it can be used only within a designated geographic area. A minister, judge, or other authorized state official performs the marriage ceremony. At the time the marriage is solemnized, the license is signed by the marrying couple, the officiating minister or state official, and the witnesses. The officiating minister or state official forwards a marriage certificate to the appropriate state office for registration. Once the marriage is registered, the original license is usually returned to the husband and wife.

§ 15.4.10 Common Law Marriage

A common law marriage is usually contracted by a couple cohabiting and representing to the public that they are husband and wife. This is the general basic requirement for a common law marriage relationship to exist in those states that recognize common law marriages.

People are often under the impression that by living together for seven years, a couple contracts a common law marriage. This is not necessarily true. In some states that recognize common law marriages, the relationship of husband and wife is deemed to exist as soon as the parties represent to the public that they are husband and wife. On the other hand, in those states which do not recognize common law marriages, neither a representation that the couple are husband and wife nor their living together for any length of time constitutes a marriage.

In many cases where common law marriages are recognized, a couple sometimes wishes to make and file in the public records a declaration of marriage to protect the putative spouse's rights in the event of the other's death or disability. These are usually in the form of affidavits by persons who have known the couple for a number of years and know that a marriage relationship exists between the couple.

§ 15.5 Methods of Termination of Marriage

Although it is intended to last for the lifetime of the couple, since marriage is a civil contract governed by state law, state law can terminate it. There are several methods by which a marriage can be terminated:

- By the death of one of the parties
- By divorce or dissolution
- By annulment or invalidity

§ 15.5.1 Grounds for Termination

The reasons for which the termination of a marriage by divorce/dissolution or annulment/invalidity may be sought are referred to as *grounds*. The grounds for termination are totally in the control of the state and therefore grounds for termination vary. It will be necessary for you to become familiar with the grounds in your state. In some states there are no grounds for dissolution except for "irretrievably broken" and in some no fault states no grounds are stated at all.

§ 15.5.2 Divorce or Dissolution and Annulment or Invalidity

Although annulment and invalidity are referred to as means of terminating marriages, in the strict sense of their definitions, that is not so. An *annulment* establishes that a marriage never existed, while a divorce or dissolution terminates a marriage. *Invalidity* is a term used for a marriage which is invalid (void) from its inception. In some states, however, the term *annulment* is used to include *invalidity*. In those states, *annulment* would mean a declaration by a competent court that the marriage never existed, regardless of the reason.

§ 15.5.3 Grounds for Annulment/Invalidity

The general circumstances for a declaration for invalidity or annulment include:

- One or both parties lacked legal capacity to consent to the marriage, *e.g.*, one of the parties is still married to another or both parties were drunk or incapacitated at the time of the marriage.
- One or both parties were under duress.
- Fraudulent pretenses were used to entice the marriage.
- Lack of capacity to physically consummate the marriage was not known to the other party prior to or at the time of the marriage (although not true in all states).
- One or both of the parties was underage and did not have proper consent or approval.
- The marriage was prohibited under state laws.

§ 15.5.4 Statute of Limitations

States have time limitations after the discovery of one or more of the above circumstances within which an annulment or invalidity action may be filed. Persons other than the parties to the marriage can file for the annulment. The classic example of this is a parent who institutes an annulment proceeding because a child was a minor and did not have consent to enter into a marriage contract. Special circumstances must exist, however, for another party to initiate the proceeding.

§ 15.5.5 Children of an Annulled or Invalid Marriage

Generally, it is recognized that children of a marriage declared invalid (or annulled) are legitimate children.

EXAMPLE:

A and *B* have been married for twenty years. They have three children. *A* discovers that he was fraudulently induced to enter into the marriage. He files an action to have the marriage declared invalid. The three children are legitimate, although the marriage is declared invalid.

Whether or not the invalidity decree is retroactive to the date of the marriage usually depends upon the circumstances involved and the wishes of the parties. Since children of the marriage and property rights are often involved, the invalidity decree may be effective on the date it is rendered rather than retroactively.

§ 15.6 Definition of Divorce/Dissolution

Divorce or dissolution is the legal termination of a marriage relationship. For simplicity the terms *dissolution* and *divorce* are used interchangeably in this chapter although there is a technical difference between the two terms in some states.

§ 15.6.1 Grounds for Divorce/Dissolution

Since each state has control over its marriage and divorce laws, the grounds for divorce vary considerably. Traditionally, the grounds may include one or all of the following:

- Cruel treatment of one spouse by the other.
- Abandonment of one spouse by the other (leaving home with no intention of returning).
- Living separate and apart from each other for a specified period of time.
- Adultery.

The foregoing list is by no means exclusive, but it is representative.

§ 15.6.2 No–Fault Divorce

No-fault divorce means that neither spouse need be accused of the traditional grounds in order for a divorce to be granted. Therefore, neither spouse carries the stigma associated with any of the traditional grounds. Consequently, the no-fault concept relieves much of the mental and emotional stress experienced by the parties, their families, and their friends during a dissolution proceeding.

One of the purposes of the Uniform Marriage and Divorce Act is to make *irretrievably broken* a basis for dissolution. Many states have adopted irretrievably broken as the sole ground for filing a dissolution action. In some states the term *irreconcilable differences* is the term used to mean irretrievably broken of the marriage relationship.

§ 15.6.3 Dissolution of Common Law Marriage

A divorce is required to terminate a common law marriage in those states that recognize common law marriages.

§ 15.6.4 Division of Property

The termination of a marriage naturally requires division of the property accumulated during the marriage. The method by which a division of the couple's property is accomplished is another matter controlled by the state. Generally, a primary consideration is the contribution made by each party, either monetary or otherwise, toward acquisition of the property. In states where the property of married couples is community property, this would not be the case. In community property states, the property of the couple is owned one-half by each. In many states the court must approve a division of the property; accordingly, it is an integral part of the proceeding for dissolution.

§ 15.6.5 Child Custody and Support

An action for separate maintenance, dissolution, or invalidity includes determination of custody (control) of any minor children (or also known as issues of the marriage) of the marriage. In addition, it is customary as part of the same proceeding to set an amount to be paid by the non-custodial parent to the other parent for support of the child.

§ 15.6.6 Jurisdiction Over Custody

For the most part, the court in which the action for dissolution is brought is the court that has jurisdiction over the custody of the children. For most states, the jurisdiction also is based on the residency requirement of the parties and/or the residency of the children.

§ 15.6.7 Determination of Custody

Many parents are able to reach an amicable agreement on which parent is to have custody of the children. If the parents are unable to reach an amicable agreement as to custody, then the court makes that determination. It would be impossible to set out detailed criteria for the award of child custody. Therefore, the general rule is that in determining custody, the court is to act in the best interests of the children. This rule leaves the court with a great deal of discretion in reaching a decision on custody, but of primary importance are the best interests of the child.

In some states, a distinction is made between legal and physical custody; either or both types can be solely vested in either parent, or be shared ("joint" custody).

§ 15.6.8 Legal and Physical Custody

There are many variations of custody: joint legal custody with sole physical custody, and vice versa. Generally speaking, the parent without physical custody has visitation rights, which may also be called access or parenting time.

Physical custody refers to the actual physical residence of the child(ren) with one or both parents. The parent having physical custody makes the day-to-day decisions for the children, including meals, clothing, playmates, bedtime, etc. Physical custody can be shared in any number of ways.

In joint physical custody arrangements, parents may alternate weeks or months with the children or the children's time may be divided equally in a manner that meets the needs of a family. Generally the parents work out physical custody arrangements, as they can be more creative than the courts. Legal custody means making important long-term decisions affecting the children's welfare, including education, religion, and medical care decisions. For example, legal custody may also be joint or divided in appropriate cases. Joint custody, legal or physical, may not always be appropriate in every case and requires the parents to work together for the welfare of their children. It is important to be aware of the specific definitions used by your state, as they may vary.

§ 15.6.9 Visitation by the Non-Custodial Parent

Regardless of which parent is awarded custody of the children, the non-custodial parent has the right to visit the children, except in rare instances. Therefore, the custody award is usually subject to the right of reasonable visitation by the non-custodial parent. The intent of a reasonable visitation provision is that the parents will cooperate and act in the best interests of the children. The court establishes specific times for parenting time if the parties cannot agree. In most states, there are guidelines that suggest reasonable parenting time, usually depending on the age(s) of the child or children, and subject to modification by the court.

§ 15.6.10 Support

In determining support for the children, the resources of both the custodial and non-custodial parent, as well as the child's resources, are considered. If the child has special problems—physical, emotional, or mental—these are also determining factors. A child who is mentally, physically, or emotionally impaired may be entitled to a higher degree of support, for a longer term, than other children, including support and maintenance for special or higher education which will allow the child to function independently in society.

§ 15.6.11 Disputed Cases

In disputed cases, the court takes testimony of the parties and their witnesses just as in any other trial. Sometimes the court requires and considers reports from investigative agencies in reaching a decision. The judge also has the discretion to interview the children to ascertain their wishes and their feelings, but the court is not bound to follow the wishes of the children. Since the primary consideration is the best interest of the children, in some jurisdictions a lawyer or a guardian *ad litem* is appointed to represent the children in the custody hearing.

§ 15.6.11.1 Mediation

In the interest of judicial economy, some states have adopted laws in which the courts order the parties to attend mediation with a court-appointed officer. This third person is to assist the parties in resolving any or all issues—whether they are child or property related. Any agreements made during this conference are submitted to the judge to become a court order.

§ 15.6.11.2 Parenting Class

Some states have now started requiring the parties with children to take a parenting information class. This class is to teach the parents how to help their children deal with the changes that come with divorce.

§ 15.6.12 Agreements

When the parties are not in dispute as to custody and are able to agree upon a support figure, they enter into a written agreement concerning both custody and support. Often the agreement recites that while both parents are fit and proper persons to have the care, custody, and control of the children, they deem it in the best interest of the children to place them in the custody of one of the parties. Visitation privileges are also provided for in this agreement. The court will generally approve an agreement reached by the parties, subject to the guidelines of the state.

§ 15.7 Definition of Alimony and Spousal Maintenance

Alimony, more commonly referred to as spousal maintenance, is an allowance which a spouse pays for the support of the other party, usually by court order. Most states have a provision for *alimony pendente lite,* that is, a temporary allowance made during the pendency of an action. Whether or not the spouse is entitled to alimony after the divorce is granted may depend upon additional criteria. However, this is an area in which the trial judge is allowed great discretion. Generally, the court considers the entire financial status of the parties, including their individual incomes, their debts, and the earning history and potential of the parties, in setting alimony.

§ 15.7.1 Who Is Entitled to Alimony or Spousal Maintenance

This is another area of family law where traditions are being changed both by courts and by husbands. Traditionally, wives were the only spouses entitled to alimony and maintenance. Some state statutes providing alimony *for wives only* have been declared unconstitutional. Most states are therefore amending their statutes to provide for alimony and separate maintenance for either spouse.

Often, if the parties reach an agreement on the division of property and child custody and support, they also reach an amicable agreement as to whether and how much alimony or maintenance is to be paid.

In some states, the following factors may be considered in awarding spousal maintenance:

1. The financial resources of the spouse seeking maintenance (payee), including marital property apportioned to the payee, and the ability to meet needs independently, including the extent to which a provision for support of a child living with the payee includes a sum for the payee as custodian.
2. The time necessary to acquire sufficient education or training to enable the payee to find appropriate employment, taking into account the payee's age, skills, and the ability to complete education or training, to become fully or partially self-supporting.
3. The standard of living before and during the marriage.
4. The duration of the marriage and, in the case of a homemaker, the length of absence from employment and the extent to which any education, skills, or experience have become outdated and earning capacity has become permanently diminished.
5. The loss of earnings, seniority, retirement benefits, and other employment opportunities forgone by the spouse seeking spousal maintenance.
6. The age and physical and emotional condition of the spouse seeking maintenance.
7. The ability of the maintenance payor to meet their own reasonable needs while meeting those of the payee.
8. The contribution of each party in the acquisition, preservation, depreciation, or appreciation in the amount or value of the marital property, as well as the contributions of a spouse as a

homemaker or in the furtherance of the payor's employment, business, or education.

§ 15.7.2 Tax Considerations

In setting alimony or maintenance and child support, there are tax consequences to be considered. Often, in an amicable settlement, a larger portion of the alimony and child support is classified as alimony in the agreement. This is because although alimony is considered income to the payee, it is deductible to the payor for income tax purposes. Therefore, if the wife is in a much lower tax bracket than the husband, for example, a higher income might not result in a substantial increase in taxes for the wife, but it might result in a substantial deduction and savings for the husband. The lawyer makes a careful study of the tax consequences facing their client in any such settlement and makes certain that the provisions of the decree or agreement will satisfy the requirements of the Internal Revenue Service. Child support is not deductible; however, arrangements must be made regarding the claiming of any child or children as dependents for tax purposes.

§ 15.8 Procedures

While the difference between a divorce and a dissolution and the difference between an annulment and an invalidity are basically a matter of semantics in many states, the procedures as far as the lawyer's assistant is concerned are generally the same regardless of whether or not the state has adopted the uniform acts or a variation of them.

The no-fault concept of dissolution of marriages has eliminated some of the paperwork that is necessary for traditional divorce actions. It also makes the task of drafting the necessary legal pleadings simpler for both the lawyer's assistant and the lawyer. The lawyer's assistant can draft a simple petition of this type for the lawyer's review.

Since the procedural anatomy of invalidity parallels that of dissolution, the procedures are not repeated here. If you keep in mind the similarities between the two types of actions, you will have no problem conforming one to the other. In instances where the parties are in agreement, the procedure is simpler than in most civil litigation. However, when there is a dispute, the litigation follows the same course as any other litigation. There is a petition, an answer, discovery, and a trial.

§ 15.8.1 Requirements of Pleadings

Each state has varying requirements as to the pleadings in these actions, and it will be up to you to learn those in your state. You can learn many of the requirements by referring to the forms manual in use in your office. If there is none, you should begin to develop your own immediately. By having a good forms file, you can relieve the lawyer of the burden of dictating the pleadings. However, be very careful not to use forms without individualizing them to the given situation. Each time a new situation arises or unique language is used, put a copy of the appropriate portion of the document in the forms manual for future reference.

§ 15.8.2 The Pleadings

In the traditional termination proceeding, just as in other civil litigation, the initiating party is the *plaintiff* and the spouse is the *defendant.* In no-fault proceedings, the initiating party is the *petitioner* and the spouse is the *respondent.*

The caption is the same as in any other civil litigation. The initial document is a *petition* or a *complaint,* and a summons is issued as in any other civil litigation. Even in no-fault dissolutions, it is still necessary to prepare a petition. Some jurisdictions do allow one of the spouses to waive service and legal delays in a no-fault proceeding.

§ 15.8.3 The Petition

The petition for a dissolution normally includes, but is not limited to, the following (but may include other statements):

1. The birth date, address, occupation, residence, and any prior names of each party and length of time residence has been continuously maintained within the state by each party.
2. A statement that at least one of the parties has resided within the state of jurisdiction for the required length of time.
3. The city, county, and state where the parties were married, the date of the marriage, and the office or governmental agency where the marriage was registered are given. This is particularly important under the uniform law, as a statistical report is sent to this office or governmental agency after the decree is entered, and in many jurisdictions the matter is also entered in the judgment docket whether or not a separate proceeding for dissolution, legal separation, or custody is pending in a court in that state or elsewhere.
4. A statement as to whether or not state conciliation laws apply to the action is made. If they do, a statement that the provisions thereof have been met by whatever action was taken is included.
5. A statement that the marriage relationship is irretrievably broken (for whatever reason) allowed by statute.
6. The names, ages, addresses, and birthdates of the children are given.
7. A statement that the wife is or is not pregnant may be required.

8. A reference to the division of property is made. If a division has been reached, it is described. The description may be included in the petition, or it may be a separate document referenced or incorporated in the petition.
9. A statement of custody, support, and visitation rights regarding minor children is required. If an agreement has been reached, refer to the provisions of the agreement. There may be an additional statement that the provisions of the agreement were made in the best interests of the children.

The prayer of the petition is typed just as in any other civil litigation and gives a summary of the relief sought by the petitioner, usually in list form.

The lawyer for the petitioner usually signs the petition. It may also be necessary that the petition be signed by the petitioner and verified. The actual form will depend upon the procedural law in your state.

Once the petition has been prepared and is ready to be filed, you will proceed just as you would in any other type of civil litigation. Refer to the chapter on Litigation for details regarding filing, summons, and service of the petition. Refer to your state laws for details on what specific documents must be included and served with the petition.

§ 15.8.4 Service

It is common in divorce proceedings for the defendant or respondent to accept service. Usually there is a separate document for this purpose. Some states allow a blurb on the summons. Either way, it is dated and signed, verified and returned to the originating lawyer for filing with the court. The respondent can handle acceptance of service through the respondent's lawyer, through the mail, or in person.

Some jurisdictions require the serving party, *e.g.*, the sheriff's office, or process server to complete the return of service on the summons or do a separate affidavit of service. It is important to learn the service requirements for each family law proceeding in your state and to make sure that you comply with them.

§ 15.8.5 Answer or Response

Just as in any other civil litigation, the defendant or respondent has a specified period of time within which to answer the petition. If the parties are in agreement, the respondent may file a verified response admitting the allegations of the petition (including admission that the marriage has irretrievably broken down) and requesting that the decree be entered as prayed for in the petition. An alternative is that the respondent makes no appearance and the petitioner takes a default judgment. The procedures vary, and you must learn the accepted procedure in your state.

Note that in the traditional divorce action, the defendant's first appearance is usually an *answer*. In a no-fault action, the appearance is a *response*. Here, again, the terminology as well as the procedures may vary.

§ 15.8.6 Importance of Calendaring

It is important that you calendar the date that a response or an answer is due as well as the date when a default judgment can be taken. This is particularly crucial if your lawyer represents the defendant or respondent, as a response of some type is essential to prevent a default judgment from being taken. If you have been instructed to prepare the entry of a default for your lawyer, it is important to verify that the lawyer has not granted an informal extension of time for a response to be filed. Lawyers sometimes forget to make such notes in the file. If your lawyer has been granted an informal extension of time, it is important to confirm it in writing. It is equally important to calendar the time from filing a default action to the time to request a hearing—especially for a respondent's lawyer—since it is a "second chance" to respond.

§ 15.9 The Decree

When the decree is entered, whether in an amicable action or a disputed one, it may set forth findings of fact, conclusions of law, and the decision of the court. Just as in any other litigation, if the matter is a disputed one, the lawyer for the prevailing party drafts the judgment and submits it to the opposing lawyer for approval before presenting it to the judge for signature and entry.

In a situation where there is no answer filed, either by intent or otherwise, one of the parties appears to testify to obtain the decree. Testimony is taken by the court, and at the conclusion of the testimony, the judge signs the decree that has been prepared by the lawyer prior to the court hearing.

Regardless of how the decree is obtained, it may contain, but is not limited to, substantially the following information:

1. The names of the parties.
2. That the summons was served and the default entered or that the summons was served and a response was filed and whatever other action resulted.
3. The date of the hearing–(in some states, the date of the decree, which may or may not be the same date as the hearing).
4. A statement that witnesses were sworn and testified and that from the evidence presented the court makes the findings of fact contained in the decree.

5. The findings of fact (generally, a basic statement of the facts of the case).
6. A statement that from the findings the court draws the conclusions set out in the decree.
7. The conclusions of law.
8. The fact that the marriage is dissolved (this is usually one of the conclusions of law, *see* paragraph 7 above).
9. That the parties have entered into an agreement regarding distribution and disposition of their property and that the agreement is incorporated by reference into the decree and approved (this is usually one of the findings of fact, *see* paragraph 5 above).
10. Full provisions for child custody, support, and visitation (this is usually one of the conclusions of law, *see* paragraph 7 above). If the noncustodial parent has not taken their parenting class, the court may order the custodial parent to automatically be awarded sole custody.
11. Provisions regarding alimony or spousal maintenance (this is usually one of the conclusions of law, *see* paragraph 7 above).

It is also possible in some states to obtain the actual marriage dissolution, reserving for further consideration the property settlement, child custody, and support matters. This is known as a "bifurcated" hearing or decree. The original decree should conform to this situation, with a final decree entered at such time as these other matters are settled or have been heard.

§ 15.9.1 Service of Decree

When the decree has been entered, copies should be served on the parties as required by appropriate state laws. Your state may require a notice of entry of decree, and it may be necessary that you prepare that notice, although it may be served by the clerk or by the sheriff. It is a good idea to see that each party receives a certified copy of the decree.

§ 15.9.2 Appeals

Appeals in these actions generally follow the same rules and procedures as in any other type of civil litigation.

§ 15.9.3 Other Special Considerations

There are several areas of special consideration in the divorce/dissolution action. The two that you are most likely to encounter are the rights of minor children and the rights of mentally disabled family members.

§ 15.10 Appointment of Lawyer to Represent Children

In some jurisdictions there are cases where there is a great deal of disparity over child custody and support. In some jurisdictions either parent may petition the court to appoint a disinterested lawyer to represent the interests of minor or disabled children who are affected by the custody, support, and property settlement of the parties. This lawyer then enters the case with the best interests of the clients (the children) in mind, and takes the role of "guardian *ad litem*."

§ 15.10.1 Petition to Appoint

The petition to appoint is a very simple one that merely requests that the court appoint a lawyer to represent special parties. Depending upon the procedural rules of the jurisdiction involved, generally the best interests of the children are sufficient to seek an appointment. The fees of the lawyer appointed are fixed by the court and taxed to the parties accordingly.

§ 15.10.2 Appointment of Guardian *Ad Litem* to Represent Mentally Disabled Party

In a situation where one of the parties to the dissolution action is mentally disabled, the court may appoint a guardian *ad litem* to act in the place of the mentally disabled spouse. The guardian *ad litem* then retains the services of a lawyer to represent the mentally disabled party.

§ 15.10.3 Mental Disability as Grounds

In most states mental disability for a specific duration does constitute grounds for a divorce or dissolution. This type of action might be utilized when a spouse has become mentally disabled to the point that the person must be institutionalized, placing a financial burden on the family. The dissolution action may enable the mentally disabled spouse to receive Medicaid or other subsidy to pay for the institutionalization and enable the family to remain financially intact.

§ 15.11 Definition of Uncontested Proceedings

In uncontested proceedings the couple have decided that they no longer wish to remain married, and they have reached an amicable decision on property, custody, child support, visitation, and alimony, if any.

§ 15.11.1 Agreement

Often the lawyer prepares a proposed agreement for execution by the parties prior to filing the action. This agreement recites basically the following facts and provisions:

1. Names of the parties.
2. Date and place of the marriage.
3. That the parties are currently husband and wife.
4. That the parties have separated or will be separated for whatever reason.
5. The name, age, sex, and birthdate of any minor children.
6. The name of each lawyer representing each party. if one is not represented by a lawyer, a statement that the unrepresented party understands they are free to seek legal representation and have been advised to do so.
7. Statement that the parties intend by the agreement to set forth in writing their mutual promises.
8. That the agreement is mutual.
9. The provisions for the division of property and debts.
10. Provisions for child custody, support, and visitation, with a statement that the parties feel these are in the best interests of the children at this particular time.
11. If joint custody, the controlling provisions.
12. Alimony or spousal maintenance provisions.
13. How tax returns for the year of dissolution will be handled, including who gets any refund and who pays any taxes due.
14. How the dependent deduction(s) for any minor child or children will be allocated.
15. Provisions for modification of the agreement.
16. Provisions for lawyers' fees—current and future.
17. Provisions for effecting transfer of title of the assets.
18. Statement that the parties have fully disclosed all property, debts, and agreements to each other and to their lawyers.
19. That the agreement has been read and is understood by the parties.
20. That the agreement is voluntary.
21. The name of the court having jurisdiction over the dissolution proceedings, any future modification of the agreement, and future child custody and support proceedings.

The agreement, when finalized, is usually signed in triplicate by the parties and notarized. Each party then retains one triplicate original and the third triplicate original is filed with the court when the petition for dissolution is filed. This eliminates the necessity of having to set forth the agreement in the petition. It also saves time when the decree is rendered, as the agreement can be made a part of the decree by reference if an original is in the court record.

§ 15.11.2 Modification of a Decree

State laws have usually recognized a minimum time within which a dissolution decree, including custody and support provisions, cannot be modified after it is entered. The uniform act recommends two years. During this time, the decree cannot be modified unless there is a substantial change in circumstances, such as severe disability of the custodial parent affecting the children; inability of non-custodial parent to continue support payments in the amount ordered; or circumstances which have changed greatly since the entry of the decree affecting the best interests of the minor children. States that order the parenting informational classes can order the parent not to modify the dissolution decree including custody and support provisions pursuant to the time restraints. They may also order the parent not to modify the same until parenting classes are taken.

§ 15.11.3 Purpose of the Uniform Interstate Family Support Act (UIFSA)

The Uniform Interstate Family Support Act (UIFSA) provides a means for enforcing duties of support in foreign jurisdictions. In this context *foreign jurisdiction* means a state other than the one where the child and custodial parent live. UIFSA has now been adopted by a majority of states.

§ 15.11.4 Jurisdiction

Actions under UIFSA are initiated in the jurisdiction of the custodial parent and child to whom support is due. It is usually the District Attorney or Attorney General's office that initiates the proceedings. The action is then transferred to the county and state where the respondent lives for service on the respondent.

§ 15.11.5 The Custodial Parent Can Initiate a UIFSA Action

Sometimes a custodial parent initiates the petition with the hope that by having support enforced, becoming dependent on state aid will be avoided. The custodial parent may have custody as a result of a divorce proceeding in which custody was awarded. Sometimes the parent seeks support even if the couple is still married, but separated—a non-custodial parent still has an obligation to support the child whether or not the parents are divorced.

§ 15.11.6 The State Department of Welfare Can Initiate a UIFSA Action

A state department of welfare that has provided support to the custodial parent often initiates a petition for enforcement of support. Usually, a condition to receiving financial aid for support from a state department is the assignment by the custodial parent of all support payments to which they are entitled. The state then initiates an action on behalf of the custodial parent to enforce support obligations and recover welfare or other payments made to the custodial parent. Sometimes the state is given custody of children because of emotional, physical, or mental disabilities or because of neglect by the parents. In those instances, the state often initiates a UIFSA action against the parents for support to offset the cost to the state for the child's care.

It is also common in cases where unwed mothers seek welfare aid for their children for the state department of welfare to file an action to enforce support from the father. In order to receive such aid, the unwed mothers are usually required to provide the name of the putative father of the child. The state then seeks to have the parentage of the child determined legally and seeks to enforce support obligations of the father. (Actions to establish paternity are discussed later in this chapter.)

§ 15.11.7 Verified Testimony

The verified testimony of the custodial parent containing the following information is an essential element to the UIFSA action:

1. Full names and addresses of both parties.
2. Date and place of marriage and dissolution or separation, or date and court where paternity was established.
3. Names, ages, and addresses of the minor children.
4. Amount of support ordered monthly.
5. Amount of arrearages, together with date and amount of last payment.
6. Respondent's employment, property, income, etc., as known to petitioner.
7. Petitioner's monthly expenses, broken down into housing, food, utilities, health care costs, gasoline, and other expenses for the petitioner and the children.
8. Whether the petitioner is currently on welfare and if petitioner will have to seek welfare assistance if support payments are not made.
9. A description of the respondent, including age and distinguishing marks.

10. Respondent's last known address and usual occupation as well as other occupations in which they have been engaged or are capable of performing.
11. Any other information which might aid authorities to find the respondent.

§ 15.11.8 Certificate of Transfer

Another essential element to a UIFSA action is a request of the court to enter a certificate for the transfer of the action to the appropriate jurisdiction. Occasionally when the action is started by the state, the petition and testimony are a combined document; the important thing is that all information required be presented.

§ 15.12 Defenses to the Action

The respondent must present testimony as to the defenses for the alleged failure to provide support. In cases where the respondent has been unemployed or otherwise unable to meet the obligations of support, the court takes the circumstances under advisement and sometimes reduces the amount of support requested in the UIFSA action.

§ 15.12.1 Action by the Court

After consideration of the evidence and the respondent's testimony, the court having jurisdiction over the respondent enters its order. The order may require the respondent to make all payments through the clerk of court in the jurisdiction where the hearing is held. When that is done, that clerk of court then forwards the funds to the clerk of court in the originating jurisdiction for disbursement. Sometimes the court simply orders that regular support payments be made to the custodial parent and a specified amount reimbursed to the welfare department. In those instances there is a specific provision in the order rendered by the court.

§ 15.12.2 The Pleadings

The only pleadings generally required by the lawyer for the petitioner are the petition, the verification of the testimony, and the certificate of the originating court to have the action transferred to the respondent's jurisdiction.

§ 15.12.3 The Petition

The petition is probably one for which your office has a standard form. If it does not, once the lawyer has dictated one to you, it will be a simple matter for you to conform future cases to the same format. The petition is verified, like other petitions, it lays out the background facts and requests of the petitioner.

§ 15.12.4 The Verified Testimony

A very important aspect of the pleading is the sworn testimony of the petitioner which sets out the information recited in the section on verified testimony. A client interview sheet will prove an invaluable aid to you in this regard.

§ 15.12.5 The Certificate for Transfer

You will also prepare the certificate that the court must sign to have the matter transferred. Depending upon jurisdictional rules and local custom, it is usually not necessary for the petitioner to appear in person when the prosecuting or state lawyer presents the matter to the court for issuance of the court certificate to transfer the case to the respondent's jurisdiction.

§ 15.13 Forwarding Pleadings to Respondent's Jurisdiction

The petition, testimony, and certified copies of UIFSA as adopted in the state of origin are forwarded to the respondent's jurisdiction. The clerk forwards the entire filing to the appropriate jurisdiction with the correct number of copies. How many copies you must prepare will depend upon your particular jurisdiction; prepare extras to be safe.

§ 15.13.1 Issuance of Citation

Upon receipt of the action in the responding jurisdiction, the matter is filed immediately and turned over to the prosecuting lawyer. A summons for the respondent to appear is issued and served, together with a complete copy of the documents on file. One set of documents is retained in the court file, the prosecuting lawyer retains one, and one is used for service on the respondent.

§ 15.13.2 Service on Respondent

The citation is served on the respondent, together with the petition and supporting documents, advising respondent of the time to appear to present a defense to the UIFSA action.

§ 15.13.3 Failure to Appear

Failure to appear before the court may cause the respondent to be held in contempt and punished accordingly. If the respondent has a history of fleeing after being served with process in a UIFSA action, the initiating court may request that the respondent be arrested and held until such time as an appearance can be made before the judge.

§ 15.13.4 Inability to Locate Respondent

In the event the parent against whom the action has been filed cannot be located within the county where the action has been transferred, the prosecuting lawyer immediately notifies the initiating court asking for any information which will lead to the location of the respondent. In this event it may be necessary for you to help locate them. You can check telephone directories, police records, income tax offices, and the Social Security Administration to trace the respondent and to effect service. These agencies usually assist to the point that they legally can in a support matter. Process service agencies also have skip tracing available for a fee, which may also be used effectively.

§ 15.13.5 Transfer to Another Jurisdiction

If it develops that the respondent is in a county other than where the action is filed, the prosecuting lawyer is notified, and an order is prepared for the court to issue transferring the action to the county where the respondent resides.

§ 15.13.6 For the Respondent

The assistant to the lawyer for the respondent has a somewhat different approach to the UIFSA action, *i.e.,* involved in the defense preparation. The secretary will help the client gather and categorize support payments made, employment records, income tax returns, and other financial records. This can be a time-consuming process and is more clerical than legal in many instances. The lawyer's assistant should verify through the court where support was due, the actual payments ordered, and the amount the client has paid.

All financial records of the respondent, as well as any medical records, and any other pertinent information that would show a change in circumstances that would substantially affect their ability to contribute to the support of the children should be categorized in a manner that can be presented to the court.

If paternity is denied, you should obtain copies of birth certificates and other public records that may substantiate the denial. You may also be responsible for seeing that DNA tests are taken and made available for use at a hearing.

§ 15.13.7 The Role of the Lawyer's Assistant in UIFSA Actions

The lawyer's assistant, under the supervision of the lawyer, can handle much of the routine work in these cases. Once the lawyer develops a workable form for the petition and the testimony, ordinary actions can be prepared; unusual circumstances, as always, will require more assistance from the lawyer for special phrasing. The court certificate will always be the same. Requests for updates of information, notification of inability to locate, requests to transfer, and subsequent orders can all be handled on a routine basis by the lawyer's assistant after several proceedings have been completed.

§ 15.13.8 Civil Liability for Support

The Uniform Civil Liability for Support Act sets forth the duties of support between spouses and parents and children. This act and UIFSA were both enacted to help enforce support obligations required under court orders.

The custodial parent may also initiate civil actions against obligors for support. These actions are filed much the same as any other civil suit, with a complaint initiating the action and the issuance of a summons. Judgments are obtained and enforced through execution and foreclosure proceedings. These, of course, will depend upon statutes applicable in the appropriate jurisdictions.

In the event the defendant to a civil support action resides in another state, the judgment entered may also be transferred to that state to ensure enforcement. It is also generally recognized that even when children have reached their majority, the non-custodial parent still owes the obligation to the custodial parent for support payments in arrears. State laws control these actions, and the procedural law for your state will have to be followed, particularly as regards the statute of limitations. Some states allow a child who has reached majority to pursue the non-custodial parent for support arrearages.

§ 15.14 Definition of Adoption

Adoption means taking into one's family the child of another and giving the child all the rights, duties, and privileges of a natural child and heir.

§ 15.14.1 Uniform Adoption Act

Although the Uniform Adoption Act has been adopted by only a few states, it still serves as a suitable basis for learning the requirements of adoption. Many of the states adopting the act have greatly modified it. As always, the lawyer's assistant should be familiar with local and state requirements.

§ 15.14.2 Jurisdiction

Adoption matters are usually filed in the probate division of a state court. However, some jurisdictions have separate family courts or juvenile courts that have jurisdiction over adoption proceedings.

§ 15.14.3 Closed Hearings

Adoption files are sealed; that is, the public is not granted access to them. In the case of adoption from an agency, even the parents are not allowed access to these files. Discretion on the part of the lawyer's assistant is imperative in adoption proceedings. Usually, adoption agencies request that the lawyer somehow prevent the adoptive parent from even seeing the last name of the child when signing the requisite documents and pleadings. The adoption hearing itself is also a closed hearing. There is continuing controversy over whether or not an adopted child should be allowed to find the biological parents or whether parents should be allowed to find their children placed for adoption. Many times whether or not a child is allowed to see the adoption file is left to the discretion of the presiding judge. In the case of a step-parent adopting a stepchild, the situation will be different.

§ 15.14.4 Adoption Procedure (Stepchildren)

When a step-parent adopts stepchildren, the procedure is relatively simple:

1. The stepparent files a petition in the proper court.
2. The spouse of the stepparent consents to the adoption by joining in the petition.
3. The non-custodial parent consents to the adoption releasing all parental rights.
4. Depending on the state, there is an investigation by a state agency, such as the Department of Social Services.
5. The agency reports to the court.
6. There is a closed court hearing, usually in the judge's chambers. Assuming the judge finds the record of the case to be in proper form, the decree is rendered.

In most states, adults may be adopted; however, the prospective adoptee and spouse, if any, must also consent to the adoption.

From the initial client interview, the lawyer determines the eligibility of the prospective adopting parent, who must receive notice, and who must consent to the adoption. If the office uses a detailed interview sheet, the lawyer's assistant should have little difficulty drafting the petition. Generally, the following information is included in the petition. Again, there will be variations from state to state.

1. Full name, age, place of, and length of residence of the petitioner.
2. Petitioner's interest (why the petition for adoption, such as marriage to the natural, custodial parent).
3. Full name of the minor child, sex, date, and place of birth, relationship to petitioner, and request for name change.
4. If petitioner is married to custodial parent, give date and place of marriage.
5. How long child has been in physical custody of petitioner.
6. That petitioner is a fit and proper person and has the capability, resources, and facilities to provide for the care, support, and maintenance of the child; that petitioner desires to do so and to establish the relationship of a natural parent and child.
7. Name of natural parent of the child and any other person from whom consent might be necessary or the reason why consent from someone else is not necessary.
8. Value and description of any property the child has.
9. Signature of the petitioner with a verification.
10. Name, address, and signature of petitioner's lawyer.

Usually the custodial parent joins in the petition for adoption. This joinder, with the consent, can be in affidavit form and should contain the following information:

1. Name of parent and relationship to child.
2. Restatement of child's full name, age, sex, date, and place of birth.
3. Former name of parent (as shown on birth certificate) if applicable.
4. Name of other natural parent, if known, or statement that other parent is deceased or other reason why consent from that parent is not necessary.
5. Statement of free consent to adoption and of joining in petition to adopt.
6. Statement that parent, by joining in adoption petition, does not relinquish rights as natural parent.

When the petition and consent have been prepared and signed, they are filed in the proper court. A certified copy of the petition and attached consent are served on the appropriate state agency, such as the Department of Social Services or other applicable agency. Since this agency conducts an investigation regarding the proposed adoption, it must be served with the petition.

§ 15.14.5 Consent to Adoption

During the time that the investigation by the state agency is being conducted, any required consents to the adoption can be obtained and filed. Even if the child is illegitimate, the natural father's consent should be obtained to avoid future actions to invalidate the adoption. If consent from someone who cannot be located is required, an order to show cause why the adoption should not be granted may be served by publication in a newspaper of general circulation in the jurisdiction where that person was last known to reside. Service of this type will vary greatly among jurisdictions, but the lawyer will supervise any such notice.

If the non-custodial parent or other person from whom consent is necessary refuses to give that consent, they may be personally served with an order to appear and show cause why the adoption should not be granted, especially if there may be a legal reason why their consent may not be necessary. Again, this is a determination that is solely in the discretion of the lawyer, who will make that decision.

After service of the petition and investigation by the investigative agency and a report by that agency to the court, the matter is set for hearing. Notice of the hearing is given in accordance with applicable state laws.

At the time of the hearing, the court, in its discretion, may enter a summary decree that waives all time requirements and declares the adoption final at that time. The court may also enter an interlocutory decree to be in effect for a specific period of time, usually six months, at which time another hearing is held prior to entry of a final decree of adoption.

It is important to know your local court rules and the attitudes of the presiding judge when time for the final hearing is set. Many times a certain judge will require that an interlocutory decree be entered in all adoptions, while another judge may usually enter a final decree at the initial hearing. As new lawyer's assistants soon learn, the judge will usually expect a decree (of whatever nature) prepared and ready for them to sign at the time of the hearing.

As the lawyer's assistant is usually responsible for seeing that the adopting parents and child are notified of the hearing date, the lawyer's assistant should also be aware of others whom the judge wishes to attend the hearing. Many judges like to have the adopting parents and their other children present in order to assess the family situation and determine the feelings of other family members toward the adoption. Of course, the lawyer should also be at the hearing. Since the hearings are closed, no one is allowed except those who are required to be present. In the event of a contested adoption, parties having a direct and vested interest are allowed to participate at the hearing.

When the adoption has been finalized, certified copies of the decree should be obtained. One copy should be given to the adoptive parent(s), one copy should be sent to the agency which conducted the investigation, and one copy should be sent (with appropriate fee) to the state bureau of vital statistics with the request to issue a new birth certificate for the child. This birth certificate should be delivered to the adopting parents, with a copy retained in the office files. A copy of the final decree is likewise retained for the office files.

Special note should be given to private or non-agency adoptions. These adoptions have come under close scrutiny because of adverse publicity. Most states have adopted legislation which either outlaws private adoptions entirely or strictly regulates as to consents required and fees or costs which may be paid to the lawyer, doctor, and/or natural mother.

§ 15.14.6 Child Custody Jurisdiction

The Uniform Child Custody Jurisdiction Enforcement Act has been adopted in a majority of states. The main purpose of this act is the protection of the child in cases of child custody litigation or abduction of a child by the non-custodial parent. The act establishes procedure on jurisdictional questions.

The actual law of child custody jurisdiction is applicable to the experienced lawyer's assistant working in litigation of this nature. If the lawyer specializes in this type of action, the beginning lawyer's assistant will soon become familiar with the procedures. This is still a changing area of the law, and new decisions are being rendered frequently in cases of this type.

§ 15.14.7 Child Custody Procedures

With certain exceptions, preparation of pleadings in a custody jurisdiction action is much the same as in any other civil suit. However, it is not uncommon in these types of cases for out-of-state service to be required. This is a decision that the lawyer makes.

Litigation can sometimes be avoided by designating in the custody and support agreement what court is to have jurisdiction over the child for future custody and support purposes.

Child custody decrees entered by foreign (out of state) courts may be filed with the clerk in another state and transferred much the same as any other decree or judgment from a foreign jurisdiction. A decree filed in this manner has the same force and effect as a decree entered in the state where the foreign decree was entered, provided the state in which it is sought to be filed has adopted statutes recognizing foreign decrees.

It is important for the lawyer's assistant to be aware of the existence of this uniform act in the event of a child custody action, especially if initial information must be elicited from a client prior to the client's being interviewed by the lawyer. This information would include:

- The court where an original order of custody was entered.
- How the client obtained custody of the child.
- Who was awarded custody in the original order, and when or how that has been changed since.
- Residence of the child since the entry of the decree.
- Any other information with regard to the custody of the child which might be helpful.

Although associated more with visitation than with custody, more and more grandparents are seeking judicial determination of their rights with grandchildren subject to a custody agreement. Some state statutes now recognize the rights of grandparents to visit with their grandchildren under custody and visitation privileges. If these rights are explained to the clients at the time of execution of the custody agreement, it might prevent future litigation by the grandparents. Setting out these rights in the original agreement, as well as in the decree, can save the client the time, money, and emotional stress involved in litigation with grandparents for visitation privileges. In some cases, persons other than grandparents or non-custodial parents may seek, and be granted, visitation rights. Check your state statutes as states vary.

§ 15.15 Alternate Birth Options

Alternate options to birth, such as *in vitro* (test tube) babies, surrogate mothering, open adoption (where the natural parents know the adoptive parents), artificial insemination, and international adoptions are becoming increasingly popular and have raised a myriad of legal issues not yet fully resolved. Some of these issues are the rights of the surrogate mother who changes her mind, malpractice involving sperm donors, and forms of contracts between the various parties. While these issues can be similar to adoption, they are presently approached in large part through aspects of contract law.

§ 15.16 Uniform Parentage Act

The Uniform Parentage Act defines, among other things, the parent/child relationship and how it is established. It also provides who may bring actions to establish paternity and when such actions may be initiated. The use of blood tests and the preservation of records are also provided for in this act.

These actions are usually brought by state prosecuting lawyers on behalf of a mother receiving welfare aid against a putative father of a child to enforce support obligations.

The child is usually made a party to the action and represented by a guardian *ad litem* (a person other than either of the child's parents). The mother and the man purported to be the natural father are also made parties to the action.

§ 15.17 Parentage and Paternity Procedure

Ordinarily, this type of action is much the same as in any other civil suit, except—as in adoption proceedings—the proceedings are confidential and closed to the public. Initial pretrial proceedings are generally informal. Some lawyers prefer to contact the putative father informally; they try to keep the proceedings completely informal and avoid a formal court action by acting through the lawyers.

The lawyer's assistant for either the prosecution or the defense may be responsible for collecting information in a paternity action. Duties may include questioning the mother about the likelihood of sexual activity with another man during the period when conception most likely occurred. Arranging for blood tests and locating experts to testify at the hearing may also be required.

The civil proceeding for determination of paternity brought by a mother or a child for support is usually also conducted in a closed courtroom with no jurors or spectators, but the evidence is similar to that brought by a prosecutor to enforce support obligations. A paternity suit can also be brought by a possible father seeking visitation and a relationship with a child.

Any judgment or order rendered by the court usually includes an order that the birth certificate be amended or reissued to conform to the order of the court.

Of course, after paternity is determined, support must be acted upon. As in other support proceedings, the abilities of both parents, the child's resources and any special needs, as well as other pertinent information, are used to determine the amount of support required for the child. Visitation is also generally established, and may, depending on the circumstances, include a "familiarization period."

§ 15.18 Duties to Disabled Persons

A disabled person is one who lacks legal capacity or one who is physically or mentally disabled from acting in their own behalf or pursuing a normal occupation. The Uniform Duties to Disabled Persons Act provides for duties of police officers, medical practitioners, and others to disabled persons; also, it provides for the use of identifying devices for these persons.

Persons with specific disabilities—epilepsy, diabetes, medicinal allergies—are encouraged (but not required) to wear identifying devices to aid police, doctors, and others in the event the person is unable in an emergency to communicate these conditions.

On the other hand, police officers and medical practitioners especially have a duty to make reasonable searches of disabled or injured persons to ascertain whether or not they are in possession of such identifying devices.

The lawyer's assistant is likely to become acquainted with this area of the law when a disabled person or their family brings suit against others for their failure to perform duties required under this act. Whether the lawyer is prosecuting or defending the action, the pleadings (complaint, summons, discovery, etc.), as well as the procedures, are in much the same form as in any other civil action.

§ 15.19 Definition of Abortion

An abortion is, simply stated, the intentional termination of a pregnancy. Abortion law is one that is still changing rapidly amidst considerable controversy. The Uniform Abortion Act was developed in an effort to standardize abortion law.

Perhaps the most common cases with which the lawyer's assistant is likely to work are those involving medical malpractice with regard to abortion, parental consent for abortion performed on minors, and the rights of the putative father in an abortion situation.

There are still, of course, criminal penalties for illegal abortions that vary from state to state.

§ 15.20 Summary

For professional advancement, the beginning lawyer's assistant may wish to read some of the uniform acts to become familiar with the subject. Both *American Jurisprudence Second* and *Corpus Juris Secundum* contain the uniform acts, and many of them are also published in the *Martindale–Hubbell Law Directory*. If the law firm specializes in this area of the law, it may subscribe to *The Family Law Reporter* published weekly by The Bureau of National Affairs. This publication highlights important cases in all areas of family law. Reading this publication will give the lawyer's assistant an opportunity to have current information on decisions affecting the principal areas of family law.

CHAPTER 16

BUSINESS ORGANIZATIONS

Table of Sections

§ 16.1 Introduction

This chapter discusses the principal structures for doing business in this country—by incorporation, by partnership, (*i.e.*, general partnership, limited partnership, limited liability partnership or limited liability limited partnership), by limited liability company, and by sole proprietorship. At time of publication, a directory of official state, county and city government websites could be found at www.statelocalgov.net. Forms and guidelines for organizing various type of business as well as other useful information may be found on the website for the respective state of domicile.

§ 16.2 Distinction Among Forms of Doing Business

A corporation, a partnership, and a limited liability company are each separate business entities. The individuals who own stock of a corporation or who are members of a limited liability company, a limited liability partnership, or limited liability limited partnership typically have no liability for the debts or obligations of the entity. A general partnership, which is an entity comprised of two or more persons, does not afford its partners this limitation of liability. The partners of any general partnership share in the losses as well as in the profits, although not necessarily on an equal basis. In a limited partnership the limited partners, but not the general partner, enjoy a limitation on their liability to the extent of their investment in the entity. In a sole proprietorship the owner bears all the losses. Legally, the obligations and liabilities of the business are not separated from personal liabilities.

The most advantageous type of entity for a business to take is dependent upon many factors. The lawyer, with the help of a Certified Public Accountant (CPA) or a tax lawyer, often helps the client make this decision. By studying these concepts and understanding them, the lawyer's assistant can better offer assistance to both the lawyer and the clients.

§ 16.3 Definition of Corporation

A corporation is a legal entity created by or under the authority of the laws of a state or (sometimes) a nation. For most legal purposes a corporation is considered a person domiciled in its state of incorporation, and is considered to be a separate and distinct legal entity from its owners. Corporations typically may enter into contracts, own property, sell property, sue, and be sued.

§ 16.3.1 Domestic Corporation

A corporation that is created or organized in the state in which it does business is known as a domestic corporation for purposes of that state.

EXAMPLE:

If a corporation is organized and is doing business in the state of Vermont, it is a domestic corporation insofar as Vermont is concerned.

§ 16.3.2 Foreign Corporation

The term "foreign corporation" is used to describe a corporation doing business in a state or country other than the state or country in which it was created.

EXAMPLE:

The corporation, which is organized and incorporated in Vermont, conducts business in the state of Kentucky. Insofar as Kentucky is concerned, such corporation would be characterized as a foreign corporation. This corporation remains a domestic corporation with respect to Vermont.

§ 16.3.3 Types of Corporations

Generally, corporations are classified as one of the following types:

- Business corporations, which are organized for any lawful purpose to make a profit. They may be "Subchapter C" corporations or "Subchapter S" corporations for tax purposes.
- Nonprofit corporations, which are organized for purposes other than making a profit such as charitable, religious, educational, scientific, and other similar purposes.
- Public corporations, which are organized for governmental purposes such as city or county governments.
- Professional corporations, which are organized to permit a professional person or group of professionals to practice a profession such as law or medicine.

The laws of the various states differ regarding the organization and operation of corporations. Because most of the corporations that you will deal with will be business corporations, the discussion in this chapter focuses on that type.

§ 16.3.4 Advantages of Incorporating

One reason for incorporating a business is the limitation of liability available to its owners. Because the corporation is itself a legal entity, it is the corporation that is legally responsible for its acts and its debts, not the people who own it. This same protection against legal liability is available to the owners of limited liability companies ("LLC"), limited liability partnerships, and the limited partners of a limited partnership.

Generally, the officers, directors, and shareholders of a corporation have no personal liability (legal responsibility) for debts and other obligations incurred by the corporation, provided they act in good faith and provided they keep their own personal business affairs completely separate from those of the corporation, treating the corporation as a separate entity at all times. Importantly, in a case where an officer, employee, or director commits a tort in the course of acting on behalf of any of these entities, both the individual committing the tort and the entity will be liable. In such a case, the limitation of liability still offers protection to other owners and individuals not involved in the tort.

Because the corporation is a separate legal entity, it can continue to do business in the event one of its officers, directors, or shareholders dies. The ownership of the corporation can change without interrupting its day-to-day business operations.

Because the corporation has the power to hold property in its own name, it is sometimes a useful vehicle for estate planning purposes. The ownership interest in an incorporated business may pass down from generation to generation through gifts of shares of stock in the corporation to family members.

Incorporation as a Subchapter C corporation might or might not be advantageous for income tax purposes. A "C" corporation is allowed certain tax deductions not available to other forms of business. However, a Subchapter C corporation's profits may be subject to double taxation (*i.e.*, the corporation's profits are taxed before being distributed to shareholders, and the shareholders are taxed on the distributed profits they receive). The tax ramifications of the selection of a business entity are very complex and require the expertise of a tax accountant or tax attorney.

§ 16.3.5 Disadvantages of Incorporating

Disadvantages of incorporation include greater expenses of organization, governmental regulation, and sometimes tax disadvantages. While the income tax structure of a corporation might be advantageous to some individuals, it could create additional tax burdens for others. For this reason, many lawyers who do not practice tax law urge their clients to discuss the advantages and disadvantages with a tax lawyer or a CPA before finalizing the incorporation and other organizational documents.

§ 16.4 Corporate Structure and Operation

The management and operation of the corporation depend upon three groups of individuals: the shareholders, the board of directors, and the officers. A data sheet is helpful. (*See* Illustration 16–1.)

Illustration 16–1
CORPORATION DATA SHEET

Name of Corporation: ______________________________

Date of Incorporation: ______________________________

Directors:	Address:	Office:
____________	____________	
____________	____________	
____________	____________	
____________	____________	
____________	____________	
____________	____________	

Maximum Number: ______ Quorum: ______ Terms: ______

Capitalization: ______________________________

Common Shares: ______ Par Value: ______

Voting Shares

Non Voting Shares

Preferred Shares

Issued Shares:

Name: ______ Number Issued: ______ Consideration: ______

Address: ______________________ Soc. Sec. No.: ______

Principal Place of Business: ______________________________

____

Purpose: ______________________________

____

Registered Agent and Office: ______________________________

____

Accountant/CPA: ______________________________

Preemptive Rights: ____________

Indemnification Allowed: ____________

Cumulative Voting Allowed: ____________

Executive Committee: ____________

Annual Meeting—Date: ____________

Place: ____________

Fiscal Year: ____________

First Meeting—Date: ____________

Place: ____________

Attendance: ____________

Bank: ______________________________

Who Signs: ______________________________

Limitations: ______________________________

Limitations on Borrowing: ______________________________

Salaries: ______________________________

1244: ______________________________

Subchapter S: ______________________________

Employer ID #: ______________________________

Actions Taken: ______________________________

Documents: (strike any not needed)	Prepared	Executed	Filed
Reservation of Corporate Name			
Articles			
Bylaws			
Minutes of 1st Directors Meeting			
Minutes of 1st Shareholders Meeting			
1244 Plan			
Subchapter S Election			
Assumed Name Certificate			
Certificate of Authority for Other States			
Shareholder Purchase Agreement			
Medical Reimbursement Plan			
Securities Filing			
Other			

Stock and Seal Ordered: ____________________

§ 16.4.1 Shareholders

The shareholders (also known as stockholders) are the persons (either individuals or other legal entities) who own shares of stock in the corporation and therefore own the corporation. A share is a proportionate ownership interest in the corporation that is evidenced by a certificate issued by the corporation. Ownership and transfers of shares are also recorded in a share register (also stock book) that is maintained as part of the corporation's records. Legal counsel sometimes issue and cancel share certificates and maintain the share register on behalf of their corporate clients.

It is the initial sale of stock by the corporation to the shareholders which often provides the initial operating capital for the corporation. Before the corporation is formed, prospective shareholders may agree to purchase a specific number of shares by executing a subscription agreement. (*See* Illustration 16–2.)

The shareholders have the right to vote on certain major issues related to the corporation, including the right to elect the board of directors, to merge with other corporations, to sell substantially all the corporation's assets, and to dissolve the corporation. Shareholders also have the right (through dividends and other distributions) to share in the profits made by the corporation, and to share in the net assets of the corporation upon dissolution of the corporation.

Illustration 16–2

SUBSCRIPTION AGREEMENT

THE UNDERSIGNED hereby subscribes to 2900 shares of the no par value common stock of A.B.C. Corporation, a ____________________ [state of incorporation] corporation. The undersigned agrees to pay the A.B.C. Corporation the sum of $________ for said shares.

Dated: ________

____
(name of subscriber)

§ 16.4.2 Board of Directors

The board of directors is the governing body of the corporation and is composed of the individuals elected by the shareholders. The board of directors establishes policies and oversees officers' actions. It acts by resolution adopted at directors' meetings or adopted by written consent.

§ 16.4.3 Officers

The officers of the corporation are elected by the board of directors and are subject to its control. Officers typically include the president, vice president(s), treasurer, and secretary. The officers conduct day-to-day business affairs of the corporation and implement the policies established by the board of directors.

§ 16.4.4 Meetings

The articles of incorporation or the bylaws provide for meetings of both the shareholders and the board of directors to be held at specified times throughout the year. Additionally, there is generally a provision under state law and/or the corporation's bylaws to permit special meetings of both the shareholders and the board of directors. It is the duty of the secretary to notify the shareholders or the board members of these meetings. The bylaws typically provide for the manner in which the notices must be sent. If your office handles these notices for your corporate clients, it is critical that you follow carefully the provisions in the bylaws and the state corporate statute.

§ 16.4.5 Notice of Meeting

Notice of meetings of directors and of shareholders must be in writing unless notice is waived or all directors or shareholders attend the meetings.

§ 16.4.6 Waivers of Notice

When you are dealing with small corporations with just a few shareholders and board members, it is not unusual for the shareholders or the board members to waive the notice of the meeting. This is perfectly acceptable as long as you remember to prepare the waiver in accordance with the articles of incorporation, bylaws, and the relevant state statute, and make certain that the waiver is signed by each director or shareholder who did not receive proper notice. Many offices include the waiver in the minutes of the meeting. This is acceptable if all people required to have notice actually sign the minutes. The method used will depend upon the preference of the lawyer.

§ 16.4.7 Quorum

A quorum is the minimum number of persons required to be in attendance in order for a meeting to be validly held. The bylaws and state statutes provide for the number of persons required to constitute a quorum for both the shareholders and the board of directors meetings. In most corporations, a majority of the stock ownership constitutes a quorum for a meeting of shareholders. This means that if a corporation has 20 shareholders, five of whom own more than half of the stock, those five shareholders at a meeting would constitute a quorum. A majority of the board of directors usually constitutes a quorum for a meeting of the board of directors.

§ 16.4.8 Proxies

A proxy is the authority given by one shareholder to another to vote the shareholder's shares of stock. This practice is particularly common in large corporations because it is difficult for all shareholders to attend meetings. In the case of those corporations listed on an exchange (such as the New York Stock Exchange or The American Stock Exchange), the Securities and Exchange Commission (SEC) requires that a proxy card be sent with the notice of meeting so that the shareholder can name a proxy. The term "proxy" is used to mean both the authority given and the form used to accomplish it.

§ 16.4.9 Securities Registration and Regulation

A corporation's stock is a type of security, the offering and sale of which is regulated by federal and state law. The Securities and Exchange Commission (SEC) administers federal securities laws and issues rules and regulations with respect to those laws. In addition, each state has its own laws that regulate the offering and sale of securities (generally referred to as "blue sky" laws). The federal and state securities laws include requirements to register securities and rules to prevent fraud. It is very important to comply with these laws. Violations of these laws can result in significant fines, and even criminal convictions, for the corporations and individuals involved, including lawyers.

Certain types of securities and certain sales of securities are exempt from various securities laws, such as the registration requirements. Such exemptions often apply to the stock of small business corporations and to sales of stock that are not made to the general public. Some exemptions require certain actions to be taken (*e.g.*, filing with the SEC and/or applicable state securities agency) before the exemption is effective. In other cases, you might require certain proof from the corporation and/or purchasers of the stock that the exemption requirements are satisfied. In cases where exemptions apply, stock certificates often bear a legend that the shares have not been registered and may not be transferred unless they are registered or an exemption from registration applies.

You should be aware that these laws are complex and may have very serious ramifications if violated. Very often, lawyers engage the services of a securities law specialist to make sure these laws are complied with.

§ 16.5 Initial Interview With Client

The lawyer generally meets with the client to determine the client's particular needs and to obtain all information necessary to begin the incorporation effort. Most lawyers use a checklist for this purpose. (*See* Illustration 16–1.) One of the items of information that the lawyer secures at the initial client interview is the name that the client proposes for the corporation.

§ 16.6 Reservation of Corporate Name

Since the name of the corporation is very important and most states do not allow a new corporation to have a name that is deceptively similar to an existing one, it is necessary to check the availability of the name in each state where the corporation will do business. Therefore, most states provide a method by which the proposed name of the corporation may be reserved for a specific time period. During that time period, no one else is allowed to use that name. One may reserve the name by filing the proper form together with the reservation fee with the state agency designated for such purpose (*e.g.*, corporation commission, secretary of state or lieutenant governor). (*See* Illustration 16–3.) Reserving the name allows the person organizing the corporation time to prepare the necessary documents without fear of losing the name. Some states have a definite period of time for which a name may be reserved. Forms and filing procedures are available on the respective state's website.

Illustration 16–3

APPLICATION FOR RESERVATION OF CORPORATE NAME

To the Secretary of State

State of ______:

Pursuant to the provisions of Section ______ of the ______ Business Corporation Act, the undersigned hereby applies for reservation of the following name for a period of ______ days: ______ ______

DATED: ______, [Year]

________________________*

Its ________________________

____
(Street Address)

____
(City and State)

Telephone: ________________

**Signature of Applicant if an individual or name of Applicant if a Corporation.*
Signature and title of officer if Applicant is a corporation.

Signature of the lawyer alone is acceptable in some states.

Note that most states require the use of the word *Corporation, Incorporated, Company, or Limited* (or an abbreviation thereof) in the name of the corporation. If the lawyer fails to designate which is to be used, be sure to ascertain which it is to be before you apply for the name reservation.

§ 16.7 Articles of Incorporation

The articles of incorporation is the legal document required to form a corporation. Some states refer to this document as the certificate of incorporation. It states what a corporation is authorized to do. A corporation has legal authority to do only what the articles of incorporation specify that it will be able to do. In some states it is allowable to form the corporation for "any legal purpose." In states where such general authority is not allowed, the articles of incorporation typically provide detail as to what the corporation may or may not do. Lawyers often prefer that this detail is stated in quite general terms, thereby not overly restricting the activities in which the corporation may be involved. Even in states where such general authority is allowed, incorporators sometimes choose to limit the corporation's permitted activities.

§ 16.7.1 Contents of Articles of Incorporation

Corporations are governed by state law, and laws regarding incorporation procedures vary from state to state. The corporation laws of each state specify just what information must be contained in the articles of incorporation. The Martindale–Hubbell Law Directory www.martindale.com contains a summary of the requirements that must be met in each state. State specific requirements may also be found on the website for the respective state. A set of typical articles would contain:

- The name of the corporation.
- The date of incorporation.
- The principal place of business.

- The duration of the corporation.
- Whether or not stockholders have cumulative rights or preemptive rights.
- The total number of shares which the corporation is allowed to issue, the classes of stock, and the par value of each share.
- The registered agent and its office address.
- A statement as to the corporation's initial capitalization, *i.e.*, stock ownership, may also be required.

There are many other provisions that may be in the articles, depending upon state law. Some states require only minimal information while others require more detail.

§ 16.7.2 Close Corporation

The incorporators may limit the sale or transfer of stock by having such a provision in the articles of incorporation. The purpose of this provision is to give the initial shareholders the right to decide whether they want to allow any additional shareholders. Usually this provision specifies that in the event a shareholder proposes a sale of their stock, they must first offer the stock on the same terms as the proposed sale to either the other shareholders or to the corporation itself. The corporation or the shareholders are allowed a specific period of time within which to exercise their right to buy the stock, and if they fail to do so, the selling shareholder has the right to sell their stock to a third person.

§ 16.7.3 Preemptive Rights

A preemptive right provision gives the shareholders the right to maintain their original, proportionate share of the corporation in the event the corporation should later issue additional shares of stock. The articles of incorporation specify the number of shares which the corporation is authorized to issue. It is possible for the corporation to increase that number at a later time either by amendment to the articles of incorporation or by any other method approved by state law. In the event of an increase in the number of authorized shares of stock issued, a preemptive right provision means that the original shareholders are given the first option to buy enough of those additional shares to maintain their proportionate share of ownership.

EXAMPLE:

If the corporation originally authorized 200 shares of stock with four shareholders each owning 50 shares and the corporation authorizes an additional 200 shares, a preemptive right provision would allow each shareholder the right to buy another 50 shares. This will allow each shareholder to maintain a 25 percent interest in the corporation. (*See* Illustration 16–4.)

Illustration 16–4

ARTICLES OF INCORPORATION OF A.B.C. CORPORATION

We, the undersigned natural persons of the age of twenty-one years or more, acting as incorporators of the corporation under the Business Corporation Act, adopt the following Articles of Incorporation for the corporation.

FIRST: (The name of the corporation; *Corporation, Incorporated,* or *Inc., Company,* or *Limited* may be required in the name)

SECOND: (The period of the corporation's duration)

THIRD: (The purposes for which the corporation is organized)

FOURTH: (The capitalization structure of the corporation, *e.g.,* dollar amount of capital stock, aggregate number of shares authorized, par value per share, voting rights of shares, designation of class or classes of shares)

FIFTH: (The corporation will not commence business until consideration of the value of at least $1,000 has been received for the issuance of the shares)

SIXTH: (Provisions limiting or denying to shareholders the preemptive right to acquire additional or treasury shares of the corporation)

SEVENTH: (Provisions pertaining to the manner of voting in the election of directors)

EIGHTH: (The post office address of the corporation and the name of its initial registered agent for service of process at said address)

NINTH: (The number, names, and addresses of the persons who shall serve as the initial Board of Directors of the corporation)

TENTH: (Provisions eliminating or limiting the liability of directors and/or officers to the corporation or its shareholders)

ELEVENTH: (Provisions pertaining to indemnification of directors and/or officers by the corporation)

TWELFTH: (The name and address of each of the incorporators of the corporation)

DATED this ______ day of ______, [year].

INCORPORATORS:

____

____

____

STATE OF __________)
) ss.
COUNTY OF ________)

On the ______ day of ______, [year], personally appeared before me John Doe, George Doe, and Charles Doe, who duly acknowledged to me that they executed the foregoing Articles of Incorporation as the incorporators of A.B.C. Corporation.

____
Notary Public
Residing at:

My Commission Expires:

§ 16.7.4 Execution and Filing of Articles

After the articles of incorporation have been prepared, they must be executed (signed) by the incorporator. If you are in a state that requires more than one incorporator, all incorporators will have to sign them. Many states require that the signatures be notarized. Once the articles are signed, they are filed with the applicable state agency (*e.g.*, the corporation commission, the secretary of state, or the lieutenant governor) together with the appropriate filing fee. It may be necessary also to file duplicate originals in the office of the county clerk where the corporation is to do business and where it will own property. The appropriate filing fees must accompany the filings. The applicable state agency issues a file-stamped copy of the articles of incorporation that evidences the incorporation.

§ 16.7.5 First or Organizational Meeting of Shareholders

Although filing the articles of incorporation with the state is the act that creates a corporation, as a practical matter there are other steps that must be taken in order for a corporation to be in a position to do business. In most states these matters are handled in an organizational meeting. The organizational meeting is known in some states as a shareholders' or stockholders' meeting or an incorporators' meeting or a subscribers' meeting. A few states do not require that an organizational meeting be held, and in those states the matters handled in the organizational meeting may be handled by the board of directors in its first meeting. A unanimous written consent may be signed by all directors or incorporators in lieu of actually holding an organizational meeting. Typical items that would be handled at this meeting include:

- Election of the initial board of directors and/or officers.
- Adoption of bylaws for the corporation.
- Issuance of the capital stock.

§ 16.7.6 First Meeting of the Board of Directors

The first meeting of the board of directors is usually held immediately following the time of the execution of the articles of incorporation and the organizational meeting if there is one. Typical items that are handled at this meeting include:

- Election of officers of the corporation.
- Adoption of the corporate seal (not a requirement in every state of domicile).
- Approval of the form of stock certificate.
- Selection of a bank for the corporation, together with a decision as to who will sign the checks for the corporation.
- Action on whether the corporation wishes to elect to be taxed as a Subchapter "S" corporation.
- Acceptance of subscriptions for shares.

(*See* Illustration 16–5.)

Illustration 16–5

MINUTES OF FIRST MEETING OF BOARD OF DIRECTORS OF A.B.C. CORPORATION

The first meeting of the Board of Directors of A.B.C. CORPORATION was held at ______ at ______ __.m. on ______, [Year], in [city and state], in accordance with the following Waiver of Notice:

WAIVER OF NOTICE FOR FIRST MEETING OF DIRECTORS

The undersigned, being all of the Directors of A.B.C. CORPORATION do hereby waive notice and publication of notice of the first meeting of the Directors of the Corporation. We do hereby assent and agree to the holding of the first meeting of the Directors of the Corporation at the offices of ______ at [Time] on the ______ day of ______, [Year], for the purposes of establishing the corporation in business, organizing the board of directors, electing officers, and the transacting of such other business as may properly come before this meeting, and we do further agree that any business transacted at this meeting shall be as valid and binding and of the same legal force and effect as though said meeting had been held after call and notice duly given.

____

____

____

PROCEEDINGS

______ called the meeting to order and upon motion duly made and seconded was appointed Temporary Chairman, and ______ was appointed Temporary Secretary.

The election of officers was thereupon declared to be in order. The following were named and duly elected:

President, TODD PAUL

Vice President, MYLES DAVID

Vice President, LOUIS BERNARD

Secretary, LISA WYNNE

Treasurer, LINDA GREEN

The Chairman announced that the Certificate of Incorporation had been filed in the office of the Secretary of State of ______ on the ______ day of ______, [year], and that a certified copy thereof would be recorded in the office of the County Clerk and Recorder of ______ County, state of ______. The Secretary was instructed to cause a copy of the Certificate of Incorporation to be inserted in the Minute Book of this Corporation.

The Secretary presented a form of bylaws for the regulation of the internal affairs of the Corporation, which were read by all present, section by section.

On motion duly made, seconded, and carried, it was:

> RESOLVED that the Bylaws submitted to and read at this meeting be, and the same hereby are, adopted as the Bylaws of this Corporation. The Secretary is instructed to cause said Bylaws to be inserted in the Minute and Bylaws Book of this Corporation which shall be held open for inspection by the shareholders at all reasonable times.

On motion duly made, seconded, and carried, it was:

> RESOLVED that the seal, an impression of which is herewith affixed, be adopted as the Corporate Seal of this Corporation.

A form of stock certificate was presented and upon motion duly made, seconded, and carried, was unanimously approved.

The Secretary was authorized and directed to procure the proper Corporate Book.

On motion duly made, seconded, and carried, it was:

> RESOLVED that the ______ Bank of ______ be designated as the depository of the Corporation and that funds deposited therein be withdrawn upon a check, draft, note, or order of the Corporation.
>
> FURTHER RESOLVED that all checks, drafts, notes, or orders drawn against said account or evidencing indebtedness of this Corporation be signed by one of the five named officers of this Corporation.

It was agreed by the Board that each person desiring to transfer equipment and property in return for stock proceed to do so through the Secretary of this Corporation with the Secretary keeping a record of all property transferred, and its agreed valuation upon transfer, said agreed valuation to be consistent with the current market value attributed to each item transferred. The Board acknowledged that the acquisition of property and equipment would be necessary and essential for Corporate operations.

Upon motion duly made, seconded, and carried unanimously, it was:

RESOLVED that the Corporation acquire property and equipment from those persons who desire to transfer property and equipment at market value as may be desired by the Corporation in exchange for the issuance of Corporate stock as payment in full, said stock to be without par value, and to constitute full payment; it being further stipulated that in the event any property transferred is encumbered by mortgage or other indebtedness, the Corporation assume such indebtedness, if any.

FURTHER RESOLVED that the Secretary be instructed to maintain a list of the property transferred and the valuation attributed thereto.

On motion duly made, seconded, and carried unanimously, it was:

RESOLVED that the proper officers of this Corporation be authorized and directed to take all steps necessary to execute and complete issuance of the stock and deliver all papers, including certificates of shares of stock of this Corporation, as such officers so acting may deem appropriate to effect the objectives and purposes of this Corporation, whether or not the same are subject to specific reference in this first meeting.

On motion duly made, seconded, and carried unanimously, it was:

RESOLVED that the Treasurer be authorized to pay all fees and expenses incident to the incorporation and organization of this Corporation.

On motion duly made, seconded, and carried unanimously, it was:

RESOLVED that ______, ______, ______, ______, and ______ constitute an executive committee in accordance with the Articles of Incorporation to act while the Board of Directors is not in session, said Executive Committee to have the same complete and unrestricted powers while so acting as would the Board of Directors acting in session.

There was discussion concerning salaries, following which, on motion duly made, seconded, and carried unanimously, it was:

RESOLVED that the following salaries be fixed to be paid to the individuals indicated until further action by the Board of Directors:

$______ per year to each officer.

There being no further business to come before the meeting, on motion duly made, seconded, and carried unanimously, the meeting adjourned at ______ __m.

____
Secretary

§ 16.7.7 Bylaws

The bylaws are the rules and regulations by which the business affairs of the corporation will be conducted. They are adopted by the shareholders or the board of directors at the organizational meeting. Unlike the articles of incorporation, the bylaws are typically not required to be filed with the state. If there is no organizational meeting, they may be adopted by the directors. The officers, directors, and shareholders are bound by these bylaws which may contain any provisions for the regulation and management of the affairs of the corporation not inconsistent with law or with the articles of incorporation. Every corporation has the power to adopt, alter, and amend bylaws. The bylaws may be a relatively brief document or they may be a long, detailed document. Most law offices have their own computer generated form of bylaws that they adapt to suit each corporation. (*See* Illustration 16–6 for the index of provisions usually contained in bylaws.)

Illustration 16–6

BYLAWS

TABLE OF CONTENTS

§ 16.7.8 Minutes and Minutes Book (Minute Book)

As part of the incorporation service to the client, you will be responsible for the preparation of the corporation's minutes book (generally referred to as a minute book). The minute book should contain copies of the articles of incorporation, the bylaws, the minutes of the first or organizational meeting of shareholders, and the minutes of the first board of directors meeting, as well as any other documents which were prepared and executed in connection with the incorporation process. The minute book will either be turned over to the secretary of the corporation so that it can be kept current or will be maintained by your law firm. Minutes are simply a written record of who attended a meeting and what transpired at the meeting. However, it is essential that the minute book be kept up to date. An incomplete minute book can result in serious tax consequences in the event of a tax audit.

§ 16.7.9 Corporate Seal

The corporate seal is an official impression utilized with the signature of an officer of the corporation to verify corporate authority. In some states it is necessary for a corporation to acquire a corporate seal, while in other states it is not. If you are in a state where a seal is required, it may be that your firm orders the seal as a part of the incorporation process.

§ 16.7.10 Issuance of Stock Certificates and Stockbook

In preparing the corporate files for your client, one of your duties may be to issue the original shares of stock and to open a stockbook (often referred to as a share or stock register). You may purchase a bound stockbook, or you may purchase individual blank stock certificates and insert the number of certificates you need into some type of binder.

The articles of incorporation provide for the number of shares that the corporation is authorized to issue. The minutes of the organizational meeting lists the number of shares of stock purchased by each stockholder. From this list you should be able to prepare the stock certificates. Each stock certificate should include:

- The name of the corporation.
- The domicile of the corporation.
- The name of the shareholder.
- The number of shares purchased by the shareholder.
- The par value of each share of stock.
- The number of the stock certificate (starting with the number 1).
- The notation that the stock is issued under section 1244 of the Internal Revenue Code (if applicable).

State law typically requires that certain information be contained in a stock certificate. Be sure to check the law of the corporation's state of incorporation to ensure that these rules are complied with. Each stock certificate is attached to a receipt that contains the identical information as on the stock certificate, together with a notation that the stock being issued is the original issue. (*See* Illustration 16–7.) The shareholder signs the receipt, which is detached from the certificate. The shareholder is given the stock certificate, and the receipt is retained in the stockbook. The stockbook contains a continuing record of the stock ownership of a corporation. It is essential that the stockbook be kept up to date and show all changes in stock ownership. Anyone should be able to look at a corporation's stockbook at any time and tell who the shareholders of the corporation are and how many shares of stock each shareholder owns.

Illustration 16–7

INCORPORATED UNDER THE LAWS OF
THE STATE OF WASHINGTON

NUMBER 004

SHARES 2,900

A. B. C. CORPORATION

COMMON STOCK

This Certifies that MYLES DAVID is the owner of 2,900 Common fully paid and non-assessable Shares of the above Corporation transferable only on the books of the Corporation by the holder hereof in person or by a duly authorized Attorney upon surrender of this Certificate properly endorsed.

In Witness Whereof, the said Corporation has caused this Certificate to be signed by its duly authorized officers and to be sealed with the Seal of the Corporation.

Dated September , [Year]

President

Secretary

© RUPERT ENTERPRISES INC. 1988

An assignment form is printed on the reverse of each stock certificate; accordingly, the shareholder may transfer their shares of stock by simply executing the assignment on the reverse of their stock certificate.

(*See* Illustration 16–7.1.) When that assigned stock certificate is handed to the secretary of the corporation, the secretary issues a new stock certificate to the new shareholder, writes "canceled" across the face of the transferred stock certificate, and attaches it to the receipt of that certificate in the stockbook. The receipt of the new stock certificate shows that it is a transfer of the shares from the original certificate.

Illustration 16–7.1

The following abbreviations, when used in the inscription on the face of this certificate, shall be construed as though they were written out in full according to applicable laws or regulations. Additional abbreviations may also be used though not in the list.

TEN COM – as tenants in common
TEN ENT – as tenants by the entireties
JT TEN – as joint tenants with right of survivorship and not as tenants in common

UNIF GIFT MIN ACT – __________ Custodian __________ (Minor)
under Uniform Gifts to Minors Act __________ (State)

PLEASE INSERT SOCIAL SECURITY OR OTHER IDENTIFYING NUMBER OF ASSIGNEE

For value received, the undersigned hereby sells, assigns and transfers unto
LOUIS BERNARD, 2424 Olive Way, Seattle, WA
PLEASE PRINT OR TYPEWRITE NAME AND ADDRESS OF ASSIGNEE

2,900-- *Shares*

represented by the within Certificate, and hereby irrevocably constitutes and appoints
LISA WYNNE
Attorney to transfer the said shares on the books of the within-named Corporation with full power of substitution in the premises.

Dated, November 25, [Year]

In presence of ______________

____

NOTICE: The signature to this assignment must correspond with the name as written upon the face of the certificate in every particular without alteration or enlargement, or any change whatever.

§ 16.7.11 Certificate of Assumed Business Name

If the corporation wishes to do business under a name other than its own, you will be asked to prepare a certificate of assumed business name. Sometimes this is referred to as a fictitious name. Forms and procedures for filing are provided on the respective Secretary of State's website.

§ 16.7.12 Application for Employer Identification Number, IRS Form No. SS–4

Depending upon the practice in your area, you may be expected to complete the corporation's application for an employer identification number. An Employer Identification Number (EIN), also known as a Federal Tax Identification Number, is a nine-digit number that the IRS assigns to business entities. The IRS uses this number to identify taxpayers that are required to file various business tax returns. EINs are used by employers, sole proprietors, corporations, partnerships, non-profit organizations, trusts and estates, government agencies, certain individuals and other business entities. You may obtain and complete the Form SS–4 online at www.irs.gov. Once you have completed all necessary fields on the online form, preliminary validation is performed and will alert you to information IRS needs that you may not have included. An EIN will be issued after the successful submission of the completed Form

SS–4 online. Online EIN is available 24/7; no registration is required to use this system; and no paper needs to be sent to the IRS. (See Illustration 16–8.)

Illustration 16–8

Form **SS-4**
(Rev. December 1995)
Department of the Treasury
Internal Revenue Service

Application for Employer Identification Number

(For use by employers, corporations, partnerships, trusts, estates, churches, government agencies, certain individuals, and others. See instructions.)
➤Keep a copy for your records.

EIN
OMB No. 1545-0003

1 Name of applicant (Legal name) (See instructions.)

2 Trade name of business (if different from name in line 1)
3 Executor, trustee, "care of" name

4a Mailing address (street address) (room, apt., or suite no.)
5a Business address (if different from address on lines 4a and 4b)

4b City, state, and ZIP code
5b City, state, and ZIP code

6 County and state where principal business is located

7 Name of principal officer, general partner, grantor, owner, or trustor--SSN required (See instructions.) ➤

8a Type of entity (Check only one box.) (See instructions.)
☐ Sole Proprietor (SSN)
☐ Partnership ☐ Personal service corp.
☐ REMIC ☐ Limited liability co.
☐ State/local government ☐ National Guard
☐ Other nonprofit organization (specify) ➤ (enter GEN if applicable)
☐ Other (specify) ➤
☐ Estate (SSN of decedent)
☐ Plan administrator-SSN
☐ Other corporation (specify) ➤
☐ Trust ☐ Farmers' cooperative
☐ Federal government/military ☐ Church or church-controlled organization

8b If a corporation, name the state or foreign country (if applicable) where incorporated ➤ | State | Foreign country

9 Reason for applying (Check only one box.)
☐ Started new business (specify) ➤
☐ Hired employees
☐ Created a pension plan (specify type) ➤
☐ Banking purpose (specify) ➤
☐ Changed type of organization (specify) ➤
☐ Purchased going business
☐ Created a trust (specify) ➤
☐ Other (specify) ➤

10 Date business started or acquired (Mo., day, year) (See instructions.)
11 Closing month of accounting year. (See instructions).

12 First date wages or annuities were paid or will be paid (Mo., day, year). **Note:** *If applicant is a withholding agent, enter date income will first be paid to nonresident alien. (Mo., day, year)* ➤

13 Highest number of employees expected in the next 12 months. **Note:** *If the applicant does not expect to have any employees during the period, enter -0-. (See instructions.)*➤ | Nonagricultural | Agricultural | Household

14 Principal activity (See instructions.) ➤

15 Is the principal business activity manufacturing? ☐ Yes ☐ No
If "Yes," principal product and raw material used ➤

16 To whom are most of the products or services sold? Please check the appropriate box. ☐ Business (wholesale)
☐ Public (retail) ☐ Other (specify) ➤ ☐ N/A

17a Has the applicant ever applied for an identification number for this or any other business? ☐ Yes ☐ No
Note: *If "Yes," please complete lines 17b and 17c.*

17b If you checked the "Yes" on line 17a, give applicant's legal name and trade name shown on prior application, if different from line 1 or 2 above.
Legal name ➤ Trade name ➤

17c Approximate date when and city and state where the application was filed. Enter previous employer identification number if known.
Approximate date when filed (Mo., day, year) | City and state where filed | Previous EIN

Under penalties of perjury, I declare that I have examined this application, and to the best of my knowledge and belief, it is true, correct, and complete.
Business telephone number (include area code)
Fax telephone number (include area code)

Name and title (Please type or print clearly.) ➤

Signature ➤ Date ➤

Note: *Do not write below this line. For official use only.*

Please leave blank ➤	Geo.	Ind.	Class	Size	Reason for applying

For Paperwork Reduction Act Notice, see page 4. Cat No. 16055N Form **SS-4** (Rev. 12-95)

§ 16.8 Miscellaneous Forms

There are other forms such as applications for state and city business and sales tax licenses, withholding tax registration, unemployment insurance, and workers' compensation forms that are often required. Most corporations handle the preparation and filing of these themselves, but there may be other documents required to complete the legal work for the corporation that your office will prepare.

§ 16.9 Professional Corporations

A professional corporation is a business corporation formed for the purpose of professional practice whose incorporators or shareholders must be natural persons, each of whom is duly licensed or admitted to practice their profession by a court, department, board, commission, or other agency of government. For example, lawyers, doctors, and certified public accountants must be licensed by the state in which they practice their profession. Many states also permit licensed professionals to form professional limited liability companies and professional partnerships (including professional LPs, LLPs, and LLLPs).

The intent of the states that have enacted professional corporation statutes is to authorize licensed persons to render professional services in the corporate forum.

§ 16.9.1 Formation, Structure, and Operation

The formation, structure, and operation of a professional corporation are similar to a business corporation as outlined earlier in this chapter.

§ 16.9.2 Differences From Business Corporations

The articles of incorporation contain a specific statement that the corporation is a professional corporation, and some states may require that the license number of the incorporator be stated.

A professional corporation is formed only for the purpose of rendering the particular professional service and may not engage in any business other than the rendering of the professional service. Nevertheless, it may generally own real estate, make investments, and do other acts incidental to its primary purpose.

Each professional corporation must acquire a certificate of registration from the state agency regulating that particular profession.

The shareholder(s) must be licensed in the profession, *e.g.*, only lawyers can be shareholders of a professional corporation organized for the practice of law. Generally, shares in a professional corporation can be delivered, issued, traded, etc., only to a third person licensed in the same profession in the same state or to the corporation.

Officers and directors of the corporation may not need to be licensed professionals, depending on state law and the corporation's organizational documents.

A professional corporation may use any name not prohibited by law, by the ethical rules of the profession in which the corporation is engaged or by a rule or regulation of the court, department, board, commission, or agency regulating such profession. For instance, a professional corporation engaged in the practice of law cannot use the name "Divorce Mill, Inc." because the Rules of Professional Conduct would not permit such a name.

Although "Corporation," "Company," "Limited,""Incorporated," or an abbreviation thereof, must be used in the name of a corporation (Section 16.6 above), the name of a professional corporation typically need not contain any of these words. The name may use the word "Associate" or consist solely of the name of one or more of the shareholders of the corporation. Some professional corporations use "P.C." in place of "Inc.," such as "Smith and Jones, P.C."

State law might provide that a shareholder may not give their proxy to another person unless it is to another licensed person who is a shareholder of the same corporation.

§ 16.9.3 Advantages and Disadvantages

The advantages and disadvantages of a professional corporation are similar to other types of corporations. However, the corporate entity will not shield the licensed professional from any actions against them for their direct breach of professional ethical standards or liability for negligence in performing services for the client.

§ 16.10 Partnerships

A partnership is a voluntary association of two or more persons to carry on a business for profit as co-owners. Partnerships are governed by each state's laws regarding partnerships. Nearly all states have adopted the Delaware Uniform Partnership Act and the Uniform Limited Partnership Act with some state-specific modifications. Specific state partnership laws can be located on the website of the respective Secretary of State.

§ 16.10.1 Types of Partnerships

There are four main types of partnerships: general partnerships (GPs), limited liability partnerships (LLPs), limited partnerships (LPs), and limited liability limited partnerships (LLLPs). Other similar associations are joint ventures, joint stock companies, syndicates, cooperatives, trading and nontrading associations, and mining partnerships. These are described more fully below.

§ 16.10.2 Legal Requirements

A partnership is a voluntary relationship based on five elements of contract law:

1. Mutual agreement of the parties (either written or oral).
2. Competency of the parties.
3. Consideration.
4. Lawful purpose.
5. Meeting formal requirements.

Partnerships are organized for profit and involve the contribution by their members of capital, labor, skills, property, or a combination thereof. The law governing formation, operation, and dissolution of partnerships is generally found in the statutes of each state.

Partnerships must be formed for a lawful purpose. Otherwise, the partners may lose their rights under the law.

§ 16.10.3 General Partnerships

General partnerships are formed by two or more persons for the purpose of carrying on a business for profit as co-owners. The Uniform Partnership Act defines a "person" as including individuals, partnerships, corporations, and other associations. A partnership may be comprised of any two or more of the foregoing, provided that the entity is properly constituted and each person is competent to enter into the partnership. The purpose for which the partnership is formed must be lawful and for the monetary gain of its partners.

§ 16.10.4 Partnership Agreement

While no formal written agreement is required by law to establish a general partnership, to avoid problems and misunderstandings among the partners as to their rights, duties, and liabilities, a written agreement is usually entered into and signed by all of the partners.

§ 16.10.5 Names of the Partners

The names and addresses of the partners are listed in the partnership agreement, and each partner also executes the agreement.

§ 16.10.6 Name of the Partnership

There are no restrictions on the name that the general partnership selects, except that it not infringe upon an existing name.

§ 16.10.7 Duration of the Partnership

Unlike corporations, partnerships cannot exist perpetually, and the partnership agreement generally states a termination date and provides that the partnership will terminate upon certain specified events including such events as the death or bankruptcy of a partner. However, the partners may desire the partnership to be formed for an indefinite period. In that event, the partnership agreement does not state a termination date and the partnership is "at will."

§ 16.10.8 Location and Nature of the Partnership Business

The nature of the business that the partnership will transact and the address from which it will operate are set forth in the partnership agreement. Sometimes there is no specific business address, and the address of one of the partners is used.

§ 16.10.9 Contributions by Partners

Contributions by a partner to the partnership may be in cash, property, skills, or services. The initial contributions are recorded in the partnership agreement. The agreement may call for additional contributions to be made at a future date or additional services to be performed.

§ 16.10.10 Method for Sharing Profits and Obligation for Losses

In the absence of different provisions in the partnership agreement, all of the partners share equally in the profits and losses of the partnership. However, provision may be made that some partners may receive a greater share of the profits and/or losses. The allocation of profits can be different from the allocation of losses. Although partnership losses will generally be apportioned among the partners according to the method by which profits are allocated. The agreement generally also sets forth the responsibilities of the partners in the event losses are sustained and additional moneys are required from the partners to sustain the partnership. Agreements specifically allocating profit and loss can be complex and require special expertise in preparation particularly with respect to the tax issues involved.

§ 16.10.11 Method of Accounting

The method of keeping the partnership account, the party responsible for keeping the account, and the location of the partnership records, are set forth in the agreement. The method of valuing a partner's contribution or their partnership interest also may be set forth in this section.

§ 16.10.12 Withdrawals From Partnership Accounts

To avoid the problem that could be caused by several partners withdrawing money from the partnership at the same time, rules and procedures are typically set forth specifying when and in what amounts partners may withdraw moneys from the partnership account. All income is deposited to and expenses paid from a central partnership account.

§ 16.10.13 Terms and Conditions for Admitting New Members to the Partnership

Additional partners may be admitted to the partnership on terms and conditions specified in the agreement. The incoming partner becomes a member upon execution of an amendment to the partnership agreement. To avoid dissolution of the partnership by operation of law, the partnership agreement must provide for its continuation in the event of the admission of a new member.

§ 16.10.14 Any Other Matters

Any other matters that the partners believe necessary for the smooth running of the partnership may be included in the agreement.

§ 16.10.15 Commencement of Existence

A general partnership commences at the time any one of the following occurs:

- Execution of the partnership agreement.
- Commencement of the partnership business.
- The filing or recording of any document required by state law to commence its existence.

The partnership agreement may provide for a different event to cause commencement of the partnership business.

§ 16.10.16 Ownership of Partnership Property

Property brought into the partnership as a contribution becomes the property of the partnership. State law and the partnership agreement govern whether a partner may assign or encumber the partner's interest in partnership property. Title to partnership property may be held in the partnership name or in the names of all of the individual partners.

§ 16.10.17 Partners' Liability

In general, all of the partners in a general partnership are each fully liable for losses or damages arising out of the partnership. A new partner is responsible for liabilities incurred prior to its admission but only to the extent of the new partner's share of partnership property not including other personal assets. If a deficit occurs, the partners are required to satisfy the deficit, generally in proportion to its share of profits. If one partner cannot completely satisfy their share, the other partners must make up the defaulting partner's share and then seek reimbursement from the defaulting partner.

§ 16.10.18 Tax Returns

The partnership itself is not taxed, but an information return must be filed by the partnership with state and federal tax authorities. The partners are taxed on the income attributed to their partnership interest under the partnership agreement, as part of their individual income tax returns, and the partners are also entitled to the benefit of any partnership losses that may occur.

§ 16.10.19 Dissolution

Dissolution under state law ends the right of a partnership to continue to do business. The partnership goes through a winding-up process and is then terminated as a legal entity. The partnership may be terminated by operation of law or by dissolution caused by the actions of the partners. Partnership agreements may express that certain actions do or do not cause dissolution of the partnership. Actions of the partners that may cause dissolution include:

- The express action of any one partner.
- The consent of all of the partners.
- The expulsion of a partner.

Events that may automatically cause dissolution of the partnership without the act of a partner or partners include:

- The occurrence of an event making it unlawful to continue the partnership business.
- The death or bankruptcy of a partner or bankruptcy of the partnership.

The partnership also automatically dissolves at the termination of the definite time for which it was formed.

After dissolution, the affairs of the partnership are wound up. The partnership agreement may provide which partner(s) will be responsible for winding up the affairs of the partnership. Winding up consists of collecting and preserving the partnership assets, paying debts, and distributing any remaining assets. Creditors of the partnership have first claim on partnership assets, with the partners sharing any remaining assets after repayment of their capital contribution. After dissolution and during the winding-up process, the liabilities of the partners are not waived or forgiven but continue, so that where dissolution of a partnership is caused by the death of a partner, their estate inherits that partner's liability. While liabilities remain, however, the authority of the partners ceases upon dissolution except for any acts they are required to perform to wind up the partnership. Notice of dissolution must be given to the partners and to any persons who have dealt with the partnership.

Certain events (such as the withdrawal of a partner or admission of a new partner) may cause a partnership to be treated as dissolved for tax purposes, even if such events do not cause the partnership to be dissolved under state law. In such cases, the partnership and partners must, however, file certain tax returns with respect to the deemed dissolution for tax purposes.

§ 16.11 Limited Liability Partnerships

A limited liability partnership ("LLP"), as opposed to a limited partnership, is a general partnership which has elected to be treated as an LLP and has adopted a name disclosing its limited liability (generally by adding "LLP" to its name, and by filing a disclosure and election document as required by the laws of the state of its organization). LLPs afford insulation for partners from liability for certain acts of the partnership or another partner. The LLP form does not generally protect partners from liability for partnership business debts or liability arising from their own actions. The extent to which such limitation of liability may be available to a limited liability partnership organized under the laws of one state for liabilities arising in another state must be determined under the applicable state law.

§ 16.11.1 Limited Partnerships

Limited partnerships ("LPs") are considerably more regulated than general partnerships and unlike general partnerships must be evidenced by an agreement. Any two or more entities may form a limited partnership, but there must be at least one general partner and at least one limited partner. The general partner has unlimited liability for the obligations of the partnership; the limited partner's liability is limited to the limited partner's initial contribution and any additional contributions to the partnership. While a general partner may contribute management services, cash and/or property, a limited partner may contribute only cash or property. A limited partner has no voice in the operation or management of the partnership, except to the extent permitted in the limited partnership agreement. Limited partners performing acts outside of a limited scope detailed in a limited partnership agreement may be considered general partners and thus forfeit their limited liability status.

Natural persons, partnerships, limited partnerships, trusts, estates, associations, or corporations may be partners in LPs.

Again, the partnership must be formed for a lawful purpose. Partnerships formed for illegal purposes are denied many of the rights granted to partners and to partnerships.

§ 16.11.2 Particular Requirements for Limited Partnerships

Limited partnerships differ from general partnerships in several areas covered by state law and the limited partnership agreement.

§ 16.11.3 Partnership Name

There are restrictions on the name under which a limited partnership does business. The word or words "Ltd.", "L.P." or "Limited Partnership" must generally be included in the name, and the name must not be deceptively similar to another business so as to confuse those with whom the partnership has dealings. In some states, the limited partnership's name may not include the name of a limited partner unless it is the same as a general partner's or unless, prior to becoming a limited partnership, the business had been carried on under a name in which the limited partner's name appeared.

§ 16.11.4 Existence

A limited partnership begins its existence on the filing or recording with the appropriate local agency of a Certificate of Limited Partnership listing specific information required by law. The name of the partnership must generally be registered or a statement filed with a local agency stating who is doing business under the partnership name and where the business is being carried on. The certificate must be amended whenever there is any change to the information contained in it. Upon dissolution of the partnership, a cancellation of the certificate must be filed for the public record alerting the public to the fact that the partnership will no longer continue its existence. Although all of the partners named in a Certificate of Limited Partnership must sign the certificate and have their signatures acknowledged if required, in the case of amendment fewer signatures may be required (or merely those of the general partners).

§ 16.11.5 Right of Inspection of Books and Records

Even though limited partners are not involved in the day-to-day activities of the partnership, they have the right to inspect and copy any of the partnership's records, which the partnership is required by law to maintain at the partnership office.

§ 16.11.6 Contributions

Limited partners must contribute cash or property, or perform certain tasks, to the extent provided by law and as agreed in the limited partnership agreement. If property or services are required but a limited partner is unable to contribute, a contribution of cash equal to the portion of the required contribution may be necessary.

§ 16.11.7 Sharing of Profits

The ratio in which the limited and general partners share in the profits and losses of the partnership is set forth in the limited partnership agreement. Also, this agreement states the amount of and manner in which future contributions will become due.

§ 16.12 Limited Liability Limited Partnerships

A limited liability limited partnership (an LLLP) is a limited partnership which has elected to be treated as a limited liability partnership in addition to being a limited partnership. To become an LLLP, the limited partnership must qualify under state law, file any necessary disclosure and election documents and adopt a name that indicates its status as an LLLP. The liability of general partners of LLLPs is limited to the same extent as the liability of partners of LLPs, as discussed in Section 16.11 above.

§ 16.12.1 Classification of Partners

Within a partnership the partners can be further classified as follows:

- A partner who takes no active part in the management of the business and is not known to the public as a partner is a dormant, sleeping, silent, or secret partner.
- A person who permits others to believe they are a partner of a partnership, or behaves in such a manner that people believe that person is a partner, may be treated by the law as a partner in terms of being required to answer for certain of the partnership's debts. Such a person is known as a partner by estoppel or an ostensible partner.

- A person who is named as a partner is a nominal partner.

§ 16.12.2 Joint Venture

A joint venture is similar to a general partnership in formation, but its duration is generally only for the accomplishment of the specific purpose for which it was formed (such as construction of a building or performance of an act). The duties owed to the public and to each other by the joint venturers are the same as those owed by general partners. While one joint venturer might perform the major portion of the management duties, all joint venturers share in the profits, losses, and obligations, typically as set forth in an agreement between the parties.

§ 16.12.3 Syndicate

A syndicate is an association of persons formed to conduct a specific, generally financial in nature, business transaction. The most common type of syndicate is that formed by investment banks for the marketing of stocks and bonds.

§ 16.12.4 Cooperative

A cooperative is comprised of a group of people who pool their products or resources for their mutual advantage. Many states have enacted regulations concerning cooperatives. In some states incorporation is permitted in accordance with state statutes.

§ 16.12.5 Business or Massachusetts Trust

A business or Massachusetts trust permits the ownership of property to be transferred by the owners to trustees who run the business for the owners' benefit. To evidence the ownership of the property, the trustees issue shares or certificates to the trustors showing their original ownership or interest in the property. The shares or certificates may be freely transferred, but the trustors do not have the control over the trustees that shareholders have over the directors. One supposed benefit of this form of organization is that the trustors avoid liability by transferring responsibility for running the trust to the trustees.

§ 16.12.6 Joint Stock Company

A joint stock company is somewhat like a combined partnership and corporation. Shares of stock are issued to evidence each partner's ownership, and the shares are transferable. Management of the business is delegated to a small group of partners because generally there are many partners in a joint stock company. There is no restriction on the transfer of the shares or who may purchase them, and any person to whom such shares are transferred or sold becomes a member of the joint stock company upon such sale or transfer.

§ 16.12.7 Trading Partnership

A trading partnership is specifically engaged in buying and selling merchandise. The partners have authority to bind the partnership and obtain loans in the partnership name.

§ 16.12.8 Nontrading Partnership

A nontrading partnership is engaged in performing services such as legal, accounting, medical, etc. The partners have no authority to bind the partnership, and the success of the partnership is more dependent upon the results of the partners than on the capital they may contribute.

§ 16.12.9 Mining Partnership

A mining partnership is formed when two or more people join together to work a mining claim to extract minerals. While similar to a general partnership, a mining partnership is not dissolved when a partner's interest is transferred; and such interest is freely transferable. The partners share in the profits and losses in the ownership ratio.

§ 16.12.10 Unincorporated Associations

Unincorporated associations are formed when persons combine either to make a profit or for a nonprofit charitable purpose. Generally, unless a member ratifies or authorizes an act, such member is not liable for the association's actions. The association has no existence apart from its members and cannot sue or be sued in its name. The association might, however, be taxable as a corporation.

§ 16.13 Limited Liability Company

A limited liability company (an LLC) seeks to blend in one business form the advantages of limited liability for equity owners found in corporations and the tax advantages found in partnerships.

The state laws generally provide that the owners and managers of an LLC are not personally liable for any debt, obligation, or liability of the LLC solely by reason of their association with it, except to the extent of their capital contribution.

Generally, a corporation must pay taxes on its income and the shareholders must pay taxes on the dividends and distributions that they receive from the corporation, which results in the taxation of the same income twice (known as "double taxation"). Entities that are treated like partnerships for tax purposes, however, are not taxed on income at the entity level because all of the partnership's income is "passed through" to the partners, and the partners pay taxes on their share of the partnership's income. The Internal Revenue Service adopted rules effective January 1, 1997 that cause an entity such as an LLC with two or more members to be treated as a partnership, unless it elects to be treated otherwise. An LLC with only one member is treated like a sole proprietorship for tax purposes.

§ 16.13.1 Formation and Operation of an LLC

Though the rules differ in the various states that have LLC legislation, generally an LLC may be formed for any business purpose. Certain states have exceptions for certain businesses such as banking and insurance. An LLC is formed by filing a certificate or other specified organizational document (*e.g.*, articles of organization) with the designated state agency that contains some basic information about the LLC. An LLC's name must typically contain one of the following: "Limited Liability Company," "Limited Liability Co.," or "LLC"

Unless an LLC's certificate of formation states otherwise, it will be managed by all of its members. The members, however, may elect to have the LLC managed by one or more managers, who need not be members. Generally, unless an LLC agreement provides otherwise, members are entitled to vote in proportion to their respective percentage interests.

§ 16.13.2 Personal Liability of Members and Managers

Generally, members and managers are not personally liable for the obligations and liabilities of the LLC solely by reason of their status as such. There are typically, however, exceptions provided under the various state acts providing situations in which members of an LLC will not enjoy limited liability. Among some typical exceptions are provisions whereby a creditor is entitled to enforce a member's contractual obligation to contribute cash, property, or perform services for the LLC to the extent that the creditor reasonably relied on such obligation. Another type of exception is provided where a member may be obligated to return an LLC distribution that the member knew was made in violation of the state law's limitations on distributions by an insolvent LLC.

Also, LLC members may be liable for the LLC's debts under circumstances that would expose a shareholder to liability in the case of a corporation. Generally, a corporation's shareholders will be liable for the corporation's obligations only if it is shown that the corporation was intentionally used to violate or evade a duty that is owed to another and such personal liability is necessary to prevent an unjustified loss to a third party.

§ 16.13.3 Contributions, Allocation of Profits and Losses, Distributions

Contributions to an LLC may be in the form of cash, property, or services rendered or an obligation for the same. Unless otherwise specified in an LLC agreement, profits and losses are allocated to the members based on each member's percentage ownership interest. Likewise, unless otherwise specified in an LLC agreement, distributions are allocated among members on the same basis. Distributions are often prohibited if, in giving effect to the distribution, the LLC would not be able to pay its debts when they became due or the LLC's liabilities would exceed the fair market value of its assets.

§ 16.13.4 Assignment of an Interest in an LLC

Like a partner's interest in a partnership, a member does not have an interest in any specific property of an LLC; they simply have an ownership interest in the entity as a whole. Generally, unless prohibited by an LLC agreement, a member may transfer its interest in the LLC's profits and losses and its right to receive distributions. An assignee, however, cannot become a member or participate in the management of the LLC until all of the other members have given their consent, unless the LLC agreement provides otherwise.

§ 16.13.5 Dissolution

State laws typically provide that an LLC will dissolve upon the occurrence of certain specified events including: (i) the expiration of its term or a period of statutorily established years from the date of formation; (ii) the happening of an event of dissociation or withdrawal with respect to any member (*e.g.*, death, incapacity, bankruptcy, etc.); (iii) the written consent of all of the members; or (iv) the entry of a decree of judicial dissolution. Often an LLC agreement may alter the events of dissociation, withdrawal, and dissolution.

§ 16.13.6 Foreign LLCs

As with foreign corporations and limited partnerships, foreign LLCs that transact business in a state are required to register with the designated state agency and maintain a registered office and agent for service of process in the state.

§ 16.13.7 Comparison of LLCs With Other Legal Entities

1. *S Corporation*. While an S Corporation is treated for tax purposes as a "pass-through" entity, the requirements for S Corporation status are rigid and a violation of any one of them at any time

terminates that status. Shareholders of an S Corporation must generally be natural persons with certain limited exceptions, thus a corporation cannot be an S Corporation shareholder. Also, an S Corporation may only have a limited number of shareholders and there are restrictions on foreign ownership.

2. *Limited Partnership ("LP")*. Unlike an LLC, at least one partner of an LP (the general partner) will be personally liable for the obligations of the partnership. While the use of a corporate general partner can reduce the risk of such liability, this practice involves another layer of complexity and expense.

3. *Limited Liability Limited Partnership (LLLP)*. Qualification as an LLLP provides limited liability protection to the general partners of limited partnerships, thus reducing or eliminating the reason to have a corporate general partner. LLLPs are comparable to LLCs in the sense that they both may be "pass-through" entities for tax purposes and both provide limited liability for all of their owners.

§ 16.14 Sole Proprietorship

A person who operates a business on their own and is solely responsible for its day-to-day operation is known as a sole proprietor. No formal documentation is required to form a sole proprietorship. A sole proprietorship is not a legal entity separate from the sole proprietor, and does not limit the sole proprietor's personal liability related to obligations of the business. On the other hand, even though a single-member LLC is treated like a sole proprietorship for tax purposes (*i.e.*, it is disregarded as a separate entity for tax purposes), it is a separate legal entity under state law and limits the sole member's personal liability as discussed in Section 16.13.2 above.

Depending on the type of business and local, state, and/or federal requirements, permits or licenses are typically required to operate the business. If the business is conducted under a name different from that of the owner, it may be necessary to file or record documents asserting the ownership of that name.

Except for licenses or permits required because of the nature of the business, there are no restrictions on transfer of ownership of the business. Upon the death of the owner, the business ceases to exist.

CHAPTER 17
REAL ESTATE

Table of Sections

---

§ 17.1 Introduction

The field of real estate law offers the lawyer's assistant an almost unlimited opportunity to assist the lawyer in the many details that are involved in a typical real estate transaction. Although the most common transaction in the law office of today may well be the transfer of residential real estate, it is likely that the lawyer's assistant will encounter various types of real estate transactions. The lawyer's assistant is in a position to relieve the lawyer of much of the detail work involved in real estate transactions. In order for the lawyer's assistant to progress to the point of handling all preliminary workup, preparing closing documents, and assembling all necessary information, the basic elements of real estate law must be understood.

The modern real estate transaction has deep roots in American history. The ownership of land is one of the oldest and most coveted forms of ownership. Owning property is a right guaranteed by the United States Constitution to all citizens of the United States—not a right guaranteed to all citizens of the world. The dream of every American is to own their own home, and accordingly, the residential real estate transaction is one that touches most of us at one time or another. Regardless of whether the lawyer's assistant is viewing the real estate transaction from a professional or personal viewpoint, innovative financing will require continually updating your knowledge.

§ 17.2 History of Real Estate Law

Many of our basic laws regarding property rights come to us from England. In medieval times, an English king would often grant real estate to an individual who supported him during a war or who performed some other valuable service for him. After the Revolutionary War, the United States found itself with a great deal of land and a large amount of debts. The government determined that it would sell land in order to retire those debts. A problem soon arose, however, for much of the land was undeveloped and in many cases totally unexplored and void of landmarks. The government had no way to describe adequately the property it was selling. Thus, in 1785, the government ordered a survey to be taken. This was the beginning of what we know as the rectangular survey system which is referred to in many legal descriptions of real estate as the United States Government Survey. A majority of the 50 states still use this system as the source of legal descriptions for real estate today. The remaining states retain control over original surveys of land which form the basis for all legal descriptions.

Legal descriptions as they relate to the preparation of real estate documents are described later in this chapter.

§ 17.3 Definition of Real Estate

Real estate, also called real property or realty, is defined as land and anything permanently attached to it. It includes items attached to the land naturally, such as grass, shrubs, or trees, and items attached to the land artificially, such as buildings, fences, certain fixtures, and other improvements.

§ 17.3.1 Fixtures

Fixtures are those items firmly affixed to buildings. Whether or not an item is a fixture has been the subject of much litigation.

EXAMPLE:

A built-in dishwasher is a fixture that has become a part of the real estate. Such an appliance has a specially created opening for its installation, and its removal would leave an obvious unfinished area in the kitchen not easily used for other purposes. On the other hand, a portable dishwasher that is moved about the kitchen on wheels would not be considered a fixture.

The distinction is often not so easily made as in this example, so great care is exercised by lawyers in defining the fixtures to be included in a given transaction.

§ 17.3.2 Improvements

Improvements include buildings, as well as such items as curbs, gutters, sidewalks, street lights, and sewer systems constructed to enhance development of real estate. More generally, any items of a permanent nature constructed upon real estate are often referred to as improvements.

§ 17.3.3 Personal Property or Chattel Property

All property that is not part of the real estate is known as personal property or chattel property. This includes everything from cars, boats, furnishings, and appliances to jewelry and clothing.

§ 17.3.4 Comparison of Property

Real property is distinguished from personal property in that real property is generally immovable, while personal property is movable. Generally, reference to real property means real estate, while reference to personal property means easily movable property such as automobiles, furniture, or jewelry. In many states the term chattel property is used interchangeably with the term personal property. The legal requirements for the sale or transfer of personal property are much less stringent than those for real property. In fact, in most states the sale of personal property for cash is accomplished by the preparation of a very simple bill of sale. In many instances it is not even necessary to have a written bill of sale.

EXAMPLE:

> If *A* wishes to sell a watch to *B* and *B* is agreeable to the price, the sale is accomplished by *A*'s handing the watch to *B* and *B*'s handing the agreed price to *A*.

This would not be the case if the sale were not for cash. If the seller were not paid the entire price, a security interest in the watch would exist. To protect that interest, the seller would have to file the appropriate security instrument in the appropriate county or state office.

In contrast, most states require that contracts for the sale of real property must be in writing.

§ 17.4 General Principles and Concepts of Real Estate Law

In the field of real estate law, the lawyer's assistant must have a good understanding of the lawyer's responsibilities in these transactions. The general principles and concepts of real estate law which play a significant role in the practice of real estate law are:

- Ownership of real estate.
- Evidence of title to real estate.
- Examination of title to real estate.
- Encumbrances of real estate.
- Transfer of real estate.

- Financing the acquisition of real estate.
- Preparation of real estate documents.
- Closing of real estate transactions.

§ 17.4.1 Ownership of Real Estate

When a seller enters into a purchase agreement for the sale of property with a prospective buyer, generally, the seller takes the position of ownership. Since the form of ownership is controlled by state law and forms of ownership vary from state to state, the lawyer's assistant will have to determine the applicable types of ownership. Although there are many forms of ownership, this chapter deals only with the most common:

- Fee simple or fee simple absolute.
- Joint tenancy.
- Tenancy in common.
- Community property.
- Tenancy by the entireties.

§ 17.4.2 Fee Simple or Fee Simple Absolute

Ownership of real estate in fee simple or fee simple absolute is that which gives the owner the absolute legal possession of the property. The vast majority of real estate transactions involve ownership in fee simple, although there are other more complicated forms of lesser ownership. The phrase "in fee simple" means that the owner named owns it all without reservation. Fee simple ownership of real estate may be acquired by corporations, partnerships, individuals, trusts, or estates. Individuals may acquire fee simple ownership either alone or with others. If two or more individuals own real estate together, they may own it either as joint tenants or as tenants in common.

§ 17.4.3 Joint Tenancy

Joint tenancy is ownership by two or more persons, with the right of survivorship. It means that upon the death of one of the joint tenants, the property automatically and immediately becomes the property of the surviving joint tenant without the necessity of probate proceedings. This right of survivorship is considered by many to be the principal advantage of joint tenancy. In some states the right of survivorship is not inherent to joint tenancy, and must be established by including additional language creating survivorship rights. A joint tenant may not change the right of survivorship in the other joint tenant by will. Neither can the heirs of a deceased joint tenant nor their creditors have any claim against property held in joint tenancy with others. The right of survivorship in joint tenancy property is absolute. Frequently, husbands and wives hold title to real estate in joint tenancy, but ownership in joint tenancy is not limited to married couples. On the other hand, just because a husband and wife have occupied certain premises jointly does not necessarily mean that they are owners in joint tenancy. The form of ownership is established not by the use of the property but by the form of ownership specified in the deed by which the owners acquired ownership of the property. Therefore, it is clearly delineated in the records. There are circumstances when the joint tenancy form of ownership is not advisable for a husband and wife, and if that is the case, the lawyer advises their client accordingly.

If it has been determined that the buyers will hold title as joint tenants, the deed contains language similar to the following:

> . . . CONVEY and WARRANT to JOHN SMITH and MARY SMITH, husband and wife, as joint tenants, with right of survivorship . . .

or

> . . . CONVEY and WARRANT to JOHN SMITH and MARY SMITH, husband and wife, as joint tenants and not as tenants in common . . .

or in the case when parties are not related:

> . . . CONVEY and WARRANT to JOHN SMITH and MARY JONES, as joint tenants and not as tenants in common . . .

In most states, if the deed does not clearly indicate how title is to be held, title passing only to "John Smith and Mary Smith" is presumed to be tenancy in common. In some states special forms are used for each form of tenancy. If this is the case, the lawyer's assistant should be extremely careful to use the correct form.

§ 17.4.4 Tenancy in Common

Tenancy in common means the tenants of the property hold undivided fractional interests in the same property, with each tenant in common having the right to possess. The interest is a fraction of the whole, as there is no tangible division of the property. Therefore, none of the tenants in common can claim any specific portion of the property, such as the north half or the east half. Interests of tenants in common may be equal or unequal, and each tenant in common has a separate legal title to their undivided fractional interest. Hence, they can sell their interest or provide for its distribution by will. In the event a tenant in common dies without a will, the undivided interest passes to tenant's heirs at law according to the laws of intestacy. These heirs become tenants in common with the other owners. The language in such a deed might read as follows:

. . . CONVEY and WARRANT to JOHN SMITH and MARY SMITH, husband and wife, as tenants in common, each to an undivided one-half interest, and not as joint tenants . . .

§ 17.4.5 Community Property

Community property exists in some states, and it is the presumption in those states that any property acquired during a marriage by either the husband or the wife, except the property acquired by gift or inheritance, belongs equally to husband and wife—one-half to each.

§ 17.4.6 Tenancy by the Entireties

Another form of ownership by a husband and wife is known as tenancy by the entireties. This form of ownership provides that neither party may convey his or her share of the property individually, and neither share can be attached by creditors. In some states this form of ownership has been abolished, while in others a conveyance to a husband and wife is presumed to be a tenancy by the entireties unless some other form of ownership is clearly indicated.

§ 17.5 Evidence of Title to Real Estate

Regardless of the form of ownership, when a parcel of real estate changes ownership, the owner, or in some instances the buyer, is required to furnish evidence of title. The form of title evidence varies from state to state, so the lawyer's assistant must determine the methods used in their area. Most commonly, evidence of title is in the form of an abstract, a Torrens certificate, or a title insurance policy.

§ 17.5.1 Abstracts

The abstract is a summary of all transactions pertaining to the parcel from the time of governmental entry (when the real estate was first recorded in formal land records) up to and including the current transaction.

Some areas deal almost exclusively with voluminous abstracts in real estate transactions. When such abstracts are used, they are updated for each transaction affecting the particular property covered by the abstract. The updating of an abstract is commonly referred to as a continuation or extension of abstract. The continuation may be attached to an existing abstract so that the abstract remains as one large document. On the other hand, the continuation might be done for each new transaction involving the real estate. The result would be several pieces of abstract, frequently referred to as stub abstracts. The cover sheet or first page of a continuation, called the caption, gives the legal description of the property covered by the abstract. The caption may sometimes describe a larger parcel of real estate from which the property involved in the transaction was taken. The final page of the continuation, called the certificate of the abstracter, contains several items of information needed for the real estate transaction. If the caption on the abstract refers to a larger parcel of land, the abstracter's certificate indicates the entry at which the legal description for which the abstract has been extended can be found.

The extension or continuation of an abstract may be done by a lawyer. More commonly, it is done by a title company specializing in such work. In some states a title company can examine and assist in the search of records, insure the title to the property, and act as an escrow or closing agent. The extent to which a title company participates in these services depends upon the laws of that particular state, as well as the custom in the area. The lawyer's assistant should become familiar with the information a title company must have in order to perform its services rapidly and efficiently. The lawyer's assistant must be aware of the special services which title companies have developed to provide specific limited title information to lawyers. Because the contribution and cooperation of the title company's staff are an integral part of the efficient real estate transaction, rapport should be developed with the staff members. The duties of the lawyer's assistant often include the responsibility of arranging for continuations of an abstract on pending real estate transactions. The lawyer's assistant must know whom to call and how to place an order for such a continuation.

An abstract must be treated as a valuable legal document, as it is very expensive and time consuming to replace. Most firms require the use of receipts in all transfers of an abstract. The lawyer's assistant should be able to draft such receipts. (*See* Illustration 17–1.)

Illustration 17–1

ABSTRACT RECEIPT

September 15, [Year]

RECEIVED OF Jones and Jones, Lawyers, the Abstract of Title to the following real estate:

Lot 2, Block 1, Red Rose Addition, Any County, Any State.

____

John K. Smith
Client/File Reference: *S–6948*

§ 17.5.2 Torrens Certificate or Owner's Duplicate Certificate of Title

Real estate having a Torrens certificate or owner's duplicate certificate of title is formally referred to as registered property. Under the

Torrens Act, which has been adopted by some states, a county may establish a system of title registration indemnified by a security or assurance fund backed by assets of the county. All transactions concerning a parcel of real estate registered under the Torrens system must be recorded in the office of the registrar of titles. The registrar of titles issues a certificate of title for each parcel of real estate registered under the Torrens system. A Torrens certificate is considered to be conclusive evidence of the present ownership and state of title. Liens, mortgages, and other encumbrances in existence are listed on the certificates. These entries are called memorials. The original certificate of title is kept in the office of the registrar of titles and may not be removed for any reason. In some states an owner's duplicate certificate of title is also issued and is delivered to the owner. This duplicate should be treated as an important legal document, as it must be surrendered to the registrar of titles upon change of ownership or when new encumbrances are memorialized (entered). If the owner cannot produce the owner's duplicate at such times, a court order must be obtained to have it replaced. In a transaction involving registered property, the lawyer's assistant may be requested to order a registered property abstract from a title company. This type of abstract summarizes the information contained on the certificate of title. In some instances the law firm may conduct an independent examination of Torrens records either in place of or as a supplement to a registered property abstract. In some states at the request of a mortgagee (a creditor who holds property as security for a debt), a mortgagee's duplicate certificate of title may also be issued. Receipts should always be used in the transfer of duplicate certificates of title.

§ 17.5.3 Title Policy

A title insurance policy is issued by a title insurance company and insures that a certain parcel of real estate is titled in certain parties. There are several kinds of title insurance available that insure different interests of different parties. In ordinary real estate transactions, however, the lawyer's assistant will be dealing with owner's and mortgagee's insurance policies. An owner's title insurance policy gives the owner the right to recover any loss suffered from a covered title defect. (*See* the section on examination of titles for an explanation of title defects.) How much the owner can recover depends upon the amount of coverage afforded by the title insurance policy. The amount of coverage on an owner's policy is usually the purchase price of the real estate.

A mortgagee's policy is separate insurance coverage that insures the mortgagee's lien on the real estate. Normally, any lending institution loaning money for the purchase of real estate will require title insurance in the amount of its loan. Mortgagee's coverage does not insure an owner's interest but guarantees only that the mortgagee (creditor) will be paid in the event of any title defect. Mortgagee's coverage may be issued in conjunction with an owner's policy or by itself. If both an owner's policy and a mortgagee's policy are issued simultaneously, the insured parties are both the owner and the mortgagee, but a separate premium is charged for each insured party. A title insurance policy may be issued by itself even when no abstract of title exists or if the abstract of title has been lost or destroyed. A title insurance policy may be issued in addition to an abstract if a title defect emerges and the title company is willing to insure over such defect. Registered property may also be covered by title insurance.

In a real estate transaction, the lawyer's assistant may be required to order the title insurance policy by telephoning or delivering the necessary information to the title insurance company. In some cases, this will be the same company which prepares the abstract. The lawyer's assistant will need to know the office practice in ordering title insurance. The names of the sellers, the names and marital status of the buyers, the amount of coverage, *i.e.,* purchase price, a legal description of the property, and in some cases the abstract of title, if one exists, are provided to the title insurance company. The title insurance company then issues a commitment for title insurance for the lawyer to examine prior to issuing the title insurance policy.

§ 17.5.4 Examination of Title

The buyer relies upon the lawyer to certify that the evidence of title reveals that the prospective seller is in a position to convey a clear, merchantable, and marketable title. Clear and merchantable title is the term applied to ownership of property that is free from any type of legal defect or encumbrance. Therefore, when a lawyer certifies to a buyer that the property has a clear and merchantable title, it means that a prudent person need have no fear of accepting it, as it would be readily transferable on the open market. If a defect in the title does exist, it is referred to as a cloud on the title or a defect in the title. Therefore, prior to the closing of a real estate transaction, the buyer has the evidence of title examined by a lawyer. In lieu of or in addition to such an examination, the buyer may secure title insurance. At the conclusion of the title examination, the lawyer issues a title opinion. In some areas, if title insurance is obtained, the lawyer does not issue a title opinion. The title opinion and/or the commitment for title insurance advises the client as to the condition of the title. If there are defects or clouds on the title, the title opinion or title insurance commitment describes what action is required to correct them. Typically, the matters which would affect the title are:

- Encumbrances
- Easements

- Encroachments
- Tax sales
- Irregularities

§ 17.5.5 Encumbrances

An encumbrance is a recorded document placing the public on notice that a third person may have a claim against the property that might diminish the value of the property to a prospective buyer. In such cases the closing lawyer would hold back sufficient funds to pay any such encumbrance so that the buyer ultimately gets full value for their purchase price. Mortgages, judgments, and liens are all encumbrances which are discussed in further detail below.

§ 17.5.6 Mortgages

A mortgage is a security instrument against real estate given by a debtor to a creditor to secure (guarantee) the payment of a debt. In some states this kind of instrument is called a deed of trust. In granting a mortgage to a creditor, a debtor pledges property to guarantee to the creditor that the debt will be paid. If the debtor does not pay, then under the terms of the mortgage the creditor may foreclose on the property. This means that upon meeting any applicable legal requirements, the creditor may seize the property and have it sold to pay the debt owed the creditor by the seller. Mortgages are quite common in real estate transactions, as most people who buy property do not have sufficient money to pay cash for the property. They borrow the money from a lending institution and grant a mortgage to secure the payment of the loan.

EXAMPLE:

> The sellers borrowed $10,000 against their home and they have not paid back any of the money. The sellers gave a mortgage as security for the loan. They immediately decided to sell the property and have found a buyer who has agreed to pay $80,000 for the property. In examining the title, the buyer's lawyer discovers the mortgage which is an encumbrance against the property. The buyer's lawyer contacts the creditor to determine how much money the sellers owe. That amount is deducted from the sellers' proceeds and the creditor is paid the amount owed through escrow in exchange for a satisfaction of mortgage.

§ 17.5.7 Judgments

A judgment is a court order or decree which represents a decision with respect to a matter that was filed in court. There are many kinds of judgments rendered by courts as a result of litigation. The type most likely to be encountered in real estate law is the money judgment which awards a sum of money due the plaintiff by the defendant. The plaintiff who is awarded the money judgment is the judgment creditor, and the debtor against whom the judgment is rendered is the judgment debtor. Plaintiffs originally file a certificate making the judgment of a lien on all of the debtor's real estate wherever located.

EXAMPLE:

The sellers in the example above might also have a judgment recorded against them and that judgment creates a lien against the property owned by the seller. Its payment is handled much the same way as payment of a mortgage is handled. The closing lawyer contacts the lawyer for the judgment creditor to find out how much money is owed on the judgment. This amount is then paid from the escrow funds in order to receive a satisfaction of judgment. (Some judgments provide for the payment of lawyer's fees, interest, and court costs in addition to the principal amount owed.)

§ 17.5.8 Materialman's or Mechanic's Liens

A materialman's or mechanic's lien is a right created in a person who has done work on or delivered materials to property which, if perfected, creates a right enforceable against the property. (The manner in which liens are perfected is governed by state law.) If such a lien is found to be recorded against the property being sold, it must be paid by the seller, and an appropriate formal satisfaction delivered at closing if the buyer is to receive clear title.

§ 17.5.9 Tax Liens

Local, state, and federal governments may utilize the tax lien as a vehicle to collect taxes. They attach by virtue of law; no action is necessary, unlike a judgment. These taxes include real estate taxes, income taxes, sales taxes, federal unemployment taxes, etc. Tax liens attach to property just as judgments do. Therefore, a seller must pay any such lien to give the buyer a clear title and deliver a formal satisfaction at closing. In many states the lien of unpaid real estate taxes is superior to all other liens.

§ 17.5.10 Easements

An easement is a right granted to someone by a property owner to come upon or use their land for a specified purpose. The terms "easement" and "servitude" are sometimes used interchangeably.

On occasion, a property owner may wish to grant to another a limited right to make use of all or a portion of their land for a specific purpose or for a definite period of time. This grant is known as an easement. An easement may be created by the act of the parties involved through negotiation and agreement. Easements are usually custom-drafted by the lawyers of the respective parties. An example of an easement would be the right of a utility company to install a gas line across an individual's property and thereafter to enter the land to maintain, repair, and service the line. The utility company would not have the right to enter the property for any other purpose.

§ 17.5.11 Encroachments

An encroachment is the unlawful intrusion of one's buildings, improvements or fixtures onto the land of another.

EXAMPLE:

> If a neighbor builds a fence or a garage which extends over the property line onto the neighbor's property, that portion extending over the property line constitutes an encroachment where the owner of the land on which the encroachment exists does not consent to the encroachment.

The encroachment is usually discovered by the engineer who makes a survey of the property, and the buyer's lawyer discovers the encroachment when examining the survey in connection with title examination. It can become a permanent right by virtue of adverse possession if unchallenged for the requisite number of years prescribed by law.

§ 17.5.12 Restrictive Covenants

When property is developed into a subdivision, the developer usually places on the property certain restrictions as to the use of the property. The restrictive covenants usually provide that the property will be used only for residential purposes and often provide for the size of the residences and the kinds of building materials permitted to be used. The reason for these covenants is to maintain the value of the property. By specifying the size and building materials, the developer ensures that the residences will cost generally the same to build.

EXAMPLE:

> If it were possible for a homebuilder to build a $100,000 house next to a $600,000 house, the $600,000 house would lose some of its value based merely on the fact that it was located next to a $100,000 house.

Although restrictive covenants are most commonly seen in the residential context, they can also be placed on commercial or other property.

§ 17.5.13 Tax Sales

As a rule, both state and local governing bodies levy taxes against property to obtain revenue. The tax is usually computed by multiplying a rate in mills ($1 per $1,000) times the assessed value of the property. (In some jurisdictions the assessed value may be some arbitrary percentage of the retail value.) Property taxes are collectible against the property. Therefore, if a property owner does not pay their taxes, the tax authority may seize the property and sell it to a purchaser who pays the taxes. The title lawyer therefore routinely verifies that property taxes on the property have been paid. If they have not been paid and the property has been sold for taxes, it is necessary for the seller to redeem (reclaim) the property within a specified time. This is done by paying the taxes due as well as interest, penalties, and costs.

§ 17.5.14 Irregularities

There are numerous other problems that could result in some type of irregularity in the title. Errors or variations in legal descriptions, errors in divorce or probate proceedings, and other types of problems must sometimes be corrected.

In most jurisdictions the seller bears the cost of furnishing the evidence of title, while the buyer secures and pays for a title examination or title insurance policy. However, this custom varies by location.

In the event that title insurance is to be used in lieu of or in addition to a lawyer's opinion, the title company examines the title and issues its commitment or binder prior to the closing. This document contains a list of all defects or clouds on the title, such as those listed above. These defects are called exceptions to the policy. The title policy does not provide coverage for any loss resulting from the listed exceptions. The commitment also lists the requirements to be met prior to closing and the issuance of its final policy. The final policy is issued once all conditions are met and the transaction has been closed, subject only to customary exceptions and any exceptions approved by the buyer. Some exceptions to title are considered customary, and they appear on most title policies. Easements, for example, are essential to proper maintenance of electric, gas, telephone, and water services. The providers of these public, as well as private, services must be able to enter upon residential property to service their lines. Therefore, most lenders accept this type of exception without question.

§ 17.6 Instruments of Conveyance

Since any legal entity may own property, an individual, a corporation, a partnership, or a limited liability company may acquire an interest in real estate. There are a number of ways to acquire real estate. Only the most common will be discussed in this chapter:

- Sale or Deed
- Devise by will or by intestate succession (Probate Deed or Deed by Personal Representative)

§ 17.6.1 Sale or Deed

In a transfer by sale or deed, the owner (called grantor, vendor, or seller) conveys title to the buyer (called grantee, vendee, or purchaser) by the delivery of a deed. A deed is a formal written contract between the parties by which the seller sells their property to the buyer for a consideration (price). There are a number of ways in which the price can be paid, and they are discussed later in this chapter.

The law of each state outlines the requirements of a deed. Printed forms containing these legal requirements are usually available through a legal stationer or through the county clerk's office. Some states require that only their forms be used, while other states allow general usage of various types of deeds. The lawyer's assistant should use the most acceptable form in the state in which the property is located, taking special care to comply with requirements for execution, such as witnesses or notary acknowledgments.

§ 17.6.2 The Warranty Deed

The warranty deed (sometimes called a general warranty deed) is the most desirable type of deed for the buyer. The seller (party conveying title) gives the following warranties to the buyer (party receiving title):

1. That at the time of the making and delivery of the deed, the seller owned a fee simple interest in the property and had the full right to convey it
2. That the title is free of all encumbrances, except any specifically listed in the deed
3. That the buyer and their successors in interest have the right to quiet and peaceable possession of the premises and are indemnified by the seller against the claims of all persons who may lawfully claim an interest other than those encumbrances

§ 17.6.3 Special Warranty Deed or Limited Warranty Deed

A special warranty deed or limited warranty deed warrants the title to the property being conveyed against any claims by, through, or under the seller or their heirs excepting encumbrances specifically listed in the deed. It does not guarantee against any claims that occurred prior to the time of the seller's acquisition.

§ 17.6.4 Quitclaim Deed

A quitclaim deed from the seller conveys any claim, right, title, or interest which seller may have to the subject property. The seller on a quitclaim deed does not warrant the condition of the title. The quitclaim deed does not even warrant that seller has any interest in the property. It merely provides that if seller does own any interest in the property, that interest is being conveyed. Quitclaim deeds are often used to correct certain types of title defects.

§ 17.6.5 Probate Deed

If property is acquired from an estate or guardianship, the buyer receives a type of special warranty deed called a probate deed or a guardian's or personal representative's deed, which generally does not contain warranties. In some states, it is also possible, however, to obtain a deed with warranties.

A transfer by devise or testate succession occurs when the owner of real estate dies and leaves such property to person(s) by a will (devise). If the owner has left no will, it is distributed by operation of law to their heirs at law (intestate succession). Each state has statutes which provide for the distribution of a decedent's property to their nearest relatives. The method of conveyance is a decree, sometimes called a certificate of transfer, from the court of jurisdiction in probate matters. The decree or certificate is then recorded with the appropriate county office for real estate documents.

§ 17.7 Legal Description of Real Estate

All real estate must have a means by which it can be uniformly described. This is known as the legal description. Do not confuse the legal description with the street address or tax identification number. A complete and accurate legal description is needed for every deed, mortgage, and other formal document required in a real estate transaction. The accuracy of a legal description is imperative, and proofreading is essential. After you have typed the description, you should check it while someone reads it to you. There are three basic types of legal descriptions:

1. Government survey
2. Metes and bounds description
3. Recorded plat of subdivision

§ 17.7.1 The Government Survey

The government survey is a description based upon the rectangular survey system which divides land into a system of squares within squares. The squares are six miles long and six miles wide. These squares are resubdivided into 36 sections (although there are some irregular sections) with each section being one mile square. Thirty-six sections make up one township. Each section contains 640 acres and is numbered from 1 to 36 running east to west. Townships are separated from each other by range lines which run north and south.

Illustration 17–2 is a diagram of the method of numbering a township.

Illustration 17–2

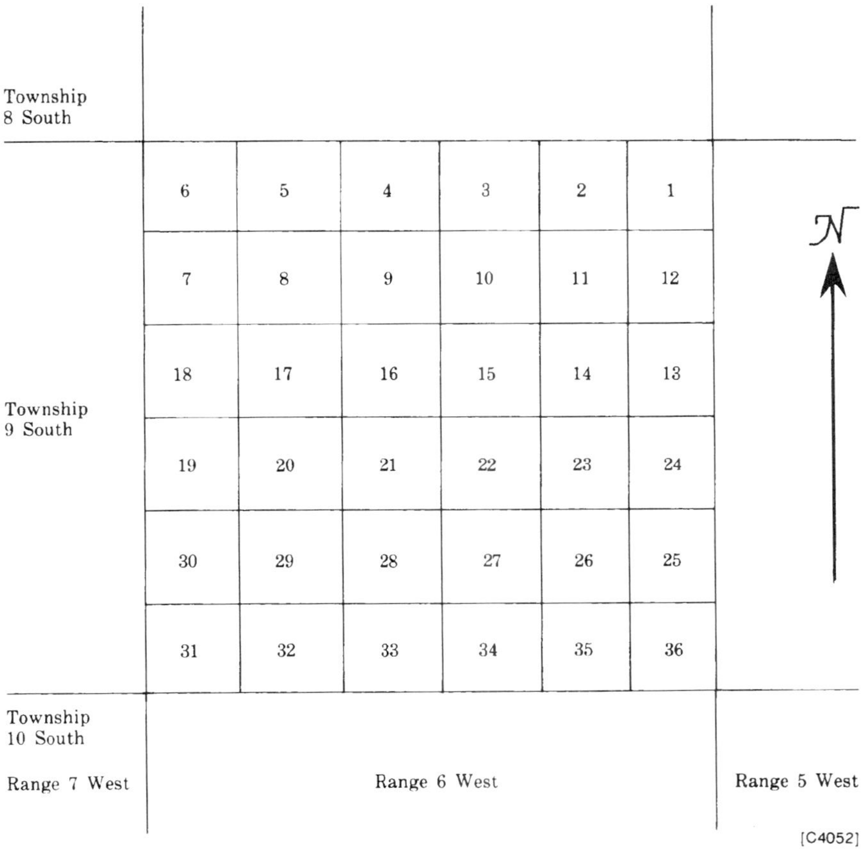

The following shows the relationships involved when the rectangular survey system is used:

1 Range = 16 Townships
1 Township = 36 Sections
1 Section = 640 Acres
¼ Section = 160 Acres

Illustration 17–3 is a diagram of a government survey section, showing two methods of division.

Illustration 17–3

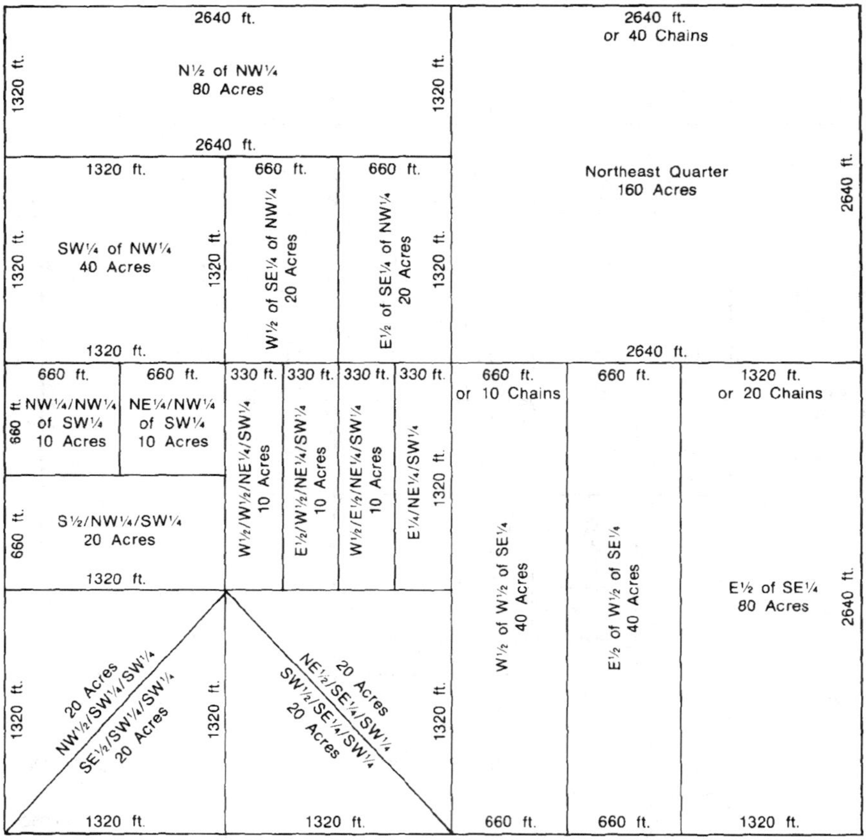

The description prescribed by these original surveys, whether government or state controlled, is the underlying basis for all legal descriptions in use today. For example, a typical original United States Government Survey description would be:

> The Northwest Quarter (NW¼) of Section Five (5), Township Fifteen (15) North, Range Three (3) West, Any County, Any State.

Illustration 17–4

Sec. 5, Twp 15N, Rge. 3W

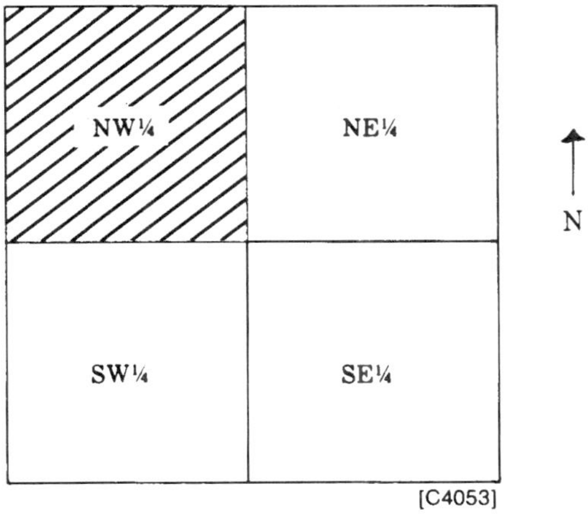

Illustration 17–4 shows the location of this property, a parcel which would consist of 160 acres (a quarter of a section or quarter section). Assume that this parcel is located in an urban area and is sold in increasingly smaller parcels.

EXAMPLE:

The description of a 40–acre tract in the northwest corner would be:

The Northwest Quarter of the Northwest Quarter (NW¼ of NW ¼) of Section Five (5), Township Fifteen (15) North, Range Three (3) West, Any County, Any State.

(*See* Illustration 17–5.)

Illustration 17–5

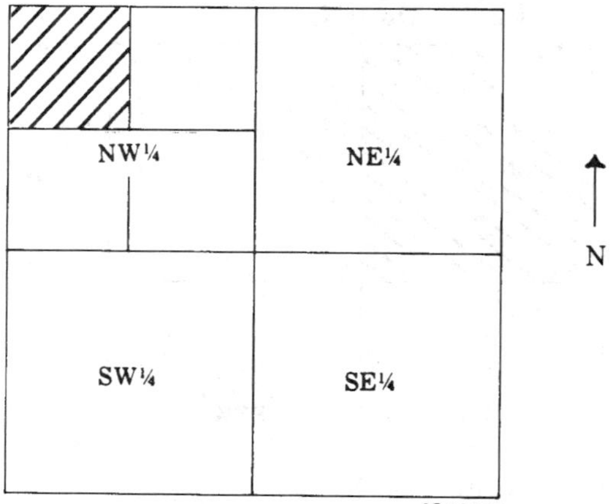

[C4054]

As increasingly smaller tracts are sold, particularly those having irregular boundaries, the legal descriptions become increasingly cumbersome. Simplified methods of describing real estate evolve. Also, as the tracts become smaller and irregularly shaped, it becomes very difficult to locate just where some of the parcels are. Therefore, it is often necessary to have a registered land surveyor actually locate the property and draw a map of the location. To do this, the surveyor makes "on site" measurements of the property being surveyed. If unable to find reference maps to help determine the physical location of the property, property records must be searched to find all sales of parcels in a section and measure those "on site" before being able to measure the property being surveyed.

In urban areas property is subdivided, measured, and mapped before sales are made. Descriptions refer to these subdivisions of property, as you will see from the discussion of subdivisions below.

§ 17.7.2 Metes and Bounds Description

The metes and bounds description is one that begins at a designated point and proceeds to describe the parcel of land by reference to units of measurement and direction.

Assume that the purchaser of the NW¼ of the NW¼ in the illustration above erected some fencing that encloses a portion of the "forty" and now wishes to sell that portion. A surveyor establishes a "point of beginning" and then follows the fencing around the property, carefully measuring distance and direction of each piece of fence until returning to the point of beginning. This description of the property would be a "metes and bounds" description and would be as follows:

> Beginning at the Southeast corner of the Northwest Quarter of the Northwest Quarter (NW¼ of NW¼) of Section Five (5), Township Fifteen (15) North, Range Three (3) West, Any County, Any State, according to the United States Government Survey thereof: thence proceed west along the south line of the NW¼ of NW¼ to an intersection with the east line of the west half of said NW¼ of NW¼; thence north along said east line 357.44 feet to a point and corner; thence south 66° 07′24″ East to an intersection with the east line of said NW¼ of NW¼; thence south along the quarter quarter line 56.7 feet to the point of beginning.

Illustration 17–6 shows where this property is located. The entire quarter section is shown only for illustrative purposes so that the reader can "piece it all together." An actual survey plat would show only the property enclosed within the fence that is being sold.

Also note that there is an arrow on the illustration. This arrow indicates the direction of north for purposes of orienting the map. Unless otherwise indicated, the arrow always points north.

Illustration 17–6

Sec. 5, Twp 15 N, Rge. 3 W

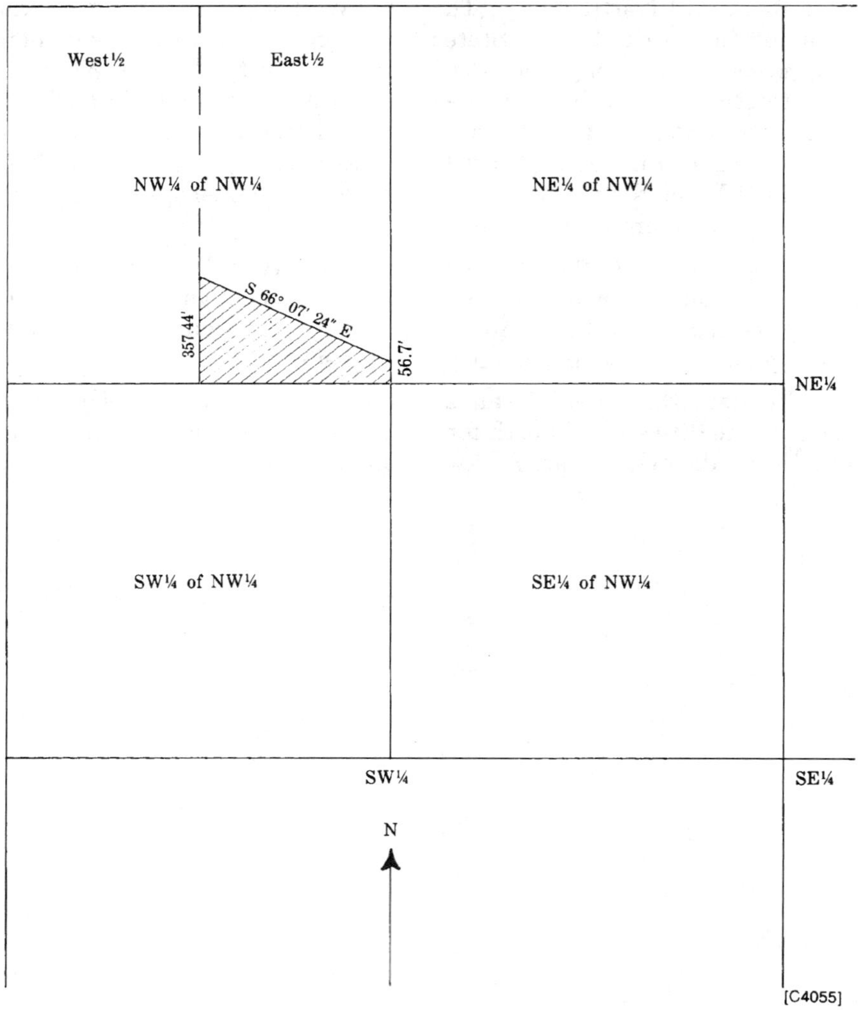

A metes and bounds description uses angles or vectors (a vector is a direction and distance of a line) to describe the line segments that represent the boundaries of the property being described. The description is actually a group of "calls," each call describing one line segment. Each call has length and direction. The length is usually given in feet, but it is not unusual to find other units of linear measurement. The direction is given in one of two ways. If the line segment's direction is exactly north, south, east, or west, then N, S, E, or W will accurately describe the direction of the line. If the direction is NE, NW, SE, or SW, then the angle between the line segment and the north-south line must be known. That angle is measured in degrees, minutes, and seconds. One degree equals 60 minutes and one minute equals 60 seconds. If, for instance, the line direction is northwest and the angle between the line and the north/south line is 40, then the description of the line is N 40° W. Note that N 40° W generally describes the direction of the line, and by including "40°" the line is identified uniquely. There is only one line that fits the description. (*See* Illustration 17–7.)

Illustration 17–7

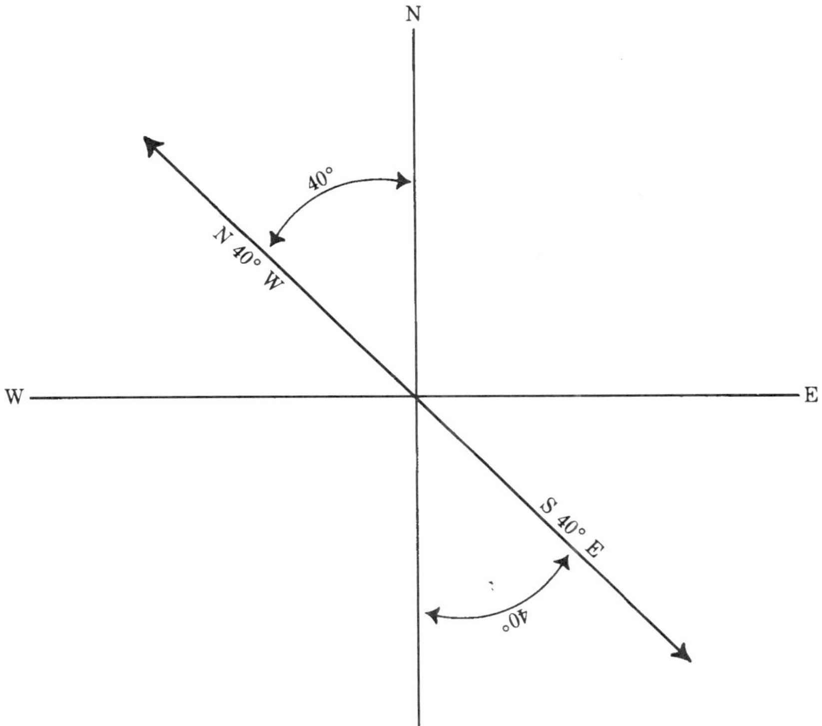

[C4056]

At this point it is interesting to note that a line can be described in either direction. The same line can also be described as S 40° E. A metes and bounds property description always proceeds from the point of beginning, around the property (usually clockwise) and back to the point of beginning, carefully and accurately describing each line segment. Once the direction of travel around the property is determined, then each line can no longer be described two ways. It must be described in the direction of travel.

In Illustration 17–6 the fencing that formed the northerly boundary of the property described made an angle of just over 66 degrees with the north/south line. Since we were going around the property clockwise, the call the surveyor used was S 66° 07′24″ E. This call did not have a dimension in feet. Nevertheless, the distance can be found because it referred to a quarter-quarter (or one-eighth of forty) line which has a specific location.

§ 17.7.3 Recorded Plat of Subdivision

A subdivision is a division of one tract into two or more smaller lots or parcels. The word "subdivision" is also used to designate a development of similar lots for the purpose of constructing residences. A property owner who decides to subdivide property for this purpose is often called a developer. The services of a civil engineer may be engaged to map out the subdivision. The map is recorded in the county clerk's office, and the recorded map is then used as the basis for describing the lots in that subdivision.

Since most urban property is now subdivided, this is the predominant means used to describe urban real estate. It is much simpler and less cumbersome than describing property by metes and bounds or by government survey. A typical subdivision plat is shown in Illustration 17–8. A typical legal description in that subdivision would be:

> Lot Twenty-five (25), Block Fourteen (14), Linden Park Addition Division No. 6 to the city of Idaho Falls, Idaho, according to the recorded plat or plan thereof.

Illustration 17–8

LINDEN PARK ADDITION

DIVISION NO. 6
TO
THE CITY OF IDAHO FALLS, IDAHO
Part of
NE 1/4 of Sec. 20 T. 2 N., R. 38 E. B.M.

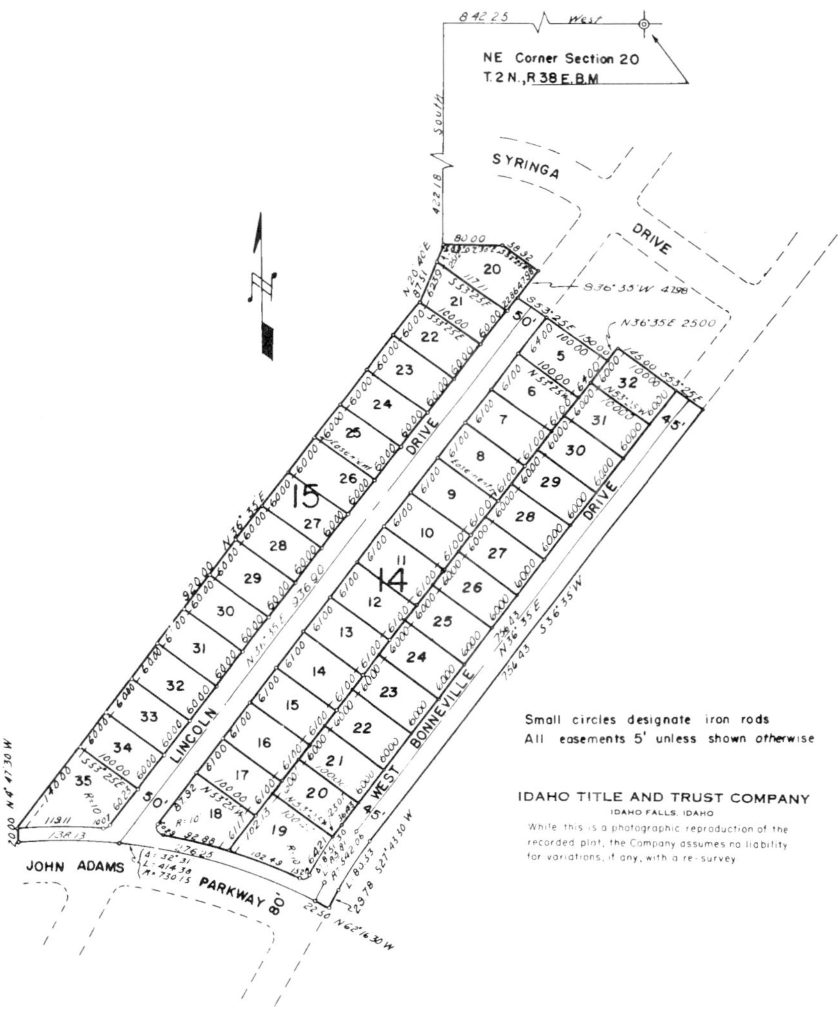

§ 17.8 The Listing Agreement

A typical real estate transaction begins when someone decides to sell property they own. The prospective seller may enlist the services of a real estate broker to help locate a buyer. Additionally, the real estate broker often helps the seller arrive at a proposed selling price for the property. The broker charges a commission (fee) for services, usually a fixed percentage of the sale price of the property, although a flat fee agreed upon by the parties is sometimes charged. Once the prospective seller and real estate broker reach an agreement on the terms of the commission, they enter into a contract, called a listing agreement, which describes in detail the real estate to be sold; the personal property to be included in the transaction, if any; the asking price; the terms of sale to which the seller is agreeable; and information concerning taxes, assessments, and existing encumbrances.

Ordinarily, this listing agreement is prepared by the real estate broker on a commercially printed form which contains the terms customary for the area involved. The seller may, however, engage a lawyer to review the proposed listing agreement before it is actually signed. Usually the listing agreement is exclusive, meaning that even if owner finds its own buyer during the term that the listing agreement is in effect, the broker must be paid a commission. Sometimes the listing agreement is non-exclusive meaning that the broker only earns commission if the broker procures the buyer.

Thereafter, the broker advertises, promotes, and shows the property to prospective buyers.

It is not unusual for prospective buyers to seek the services of a real estate broker to help them find property. This is particularly true in instances when people are moving to another state or are interested in a particular kind of property for investment purposes. In many areas, real estate brokers exchange information concerning all listings in the area (sometimes called a multiple listing service [MLS]), thus broadening the exposure of the property. If the property is ultimately sold to a client of another broker, that broker is said to be the selling broker while the original broker is the listing broker. The broker may act as the buyer's agent or as another agent of the seller. If no broker is involved, the seller must locate a buyer through their own efforts.

§ 17.8.1 The Purchase Agreement (Earnest Money Contract)

When a prospective buyer becomes interested in the property, an offer is made to the seller. If the property is exclusively listed with a real estate broker, the prospective buyer makes the offer through the broker, who then relays the offer to the seller. The purchaser's offer usually includes a proposed price and a method of proposed payment. If the prospective buyer and seller reach an agreement, that agreement is reduced to writing in the form of a purchase agreement, also referred to as a memorandum sale agreement, purchase offer, or earnest money contract. This document may be prepared by a lawyer, a real estate broker, or by the parties themselves. The purchase agreement is a contract, and it must meet all legal requirements for a contract. (*See* the chapter on Contracts.) It includes such information as:

- Full names and marital status of the seller(s).
- Full names of the buyer(s).
- Addresses of the parties.
- Legal and common (street address) description of the property.
- Personal property to be included in the transaction (draperies, appliances, or similar items).
- Sale price.
- Terms and conditions of the sale including financing arrangements or contingencies.
- Type of deed required.
- Evidence of title to be provided.

The closing and possession dates and any other special provisions or conditions of the transaction should be clearly set forth in the purchase agreement. A down payment, referred to as earnest money, is usually required from the buyer. The down payment typically is deposited in the trust account of either the lawyer for the seller or the broker or in an escrow account at an escrow or title company pending the closing of the transaction. As the parties negotiate the terms, the purchase agreement may be revised extensively before its final execution, since this document controls the consummation of the transaction. Frequently, lawyers for both parties review it and suggest changes. If a real estate broker is involved in the transaction, most of the basic information concerning the property will be provided by the broker. A broker may also assist the buyer with financing arrangements if the buyer is not able to pay for the property in cash.

§ 17.8.2 Financing Arrangements

Once a seller and buyer have reached an agreement on the terms of the transaction, the buyer must get the money to buy the property. Ours is a credit-oriented society and rarely is a prospective homeowner able to accumulate the substantial cash necessary to buy property. It is not uncommon for a purchase agreement to be conditioned upon the purchaser's ability to secure financing for the property. The buyer usually arranges financing either through a commercial institution in the business of residential financing or through satisfactory arrangements with the seller. This chapter discusses only these two types of financing.

§ 17.8.3 Conventional Financing

There are many factors which control the availability of commercial money for residential financing, many of which are controlled by the general state of the economy. Local banks and savings institutions often have funds available for residential financing. This type of financing is referred to as conventional financing. Some conventional financing allows for assumption of the financing by a subsequent purchaser of the property, subject to the bank's approval.

§ 17.8.4 FHA and VA Financing

Assuming a buyer qualifies, certain types of financing through government agencies can be secured, such as the Department of Veterans Affairs (VA) or the Federal Housing Administration (FHA). These loans require little or no cash down payment and have less restrictive financial qualifications than conventional loans. VA loans are available only to veterans and to surviving spouses of servicemen who died while they were on active duty.

VA and FHA loans are processed through local lending institutions, but the guarantee extended by the VA or FHA insures that the local lender suffers no financial loss in the event the buyer defaults on the loan. The Federal National Mortgage Association (FNMA) offers a similar guarantee to local lenders on qualified conventional loans.

§ 17.8.5 The Loan Application

Regardless of the type of loan, the buyer's application for the loan is processed through a lending institution. To process a homebuyer's application, the lender accumulates financial and personal data about the buyer to determine whether the homebuyer qualifies for the kind and amount of loan desired.

§ 17.8.6 Private Financing

It is possible for the buyer to arrange for payment of the purchase price without the necessity of securing commercial financing. Sometimes the seller is in a position to help with the financing. It is common for some type of financing already to be in existence on the property. In such a case, the buyer may be able to utilize or "assume" the existing financing. The existing financing is most commonly found in the form of a commercial loan which the seller made when originally purchasing the property. That loan would be secured (guaranteed) by a mortgage on the property. A mortgage is a security instrument which allows a lender to foreclose on the property (seize it) and cause it to be sold at public sale if the loan is not repaid according to the terms of the mortgage.

The most common methods of private financing are:

- Assumption of an existing mortgage.
- Installment real estate contract, either with or without an escrow.
- Purchase money mortgage.
- Deed of trust.

§ 17.9 Types of Real Estate Transactions and Requisite Documents

The documents required in real estate transactions vary greatly. The lawyer's assistant must learn to develop a checklist of items that are required in various types of transactions. A commercial real estate transaction, such as an apartment complex or office building could easily require more than 25 different documents, while a transaction involving a home or vacant land could involve fewer than five documents. All real estate transactions require some form of conveyance document and closing statement. All, except cash transactions, require documents relating to the financing.

If a real estate broker is involved, their firm may have a closing department which submits drafts of documents to lawyers for both the buyer and the seller. The real estate firm may also act as an intermediary with any lending institution. In some states lending institutions or title insurance companies prepare the loan documentation, while in other states lawyers prepare all loan documents.

§ 17.9.1 The Cash Transaction

If a purchaser is buying the property for cash, no financing documents need to be prepared. As was discussed earlier, most deeds are warranty deeds. This is a "fill in the blanks" form that can be computer generated or can be purchased at a legal stationer. The printed language in the form is important, and the lawyer should verify that the correct form is used.

The other key document which you will need to prepare for the cash transaction is the closing statement. It will be a much simpler form than the example shown in Illustration 17–9 because of the nature of a cash transaction, but the same principles apply to the preparation of all closing statements.

§ 17.9.2 The Sale With Assumption of Mortgage

In a transaction involving an assumption, the buyer pays cash down equal to the sales price less the balance of the existing mortgage and thereafter makes all payments under the terms of the mortgage. For example, if a buyer pays $50,000 for a house having a $15,000 mortgage, their earnest money and cash at closing total $35,000.

If an assumption is planned, the lawyer and/or broker (depending upon the practice in your area) verifies prior to the closing that an assumption is possible. Most commercial mortgages specifically prohibit assumption and, even if the purchase agreement provides for assumption of the mortgage, the sale may not be possible if this is the case. Although the lawyer often determines this fact in their examination of the title, it may come to light when your office or the realtor's office contacts the mortgage company for assumption information.

If you are responsible for helping to process this type of sale to closing, you will contact the mortgage company for the necessary assumption information. Your office may have a form letter developed for this purpose, but if it does not, you should ask the lawyer to help you develop such a form. You will ask the mortgage company for the balance due on the loan, the amount of the monthly payments, the balance being held by the company in any escrow accounts, and the status of both the monthly payment and any escrow accounts. Since you cannot prepare the sale documents until you have this information, you should do this as soon as possible. A good rule of thumb is to write the mortgage company when you open the file and order whatever abstract work must be done. (The lawyer will probably order the abstract work until you are familiar with the procedures, or will give you instructions on how to do this.) If the mortgage cannot be assumed, the mortgage company will advise you of this in response to your letter. With most mortgages, the balance owed under the mortgage is "due on sale" of the property, and the lender reserves the right to approve any prospective buyer in the event of a sale with an assumption of mortgage. Most real estate brokers are familiar with the local lenders that make this requirement and often coordinate securing lender approval of the prospective buyer before the file reaches your office. If the realtor does not do this, the lender will notify you of this requirement in response to your letter asking for an assumption statement.

§ 17.9.3 The Assumption Closing Statement

In preparing the closing statement for an assumption, there are a few items peculiar to this type of sale.

- Most lenders charge an assumption or transfer fee. The amount of the fee varies greatly and the lender's assumption statement will indicate the amount.
- It is very important to verify that the monthly installments on the loan are up to date and, if they are not, you must collect those payments from the seller.
- The escrow account is an account for the payment of property taxes and hazard and extended insurance (protection against fire,

wind damage, hail, and other perils of nature). The monthly payments include the amount of one-twelfth of the property taxes and one-twelfth of the insurance policy premium. The lender directs the payment of property taxes and insurance from the money in the escrow account. Sometimes there is not enough money in the escrow account to pay the amount of the taxes or insurance, so the lender overdraws the account. This creates an escrow shortage, and the lender usually requires funds to bring this account current in the event of an assumption.

Although the buyer usually pays the transfer fee and lawyer's fees for an assumption and the seller must pay to bring the loan and escrow account current, all closing costs in connection with an assumption of mortgage are negotiable; therefore, it is necessary for you to refer to the purchase agreement to determine who is paying which costs. Since insurance is usually paid in advance, sometimes the amount of the insurance premium is prorated, and the buyer pays the seller for the unused portion of the insurance premium if the insurance policy is being transferred in the sale. Property taxes are handled the same way; but in most areas, property taxes are paid after they have accrued, and the taxes will be prorated accordingly. In handling these items, you will need to become familiar with the practice in your area, and you will have to work very closely with the lawyer on the preparation of this type of closing statement.

§ 17.9.4 Purchase Money Mortgage, Credit Sale, Sale With Mortgage

A purchase money mortgage is a mortgage given by a buyer to a seller in partial payment of the purchase price. Although the buyer pays an agreed portion of the price in cash, this kind of sale is generally referred to as a credit sale. Since the seller does not receive money for the property until later, the property is considered sold on credit. The transaction is directly between the buyer and seller. The seller gives a deed to the buyer at closing, and the buyer gives the seller a mortgage just as if the loan was obtained from a commercial lending institution.

If the financing on the transaction is being handled by the seller, you will likely prepare the documentation for both the deed and the mortgage. The kind of instrument which is used in this kind of transaction varies a great deal, but here again, your firm will already have on hand the kind of form it prefers to use. As was discussed earlier, in this kind of sale the buyer pays some of the purchase price in cash and handles the remainder of the purchase price on credit with the seller. Generally, the buyer pays the seller in monthly installments over a specified period of time just as if dealing with a commercial lender. The buyer executes a promissory note (promise to pay) and a mortgage (security instrument) in favor of the seller. These evidence the debt to the seller and also provide the seller with security on the debt.

§ 17.9.5 Installment Real Estate Contract

An installment real estate contract (also called a land contract or a contract for deed) is an agreement between the seller and the buyer for the purchase of certain real estate over a period of time by making installment payments with interest. The contract buyer takes possession of the property and becomes responsible for payment of taxes, insurance coverage, maintenance of the property, and any other conditions set forth in the contract, but the contract seller retains title to the premises until the price is paid in full. The contract is recorded in order that anyone searching title can ascertain the buyer's interest in the property. Upon the buyer's completion of the contract, the buyer receives a deed giving them title to the property. In some states, to ensure the performance of the seller, the signed deed is placed in escrow until consummation of the contract.

The use of the installment contract provides the parties with a great deal of flexibility in structuring the financing for the real estate transaction. It often provides the seller with the opportunity for more favorable income tax treatment. Advantages to the buyer may include a lower interest rate than that available from commercial lending institutions and lower payments in the early years of ownership through the use of a balloon payment. A balloon payment is a provision that provides for payment in full of any unpaid balance a certain number of years from the date of the contract, typically 5–10 years, but the payments are calculated as though the loan were for a longer period of time.

§ 17.9.6 Escrow Agreement for Installment Real Estate Contract

The escrow agent (usually a bank) serves as a trustee for certain documents (warranty deed executed by the seller, fire and extended coverage insurance policy, or abstract of title). The escrow agent collects payments from the buyer and puts them in the seller's account. When the total due the seller by the buyer has been paid, all documents are delivered to the buyer, and the warranty deed which the agent was holding in trust is recorded. The escrow agent charges a monthly fee for this service. Who pays the fee is negotiable, but it is often paid one-half by the seller and one-half by the buyer. If payments are not made as required, the escrow agent gives notice of default to the buyer upon the request of the seller. The agreement often provides that if a lawyer is retained by the seller or the escrow agent to collect on the default, the buyer must pay the lawyer's fee.

All provisions of the agreement between the buyer and the seller are set out in an escrow agreement signed by all parties and acknowledged before a notary public.

The escrow agreement contains provisions that generally protect both the seller and the buyer. When the contract is paid, the buyer does not have to locate the seller for execution of a deed. The seller is protected because title is retained until full payment for the property has been received.

§ 17.9.7 Mortgage and Note for Purchase Money Mortgage

Once a buyer's loan application has been approved, the lender issues closing instructions which advise the closing lawyer or title company (if the title company handles the closing as escrow agent) of its requirements in connection with the loan. The duties of the closing lawyer may include preparation of the security instruments required by the lender. The promissory note and mortgage are prepared on preprinted or computer generated forms provided by the lending institution or on commercially prepared forms. In the case of FHA or VA insured loans, the note and mortgage are prepared on forms provided by the FHA or the VA. Until you are able to differentiate among these various forms, you should request the lawyer to specify the kind of forms needed for a particular transaction.

The person obligated to pay the amount specified in the promissory note is the maker, while the person or entity to whom the payment is made is the payee. Many of the terms of the promissory note are requirements of the lending institution and are provided to the lawyer in writing. The mortgage is prepared using the information contained in the promissory note, as well as information provided by the deed as to the names of the parties and the legal description. The mortgage secures payment of the promissory note by the maker. The person executing the mortgage and granting the security in their real estate is called the mortgagor while the lending institution is the mortgagee. A lending institution usually requires that its mortgage be the first lien against the premises, so the mortgage is generally recorded immediately after the deed is recorded. Should the mortgagor grant a subsequent or second mortgage on the premises, another promissory note and mortgage would be executed in compliance with the terms set forth by the lending institution or the individual taking the second mortgage.

The preparation of the mortgage documents follows the same principles as set forth below for the preparation of deeds. In addition, the mortgage may contain the terms of the loan as they appear in the promissory note. A mortgage and promissory note are executed only by the mortgagor in the same manner as deeds are executed.

§ 17.9.8 Deed of Trust

In some states, lending institutions hold a deed of trust to the property rather than a mortgage. They lend the money to the buyer. The buyer executes a deed of trust transferring the property in trust to the lending institution as security for the loan. In many states, only certain individuals or entities, such as a title company, bank or lending institution, or lawyer can serve as trustee. Normally the trustee is either an officer of or the lawyer for the lending institution. When the institution has been paid in full, the trustee executes a deed of release and reconveyance, returning title of the property to the buyer.

§ 17.9.9 Preparation of Deeds

In any transfer of real property, a deed (normally a warranty deed in residential transactions) is required. Regardless of the type of deed to be used in a given transaction, the preparation of deeds must be done precisely and with great attention to detail. Deeds should not contain any visible typographical corrections or "white-outs." In some jurisdictions, deeds containing such corrections are not recordable. The guidelines to be followed in the preparation of all deeds are:

1. The name of the seller must appear on the deed exactly as title was taken to the property. If the name of a seller appears in a different form on different documents, the preferred usage should be followed by the variant.

   EXAMPLE:

   John A. Smith a.k.a. Jon A. Smith; or Florence A. Jones formerly Florence A. Smith.

2. It may be necessary for the spouse of the seller to join in the conveyance and execute the deed even if the spouse is not listed as the title holder in the title evidence. (This requirement may vary from state to state, depending upon whether the state recognizes rights of dower or curtesy, or the property is homestead or non-homestead.)

3. The marital status of the seller must be shown.

   EXAMPLE:

   John A. Smith and Florence A. Smith, husband and wife; or John A. Smith, a single person.

4. If the seller is a corporation or a partnership, its name should be used as set forth in its articles of incorporation or articles of partnership.

   EXAMPLE:

   A.B.C. Inc., an Any State corporation; or Jones and Smith Company, an Any State general partnership.

5. If the seller is a trust, that fact should be shown.

   EXAMPLE:

   Jack Smith, Trustee under Agreement with Donald Smith, dated January 15, 1986.

6. The buyer's name should appear exactly as the buyer desires to take title. The lawyer's assistant should verify the correct spelling of the names of all buyers.

7. The deed must contain the exact legal description of the property being conveyed. The legal description should be taken from the title opinion or title insurance binder or commitment. Never rely upon a legal description taken from a tax statement. The legal description should be carefully proofread, preferably by reading it out loud to another lawyer's assistant, and all punctuation and capitalization must be exact. Legal descriptions should have lot and block numbers written followed by the numerals in parentheses.

   EXAMPLES:

   Lot Two (2), Block One (1), Easy Street Addition to Jonestown, Any County, Any State;

   or in the case of a metes and bounds description:

   The Southwest Quarter of the Northwest Quarter (SW¼ of the NW¼), Section One (1), Township Two (2) South, Range Three (3) West, Any City, Any County, Any State.

8. A deed is signed only by the seller. The name of the seller should be typed beneath the appropriate signature line. In some states this is mandatory.

9. Some states require that witnesses sign the deed as well. It is helpful if the witnesses' names are printed beneath their signatures.

10. A deed must be acknowledged by a notary public or other authorized person. The name of the grantor must appear in the acknowledgment exactly as it appears in the body of the deed. The notary public must date, sign, and affix his official seal to the deed. Some states also require that the notary's area of commission and the expiration date of the commission appear on the deed.

11. Many states require that the deed indicate the name and address of the person or firm drafting the deed and the name and address of the person or entity to whom future tax statements should be directed. (Since this is often the buyer, the address can be placed after the buyer's name.)

12. Some states require that the consideration shown on the warranty deed be the amount of the purchase price. In other states, a nominal consideration (usually $10) is stated along with the phrase "and other good and valuable consideration."

13. Consideration on a quitclaim deed is usually a nominal amount, such as $1.

§ 17.10 The Real Estate Closing

The closing is the formal meeting of all parties to the transaction at which documents are executed and funds disbursed. The location and mode of closing also vary greatly, depending upon local practice. In some states most closings are handled by title companies in their offices. In other states they are handled by law firms, lending institutions, or closers in the employ of the real estate broker. In still other states, a formal closing with all parties is not held; rather the parties individually deposit other closing deliveries, together with a closing instruction letter addressed to the title company or lawyers handling the transaction, which letter details the conditions under which the deliveries may be released to other party, and/or for filing. When all title matters are resolved, documents prepared, and financing arrangements finalized, a time for the closing is set. The lawyer carefully explains the meaning of each of the documents, supervises the execution thereof, and sometimes disburses the sale funds to the client through the trust account if a closing or escrow agent is not involved.

The closing statement is a detailed accounting of the credits and charges to the buyer and seller. In preparing the closing statement, the purchase agreement serves as the guideline for determining prorations and payoff figures. Illustrations 17–9 and 17–10 are sample buyer's and seller's closing statements for study and use. It should be noted that the earnest money or down payment is deducted from the purchase price. It is held in the trust account of the real estate broker or by the lawyer for the seller if no real estate broker is involved, or by the title company, and released to seller or buyer in accordance with the terms of the purchase agreement.

Probably the most commonly used closing statement form is the HUD–1 Settlement Statement issued by the United States Department of Housing and Urban Development. It is designed to meet the requirements of the federal Real Estate Procedures Act (RESPA). (*See* Illustration 17–11.)

Illustration 17–9

BUYER'S CLOSING STATEMENT

Seller: John Doe
Buyer: David Smith
Property: Lot 1, Block 2, Marigold Addition
Date: September 15, 20xx

Item	Debits	Credits
Purchase Price	$50,000.00	$
Earnest Money		5,000.00
First Mortgage Assumed		35,000.00
Interest		

Item	Debits	Credits
15 days at $7.67		115.05
Transfer tax		33.00
Abstracting charges		56.00
20xx real estate tax adjustment		
$750.00 ÷ 365 × 107 days =		219.35
Cash at closing		9,576.60
	$50,000.00	$50,000.00

Accepted:

________________________ ________________________

Buyer Seller

Note: The foregoing represents a simple buyer's closing statement and accordingly would not reflect such items as broker's commissions, etc. These would be contained in a separate seller's closing statement.

Buyer's credits against the purchase price may include adjustments for:

- Accrued real estate taxes for the year in which the transaction occurs (formula to be used in making this computation designated in the purchase agreement).
- Special assessments (again as provided for in the purchase agreement).
- Unearned rent for the remainder of the month (if the property is a rental unit).
- The amount to be carried on contract or the balance of the mortgage (if the transaction involves an installment contract or a mortgage assumption).
- Services rendered in repairing certain items on the premises or improvements made prior to closing.
- Discount points which the seller may be required to pay in order for buyer to obtain financing.

Buyer's expenses (debits) may include adjustments for:

- Lawyer's fees for examination of the title and preparation of title opinion.
- Preparation of the promissory note, mortgage, and other financing documents required for the closing.
- Closing services.
- Recording fees for the deed and mortgage.
- Mortgage registration tax.
- Abstracting expenses.

- Origination charge or service fee imposed by the lending institution according to the terms of the loan.
- Interest on the new loan should the lending institution require it.

EXAMPLE:

A transaction is closed on January 20. The first mortgage payment is due on March 1. The lender may require that interest accruing on the loan from January 20 through January 31 be paid at closing. (February interest is paid in the March 1 payment.)

- Any other expenses incurred by the buyer prior to closing

Illustration 17–10

SELLER'S CLOSING STATEMENT

Seller: John Doe
Buyer: David Smith
Property: Lot 1, Block 2, Marigold Addition, Street Address, City, State
Date: September 15, 20xx

Item	Debits	Credits
Purchase Price	$	$50,000.00
Existing Mortgage Assumed	35,000.00	
Interest adjustment		
15 days at $7.67	115.05	
Transfer tax	33.00	
Abstracting charges	56.00	
20xx real estate tax adjustment		
$750.00 ÷ 365 × 107 days =	219.35	
Real estate commission	3,500.00	
Balance due Seller	11,076.60	
	$50,000.00	$50,000.00

Accepted:

____________________ ____________________

Buyer Seller

Note: Earnest money paid by buyer is normally held in the broker's trust account pending closing. In this example, the seller will receive $9,576.60 from the buyer and the balance from the broker's trust account after deduction is made for the real estate commission.

The seller might receive credit for:

- Unearned insurance premiums (should a buyer assume existing insurance coverage on the property).

- Insurance reserves or escrows being held by a lending institution (which the buyer assumes by virtue of a mortgage assumption).

The seller's expenses usually include:

- The broker's commission (usually a percentage of the purchase price unless a flat sum has previously been agreed upon) (earnest money deposit may have already been credited).
- Abstracting charges.
- Recording charges for a release of mortgage or any documents necessary to clear title defects.
- Lawyer's fees applicable to seller for preparing a contract, deed, closing statement, and attendance at the closing.
- Transfer tax, if required by the city, county, or state in which the transaction is being closed.
- The balance due on any outstanding contract, including interest up to the date of payment, or the balance due on a mortgage, including interest up to the date of payoff.
- Any other expenses or liens as outlined or required by the purchase agreement, such as inspection fees, repair costs, and similar items.

A contract payoff is obtained from the contract seller or the seller's agent, and a mortgage payoff with per diem (daily) interest is available from the lending institution holding the mortgage.

Other adjustments might be necessary to a closing statement, depending upon the particular transaction and the terms of the purchase agreement.

Illustration 17–11

A. **Settlement Statement**

U.S. Department of Housing
and Urban Development

OMB No. 2502-0265

B. Type of Loan

1.☐ FHA 2.☐ FmHA 3.☐ Conv. Unins 4.☐ VA 5.☐ Conv. Ins.	6. File Number	7. Loan Number	8. Mortgage Insurance Case Number

C. Note: This form is furnished to give you a statement of actual settlement costs. Amounts paid to and by the settlement agent are shown. Items marked "(p.o.c.)" were paid outside the closing; they are shown here form information purposes and are not included in the totals.

D. Name and Address of Borrower	E. Name and Address of Seller	F. Name and Address of Lender

G. Property of Location	H. Settlement Agent	
	Place of Settlement	I. Settlement Date

J. Summary of Borrower's Transactions		K. Summary of Seller's Transaction	
100. Gross Amount Due from Borrower		**400. Gross Amount Due To Seller**	
101. Contract sales price		401. Contract Sales Price	
102. Personal Property		402. Personal Property	
103. Settlement Charges to Borrower (line 1400)		403.	
104.		404.	
105.		405.	
Adjustments for items paid by seller in advance		**Adjustments for items paid by seller in advance**	
106. City/town taxes		406. City/town taxes to	
107. County taxes to		407. County taxes to	
108. Assessments to		408. Assessments to	
109.		409.	
110.		410.	
111.		411.	
112.		412.	
120. Gross Amount Due From Borrower		**420. Gross Amount Due To Seller**	
200. Amount Paid By or in Behalf of Borrower		**500. Reductions in Amount Due To Seller**	
201. Deposit or earnest money		501. Excess deposit (see instructions)	
202. Prinicpal amount of new loan(s)		502. Settlement charges to seller (line 1400)	
203. Existing loan(s) taken subject to		503. Existing loan(s) taken subject to	
204.		504. Payoff of first mortgage loan	
205.		505. Payoff of second mortgage loan	
206.		506.	
207.		507.	
208.		508.	
209.		509.	
Adjustments for items unpaid by seller		**Adjustments for items unpaid by seller**	
210. City/town taxes to		510. City/town taxes to	
211. County taxes to		511. County taxes to	
212. Assessments to		512. Assessments to	
213.		513.	
214.		514.	
215.		515.	
216.		516.	
217.		517.	
218.		518.	
219.		519.	
220. Total Paid By/For Borrower		**520. Total Reduction Amount Due Seller**	
300. Cash At Settlement From/To Borrower		**600. Cash At Settlement To/From Seller**	
301. Gross Amount due from borrower (line 120)		601. Gross amount due to Seller (420)	
302. Less amounts paid by/for borrower (line 220)	( )	602 Less reductions in amt. due seller (line 520)	( )
303. Cash ☐ From ☐ To Borrower		603. Cash ☐ To ☐ From Seller	

Previous Edition Is Obsolete
ITEM 2384 (9301)

HUD-1 (3-86)
RESPA, HB 4305.2

L. Settlement Charges		
700. Total Sales/Broker's Commission based on Price @ =	Paid From Borrower's Funds at Settlement	Paid From Seller's Funds at Settlement
Division of Commission (line 700) as follows:		
701. to		
702. to		
703. Commission paid at Settlement		
704.		
800. Items Payable in Connection With Loan		
801. Loan Origination Fee		
802. Loan Discount		
803. Appraisal Fee to		
804. Credit Report to		
805. Lender's Inspection fee		
806. Mortgage Insurance Application Fee to		
807. Assumption Fee		
808.		
809.		
810.		
811.		
812.		
813.		
814.		
815.		
900. Items Required By Lender To Be Paid in Advance		
901. Interest from to @ /day		
902. Mortgage Insurance Premium for months to		
903. Hazard Insurance Premium for years to		
904. years to		
905.		
1000. Reserves Deposited With Lender		
1001. Hazard Insurance months @ per month		
1002. Mortgage Insurance months @ per month		
1003. City property taxes months @ per month		
1004. County property taxes months @ per month		
1005. Annual Assessments months @ per month		
1006. months @ per month		
1007. months @ per month		
1008. months @ per month		
1100. Title Charges		
1101. Settlement or closing fee to		
1102. Abstract or title search to		
1103. Title examination to		
1104. Title insurance binder to		
1105. Document preparation to		
1106. Notary fees to		
1107. Attorney's fees to		
(includes above items numbers:)		
1108. Title Insurance to		
(includes above items numbers:)		
1109. Lender's coverage		
1110. Owner's coverage		
1111.		
1112.		
1113.		
1200. Government Recording and Transfer Charges		
1201. Recording fees: Deed ; Mortgage Releases		
1202. City/county tax/stamps: Deed ; Mortgage		
1203. State tax/stamps: Deed ; Mortgage		
1204.		
1205.		
1300. Additional Settlement Charges		
1301. Survey to		
1302. Pest Inspection to		
1303.		
1304.		
1305.		
1400. Total Settlement Charges (enter on lines 103, Section J and 502, Section K)		

I have carefully reviewed the HUD-1 Settlement Statement and to the best of my knowledge and belief, it is true and accurate statement of all receipts and disbursements made on my account or by me in this transaction. I further certify that I have received a copy of HUD-1 Settlement Statement

Borrowers

Sellers

The HUD-1 Settlement Statement which I have prepared is a true and accurate account of this transaction. I have caused or will cause the funds to be disbursed in accordance with this statement.

Settlement Agent

Date

WARNING: It is a crime to knowingly make false statements to the United States on this or any other similar form. Penalties upon conviction can include a fine or imprisonment. For details see: Title 18 U.S. Code Section 1001 and Section 1010.

§ 17.10.1 Recording of Documents

Transfer of title occurs at the time an executed deed is delivered to and accepted by the buyer or agent. A security interest (mortgage or other financing arrangement) becomes effective at the time the documents are executed and the funds disbursed. Recording is not necessary to complete the transfer of title between the parties; however, it is necessary to protect the buyer against a second fraudulent sale by the seller and against any liens which may accrue against the property while it is still recorded in the seller's name. Likewise, the mortgagee will want to have its security interest placed of record to protect it from subsequent security interests. Hence, the time of recording becomes essential in determining the priority of each of the liens or claims against the real estate. It is important, therefore, to record documents as soon as possible after the completion of a transaction.

The recording of documents is a function which will frequently be delegated to the lawyer's assistant. The requirements for recording and fees charged for recording vary greatly from state to state and from county to county. In some states documents are returned to the person filing them after the recording process is complete, while in other states they are not. Documents filed under the Torrens system are never returned to the filer.

§ 17.10.2 Exchanges of Real Estate

To delay the payment of taxes, sometimes owners of real estate will exchange one piece of real estate for another. These transactions are referred to as "like kind exchanges" or "1031 exchanges." Real estate can be exchanged directly between owners, but more often an intermediary is used to facilitate a like kind exchange. The tax code governs the timing and methods of like kind exchanges.

§ 17.10.3 The Role of the Investor

Although the majority of residential financing is originated on the local level, unless the financing is arranged through a local savings and loan association (and sometimes certain banks), once the loan has been made and the legal work completed, the loan is often sold to an investor who is in the business of buying these loans. This is particularly common with VA and FNMA loans. In this instance the investor may, for a fee, retain the local lender to service the loan, that is, the local lender collects the monthly payment from the buyer and handles any day-to-day problems that might arise. Most mortgagors are not even aware that their loans are not owned by the lender servicing them.

§ 17.10.4 Miscellaneous Matters

The practice of real estate law is not limited to the representation of clients buying or selling property.

§ 17.10.5 Leases

A lease is a contract between the landlord (lessor) and the tenant (lessee) whereby the landlord conveys the use of real estate to another for a specific term at a particular rent subject to certain conditions. Many commercially printed lease forms are available from legal stationers. These forms may be used in their entirety or adjusted to use only particular sections in preparation of custom-drafted instruments, depending upon the needs of the client. A lawyer drafts the lease to protect their client and includes those clauses and phrases beneficial to the client. Commercially printed lease forms generally favor the landlord. Certain statutory provisions and court decisions also govern the rights of the landlord and tenant in such contracts.

A lease also contains specific provisions relating to the permitted use(s) of the premises during the term of the lease, which vary depending upon the circumstances.

§ 17.10.6 Real Estate in Litigation

Real estate may also become the subject of litigation for a variety of reasons. One of the most common reasons is a lawsuit brought to establish the proper ownership of a parcel of real estate that has not been registered (i.e. there is no Certificate of Title). Usually such a lawsuit has its basis in a title defect. A lawsuit of this kind is called an action to quiet title. Lawsuits may also result from boundary disputes, fraudulent conveyances, or misrepresentations made during a sale, as well as many other reasons.

§ 17.11 Summary

The foregoing is by no means exhaustive of all real estate matters that will confront the lawyer's assistant. Additional information will be acquired from each transaction in which a lawyer's assistant is involved; and, as skill and knowledge increase, the lawyer's assistant will become increasingly valuable in this area of law.

CHAPTER 18

ESTATE PLANNING

Table of Sections

---

§ 18.1 Introduction

The area of law dealing with the disposition of a person's property after their death is known as estate planning. There are many techniques available to a lawyer to tailor a plan to achieve the client's desired distribution of property while minimizing death taxes and administration expenses. The most common document utilized in estate planning is the last will and testament, or more simply, a will. However, many people create living trusts that will enable them to avoid probate of their assets upon death and also avoid the necessity of having to establish a guardianship or conservatorship during their lifetime, should they become incapacitated. Of course, the trust agreement can have many technical features to minimize death taxes and take care of the special needs of the trustor or the trustor's family. Wills and trusts both have their places in the estate planning field. Even if a trust is executed and funded, it is still important for the testator to execute a will to take care of any assets that may not have been transferred to the trust.

§ 18.2 Importance of Accuracy and Proper Execution

A will or trust agreement is one of the most important legal documents that is prepared in the law office. Not only is it extremely important that the document be prepared properly, it must be executed with extreme care to protect the party making the will or trust. An error or omission could result in a lawsuit and expenditures of large sums of money for lawyer's fees and court costs, and even more important, the wishes of the decedent might not be carried out.

§ 18.3 Definitions

A will is a legal document in which a person provides for the disposition of their property (estate) to take effect after their death. A testator is the person (male or female) who makes a will.

A trust creates a fiduciary relationship with regards to property, where the legal title is with the trustee, but the benefit of ownership is with another person. A trust must be intentionally created. The person who benefits from the trust is called the "beneficiary." The maker of the trust is called a "grantor," "trustor," or "settlor." The relationship of the trust imposes "fiduciary" duties on the trustee.

§ 18.4 Power and Capacity to Make a Will

In order for a will to be valid, the testator must have both the power and capacity to make a will. In most states the testator has the power to make a will if he or she has reached legal age. (*See* the chapter on Courts for a more complete discussion of legal age.) The age at which a minor may make a will varies from state to state. Generally, minors and adults under legal disability (incapacitated or incompetent) do not possess the power to make a will. Possession of the requisite capacity to make a will means that the testator is of sound mind, knows the extent of their assets, who their natural heirs are, knows the disposition they want to make of any personal assets, and that they intend to make a will.

§ 18.5 Terminology

Those persons named in a will to receive property are beneficiaries. Gifts of real estate by a will are devises, and the recipients of such gifts are devisees. A person may gift personal property by will also, and the personal property that is transferred is known as a bequest. Money passing under a will is known as a legacy and the recipient as a legatee. The words "legacy" and "legatee" are commonly used to designate other kinds of personal property as well. In states that have adopted the Uniform Probate Code (UPC), all recipients of property under a will are referred to as devisees, regardless of whether they receive real or personal property. More information concerning the UPC is given in the chapter on Estates and Guardianships.

If a testator gives specific property in their will but no longer owns the property at the time of their death, an ademption occurs. This simply means that the particular legacy is extinguished, and that provision of the will can be ignored. The remainder of the will is not affected by the ademption.

In addition to the distribution of the property, the testator also names a person(s) or entity (usually a bank with a trust department or independent trust company) to administer the terms of their will and distribute their estate. That person or entity is called the executor. Under the UPC, the person or entity is referred to as the personal representative. If the testator has minor children, they may also designate a guardian for those children.

The supervision of an estate by an administrator or executor is called "administration."

If a person dies without a will the court probate process is called an administration and the fiduciary appointed by the court is called an administrator.

§ 18.6 Characteristics of a Will

Regardless of the type of will you are preparing, there are certain requirements that control the preparation of all wills:

- Opening clause (preamble) stating domicile and declaring the document to be the testator's last will.
- Clause identifying spouse and children.

- Clause(s) relating to the payment of testator's debts, death taxes, expenses of administration, etc.
- Clause(s) directing the disposition of the testator's property.
- Clause nominating the estate's personal representative.
- Signature and attestation clause (for testator and witnesses.)

All wills prepared by lawyers will contain these basic elements. There may be many additional provisions, and these basic elements may be expanded to accommodate the testator's individual needs.

§ 18.6.1 Opening and Domicile Clause of a Will (Preamble)

The opening clause of a will gives the testator's name and domicile, and it revokes any earlier wills or codicils that may exist. The revocation clause (revoking earlier wills and codicils) should be a part of every will whether or not the testator remembers executing a previous will. A will, of course, does not become effective until the death of the testator, and, until that time, a competent testator may take any action or make any changes desired.

The place of the decedent's domicile should not be confused with the place of residence. It is quite possible to have several residences, but one may have only one domicile. The place of domicile at the time of death determines the location of the primary probate proceeding as well as the state that collects the major portion of state death taxes. A classic example of a dilemma that can be created relating to domicile is the estate of the late billionaire, Howard Hughes. Mr. Hughes died without a will and lived in several states, apparently without firmly establishing domicile in any one. Three different states alleged that his domicile was in their state. Millions of dollars in state death taxes were at stake, and the matter was in litigation for several years.

§ 18.6.2 Identification of Family

In some states, if the testator fails to name and specifically make provisions for one's spouse, this voids the will as to the spouse, who then takes by intestate succession according to the laws of descent in the state of domicile. If children are not named, they may claim a portion of the estate as a pretermitted heir if there is no surviving spouse.

§ 18.6.3 Payment of Debts Clause of a Will

The clause(s) relating to the payment of debts, expenses, and taxes, gives the estate's personal representative specific direction as to whether the general estate or specific gifts will pay these items. The direction relating to death taxes (inheritance, estate, etc.) is of particular importance, as it determines whether such taxes will be paid from estate funds or charged to the beneficiaries of the estate.

§ 18.6.4 Disposition of Property Clause of a Will

The disposition of property is divided into two basic kinds—specific bequests or devises (also called preresiduary gifts) and residuary bequests or devises.

§ 18.6.5 Specific Bequest Clause of a Will

A specific bequest is a gift of an identified asset or stated amount of money.

EXAMPLE:

> I give and bequeath to my daughter, Jane Doe, my sterling silver flatware.
>
> I give and bequeath to my friend, John Smith, the sum of $10,000.

Some states allow the disposition of tangible personal property by reference in the will to a separate written document.

§ 18.6.6 Residuary Bequest Clause of a Will

A residuary bequest is a gift of the remaining assets of the estate.

EXAMPLE:

> All of the rest, residue, and remainder of my property, real, personal, or mixed, wherever situated, I give, devise, and bequeath to my daughters, Jane Doe and Mary Doe, in equal shares, or to the survivor of them.

The residue of an estate is what is left over after the payment of debts, expenses, taxes, and specific bequests. If the estate's assets are depleted entirely by payment of the debts, expenses, taxes, and specific bequests, there is no residue to distribute, so the residuary beneficiaries receive nothing.

§ 18.6.7 Appointment of Personal Representative

The clause relating to the testator's choice of personal representative (and frequently an alternate) may also include statements as to the specific powers granted to the representative. A testator may want to give the representative a great deal of leeway and may fully outline the powers. This enables the representative to go about the business of administering the estate without requesting the power from the Court for each transaction. A will may designate that the representative need not provide a bond with surety. Some states now provide that representatives have statutory powers regardless of whether or not they are set forth in the will. (More information on the administration of wills is given in the chapter on Estates and Guardianships.)

§ 18.6.8 Signature Lines of a Will

The signature area of the will is an important one, since virtually all jurisdictions require that a will be signed by the testator. The date of the signing is also important since, if more than one will is found after the testator's death, the one bearing the most recent date controls.

§ 18.6.9 Attestation Clause of a Will

The attestation clause of the will is the section where the witnesses sign the will. Most states require that wills be executed in the presence of at least two witnesses. In addition to the act of witnessing the execution, the witnesses also usually attest to the fact that the testator declared that this was their will and requested the individuals present to witness it.

All wills drafted by lawyers contain these basic elements, although many are a great deal more sophisticated than the illustration in § 18.19.

§ 18.6.10 Self–Proving Affidavit

Most states acknowledge the addition of an affidavit at the end of the will that is signed by the witnesses and acknowledged by a notary at the time the will is signed by the testator. This affidavit, in most states, will allow the will to be admitted into probate without having to have one of the attesting witnesses sign and file a separate affidavit or testify in court. In some states this may be accomplished by attaching a separate affidavit of attesting witnesses to the will.

§ 18.6.11 Possession of the Will

One important characteristic of a will is that it is the personal possession of the testator. The testator may designate who shall hold the will, and may request possession of the document at any time. Because of the very personal nature of a will, should the testator desire to revoke the will, they must do so personally. A will may be revoked by mutilation, cancellation, destruction, or execution of a new will. A revoked will must be destroyed by the person making the will.

§ 18.7 Types of Wills

There are many types of wills that are used for different purposes. Many of the more sophisticated wills are written to achieve favorable death tax consideration and will involve the use of various kinds of trusts. A will may also contain trust provisions for minor children to avoid distributing estate assets into a guardianship for a minor child or to a child when the child attains majority (18 or 21 years of age, depending upon state law) because the testator may feel that a child is not ready to handle such sums of money at their present age.

§ 18.7.1 Simple Will

Most wills that the lawyer's assistant prepares will be drafted by lawyers. This chapter deals primarily with those types of wills, although more unusual kinds of wills are defined. A typical simple will is shown in Illustration 18–1. This will contains all of the necessary elements mentioned earlier in the chapter.

Illustration 18–1

LAST WILL AND TESTAMENT OF JANE A. DOE

I, Jane A. Doe, domiciled in Any County, State of Anystate, do hereby make, with complete testamentary intent and capacity, my Last Will and Testament, hereby revoking all former wills and codicils.

ARTICLE I

Identification of Family

My immediate family now consists of my husband, John J. Doe, and my three (3) children: Paul Doe, born March 3, 1973; Elizabeth Doe, born July 14, 1975; and Ryan Doe, born October 7, 1977.

ARTICLE II

I direct my executor to pay all funeral expenses, expenses of administration, and my just debts, if any, except such as are at the time of my death specific liens upon property holdings, which my executor is authorized to continue in force if and for so long as, in his judgment, it is necessary or desirable.

ARTICLE III

I direct that all estate, inheritance, legacy, and death taxes imposed on account of my death, whether or not accruing against property or insurance proceeds not part of my probate estate, be paid from the residue of my estate passing under Article VI, without apportionment. There shall be no obligation resting on anyone to contribute to the payment of said taxes, and my Personal Representative shall have no duty to secure reimbursement to my estate on account of taxes so paid.

ARTICLE IV

I give and devise any homestead, including contiguous land used in connection therewith, which I may own at the time of my death to my husband, John J. Doe, outright. Should my husband not survive me, this devise shall lapse, and said homestead shall be added to and be distributed with the residue of my estate. [Optional unless required by statute.]

ARTICLE V

I give and bequeath to my husband, John J. Doe, all of the household furniture and furnishings, automobiles, musical instruments, books, pictures, jewelry, watches, silverware, wearing apparel, and all other articles of household or personal use or adornment that I own at my date of death. In the event he shall not survive me, then I give all of said property to my children or to the survivor or survivors of them, in equal shares.

ARTICLE VI

All the rest, residue, and remainder of my property, real, personal or mixed, wheresoever situated, I give and devise to my husband, John J. Doe; but if he does not survive me, I direct that my Personal Representative distribute said property to my children, Paul Doe, Elizabeth Doe, and Ryan Doe, in equal shares, or to their issue by right of representation.

ARTICLE VII

I nominate, constitute, and appoint my husband, John J. Doe, personal representative of my estate to serve without bond. If my husband predeceases me or is unable or unwilling to serve, then I appoint Brian Doe as personal representative. I grant my personal representative the power to do without court order any of the acts permitted a personal representative pursuant to the statutes of that state of Anywhere.

ARTICLE VIII

In the event my husband and I die under such circumstances that the order of our deaths may not be conveniently determined, I direct that the distribution of my estate under this Will shall be made as if my husband predeceased me.

IN WITNESS WHEREOF, I have hereunto set my hand to this my Last Will and Testament this ______ day of ______, [*year*].

____

Jane A. Doe

This instrument, consisting of ______ typewritten pages, including this certificate, each bearing the signature of the above named, Jane A. Doe, was by her on the date hereof signed. We believe her to be of sound and disposing mind and memory and have hereunto subscribed our names as witnesses.

______________________ Residing at ______________________
____

______________________ Residing at ______________________
____

STATE OF __________
COUNTY OF __________

We, Jane A. Doe, ______, and ______, the Testator and the witnesses, respectively, whose names are signed to the attached or foregoing instrument, being first duly sworn, do hereby declare to the undersigned authority that the Testator signed and executed this instrument as her last will and that she had signed willingly or directed another to sign for her, and that she executed it as her free and voluntary act for the purposes therein expressed; and that each of the witnesses, in the presence and hearing of the Testator, signed the will as witness and that to the best of their knowledge, the Testator was at that time 18 or more years of age, of sound mind, and under no constraint or undue influence.

____
Testator

____
Witness

____
Witness

[Signature of Testator not required on the affidavit in many states.]

Subscribed, sworn to and acknowledged before me by Jane A. Doe, the Testator, and subscribed and sworn to before me by ______ and ______ witnesses, this ______ day of ______, *[year]*.

____
Notary Public

The foregoing will is a sample of a simple will. Many times additional paragraphs will be added to wills to provide for the appointment of a guardian or a trust for minor children. Trust provisions for minor children do not have to be complicated and can continue beyond the time a minor child becomes of age. If funds are not left to a trust but are distributed to a guardianship for the estate of a minor child, then the funds must be distributed to said child upon attaining majority, even though that child may not have a full understanding of handling money, business, etc.

§ 18.7.2 Holographic Will

A holographic will is one completely handwritten by the testator and signed without the benefit of statutory formalities. State law regarding the circumstances under which holographic wills are valid vary greatly, although many states make provision for holographic wills under certain circumstances.

§ 18.7.3 Oral Wills (Nuncupative and Soldiers' and Sailors')

Two kinds of oral wills are recognized by some states—nuncupative wills and soldiers' and sailors' wills. A nuncupative will is a will spoken by a person in peril of imminent death. Usually, the witnesses to whom it was spoken must reduce it to writing within a limited time frame. Soldiers' and sailors' wills are oral dispositions made by soldiers in actual military service or sailors at sea.

Again, the requirements and recognition of these wills vary greatly in the states in which they are permitted. Since oral wills offer the open opportunity for fraud, all states in which they are recognized restrict severely the value of assets to pass under them and restrict it to personal property. In those states in which the Uniform Probate Code has been adopted only written wills are permitted.

§ 18.7.4 Contingent or Conditional Wills

Contingent or conditional wills do not take effect unless a specific event occurs. Therefore, if the event does not occur, it is as though there is no will. Most states do not recognize contingent wills.

§ 18.7.5 Joint Wills

Sometimes two or more persons execute a joint will, that is, two or more people execute the same document. These are not widely used since problems often arise if circumstances change and one testator desires to change the terms or revoke the instrument. Many states do not favor joint wills.

§ 18.7.6 Codicils

A codicil to a will literally means a "little will." It is an amendment, afterthought, postscript, addition, supplement, or change to the original will. It must be prepared, executed, and witnessed with all the formality of the original will.

§ 18.8 Preparation of Wills

A person's will is a very personal matter, and it must be drafted to meet the individual needs of the client. Most law offices will have a compilation of standard will clauses in their computer forms file. Some clauses are not standard and need to be dictated by the lawyer.

§ 18.8.1 Will Paper

Many law firms use special paper, manuscript covers, and envelopes in preparing wills. If your office does not, you should prepare wills on non-erasable bond paper.

§ 18.8.2 Printed Forms

Occasionally, the lawyer's assistant may encounter a homemade or printed form of will. Such wills should be used with caution as the forms available at the drugstore or through mail order houses obviously cannot be adapted carefully to a particular case. Such wills, by their very nature, must be general and may not be in accordance with the statutes of the state in which they are executed. It is very important that the will that is executed be entirely valid so that the testator's wishes will be honored after death. A will that is successfully contested or proved invalid is inadmissible to probate, and the decedent's assets will be disposed of according to the laws of descent in the state of domicile.

§ 18.8.3 Corrections to Wills

Take special care in the spelling of names, figures, and words that could change the meaning of the will provisions. If you are setting forth percentages or fractions, make sure they equal 100 percent or a whole unit. If a correction must be made at the time the will is signed, the correction should be written out by the testator and then initialed by the testator and the witnesses. This type of correction could include changing the year at the beginning of a new year, a middle initial, etc. The best way to make corrections, however, is to revise and reprint the page before the testator signs.

§ 18.8.4 Numbering Paragraphs and Pages

Within the body of the will, each clause should be numbered with a Roman numeral or other designation used in your locality. The pages should be numbered. At the bottom of each page there may be a signature line for the testator or there may be places for the testator and witnesses to initial each page. If this is the practice of your firm, you should include the appropriate line(s) for the testator's signature, initials, etc., in the footer of your document.

§ 18.8.5 Ending a Page

It is best not to complete an item at the bottom of a page. Never type the signature or attestation clause on a page separate from the remainder of the will. While no one anticipates that a person would attempt to substitute pages in a will after it has been executed, following this procedure will make such an attempt more difficult. The self-proving affidavit of attesting witnesses can be on a separate page as long as they will be signing the affidavit.

§ 18.8.6 Execution of Wills

Wills should be executed under the supervision of a lawyer. The lawyer's assistant may, however, be called upon to serve as a witness. The number of witnesses necessary will vary from state to state as mentioned earlier.

The testator should declare that the instrument is, in fact, their will. It is preferable, and in some states mandatory, that none of the witnesses be beneficiaries or parties with a financial interest in the estate. Usually, they need not be aware of the contents of the will. Each witness should sign their name and address in the presence of the testator and should initial each page, if requested. Most states require that the witnesses and the testator sign in the presence of each other, so it is a good practice not to leave the room or attend to other business while executing a will. Only the necessary parties, *i.e.*, the testator, the lawyer, the witnesses, and the notary public should be in the room during the execution process. Once these people enter the room, the door should be closed, and no one should be permitted to leave until the task of execution is complete. The will should be dated correctly and checked after execution as to the accuracy and completeness of the execution. Only the original of the will should be executed, although file copies should be conformed to reflect the date of execution, witnesses, etc., or copies made for the lawyer's file. Lawyer's assistants should be aware that the procedures described here are merely illustrative and should learn the formal requirements for execution of wills in their state. The formal requirements do vary and are important, as a will could be contested for failure to meet those requirements.

§ 18.9 Intestate

Intestate means having made no will. A person who dies having made no will is referred to as having died intestate.

§ 18.10 Types of Trusts

There are two types of trusts—revocable and irrevocable. A revocable trust is one that can be revoked or amended by the trustor at any time prior to death. An irrevocable trust cannot be revoked by the trustor and cannot be materially changed once it is executed. A trust is presumed to be irrevocable unless it is expressly stated to be revocable. A trust can be established between the trustor and the trustee during the lifetime of the trustor, or it can be established through the trustor's will to take effect upon the trustor's death. In order to establish a trust, the trustor must have the legal capacity to transfer the property to the trustee.

Irrevocable trusts are generally made for tax reasons, and the trustor transfers all ownership rights in and all power over their property to the trustee so that the assets in the trust will not be included as part of the taxable estate for estate tax purposes at the time of the trustor's death. There are numerous types of irrevocable trusts used in sophisticated estate planning techniques beyond the scope of this chapter.

In a revocable trust, the trustor generally maintains some power over the trust as long as they are alive and not incapacitated. Once the maker dies or becomes incapacitated, the terms of the trust become irrevocable and cannot be changed without court order.

The trustor can be more than one person, and the trustee can be more than one person, or it can be an entity, such as the trust department of a bank.

§ 18.10.1 Classifications of Trusts

Most trusts are active trusts in which the trustee has some additional duty other than just transferring the property to the beneficiary.

Testamentary trusts are created under a will, and *inter vivos* or living trusts are created during the lifetime of the trustor.

Express restrictions are usually included in a trust to limit access to trust assets by a beneficiary and existing creditors. These restrictions are referred to as spendthrift provisions.

In revocable trusts, standby trust provisions permit the trustor to retain control over the trust assets during their lifetime, unless they become disabled or request the trustee to assume management of the trust. Income is taxed to the trustor, and the assets are included in the trustor's estate for federal estate tax purposes at the time of death. No gift tax liability is created.

A joint interest trust is created when two trustors place jointly held assets in a trust. The income and principal are distributed by the trustee according to the terms of the trust. This type of trust is quite often used for a husband and wife so that they do not have to establish two separate trusts. When one of the trustors dies, that share of the trust property passes as the trust agreement dictates.

In a revocable trust where the trustor and trustee are the same person, the trust does not need to file separate fiduciary income tax returns, and the income is included on the trustor's individual income tax returns. If the trustor and trustee are not the same person, the Internal Revenue Code requires that the trust obtain a federal identification number and file its own fiduciary income tax returns.

A qualified terminable interest provision in a trust (or even in a will) permits property to qualify for a marital deduction, if the spouse has use of the property for life and other Internal Revenue Code requirements are met. The personal representative or trustee is given the option to make this election, and the election is made on the decedent's federal estate tax return. If the election is not made on a return which is timely filed, the election is lost and not available.

§ 18.10.2 Powers and Duties of Trustee

The powers, duties, and liabilities of a trustee are interrelated. The trust instrument usually sets forth the trustee's powers. Most states have statutory laws that regulate a trustee's powers, duties, and liabilities. Generally it is not necessary for a trustee to post a bond or make accountings to a court, such as may be required by a personal representative. A trustee is accountable to the trustor and beneficiaries during the trustor's lifetime and to the beneficiaries after the trustor's death.

§ 18.10.3 Funding the Trust

A trust agreement can be executed by the trustor, but until the assets are actually placed in the trustee's name and delivered to the trustee, the trust is not activated. In other words, if the trustor makes a trust agreement but does not deed any real property to the trust or place existing bank accounts, securities, and other personal property in the trustee's name, then these assets remain in the individual's name and are not subject to the terms of the trust. If these assets have not been transferred to the trust, they are treated like any other asset at the time of the trustor's death and may have to be probated. That is why it is important that a trustor also execute a will, so that in the event there are any assets that are not in the trust they can be distributed to the trust and become a part of the trust estate. This type of will is often referred to as a "pourover" will because it simply pours the decedent's assets over to the trust.

It is a good idea for the lawyer to keep in a client's file a letter, memorandum, or other written evidence of what assets the lawyer has assisted the client in transferring to the trust and what assets the client is going to handle personally. This could be very beneficial to the lawyer after the trustor's death if the beneficiaries bring a claim against the lawyer for not transferring estate assets to the trust.

§ 18.10.4 Trust Termination

The trustor can revoke a trust, so long as the power of revocation is according to the trust terms. Generally a trust is terminated in accordance with the trust provisions, although it can be terminated differently, with the consent of all of the beneficiaries, if no material trust purpose is defeated by such termination.

§ 18.11 Other Estate Planning Documents

Many other documents may be executed by the client at the time of the signing of the will or trust agreement. Many people now desire to execute health care powers of attorney. This kind of power of attorney permits the attorney-in-fact to make health care decisions on behalf of the maker in the event the maker is unable to make these decisions personally. A health care power of attorney should not be confused with a living will. In a living will, the maker instructs the physician or medical supplier not to keep the maker alive by the use of life-supporting procedures. The living will is an essential document as most courts will enforce the provisions of a valid living will.

A durable power of attorney is used quite often in estate planning. A durable power of attorney is given to another, usually a spouse, child, or entity, which empowers that person to act on behalf of the maker, even if the maker has become incapacitated. If the maker has established a trust and has not transferred all existing assets to the trust, a general durable power of attorney would permit the agent to transfer the assets, so that the assets would become part of the trust estate and subject to the trust provisions. It is important that the power of attorney include language that it will be effective even if the maker is incapacitated, or it will not qualify as a durable power of attorney, and the agent will not be able to continue to act under the provisions of the power of attorney.

§ 18.12 Elder Law

The area of elder law developed as a response to the changing demographics of American society. It is sometimes defined as a practice of law focused on the unique concerns of that particular segment of the population over the age of 50. Lawyers who practice in this area are attuned to the social, medical, and legal aspects of complex issues facing the elderly and their families. Such issues include:

- Planning for disability.
- Estate planning and management.
- Estate tax and gift tax issues.
- Medicaid and Medicare issues.
- Age discrimination in housing and employment.
- Personal injury.
- Guardianships.
- Living wills or advance health care directives.
- Durable power of attorney.

- Health care power of attorney.

§ 18.13 Meeting the Needs of Clients and the Community

As you can see, estate planning is not something to take lightly. The client trusts the lawyer to do what is best, and the lawyer needs to be knowledgeable in order to help the client. If the lawyer is not trained in this area, the best thing for the client and for the legal profession in general, is to refer the client to a lawyer who can provide the client with the best estate planning results. Just like other areas of the law, because there are many things to be considered for some estate plans, it is impossible for all lawyers to know what will work best unless they specialize in estate and tax planning.

What can you do, as a lawyer's assistant, to help the lawyer? You can make sure that the documents are prepared as accurately as possible and that the file contains documents and written data as to what the lawyer is to do for the client and also stating what is not to be done. If you think a paragraph in a will or trust agreement does not make sense, bring this to the lawyer's attention. If you do not believe the will or trust agreement includes all of the provisions it should, ask the lawyer about it. This is just a way of double checking to make sure that the documents contain all of the necessary language in order to carry out the wishes of the client. Remember, most of the time these documents are not used until the client is either deceased or incapacitated, and then it is too late to make the corrections that should have been included prior to signing.

CHAPTER 19

ESTATES AND GUARDIANSHIPS

Table of Sections

---

§ 19.1 Introduction

When a person dies, it is necessary that an orderly disposition be made of that person's property. The person who dies is called the decedent or the deceased. The property the decedent owned at death is referred to as the decedent's estate or probate property.

Probate assets are those assets that generally require some type of proceeding in the appropriate court of jurisdiction to determine their proper distribution. Probate property consists of those items of property owned solely by the decedent or in which the decedent owned an interest as a tenant in common, or an interest in community property, and life insurance proceeds payable to the executor, administrator, or personal representative of the decedent's estate.

Estate administration or probate proceedings are the terms most often used to refer to proceedings that are brought for the purpose of distribution of the estate. The persons or entities that become owners of the decedent's probate estate after the completion of probate proceedings are called the beneficiaries. The persons or institutions who manage money or property for another and who must exercise a standard of care imposed by law, *i.e.,* personal representative or executor of an estate, trustee, etc., are called fiduciaries. It should be noted that fiduciaries also handle the affairs of living persons, *i.e.,* wards, minors, etc.

Non-probate property consists of those assets owned by the decedent and others in joint tenancy, life insurance, and other property payable under a contract to specific beneficiaries other than the decedent's estate, and property titled in *inter vivos* and Totten trusts, all of which are transferred automatically to the recipient without passing through probate. An *inter vivos* trust is one created by, and which becomes operative during, the decedent's lifetime. A Totten trust is a trust created upon the deposit by the decedent of money in their own name as trustee for another. It may be revoked at will until decedent's death, when it automatically becomes the property of the named beneficiary.

The legal process involved in handling a decedent's estate is one that laymen tend to find tedious and burdensome. In fact, laymen sometimes face estate administration with a great deal of apprehension because of the misinformation they have received that avoiding probate is desirable. Actually, the legal process is a very orderly one that can save the heirs many tax dollars. It is often the first contact that the survivors have with the court system. Also, the event that necessitates this kind of proceeding is one of the most traumatic in any of our lives—the death of a loved one. It is very important that the lawyer's assistant have an understanding of estate administration, so as to deal intelligently and compassionately with the client who is a member of the decedent's family.

§ 19.2 The Uniform Probate Code

The Uniform Probate Code (UPC) adopted by the National Conference of Commissioners on Uniform State Laws has been adopted by most states. Some states have adopted the Code with some modifications or have adopted only certain parts of it. The purpose of the Uniform Probate Code is to make it possible for estates to be administered in the same fashion in all states and to streamline the entire procedure. There has been a great deal of criticism from the public that the probate process is too involved and bureaucratic and permits the courts to become involved in matters in which they need not be involved.

The Uniform Probate Code provides for informal proceedings in some cases that can be handled without the assistance of a lawyer or with only minimal lawyer involvement. This greatly reduces the expenses of administering an estate. The Uniform Probate Code also provides for totally supervised court proceedings in the traditional manner. Accordingly, the heirs, representative, lawyer, and court have the option of determining whether or not the estate should be administered under the informal proceedings or under the formal provisions of the Code.

§ 19.3 Classification

For purposes of handling the decedent's probate estate, the estate is classified in one of two ways: testate or intestate.

If the decedent had a will, the decedent died testate. A will is a document by which an individual can provide for the disposition of property after death. Those persons named in the will to receive some portion of the estate are beneficiaries. Gifts of real estate by a will are known as devises, and the recipient of such gifts are devisees. A person may bequeath personal property (movable property as distinguished from real estate) to another by will. Personal property so transferred is a legacy, and the recipient of the property is a legatee. The terms "legacy" and "devise" and "legatee" and "devisee" are now used interchangeably in many jurisdictions. Under the Uniform Probate Code all gifts made by will are known as devises, and the recipient is the devisee, regardless of whether or not the gifts consist of real or personal property.

§ 19.3.1 Locating the Will

If the decedent died testate, it is necessary to locate the original will so it can be presented to the appropriate court for probate. Probate of the will is its presentation to the court to have it declared valid. It is important to note, however, that the word "probate" is now used to mean all proceedings concerning the administration of estates.

If the decedent was a client of the law firm, you should review all of the client's files, as they frequently contain information that will be necessary in the administration of the estate. The files may contain a copy of the decedent's will. If they do, you should have copies available at the initial conference with the personal representative, together with any information as to the location of the original.

It is the custom for the lawyer to hold the original will for the client. Some lawyers are hesitant to do this since a will belongs to the testator (person who makes the will), and one important characteristic of a will is that it is a personal possession of the testator. The testator may designate who will hold the will and may request possession of the document at any time. Because of the very personal nature of a will, should the testator desire to revoke the will, it must be done personally. A will may be revoked by mutilation, cancellation, destruction, or execution of a new will. A will must be destroyed by the testator. In many wills, the first paragraph is a revocation of all prior wills. A will, which was unintentionally destroyed by the testator, may still be probated if the contents can be established to the satisfaction of the jurisdictional court. Marriage or divorce subsequent to the date of the will, however, may modify the terms of the will.

Some people place their wills in their safe deposit boxes, in home safes, or even in desk drawers at home. If the family believes that the decedent left a will, it is incumbent upon them to search through decedent's personal belongings until they find it. Sometimes the decedent's will is stored in a safe deposit box, which may be sealed by state law upon decedent's death, requiring that the lawyer and family follow special procedures to obtain access to the will.

An amendment, addition, or supplement to a will is known as a codicil or literally a "little will." If there are one or more codicils in existence, they will be subject to the same rules and treatment as wills in the probate proceedings.

If the decedent did not leave a will, the decedent died intestate. The estate is then administered and distributed according to the laws of the state of domicile.

§ 19.3.2 Determination of Heirship

Proof of heirship is the judicial determination of the identity of those persons who are entitled to inherit the decedent's property under state law if the decedent dies intestate. In many states this proof is an essential part of the probate proceeding. It is also necessary in some states to notify all possible heirs of the pending probate proceeding regardless of whether or not they are named as beneficiaries in the will. This notice is extremely important, since it affords any heir at law not named as a beneficiary an opportunity to object to the admission of the will to probate. There is a statutory time period within which an objection to the will must be made. In the case of an intestate proceeding, the heirs at law must be notified, since they will ultimately share in the distribution of the estate.

§ 19.3.3 Proof of Heirship

In many jurisdictions heirship is proved by the filing of an affidavit of death and heirship. This is simply an affidavit executed by one or two family members (heirs are not allowed to sign this affidavit in some states) or close friends who attest to their knowledge of:

- The date of the decedent's death;

- The decedent's address at the time of death;
- The decedent's age at the time of death; and
- Facts about the decedent's marriages, surviving spouse, and children.

The affidavit is specific about the number of times the decedent was married and the children who were born of each marriage. Additionally, if there were any children who died before (predeceased) the decedent, the names of these children as well as their issue are listed. In the case of intestacy, these children would probably inherit their parent's share.

§ 19.3.4 Minor Heirs

Should there be minor heirs, that is, persons who are under the statutory age of legal competence, the court in most states appoints a guardian to protect the minor's interests during any court proceedings. The court is concerned with the minor child or ward who cannot represent himself. The appointment of a guardian of the estate varies from jurisdiction to jurisdiction and may be a lawyer disinterested in the proceeding, the natural guardian (parent), or the legally appointed guardian of the child. The court may also require that the inherited funds of a minor be deposited with the court until the minor becomes of legal age.

§ 19.4 Functions of Estate Administration or Probate

Probate serves three main functions:

1. Identification of assets so they can be distributed to beneficiaries of the decedent;
2. Protection of creditors of the decedent; and
3. Determination of the tax liability of the estate.

§ 19.4.1 Protection of Creditors

Since distribution cannot be made to heirs without paying debts of the decedent, it is necessary to also determine what debts exist. Usually, the family members are aware of the debts, and if they are not, creditors notify either the lawyer for the estate or a family member of their claim. Most states also have a procedure by which creditors may protect their claims against estates. Also, most states require the personal representative to publish notice to creditors and give actual notice of the claims filing procedure to known creditors.

All states make provisions in their laws to protect claims of creditors of an estate. While the method for making the claim varies from state to state, there is always a specific time period within which a creditor must assert a claim in order to protect it. Generally, a claim is filed by presenting it either to the court or to the executor or representative of the estate or their lawyer.

In some states, a claim must be made for such items as expenses of the last illness and funeral expenses, as well as for ordinary debts. In other states expenses of last illness and funeral expenses are paid routinely as expenses of administration.

In some states the executor or representative may pay any debts presented on a routine basis, while in other states the executor must advertise intent to pay the debts and must have court approval. Generally, if an executor or representative wishes to disallow a particular debt submitted by a creditor, it is necessary to file an intent to disallow the claim with the court within a specific period of time after the claim is presented. The principal purpose of these provisions is to ensure that the creditor does not suffer a loss from having extended credit to the decedent.

§ 19.4.2 Death Taxes

The federal government, the District of Columbia, and most states have some form of death tax. This means that either the decedent's estate or its beneficiaries are taxed in connection with the distribution of the decedent's property. There are three types of death taxes:

1. Estate taxes, a tax on the property constituting the estate;
2. Inheritance (or succession) taxes, a tax on the transfer of property; and
3. "Pickup" taxes equal to the state death tax credit allowed on the federal estate tax return.

§ 19.4.3 Estate Tax

An estate tax is a tax imposed upon the privilege of transmitting property at death and thus is payable upon the entire amount of the taxable estate; that is, the gross estate consisting of probate and non-probate assets less certain allowable deductions and exemptions. The federal government imposes an estate tax. The Economic Growth and Tax Relief Reconciliation Act of 2001 was enacted into law on June 7, 2001 (the "Act"). The Act revises the amount exempt from the federal estate tax as follows:

No federal estate tax return is required to be filed if the gross estate is:

- $1 million or less in 2002 and 2003.
- $1.5 million or less in 2004 and 2005.
- $2 million or less in 2006, 2007, and 2008.

- $3.5 million or less in 2009.

In the year 2010, the Act repeals the estate tax. In the year 2011, the changes contained in the 2001 Act disappear and the estate tax reverts back to the law in effect prior the 2001 Act.

If a return must be filed, it is filed within nine months from the date of death. It is very important that the lawyer's assistant calendar the date that the Federal Estate Tax Return is due because severe penalties and interest are imposed if the estate tax return is not filed and the taxes paid timely. Deferral of payment and/or an extension of time within which to file the return are available in special circumstances upon proper application.

States also levy an estate or inheritance tax, either alone or in conjunction with a "pickup" tax.

§ 19.4.4 Inheritance Tax

An inheritance tax is a frequently encountered state death tax. Inheritance taxes are imposed upon the amount received by each beneficiary. Generally, each beneficiary is granted an exemption based upon their family relationship to the decedent (the closer the relationship the larger the exemption). The balance is taxed in accordance with a rate schedule provided by that state's laws. Frequently, the rates also vary depending upon the closeness of the relationship between the beneficiary and the decedent. The deadline for this return, if required, should also be calendared.

§ 19.4.5 "Pickup" Tax

Some states have what is commonly referred to as a "pickup" tax. In computing federal estate taxes, the government allows a credit for state death taxes based on a graduated table. In the states having a "pickup" tax, this credit then becomes the required amount of state death taxes paid to the state. Under Federal law, the state death tax credit will be reduced and eventually eliminated in future years. Changes to the various state "pickup" tax statutes should be closely monitored as states decide how to deal with this federal change which directly affects the state "pickup" tax.

§ 19.4.6 Final Personal Income Tax Return

The decedent's final personal income tax year ends on the date of death. The decedent's spouse, if any, is entitled to file a joint return for the year in which the decedent dies if that spouse remains unmarried at the end of the year. The representative of the estate is responsible for assisting the surviving spouse in the preparation of this return.

§ 19.4.7 Fiduciary Income Tax Returns

At the time of death, the decedent's estate becomes a separate entity for income tax purposes, and all income derived from probate assets must be reported on a Fiduciary Income Tax Return. The first tax year starts on the date of decedent's death and may end on any date chosen by the representative; provided that the first tax year may be no more than 12 months in length and must end on the last day of a month. The choice of a tax year for the estate depends upon when the most favorable tax treatment of the income can be obtained. For second and subsequent years, the tax year starts on the first of the month following the end of the first return, and is a 12–month period.

§ 19.5 Identification of Assets

The assets of the decedent are things of value that decedent owned. Not all of a decedent's assets are necessarily included in the probate estate. The decedent's property that forms the probate estate is specifically set forth by law. It is dependent also upon the form of ownership of the property.

EXAMPLES:

A. If a decedent owned property with anyone else in joint tenancy with right of survivorship, that property would automatically belong to the other owner upon the decedent's death. It would not form a part of the probate estate, but all or part of it may be a part of his gross estate for death tax purposes. On the other hand, if the decedent owned property as a tenant in common with someone else, or as community property with his spouse, then the undivided interest that the decedent owned in the property would form a part of his probate estate.

B. If the decedent owned a life insurance policy payable to a named beneficiary upon his death, that policy would not be part of his probate estate, but would be part of the estate for death tax purposes. On the other hand, if the decedent owned a life insurance policy payable to his estate, that policy would form part of the probate estate.

C. If the decedent owned property which was titled in beneficiaries other than his estate, particularly in certain types of trusts (property held by one party for the benefit of another), that property would not be included in his probate estate, but may be included for death tax purposes.

Regardless of whether the decedent died testate or intestate, it is necessary for the lawyer to develop a list of the decedent's assets, both probate and non-probate. The lawyer needs to know whether at the time of death the decedent owned or had an interest in any of the following:

- Real estate, as well as the form of ownership of each parcel.
- Mortgages, promissory notes, or real estate installment sale contracts payable to decedent.
- Stocks, bonds, and other types of securities.
- Life insurance on decedent's life.
- Life insurance owned by decedent on the life of another.
- Oil, mineral, timber, and gas interests.
- Cash, bank accounts, savings certificates, etc..
- Interests in unincorporated businesses or partnerships.
- Annuities, IRA, and Keogh plans.
- Pension, profit sharing, and other employee benefit plans.
- Assets in certain types of trusts.
- Farm equipment, livestock, and crops.
- Gifts made by decedent in excess of $10,000 per year for each donee.
- Powers of appointment.
- Large amounts of jewelry.
- Coin or stamp collections.
- Antiques.
- Art objects.
- Household goods.
- Vehicles.
- Death benefits.
- Uncashed checks in decedent's possession.
- Payroll checks receivable.
- Accounts receivable.
- Tax refunds for decedent's final tax year.
- Military benefits.

The foregoing is by no means inclusive of all types of assets that may be encountered but is shown to give some idea of the many different kinds of assets.

The form of ownership of each item must be ascertained to determine whether it is a probate asset or a non-probate asset. Often, compiling an accurate list of all assets of the decedent that comprises the gross estate is the most time-consuming step in the administration of the estate. It may be necessary to have several conferences with the family members before a complete list is compiled. It is also usually necessary to correspond with banks, savings and loan associations, stockbrokers, the former employer of the decedent, and insurance companies to get all of the information you need to handle the estate.

Not only is it necessary to compile a list of assets, but it is also necessary to determine the values of the various assets as of the date of death. This process can become quite complicated. For some assets, such as bank accounts, this can be accomplished quite simply by writing to the bank and requesting that it furnish you with the date of death balance plus accrued interest to that date. However, many assets do not have such a clearly obtainable value and require the use of formulas and guidelines used by the Internal Revenue Service or professional appraisers. The exact procedures may also vary depending upon the jurisdiction and the size of the estate.

§ 19.6 The Estate Representative

The person who handles this administration is known as the personal representative (representative). This term is used in the Uniform Probate Code to mean anyone who handles the administration regardless of whether the appointment is by will or by the court in cases of intestacy. In many jurisdictions the formal designation of the personal representative depends upon whether the estate is testate or intestate or whether a representative is named in the will.

In the case of testate succession, the will usually designates someone to serve as the estate's representative. That person is referred to as the executor, whether male or female.

However, if the executor so named is unable or unwilling to serve and no alternative is designated in the will, the court appoints a representative, and that representative is known as the administrator c.t.a. (the Latin abbreviation for *cum testamento annexo* meaning *with will annexed*), or an administrator *de bonis non*, meaning of the goods not administered. If the decedent died intestate, then the representative appointed by the court is the administrator. Each of these persons serves the same function and has basically the same duties. In the legal field, many use all of these terms interchangeably, although in the actual legal documents the appropriate designation should be used.

A testator may give the executor a great deal of leeway and fully outline in the will the powers accorded the executor. This enables the executor to go about the business of administering the estate without requesting authority from the court to handle transactions such as the sale of estate assets. A will may also provide that the executor need not provide a surety bond. The surety bond is required for the protection of both the heirs and the creditors. The surety bond is often in the form of a commercial bond (similar to an insurance policy) issued by an insurance company which, for a premium, insures that the executor will properly perform all duties. The court may in some states override the waiver of the bond by the testator and require the executor to post bond.

Some states now give executors certain statutory powers whether or not they are specifically set out in the will.

There are certain requirements (in addition to posting bond) that the representative must meet to be qualified to serve as the representative. Once the requirements are met, the court issues letters testamentary (in testate matters) or letters of administration (in intestate matters) to the representative. These letters give the representative authority to act.

Usually, the representative acts under court supervision. The will or state statute may give the representative some freedom as to how much court authority is necessary to perform certain acts (such as paying bills or selling assets). These powers are referred to as nonintervention powers in some states. However, it may be necessary for the representative to make periodic accountings to the court concerning the administration of the estate.

There are alternatives to probate that do not require the appointment of a representative. These kinds of proceedings are usually reserved for small estates passing to close relatives or having certain limited types of assets or community property agreements in community property states. It is not possible to discuss every conceivable alternative in this chapter, but the important thing to realize is that there are many alternatives available to the beneficiaries in the administration of estates.

§ 19.7 Initial Client Interview

One or more of the decedent's closest relatives generally make the initial contact with the law firm. An appointment is usually scheduled for a time as soon as practicable following the funeral.

The initial interview generally includes the lawyer, the decedent's spouse, children, or other close relatives. It may also include the person named as executor of the decedent's will if it is someone other than a family member. The executor is the person named in the will to carry out the terms of the will. The lawyer's assistant should also be included in the initial conference to take notes as information is obtained.

Most firms have developed client interview forms for probate matters that they use to ensure that they secure all needed information. (*See* Illustration 19–1.)

If the will is available for the initial conference, it is read at that time. The reading of the will, however, is not nearly so dramatic as is depicted in the movies. In fact, the family usually is familiar with the contents of the will before the conference with the lawyer. At that time the lawyer answers any questions any member of the family might have concerning the terms of the will and the probate process.

It may also be useful for you to locate a copy of any printed obituaries appearing in the local newspapers, as they will list survivors and relationships. This will help both the legal assistant and the lawyer to become familiar with the family structure prior to the interview. Since it is necessary for the lawyer to secure biographical data concerning the decedent's family, both the lawyer and the decedent's family will appreciate it if some of the information can be obtained from the files.

Illustration 19–1

CLIENT INTERVIEW FORM

GENERAL INFORMATION

Estate of ______________________________
Known aliases ______________________________
Date of birth ______ Place of birth ______________________________
Date of death ______ Place of death ______________________________
Name of spouse ______ Date of birth of spouse ______________________________
If spouse is deceased, state date of death ______________________________
Decedent's social security no. ______________________________
Spouse's social security no. ______________________________
Date of marriage to surviving spouse ______________________________
Domicile at date of marriage ______________________________
Year domicile established in this state ______________________________
For each devisee, heir or other interested person, state:

Full name and relationship to decedent	**Address**	**Date of birth**	**Social Security No.**

Decedent's business or occupation ______________________________
Employer identification number, if any ______________________________
Name and address of personal representative ______________________________
____
Business phone ______ Home phone ______________________________
Address of decedent at date of death ______________________________
____
Did the decedent have a safe deposit box? ______________________________
____
If so, state: Name of bank ______ and joint depositor(s), if any
____

ASSET INFORMATION

It is suggested that sheets similar to the following should be prepared for each type of asset. In some cases you will need a separate sheet for every item of property within that category while for others you will be able to list several on the same sheet. These forms can be easily modified to meet specific information requirements of your state. If all information is not available, the forms can be given to the personal representative and family members to gather the information.

REAL ESTATE

Estate of ______

Probate ______
Non–Probate ______
Legal description of property ____

____

Name or names in which title stands and form of ownership ______________

____

Homestead? Yes ______ No ______
Abstract ______ Torrens ______
Location of abstract of title or Torrens certificate ______________

____

Date of death value $____
Mortgages or other encumbrances:
Payee ______________________ Loan No. ______________
Balance of encumbrance on date of death $______________
Payee ______________________ Loan No. ______________
Property identification number ______________
NOTE: It is helpful to obtain a copy of the most recent real estate tax statement and the deed to the present owner.

BANK ACCOUNTS

Estate of ____
Probate ______
Non–Probate ______
Name of bank ____
Type of account ______ No. of account ______
Approximate balance $______ Date of death balance $______
Name or names in which account stands and form of ownership ______________

____

LIFE INSURANCE

Estate of ____
Probate ______
Non–Probate ______
Name of company ______________ Policy No. ______________
Date of issuance ______________ Face amount of policy ______________
Date of death value ____
Beneficiary and relationship ______________________________
Policy owner ______________ Date established ______________
Any known loans ____

NOTE: Form 712 should be requested from the insurance company for each policy of life insurance on the decedent's life.

NOTE: Form 712 should be requested from the insurance company for each policy of life insurance on the decedent's life.

STOCKS AND BONDS

Estate of ____
Probate ______
Non–Probate ______
Name of company ____
Certificate No. ______________ Dated ______________
Issued to ______________ for ______________ shares
Transfer Agent ____
Date of death value $______ Source ______________
Cusip number ____

U.S. SAVINGS BONDS

Estate of ______
Probate ______
Non–Probate ______ Joint Owner ______

Date of issuance	Denomination	Serial number	Date of death value

MISCELLANEOUS SECURITIES & INVESTMENTS

Estate of ______
Probate ______
Non–Probate ______
Complete description of security, including type, numbers, date, approximate value, maturity date, if any, etc.

______
______
______

Name or names in which security stands and form of ownership ______
______

MISCELLANEOUS PERSONAL PROPERTY

Estate of ______
Probate ______

Description	Joint owner or beneficiary, if any	Value
Federal income tax refund		
State income tax refund		
Household goods and furnishings		
Automobile		
______ Year and make		
______ Vehicle ID or serial #		
Final payroll check		
______ Company ______		
Cash in decedent's possession		

Uncashed checks in decedent's possession (List) ______
______
Jewelry or other personal property of intrinsic value (List) ______
______
Retirement and/or deferred compensation plans (obtain copy of plan)
Interests in partnerships
IRA and Keogh Plans

PROPERTY TRANSFERRED PRIOR TO DEATH

Estate of ______

Description ____
____
____
Transferee ____________________ Relationship to decedent ____________________
Date of transfer ____
Value of transfer ____
Were gift tax returns filed? ______________________________________
NOTE: If gift tax returns were filed, copies should be obtained.

EXPENSES OF ADMINISTRATION

Estate of ____
Expenses of last illness:
____ $______
____ ______
____ ______
____ ______

Funeral expenses:
Mortuary ______________________________ $______
Cemetery ______________________________ $______
Flowers ______________________________ $______
Marker ______________________________ $______
Honorariums ______________________________ $______
Other ______________________________ $______

Debts of decedent:
____ $______
____ ______
____ ______

Taxes:
____ $______

Attorney's fees: ______________________________
____ $______

Miscellaneous: ______________________________
____ $______

§ 19.8 Method of Handling Estate Administration

In most jurisdictions, there is usually a choice as to the type of probate proceeding to use to handle the estate. This is true of both testate and intestate successions. After the lawyer has compiled a list of the items that comprise the estate of the decedent and determined who the heirs and beneficiaries are, the lawyer is then in a position to make a recommendation as to what is believed to be the most efficient method of probate. Often, if some of the heirs or beneficiaries are minor children, there is less choice of the method of probate, and the proceedings may be more complicated. In some jurisdictions abbreviated or summary proceedings are available for estates that are valued up to a specific amount of money. It will be up to you to learn the methods that are available in your state. Ask the lawyer, a senior lawyer's assistant, or a legal assistant to help you find the applicable statutes for your state.

The value of the gross estate determines whether a state death tax return and a federal estate tax return are required. Based on the value of the gross estate, the lawyer can also estimate the tax liability.

§ 19.9 Probate Procedures

The domicile of the decedent at the time of death generally controls where a proceeding must be commenced. A domicile does not have the same legal meaning as a residence. A person may maintain many residences, but can be domiciled at only one address. The necessary pleadings will depend upon whether you are dealing with a testate or intestate estate and whether informal proceedings may be utilized. The pleadings vary with the jurisdiction. It is up to you to familiarize yourself with the pleadings used in your state for each kind of proceeding. You probably will have sample forms of pleadings in a forms file or procedures manual.

In most instances, some kind of petition is necessary to begin the proceeding. Whether you utilize a printed form or have to prepare the complete pleading depends upon the procedures in your state. Probably the affidavit of death and heirship, if required, will be filed at the same time the initial petition is filed. You may also file pleadings regarding proof of the will and notice to creditors and heirs at that time.

In the event there is more than one validly executed will in existence at the time of a decedent's death, the will bearing the most recent date usually controls.

In most states at least one court hearing is required to admit the will to probate, establish heirship, and appoint a representative for the estate. The major exception to the hearing requirement is in informal proceedings under the Uniform Probate Code where only a conference with a registrar is necessary. The registrar is either a judge or a person such as the clerk of court designated as a registrar by the court.

§ 19.9.1 Proof of Will

Proof of will is the process by which a decedent's will is validated (proved) and admitted to probate. In some states, this is done by one or more of the witnesses to the will filing an affidavit that they were in fact witnesses to the will and that the testator was of sound mind at the time the will was made. In other states, it is necessary that one or more of the witnesses appear in open court and give oral testimony as to the circumstances under which they witnessed the execution of the will.

§ 19.9.2 The Self–Proved Will

The concept of the self-proved will was introduced by the Uniform Probate Code. A self-proved will contains not only the signatures of the testator and witnesses but also the acknowledgment of a notary public attesting to the signatures of the testator and witnesses, the soundness of the testator's mind, and the testator's intention to declare the will to be their last will and testament. In those states in which the Uniform

Probate Code has been adopted, a self-proved will needs no further proof. This does not mean that a state cannot make statutory provision for self-proved wills without adopting the Uniform Probate Code.

§ 19.9.3 Contesting the Will

Any heir who is disgruntled because they either were omitted from the will or did not receive the full bequest to which they thought they were entitled may file a petition to contest the will. Most states have a specific time period within which this must be done. Such a contest follows the standard procedures of civil litigation. Notice and service on the parties involved are required. The petitioner must allege to the court the reasons for the contest and must prove undue influence, fraud, or mistake in the making of the will. Should the petitioner receive a favorable decision in a will contest, the will is declared invalid, is not admitted to probate, and the laws of intestacy apply.

§ 19.9.4 Administering the Assets

The process of administering an estate is just what the name implies. The representative collects assets; liquidates assets if necessary or prudent; pays debts, funeral and administration expenses, taxes, and claims; and determines the distributions to be made. Liquidation is simply the process of converting assets of whatever form into cash for easier distribution when the estate is closed. If property is not liquidated and is distributed in the same form received, it is said to have been distributed in kind.

The estate of a decedent is generally administered in the state of domicile; however, if the decedent owned any real estate or tangible property in another state, a probate proceeding may be required in that state. This procedure is known as an ancillary proceeding.

As soon as feasible after appointment and prior to the statutory deadline date, the representative must file a complete inventory of the property owned by the decedent, including appraised or approximate values as required by law. An accurate inventory is important, as it serves as the basis for taxation purposes as well as subsequent accounting purposes. For this reason it is sometimes necessary to file an addendum to the inventory or to amend it if additional property is discovered after preparation and filing of the inventory.

§ 19.9.5 Accounting and Distribution

In all except informal probate matters, settlement of the estate is accomplished by the representative's filing a final account with the court; this account summarizes all of the transactions involved in the administration. This would include the payment of all claims, taxes, expenses of administration, liquidation of assets as necessary or prudent, and any other transactions that may have taken place. At the same time, the representative petitions the court for distribution of the remaining assets. In some states a hearing is required on this account, while in others the hearing may be waived by consent of the heirs or by statute. The court, after submission of these documents and the hearing (if required), approves the account and orders the distribution of assets. At the time distribution is made, the representative must obtain a receipt from each devisee or legatee to file with the court. Thereafter, the representative is discharged from all responsibilities. If there was a surety bond required, it is ordered terminated.

In informal proceedings, generally a statement is filed to close the estate. No discharge is given but a statutory time frame begins to run on the liability of the personal representative for his actions.

§ 19.10 Guardianships or Conservatorships

You learned in the chapter on Litigation that minors do not have the legal capacity to act for themselves. Therefore the court appoints someone to act for them concerning their legal affairs. The same is true of persons of adult age who do not possess either the mental or physical capacity to care for their own affairs or who may be deemed to be "vulnerable adults" in some states. Someone must be appointed to handle their affairs for them. These persons are sometimes considered as wards of the court, and the court appoints one or more guardians or conservators to protect the ward's personal needs and/or preserve any financial resources.

Terminology, when referring to these persons, varies from jurisdiction to jurisdiction. The term "minor" usually means someone under the age of legal majority in a particular state (usually 18 to 21 years of age). The term "incompetent," "incapacitated," or "disabled adult" is applied to persons of adult age. Although state laws vary, guardianships generally may be initiated for both minors and adults while conservatorships are generally limited to disabled adults.

When it is necessary to appoint a guardian for a minor, a parent is often appointed since a parent is usually the natural guardian of the child. In some instances, if the court determines that the interests of the natural guardian may conflict with the interests of the minor, the court may appoint a guardian *ad litem* to represent the minor in that particular legal proceeding. It is for that particular purpose only.

When it is necessary to appoint a guardian or conservator for a disabled adult, it is necessary to present detailed proof to the court that the adult is in fact disabled. The disabled adult is usually served with a copy of the petition seeking the guardianship, limited guardianship, or conservatorship, although in some states physically disabled adults may petition for conservatorship on their own behalf voluntarily. A lawyer or a guardian *ad litem* may be appointed to represent the disabled adult. Once the statutory delays have run, the court receives testimony from a physician, as well as from the lawyer appointed to represent the adult, as to the adult's inability to handle their own affairs and/or to care for their physical needs. Some states use the terms guardianship and conservatorship interchangeably. In other states guardianships and conservatorships are separate and distinct proceedings. The basic difference in these states is that a person under guardianship is declared incompetent to manage their own affairs. A person under conservatorship or limited guardianship does not lose any civil rights and, thus, is free to execute a will, marry, vote, etc. Conservatorships and guardianships of adults can be terminated when the ward regains mental or physical capacity or upon death. Guardianships of minors terminate when the ward reaches legal age. In both instances, a final accounting and hearing are usually required before termination.

In both guardianships and conservatorships, bonds are usually required of the guardian or conservator. These bonds are usually in the form of commercial insurance policies and guarantee the property of the ward under the guardian's or conservator's control.

It is necessary for the guardian or conservator to file an inventory of the assets of the ward, obtain court authorization to make expenditures, and to keep detailed accounts of administration. Periodic accountings must be filed with the court; and, when the guardianship or conservatorship terminates, a final accounting must be filed before discharge bond termination.

§ 19.11 Summary

The foregoing, very generally, covers the proper procedures to be taken in the administration of estates, guardianships, and conservatorships. The value of the lawyer's assistant will increase as procedures become familiar, and checklists of statutory requirements and proper procedures are established.

CHAPTER 20

BANKRUPTCY

Table of Sections

---

§ 20.1 Definition and Areas Covered in This Chapter

A bankruptcy is a proceeding under Title 11 of the United States Code whereby an individual or a legal entity requests protection under the terms of that law. The protection given a debtor under the Bankruptcy Code is the opportunity for financial rehabilitation and a "fresh start." Most bankruptcies are voluntary Chapter 7 cases. Consequently, the information contained in this chapter is primarily applicable to Chapter 7 cases. Since Chapters 9, 11, 12, and 13 are administered differently from Chapter 7, those rules and procedures should be consulted before undertaking work on those types of cases.

§ 20.2 History

The Bankruptcy Code is federal law. Under the Constitution, Congress has the power to establish "uniform laws on the subject of bankruptcies throughout the United States" (Article 1, Section 8). In 2005, bankruptcy reform legislation called Bankruptcy Abuse Prevention and Consumer Protection Act (BAPCPA) was passed which took effect for cases filed on and after October 17, 2005. BAPCPA made significant changes. Prior to the current law, bankruptcy law encompassed several bankruptcy acts. Then, the Bankruptcy Code was enacted November 6, 1978, with principal provisions effective October 1, 1979. The Bankruptcy Code was amended several times since then.

§ 20.3 Terminology Differences in the 1978 Code

When the first bankruptcy law was established, a person seeking relief under the law was known as a bankrupt, and the proceeding was known as bankruptcy. Cases governed by the pre–1978 law are generally called "Act" cases. The 1978 Code abolished the term bankrupt. A person or entity filing for relief under the Bankruptcy Code now is called a debtor. Persons who are owed money by the debtor are generally called claimants or creditors.

§ 20.3.1 Options Available Under Code

Under the Bankruptcy Code, a debtor can obtain a "fresh start" through liquidation of its assets (Chapter 7) or make arrangements to repay its creditors from income in future years (Chapters 11, 12, and 13). A person or entity may file for relief under Chapter 7 (straight liquidation as discussed herein), Chapter 11 (reorganization), Chapter 13 (wage earner payment plan), or Chapter 12 (family farmer or fisherman plan). *See* discussion at §§ 20.10 through 20.12 below. There is also a chapter for bankrupt municipalities (Chapter 9).

§ 20.4 Purpose of Seeking Bankruptcy Protection

One main purpose of bankruptcy is to give a debtor a chance to make a fresh start in life by relieving them of the burden of their debts. When filing Chapter 7 (liquidation), as a condition for receiving this relief, the debtor must turn over to the bankruptcy court all property which it owns which is not exempt by law. (Exempt property the debtor is generally entitled to keep and is discussed more fully later in this chapter.) This property is converted into money and is used to pay costs of administration and creditors to the extent there are funds available.

§ 20.4.1 Need for a Lawyer

A debtor contemplating filing for relief under the Bankruptcy Code will generally benefit by the services of a lawyer. A lawyer can:

1. Advise a client whether bankruptcy is the best solution, which chapter would be best to solve their financial problems;
2. Prepare the necessary legal papers for filing bankruptcy;
3. Provide representation during the course of the bankruptcy proceedings; and
4. Give advice on exemption, tax, and other rights

If a person encounters difficulty in securing the services of a lawyer, a list of names of lawyers who accept bankruptcy cases is generally available from the bar association or Legal Aid Society.

§ 20.5 Bankruptcy Courts and Jurisdiction

Bankruptcy cases may not be filed in state court. The court of exclusive jurisdiction is the United States Bankruptcy Court for each United States District Court. This court has exclusive jurisdiction over the debtor, all of its property no matter where it is located, and over any and all lawsuits by or against the debtor. Bankruptcy law, as federal law, has supremacy over state law on the same issues; however, the bankruptcy court can look to state law when there is no express governing bankruptcy law.

§ 20.5.1 Venue

A debtor can file for bankruptcy only in the district where that debtor has resided or had their main place of business for the preceding six months or the majority of the preceding six months. *See* 28 U.S.C. § 1408.

§ 20.5.2 Bankruptcy Court Officers

The bankruptcy court has, as its officers, certain persons whose job it is to administer an estate. They include:

- Bankruptcy Judge—The judge presides over the bankruptcy court and hears all litigation pertaining to the case. It is the bankruptcy judge who determines whether a debtor is entitled to a discharge.

- Clerk of Court—The clerk has the identical duties of a federal district clerk of court; and in addition, in some districts the clerk is the presiding officer at the first meeting of creditors of a debtor.
- Chapter 7 Trustee—A trustee is appointed at the commencement of a bankruptcy case and serves in the capacity of trustee at least until the first meeting of creditors of the debtor. It is the duty of the trustee to recover all assets of the debtor not exempt under the law and to liquidate those assets for the benefit of the debtor's creditors. Trustees in most districts are chosen from a panel of private individuals appointed by the United States Trustee.
- Chapter 13 Trustee—A trustee is appointed at the commencement of a bankruptcy case and serves in the capacity of trustee. It is the duty of the trustee to collect monthly plan payment from the debtor and distribute the funds to the debtor's creditors. Most districts have one or two standing chapter 13 trustees.

§ 20.6 Definitions

A familiarity with the following terms should help the novice lawyer's assistant better understand this chapter. A list of defined words and their legal definition under the Bankruptcy Code can be found at 11 U.S.C. § 101.

- Adversary Proceedings—any individual lawsuits brought within a bankruptcy case.
- Assisted Person—consumer debtors with non-exempt property below $150,000.00 in value.
- Automatic Stay—An injunction or court order that takes effect when a bankruptcy petition is filed, prohibiting all entities and individuals from any action against the debtor, property of the debtor, or property of the bankruptcy estate.
- Business Bankruptcy—a bankruptcy filed by a business entity—a sole proprietorship, corporation, partnership, or other such business entity.
- Case—the entire bankruptcy proceedings of a debtor.
- Claim—a right to payment asserted by another.
- Consumer Bankruptcy—a bankruptcy filed by an individual (or husband and wife) who is not in business.
- Consumer Debt—a debt incurred by an individual or family primarily for a personal, household, or family use.
- Creditor—a person or entity claiming it is owed money by the debtor.

- Debt Relief Agency—anyone who provides bankruptcy assistance to an assisted person.
- Debtor—the person or entity seeking relief under the Bankruptcy Code.
- Debtor in Possession—the entity or individual retaining possession of the assets of the bankruptcy estate in a Chapter 11 bankruptcy case.
- Discharge—the conclusion of the bankruptcy case when all payments under a plan have been made or the debtor has been relieved of its debts.
- Entity—a person or legally recognized organization.
- Estate—all of a debtor's nonexempt property.
- Exempt Property—all of the property of a debtor which is, by virtue of the Bankruptcy Code or state statute, not attachable in a bankruptcy.
- Family Farmer—an individual engaged in a farming operation with a regular annual income.
- Family Fisherman—an individual engaged in a fishing operation with a regular annual income.
- Insolvent—when the total debt of a person or entity is greater than the total value of its property or when a person or entity is unable to pay its debts as they come due.
- Judicial Lien—a lien obtained by judgment or other judicial process.
- Lien—a legally enforceable claim against property of a debtor to secure repayment of a debt or obligation.
- Liquidation—the sale of all of a debtor's nonexempt property.
- Median Family Income—the median family income calculated and reported by the Bureau of the Census in the most recent year.
- Trustee—the individual charged with the duty of liquidating a debtor's estate and seeing that creditors receive as much of their claims as possible.
- United States Trustee—the division of the Department of Justice established to monitor bankruptcy cases.

§ 20.7 Methods of Filing Bankruptcy

There are two ways in which a bankruptcy case can be started:

1. By the filing of a voluntary petition; or
2. By the filing of an involuntary petition.

The terms *voluntary* and *involuntary* mean just that. In a voluntary case, a debtor decides to seek relief under the Code. In an involuntary case, creditors ask the court to place a debtor in bankruptcy. To accomplish that, the creditors must satisfy certain requirements, depending on the size and nature of the debtor.

§ 20.7.1 Conditions to Be Met by Debtor in Voluntary Chapter 7 Cases

An individual voluntarily seeking a discharge of any debts under Chapter 7 of the Bankruptcy Code must meet certain conditions:

- Only a person who resides in, has a place of business, or owns property in the United States can file bankruptcy.
- One or more debts must be owed, although there is no minimum or maximum as to the amount of debts which are owed. (Interestingly, there is no requirement that the individual be insolvent. Normally, however, the individual seeking a discharge in bankruptcy is insolvent or is unable to pay debts as they come due.) In 1998, Congress was considering a form of "means testing" that can limit a debtor's ability to seek protection under Chapter 7.
- BAPCPA requires a debtor to pass a "means testing." The means test formula is base on the median family income for the area and household size of the debtor. It is complex. It is a major part of BAPCPA.
- BAPCPA requires a debtor to receive approved credit counseling before filing and take an approved financial management instructional course after filing.
- A debtor may not file for Chapter 7 bankruptcy if previously granted a discharge in a proceeding commenced within eight years prior to the date of the filing of the petition in bankruptcy. However, in limited instances, a debtor could file a Chapter 13 petition in that time period. In addition, a debtor who has been a debtor in a case pending in bankruptcy within the last 180 days may be prohibited from filing bankruptcy.

§ 20.7.2 Filing the Petition in Voluntary Cases

Bankruptcy begins with the filing of a petition for an order for relief with the Clerk of the United States Bankruptcy Court having jurisdiction.

Additional pleadings must also be filed by the debtor seeking relief under the Bankruptcy Code, generally called *schedules*. The information required to be in the schedules is set forth by the Bankruptcy Code in official forms. *See* Illustration 20–1. The necessary forms are generally available online. They are also commercially available. The debtor's lawyer is responsible for proper preparation of the forms, but of course, the information must first be obtained from the debtor. The lawyer's assistant prepares these forms under the supervision of the lawyer, and careful attention in preparation of the forms is very important. Errors or omissions often necessitate amendments to the pleadings and cause delays in the discharge. This is both expensive and time-consuming. In addition, the debtor must swear, under penalty of perjury, to the accuracy of the schedule.

The number of copies of a petition and supporting documents that must be filed is a matter of local rule, which usually provides for filing sufficient copies for the court's files and for a trustee. A husband and wife may file a joint petition. The schedules and statements are filed with the petition in a voluntary case. Bankruptcy courts now accept electronic filings; some require all documents be filed electronically. Consult the local rules to ensure compliance.

If an individual debtor's schedule of assets and liabilities includes consumer debts which are secured by property of the estate, the debtor must also file a Statement of Intention (*see* Illustration 20–2) within 30 days after the filing of the petition or on or before the date of the meeting of creditors, whichever is earlier, and must serve a copy on the trustee and the creditors named in the statement on or before the filing of the statement.

Preparation of the petition, schedules, and other supporting documents should be completed with as much information as possible. The more detail and information presented in the filed documents, the less time the debtor will need to spend with the trustee, and the proceeding will run much smoother.

The Voluntary Petition (*see* Illustration 20–1, Form 1) is completed for all types of bankruptcies with the appropriate type of proceeding indicated on the form, and is signed and dated by the lawyer and debtor.

Exhibit "A" to the Voluntary Petition is only used by corporations filing under Chapter 11 of the Code and is signed by an authorized officer of the debtor corporation or a member or an authorized agent of the partnership debtor under penalty of perjury. (Note: a partnership may be comprised of corporations who are the partners.)

Exhibit "D" to the Voluntary Petition is the Individual Debtor's Statement of Compliance with Credit Counseling Requirement.

The Summary of Schedules and the schedules include general instructions at the beginning of each form, which should be reviewed before starting to complete the forms to ensure that all the necessary information is available to the lawyer's assistant.

The first page of the debtor's schedules and the first page of any amendments thereto must contain the caption in the petition, *i.e.*, name of the court, debtor, and case number. Subsequent pages should be identified with the debtor's name and case number. If the schedules are filed with the petition, the case number is left blank.

The Summary of Schedules indicates which schedules are attached and states the number of pages in each schedule. The totals from each schedule are listed in the appropriate box. The total number of sheets of all schedules is added and inserted in the box at the bottom of the column entitled "No. of Sheets."

Schedule A lists all real property in which the debtor has any legal, equitable, or future interest, including all property owned as a co-tenant, community property, or in which the debtor has a life estate. The values of the property should reflect the best estimate as to the property's true market value.

Schedule B lists all personal property of the debtor of whatever kind and is separated into 35 different categories. If the debtor does not own any property in a category, the column entitled "None" is checked. The values of the tangible property should reflect the best estimate of the debtor as to the true market value.

Schedule C lists the property claimed as exempt by the debtor. It is important that the correct law for exemptions be used. In some states, it may be in the best interest of the debtor to select the state exemptions instead of the federal exemptions. The lawyer's assistant should check with the lawyer to determine the correct exemption law to use. The property claimed as exempt should be listed individually, each item should be valued separately, and the specific exemption, by subsection, should be indicated.

Some bankruptcy courts take a stringent approach to exemptions, ruling that if all exemptions to which a debtor is entitled are not requested in the initial filing by the debtor, those not claimed will not be allowed to the debtor. Other courts do allow amendments.

Schedule D lists all creditors holding secured claims. If the debtor has no secured creditors, the box provided on the form must be checked to indicate that there are no such creditors. If the continuation page is used, the number of continuation pages must be entered on the appropriate line at the bottom of the first page. At the bottom of each continuation page, the sheet number and the total number of continuation sheets must be completed. For example, if there are three continuation sheets, on the first continuation sheet you would insert "1 of 3," on the second sheet you would insert "2 of 3," and so on.

Schedule E lists creditors holding unsecured priority claims. The types of priority claims are listed on Schedule E. If the debtor has no unsecured creditors holding priority claims, the box provided on the first page must be checked to indicate that there are no such creditors. The first page also contains other statements that must be answered, and on the next page, or the continuation page, the creditors are listed. The number of continuation pages must be entered on the appropriate line at the bottom of the first page. Again, the sheet number and the number of continuation sheets must be inserted at the bottom of each continuation sheet.

Schedule F lists creditors holding unsecured non-priority claims. For each creditor listed, the amount of the claim, the date incurred, and the reason for the claim (*e.g.*, credit card debt, medical service, etc.) must be identified. If the debtor has no unsecured creditors, the box provided on the first page must be checked to indicate that there are no such creditors. If continuation sheets are used, the same numbering of continuation sheets must be used.

It is important that all creditors be listed on the appropriate schedules. Any creditor omitted from the schedule by the debtor, lawyer, or staff, may not be discharged; and, if the omission is a result of error in preparation by the lawyer or support staff, the error could result in a claim against the lawyer.

Schedule G lists executory contracts and unexpired leases. If the debtor does not own any such contracts, the box must be checked to indicate this fact.

Schedule H lists co-debtors (an entity that may also be liable on any debts listed by the debtor in the Schedule of Creditors), other than a spouse in a joint proceeding. Again, if there are no co-debtors, the box must be checked to indicate this fact.

Schedule I lists the current income of the debtor. If the debtor is self-employed, a detailed listing of the debtor's business income and expenses must be submitted with Schedules I and J.

Schedule J lists the current expenditures of the debtor.

The Declaration Concerning Debtor's Schedules is signed by the debtor or an officer or authorized agent of the debtor corporation or a member or authorized agent of a partnership debtor under penalty of perjury. If it is a husband and wife petition, both spouses must sign.

Every debtor must complete the Statement of Financial Affairs. It contains instructions and definitions at the beginning of the form which should be reviewed prior to completion of the form. Each question must be answered. If the answer is "None" or the question is not applicable, mark the box labeled "None." If the answer space provided is not sufficient, attach a separate sheet properly identified with the case name, case number (if known), and the number of the question. It is signed by the debtor or an officer or authorized agent of the debtor corporation or a member or authorized agent of a partnership debtor under penalty of perjury. If it is a husband and wife petition, both spouses must sign.

The Statement of Current Monthly Income and Means–Test Calculation must be completed and filed which is used to determine if a debtor is eligible for Chapter 7.

The Notice to Individual Consumer Debtor under section 342(b) must be filed. It gives notice of Credit Counseling Agencies, available bankruptcy chapters, and bankruptcy crimes.

The Statement Pursuant to Rule 2016(b), Disclosure of Compensation of Attorney for Debtor(s), form is signed by the lawyer and is filed and transmitted to the United States Trustee within 15 days after the order for relief, or at another time as the court may direct.

§ 20.7.3 Filing Fee in Voluntary Cases

A filing fee must be paid to the clerk at the time the petition is filed unless by local court rule it may be paid in installments, upon application to the court by the debtor. This fee is in addition to the fees charged by the lawyer, and generally cannot be advanced by the lawyer. The debtor may not receive a discharge unless the filing fee is paid in full. Under the Bankruptcy Code, a husband and wife may file under a single petition and pay one filing fee. (Local rules of court are very important in bankruptcy matters and must be followed very carefully. If your office does not have a copy of the rules, request a copy from the clerk of the bankruptcy court.)

§ 20.7.4 Effect of Filing a Petition in Voluntary Cases

The act of the debtor in filing a petition in bankruptcy has far-reaching significance:

- The petition serves as the application by the debtor for an order of relief, *i.e.,* for a discharge of any debts.
- The petition operates as an automatic stay, applicable to almost all creditors of the debtor, prohibiting further collection efforts.
- An estate is created by law consisting of any property and interests possessed by the debtor which are not exempt under applicable federal or state law. The estate is used for repayment to creditors.

§ 20.7.5 Notice to Creditors

Within a reasonable time after the petition is filed, the bankruptcy court sends out notice (with at least 20 days' notice) by mail to all creditors listed by the debtor on the schedules of a meeting of creditors (the "341 Notice"). Creditors are entitled, but not required, to attend this meeting, elect a trustee, and question the debtor. In the same notice they are given information about filing claims, as well as deadlines for filing objections to discharge and to exemptions claimed by the debtor.

§ 20.7.6 First Meeting of Creditors

The debtor must attend this Section 341 meeting. The bankruptcy judge is not permitted to attend the meeting of creditors. The Chapter 7 trustee usually presides over the meeting. At this first meeting of creditors, the debtor is questioned under oath by the presiding clerk or trustee and by any interested creditors who wish to do so. The debtor is required to be completely truthful and cooperative in answering questions concerning personal financial matters. Failure to cooperate or providing inaccurate information can be the basis for dismissal of the case, denial of discharge, or under the most egregious circumstances, referral to the United States Attorney for prosecution as a bankruptcy crime.

§ 20.7.7 Types of Claims

Creditors' claims are generally classified as secured or unsecured. Secured debts are those which are supported by some kind of collateral. Most voluntary liens are not affected by the bankruptcy filing.

EXAMPLE:

The debtor bought a car, borrowing the money from a bank. The bank took a security interest in the car, reflected by a lien. The debtor purchased a home, again borrowing the money from the bank. The bank took a mortgage on the house as security. The debtor borrowed money from a finance company to consolidate other debts. The finance company took a security interest in all of the furniture and appliances. The bank and finance company are secured creditors.

Unsecured claims are all of those claims that have no collateral or other lien, *e.g.*, open accounts such as credit card or trade accounts, personal loans, or claims where the amount of security is less than the debt (for instance, $10,000 is owed on a car worth $7,000).

EXAMPLE:

The debtor has charge cards at a number of local department stores. The debtor has an American Express card and a MasterCard. The debtor has outstanding obligations to a plumber.

These are unsecured debts and the creditors are unsecured creditors, since none of the obligations are secured by collateral.

A third classification of claim is an administrative claim. Generally, it is related to the bankruptcy administration, *e.g.*, payment of taxes, accountants, or lawyers. The administrative claim is given priority treatment.

When the debtor files its petition, it is required to list all of its creditors, identifying whether the claim is secured, unsecured, or administrative. If the creditor disagrees with either the classification or the amount of the debt listed by the debtor, it must notify the court by filing a claim.

§ 20.7.8 Filing of Claims by Creditors

Creditors in Chapter 7 cases must file their claims with the bankruptcy court within the time set by the court or be barred from participating in any dividend (distribution) which might be declared. There is a prescribed form for submitting proofs of claim. *See* Illustration 20–3. If the creditor fails to file a claim, the trustee or a co-debtor may file a claim for the creditor. Often a creditor is advised in the Notice of Bankruptcy (341 Notice) not to file a claim at that time, awaiting a determination of whether there are any nonexempt assets available to pay creditors. In that case, the creditor must remain alert, awaiting a subsequent notice to file a claim.

§ 20.8 The Debtor's Estate

At the time a Chapter 7 bankruptcy petition is filed, the debtor's nonexempt property comes under the control of the bankruptcy court. It is the responsibility of the trustee to liquidate the estate in the best interests of the creditors. There are many factors which the trustee must consider in liquidation of the estate, and in many consumer cases, the trustee will determine that there are in fact no assets available to pay creditors, because the debtor has only exempt assets, or the value of the debtor's non-exempt assets is so low, it is uneconomical to liquidate. This is called a "no asset" case. Most cases are no asset cases.

§ 20.8.1 Liquidation of the Estate

As discussed earlier, the trustee examines the economics of the debtor's entire financial situation. The trustee is interested in how much money can be raised for the benefit of creditors and at what cost. In determining whether there are assets to liquidate, the trustee will consider if assets are exempt and if equity exists in the asset.

§ 20.8.2 Exempt Property

Although in theory the debtor surrenders all property for the benefit of the creditors, the debtor is entitled by law to keep certain items of property. Such property is called exempt property. The Bankruptcy Code identifies certain exemptions under federal law. Most states have their own exemption system. Unless dictated by state law, a debtor must choose whether to use the federal or state exemption system. Under BAPCPA, debtors usually must claim the exemptions allowed under the law of the state where they lived two years prior to the filing of the voluntary petition. Sometimes this will be different from the state in which they are required to file. This is a very important change in the law. Knowing what property is allowed to be exempted can now be very difficult to determine.

The federal exemption law is adjusted every three years. As of April 1, 2004, the federal exemptions allow a debtor to keep:

- Up to a maximum of $18,450 of equity in residential real estate or personal property, such as a mobile home, used by the debtor as a residence (homestead) (per debtor)
- Up to $2,950 equity in a vehicle
- Up to $475 per item of personal property used in the household of the debtor up to $9,850
- Up to $1,225 equity in jewelry of the debtor
- Up to $1,850 in tools of trade of the debtor
- The debtor's aggregate interest in any property, not to exceed in value $975 plus any unused portion of the real estate exemption up to $9,250, which can be applied to any property of the debtor.

There are various other exempt items—insurance, retirement, alimony, and the like—specifically itemized in section 522 of the Code. State exemptions can vary significantly, and should be evaluated by the debtor and the lawyer to determine whether state or federal exemptions are more favorable.

§ 20.8.3 Equity

What is equity? Generally it is the value of a property or of an interest in it in excess of claims against it.

EXAMPLE:

> The debtor has a house worth $130,000. The mortgage balance is $115,000. The debtor's equity is $15,000, assuming there are no other liens (judgment, tax, etc.) on the house.

It would seem as a practical matter that if the trustee sold the house, the debtor's estate would realize a profit of $15,000. However, the net amount available to pay creditors is reduced both by the cost of sale (often estimated at ten percent of the sale price), plus the debtor's homestead exemption, if the property sold qualifies as a homestead. The value of the homestead (whether state or federal) is generally distributed to the debtor on sale, reducing the net benefit to the estate. Accordingly, the trustee, when analyzing equity, may determine that there is no value available to creditors, and thus no point to liquidating the property. In this example, the house sells for $120,000, the underlying mortgage is $150,000, and the cost to sell is $13,000, leaving net proceeds on $12,000. Since the debtor's federal homestead exemption is $18,450, the estate would receive nothing. Alternatively, in areas where property values have increased, a debtor may have accumulated significant equity in property, which can be liquidated to pay creditors.

§ 20.8.4 Abandoned Property

When, as in the example above, the estate will receive nothing from the sale of an asset, the asset will generally be abandoned by the trustee, so that the trustee has no further responsibility regarding the property. When the trustee abandons the property, the debtor becomes the owner again, subject to the valid liens against it. The debtor must then decide whether to keep it subject to the mortgage. If so, the debtor must continue to make the regular mortgage payments and pay any arrearage. The same is true for other debts secured by liens on property. The debt does not need to be reaffirmed (discussed at § 20.30) since, so long as the debtor is making the payments and complying with the other terms of the mortgage, it is not in default. The trustee may abandon any property that is burdensome to the estate or of inconsequential value to the estate. In addition, a party in interest may request the court to order the trustee to abandon property that is burdensome or of inconsequential value to the estate.

§ 20.8.5 Sale of Property

There are many instances, of course, when there is sufficient equity in property over and above any exemptions to which the debtor is entitled to make a sale profitable for the estate. In those instances, the trustee offers the property for sale. Sales of property have to be approved by the court.

§ 20.9 Dischargeable and Non–Dischargeable Debts

The filing of a petition for relief under Chapter 7 acts as a request for a discharge of all of a person's debts. If no objection to the discharge of a debt owed by the debtor is made by a creditor or by the trustee within the time set by the bankruptcy court, then a discharge will be entered, relieving the debtor of all pre-bankruptcy debts except those debts that are secured by a lien (to the extent of the value of the lien), and certain obligations that the legislature has determined for public policy reasons, should not be able to be discharged.

§ 20.9.1 Non–Dischargeable Debts

Debts which are not discharged by the Chapter 7 bankruptcy are itemized in the Code in Section 523 and most are included below:

- Certain taxes and loans to pay taxes
- Alimony, child support, and maintenance obligations

- Certain debts related to luxury goods
- Debts arising from fines, penalties, or forfeitures payable to a governmental unit
- Personal injury or other claims arising from drunk driving or for willful or malicious injury
- Educational loan and educational benefits overpayment, absent a showing of undue hardship
- Debts incurred through false pretenses, false representation, or fraud
- Debts not listed by the debtor on the schedules filed with the bankruptcy court (though a case can be reopened to include debts inadvertently omitted)

Some of the obligations non-dischargeable in Chapter 7 may be discharged in a Chapter 13 proceeding.

§ 20.9.2 Complaint to Have Debt Declared Non-Dischargeable

Some debts are automatically non-dischargeable while others are discharged unless an objection to discharge is timely filed. If a creditor or the trustee believes that a debt is not dischargeable, it has the right to file a complaint with the court to find either a particular debt non-dischargeable under section 523 of the Code or that the debtor should be denied a discharge in its entirety under section 727 of the Code. The complaint is called an adversary proceeding and is conducted as a separate lawsuit within the bankruptcy proceeding. If the bankruptcy court agrees that discharge should be denied, then the case might be dismissed or, in the event only one debt is found non-dischargeable, the creditor can seek a judgment for the amount owed, which will survive the bankruptcy.

§ 20.9.3 Discharge

A debtor will generally be granted a discharge under Chapter 7 absent an objection as discussed. The Bankruptcy Code requires the bankruptcy court to hold a hearing to inform the debtor why a discharge has not been granted, if discharge is denied.

Once a debtor has been granted a discharge, all creditors are enjoined from commencing or continuing any action against the debtor or the exempt property to collect their debt, with the exception of debts reaffirmed which are subsequently defaulted on by the debtor or specific non-dischargeable debts. Debtors can voluntarily repay a discharged debt at any time.

§ 20.9.4 Reaffirmation of a Debt

Debtors are often encouraged by creditors to "reaffirm" a debt, effectively negating the benefit of the discharge granted by a bankruptcy. Reaffirmation is appropriate only in limited situations and courts will often refuse to allow a debtor to reaffirm a debt if the court believes it will interfere with the debtor's fresh start. When seeking reaffirmation, either the lawyer for the debtor must sign the reaffirmation stating that the debtor fully understood what they were doing *and* that the lawyer believes that the reaffirmation does not impose an undue hardship on the debtor or any dependents, *or* the debtor must appear in court and explain to the bankruptcy judge why it is in the debtor's best interests to do so. Many courts have local rules and requirements for reaffirmation agreements, so the local rules should be checked before any agreement is executed or submitted to the court.

§ 20.9.5 Closing Out the Estate

The administration of the estate is carried on by the trustee, in accordance with specific duties which are set forth in the Bankruptcy Code. Additionally, the trustee makes periodic accountings to the bankruptcy court as well as a final report to the bankruptcy court of the liquidation, including a detailed accounting of the money realized and disbursed and all property sold. At a final hearing, the trustee presents a final accounting to the court and disburses all funds on hand to the creditors in accordance with the bankruptcy court's order.

§ 20.10 Chapter 11 Reorganization

Chapter 11 of the Bankruptcy Code is available to businesses and individual debtors who seek to reorganize their affairs, rather than liquidate. Many major United States' corporations have sought protection under Chapter 11 at one time or another. In Chapter 11, the business continues to be operated by the debtor and its management, a "Debtor in Possession" rather than a trustee, unless the court rules a trustee is necessary. Procedures under Chapter 11 are quite different from those described in this chapter and so other sources should be used for assistance in Chapter 11 practice.

§ 20.11 Chapter 12 Relief—Adjustment of Debts of a Family Farmer or Fisherman With Regular Annual Income

The 1986 amendments to the Bankruptcy Code created a new chapter, Chapter 12, for use by true family farmers, including partnerships consisting of farmers and corporations consisting of owner farmers operating a farming operation. Only a "family farmer" with regular annual income may be a debtor under Chapter 12. A Chapter 12 case may only be initiated voluntarily by the debtor; there cannot be an involuntary Chapter 12 proceeding.

Once a reorganization plan has been filed, a Chapter 12 trustee will supervise the debtor's operation for a period of from three to five years, but once the plan has been confirmed the debtor retains possession of the assets of the estate, including operating the debtor's farm.

BAPCA makes this chapter permanent and added fishermen as eligible debtors.

§ 20.12 Chapter 13 Relief—Adjustments of Debts of an Individual Regular Income

Under this chapter of the Bankruptcy Code, the debtor files a plan agreeing to pay a certain percentage of future earnings or cash from sales of assets to a trustee to pay off the debts within a reasonable period of time, 3–5 years. BAPCPA requires some individuals to pay for 5 years, or the amount the court determines their disposable income would add up to over five years. If the court accepts the plan as being feasible, the debtor has the protection of the court while the debts are paid. At the conclusion of the plan, all debts that have not been repaid are discharged. Thus, in Chapter 13, a debtor uses future earnings, not current assets, to satisfy creditors.

Further advantages in a Chapter 13 plan are:

- Discharge of criminal fines and penalties (but not restitution)
- Discharge of debts for fraud and malicious injury (excluding death or personal injury caused while driving intoxicated)
- Payment of tax arrearages without further penalties and interest
- Payment of mortgage arrearages over the objection of the mortgage lender
- Ability to change the terms of a secured loan (other than a mortgage secured only by the residence). A debtor can sometimes change the interest rate, length of loan, monthly payment, etc.

Chapter 13 bankruptcy or "wage earner" bankruptcies are an alternative to liquidation for an individual consumer with a regular source of income. Also, the debtor must have non-contingent, liquidated, unsecured debt of less than $307,675, and non-contingent, liquidated, secured debt of less than $922,975. These amounts are adjusted every three years. These amounts are as of April 1, 2004.

Illustration 20–1 Petition and Schedules & Statement of Financial Affairs (Official Forms 1, 6, and 7).

FORM 1 VOLUNTARY PETITION

Official Form 1 (10/06)

United States Bankruptcy Court
______________ DISTRICT OF ______________

Voluntary Petition

Name of Debtor (if individual, enter Last, First, Middle):	Name of Joint Debtor (Spouse) (Last, First, Middle):
All Other Names used by the Debtor in the last 8 years (include married, maiden, and trade names):	All Other Names used by the Joint Debtor in the last 8 years (include married, maiden, and trade names):
Last four digits of Soc. Sec./Complete EIN or other Tax I.D. No. (if more than one, state all):	Last four digits of Soc. Sec./Complete EIN or other Tax I.D. No. (if more than one, state all):
Street Address of Debtor (No. and Street, City, and State): ZIP CODE	Street Address of Joint Debtor (No. and Street, City, and State): ZIP CODE
County of Residence or of the Principal Place of Business:	County of Residence or of the Principal Place of Business:
Mailing Address of Debtor (if different from street address): ZIP CODE	Mailing Address of Joint Debtor (if different from street address): ZIP CODE
Location of Principal Assets of Business Debtor (if different from street address above): ZIP CODE	

Type of Debtor
(Form of Organization)
(Check **one** box.)

☐ Individual (includes Joint Debtors)
See Exhibit D on page 2 of this form.
☐ Corporation (includes LLC and LLP)
☐ Partnership
☐ Other (If debtor is not one of the above entities, check this box and state type of entity below.)
____

Nature of Business
(Check **one** box.)

☐ Health Care Business
☐ Single Asset Real Estate as defined in 11 U.S.C. § 101(51B)
☐ Railroad
☐ Stockbroker
☐ Commodity Broker
☐ Clearing Bank
☐ Other

Tax-Exempt Entity
(Check box, if applicable.)

☐ Debtor is a tax-exempt organization under Title 26 of the United States Code (the Internal Revenue Code).

Chapter of Bankruptcy Code Under Which the Petition is Filed (Check **one** box.)

☐ Chapter 7
☐ Chapter 9
☐ Chapter 11
☐ Chapter 12
☐ Chapter 13
☐ Chapter 15 Petition for Recognition of a Foreign Main Proceeding
☐ Chapter 15 Petition for Recognition of a Foreign Nonmain Proceeding

Nature of Debts
(Check one box.)

☐ Debts are primarily consumer debts, defined in 11 U.S.C. § 101(8) as "incurred by an individual primarily for a personal, family, or house-hold purpose."
☐ Debts are primarily business debts.

Filing Fee (Check one box.)

☐ Full Filing Fee attached.

☐ Filing Fee to be paid in installments (applicable to individuals only). Must attach signed application for the court's consideration certifying that the debtor is unable to pay fee except in installments. Rule 1006(b). See Official Form 3A.

☐ Filing Fee waiver requested (applicable to chapter 7 individuals only). Must attach signed application for the court's consideration. See Official Form 3B.

Chapter 11 Debtors

Check one box:
☐ Debtor is a small business debtor as defined in 11 U.S.C. § 101(51D).

☐ Debtor is not a small business debtor as defined in 11 U.S.C. § 101(51D).

Check if:
☐ Debtor's aggregate noncontingent liquidated debts (excluding debts owed to insiders or affiliates) are less than $2 million.

Check all applicable boxes:
☐ A plan is being filed with this petition.
☐ Acceptances of the plan were solicited prepetition from one or more classes of creditors, in accordance with 11 U.S.C. § 1126(b).

Statistical/Administrative Information

☐ Debtor estimates that funds will be available for distribution to unsecured creditors.
☐ Debtor estimates that, after any exempt property is excluded and administrative expenses paid, there will be no funds available for distribution to unsecured creditors.

THIS SPACE IS FOR COURT USE ONLY

Estimated Number of Creditors

1-49	50-99	100-199	200-999	1,000-5,000	5,001-10,000	10,001-25,000	25,001-50,000	50,001 100,000	Over 100,000
☐	☐	☐	☐	☐	☐	☐	☐	☐	☐

Estimated Assets

☐ $0 to $10,000 ☐ $10,000 to $100,000 ☐ $100,000 to $1 million ☐ $1 million to $100 million ☐ More than $100 million

Estimated Liabilities

☐ $0 to $50,000 ☐ $50,000 to $100,000 ☐ $100,000 to $1 million ☐ $1 million to $100 million ☐ More than $100 million

Official Form 1 (10/06) **Form B1, Page 2**

Voluntary Petition *(This page must be completed and filed in every case.)*	Name of Debtor(s):	
All Prior Bankruptcy Cases Filed Within Last 8 Years (If more than two, attach additional sheet.)		
Location Where Filed:	Case Number:	Date Filed:
Location Where Filed:	Case Number:	Date Filed:
Pending Bankruptcy Case Filed by any Spouse, Partner, or Affiliate of this Debtor (If more than one, attach additional sheet.)		
Name of Debtor:	Case Number:	Date Filed:
District:	Relationship:	Judge:

Exhibit A

(To be completed if debtor is required to file periodic reports (e.g., forms 10K and 10Q) with the Securities and Exchange Commission pursuant to Section 13 or 15(d) of the Securities Exchange Act of 1934 and is requesting relief under chapter 11.)

☐ Exhibit A is attached and made a part of this petition.

Exhibit B

(To be completed if debtor is an individual whose debts are primarily consumer debts.)

I, the attorney for the petitioner named in the foregoing petition, declare that I have informed the petitioner that [he or she] may proceed under chapter 7, 11, 12, or 13 of title 11, United States Code, and have explained the relief available under each such chapter. I further certify that I have delivered to the debtor the notice required by 11 U.S.C. § 342(b).

X ______________________________

Signature of Attorney for Debtor(s) (Date)

Exhibit C

Does the debtor own or have possession of any property that poses or is alleged to pose a threat of imminent and identifiable harm to public health or safety?

☐ Yes, and Exhibit C is attached and made a part of this petition.

☐ No.

Exhibit D

(To be completed by every individual debtor. If a joint petition is filed, each spouse must complete and attach a separate Exhibit D.)

☐ Exhibit D completed and signed by the debtor is attached and made a part of this petition.

If this is a joint petition:

☐ Exhibit D also completed and signed by the joint debtor is attached and made a part of this petition.

Information Regarding the Debtor - Venue
(Check any applicable box.)

☐ Debtor has been domiciled or has had a residence, principal place of business, or principal assets in this District for 180 days immediately preceding the date of this petition or for a longer part of such 180 days than in any other District.

☐ There is a bankruptcy case concerning debtor's affiliate, general partner, or partnership pending in this District.

☐ Debtor is a debtor in a foreign proceeding and has its principal place of business or principal assets in the United States in this District, or has no principal place of business or assets in the United States but is a defendant in an action or proceeding [in a federal or state court] in this District, or the interests of the parties will be served in regard to the relief sought in this District.

Statement by a Debtor Who Resides as a Tenant of Residential Property
(Check all applicable boxes.)

☐ Landlord has a judgment against the debtor for possession of debtor's residence. (If box checked, complete the following.)

____
(Name of landlord that obtained judgment)

____
(Address of landlord)

☐ Debtor claims that under applicable nonbankruptcy law, there are circumstances under which the debtor would be permitted to cure the entire monetary default that gave rise to the judgment for possession, after the judgment for possession was entered, and

☐ Debtor has included with this petition the deposit with the court of any rent that would become due during the 30-day period after the filing of the petition.

Official Form 1 (10/06) **Form B1, Page 3**

Voluntary Petition
(This page must be completed and filed in every case.)

Name of Debtor(s):

Signatures

Signature(s) of Debtor(s) (Individual/Joint)

I declare under penalty of perjury that the information provided in this petition is true and correct.
[If petitioner is an individual whose debts are primarily consumer debts and has chosen to file under chapter 7] I am aware that I may proceed under chapter 7, 11, 12 or 13 of title 11, United States Code, understand the relief available under each such chapter, and choose to proceed under chapter 7.
[If no attorney represents me and no bankruptcy petition preparer signs the petition] I have obtained and read the notice required by 11 U.S.C. § 342(b).

I request relief in accordance with the chapter of title 11, United States Code, specified in this petition.

X ______________________________
Signature of Debtor

X ______________________________
Signature of Joint Debtor

____
Telephone Number (if not represented by attorney)

____
Date

Signature of a Foreign Representative

I declare under penalty of perjury that the information provided in this petition is true and correct, that I am the foreign representative of a debtor in a foreign proceeding, and that I am authorized to file this petition.

(Check only **one** box.)

☐ I request relief in accordance with chapter 15 of title 11, United States Code. Certified copies of the documents required by 11 U.S.C. § 1515 are attached.

☐ Pursuant to 11 U.S.C. § 1511, I request relief in accordance with the chapter of title 11 specified in this petition. A certified copy of the order granting recognition of the foreign main proceeding is attached.

X ______________________________
(Signature of Foreign Representative)

____
(Printed Name of Foreign Representative)

____
Date

Signature of Attorney

X ______________________________
Signature of Attorney for Debtor(s)

____
Printed Name of Attorney for Debtor(s)

____
Firm Name

____
Address

____
____
____
Telephone Number

____
Date

Signature of Non-Attorney Bankruptcy Petition Preparer

I declare under penalty of perjury that: (1) I am a bankruptcy petition preparer as defined in 11 U.S.C. § 110; (2) I prepared this document for compensation and have provided the debtor with a copy of this document and the notices and information required under 11 U.S.C. §§ 110(b), 110(h), and 342(b); and, (3) if rules or guidelines have been promulgated pursuant to 11 U.S.C. § 110(h) setting a maximum fee for services chargeable by bankruptcy petition preparers, I have given the debtor notice of the maximum amount before preparing any document for filing for a debtor or accepting any fee from the debtor, as required in that section. Official Form 19B is attached.

____
Printed Name and title, if any, of Bankruptcy Petition Preparer

____
Social Security number (If the bankruptcy petition preparer is not an individual, state the Social Security number of the officer, principal, responsible person or partner of the bankruptcy petition preparer.) (Required by 11 U.S.C. § 110.)

____
Address

____
X ______________________________

____
Date

Signature of bankruptcy petition preparer or officer, principal, responsible person, or partner whose Social Security number is provided above.

Names and Social Security numbers of all other individuals who prepared or assisted in preparing this document unless the bankruptcy petition preparer is not an individual.

If more than one person prepared this document, attach additional sheets conforming to the appropriate official form for each person.

A bankruptcy petition preparer's failure to comply with the provisions of title 11 and the Federal Rules of Bankruptcy Procedure may result in fines or imprisonment or both. 11 U.S.C. § 110; 18 U.S.C. § 156.

Signature of Debtor (Corporation/Partnership)

I declare under penalty of perjury that the information provided in this petition is true and correct, and that I have been authorized to file this petition on behalf of the debtor.

The debtor requests the relief in accordance with the chapter of title 11, United States Code, specified in this petition.

X ______________________________
Signature of Authorized Individual

____
Printed Name of Authorized Individual

____
Title of Authorized Individual

____
Date

Official Form 1, Exhibit D (10/06)

UNITED STATES BANKRUPTCY COURT

_______________District of_______________

In re___________________________ Case No.____________
Debtor(s) (if known)

EXHIBIT D - INDIVIDUAL DEBTOR'S STATEMENT OF COMPLIANCE WITH CREDIT COUNSELING REQUIREMENT

Warning: You must be able to check truthfully one of the five statements regarding credit counseling listed below. If you cannot do so, you are not eligible to file a bankruptcy case, and the court can dismiss any case you do file. If that happens, you will lose whatever filing fee you paid, and your creditors will be able to resume collection activities against you. If your case is dismissed and you file another bankruptcy case later, you may be required to pay a second filing fee and you may have to take extra steps to stop creditors' collection activities.

Every individual debtor must file this Exhibit D. If a joint petition is filed, each spouse must complete and file a separate Exhibit D. Check one of the five statements below and attach any documents as directed.

☐ 1. Within the 180 days **before the filing of my bankruptcy case,** I received a briefing from a credit counseling agency approved by the United States trustee or bankruptcy administrator that outlined the opportunities for available credit counseling and assisted me in performing a related budget analysis, and I have a certificate from the agency describing the services provided to me. *Attach a copy of the certificate and a copy of any debt repayment plan developed through the agency.*

☐ 2. Within the 180 days **before the filing of my bankruptcy case,** I received a briefing from a credit counseling agency approved by the United States trustee or bankruptcy administrator that outlined the opportunities for available credit counseling and assisted me in performing a related budget analysis, but I do not have a certificate from the agency describing the services provided to me. *You must file a copy of a certificate from the agency describing the services provided to you and a copy of any debt repayment plan developed through the agency no later than 15 days after your bankruptcy case is filed.*

Official Form 1, Exh. D (10/06) – Cont.

☐ 3. I certify that I requested credit counseling services from an approved agency but was unable to obtain the services during the five days from the time I made my request, and the following exigent circumstances merit a temporary waiver of the credit counseling requirement so I can file my bankruptcy case now. *[Must be accompanied by a motion for determination by the court.][Summarize exigent circumstances here.]* ______________________________
____.

If the court is satisfied with the reasons stated in your motion, it will send you an order approving your request. You must still obtain the credit counseling briefing within the first 30 days after you file your bankruptcy case and promptly file a certificate from the agency that provided the briefing, together with a copy of any debt management plan developed through the agency. Any extension of the 30-day deadline can be granted only for cause and is limited to a maximum of 15 days. A motion for extension must be filed within the 30-day period. Failure to fulfill these requirements may result in dismissal of your case. If the court is not satisfied with your reasons for filing your bankruptcy case without first receiving a credit counseling briefing, your case may be dismissed.

☐ 4. I am not required to receive a credit counseling briefing because of: *[Check the applicable statement.] [Must be accompanied by a motion for determination by the court.]*

☐ Incapacity. (Defined in 11 U.S.C. § 109(h)(4) as impaired by reason of mental illness or mental deficiency so as to be incapable of realizing and making rational decisions with respect to financial responsibilities.);

☐ Disability. (Defined in 11 U.S.C. § 109(h)(4) as physically impaired to the extent of being unable, after reasonable effort, to participate in a credit counseling briefing in person, by telephone, or through the Internet.);

☐ Active military duty in a military combat zone.

☐ 5. The United States trustee or bankruptcy administrator has determined that the credit counseling requirement of 11 U.S.C. § 109(h) does not apply in this district.

I certify under penalty of perjury that the information provided above is true and correct.

Signature of Debtor: ______________________________

Date: ________________

2

FORM 6 SCHEDULES

Official Form 6 - Summary (10/06)

United States Bankruptcy Court

_______________ District Of _______________

In re ______________________________,
Debtor

Case No. ________________

Chapter ___________

SUMMARY OF SCHEDULES

Indicate as to each schedule whether that schedule is attached and state the number of pages in each. Report the totals from Schedules A, B, D, E, F, I, and J in the boxes provided. Add the amounts from Schedules A and B to determine the total amount of the debtor's assets. Add the amounts of all claims from Schedules D, E, and F to determine the total amount of the debtor's liabilities. Individual debtors also must complete the "Statistical Summary of Certain Liabilities and Related Data" if they file a case under chapter 7, 11, or 13.

NAME OF SCHEDULE	ATTACHED (YES/NO)	NO. OF SHEETS	ASSETS	LIABILITIES	OTHER
A - Real Property			$		
B - Personal Property			$		
C - Property Claimed as Exempt					
D - Creditors Holding Secured Claims				$	
E - Creditors Holding Unsecured Priority Claims (Total of Claims on Schedule E)				$	
F - Creditors Holding Unsecured Nonpriority Claims				$	
G - Executory Contracts and Unexpired Leases					
H - Codebtors					
I - Current Income of Individual Debtor(s)					$
J - Current Expenditures of Individual Debtors(s)					$
TOTAL			$	$	

Official Form 6 - Statistical Summary (10/06)

United States Bankruptcy Court

______________ District Of ______________

In re ____,
Debtor

Case No. __________________

Chapter ___________

STATISTICAL SUMMARY OF CERTAIN LIABILITIES AND RELATED DATA (28 U.S.C. § 159)

If you are an individual debtor whose debts are primarily consumer debts, as defined in § 101(8) of the Bankruptcy Code (11 U.S.C. § 101(8)), filing a case under chapter 7, 11 or 13, you must report all information requested below.

☐ Check this box if you are an individual debtor whose debts are NOT primarily consumer debts. You are not required to report any information here.

This information is for statistical purposes only under 28 U.S.C. § 159.

Summarize the following types of liabilities, as reported in the Schedules, and total them.

Type of Liability	Amount
Domestic Support Obligations (from Schedule E)	$
Taxes and Certain Other Debts Owed to Governmental Units (from Schedule E) (whether disputed or undisputed)	$
Claims for Death or Personal Injury While Debtor Was Intoxicated (from Schedule E)	$
Student Loan Obligations (from Schedule F)	$
Domestic Support, Separation Agreement, and Divorce Decree Obligations Not Reported on Schedule E	$
Obligations to Pension or Profit-Sharing, and Other Similar Obligations (from Schedule F)	$
TOTAL	$

State the following:

Average Income (from Schedule I, Line 16)	$
Average Expenses (from Schedule J, Line 18)	$
Current Monthly Income (from Form 22A Line 12; **OR**, Form 22B Line 11; **OR**, Form 22C Line 20)	$

State the following:

1. Total from Schedule D, "UNSECURED PORTION, IF ANY" column		$
2. Total from Schedule E, "AMOUNT ENTITLED TO PRIORITY" column.	$	
3. Total from Schedule E, "AMOUNT NOT ENTITLED TO PRIORITY, IF ANY" column		$
4. Total from Schedule F		$
5. Total of non-priority unsecured debt (sum of 1, 3, and 4)		$

Form B6A
(10/05)

In re ______________________________________,
Debtor

Case No. ______________________________
(If known)

SCHEDULE A - REAL PROPERTY

Except as directed below, list all real property in which the debtor has any legal, equitable, or future interest, including all property owned as a co-tenant, community property, or in which the debtor has a life estate. Include any property in which the debtor holds rights and powers exercisable for the debtor's own benefit. If the debtor is married, state whether husband, wife, or both own the property by placing an "H," "W," "J," or "C" in the column labeled "Husband, Wife, Joint, or Community." If the debtor holds no interest in real property, write "None" under "Description and Location of Property."

Do not include interests in executory contracts and unexpired leases on this schedule. List them in Schedule G - Executory Contracts and Unexpired Leases.

If an entity claims to have a lien or hold a secured interest in any property, state the amount of the secured claim. See Schedule D. If no entity claims to hold a secured interest in the property, write "None" in the column labeled "Amount of Secured Claim."

If the debtor is an individual or if a joint petition is filed, state the amount of any exemption claimed in the property only in Schedule C - Property Claimed as Exempt.

DESCRIPTION AND LOCATION OF PROPERTY	NATURE OF DEBTOR'S INTEREST IN PROPERTY	HUSBAND, WIFE, JOINT, OR COMMUNITY	CURRENT VALUE OF DEBTOR'S INTEREST IN PROPERTY, WITHOUT DEDUCTING ANY SECURED CLAIM OR EXEMPTION	AMOUNT OF SECURED CLAIM
		Total➤		

(Report also on Summary of Schedules.)

Form B6B
(10/05)

In re ______________________________, Case No. ____________________
Debtor (If known)

SCHEDULE B - PERSONAL PROPERTY

Except as directed below, list all personal property of the debtor of whatever kind. If the debtor has no property in one or more of the categories, place an "x" in the appropriate position in the column labeled "None." If additional space is needed in any category, attach a separate sheet properly identified with the case name, case number, and the number of the category. If the debtor is married, state whether husband, wife, or both own the property by placing an "H," "W," "J," or "C" in the column labeled "Husband, Wife, Joint, or Community." If the debtor is an individual or a joint petition is filed, state the amount of any exemptions claimed only in Schedule C - Property Claimed as Exempt.

Do not list interests in executory contracts and unexpired leases on this schedule. List them in Schedule G - Executory Contracts and Unexpired Leases.

If the property is being held for the debtor by someone else, state that person's name and address under "Description and Location of Property." In providing the information requested in this schedule, do not include the name or address of a minor child. Simply state "a minor child."

TYPE OF PROPERTY	NONE	DESCRIPTION AND LOCATION OF PROPERTY	HUSBAND, WIFE, JOINT, OR COMMUNITY	CURRENT VALUE OF DEBTOR'S INTEREST IN PROPERTY, WITH-OUT DEDUCTING ANY SECURED CLAIM OR EXEMPTION
1. Cash on hand.				
2. Checking, savings or other financial accounts, certificates of deposit, or shares in banks, savings and loan, thrift, building and loan, and homestead associations, or credit unions, brokerage houses, or cooperatives.				
3. Security deposits with public utilities, telephone companies, landlords, and others.				
4. Household goods and furnishings, including audio, video, and computer equipment.				
5. Books; pictures and other art objects; antiques; stamp, coin, record, tape, compact disc, and other collections or collectibles.				
6. Wearing apparel.				
7. Furs and jewelry.				
8. Firearms and sports, photographic, and other hobby equipment.				
9. Interests in insurance policies. Name insurance company of each policy and itemize surrender or refund value of each.				
10. Annuities. Itemize and name each issuer.				
11. Interests in an education IRA as defined in 26 U.S.C. § 530(b)(1) or under a qualified State tuition plan as defined in 26 U.S.C. § 529(b)(1). Give particulars. (File separately the record(s) of any such interest(s). 11 U.S.C. § 521(c); Rule 1007(b)).				

Form B6B-Cont.
(10/05)

In re ______________________________, Case No. ____________________
Debtor (If known)

SCHEDULE B - PERSONAL PROPERTY
(Continuation Sheet)

TYPE OF PROPERTY	N O N E	DESCRIPTION AND LOCATION OF PROPERTY	HUSBAND, WIFE, JOINT, OR COMMUNITY	CURRENT VALUE OF DEBTOR'S INTEREST IN PROPERTY, WITH-OUT DEDUCTING ANY SECURED CLAIM OR EXEMPTION
12. Interests in IRA, ERISA, Keogh, or other pension or profit sharing plans. Give particulars.				
13. Stock and interests in incorporated and unincorporated businesses. Itemize.				
14. Interests in partnerships or joint ventures. Itemize.				
15. Government and corporate bonds and other negotiable and non-negotiable instruments.				
16. Accounts receivable.				
17. Alimony, maintenance, support, and property settlements to which the debtor is or may be entitled. Give particulars.				
18. Other liquidated debts owed to debtor including tax refunds. Give particulars.				
19. Equitable or future interests, life estates, and rights or powers exercisable for the benefit of the debtor other than those listed in Schedule A – Real Property.				
20. Contingent and noncontingent interests in estate of a decedent, death benefit plan, life insurance policy, or trust.				
21. Other contingent and unliquidated claims of every nature, including tax refunds, counterclaims of the debtor, and rights to setoff claims. Give estimated value of each.				

Form B6B-cont.
(10/05)

In re ______________________________________, Case No. ____________________
Debtor (If known)

SCHEDULE B -PERSONAL PROPERTY

(Continuation Sheet)

TYPE OF PROPERTY	N O N E	DESCRIPTION AND LOCATION OF PROPERTY	HUSBAND, WIFE, JOINT, OR COMMUNITY	CURRENT VALUE OF DEBTOR'S INTEREST IN PROPERTY, WITH-OUT DEDUCTING ANY SECURED CLAIM OR EXEMPTION
22. Patents, copyrights, and other intellectual property. Give particulars.				
23. Licenses, franchises, and other general intangibles. Give particulars.				
24. Customer lists or other compilations containing personally identifiable information (as defined in 11 U.S.C. § 101(41A)) provided to the debtor by individuals in connection with obtaining a product or service from the debtor primarily for personal, family, or household purposes.				
25. Automobiles, trucks, trailers, and other vehicles and accessories.				
26. Boats, motors, and accessories.				
27. Aircraft and accessories.				
28. Office equipment, furnishings, and supplies.				
29. Machinery, fixtures, equipment, and supplies used in business.				
30. Inventory.				
31. Animals.				
32. Crops - growing or harvested. Give particulars.				
33. Farming equipment and implements.				
34. Farm supplies, chemicals, and feed.				
35. Other personal property of any kind not already listed. Itemize.				

_________continuation sheets attached Total➤ $

(Include amounts from any continuation sheets attached. Report total also on Summary of Schedules.)

Form B6C
(10/05)

In re ______________________________, Case No. ____________________
Debtor (If known)

SCHEDULE C - PROPERTY CLAIMED AS EXEMPT

Debtor claims the exemptions to which debtor is entitled under:
(Check one box)
☐ 11 U.S.C. § 522(b)(2)
☐ 11 U.S.C. § 522(b)(3)

☐ Check if debtor claims a homestead exemption that exceeds $125,000.

DESCRIPTION OF PROPERTY	SPECIFY LAW PROVIDING EACH EXEMPTION	VALUE OF CLAIMED EXEMPTION	CURRENT VALUE OF PROPERTY WITHOUT DEDUCTING EXEMPTION

Official Form 6D (10/06)

In re _________________________________, **Case No.** ______________________________
Debtor **(if known)**

SCHEDULE D - CREDITORS HOLDING SECURED CLAIMS

State the name, mailing address, including zip code, and last four digits of any account number of all entities holding claims secured by property of the debtor as of the date of filing of the petition. The complete account number of any account the debtor has with the creditor is useful to the trustee and the creditor and may be provided if the debtor chooses to do so. List creditors holding all types of secured interests such as judgment liens, garnishments, statutory liens, mortgages, deeds of trust, and other security interests.

List creditors in alphabetical order to the extent practicable. If a minor child is a creditor, indicate that by stating "a minor child" and do not disclose the child's name. See 11 U.S.C. § 112. If "a minor child" is stated, also include the name, address, and legal relationship to the minor child of a person described in Fed. R. Bankr. P. 1007(m). If all secured creditors will not fit on this page, use the continuation sheet provided.

If any entity other than a spouse in a joint case may be jointly liable on a claim, place an "X" in the column labeled "Codebtor," include the entity on the appropriate schedule of creditors, and complete Schedule H – Codebtors. If a joint petition is filed, state whether the husband, wife, both of them, or the marital community may be liable on each claim by placing an "H," "W," "J," or "C" in the column labeled "Husband, Wife, Joint, or Community."

If the claim is contingent, place an "X" in the column labeled "Contingent." If the claim is unliquidated, place an "X" in the column labeled "Unliquidated." If the claim is disputed, place an "X" in the column labeled "Disputed." (You may need to place an "X" in more than one of these three columns.)

Total the columns labeled "Amount of Claim Without Deducting Value of Collateral" and "Unsecured Portion, if Any" in the boxes labeled "Total(s)" on the last sheet of the completed schedule. Report the total from the column labeled "Amount of Claim Without Deducting Value of Collateral" also on the Summary of Schedules and, if the debtor is an individual with primarily consumer debts, report the total from the column labeled "Unsecured Portion, if Any" on the Statistical Summary of Certain Liabilities and Related Data.

☐ Check this box if debtor has no creditors holding secured claims to report on this Schedule D.

CREDITOR'S NAME AND MAILING ADDRESS INCLUDING ZIP CODE AND AN ACCOUNT NUMBER (*See Instructions Above.*)	CODEBTOR	HUSBAND, WIFE, JOINT, OR COMMUNITY	DATE CLAIM WAS INCURRED, NATURE OF LIEN, AND DESCRIPTION AND VALUE OF PROPERTY SUBJECT TO LIEN	CONTINGENT	UNLIQUIDATED	DISPUTED	AMOUNT OF CLAIM WITHOUT DEDUCTING VALUE OF COLLATERAL	UNSECURED PORTION, IF ANY
ACCOUNT NO.			VALUE $					
ACCOUNT NO.			VALUE $					
ACCOUNT NO.			VALUE $					
____continuation sheets attached			Subtotal ► (Total of this page)				$	$
			Total ► (Use only on last page)				$	$
							(Report also on Summary of Schedules.)	(If applicable, report also on Statistical Summary of Certain Liabilities and Related Data.)

Official Form 6D (10/06) – Cont.
In re ______________________________, Case No. ______________________________
Debtor **(if known)**

SCHEDULE D - CREDITORS HOLDING SECURED CLAIMS
(Continuation Sheet)

CREDITOR'S NAME AND MAILING ADDRESS INCLUDING ZIP CODE AND AN ACCOUNT NUMBER (*See Instructions Above.*)	CODEBTOR	HUSBAND, WIFE, JOINT, OR COMMUNITY	DATE CLAIM WAS INCURRED, NATURE OF LIEN , AND DESCRIPTION AND VALUE OF PROPERTY SUBJECT TO LIEN	CONTINGENT	UNLIQUIDATED	DISPUTED	AMOUNT OF CLAIM WITHOUT DEDUCTING VALUE OF COLLATERAL	UNSECURED PORTION, IF ANY
ACCOUNT NO.			VALUE $					
ACCOUNT NO.			VALUE $					
ACCOUNT NO.			VALUE $					
ACCOUNT NO.			VALUE $					
ACCOUNT NO.			VALUE $					
Sheet no.___of___continuation sheets attached to Schedule of Creditors Holding Secured Claims			Subtotal (s)► (Total(s) of this page)				$	$
			Total(s) ► (Use only on last page)				$	$
							(Report also on Summary of Schedules.)	(If applicable, report also on Statistical Summary of Certain Liabilities and Related Data.)

Official Form 6E (10/06)

In re ______________________________, Case No.______________________
Debtor (if known)

SCHEDULE E - CREDITORS HOLDING UNSECURED PRIORITY CLAIMS

A complete list of claims entitled to priority, listed separately by type of priority, is to be set forth on the sheets provided. Only holders of unsecured claims entitled to priority should be listed in this schedule. In the boxes provided on the attached sheets, state the name, mailing address, including zip code, and last four digits of the account number, if any, of all entities holding priority claims against the debtor or the property of the debtor, as of the date of the filing of the petition. Use a separate continuation sheet for each type of priority and label each with the type of priority.

The complete account number of any account the debtor has with the creditor is useful to the trustee and the creditor and may be provided if the debtor chooses to do so. If a minor child is a creditor, indicate that by stating "a minor child" and do not disclose the child's name. See 11 U.S.C. § 112. If "a minor child" is stated, also include the name, address, and legal relationship to the minor child of a person described in Fed. R. Bankr. P. 1007(m).

If any entity other than a spouse in a joint case may be jointly liable on a claim, place an "X" in the column labeled "Codebtor," include the entity on the appropriate schedule of creditors, and complete Schedule H-Codebtors. If a joint petition is filed, state whether the husband, wife, both of them, or the marital community may be liable on each claim by placing an "H," "W," "J," or "C" in the column labeled "Husband, Wife, Joint, or Community." If the claim is contingent, place an "X" in the column labeled "Contingent." If the claim is unliquidated, place an "X" in the column labeled "Unliquidated." If the claim is disputed, place an "X" in the column labeled "Disputed." (You may need to place an "X" in more than one of these three columns.)

Report the total of claims listed on each sheet in the box labeled "Subtotals" on each sheet. Report the total of all claims listed on this Schedule E in the box labeled "Total" on the last sheet of the completed schedule. Report this total also on the Summary of Schedules.

Report the total of amounts entitled to priority listed on each sheet in the box labeled "Subtotals" on each sheet. Report the total of all amounts entitled to priority listed on this Schedule E in the box labeled "Totals" on the last sheet of the completed schedule. Individual debtors with primarily consumer debts who file a case under chapter 7 or 13 report this total also on the Statistical Summary of Certain Liabilities and Related Data.

Report the total of amounts not entitled to priority listed on each sheet in the box labeled "Subtotals" on each sheet. Report the total of all amounts not entitled to priority listed on this Schedule E in the box labeled "Totals" on the last sheet of the completed schedule. Individual debtors with primarily consumer debts who file a case under chapter 7 report this total also on the Statistical Summary of Certain Liabilities and Related Data.

☐ Check this box if debtor has no creditors holding unsecured priority claims to report on this Schedule E.

TYPES OF PRIORITY CLAIMS (Check the appropriate box(es) below if claims in that category are listed on the attached sheets)

☐ **Domestic Support Obligations**

Claims for domestic support that are owed to or recoverable by a spouse, former spouse, or child of the debtor, or the parent, legal guardian, or responsible relative of such a child, or a governmental unit to whom such a domestic support claim has been assigned to the extent provided in 11 U.S.C. § 507(a)(1).

☐ **Extensions of credit in an involuntary case**

Claims arising in the ordinary course of the debtor's business or financial affairs after the commencement of the case but before the earlier of the appointment of a trustee or the order for relief. 11 U.S.C. § 507(a)(3).

☐ **Wages, salaries, and commissions**

Wages, salaries, and commissions, including vacation, severance, and sick leave pay owing to employees and commissions owing to qualifying independent sales representatives up to $10,000* per person earned within 180 days immediately preceding the filing of the original petition, or the cessation of business, whichever occurred first, to the extent provided in 11 U.S.C. § 507(a)(4).

☐ **Contributions to employee benefit plans**

Money owed to employee benefit plans for services rendered within 180 days immediately preceding the filing of the original petition, or the cessation of business, whichever occurred first, to the extent provided in 11 U.S.C. § 507(a)(5).

Official Form 6E (10/06) - Cont.

In re ______________________________________,   Case No.______________________
Debtor   (if known)

☐ **Certain farmers and fishermen**

Claims of certain farmers and fishermen, up to $4,925* per farmer or fisherman, against the debtor, as provided in 11 U.S.C. § 507(a)(6).

☐ **Deposits by individuals**

Claims of individuals up to $2,225* for deposits for the purchase, lease, or rental of property or services for personal, family, or household use, that were not delivered or provided. 11 U.S.C. § 507(a)(7).

☐ **Taxes and Certain Other Debts Owed to Governmental Units**

Taxes, customs duties, and penalties owing to federal, state, and local governmental units as set forth in 11 U.S.C. § 507(a)(8).

☐ **Commitments to Maintain the Capital of an Insured Depository Institution**

Claims based on commitments to the FDIC, RTC, Director of the Office of Thrift Supervision, Comptroller of the Currency, or Board of Governors of the Federal Reserve System, or their predecessors or successors, to maintain the capital of an insured depository institution. 11 U.S.C. § 507 (a)(9).

☐ **Claims for Death or Personal Injury While Debtor Was Intoxicated**

Claims for death or personal injury resulting from the operation of a motor vehicle or vessel while the debtor was intoxicated from using alcohol, a drug, or another substance. 11 U.S.C. § 507(a)(10).

* Amounts are subject to adjustment on April 1, 2007, and every three years thereafter with respect to cases commenced on or after the date of adjustment.

____ **continuation sheets attached**

Official Form 6E (10/06) - Cont.

In re ______________________________, Case No. ______________________
Debtor (If known)

SCHEDULE E - CREDITORS HOLDING UNSECURED PRIORITY CLAIMS

(Continuation Sheet)

Type of Priority for Claims Listed on This Sheet

CREDITOR'S NAME, MAILING ADDRESS INCLUDING ZIP CODE, AND ACCOUNT NUMBER (*See instructions above.*)	CODEBTOR	HUSBAND, WIFE, JOINT, OR COMMUNITY	DATE CLAIM WAS INCURRED AND CONSIDERATION FOR CLAIM	CONTINGENT	UNLIQUIDATED	DISPUTED	AMOUNT OF CLAIM	AMOUNT ENTITLED TO PRIORITY	AMOUNT NOT ENTITLED TO PRIORITY, IF ANY
Account No.									
Account No.									
Account No.									
Account No.									
Sheet no. ___ of ___ continuation sheets attached to Schedule of Creditors Holding Priority Claims						Subtotals➤ (Totals of this page)	$	$	
						Total➤ (Use only on last page of the completed Schedule E. Report also on the Summary of Schedules.)	$		
						Totals➤ (Use only on last page of the completed Schedule E. If applicable, report also on the Statistical Summary of Certain Liabilities and Related Data.)		$	$

Official Form 6F (10/06)

In re ______________________________, Debtor   Case No. ______________________ (if known)

SCHEDULE F - CREDITORS HOLDING UNSECURED NONPRIORITY CLAIMS

State the name, mailing address, including zip code, and last four digits of any account number, of all entities holding unsecured claims without priority against the debtor or the property of the debtor, as of the date of filing of the petition. The complete account number of any account the debtor has with the creditor is useful to the trustee and the creditor and may be provided if the debtor chooses to do so. If a minor child is a creditor, indicate that by stating "a minor child" and do not disclose the child's name. See 11 U.S.C. § 112. If "a minor child" is stated, also include the name, address, and legal relationship to the minor child of a person described in Fed. R. Bankr. P. 1007(m). Do not include claims listed in Schedules D and E. If all creditors will not fit on this page, use the continuation sheet provided.

If any entity other than a spouse in a joint case may be jointly liable on a claim, place an "X" in the column labeled "Codebtor," include the entity on the appropriate schedule of creditors, and complete Schedule H - Codebtors. If a joint petition is filed, state whether the husband, wife, both of them, or the marital community may be liable on each claim by placing an "H," "W," "J," or "C" in the column labeled "Husband, Wife, Joint, or Community."

If the claim is contingent, place an "X" in the column labeled "Contingent." If the claim is unliquidated, place an "X" in the column labeled "Unliquidated." If the claim is disputed, place an "X" in the column labeled "Disputed." (You may need to place an "X" in more than one of these three columns.)

Report the total of all claims listed on this schedule in the box labeled "Total" on the last sheet of the completed schedule. Report this total also on the Summary of Schedules and, if the debtor is an individual with primarily consumer debts filing a case under chapter 7, report this total also on the Statistical Summary of Certain Liabilities and Related Data..

☐ Check this box if debtor has no creditors holding unsecured claims to report on this Schedule F.

CREDITOR'S NAME, MAILING ADDRESS INCLUDING ZIP CODE, AND ACCOUNT NUMBER *(See instructions above.)*	CODEBTOR	HUSBAND, WIFE, JOINT, OR COMMUNITY	DATE CLAIM WAS INCURRED AND CONSIDERATION FOR CLAIM. IF CLAIM IS SUBJECT TO SETOFF, SO STATE.	CONTINGENT	UNLIQUIDATED	DISPUTED	AMOUNT OF CLAIM
ACCOUNT NO.							
ACCOUNT NO.							
ACCOUNT NO.							
ACCOUNT NO.							
						Subtotal➤	$
____continuation sheets attached						Total➤ (Use only on last page of the completed Schedule F.) (Report also on Summary of Schedules and, if applicable, on the Statistical Summary of Certain Liabilities and Related Data.)	$

Official Form 6F (10/06) - Cont.

In re ______________________________, Case No. ______________________
Debtor (if known)

SCHEDULE F - CREDITORS HOLDING UNSECURED NONPRIORITY CLAIMS

(Continuation Sheet)

CREDITOR'S NAME, MAILING ADDRESS INCLUDING ZIP CODE, AND ACCOUNT NUMBER (See instructions above.)	CODEBTOR	HUSBAND, WIFE, JOINT, OR COMMUNITY	DATE CLAIM WAS INCURRED AND CONSIDERATION FOR CLAIM. IF CLAIM IS SUBJECT TO SETOFF, SO STATE.	CONTINGENT	UNLIQUIDATED	DISPUTED	AMOUNT OF CLAIM
ACCOUNT NO.							
ACCOUNT NO.							
ACCOUNT NO.							
ACCOUNT NO.							
ACCOUNT NO.							

Sheet no.___of___continuation sheets attached to Schedule of Creditors Holding Unsecured Nonpriority Claims

Subtotal➤ $

Total➤ $
(Use only on last page of the completed Schedule F.)
(Report also on Summary of Schedules and, if applicable on the Statistical Summary of Certain Liabilities and Related Data.)

Form B6G
(10/05)

In re ______________________________, Case No.____________________
Debtor (if known)

SCHEDULE G - EXECUTORY CONTRACTS AND UNEXPIRED LEASES

Describe all executory contracts of any nature and all unexpired leases of real or personal property. Include any timeshare interests. State nature of debtor's interest in contract, i.e., "Purchaser," "Agent," etc. State whether debtor is the lessor or lessee of a lease. Provide the names and complete mailing addresses of all other parties to each lease or contract described. If a minor child is a party to one of the leases or contracts, indicate that by stating "a minor child" and do not disclose the child's name. See 11 U.S.C. § 112; Fed.R. Bankr. P. 1007(m).

☐ Check this box if debtor has no executory contracts or unexpired leases.

NAME AND MAILING ADDRESS, INCLUDING ZIP CODE, OF OTHER PARTIES TO LEASE OR CONTRACT.	DESCRIPTION OF CONTRACT OR LEASE AND NATURE OF DEBTOR'S INTEREST. STATE WHETHER LEASE IS FOR NONRESIDENTIAL REAL PROPERTY. STATE CONTRACT NUMBER OF ANY GOVERNMENT CONTRACT.

Form B6H
(10/05)

In re ____________________________________,
Debtor

Case No. __________________________
(if known)

SCHEDULE H - CODEBTORS

Provide the information requested concerning any person or entity, other than a spouse in a joint case, that is also liable on any debts listed by debtor in the schedules of creditors. Include all guarantors and co-signers. If the debtor resides or resided in a community property state, commonwealth, or territory (including Alaska, Arizona, California, Idaho, Louisiana, Nevada, New Mexico, Puerto Rico, Texas, Washington, or Wisconsin) within the eight year period immediately preceding the commencement of the case, identify the name of the debtor's spouse and of any former spouse who resides or resided with the debtor in the community property state, commonwealth, or territory. Include all names used by the nondebtor spouse during the eight years immediately preceding the commencement of this case. If a minor child is a codebtor or a creditor, indicate that by stating "a minor child" and do not disclose the child's name. See 11 U.S.C. § 112; Fed. Bankr. P. 1007(m).

☐ Check this box if debtor has no codebtors.

NAME AND ADDRESS OF CODEBTOR	NAME AND ADDRESS OF CREDITOR

Official Form 6I (10/06)

In re ______________________________ , Case No.______________________
Debtor (if known)

SCHEDULE I - CURRENT INCOME OF INDIVIDUAL DEBTOR(S)

The column labeled "Spouse" must be completed in all cases filed by joint debtors and by every married debtor, whether or not a joint petition is filed, unless the spouses are separated and a joint petition is not filed. Do not state the name of any minor child.

Debtor's Marital Status:	DEPENDENTS OF DEBTOR AND SPOUSE	
	RELATIONSHIP(S):	AGE(S):

Employment:	DEBTOR	SPOUSE
Occupation		
Name of Employer		
How long employed		
Address of Employer		

INCOME: (Estimate of average or projected monthly income at time case filed)	DEBTOR	SPOUSE
1. Monthly gross wages, salary, and commissions (Prorate if not paid monthly)	$________	$________
2. Estimate monthly overtime	$________	$________
3. SUBTOTAL	$________	$________
4. LESS PAYROLL DEDUCTIONS		
a. Payroll taxes and social security	$________	$________
b. Insurance	$________	$________
c. Union dues	$________	$________
d. Other (Specify): ________________	$________	$________
5. SUBTOTAL OF PAYROLL DEDUCTIONS	$________	$________
6. TOTAL NET MONTHLY TAKE HOME PAY	$________	$________
7. Regular income from operation of business or profession or farm (Attach detailed statement)	$________	$________
8. Income from real property	$________	$________
9. Interest and dividends	$________	$________
10. Alimony, maintenance or support payments payable to the debtor for the debtor's use or that of dependents listed above	$________	$________
11. Social security or government assistance (Specify): ________________	$________	$________
12. Pension or retirement income	$________	$________
13. Other monthly income (Specify): ________________	$________	$________
14. SUBTOTAL OF LINES 7 THROUGH 13	$________	$________
15. AVERAGE MONTHLY INCOME (Add amounts shown on lines 6 and 14)	$________	$________
16. COMBINED AVERAGE MONTHLY INCOME: (Combine column totals from line 15; if there is only one debtor repeat total reported on line 15)	$________	

(Report also on Summary of Schedules and, if applicable, on Statistical Summary of Certain Liabilities and Related Data)

17. Describe any increase or decrease in income reasonably anticipated to occur within the year following the filing of this document:

____

____

Official Form 6J (10/06)

In re ______________________________, Case No.______________________
Debtor (if known)

SCHEDULE J - CURRENT EXPENDITURES OF INDIVIDUAL DEBTOR(S)

Complete this schedule by estimating the average or projected monthly expenses of the debtor and the debtor's family at time case filed. Prorate any payments made bi-weekly, quarterly, semi-annually, or annually to show monthly rate.

Check this box if a joint petition is filed and debtor's spouse maintains a separate household. Complete a separate schedule of expenditures labeled "Spouse."

1. Rent or home mortgage payment (include lot rented for mobile home) $__________
   a. Are real estate taxes included? Yes ______ No ______
   b. Is property insurance included? Yes ______ No ______
2. Utilities: a. Electricity and heating fuel $__________
   b. Water and sewer $__________
   c. Telephone $__________
   d. Other ______________________________ $__________
3. Home maintenance (repairs and upkeep) $__________
4. Food $__________
5. Clothing $__________
6. Laundry and dry cleaning $__________
7. Medical and dental expenses $__________
8. Transportation (not including car payments) $__________
9. Recreation, clubs and entertainment, newspapers, magazines, etc. $__________
10. Charitable contributions $__________
11. Insurance (not deducted from wages or included in home mortgage payments)
   a. Homeowner's or renter's $__________
   b. Life $__________
   c. Health $__________
   d. Auto $__________
   e. Other ______________________________ $__________
12. Taxes (not deducted from wages or included in home mortgage payments)
(Specify) ______________________________ $__________
13. Installment payments: (In chapter 11, 12, and 13 cases, do not list payments to be included in the plan)
   a. Auto $__________
   b. Other ______________________________ $__________
   c. Other ______________________________ $__________
14. Alimony, maintenance, and support paid to others $__________
15. Payments for support of additional dependents not living at your home $__________
16. Regular expenses from operation of business, profession, or farm (attach detailed statement) $__________
17. Other ______________________________ $__________
18. AVERAGE MONTHLY EXPENSES (Total lines 1-17. Report also on Summary of Schedules and, if applicable, on the Statistical Summary of Certain Liabilities and Related Data.) $__________
19. Describe any increase or decrease in expenditures reasonably anticipated to occur within the year following the filing of this document:
____
____
____

20. STATEMENT OF MONTHLY NET INCOME
   a. Average monthly income from Line 15 of Schedule I $__________
   b. Average monthly expenses from Line 18 above $__________
   c. Monthly net income (a. minus b.) $__________

Official Form 6 - Declaration (10/06)

In re ______________________________ ,
Debtor

Case No. ______________________________
(if known)

DECLARATION CONCERNING DEBTOR'S SCHEDULES

DECLARATION UNDER PENALTY OF PERJURY BY INDIVIDUAL DEBTOR

I declare under penalty of perjury that I have read the foregoing summary and schedules, consisting of ____ sheets (*total shown on summary page plus 2*), and that they are true and correct to the best of my knowledge, information, and belief.

Date ______________________________ Signature: ______________________________
Debtor

Date ______________________________ Signature: ______________________________
(Joint Debtor, if any)

[If joint case, both spouses must sign.]

DECLARATION AND SIGNATURE OF NON-ATTORNEY BANKRUPTCY PETITION PREPARER (See 11 U.S.C. § 110)

I declare under penalty of perjury that: (1) I am a bankruptcy petition preparer as defined in 11 U.S.C. § 110; (2) I prepared this document for compensation and have provided the debtor with a copy of this document and the notices and information required under 11 U.S.C. §§ 110(b), 110(h) and 342(b); and, (3) if rules or guidelines have been promulgated pursuant to 11 U.S.C. § 110(h) setting a maximum fee for services chargeable by bankruptcy petition preparers, I have given the debtor notice of the maximum amount before preparing any document for filing for a debtor or accepting any fee from the debtor, as required by that section.

______________________________ ______________________________
Printed or Typed Name and Title, if any, of Bankruptcy Petition Preparer
Social Security No. *(Required by 11 U.S.C. § 110.)*

If the bankruptcy petition preparer is not an individual, state the name, title (if any), address, and social security number of the officer, principal, responsible person, or partner who signs this document.

____
____
____
Address

X ______________________________ ______________________________
Signature of Bankruptcy Petition Preparer Date

Names and Social Security numbers of all other individuals who prepared or assisted in preparing this document, unless the bankruptcy petition preparer is not an individual:

If more than one person prepared this document, attach additional signed sheets conforming to the appropriate Official Form for each person.

A bankruptcy petition preparer's failure to comply with the provisions of title 11 and the Federal Rules of Bankruptcy Procedure may result in fines or imprisonment or both. 11 U.S.C. § 110; 18 U.S.C. § 156.

DECLARATION UNDER PENALTY OF PERJURY ON BEHALF OF A CORPORATION OR PARTNERSHIP

I, the ______________________________ [the president or other officer or an authorized agent of the corporation or a member or an authorized agent of the partnership] of the ______________________________ [corporation or partnership] named as debtor in this case, declare under penalty of perjury that I have read the foregoing summary and schedules, consisting of ____ sheets (*total shown on summary page plus 1*), and that they are true and correct to the best of my knowledge, information, and belief.

Date ______________________________ Signature: ______________________________

____
[Print or type name of individual signing on behalf of debtor.]

[An individual signing on behalf of a partnership or corporation must indicate position or relationship to debtor.]

Penalty for making a false statement or concealing property: Fine of up to $500,000 or imprisonment for up to 5 years or both. 18 U.S.C. §§ 152 and 3571.

FORM 7 STATEMENT OF FINANCIAL AFFAIRS

Official Form 7
(10/05)

UNITED STATES BANKRUPTCY COURT

__________________________ DISTRICT OF __________________________

In re: ______________________________, Case No. ______________________________
Debtor (if known)

STATEMENT OF FINANCIAL AFFAIRS

This statement is to be completed by every debtor. Spouses filing a joint petition may file a single statement on which the information for both spouses is combined. If the case is filed under chapter 12 or chapter 13, a married debtor must furnish information for both spouses whether or not a joint petition is filed, unless the spouses are separated and a joint petition is not filed. An individual debtor engaged in business as a sole proprietor, partner, family farmer, or self-employed professional, should provide the information requested on this statement concerning all such activities as well as the individual's personal affairs. Do not include the name or address of a minor child in this statement. Indicate payments, transfers and the like to minor children by stating "a minor child." See 11 U.S.C. § 112; Fed. R. Bankr. P. 1007(m).

Questions 1 - 18 are to be completed by all debtors. Debtors that are or have been in business, as defined below, also must complete Questions 19 - 25. **If the answer to an applicable question is "None," mark the box labeled "None."** If additional space is needed for the answer to any question, use and attach a separate sheet properly identified with the case name, case number (if known), and the number of the question.

DEFINITIONS

"In business." A debtor is "in business" for the purpose of this form if the debtor is a corporation or partnership. An individual debtor is "in business" for the purpose of this form if the debtor is or has been, within six years immediately preceding the filing of this bankruptcy case, any of the following: an officer, director, managing executive, or owner of 5 percent or more of the voting or equity securities of a corporation; a partner, other than a limited partner, of a partnership; a sole proprietor or self-employed full-time or part-time. An individual debtor also may be "in business" for the purpose of this form if the debtor engages in a trade, business, or other activity, other than as an employee, to supplement income from the debtor's primary employment.

"Insider." The term "insider" includes but is not limited to: relatives of the debtor; general partners of the debtor and their relatives; corporations of which the debtor is an officer, director, or person in control; officers, directors, and any owner of 5 percent or more of the voting or equity securities of a corporate debtor and their relatives; affiliates of the debtor and insiders of such affiliates; any managing agent of the debtor. 11 U.S.C. § 101.

---

1. Income from employment or operation of business

None ☐

State the gross amount of income the debtor has received from employment, trade, or profession, or from operation of the debtor's business, including part-time activities either as an employee or in independent trade or business, from the beginning of this calendar year to the date this case was commenced. State also the gross amounts received during the **two years** immediately preceding this calendar year. (A debtor that maintains, or has maintained, financial records on the basis of a fiscal rather than a calendar year may report fiscal year income. Identify the beginning and ending dates of the debtor's fiscal year.) If a joint petition is filed, state income for each spouse separately. (Married debtors filing under chapter 12 or chapter 13 must state income of both spouses whether or not a joint petition is filed, unless the spouses are separated and a joint petition is not filed.)

AMOUNT SOURCE

2. Income other than from employment or operation of business

None ☐ State the amount of income received by the debtor other than from employment, trade, profession, operation of the debtor's business during the **two years** immediately preceding the commencement of this case. Give particulars. If a joint petition is filed, state income for each spouse separately. (Married debtors filing under chapter 12 or chapter 13 must state income for each spouse whether or not a joint petition is filed, unless the spouses are separated and a joint petition is not filed.)

AMOUNT	SOURCE

3. Payments to creditors

Complete a. or b., as appropriate, and c.

None ☐ a. *Individual or joint debtor(s) with primarily consumer debts:* List all payments on loans, installment purchases of goods or services, and other debts to any creditor made within **90 days** immediately preceding the commencement of this case if the aggregate value of all property that constitutes or is affected by such transfer is not less than $600. Indicate with an asterisk (*) any payments that were made to a creditor on account of a domestic support obligation or as part of an alternative repayment schedule under a plan by an approved nonprofit budgeting and creditor counseling agency. (Married debtors filing under chapter 12 or chapter 13 must include payments by either or both spouses whether or not a joint petition is filed, unless the spouses are separated and a joint petition is not filed.)

NAME AND ADDRESS OF CREDITOR	DATES OF PAYMENTS	AMOUNT PAID	AMOUNT STILL OWING

None ☐ b. *Debtor whose debts are not primarily consumer debts:* List each payment or other transfer to any creditor made within **90** days immediately preceding the commencement of the case if the aggregate value of all property that constitutes or is affected by such transfer is not less than $5,000. (Married debtors filing under chapter 12 or chapter 13 must include payments and other transfers by either or both spouses whether or not a joint petition is filed, unless the spouses are separated and a joint petition is not filed.)

NAME AND ADDRESS OF CREDITOR	DATES OF PAYMENTS/ TRANSFERS	AMOUNT PAID OR VALUE OF TRANSFERS	AMOUNT STILL OWING

None ☐ c. *All debtors:* List all payments made within **one year** immediately preceding the commencement of this case to or for the benefit of creditors who are or were insiders. (Married debtors filing under chapter 12 or chapter 13 must include payments by either or both spouses whether or not a joint petition is filed, unless the spouses are separated and a joint petition is not filed.)

NAME AND ADDRESS OF CREDITOR AND RELATIONSHIP TO DEBTOR	DATE OF PAYMENT	AMOUNT PAID	AMOUNT STILL OWING

4. Suits and administrative proceedings, executions, garnishments and attachments

3

None ☐ a. List all suits and administrative proceedings to which the debtor is or was a party within **one year** immediately preceding the filing of this bankruptcy case. (Married debtors filing under chapter 12 or chapter 13 must include information concerning either or both spouses whether or not a joint petition is filed, unless the spouses are separated and a joint petition is not filed.)

CAPTION OF SUIT AND CASE NUMBER	NATURE OF PROCEEDING	COURT OR AGENCY AND LOCATION	STATUS OR DISPOSITION

None ☐ b. Describe all property that has been attached, garnished or seized under any legal or equitable process within **one year** immediately preceding the commencement of this case. (Married debtors filing under chapter 12 or chapter 13 must include information concerning property of either or both spouses whether or not a joint petition is filed, unless the spouses are separated and a joint petition is not filed.)

NAME AND ADDRESS OF PERSON FOR WHOSE BENEFIT PROPERTY WAS SEIZED	DATE OF SEIZURE	DESCRIPTION AND VALUE OF PROPERTY

5. **Repossessions, foreclosures and returns**

None ☐ List all property that has been repossessed by a creditor, sold at a foreclosure sale, transferred through a deed in lieu of foreclosure or returned to the seller, within **one year** immediately preceding the commencement of this case. (Married debtors filing under chapter 12 or chapter 13 must include information concerning property of either or both spouses whether or not a joint petition is filed, unless the spouses are separated and a joint petition is not filed.)

NAME AND ADDRESS OF CREDITOR OR SELLER	DATE OF REPOSSESSION, FORECLOSURE SALE, TRANSFER OR RETURN	DESCRIPTION AND VALUE OF PROPERTY

6. **Assignments and receiverships**

None ☐ a. Describe any assignment of property for the benefit of creditors made within **120 days** immediately preceding the commencement of this case. (Married debtors filing under chapter 12 or chapter 13 must include any assignment by either or both spouses whether or not a joint petition is filed, unless the spouses are separated and a joint petition is not filed.)

NAME AND ADDRESS OF ASSIGNEE	DATE OF ASSIGNMENT	TERMS OF ASSIGNMENT OR SETTLEMENT

None ☐ b. List all property which has been in the hands of a custodian, receiver, or court-appointed official within **one year** immediately preceding the commencement of this case. (Married debtors filing under chapter 12 or chapter 13 must include information concerning property of either or both spouses whether or not a joint petition is filed, unless the spouses are separated and a joint petition is not filed.)

NAME AND ADDRESS OF CUSTODIAN	NAME AND LOCATION OF COURT CASE TITLE & NUMBER	DATE OF ORDER	DESCRIPTION AND VALUE OF PROPERTY

7. **Gifts**

None ☐ List all gifts or charitable contributions made within **one year** immediately preceding the commencement of this case except ordinary and usual gifts to family members aggregating less than $200 in value per individual family member and charitable contributions aggregating less than $100 per recipient. (Married debtors filing under chapter 12 or chapter 13 must include gifts or contributions by either or both spouses whether or not a joint petition is filed, unless the spouses are separated and a joint petition is not filed.)

NAME AND ADDRESS OF PERSON OR ORGANIZATION	RELATIONSHIP TO DEBTOR, IF ANY	DATE OF GIFT	DESCRIPTION AND VALUE OF GIFT

8. **Losses**

None ☐ List all losses from fire, theft, other casualty or gambling within **one year** immediately preceding the commencement of this case **or since the commencement of this case**. (Married debtors filing under chapter 12 or chapter 13 must include losses by either or both spouses whether or not a joint petition is filed, unless the spouses are separated and a joint petition is not filed.)

DESCRIPTION AND VALUE OF PROPERTY	DESCRIPTION OF CIRCUMSTANCES AND, IF LOSS WAS COVERED IN WHOLE OR IN PART BY INSURANCE, GIVE PARTICULARS	DATE OF LOSS

9. **Payments related to debt counseling or bankruptcy**

None ☐ List all payments made or property transferred by or on behalf of the debtor to any persons, including attorneys, for consultation concerning debt consolidation, relief under the bankruptcy law or preparation of a petition in bankruptcy within **one year** immediately preceding the commencement of this case.

NAME AND ADDRESS OF PAYEE	DATE OF PAYMENT, NAME OF PAYER IF OTHER THAN DEBTOR	AMOUNT OF MONEY OR DESCRIPTION AND VALUE OF PROPERTY

10. **Other transfers**

None ☐ a. List all other property, other than property transferred in the ordinary course of the business or financial affairs of the debtor, transferred either absolutely or as security within **two years** immediately preceding the commencement of this case. (Married debtors filing under chapter 12 or chapter 13 must include transfers by either or both spouses whether or not a joint petition is filed, unless the spouses are separated and a joint petition is not filed.)

NAME AND ADDRESS OF TRANSFEREE, RELATIONSHIP TO DEBTOR	DATE	DESCRIBE PROPERTY TRANSFERRED AND VALUE RECEIVED

None ☐ b. List all property transferred by the debtor within **ten years** immediately preceding the commencement of this case to a self-settled trust or similar device of which the debtor is a beneficiary.

NAME OF TRUST OR OTHER DEVICE	DATE(S) OF TRANSFER(S)	AMOUNT OF MONEY OR DESCRIPTION AND VALUE OF PROPERTY OR DEBTOR'S INTEREST IN PROPERTY

11. Closed financial accounts

None ☐ List all financial accounts and instruments held in the name of the debtor or for the benefit of the debtor which were closed, sold, or otherwise transferred within **one year** immediately preceding the commencement of this case. Include checking, savings, or other financial accounts, certificates of deposit, or other instruments; shares and share accounts held in banks, credit unions, pension funds, cooperatives, associations, brokerage houses and other financial institutions. (Married debtors filing under chapter 12 or chapter 13 must include information concerning accounts or instruments held by or for either or both spouses whether or not a joint petition is filed, unless the spouses are separated and a joint petition is not filed.)

NAME AND ADDRESS OF INSTITUTION	TYPE OF ACCOUNT, LAST FOUR DIGITS OF ACCOUNT NUMBER, AND AMOUNT OF FINAL BALANCE	AMOUNT AND DATE OF SALE OR CLOSING

12. Safe deposit boxes

None ☐ List each safe deposit or other box or depository in which the debtor has or had securities, cash, or other valuables within **one year** immediately preceding the commencement of this case. (Married debtors filing under chapter 12 or chapter 13 must include boxes or depositories of either or both spouses whether or not a joint petition is filed, unless the spouses are separated and a joint petition is not filed.)

NAME AND ADDRESS OF BANK OR OTHER DEPOSITORY	NAMES AND ADDRESSES OF THOSE WITH ACCESS TO BOX OR DEPOSITORY	DESCRIPTION OF CONTENTS	DATE OF TRANSFER OR SURRENDER, IF ANY

13. Setoffs

None ☐ List all setoffs made by any creditor, including a bank, against a debt or deposit of the debtor within **90 days** preceding the commencement of this case. (Married debtors filing under chapter 12 or chapter 13 must include information concerning either or both spouses whether or not a joint petition is filed, unless the spouses are separated and a joint petition is not filed.)

NAME AND ADDRESS OF CREDITOR	DATE OF SETOFF	AMOUNT OF SETOFF

---

14. Property held for another person

None ☐ List all property owned by another person that the debtor holds or controls.

NAME AND ADDRESS OF OWNER	DESCRIPTION AND VALUE OF PROPERTY	LOCATION OF PROPERTY

---

15. Prior address of debtor

None ☐ If debtor has moved within **three years** immediately preceding the commencement of this case, list all premises which the debtor occupied during that period and vacated prior to the commencement of this case. If a joint petition is filed, report also any separate address of either spouse.

ADDRESS	NAME USED	DATES OF OCCUPANCY

---

16. Spouses and Former Spouses

None ☐ If the debtor resides or resided in a community property state, commonwealth, or territory (including Alaska, Arizona, California, Idaho, Louisiana, Nevada, New Mexico, Puerto Rico, Texas, Washington, or Wisconsin) within **eight years** immediately preceding the commencement of the case, identify the name of the debtor's spouse and of any former spouse who resides or resided with the debtor in the community property state.

NAME

17. Environmental Information.

For the purpose of this question, the following definitions apply:

"Environmental Law" means any federal, state, or local statute or regulation regulating pollution, contamination, releases of hazardous or toxic substances, wastes or material into the air, land, soil, surface water, groundwater, or other medium, including, but not limited to, statutes or regulations regulating the cleanup of these substances, wastes, or material.

"Site" means any location, facility, or property as defined under any Environmental Law, whether or not presently or formerly owned or operated by the debtor, including, but not limited to, disposal sites.

"Hazardous Material" means anything defined as a hazardous waste, hazardous substance, toxic substance, hazardous material, pollutant, or contaminant or similar term under an Environmental Law.

None ☐ a. List the name and address of every site for which the debtor has received notice in writing by a governmental unit that it may be liable or potentially liable under or in violation of an Environmental Law. Indicate the governmental unit, the date of the notice, and, if known, the Environmental Law:

SITE NAME AND ADDRESS	NAME AND ADDRESS OF GOVERNMENTAL UNIT	DATE OF NOTICE	ENVIRONMENTAL LAW

None ☐ b. List the name and address of every site for which the debtor provided notice to a governmental unit of a release of Hazardous Material. Indicate the governmental unit to which the notice was sent and the date of the notice.

SITE NAME AND ADDRESS	NAME AND ADDRESS OF GOVERNMENTAL UNIT	DATE OF NOTICE	ENVIRONMENTAL LAW

None ☐ c. List all judicial or administrative proceedings, including settlements or orders, under any Environmental Law with respect to which the debtor is or was a party. Indicate the name and address of the governmental unit that is or was a par to the proceeding, and the docket number.

NAME AND ADDRESS OF GOVERNMENTAL UNIT	DOCKET NUMBER	STATUS OR DISPOSITION

---

18 . Nature, location and name of business

None ☐ a. *If the debtor is an individual*, list the names, addresses, taxpayer identification numbers, nature of the businesses, and beginning and ending dates of all businesses in which the debtor was an officer, director, partner, or managing executive of a corporation, partner in a partnership, sole proprietor, or was self-employed in a trade, profession, or other activity either full- or part-time within **six years** immediately preceding the commencement of this case, or in which the debtor owned 5 percent or more of the voting or equity securities within **six years** immediately preceding the commencement of this case.

If the debtor is a partnership, list the names, addresses, taxpayer identification numbers, nature of the businesses, and beginning and ending dates of all businesses in which the debtor was a partner or owned 5 percent or more of the voting or equity securities, within **six years** immediately preceding the commencement of this case.

If the debtor is a corporation, list the names, addresses, taxpayer identification numbers, nature of the businesses, and beginning and ending dates of all businesses in which the debtor was a partner or owned 5 percent or more of the voting or equity securities within **six years** immediately preceding the commencement of this case.

NAME	LAST FOUR DIGITS OF SOC. SEC. NO./ COMPLETE EIN OR OTHER TAXPAYER I.D. NO.	ADDRESS	NATURE OF BUSINESS	BEGINNING AND ENDING DATES

None ☐ b. Identify any business listed in response to subdivision a., above, that is "single asset real estate" as defined in 11 U.S.C. § 101.

NAME	ADDRESS

The following questions are to be completed by every debtor that is a corporation or partnership and by any individual debtor who is or has been, within **six years** immediately preceding the commencement of this case, any of the following: an officer, director, managing executive, or owner of more than 5 percent of the voting or equity securities of a corporation; a partner, other than a limited partner, of a partnership, a sole proprietor, or self-employed in a trade, profession, or other activity, either full- or part-time.

*(An individual or joint debtor should complete this portion of the statement **only** if the debtor is or has been in business, as defined above, within six years immediately preceding the commencement of this case. A debtor who has not been in business within those six years should go directly to the signature page.)*

19. Books, records and financial statements

None ☐ a. List all bookkeepers and accountants who within **two years** immediately preceding the filing of this bankruptcy case kept or supervised the keeping of books of account and records of the debtor.

NAME AND ADDRESS	DATES SERVICES RENDERED

None ☐ b. List all firms or individuals who within **two years** immediately preceding the filing of this bankruptcy case have audited the books of account and records, or prepared a financial statement of the debtor.

NAME	ADDRESS	DATES SERVICES RENDERED

None ☐ c. List all firms or individuals who at the time of the commencement of this case were in possession of the books of account and records of the debtor. If any of the books of account and records are not available, explain.

NAME	ADDRESS

None ☐ d. List all financial institutions, creditors and other parties, including mercantile and trade agencies, to whom a financial statement was issued by the debtor within **two years** immediately preceding the commencement of this case.

NAME AND ADDRESS	DATE ISSUED

---

20. Inventories

None ☐ a. List the dates of the last two inventories taken of your property, the name of the person who supervised the taking of each inventory, and the dollar amount and basis of each inventory.

DATE OF INVENTORY	INVENTORY SUPERVISOR	DOLLAR AMOUNT OF INVENTORY (Specify cost, market or other basis)

None ☐ b. List the name and address of the person having possession of the records of each of the inventories reported in a., above.

DATE OF INVENTORY	NAME AND ADDRESSES OF CUSTODIAN OF INVENTORY RECORDS

---

21. Current Partners, Officers, Directors and Shareholders

None ☐ a. If the debtor is a partnership, list the nature and percentage of partnership interest of each member of the partnership.

NAME AND ADDRESS	NATURE OF INTEREST	PERCENTAGE OF INTEREST

None ☐ b. If the debtor is a corporation, list all officers and directors of the corporation, and each stockholder who directly or indirectly owns, controls, or holds 5 percent or more of the voting or equity securities of the corporation.

NAME AND ADDRESS	TITLE	NATURE AND PERCENTAGE OF STOCK OWNERSHIP

---

22. Former partners, officers, directors and shareholders

None ☐ a. If the debtor is a partnership, list each member who withdrew from the partnership within **one year** immediately preceding the commencement of this case.

NAME	ADDRESS	DATE OF WITHDRAWAL

None ☐ b. If the debtor is a corporation, list all officers, or directors whose relationship with the corporation terminated within **one year** immediately preceding the commencement of this case.

NAME AND ADDRESS	TITLE	DATE OF TERMINATION

23. Withdrawals from a partnership or distributions by a corporation

None ☐ If the debtor is a partnership or corporation, list all withdrawals or distributions credited or given to an insider, including compensation in any form, bonuses, loans, stock redemptions, options exercised and any other perquisite during **one year** immediately preceding the commencement of this case.

NAME & ADDRESS OF RECIPIENT, RELATIONSHIP TO DEBTOR	DATE AND PURPOSE OF WITHDRAWAL	AMOUNT OF MONEY OR DESCRIPTION AND VALUE OF PROPERTY

24. Tax Consolidation Group.

None ☐ If the debtor is a corporation, list the name and federal taxpayer identification number of the parent corporation of any consolidated group for tax purposes of which the debtor has been a member at any time within **six years** immediately preceding the commencement of the case.

NAME OF PARENT CORPORATION	TAXPAYER IDENTIFICATION NUMBER (EIN)

25. Pension Funds.

None ☐ If the debtor is not an individual, list the name and federal taxpayer identification number of any pension fund to which the debtor, as an employer, has been responsible for contributing at any time within **six years** immediately preceding the commencement of the case.

NAME OF PENSION FUND	TAXPAYER IDENTIFICATION NUMBER (EIN)

* * * * * *

11

[If completed by an individual or individual and spouse]

I declare under penalty of perjury that I have read the answers contained in the foregoing statement of financial affairs and any attachments thereto and that they are true and correct.

Date ____________________ Signature of Debtor ______________________________

Date ____________________ Signature of Joint Debtor (if any) ______________________________

[If completed on behalf of a partnership or corporation]

I, declare under penalty of perjury that I have read the answers contained in the foregoing statement of financial affairs and any attachments thereto and that they are true and correct to the best of my knowledge, information and belief.

Date ____________________ Signature ______________________________

____
Print Name and Title

[An individual signing on behalf of a partnership or corporation must indicate position or relationship to debtor.]

____ continuation sheets attached

Penalty for making a false statement: Fine of up to $500,000 or imprisonment for up to 5 years, or both. 18 U.S.C. §§ 152 and 3571

DECLARATION AND SIGNATURE OF NON-ATTORNEY BANKRUPTCY PETITION PREPARER (See 11 U.S.C. § 110)

I declare under penalty of perjury that: (1) I am a bankruptcy petition preparer as defined in 11 U.S.C. § 110; (2) I prepared this document for compensation and have provided the debtor with a copy of this document and the notices and information required under 11 U.S.C. §§ 110(b), 110(h), and 342(b); and, (3) if rules or guidelines have been promulgated pursuant to 11 U.S.C. § 110(h) setting a maximum fee for services chargeable by bankruptcy petition preparers, I have given the debtor notice of the maximum amount before preparing any document for filing for a debtor or accepting any fee from the debtor, as required by that section.

______________________________ ______________________________
Printed or Typed Name and Title, if any, of Bankruptcy Petition Preparer Social Security No.(Required by 11 U.S.C. § 110.)

If the bankruptcy petition preparer is not an individual, state the name, title (if any), address, and social security number of the officer, principal, responsible person, or partner who signs this document.

____

____
Address

X ______________________________ ____________________
Signature of Bankruptcy Petition Preparer Date

Names and Social Security numbers of all other individuals who prepared or assisted in preparing this document unless the bankruptcy petition preparer is not an individual:

If more than one person prepared this document, attach additional signed sheets conforming to the appropriate Official Form for each person.

A bankruptcy petition preparer's failure to comply with the provisions of title 11 and the Federal Rules of Bankruptcy Procedure may result in fines or imprisonment or both. 18 U.S.C. § 156.

B 201 (04/09/06)

UNITED STATES BANKRUPTCY COURT

NOTICE TO INDIVIDUAL CONSUMER DEBTOR UNDER § 342(b) OF THE BANKRUPTCY CODE

In accordance with § 342(b) of the Bankruptcy Code, this notice: (1) Describes briefly the services available from credit counseling services; (2) Describes briefly the purposes, benefits and costs of the four types of bankruptcy proceedings you may commence; and (3) Informs you about bankruptcy crimes and notifies you that the Attorney General may examine all information you supply in connection with a bankruptcy case. You are cautioned that bankruptcy law is complicated and not easily described. Thus, you may wish to seek the advice of an attorney to learn of your rights and responsibilities should you decide to file a petition. Court employees cannot give you legal advice.

1. Services Available from Credit Counseling Agencies

With limited exceptions, § 109(h) of the Bankruptcy Code requires that all individual debtors who file for bankruptcy relief on or after October 17, 2005, receive a briefing that outlines the available opportunities for credit counseling and provides assistance in performing a budget analysis. The briefing must be given within 180 days **before** the bankruptcy filing. The briefing may be provided individually or in a group (including briefings conducted by telephone or on the Internet) and must be provided by a nonprofit budget and credit counseling agency approved by the United States trustee or bankruptcy administrator. The clerk of the bankruptcy court has a list that you may consult of the approved budget and credit counseling agencies.

In addition, after filing a bankruptcy case, an individual debtor generally must complete a financial management instructional course before he or she can receive a discharge. The clerk also has a list of approved financial management instructional courses.

2. The Four Chapters of the Bankruptcy Code Available to Individual Consumer Debtors

Chapter 7: Liquidation ($245 filing fee, $39 administrative fee, $15 trustee surcharge: Total fee $299)

1. Chapter 7 is designed for debtors in financial difficulty who do not have the ability to pay their existing debts. Debtors whose debts are primarily consumer debts are subject to a "means test" designed to determine whether the case should be permitted to proceed under chapter 7. If your income is greater than the median income for your state of residence and family size, in some cases, creditors have the right to file a motion requesting that the court dismiss your case under § 707(b) of the Code. It is up to the court to decide whether the case should be dismissed.

2. Under chapter 7, you may claim certain of your property as exempt under governing law. A trustee may have the right to take possession of and sell the remaining property that is not exempt and use the sale proceeds to pay your creditors.

3. The purpose of filing a chapter 7 case is to obtain a discharge of your existing debts. If, however, you are found to have committed certain kinds of improper conduct described in the Bankruptcy Code, the court may deny your discharge and, if it does, the purpose for which you filed the bankruptcy petition will be defeated.

4. Even if you receive a general discharge, some particular debts are not discharged under the law. Therefore, you may still be responsible for most taxes and student loans; debts incurred to pay nondischargeable taxes; domestic support and property settlement obligations; most fines, penalties, forfeitures, and criminal restitution obligations; certain debts which are not properly listed in your bankruptcy papers; and debts for death or personal injury caused by operating a motor vehicle, vessel, or aircraft while intoxicated from alcohol or drugs. Also, if a creditor can prove that a debt arose from fraud, breach of fiduciary duty, or theft, or from a willful and malicious injury, the bankruptcy court may determine that the debt is not discharged.

Chapter 13: Repayment of All or Part of the Debts of an Individual with Regular Income ($235 filing fee, $39 administrative fee: Total fee $274)

1. Chapter 13 is designed for individuals with regular income who would like to pay all or part of their debts in installments over a period of time. You are only eligible for chapter 13 if your debts do not exceed certain dollar amounts set forth in the Bankruptcy Code.

B 201 Page 2

2. Under chapter 13, you must file with the court a plan to repay your creditors all or part of the money that you owe them, using your future earnings. The period allowed by the court to repay your debts may be three years or five years, depending upon your income and other factors. The court must approve your plan before it can take effect.

3. After completing the payments under your plan, your debts are generally discharged except for domestic support obligations; most student loans; certain taxes; most criminal fines and restitution obligations; certain debts which are not properly listed in your bankruptcy papers; certain debts for acts that caused death or personal injury; and certain long term secured obligations.

Chapter 11: Reorganization ($1000 filing fee, $39 administrative fee: Total fee $1039)

Chapter 11 is designed for the reorganization of a business but is also available to consumer debtors. Its provisions are quite complicated, and any decision by an individual to file a chapter 11 petition should be reviewed with an attorney.

Chapter 12: Family Farmer or Fisherman ($200 filing fee, $39 administrative fee: Total fee $239)

Chapter 12 is designed to permit family farmers and fishermen to repay their debts over a period of time from future earnings and is similar to chapter 13. The eligibility requirements are restrictive, limiting its use to those whose income arises primarily from a family-owned farm or commercial fishing operation.

3. Bankruptcy Crimes and Availability of Bankruptcy Papers to Law Enforcement Officials

A person who knowingly and fraudulently conceals assets or makes a false oath or statement under penalty of perjury, either orally or in writing, in connection with a bankruptcy case is subject to a fine, imprisonment, or both. All information supplied by a debtor in connection with a bankruptcy case is subject to examination by the Attorney General acting through the Office of the United States Trustee, the Office of the United States Attorney, and other components and employees of the Department of Justice.

WARNING: Section 521(a)(1) of the Bankruptcy Code requires that you promptly file detailed information regarding your creditors, assets, liabilities, income, expenses and general financial condition. Your bankruptcy case may be dismissed if this information is not filed with the court within the time deadlines set by the Bankruptcy Code, the Bankruptcy Rules, and the local rules of the court.

Certificate of [Non-Attorney] Bankruptcy Petition Preparer

I, the [non-attorney] bankruptcy petition preparer signing the debtor's petition, hereby certify that I delivered to the debtor this notice required by § 342(b) of the Bankruptcy Code.

____
Printed name and title, if any, of Bankruptcy Petition Preparer

Address:
____

X______________________________
Signature of Bankruptcy Petition Preparer or officer, principal, responsible person, or partner whose Social Security number is provided above.

____
Social Security number (If the bankruptcy petition preparer is not an individual, state the Social Security number of the officer, principal, responsible person, or partner of the bankruptcy petition preparer.) (Required by 11 U.S.C. § 110.)

Certificate of the Debtor

I (We), the debtor(s), affirm that I (we) have received and read this notice.

____
Printed Name(s) of Debtor(s)

Case No. (if known) ______________

X______________________________
Signature of Debtor Date

X______________________________
Signature of Joint Debtor (if any) Date

United States Bankruptcy Court
Southern District of Mississippi

In re ______________________________ Case No. ______________
Debtor(s) Chapter ______________

VERIFICATION OF CREDITOR MATRIX

The above-named Debtor hereby verifies that the attached list of creditors is true and correct to the best of his/her knowledge.

Date: ____________________ ______________________________

Signature of Debtor

Form B 21 Official Form 21
(12/03)

FORM 21. STATEMENT OF SOCIAL SECURITY NUMBER

[*Caption as in Form 16A.*]

STATEMENT OF SOCIAL SECURITY NUMBER(S)

1.Name of Debtor (enter Last, First, Middle):______________________________
(Check the appropriate box and, if applicable, provide the required information.)

/ /Debtor has a Social Security Number and it is: _ _ _-_ _-_ _ _ _
(*If more than one, state all.*)
/ /Debtor does not have a Social Security Number.

2.Name of Joint Debtor (enter Last, First, Middle):________________________
(Check the appropriate box and, if applicable, provide the required information.)

/ /Joint Debtor has a Social Security Number and it is: _ _ _-_ _-_ _ _ _
(*If more than one, state all.*)
/ /Joint Debtor does not have a Social Security Number.

I declare under penalty of perjury that the foregoing is true and correct.

X ____
Signature of Debtor Date

X ____
Signature of Joint Debtor Date

**Joint debtors must provide information for both spouses.*
Penalty for making a false statement: Fine of up to $250,000 or up to 5 years imprisonment or both. 18 U.S.C. §§ 152 and 3571.

Illustration 20–2 Statement of Intentions (Official Form 8)

FORM 8 STATEMENT OF INTENTIONS

Form 8
(10/05)

United States Bankruptcy Court
_______________ District Of _______________

In re ______________________________,
Debtor

Case No. ________________
Chapter 7

CHAPTER 7 INDIVIDUAL DEBTOR'S STATEMENT OF INTENTION

☐ I have filed a schedule of assets and liabilities which includes debts secured by property of the estate.
☐ I have filed a schedule of executory contracts and unexpired leases which includes personal property subject to an unexpired lease.
☐ I intend to do the following with respect to the property of the estate which secures those debts or is subject to a lease:

Description of Secured Property	Creditor's Name	Property will be Surrendered	Property is claimed as exempt	Property will be redeemed pursuant to 11 U.S.C. § 722	Debt will be reaffirmed pursuant to 11 U.S.C. § 524(c)

Description of Leased Property	Lessor's Name	Lease will be assumed pursuant to 11 U.S.C. § 362(h)(1)(A)

Date: ______________

____
Signature of Debtor

DECLARATION OF NON-ATTORNEY BANKRUPTCY PETITION PREPARER (See 11 U.S.C. § 110)

I declare under penalty of perjury that: (1) I am a bankruptcy petition preparer as defined in 11 U.S.C. § 110; (2) I prepared this document for compensation and have provided the debtor with a copy of this document and the notices and information required under 11 U.S.C. §§ 110(b), 110(h), and 342(b); and, (3) if rules or guidelines have been promulgated pursuant to 11 U.S.C. § 110(h) setting a maximum fee for services chargeable by bankruptcy petition preparers, I have given the debtor notice of the maximum amount before preparing any document for filing for a debtor or accepting any fee from the debtor, as required in that section.

____
Printed or Typed Name of Bankruptcy Petition Preparer

____
Social Security No. (Required under 11 U.S.C. § 110.)

If the bankruptcy petition preparer is not an individual, state the name, title (if any), address, and social security number of the officer, principal, responsible person or partner who signs this document.

____

____
Address

X______________________________ ______________
Signature of Bankruptcy Petition Preparer Date

Names and Social Security Numbers of all other individuals who prepared or assisted in preparing this document unless the bankruptcy petition preparer is not an individual:

If more than one person prepared this document, attach additional signed sheets conforming to the appropriate Official Form for each person.

A bankruptcy petition preparer's failure to comply with the provisions of title 11 and the Federal Rules of Bankruptcy Procedure may result in fines or imprisonment or both. 11 U.S.C. § 110; 18 U.S.C. § 156.

B 203
(12/94)

United States Bankruptcy Court

_______________ District Of _______________

In re

Case No. __________

Debtor

Chapter ________

DISCLOSURE OF COMPENSATION OF ATTORNEY FOR DEBTOR

1. Pursuant to 11 U.S.C. § 329(a) and Fed. Bankr. P. 2016(b), I certify that I am the attorney for the above-named debtor(s) and that compensation paid to me within one year before the filing of the petition in bankruptcy, or agreed to be paid to me, for services rendered or to be rendered on behalf of the debtor(s) in contemplation of or in connection with the bankruptcy case is as follows:

   For legal services, I have agreed to accept . . . . $__________

   Prior to the filing of this statement I have received . . . . $__________

   Balance Due . . . . $__________

2. The source of the compensation paid to me was:

   ☐ Debtor ☐ Other (specify)

3. The source of compensation to be paid to me is:

   ☐ Debtor ☐ Other (specify)

4. ☐ I have not agreed to share the above-disclosed compensation with any other person unless they are members and associates of my law firm.

   ☐ I have agreed to share the above-disclosed compensation with a other person or persons who are not members or associates of my law firm. A copy of the agreement, together with a list of the names of the people sharing in the compensation, is attached.

5. In return for the above-disclosed fee, I have agreed to render legal service for all aspects of the bankruptcy case, including:

   a. Analysis of the debtor's financial situation, and rendering advice to the debtor in determining whether to file a petition in bankruptcy;

   b. Preparation and filing of any petition, schedules, statements of affairs and plan which may be required;

   c. Representation of the debtor at the meeting of creditors and confirmation hearing, and any adjourned hearings thereof;

DISCLOSURE OF COMPENSATION OF ATTORNEY FOR DEBTOR (Continued)

d. Representation of the debtor in adversary proceedings and other contested bankruptcy matters;

e. [Other provisions as needed]

6. By agreement with the debtor(s), the above-disclosed fee does not include the following services:

CERTIFICATION

I certify that the foregoing is a complete statement of any agreement or arrangement for payment to me for representation of the debtor(s) in this bankruptcy proceedings.

______________________ ______________________________

Date Signature of Attorney

____

Name of law firm

Official Form 22A (Chapter 7) (10/06)

In re ______________________
Debtor(s)

Case Number: ______________
(If known)

According to the calculations required by this statement:
☐ **The presumption arises.**
☐ **The presumption does not arise.**
(Check the box as directed in Parts I, III, and VI of this statement.)

CHAPTER 7 STATEMENT OF CURRENT MONTHLY INCOME AND MEANS-TEST CALCULATION

In addition to Schedule I and J, this statement must be completed by every individual Chapter 7 debtor, whether or not filing jointly, whose debts are primarily consumer debts. Joint debtors may complete one statement only.

Part I. EXCLUSION FOR DISABLED VETERANS

1	If you are a disabled veteran described in the Veteran's Declaration in this Part I, (1) check the box at the beginning of the Veteran's Declaration, (2) check the box for "The presumption does not arise" at the top of this statement, and (3) complete the verification in Part VIII. Do not complete any of the remaining parts of this statement. ☐ **Veteran's Declaration.** By checking this box, I declare under penalty of perjury that I am a disabled veteran (as defined in 38 U.S.C. § 3741(1)) whose indebtedness occurred primarily during a period in which I was on active duty (as defined in 10 U.S.C. § 101(d)(1)) or while I was performing a homeland defense activity (as defined in 32 U.S.C. §901(1)).

Part II. CALCULATION OF MONTHLY INCOME FOR § 707(b)(7) EXCLUSION

2	**Marital/filing status.** Check the box that applies and complete the balance of this part of this statement as directed. a. ☐ Unmarried. **Complete only Column A ("Debtor's Income") for Lines 3-11.** b. ☐ Married, not filing jointly, with declaration of separate households. By checking this box, debtor declares under penalty of perjury: "My spouse and I are legally separated under applicable non-bankruptcy law or my spouse and I are living apart other than for the purpose of evading the requirements of § 707(b)(2)(A) of the Bankruptcy Code." **Complete only Column A ("Debtor's Income") for Lines 3-11.** c. ☐ Married, not filing jointly, without the declaration of separate households set out in Line 2.b above. **Complete both Column A ("Debtor's Income") and Column B (Spouse's Income) for Lines 3-11.** d. ☐ Married, filing jointly. **Complete both Column A ("Debtor's Income") and Column B ("Spouse's Income") for Lines 3-11.**		
	All figures must reflect average monthly income received from all sources, derived during the six calendar months prior to filing the bankruptcy case, ending on the last day of the month before the filing. If the amount of monthly income varied during the six months, you must divide the six-month total by six, and enter the result on the appropriate line.	**Column A Debtor's Income**	**Column B Spouse's Income**
3	**Gross wages, salary, tips, bonuses, overtime, commissions.**	$	$
4	**Income from the operation of a business, profession or farm.** Subtract Line b from Line a and enter the difference in the appropriate column(s) of Line 4. Do not enter a number less than zero. **Do not include any part of the business expenses entered Line b as a deduction in Part V.** a. Gross receipts — $ b. Ordinary and necessary business expenses — $ c. Business income — Subtract Line b from Line a	$	$
5	**Rent and other real property income.** Subtract Line b from Line a and enter the difference in the appropriate column(s) of Line 5. Do not enter a number less than zero. **Do not include any part of the operating expenses entered on Line b as a deduction in Part V.** a. Gross receipts — $ b. Ordinary and necessary operating expenses — $ c. Rent and other real property income — Subtract Line b from Line a	$	$
6	**Interest, dividends and royalties.**	$	$
7	**Pension and retirement income.**	$	$
8	**Any amounts paid by another person or entity, on a regular basis, for the household expenses of the debtor or the debtor's dependents, including child or spousal support.** Do not include amounts paid by the debtor's spouse if Column B is completed.	$	$

Official Form 22A (Chapter 7) (10/06) – Cont. 2

9	**Unemployment compensation.** Enter the amount in the appropriate column(s) of Line 9. However, if you contend that unemployment compensation received by you or your spouse was a benefit under the Social Security Act, do not list the amount of such compensation in Column A or B, but instead state the amount in the space below: Unemployment compensation claimed to be a benefit under the Social Security Act · Debtor $ ______ · Spouse $ ______	$	$
10	**Income from all other sources.** If necessary, list additional sources on a separate page. **Do not include** any benefits received under the Social Security Act or payments received as a victim of a war crime, crime against humanity, or as a victim of international or domestic terrorism. Specify source and amount. a. ______ $ b. ______ $ Total and enter on Line 10	$	$
11	**Subtotal of Current Monthly Income for § 707(b)(7).** Add Lines 3 thru 10 in Column A, and, if Column B is completed, add Lines 3 through 10 in Column B. Enter the total(s).	$	$
12	**Total Current Monthly Income for § 707(b)(7).** If Column B has been completed, add Line 11, Column A to Line 11, Column B, and enter the total. If Column B has not been completed, enter the amount from Line 11, Column A.	$	

	Part III. APPLICATION OF § 707(b)(7) EXCLUSION	
13	**Annualized Current Monthly Income for § 707(b)(7).** Multiply the amount from Line 12 by the number 12 and enter the result.	$
14	**Applicable median family income.** Enter the median family income for the applicable state and household size. (This information is available by family size at www.usdoj.gov/ust/ or from the clerk of the bankruptcy court.) a. Enter debtor's state of residence: ______ b. Enter debtor's household size: ______	$
15	**Application of Section 707(b)(7).** Check the applicable box and proceed as directed. ☐ **The amount on Line 13 is less than or equal to the amount on Line 14.** Check the box for "The presumption does not arise" at the top of page 1 of this statement, and complete Part VIII; do not complete Parts IV, V, VI or VII. ☐ **The amount on Line 13 is more than the amount on Line 14.** Complete the remaining parts of this statement.	

Complete Parts IV, V, VI, and VII of this statement only if required. (See Line 15.)

	Part IV. CALCULATION OF CURRENT MONTHLY INCOME FOR § 707(b)(2)	
16	**Enter the amount from Line 12.**	$
17	**Marital adjustment.** If you checked the box at Line 2.c, enter the amount of the income listed in Line 11, Column B that was NOT paid on a regular basis for the household expenses of the debtor or the debtor's dependents. If you did not check box at Line 2.c, enter zero.	$
18	**Current monthly income for § 707(b)(2).** Subtract Line 17 from Line 16 and enter the result.	$

	Part V. CALCULATION OF DEDUCTIONS ALLOWED UNDER § 707(b)(2)	
	Subpart A: Deductions under Standards of the Internal Revenue Service (IRS)	
19	**National Standards: food, clothing, household supplies, personal care, and miscellaneous.** Enter "Total" amount from IRS National Standards for Allowable Living Expenses for the applicable family size and income level. (This information is available at www.usdoj.gov/ust/ or from the clerk of the bankruptcy court.)	$
20A	**Local Standards: housing and utilities; non-mortgage expenses.** Enter the amount of the IRS Housing and Utilities Standards; non-mortgage expenses for the applicable county and family size. (This information is available at www.usdoj.gov/ust/ or from the clerk of the bankruptcy court).	$

Official Form 22A (Chapter 7) (10/06) – Cont. 3

20B	**Local Standards: housing and utilities; mortgage/rent expense.** Enter, in Line a below, the amount of the IRS Housing and Utilities Standards; mortgage/rent expense for your county and family size (this information is available at www.usdoj.gov/ust/ or from the clerk of the bankruptcy court); enter on Line b the total of the Average Monthly Payments for any debts secured by your home, as stated in Line 42; subtract Line b from Line a and enter the result in Line 20B. **Do not enter an amount less than zero.** a. IRS Housing and Utilities Standards; mortgage/rental expense — $ b. Average Monthly Payment for any debts secured by your home, if any, as stated in Line 42 — $ c. Net mortgage/rental expense — Subtract Line b from Line a.	$
21	**Local Standards: housing and utilities; adjustment.** if you contend that the process set out in Lines 20A and 20B does not accurately compute the allowance to which you are entitled under the IRS Housing and Utilities Standards, enter any additional amount to which you contend you are entitled, and state the basis for your contention in the space below: __________ __________ __________	$
22	**Local Standards: transportation; vehicle operation/public transportation expense.** You are entitled to an expense allowance in this category regardless of whether you pay the expenses of operating a vehicle and regardless of whether you use public transportation. Check the number of vehicles for which you pay the operating expenses or for which the operating expenses are included as a contribution to your household expenses in Line 8. ☐ 0 ☐ 1 ☐ 2 or more. Enter the amount from IRS Transportation Standards, Operating Costs & Public Transportation Costs for the applicable number of vehicles in the applicable Metropolitan Statistical Area or Census Region. (This information is available at www.usdoj.gov/ust/ or from the clerk of the bankruptcy court.)	$
23	**Local Standards: transportation ownership/lease expense; Vehicle 1.** Check the number of vehicles for which you claim an ownership/lease expense. (You may not claim an ownership/lease expense for more than two vehicles.) ☐ 1 ☐ 2 or more. Enter, in Line a below, the amount of the IRS Transportation Standards, Ownership Costs, First Car (available at www.usdoj.gov/ust/ or from the clerk of the bankruptcy court); enter in Line b the total of the Average Monthly Payments for any debts secured by Vehicle 1, as stated in Line 42; subtract Line b from Line a and enter the result in Line 23. **Do not enter an amount less than zero.** a. IRS Transportation Standards, Ownership Costs, First Car — $ b. Average Monthly Payment for any debts secured by Vehicle 1, as stated in Line 42 — $ c. Net ownership/lease expense for Vehicle 1 — Subtract Line b from Line a.	$
24	**Local Standards: transportation ownership/lease expense; Vehicle 2.** Complete this Line only if you checked the "2 or more" Box in Line 23. Enter, in Line a below, the amount of the IRS Transportation Standards, Ownership Costs, Second Car (available at www.usdoj.gov/ust/ or from the clerk of the bankruptcy court); enter in Line b the total of the Average Monthly Payments for any debts secured by Vehicle 2, as stated in Line 42; subtract Line b from Line a and enter the result in Line 24. **Do not enter an amount less than zero.** a. IRS Transportation Standards, Ownership Costs, Second Car — $ b. Average Monthly Payment for any debts secured by Vehicle 2, as stated in Line 42 — $ c. Net ownership/lease expense for Vehicle 2 — Subtract Line b from Line a.	$
25	**Other Necessary Expenses: taxes.** Enter the total average monthly expense that you actually incur for all federal, state and local taxes, other than real estate and sales taxes, such as income taxes, self employment taxes, social security taxes, and Medicare taxes. **Do not include real estate or sales taxes.**	
26	**Other Necessary Expenses: mandatory payroll deductions.** Enter the total average monthly payroll deductions that are required for your employment, such as mandatory retirement contributions, union dues, and uniform costs. **Do not include discretionary amounts, such as non-mandatory 401(k) contributions.**	$

Official Form 22A (Chapter 7) (10/06) - Cont. 4

27	**Other Necessary Expenses: life insurance.** Enter average monthly premiums that you actually pay for term life insurance for yourself. **Do not include premiums for insurance on your dependents, for whole life or for any other form of insurance.**	$
28	**Other Necessary Expenses: court-ordered payments.** Enter the total monthly amount that you are required to pay pursuant to court order, such as spousal or child support payments. **Do not include payments on past due support obligations included in Line 44.**	$
29	**Other Necessary Expenses: education for employment or for a physically or mentally challenged child.** Enter the total monthly amount that you actually expend for education that is a condition of employment and for education that is required for a physically or mentally challenged dependent child for whom no public education providing similar services is available.	$
30	**Other Necessary Expenses: childcare.** Enter the average monthly amount that you actually expend on childcare—such as baby-sitting, day care, nursery and preschool. **Do not include other educational payments.**	$
31	**Other Necessary Expenses: health care.** Enter the average monthly amount that you actually expend on health care expenses that are not reimbursed by insurance or paid by a health savings account. **Do not include payments for health insurance or health savings accounts listed in Line 34.**	$
32	**Other Necessary Expenses: telecommunication services.** Enter the average monthly amount that you actually pay for telecommunication services other than your basic home telephone service—such as cell phones, pagers, call waiting, caller id, special long distance, or internet service—to the extent necessary for your health and welfare or that of your dependents. **Do not include any amount previously deducted.**	$
33	**Total Expenses Allowed under IRS Standards.** Enter the total of Lines 19 through 32.	$
	Subpart B: Additional Expense Deductions under § 707(b) **Note: Do not include any expenses that you have listed in Lines 19-32**	
34	**Health Insurance, Disability Insurance, and Health Savings Account Expenses.** List and total the average monthly amounts that you actually pay for yourself, your spouse, or your dependents in the following categories. a. Health Insurance $ b. Disability Insurance $ c. Health Savings Account $ Total: Add Lines a, b and c	$
35	**Continued contributions to the care of household or family members.** Enter the actual monthly expenses that you will continue to pay for the reasonable and necessary care and support of an elderly, chronically ill, or disabled member of your household or member of your immediate family who is unable to pay for such expenses.	$
36	**Protection against family violence.** Enter any average monthly expenses that you actually incurred to maintain the safety of your family under the Family Violence Prevention and Services Act or other applicable federal law. The nature of these expenses is required to be kept confidential by the court.	$
37	**Home energy costs.** Enter the average monthly amount, in excess of the allowance specified by IRS Local Standards for Housing and Utilities, that you actually expend for home energy costs. **You must provide your case trustee with documentation demonstrating that the additional amount claimed is reasonable and necessary**.	$
38	**Education expenses for dependent children less than 18.** Enter the average monthly expenses that you actually incur, not to exceed $125 per child, in providing elementary and secondary education for your dependent children less than 18 years of age. **You must provide your case trustee with documentation demonstrating that the amount claimed is reasonable and necessary and not already accounted for in the IRS Standards**.	$
39	**Additional food and clothing expense.** Enter the average monthly amount by which your food and clothing expenses exceed the combined allowances for food and apparel in the IRS National Standards, not to exceed five percent of those combined allowances. (This information is available at www.usdoj.gov/ust/ or from the clerk of the bankruptcy court.) **You must provide your case trustee with documentation demonstrating that the additional amount claimed is reasonable and necessary**.	$
40	**Continued charitable contributions.** Enter the amount that you will continue to contribute in the form of cash or financial instruments to a charitable organization as defined in 26 U.S.C. § 170(c)(1)-(2).	$
41	**Total Additional Expense Deductions under § 707(b).** Enter the total of Lines 34 through 40	$

Official Form 22A (Chapter 7) (10/06) - Cont. 5

	Subpart C: Deductions for Debt Payment	
42	**Future payments on secured claims.** For each of your debts that is secured by an interest in property that you own, list the name of the creditor, identify the property securing the debt, and state the Average Monthly Payment. The Average Monthly Payment is the total of all amounts contractually due to each Secured Creditor in the 60 months following the filing of the bankruptcy case, divided by 60. Mortgage debts should include payments of taxes and insurance required by the mortgage. If necessary, list additional entries on a separate page.	

	Name of Creditor	Property Securing the Debt	60-month Average Payment
a.			$
b.			$
c.			$
			Total: Add Lines a, b and c.

Line 42 total: $

43	**Other payments on secured claims.** If any of debts listed in Line 42 are secured by your primary residence, a motor vehicle, or other property necessary for your support or the support of your dependents, you may include in your deduction 1/60th of any amount (the "cure amount") that you must pay the creditor in addition to the payments listed in Line 42, in order to maintain possession of the property. The cure amount would include any sums in default that must be paid in order to avoid repossession or foreclosure. List and total any such amounts in the following chart. If necessary, list additional entries on a separate page.	

	Name of Creditor	Property Securing the Debt	1/60th of the Cure Amount
a.			$
b.			$
c.			$
			Total: Add Lines a, b and c

Line 43 total: $

44	**Payments on priority claims.** Enter the total amount of all priority claims (including priority child support and alimony claims), divided by 60.	$
45	**Chapter 13 administrative expenses.** If you are eligible to file a case under Chapter 13, complete the following chart, multiply the amount in line a by the amount in line b, and enter the resulting administrative expense.	

a.	Projected average monthly Chapter 13 plan payment.	$
b.	Current multiplier for your district as determined under schedules issued by the Executive Office for United States Trustees. (This information is available at www.usdoj.gov/ust/ or from the clerk of the bankruptcy court.)	x
c.	Average monthly administrative expense of Chapter 13 case	Total: Multiply Lines a and b

Line 45 total: $

46	**Total Deductions for Debt Payment.** Enter the total of Lines 42 through 45.	$
	Subpart D: Total Deductions Allowed under § 707(b)(2)	
47	**Total of all deductions allowed under § 707(b)(2).** Enter the total of Lines 33, 41, and 46.	$

	Part VI. DETERMINATION OF § 707(b)(2) PRESUMPTION	
48	**Enter the amount from Line 18 (Current monthly income for § 707(b)(2))**	$
49	**Enter the amount from Line 47 (Total of all deductions allowed under § 707(b)(2))**	$
50	**Monthly disposable income under § 707(b)(2).** Subtract Line 49 from Line 48 and enter the result	$
51	**60-month disposable income under § 707(b)(2).** Multiply the amount in Line 50 by the number 60 and enter the result.	$

Official Form 22A (Chapter 7) (10/06) – Cont. 6

52	**Initial presumption determination.** Check the applicable box and proceed as directed. ☐ **The amount on Line 51 is less than $6,000** Check the box for "The presumption does not arise" at the top of page 1 of this statement, and complete the verification in Part VIII. Do not complete the remainder of Part VI. ☐ **The amount set forth on Line 51 is more than $10,000**. Check the box for "The presumption arises" at the top of page 1 of this statement, and complete the verification in Part VIII. You may also complete Part VII. Do not complete the remainder of Part VI. ☐ **The amount on Line 51 is at least $6,000, but not more than $10,000.** Complete the remainder of Part VI (Lines 53 through 55).
53	**Enter the amount of your total non-priority unsecured debt** — $
54	**Threshold debt payment amount.** Multiply the amount in Line 53 by the number 0.25 and enter the result. — $
55	**Secondary presumption determination.** Check the applicable box and proceed as directed. ☐ **The amount on Line 51 is less than the amount on Line 54.** Check the box for "The presumption does not arise" at the top of page 1 of this statement, and complete the verification in Part VIII. ☐ **The amount on Line 51 is equal to or greater than the amount on Line 54.** Check the box for "The presumption arises" at the top of page 1 of this statement, and complete the verification in Part VIII. You may also complete Part VII.

Part VII: ADDITIONAL EXPENSE CLAIMS

56 **Other Expenses.** List and describe any monthly expenses, not otherwise stated in this form, that are required for the health and welfare of you and your family and that you contend should be an additional deduction from your current monthly income under § 707(b)(2)(A)(ii)(I). If necessary, list additional sources on a separate page. All figures should reflect your average monthly expense for each item. Total the expenses.

	Expense Description	Monthly Amount
a.		$
b.		$
c.		$
	Total: Add Lines a, b and c	$

Part VIII: VERIFICATION

57 I declare under penalty of perjury that the information provided in this statement is true and correct. *(If this is a joint case, both debtors must sign.)*

Date: ____________ Signature: ____________ (Debtor)

Date: ____________ Signature: ____________ (Joint Debtor, if any)

Illustration 20–3 Proof of Claim (Official Form 10)

FORM 10 PROOF OF CLAIM

FORM 10 (Official Form 10) (10/05)

UNITED STATES BANKRUPTCY COURT ____________ DISTRICT OF ____________

PROOF OF CLAIM

Name of Debtor | Case Number

NOTE: This form should not be used to make a claim for an administrative expense arising after the commencement of the case. A "request" for payment of an administrative expense may be filed pursuant to 11 U.S.C. § 503.

Name of Creditor (The person or other entity to whom the debtor owes money or property):

□ Check box if you are aware that anyone else has filed a proof of claim relating to your claim. Attach copy of statement giving particulars.

Name and address where notices should be sent:

□ Check box if you have never received any notices from the bankruptcy court in this case.

Telephone number:

□ Check box if the address differs from the address on the envelope sent to you by the court.

THIS SPACE IS FOR COURT USE ONLY

Last four digits of account or other number by which creditor identifies debtor:

Check here if this claim □ replaces □ amends a previously filed claim, dated: ____________

1. Basis for Claim
- □ Goods sold
- □ Services performed
- □ Money loaned
- □ Personal injury/wrongful death
- □ Taxes
- □ Other ____________
- □ Retiree benefits as defined in 11 U.S.C. § 1114(a)
- □ Wages, salaries, and compensation (fill out below)

Last four digits of your SS #: ____

Unpaid compensation for services performed

from ____________ (date) to ____________ (date)

2. Date debt was incurred:

3. If court judgment, date obtained:

4. Classification of Claim. Check the appropriate box or boxes that best describe your claim and state the amount of the claim at the time the case was filed. See reverse side for important explanations.

Unsecured Nonpriority Claim $____________

□ Check this box if: a) there is no collateral or lien securing your claim, or b) your claim exceeds the value of the property securing it, or c) none or only part of your claim is entitled to priority.

Unsecured Priority Claim

□ Check this box if you have an unsecured claim, all or part of which is entitled to priority.

Amount entitled to priority $____________

Secured Claim

□ Check this box if your claim is secured by collateral (including a right of setoff).

Brief Description of Collateral:
□ Real Estate □ Motor Vehicle □ Other ____________

Value of Collateral: $____________

Amount of arrearage and other charges at time case filed included in secured claim, if any: $____________

Specify the priority of the claim:

□ Domestic support obligations under 11 U.S.C. § 507(a)(1)(A) or (a)(1)(B).

□ Wages, salaries, or commissions (up to $10,000),* earned within 180 days before filing of the bankruptcy petition or cessation of the debtor's business, whichever is earlier - 11 U.S.C. § 507(a)(4).

□ Contributions to an employee benefit plan - 11 U.S.C. § 507(a)(5).

□ Up to $2,225* of deposits toward purchase, lease, or rental of property or services for personal, family, or household use - 11 U.S.C. § 507(a)(7).

□ Taxes or penalties owed to governmental units - 11 U.S.C. § 507(a)(8).

□ Other – Specify applicable paragraph of 11 U.S.C. § 507(a)(___).

**Amounts are subject to adjustment on 4/1/07 and every 3 years thereafter with respect to cases commenced on or after the date of adjustment.*

5. Total Amount of Claim at Time Case Filed: $__________ (unsecured) __________ (secured) __________ (priority) __________ (total)

□ Check this box if claim includes interest or other charges in addition to the principal amount of the claim. Attach itemized statement of all interest or additional charges.

6. Credits: The amount of all payments on this claim has been credited and deducted for the purpose of making this proof of claim.

7. Supporting Documents: *Attach copies of supporting documents,* such as promissory notes, purchase orders, invoices, itemized statements of running accounts, contracts, court judgments, mortgages, security agreements, and evidence of perfection of lien. DO NOT SEND ORIGINAL DOCUMENTS. If the documents are not available, explain. If the documents are voluminous, attach a summary.

8. Date-Stamped Copy: To receive an acknowledgment of the filing of your claim, enclose a stamped, self-addressed envelope and copy of this proof of claim.

THIS SPACE IS FOR COURT USE ONLY

Date | Sign and print the name and title, if any, of the creditor or other person authorized to file this claim (attach copy of power of attorney, if any):

Penalty for presenting fraudulent claim: Fine of up to $500,000 or imprisonment for up to 5 years, or both. 18 U.S.C. §§ 152 and 3571.

FORM 10 (Official Form 10) (10/05)

INSTRUCTIONS FOR PROOF OF CLAIM FORM

The instructions and definitions below are general explanations of the law. In particular types of cases or circumstances, such as bankruptcy cases that are not filed voluntarily by a debtor, there may be exceptions to these general rules.

------ DEFINITIONS ------

Debtor

The person, corporation, or other entity that has filed a bankruptcy case is called the debtor.

Creditor

A creditor is any person, corporation, or other entity to whom the debtor owed a debt on the date that the bankruptcy case was filed.

Proof of Claim

A form telling the bankruptcy court how much the debtor owed a creditor at the time the bankruptcy case was filed (the amount of the creditor's claim). This form must be filed with the clerk of the bankruptcy court where the bankruptcy case was filed.

Secured Claim

A claim is a secured claim to the extent that the creditor has a lien on property of the debtor (collateral) that gives the creditor the right to be paid from that property before creditors who do not have liens on the property.

Examples of liens are a mortgage on real estate and a security interest in a car, truck, boat, television set, or other item of property. A lien may have been obtained through a court proceeding before the bankruptcy case began; in some states a court judgment is a lien. In addition, to the extent a creditor also owes money to the debtor (has a right of setoff), the creditor's claim may be a secured claim. (See also *Unsecured Claim*.)

Unsecured Claim

If a claim is not a secured claim it is an unsecured claim. A claim may be partly secured and partly unsecured if the property on which a creditor has a lien is not worth enough to pay the creditor in full.

Unsecured Priority Claim

Certain types of unsecured claims are given priority, so they are to be paid in bankruptcy cases before most other unsecured claims (if there is sufficient money or property available to pay these claims). The most common types of priority claims are listed on the proof of claim form. Unsecured claims that are not specifically given priority status by the bankruptcy laws are classified as *Unsecured Nonpriority Claims*.

Items to be completed in Proof of Claim form (if not already filled in)

Court, Name of Debtor, and Case Number:
Fill in the name of the federal judicial district where the bankruptcy case was filed (for example, Central District of California), the name of the debtor in the bankruptcy case, and the bankruptcy case number. If you received a notice of the case from the court, all of this information is near the top of the notice.

Information about Creditor:
Complete the section giving the name, address, and telephone number of the creditor to whom the debtor owes money or property, and the debtor's account number, if any. If anyone else has already filed a proof of claim relating to this debt, if you never received notices from the bankruptcy court about this case, if your address differs from that to which the court sent notice, or if this proof of claim replaces or changes a proof of claim that was already filed, check the appropriate box on the form.

1. **Basis for Claim:**
   Check the type of debt for which the proof of claim is being filed. If the type of debt is not listed, check "Other" and briefly describe the type of debt. If you were an employee of the debtor, fill in the last four digits of your social security number and the dates of work for which you were not paid.

2. **Date Debt Incurred:**
   Fill in the date when the debt first was owed by the debtor.

3. **Court Judgments:**
   If you have a court judgment for this debt, state the date the court entered the judgment.

4. **Classification of Claim:**
   Secured Claim:
   Check the appropriate place if the claim is a secured claim. You must state the type and value of property that is collateral for the claim, attach copies of the documentation of your lien, and state the amount past due on the claim as of the date the bankruptcy case was filed. A claim may be partly secured and partly unsecured. (See DEFINITIONS, above).

   Unsecured Priority Claim:
   Check the appropriate place if you have an unsecured priority claim, and state the amount entitled to priority. (See DEFINITIONS, above). A claim may be partly priority and partly nonpriority if, for example, the claim is for more than the amount given priority by the law. Check the appropriate place to specify the type of priority claim.

   Unsecured Nonpriority Claim:
   Check the appropriate place if you have an unsecured nonpriority claim, sometimes referred to as a "general unsecured claim." (See DEFINITIONS, above.) If your claim is partly secured and partly unsecured, state here the amount that is unsecured. If part of your claim is entitled to priority, state here the amount **not** entitled to priority.

5. **Total Amount of Claim at Time Case Filed:**
   Fill in the total amount of the entire claim. If interest or other charges in addition to the principal amount of the claim are included, check the appropriate place on the form and attach an itemization of the interest and charges.

6. **Credits:**
   By signing this proof of claim, you are stating under oath that in calculating the amount of your claim you have given the debtor credit for all payments received from the debtor.

7. **Supporting Documents:**
   You must attach to this proof of claim form copies of documents that show the debtor owes the debt claimed or, if the documents are too lengthy, a summary of those documents. If documents are not available, you must attach an explanation of why they are not available.

BIBLIOGRAPHY

Black's Law Dictionary With Pronunciations, Seventh Edition, West Publishing Company, St. Paul, Minnesota, 1999.

Cline and Strong, *Law Office Management,* West Publishing Company.

Code of Judicial Ethics, American Bar Association, Chicago, Illinois.

NALS, *Advanced Manual for the Lawyer's Assistant,* Eighth Edition, West, a Thomson business, 2006.

Martindale–Hubbell Law Directory, Reed Publishing (USA), Inc., 2002.

Model Rules of Professional Conduct, American Bar Association.

Professional Responsibility, 7th ed., West, a Thomson business, 2004.

Sabin, William A., *The Gregg Reference Manual,* 10th ed., Glencoe/McGrawHill, Westerville, Ohio, 2001.

The Bluebook, A Uniform System of Citation, 18th ed., The Harvard Law Review Association, Gannet House, Cambridge, Massachusetts, 2005.

United States Government Manual, U. S. Government Printing Office, Washington, D.C., 1996.

West's Law Finder, West Publishing Company, 1987.

GLOSSARY

A

Abandoned property	In bankruptcy, property belonging to the debtor whom a trustee decides would bring in no money for creditors in a bankruptcy proceeding.
Abortion	Intentional termination of a pregnancy.
Abstract extension	The act of having the abstract of title brought to a current date through search of title records.
Abstract of Title	A condensed history of the title to the land.
Abstracter's certificate	A certificate that is made a part of the abstract and signed by the abstracter verifying what the abstract covers.
Accelerated depreciation	A method of depreciating buildings, furniture or equipment that provides for larger charges to expense in the early years of asset's life.
Acceptance	In contracts, the situation occurring when the offeree is in total agreement with the offer.
Accord and satisfaction	Accord is accepting another thing (substitution) in place of the thing promised in the original contract. Satisfaction occurs when the substitution is accepted.
Account Stated	A summarized statement of a debtor's account.
Accounting cycle	The steps involved in handling all of the transactions completed during the fiscal period beginning with recording in a book of original entry and ending with a post-closing trial balance.
Accounting equation	Assets = liabilities + owner's equity.
Accounts payable	All accounts owed.
Accounts payable ledger	Accounts for creditors, arranged in alphabetical order showing the amounts owed.
Accounts receivable	Amounts owed by the clients to the law firm.
Accounts receivable ledger	The accounts for clients arranged in alphabetical order, showing the amounts owed to the law firm.
Accrual basis	Recording revenue and expenses in the period in which it is earned.
Accumulated depreciation	Contra asset account to which periodic depreciation expense is recorded.

GLOSSARY

Acknowledgment	(1) A formal declaration by the person who executed the instrument before an authorized official that it is a free act and deed. (2) The certificate of the official on such instrument attesting that it was so acknowledged.
Acquittal	(1) A release, absolution, or discharge of an obligation or liability. (2) In criminal law the finding of not guilty.
Action to quiet title	Legal action taken by a property owner to have a court declare the owner of a particular parcel.
Active files	Files in which there is work to be done and in which there may be unbilled time.
Actus reus	The "guilty act." The *actus reus* is the physical aspect of a crime.
Adjective	Words which modify, describe or limit nouns, pronouns and gerunds.
Adjudicate	To settle controversies and disputes between parties.
Adjudication	The formal giving or pronouncing a judgment or decree in a cause.
Adjustments (adjusting journal entries)	General journal entries that are required specifically for the purpose of adjusting balances or correcting errors.
Administration	In estates, the supervision of an estate by an administrator or executor.
Administrative agencies	Agencies created by the legislative branch of government to administer laws pertaining to specific areas, such as the environment, taxes, transportation, and labor.
Administrator	A person appointed by a court to administer an intestate estate.
Adoption	The legal process under a state statute by which a child is taken into one's family and given all rights and privileges of a natural child and heir.
Advance health care directive	A written form appointing agent(s) to make health-care decisions for the maker and/or expressing the maker's wishes regarding health-care decisions.
Advance sheets	Paperback pamphlets published weekly which contain reporter cases, including correct volume number and page number.
Adverb	Words used to describe or limit a verb, adjective or another adverb.

GLOSSARY

Adversary proceeding	(1) One having opposing parties, such as a plaintiff and a defendant. (2) Individual lawsuit(s) brought within a bankruptcy proceeding.
Adverse possession	A method of acquiring title to real property under certain conditions by possession for a statutory period.
Advocate	One who assists, defends or pleads for another. One who renders legal advice and aid and pleads the cause of another before a court or a tribunal.
Affiant	The person who makes and subscribes to an affidavit.
Affidavit	A written or printed declaration of facts made voluntarily and confirmed by oath of the maker to a person with authority to administer the oath.
Affirmation	A solemn and formal declaration that an affidavit is true. This is substituted for an oath in certain instances.
Affirmative defense	A defense raised in a responsive pleading (answer) relating a new matter as a defense to the complaint.
Agent	A person authorized by another to act for or in the place of the person.
Agreement	Mutual consent.
aka	"Also known as."
Alford plea	Name derived from *North Carolina v. Alford* in which the Supreme Court held that a guilty plea which represented a voluntary and intelligent choice among alternatives available to defendant, especially where defendant was represented by competent counsel, was not compelled within the meaning of the Fifth Amendment merely because the plea was entered to avoid the possibility of the death penalty.
Alien	A foreign-born person who has not qualified as a citizen of a particular country.
Alimony	Also, spousal maintenance. Allowance which a spouse pays for the support of the other spouse after final divorce decree.
Allegations	Numbered paragraphs setting forth the background and reasons for filing a suit.
Alphabetic filing	A system of filing where files are labeled and stored in alphabetical order following standard filing procedures; generally by name of client.

GLOSSARY

Alphanumeric filing	A combination of an alphabetic filing system and a numeric system where numbers are assigned to files in blocks according to the letter of the alphabet which identifies the client.
Alternative relief	A remedy sought in a lawsuit other than a monetary award, *e.g.*, specific performance.
American Bar Association	A national association of lawyers whose primary purpose is improvement of lawyers and the administration of justice.
American Law Reports	Reports cases from all United States jurisdictions by subject matter.
Amicus curiae	Friend of the court.
Ancillary	Describes a proceeding that is auxiliary or subordinate to another proceeding.
Annotations	Remarks, notes, case summaries, or commentaries following a statute which describe interpretations of the statute.
Annual meeting	The meeting of stockholders each year called to elect officers and directors, to ratify actions of officers and directors and to vote on corporate matters which come before it.
Annual report	A report for stockholders and other interested parties prepared by the corporation once a year.
Annulment	(1) The act of making void. (2) That which establishes that marital status never existed.
Answer	A formal, written statement by the defendant in a lawsuit that answers each allegation contained in the complaint.
Answers to interrogatories	A formal, written statement by a party to a lawsuit that answers each question or interrogatory propounded by the other party.
Appeal	A proceeding brought to a higher court to review a lower court's decision.
Appeal bond	A guaranty by the appealing party insuring that court costs will be paid.
Appearance	Coming into court as a party to a suit, either in person or through a lawyer.
Appellant	The party who takes an appeal from one court or jurisdiction to another.
Appellate court	A court having jurisdiction of appeal and review.
Appellate jurisdiction	Authority of a court to review cases tried in lower courts.
Appellee	The party in a cause against whom an appeal is taken. Sometimes called the respondent.

GLOSSARY

Application	Term used to refer to the specific uses of a computer and the functions or operations it can perform.
Appurtenant	That which belongs to something else; an adjunct; an appendage. Something annexed to another thing more worthy as principal, and which passes as incident to it, as a right of way or other easement to land.
Arbitration	The reference of a dispute to an impartial (third) person chosen by the parties to the dispute who agree in advance to abide by the arbitrator's award issued after a hearing at which both parties have an opportunity to be heard.
Arraignment	The hearing at which the accused is brought before the court to plead to the criminal charge in the indictment.
Arrears	Money which is overdue and unpaid.
Arrest	The actual restraint of a person for submission to custody.
Arson	The malicious burning of the property of another.
Articles of Incorporation	The basic instrument filed with the appropriate government agency to form a corporation.
Assault	An act that creates in a person immediate fear of an attempted battery.
Assessed value	Assets value as determined by tax authorities for the purpose of assessing (*ad valorem*) taxes.
Assets	In bookkeeping, the entries on a balance sheet that express in terms of money the value of tangible things or intangible rights which constitute the resources of a person or business as of a given date. In estates, the property owned by the decedent.
Assignee	A person to whom an assignment is made.
Assignor	A person who assigns a right, whether or not he is the original owner thereof.
Assumed business name	A name other than its own by which a person or entity does business. Also known as a fictitious name.
Assumption of risk	The legal rule under which a person may not recover for an injury received when voluntarily exposed to a known danger.
At issue	The term used when the complaint and a responsive pleading have been filed.

Attention line	A line placed two lines below the inside address (or on the second line of the inside address) when writing to a company or institution to ensure that a specific person sees the letter.
Attestation clause	The clause of a will immediately following the signature of a testator and usually beginning "Signed, sealed, published, and declared. . . ."
Attorney-client privilege	Confidential communications, whether oral or written, between the attorney and a client in the course of the professional relationship that cannot be disclosed without the consent of the client.
Auto centering	The ability to center a word or text segment automatically.
Auto headers/footers	The ability to place header/footer text at the top or bottom of each page of a multi-page document.
Auto pagination	The ability to take a multi-page document and divide it into pages of a specified length (in number of lines) and to generate page numbers automatically.
Auto repagination	The ability to change page endings automatically if text is inserted or deleted within a document or if a new page length is desired.
Automatic measured review	A feature of certain dictation systems that permits the machine to back up a certain number of words automatically.
Automatic stay	An injunction or court order that takes effect when a bankruptcy petition is filed prohibiting all entities and individuals from any action against the debtor, property of the debtor or property of the estate.
Award	To grant, concede, or adjudge to. To give or assign by sentence or judicial determination after careful weighing of evidence.

B

Bail	Security given for the release of a jailed person that guarantees attendance at all required court appearances.
Bail bond	A written guaranty executed by a defendant and a surety to ensure the defendant will appear and make oneself available to the court.
Bailiff	The peace officer of the court responsible for keeping order and maintaining appropriate courtroom decorum.

Balance	In bookkeeping, the difference between the total debits and credits in an account.
Balance sheet	Provides information regarding the status of assets, liabilities, and owner's equity as of a specified time or date.
Bank draft	A check issued by a bank upon its funds in another bank usually located in another city.
Bankruptcy	The means by which a person may gain protection under the law for unpaid debts.
Bankruptcy judge	The judge who determines whether a debtor is entitled to a discharge in bankruptcy.
Bankruptcy law	The area of federal law dealing with persons or businesses that file for protection under the Bankruptcy Code.
Battery	A harmful offensive touching of another's person.
Beneficiary	(1) A person who benefits from the act of another. (2) A person named to receive property in a will or trust.
Bequest	A gift by will of personal property; a legacy.
Beyond a reasonable doubt	In evidence means fully satisfied, entirely convinced, satisfied to a moral certainty; and the phrase is the equivalent of the words "clear, precise and indubitable."
Bigamy	The criminal offense of willfully and knowingly contracting a second marriage while the first marriage is still subsisting and undissolved.
Bilateral contract	One where both parties make a promise.
Bill of Costs	A certified, itemized statement of the amount of costs in an action or suit.
Bill of Particulars	A motion by a criminal defendant that requests details concerning the offense charged.
Binder	Also, title commitment.
Bind over	Transfer of jurisdiction of an accused person from one court to another court.
BIOS	Basic Input Output System.
Bit	The smallest unit of information recognized by a computer. Also, an abbreviation for "binary digit."
Blank endorsement	Check endorsement consisting of only the endorser's signature.
Block move/copy	The ability to designate a block of text (generally with some maximum number of characters and related to buffer size) and to move it within the document or to another document.

Board of Directors	Governing body of a corporation elected by the shareholders.
Boilerplate	An initial prerecorded document combined with variable information to produce another document.
Bond	A written agreement by which a person agrees to pay a certain sum of money if the person bonded does not perform certain duties properly.
Book of Original Entry	A book in which transactions are recorded in the order in which they occur.
Booting	Starting or restarting the computer.
Bound supplement	A supplement to a book or books to update the service bound in permanent form.
Breach	(1) The breaking or violating of a law, right, or duty, either by commission or omission. (2) The failure of one party to carry out any condition of a contract.
Breach of duty	Any violation or omission of a legal or moral duty.
Brief	A memorandum of material facts, points of law, precedents, etc., prepared to familiarize the court with the facts and the law of a particular case.
Bureau of Land Management (BLM)	An agency within the U.S. Department of the Interior, administers 262 million surface acres of America's public lands, located primarily in 12 Western states. These lands are managed for multiple uses in three broad categories: commercial activities, recreation, and conservation. The BLM provides for acquisition, use, disposal, and adjustment of land resources; determines the boundaries of federal land; and maintains historic records for these ownership transactions.
Burden of proof	The obligation of a party to establish by evidence a requisite degree of belief concerning a fact in the mind of the trier of fact or the court.
Burglary	The act of illegal entry with the intent to steal.
Business bankruptcy	The proceeding under the Bankruptcy Code filed by a business entity.
Bylaws	Rules or laws adopted by an association or corporation to govern its actions.
Byte	A unit that measures data. One byte is the equivalent of one letter, number, or punctuation mark. A KB is one thousand bytes; a MG

	is one million bytes; a GB is one billion bytes. A sequence of adjacent binary digits operated upon as a unit and usually shorter than a word (eight adjacent binary digits).

C

Canon	A rule or standard of conduct adopted by a professional group to guide or discipline the professional conduct of its members.
Capacity	Having legal authority or mental ability; being of sound mind.
Capital case	A felony case punishable by death.
Capital statement	A financial statement that summarizes the changes in capital during a fiscal period.
Caption	The title of the case that usually includes the name of the court, the names of the parties, and the court number.
Cash basis	In bookkeeping, the method by which no record is made of revenue until cash is received and expenses are not recorded in the records until they are paid.
Cash journal	Book of original entry for recording daily transactions.
Cashier's check	A check drawn by a bank on its own funds.
Cause of action	The incident or facts that give a person a right to relief in court.
CD–ROM	Compact Disk–Read Only Memory
Censure	The official reprimand by a legislative or other formal body of one of its own members.
Central Processor Unit (CPU)	The part of a computer system where all computations, sorting, selecting, and data manipulation take place; oversees the use of the main memory and monitors input and output operations.
Central recording system	Dictation system with the recorded located in one main area but with dictation and transcription units in several locations.
Ceremonial marriage	A marriage authorized by legislative action and validated according to statutes for licensing, solemnization, and registration.
Certificate of Abstracter	Final page of an updated abstract containing several items of information needed for the real estate transaction.
Certificate of Title	*See* title insurance.

Certification	The formal assertion in writing of some fact.
Certified check	A check issued by a bank that reduces the drawer's account by the amount of the check. The bank holds those funds for payment of the check and becomes responsible for its payment.
Certiorari	A writ of review issued by a higher court to a lower court.
Cessation	Termination.
Challenge for cause	A request by a plaintiff or a defendant to a judge that a certain prospective juror not be allowed to be a member of the jury because of specified causes or reasons. *See* peremptory challenge.
Change of venue	A change in the location of a trial.
Chapter 13 Plan	A plan in bankruptcy which gives a salaried debtor or wage earner the protection of the court from creditors while paying a percentage of wages to a trustee to pay off debts.
Chart of accounts	An outline of the business accounts used in the bookkeeping system.
Chattel	An article of personal property; not real estate.
Check register	Cash disbursements journal.
Child support	The legal obligation of parents to contribute to the economic maintenance, including education, of their children.
Chronological	Arranged in the order in which events happened; according to date.
Circular E—Employer's Tax Guide	A booklet published periodically by the Internal Revenue Service as a guide for the bookkeeper regarding tax law.
Citation	A legal authority, such as a constitution, statute, case, or other authoritative source, which is used to support a written legal document.
Citators	A set of books used to verify legal authorities and locate additional, more recent cases.
Civil	Relating to private rights and remedies sought by civil actions as contrasted with criminal proceedings.
Civil action	An action brought by one party against another to resolve a controversy.
Civil law	Law that is based on a series of written codes or laws.
Claim	A debt owing by a debtor to another person or business.
Claimant	One who claims or asserts a right.

Clear and merchantable title	The term used to indicate that there are no outstanding liens or encumbrances of record against the property excepting only those of the type normally associated with the property to which most lawyers would not object.
Clerk of court	Administrator or chief clerical officer of the court.
Click	To press and quickly release a mouse button in order to activate a function of the computer.
Client/matter number	A number assigned to a client to use in accounting and records management.
Close corporation	Corporation whose shares are held by a single shareholder or a closely knit group of shareholders.
Closed file	A file where all work has been done and the file has been billed, collected, culled and marked for destruction if it can be destroyed or for permanent retention if it cannot.
Closed hearing	Hearings at which members of the general public are not allowed as spectators.
Closing agent	A person who handles a closing of sale of real estate.
Closing entries	Bookkeeping totals made to close out accounting entries at the end of a given time period.
Closing Instructions	Instructions supplied by a mortgage company, bank or other lender listing the procedures required in closing a real estate transaction, including a loan.
Closing Statement	Detailed accounting of the credits and charges to the buyer and seller.
Code of Ethics	The principles of conduct governing an individual or professional conduct.
Code of Federal Regulations	Publication that contains federal administrative rules and regulations.
Code of Judicial Ethics	Standards of ethical conduct for judges.
Codicil	An amendment to a will, either to add provisions or delete provisions of a will, which is executed with all the formalities of a will.
Codification	The process of collecting and arranging the laws (federal, county, or state) into a code.
Collate	The process of placing the pages of a document in proper sequence.
Collateral attack	The means by which a criminal defendant, after exhausting all direct appellate remedies,

seeks to attack the conditions of confinement or otherwise indirectly attack conviction.

Commingling of funds	The act of a fiduciary or trustee, including a lawyer, in mixing personal funds with those belonging to a client or customer; generally prohibited unless the fiduciary maintains an exact accounting of the client's funds and how they have been used.
Common law	Law based on precedent; case law.
Common stock	A class of corporate stock that represents the ownership of the corporation and normally has voting rights.
Community property	Property acquired during a marriage that is owned by husband and wife, each having an undivided one-half interest, except gifts of inheritances.
Comparative negligence	The rule under which negligence is measured by percentage and damages are diminished in proportion to the amount of negligence attributable to the person seeking recovery.
Compatibility	A characteristic of word or data processing equipment which permits one machine to accept and process data prepared by another machine without conversion or code modification.
Compensatory damages	Compensation to the injured party for the injury sustained.
Complaint	The original or initial pleading by which an action is filed in court.
Complimentary closing	A word or group of words placed two spaces below the body of the letter and preceding the signature as a courteous note.
Compound journal entry	A journal entry that is necessary to show a distribution of an amount to more than one account.
Concurrent jurisdiction	Jurisdiction granted in different courts at the same time over the same matters and within the same territorial limit.
Conditional will	Also, contingent will. One which does not take effect unless a specific event occurs. If the event does not occur, it is as though there is no will.
Conflict of Interest	A situation in which a person, either intentionally or unintentionally, is in a position where that person's own needs and desires might lead one to violate one's duty to another who has a right to depend on that person.

Conforming	The process of inserting on all copies of a document the information shown on the original so the copy will reflect dates, signatures, and corrections that were placed on the original.
Conjunction	Word used to connect two or more words, phrases or clauses.
Consent	Agreement; voluntary acceptance of the wish of another.
Conservator	A person appointed by a court to manage the estate of a protected person.
Consideration	In contracts, the price bargained for and paid for a promise, goods, or real estate.
Constitution	The fundamental laws of a nation or states which establish the character and basic principles of the government.
Constitutional law	Law set forth in the Constitution of the United States and in state constitutions.
Consumer bankruptcy	A proceeding under the Bankruptcy Code filed by an individual (or husband and wife) who is not in business.
Consumer debt	A debt incurred by an individual or family for personal, household, or family use.
Consumer Product Safety Commission	Commission which protects against unreasonable risks of injury from consumer products and assists in the evaluation of the comparative safety of consumer products.
Contempt of court	The term applied to an individual's refusal to obey either a written or an oral order of the court.
Contested	Challenged; opposed.
Contingent will	*See* conditional will.
Continuation or extension of abstract	*See* abstract extension.
Contra account	Account that reduces or offsets a related account on financial statements.
Contract	An enforceable agreement between two or more competent parties, which creates an obligation to do or not to do a particular thing.
Contract for deed	A contract to sell real estate upon installment payment. *See* land contract.
Contributory negligence	An affirmative defense which asserts that the injuries and damages complained of by the plaintiff were caused in whole or in part, or were contributed to as a result of plaintiff's own negligence.

Term	Definition
Conversion	Taking property that belongs to another and using it as one's own.
Conveyance	Transfer of title to land from one person or entity or group of persons or entities to another by deed.
Corporate seal	A seal used by a corporation for authenticating its corporate acts and executing legal instruments.
Corporation	A legal entity created by authority of the laws of a state or nation.
Costs advanced	Costs paid by a lawyer on the client's behalf.
Counselor	An attorney or lawyer.
Counterclaim	A claim presented by a defendant in opposition to or for deduction from the claim of plaintiff.
Counteroffer	Response to an offer with different terms than the original offer; counterproposal.
Court	Tribunal with judicial authority to handle the administration of justice.
Court-appointed lawyer	A lawyer appointed by the court to represent a defendant, usually with respect to criminal charges and without the defendant's having to pay for the representation.
Court of original jurisdiction	A court where a matter is initiated and heard in the first instance.
Court reporter	A person who usually sits in court while it is in session and records all proceedings verbatim.
Court rules	Regulations with the force of law governing practice and procedure in the various courts.
Credit	In bookkeeping, (1) to record on the right or credit side of an account; (2) those items recorded on the right side of an account.
Credit sale, sale with mortgage, or purchase money mortgage	Sale of real estate for credit. The seller receives a mortgage on the property to secure the unpaid portion of the purchase price.
Creditor	A person or entity to whom a debt is owed by another.
Creditors' meeting	In bankruptcy, first meeting of creditors and equity security holders, at which time a trustee may be elected and the debtor examined under oath.
Crime	An act in violation of the penal laws of a state or the United States and for which a specific punishment is prescribed.
Criminal action	Generally brought by the people through a government (either federal or state) against the person or persons accused of a crime.

Criminal Justice System	The network of courts and tribunals which deal with criminal law and its enforcement.
Cross-claim	A pleading filed by a defendant which asserts a claim against another defendant arising out of the same action as the original complaint.
Current asset	Cash and assets that will be converted to cash within one year.
Cursor	A symbol on the monitor that indicates the position where the next character will appear.
Cursor movement	Describes the movement of a cursor. Arrow keys are used to move the cursor up, down, left, and right.
Custody	The care and keeping of anything; in divorce (dissolution), the physical care and control of minors.

D

Damages	Pecuniary compensation which may be recovered in the courts by any person who has suffered loss, detriment or injury, whether to his person, property or rights through the unlawful act or omission or negligence of another.
dba	"Doing business as."
Database	A compilation of data fields and records that is collected, stored, and organized for later retrieval through sorting, searches, queries, etc.
Debit	In bookkeeping, (1) to record an amount on the left or debit side of an account; (2) those items recorded on the left side of an account.
Debtor	One who owes a debt to another; a person or entity filing for relief under the Bankruptcy Code.
Debtor in possession	Entity or individual retaining possession of the assets of the bankruptcy estate in a Chapter 11 bankruptcy case.
Decedent	Also, deceased. A person who has died.
Decimal tab	A feature that automatically keeps decimal points in vertical alignment while columns of numbers are being typed.
Decision	The opinion of the court.
Decree	Document issued by a court evidencing final judgment.
Deed	A formal written contract effectuating the sale and conveyance of property by the seller to the buyer for a price.

Deed of Trust	An instrument given to a lending institution to secure a loan whereby the institution holds title to the property in trust until the debt has been paid; it is similar to a mortgage, but the lender holds title to the property in trust rather than the property owner holding title outright.
Defamation	An intentional false communication, either published or publicly spoken, that injures another's reputation or good name.
Default	(1) Failure of the defendant to appear and answer the summons and complaint. (2) Failure to comply with the terms of a contract.
Default settings	The standard settings of a computer program such as for margins, tabs, paper size, and line spacing.
Defendant	(1) The person or entity defending or denying a suit. (2) The party against whom recovery is sought or the accused in a criminal case.
Defense of property	Affirmative defense in criminal law or tort law where force was used to protect one's property.
Deficiency	A lack, shortage, or insufficiency.
Deficient	Incomplete; defective; not sufficient in quantity or force.
Defunct	With reference to corporations, a corporation no longer operative; having ceased to exist.
Degrees of crime	A term used to refer to similar conduct that is punished to a great or a lesser extent depending on the existence of one or more factors.
Delete	A feature that removes a specified section of text (either a space, character, group of words, paragraph, or page).
Department of Veterans Affairs (VA)	The department of the executive branch of the United States Government which administers veterans' benefits.
Deposition	Testimony of a witness or a party taken under oath outside the courtroom.
Depository resolution	A resolution by a corporation that designates a bank to be the depository of the corporate funds.
Depreciation	Decrease in value of an asset because of use and passage of time.
Descendants	Those persons who are in the blood stream of the ancestor.

Term	Definition
Desktop Publishing	A software program that provides a means to create and produce documents of typeset quality.
Determination of heirship	The judicial determination of the identity of those persons who are entitled to inherit the decedent's property under state law if the decedent dies intestate.
Devise	Also, preresiduary gift. A gift of real property by will. Under the Uniform Probate Code, a gift of personal or real property by will.
Devisee	The person to whom land or real property is given by will.
Diary	A book used to keep track of appointments with clients, court dates and other important dates so that action will be taken when required.
Digest	A detailed index by subject on points of law covered by reported cases.
Digital camera	A camera that formats photographs into files that computer programs can use.
Digital Video Disk	A compact disk that stores greater amounts of data than a CD–ROM.
Directed Verdict	Also, instructed verdict. In a case in which the plaintiff has failed to present on the face of the case proper evidence for jury consideration, the trial judge may order the entry of a verdict without allowing the jury to consider it.
Directors	Persons appointed or elected by shareholders that are authorized to manage and direct the affairs of the corporation.
Directory	A subdivision created on a disk by the user that is used as part of the filename of a document so it can be stored in an organized manner.
Disabled person	One who lacks legal capacity; one who is physically or mentally unable to act in one's own behalf or pursue one's normal occupation.
Disbar	To deprive an attorney of the right to practice law by rescinding the license to so practice, as a result of illegal or unethical conduct by the attorney.
Disbursement	The act of paying out; money paid out; expenditure.
Discharge	In bankruptcy, the relief sought by a person who files a petition in bankruptcy.
Disciplinary procedures	Procedures by which rules of professional conduct are enforceable.

Disciplinary rules	Those regulations of the ABA Code of Professional Responsibility stating the minimum level of conduct below which no lawyer can fall without being subject to disciplinary action.
Disclaimer	The refusal, or rejection, of an estate or right offered to a person.
Discovery	The vehicle by which a party to a lawsuit is entitled to obtain facts, documents, and information about the case.
Dishonored check	Check a bank refuses to pay.
Disk drive	Apparatus that reads floppy or fixed disks.
Disks	The medium for storing data. Magnetic disk that can be removed from the computer.
Disk Operating System (DOS)	Software used to operate the computer which is installed in the computer before application software can be used.
Dismissal	An order or judgment finally disposing of an action, suit, motion, etc., without trial of the issues involved.
Disposition	In estate and probate matters, the handling of a person's property in accordance with the terms of the will.
Dispositive provisions	The provisions of a will or trust agreement relating to the disposition and distribution of property in the estate or trust.
Dissolution/divorce	(1) Dissolving the business entity and winding up its affairs. (2) The termination process of dissolving or winding up something. (3) Legal termination of a marriage.
Diversity of citizenship	A term used to mean that the party on one side of a lawsuit is a citizen of one state and the other party is a citizen of another state.
Dividends	Payments designated by the board of directors of a corporation to be distributed pro rata among shareholders.
Docket	(1) An abstract or brief entry or the book containing such entries. (2) Trial docket is a list or calendar of cases to be tried in a certain term of court.
Docket control	A system for keeping track of deadlines and court dates for both litigation and non-litigation matters.
Doctrine of *stare decisis*	That doctrine requiring courts to stand by earlier court decisions when hearing cases with similar fact situations.

Term	Definition
Document assembly/ merge	(1) The manner in which a system assembles new documents from previously recorded text. (2) The system's ability to join a document to such variable information as names and addresses to create a number of nearly identical documents.
Document management	A well-organized and managed filing system for computer documents through the use of a well-defined, uniform method for naming, storing, controlling, and retrieving documents.
Domestic corporation	Corporation created or organized in the state in which it does business.
Domestic relations	That branch or discipline of law which deals with matters of the household or family, including divorce, separation, custody, support and adoption.
Domicile	The place where a person has true, fixed, and permanent home and principal establishment, and to which whenever absent the person has the intention of returning.
Donation	A gift; something given to another in which no consideration was given or accepted.
Dormant partner	A partner who takes no active part in the management of a business and is not known to the public as a partner.
DOS prompt	A prompt that indicates that the computer is ready for the operator's command(s).
Dot pitch	The size of the smallest dot that a monitor can display onscreen.
Double click	To quickly press and release a mouse button twice.
Double-entry bookkeeping	A bookkeeping system where each entry has a dual effect. A change in any asset, liability, or in owner's equity is always accompanied by an offsetting change within the basic accounting elements.
Dower	The interest in a husband's real estate granted by law to his widow for her lifetime.
Dragging	A term for moving text or icons on a computer screen.
Drawing account	Account of withdrawals by owner for personal use.
Due care	That care which a reasonable, prudent person would exercise in a particular situation.
Duplicate original	A term frequently used when an original and duplicate copy are both executed as originals.

Durable power of attorney	A power given to another which empowers that person to act on behalf of the maker, even if the maker has become incapacitated.
Duress	Use of force or threatened force to gain consent.
Duty	Legal or moral obligation.

E

Earnest money	Deposit made by buyer indicating the buyer is entering into a contract in good faith.
Earnest Money Contract	Purchase agreement accompanied by earnest money to guarantee performance of buyer.
Easement	A right to use the lands of another. (*See* right of way.)
Editing	The act of revising text prior to its production as a final document.
Elder Law	A practice of law focused on the unique concerns of a segment of the population over the age of 50.
Ellipses marks	Omission marks; used to denote omission of a word or words in quoted material.
E-mail	The system of delivering and receiving messages electronically using a modem, telephone line, and communications software.
Emancipated	One who is set free and made one's own master. The term principally used as an emancipated minor, a person under legal age who is given legal capacity by court order or by operation of law.
Eminent domain	The power to take private property for public use by the state, municipalities, and private persons or corporations authorized to exercise functions of public character.
Employer Identification Number (EIN- or FEIN)	A number assigned to an employer by the Internal Revenue Service that must be used on all reports submitted to the IRS.
Encroachment	An intrusion on the property of another.
Encumbrance	A claim or lien on real property (real estate).
Encyclopedia	In law, a series of topics in book form arranged alphabetically containing information on legal matters.
Entity	A person or legally recognized organization.

Entrapment	The act of inducing a person to commit a crime so that a criminal charge will be brought against him.
Environmental Protection Agency (EPA)	The federal agency which works to abate and control pollution.
Ergonomics	Equipment and behavior modification techniques that aid in the prevention/reduction of repetitive strain injuries.
Equal Employment Opportunity Commission (EEOC)	A federal commission whose purpose is to eliminate employment discrimination in all areas and to promote voluntary compliance by employers.
Equity	The money value of property or an interest in a property in excess of claims or liens against that property.
Escrow	Something of value delivered to a disinterested third party to be held pending performance of certain conditions and delivered upon performance.
Escrow agent	The person designated to hold escrow property.
Escrow Agreement	Contains provisions that generally protect both the seller and the buyer. The escrow agent collects the purchase price and records the sale when all payments are made.
Estate	A person's property.
Estate planning	The area of the law dealing with arranging a person's property and estate by taking into account the laws of wills, taxes, property, and trusts to gain a maximum benefit under all laws while carrying out the person's own wishes for disposition of property upon one's death.
Estate tax	A tax imposed by the federal government and some states on the right to transfer property by death based upon decedent's assets on date of death or an alternate valuation date.
Estoppel	A principle that an individual is barred from denying or alleging a certain fact or state facts because of that individual's previous conduct, allegation or denial.
Ethernet Cable	A common cable used to connect computers on a Local Area Network.
Ethical considerations	Objectives toward which lawyers should strive.
Ethics	Of or relating to moral action and conduct; professionally right; conforming to professional standards.

Evidence	Testimony, writings, or material objects offered in proof of an alleged fact or proposition.
Evidence of title	A document evidencing title to property.
Ex parte	A court order rendered without the presence of a lawyer from both sides of the case.
Exceptions to title	Those things that are listed as exceptions to the title in a title policy or title opinion letter, *e.g.,* taxes not yet due, instrument affecting title, including those that are recorded and those that are not of public record.
Exclusionary rule	The rule commands that where evidence has been obtained in violation of the search and seizure protections guaranteed by the U.S. Constitution, the illegally obtained evidence cannot be used at the trial of the defendant.
Exclusive jurisdiction	The authority granted to a court to hear certain matters to the exclusion of all other courts.
Execute	To complete; to sign; to carry out according to its terms.
Executed contract	A contract that has been fully performed by both parties.
Executor	A person or an entity appointed by a person to administer the terms of one's will.
Executory contract	A contract which has been partially performed but with something remaining to be done by one or both parties.
Exempt property	All the property of a debtor that is not attachable under the Bankruptcy Code or state statute.
Exhibit	A paper or document produced and exhibited in court during a trial or hearing, or a person taking deposition, or to auditors, arbitrators, etc., as a voucher, or in proof of facts, or as otherwise connected with the subject matter and which, on being accepted, is marked for identification and annexed to the deposition, report, or other principal document, or file of record, or otherwise made a part of the case.
Expert witness	One who by reason of education or specialized experience possesses superior knowledge respecting a subject about which persons having no particular training are incapable of forming an accurate opinion or deducing correct conclusions.
Express contract	A contract in which the terms are specifically stated and agreed to by both parties.

Extrahazardous activity	One that carries that likelihood of causing some types of damage even if reasonable care is exercised.

F

Facsimile (fax)	An exact reproduction of a document or image sent or received to and from any location where there is phone service and a compatible fax machine.
Facsimile machine	A machine that scans a printed sheet of paper and converts its image into an electrical form that can be transmitted through a modem to another fax machine that decodes the transmission and prints out the electronic form onto paper.
Fair Labor Standards Act	Minimum wage laws.
Family law (aka domestic relations)	Those areas of the law pertaining to families, *e.g.,* marriage, divorce, child custody, juvenile laws, paternity, etc.
Fault	Negligence; an error or defect of judgment or of conduct.
Federal Aviation Administration (FAA)	The federal agency which regulates air commerce to foster aviation safety.
Federal Bureau of Investigation (FBI)	The federal agency that investigates all violations of federal laws, except those assigned to other federal agencies.
Federal Communications Commission (FCC)	The federal agency which licenses and regulates interstate and foreign communications by radio and television broadcast, wire, telephone, telegraph, cable television operation, two-way radio and radio operators, microwave, and satellite communications.
Federal Deposit Insurance Corporation (FDIC)	An independent agency within the executive branch of the federal government, which insures, up to statutory limitations, the deposits in national banks, in state banks which are members of the Federal Reserve System, and in state banks which apply for Federal Deposit Insurance and meet certain prescribed qualifications.
Federal Estate Tax	A federal tax imposed upon the privilege of transmitting property at death—IRS Form 706.
Federal Mediation and Conciliation Service	The federal agency that provides mediators to assist in labor-management disputes.

Federal Register	Published daily and contains federal administrative rules and regulations.
Federal Reporter	Reports of decisions of the United States Courts of Appeals.
Federal Supplement	Contains reported decisions of the United States District Courts.
Federal Trade Commission (FTC)	The federal agency which promotes free and fair competitive enterprise in interstate commerce.
Federal Unemployment Tax Act (FUTA)	A federal unemployment tax based on wages.
Fee simple	Absolute ownership of real property (real estate).
Felony	(1) A serious criminal offense. (2) Under federal law any offense punishable by death or imprisonment for a term exceeding one year.
FHA	Federal Housing Administration.
Fiduciary	A person or institution who manages money or property of another and who must exercise a standard of care imposed by law, *e.g.*, personal representatives or executor of an estate, a trustee, etc.
Fiduciary Income Tax Return	A federal tax return filed by the fiduciary for an estate or trust—IRS Form 1041.
Field	Predefined area where one or more characters of specific information may be entered or modified.
Filename	Term used to identify the storage area where a document is saved, its path and the name of the document.
Filename Extension	An extra set of characters, usually three, appended to a filename that can be used to determine the type of data stored in the file.
Files management	The control of each file in the office from the time it is opened to the time that it is ultimately closed and destroyed.
Filing fee	The fee required for filing various documents.
Final individual tax return	Final return for a decedent due on April 15 of year following taxable year—IRS Form 1040.
Findings of Fact and Conclusions of Law	A court's decision is a finding of fact in a case. The judge's written reasons for the findings are conclusions of law.
Fiscal year	(1) A period of 12 consecutive months chosen as an accounting period for a business; (2) A year from date of death for an estate.

Fixture	An article of personal property permanently attached to real estate.
Font	The style or design of a collection of letters, numerals, symbols, and punctuation marks.
Food and Drug Administration (FDA)	The federal agency which sets safety and quality standards for food, drugs, cosmetics, and household substances.
Foreclosure	To shut out; A termination of all rights of the mortgagor or grantee in the property covered by the mortgage.
Foreign corporation	A corporation that does business in a state or country other than the state or country in which it was created.
Foreign jurisdiction	A state other than the one where the child and custodial parent live.
Foreseeability	In tort law, the foreseeability element of proximate cause is established by proof that an actor or person of ordinary intelligence should have anticipated danger to others created by a negligent act.
Form letter	A standard form used to generate letters that have similar content.
Form paragraphs	Paragraphs that are keyboarded, stored, and coded for easy access.
Format	Includes margin and tab settings, line length and spacing, page length, etc.
Fraud	A false statement of a material fact with the intent to deceive, which statement is relied upon and is intended to be relied upon to cause a loss to the victim.
Function keys	Keys located at the top of the keyboard labeled F1–F2, etc. that are used to perform tasks in software programs.

G

Garnishment	A proceeding whereby a plaintiff creditor seeks to subject to claim the property or money of a third party; an ancillary remedy in aid of execution to obtain payment of a judgment.
General jurisdiction	Court with no limitation as to the types of cases it can hear and no limitation as to monetary jurisdiction (sometimes referred to as unlimited jurisdiction).
General ledger	A group of accounts.

General partnership	A partnership in which the parties carry on their trade or business for the joint benefit and profit of all parties.
Geographic filing	A system of filing by geographic area, such as state or region.
Gerund	Present participle form of the verb used in the sentence as a noun or part of a noun phrase.
Gigabytes (GB)	Approximately one billion bytes.
Government Printing Office (GPO)	The federal agency in charge of printing, binding, and sales of all government communications.
Government Survey	System adopted by government in 1785 for mapping out tracts of ground in townships and sections.
Grand jury	A body of citizens assembled to receive complaints and accusations in criminal cases, to hear evidence, and to determine whether probable cause exists that a crime has been committed, and whether an indictment should be issued.
Grantee	Person who receives a grant of property; the buyer.
Grantor	Person who transfers property; the seller; maker of a trust.
Graphics	Pictures, images and illustrations scanned from a hard copy or created on a computer.
Grounds	The reason for which the termination of a marriage may be sought.
Guardian *ad litem*	Person appointed by a court to represent a minor or incapacitated person in a legal proceeding.
Guardian of the estate	Person appointed by the court to be responsible for preserving the estate of a minor or disabled person.
Guardian of the person	Person appointed by the court to be responsible for the physical well-being, education, and general welfare of a minor or disabled person.

H

Hard copy	Written or printed matter.
Hardware	The physical elements of a computer, such as a keyboard, monitor, printer, case or chassis, modem, scanner, and/or joy stick.
Headnote	Summary of each point of law contained in the court decision of a reported case.

Health care power of attorney	A power given to another permitting that person to make health care decisions on behalf of the maker.
Hearing	A formal proceeding (generally less formal than a trial) with definite issues of law or of fact to be tried.
Heir	One who inherits property, either real or personal, from a relative.
Highlighting	The ability of the system to intensify certain portions of the display screen—either the characters themselves or the screen area behind the characters—to emphasize a text segment.
Holographic will	A will that is entirely handwritten, dated, and signed by the testator.
Homestead property	The dwelling house and the adjoining land where the head of the family lives.
Homicide	The killing of one human being by the act, procurement or omission of another.

I

I-beam	An image such as an arrow, hourglass, or hand that appears on a computer screen when a mouse is moved.
Illegitimate	Term applied to children born out of lawful wedlock.
Immigrant	Person who comes into a foreign country or region to live.
Immigration and Naturalization Service (INS)	The federal agency which regulates immigration and naturalization of aliens. Now under the Department of Homeland Security.
Implied contract	A contract created by law and imposed upon parties because of their actions or because of their relationships.
Imprest fund	Also, petty cash fund.
Improvements	Such items as curbs, gutters, sidewalks, street lights, and sewer systems constructed to enhance development of real estate.
Inactive files	Files in which there has been no activity for some time but for which all time has been billed.
Incapacitated	Physically or mentally disabled.
Incarceration	Imprisonment in a jail or penitentiary.
Income statement	Profit and loss statement.

Term	Definition
Income tax	A tax levied by the federal (and in some cases, state and local) government on the income of individuals which an employer may be required to withhold from the wages of an employee.
Incompetent	One who lacks ability, legal qualification, or fitness to manage one's own affairs.
Incorporation	The act or process of forming a corporation.
Incorporator	A person signing the articles of incorporation.
Indictment	A written accusation issued by a grand jury against a defendant.
Infinitive	Created by placing the word to in front of the verb. An infinitive may be used as a noun, adjective or adverb.
Information	A written accusation against the defendant.
Information management	A system of processing all types of information (written text, statistics, voice communications, and any other form of data) at top speed with the highest accuracy, least effort, and lowest cost utilizing automated equipment, standardized procedures, and specialized personnel.
Inheritance tax	A tax imposed by some states upon persons receiving property from an estate based upon individual shares, less exemptions, depending upon familial relationship between the decedent and recipient.
Injunction	A court order prohibiting someone from doing some specified act or commanding someone to undo some wrong or injury.
Input	(1) Information or ideas in raw form. (2) Term used when referring to the submission of work to a word processing center. (3) To keyboard material.
Input devices	Keyboard, mouse, optical character reader, imaging scanner, and voice recognition system.
Inside address	Name and address of person to whom a letter is to be sent, placed 2 lines following the date in a letter.
Insider	With respect to federal regulation of purchase and sale of securities, refers to anyone who has knowledge of facts not available to the general public.
Insolvent	When the total debt of an entity is greater than all of its property.
Installment real estate contract	Agreement between seller and buyer for the sale and purchase of certain real estate over a period of time by making installment payments with interest. The buyer takes possession of

	the property and maintains the property, but the seller retains title to the property until the buyer has paid the entire price.
Intent	(1) A clearly formulated or planned intention. (2) That which a plaintiff must prove to recover damages for an intentional tort.
Intentional tort	Wrong perpetrated by one who intends to break the law.
Interim trustee	The individual who serves until a trustee is appointed.
Interjection	A word used to express strong feeling or emotion.
Interlocutory	Temporary; provisional; interim, not final.
Internal Revenue Service (IRS)	The federal agency which administers the tax laws of the United States, except tax on alcohol, firearms, explosives, and tobacco.
Interpleader	An equitable proceeding to determine the rights of rival claimants to property held by a third person having no interest therein.
Interrogatories	A set or series of written questions propounded to a party, witness, or other person having information or interest in a case; a discovery device.
Interstate Commerce Commission (ICC)	The federal agency which regulates all transportation in interstate commerce.
Inter vivos trust	A trust created during a decedent's lifetime that becomes operative during one's lifetime.
Intestate	Having died without making a will.
Intestate succession	The statutory acquisition of title to property when the deceased left no will or an invalid will.
Invalid marriage	A marriage that is void from its inception.
Invalidity	In marriage, one which is invalid from its inception.
Inventory	In estates, a list of the assets that comprise the estate, including values.
Involuntary bankruptcy	A proceeding initiated by creditors requesting the bankruptcy court to place a debtor in liquidation.
Involuntary petition	One in which the creditors ask the court to place a debtor in liquidation.
Irrevocable trust	A trust which may not be revoked by the maker after its creation; generally made for tax reasons.
Issue	Child of a marriage.

J

Joint and several liability	Describes the liability of co-promisors of the same performance when each of them, individually, has the duty of fully performing the obligation, and the obligee can sue all or any of them upon breach of performance.
Joint custody	In a divorce/dissolution, the situation occurring when both parents are awarded custody of a child, often for specified periods of time during any one year.
Joint Interest Trust	A trust that is created by two persons placing their jointly held assets in trust.
Joint Stock Company	An unincorporated business enterprise with ownership represented by shares of stock.
Joint Tenancy	Property held by two or more persons, each with the same undivided interest in the property.
Joint Venture	A legal entity in the nature of a partnership engaged in a joint undertaking of a commercial enterprise.
Joint will	A single will made by two or more persons.
Journal	A chronological record of all transactions completed, showing date, titles of accounts to be debited or credited, and amounts of the debits and credits.
Journalizing	The act of recording transactions in a journal.
Judgment	The written decision of a court to an action or suit submitted to the court for determination.
Judgment debtor	One who owes money as a result of a judgment in favor of a creditor.
Judiciary	The branch of government vested with judicial power to interpret and apply the law; the court system; the body of judges; the bench.
Jurat	Certification of person or officer before whom a writing was sworn to.
Jurisdiction	The power and authority of a court to hear and try a case.
Jurisdiction *in personam*	The authority of a court to render a judgment against a person or to subject the disputing parties to the decisions and rulings made by it.
Jurisdiction *in rem*	The authority of a court to render a judgment concerning property over which it has jurisdiction.

Jury — A certain number of men and women selected according to law and sworn to try a question of fact or indict a person for public offense.

Justification — The term that refers to the four types of text alignment (left justification, right justification, center justification, and full justification).

K

Key Number System — A research aid developed by West Publishing Company which divides the law into primary sections, subsections, and topics. The key number for a given topic will help the researcher find all references to that subject quickly.

Keyboarding — Inputting information into a computer.

Kilobytes (KB) — Approximately one thousand bytes (1,024 characters).

L

LAN — Local Area Network. The linking of computers within close proximity.

Land contract — Contract for purchase and sale of real property.

Landlord — Also, lessor. The owner of property who leases it to a person or business entity.

Last Will and Testament — Also, will. An instrument by which a person makes a disposition of property, to take effect after death, and which by its own nature is ambulatory and revocable during one's lifetime.

Law blank — A printed legal form available for preparing documents.

Law of Descent — Controls who shall inherit under a will which has been proved invalid or when there is no will.

Lawsuit — (1) An action or proceeding in a civil court. (2) Term used for a suit or action between two private parties in a court of law.

Lease — (1) A contract between owner and lessee for possession and use of property. (2) An agreement that gives rise to a landlord and tenant relationship.

Leave of court — Permission of court to take some action.

Ledger	The book of final entry in bookkeeping, where a complete record of all assets, liabilities, and proprietorship items is kept.
Legacy	A disposition of personal property by will; a bequest.
Legal cap	White paper, 8 1/2″ x 13″ or 8 1/2″ x 14″, with a ruled left margin and a narrow ruled right margin.
Legal capacity	Refers to whether a person may sue in one's own right without being represented by someone else.
Legal consideration	The price, motive, or act that leads a party to do something the party would not be obliged to do otherwise.
Legal description	A detailed specification of real property which must be complete enough that the parcel can be located and identified (by metes and bounds or lot numbers of a recorded plat).
Legal encyclopedia	Books that state principles of law supported by footnote references to pertinent cases throughout the US.
Legal process	(1) A formal paper that is legally valid. (2) Something issuing from the court, usually a command such as a writ or mandate.
Legal texts	Books that cover specific areas of the law, usually dealing with a single topic.
Legatee	The person to whom a legacy is given in a will.
Legislation	(1) The act of giving or enacting laws. (2) The power to make laws via legislation in contrast to court-made laws.
Legitimate	That which is legal, lawful, recognized by law, or according to law. A child or children born of persons in lawful wedlock.
Lessee	Also, tenant. Person who rents property from another.
Lessor	Also, landlord. Owner who rents property to another.
Letters of Administration	Formal document issued by probate court appointing the administrator of an estate.
Letters Testamentary	The formal instrument of authority and administration given to a personal representative by the court in a testacy situation, empowering the personal representative to enter upon the discharge of one's office as the personal representative.

Liabilities	In bookkeeping, the debts or other financial obligations of a business for money, goods, services, etc., received.
Liability	(1) A debt or obligation to another person or entity. (2) Legal responsibility to another.
Libel	In torts, damage to a person's reputation by written or published information.
Licensing boards	State agencies created to regulate the issuance of licenses, *e.g.,* contractors, cosmetologists, realtors, etc.
Lien	An encumbrance or legal burden upon property.
Limited jurisdiction	Where a court is restricted in the type of case it can hear or in the amount of money involved in the litigation.
Limited Liability Company (LLC)	A business entity giving advantages of limited liability to equity owners and control persons.
Limited Liability Limited Partnership	A limited partnership which has elected to be treated as a limited liability partnership in addition to being a limited partnership.
Limited Partnership	A partnership consisting of one or more general partners who conduct the business and one or more limited partners who contribute cash payments as capital and who are not liable for the debts of the partnership beyond the amount each contributes.
Limited Warranty Deed	Also, special warranty deed. Guaranty clause in deed by which grantor pledges that grantor has done nothing to cloud or encumber the title. Grantor does not guarantee against any defects that occurred before he owned the property.
Liquidation	The conversion by sale of all of a debtor's nonexempt property in a bankruptcy proceeding.
Lis pendens	A pending suit. Jurisdiction, power or control which courts acquire over property in litigation pending action and until final judgment.
Listing Agreement	Agreement whereby owners of real estate agree to have a broker represent them in the sale of real estate.
Litigation	A lawsuit; a legal action, including all proceedings therein.
Living Will	The document by which the maker instructs the physician or medical supplier not to keep the maker alive by use of life-supporting procedures.

Looseleaf Services	Looseleaf replacement pages provided by a publisher in areas of the law where changes occur at a rapid rate.

M

Macro	A format that is created by recording a number of keystrokes, storing them, and playing them back by using fewer keystrokes.
Magistrate	An official or officer with limited judicial authority; a public officer.
Majority (age of)	Full age, legal age; age at which a person is no longer a minor.
Malicious prosecution	One begun in malice without probable cause to believe the charges can be sustained.
Malpractice	Professional misconduct or unreasonable lack of skill; a violation of a standard of care.
Marriage	A civil contract governed by state law.
Martindale–Hubbell Law Directory	A publication of several volumes that contains names, addresses, specialties, and ratings of lawyers.
Massachusetts Trust	A business organization wherein property is conveyed to trustees and managed for the benefit of the holders of certificates similar to corporate stock certificates.
Materialman's Lien	Also, mechanic's lien. An instrument filed by a materialman or a mechanic who has furnished material or performed labor for improvements to property but has not been paid for that work. Such a lien creates an enforceable right against the property which may be enforced by foreclosure to recover payment.
Maturity value	Principal plus interest that will be due on a note on its due date.
Mediation	Non-binding settlement discussions between the parties.
Megabytes (MB)	Approximately one million bytes (1,048,576 characters).
Memorial	In real estate, entries on a Torrens certificate which describe encumbrances (such as mortgages or liens) in existence on the property.
Mens reus	A guilty mind; a criminal intent.
Merger	The fusion or absorption of one thing or right into another.
Metes and bounds	A way of describing land by listing compass directions and distances of boundaries.

Mining Partnership	An association of several mine owners for cooperation in working the mine.
Minor	A person under the age of legal competence.
Minute Book	The official book of corporate minutes kept by the secretary of the corporation.
Minute Clerk	The person who sits in court while it is in session and keeps track of files, exhibits, and proceedings and administers oaths.
Minutes	Memorandum of a transaction or proceeding.
Miranda rule	Prior to any custodial interrogation, the person must be warned: (1) that he has a right to remain silent, (2) that any statement made may be used as evidence against the person, (3) that the person has a right to the presence of an attorney, (4) that if he cannot afford an attorney, one will be appointed prior to any questioning if the person so desires.
Misdemeanor	A criminal offense lesser than a felony and generally punishable by fine or by imprisonment other than in a penitentiary.
Misrepresentation	A false statement of material fact which is relied upon and is intended to be relied upon to cause a loss to the victim.
Mistake	Genuine misunderstanding that brings about the end result the parties did not intend.
Mitigation	Reducing money damages to the amount of the actual loss.
Mixed punctuation	In correspondence, a colon follows the salutation and a comma follows the complimentary closing.
Model Rules of Professional Conduct	The guidelines that define the relationship of the lawyer to the legal system.
Modem	A device that allows for the exchange of data from one computer to another by transmission through cables, telephone lines, fiber optics, or satellite links.
Modification of decree	A procedure whereby a decree can be changed after a period of time due to a substantial change in circumstances.
Monetary jurisdiction	The limitation on dollar amounts that a court may award.
Mortgage	A written instrument that grants an interest in real property to provide security for the repayment of a debt.
Mortgagee	Person who receives the mortgage (the creditor).

Mortgagee's title policy	A policy of insurance issued by a title insurance company to a lender insuring the lender from loss resulting from a defect of title.
Mortgagor	Person with legal title who gives a lien on property to secure a loan (the debtor).
Motion	An application made to a court or judge that requests specific relief.
Motion to Quash Service	A motion seeking to have service declared invalid on the basis that service was improperly made, that the wrong party was served, or that the summons does not show the date of service.
Mouse	Device used to move the insertion point or icons in a windows product.
Movant	The moving party.
Multicolumn cash journal	A multicolumn journal in which all transactions of a business are recorded.
Multitasking	Ability to perform one or more application programs at the same time.
Mutual and reciprocal will	Sometimes also called a double will. A will executed jointly by two persons containing reciprocal provisions and language to the effect that the devises are made one in consideration of the other.

N

NALS	An association for legal professionals.
National Labor Relations Board (NLRB)	The NLRB is vested with the power to safeguard employees' rights to form bargaining units and to prevent and remedy unfair labor practices.
Naturalization	Process by which a person acquires nationality after birth and becomes entitled to privileges of citizenship.
Negligence	Failure to use care which a reasonable and prudent person would use under similar circumstances.
Net income	Total income less expenses equals net income.
Net loss	If total expenses exceed net income, a net loss results.
Net profit	Excess of total revenue over total expenses.
No-fault divorce	The dissolution of a marriage on the grounds of irreconcilable differences; a divorce under which neither spouse is accused of the traditional grounds upon which divorces are usually granted.

Nolo contendere	Latin phrase meaning "I will not contest it." Type of plea which may be entered with leave of court to a criminal complaint or indictment by which the defendant does not admit or deny the charges, though a fine or sentence may be imposed pursuant to it.
Nominal partner	A person who permits others to believe the person is a partner, or acts in a manner so that people believe the person is a partner.
Non-custodial parent	The parent who does not have physical care and control of the child.
Non-jury trial	Trial before the court but without a jury.
Non-probate assets	Assets owned by decedent and others in joint tenancy, life insurance, and other property payable to others instead of to the estate, and property held in inter vivos and Totten trusts.
Non-trading partnership	A partnership engaged in performing services; dependent on the work results of the partners rather than on capital contributed.
Notary public	A public officer whose function it is to administer oaths, to attest and certify documents, and to take acknowledgments.
Notes payable	Promissory notes given to creditors.
Notes receivable	Promissory notes a business accepts from customers.
Notice	Written notification to parties in a lawsuit of the date, time, place, and subject matter of a hearing.
Notice to Creditors	A notice given by the bankruptcy court to all creditors of a meeting of creditors.
Noun	Word that names a person, place, thing or idea.
Novation	In contracts, the removal of one of the original parties to a contract and the substitution of a newcomer (all parties must consent).
Nuisance	Activity which arises from unreasonable, unwarranted or unlawful use by a person of the person's own property, working obstruction or injury to right of another or to the public, and producing such material annoyance, inconvenience and discomfort that law will presume resulting damage.
Numeric filing	An indirect method of assigning numbers to client files and filing them in numerical order with the most recent files being given the latest number.
Nuncupative will	A will spoken by a person in peril of imminent death.

O

Oath	A solemn pledge by which a person signifies that he is bound in conscience to perform an act faithfully and truthfully.
Occupational Safety and Health Act (OSHA)	OSHA's mission is to assure the safety and health of America's workers by setting and enforcing standards; providing training, outreach, and education; establishing partnerships; and encouraging continual improvement in workplace safety and health.
Offeree	The party to whom the offer is made.
Offeror	The party making the offer.
Officers	In corporations, the persons elected by the directors of said corporation to be responsible for the day-to-day operation and management of the corporation.
One write accounting system	Figures are entered on the system only once.
Open court	Hearings conducted in the courtroom at which members of the general public may be present as spectators.
Open punctuation	In correspondence, no punctuation is used following the salutation or the complimentary closing.
Operating System	Software that controls the flow of information to and from the CPU and to and from the input/output devices.
Optical Character Reader	A scanner that converts an image into a character-based text file.
Oral argument	Verbal presentation before a court of the merits and law relating to a case or an aspect of the case. In appellate court, a time limit is usually set; in other courts, the judge has discretion to set or waiver time limits.
Order	Direction of a court or judge made in writing.
Order to show cause	An order to a person or corporation, on motion of opposing party, to appear in court and explain why the court should not take a proposed action.
Ordinance	A rule established by authority; may be a municipal statute of a city council regulating such matters as zoning, building, safety, matters of municipality, etc.

Organizational meeting	Meeting of shareholders, etc. held as part of the incorporation process to handle routine matters necessary for the corporation to commence business.
Original jurisdiction	The authority granted to a court to hear and determine a matter for the first time.
Output	In word processing, (1) the final results after recorded "input" is processed, revised, and printed out; (2) the final documents or other information produced by an automated system.
Output devices	Computer peripherals such as monitors and printers.
Owner's equity	The amount by which the assets of a business exceed the liabilities of a business (assets = liabilities + owner's equity).
Owner's Title Policy	A policy of insurance issued by a title insurance company to a property owner that insures the owner from loss resulting from a defect of title.

P

Parole	Release from jail, prison, or other confinement after actually serving part of sentence.
Partner	Member of a partnership.
Partnership	A voluntary association of two or more persons or entities to place money, effects, labor, and skill in lawful commerce or business and to have a proportional share in profits and losses.
Par value	Value printed on a stock certificate.
Patent and Trademark Office	The federal agency that examines and issues patents and registers trademarks.
Paternity	State of being a father.
Payee	Person to whom a promissory note, bank draft or check is issued.
Payroll records	The records that are the accounting of employees' earnings and deductions.
Payroll register	A register on which all payroll information is recorded.
Per capita	According to the number of individuals, share and share alike.
Peremptory challenge	Request by a party that a judge not allow a certain prospective juror as a member of the jury. No reason or cause need be given.

Performance	The doing of all the contractual terms by both parties.
Periodical	A publication which appears regularly but less often than daily.
Peripherals	Devices that are connected to a computer such as terminals, tape drives, disk drives, modems, and printers.
Permanent memory devices	Storage media such as floppy disks, hard drives, magnetic tapes, or CD–ROMs.
Perpetual calendar	A set of index cards or file folders that are used to keep track of events. Also known as a tickler system.
Per stirpes	By roots or stocks; by representation. Denotes that method of dividing an intestate estate where a class or group of distributees take the share which deceased would have been entitled to, had the deceased lived, taking thus by their right of representing such ancestor, and not as so many individuals.
Personal income tax	A tax levied by the government on the income of individuals which an employer may be required to withhold from the earnings of an employee.
Personal information management (PIM)	Database software that aids in organizing, scheduling time and keeping track of clients and events.
Personal injury	The term that usually describes the kind of suit filed to recover damages for a physical injury.
Personal property	All property not classified as real property.
Personal representative	Term used by the Uniform Probate Code to designate the representative of an estate, replacing the terms executor, administrator, etc.
Petition	First pleading filed in any lawsuit; also called complaint.
Petition for dissolution	Initial document in a dissolution of marriage proceeding.
Petitioner	Initiating party or plaintiff in a dissolution of marriage proceeding.
Petty cash fund	Fund for paying small expenses to eliminate necessity of writing checks for small amounts. Sometimes referred to as an imprest fund.
Petty cash ledger	A subsidiary ledger in which all expenditures and reimbursements of the petty cash fund are listed.

Piercing the corporate veil	Judicial process whereby court will disregard usual immunity of corporate officers or entities from liability for wrongful corporate activities.
PIM	Personal Information Management.
Pixel	One of the individual dots that constitute the graphical image on the computer screen.
PKPA	Parental Kidnapping Prevention Act.
Plaintiff	A person or entity who brings the action; the party who complains or sues in a civil action.
Plat	A map of a subdivided area, usually drawn to scale.
Plea	The first pleading by a criminal defendant.
Plea bargaining	Process where the accused in a criminal case and the prosecutor work out a satisfactory disposition of the case, usually by the defendant's agreeing to plead guilty to a lesser offense.
Pleading	Written statement made by each side of a lawsuit concerning the various claims and defenses to be decided in court.
Pocket parts	Supplements to law books in pamphlet form which are inserted in a pocket inside the back cover of the books to keep them current.
Postal notation	Remarks on a letter regarding special mail handling.
Post–Closing Trial Balance	A trial balance prepared after the closing entries are posted to the general ledger.
Posting	The process of recording information in the ledger from the journal.
Post-trial	Refers to items happening after the trial, *e.g.*, posttrial motions or posttrial discovery.
Prayer	A summary in the complaint or petition which states what the plaintiff or petitioner is asking the court to do.
Preemptive right	The original shareholders are given the first option to buy enough of additional issued shares of stock to maintain their proportionate share of ownership.
Preference	The paying or securing to one or more creditors, by an insolvent debtor, the whole or a part of their claim, to the exclusion or detriment of the rest.
Preliminary hearing	Also, preliminary examination. A hearing by a judge to determine whether a person charged with a crime should be held for trial.

Term	Definition
Prenuptial or antinuptial agreement	One entered into by prospective spouses prior to marriage but in contemplation and in consideration thereof.
Preponderance of the evidence	As standard of proof in civil cases, is evidence which is of greater weight or more convincing than the evidence which is offered in opposition to it; that is, evidence which as a whole shows that the fact sought to be proved is more probable than not.
Preposition	Word used to show the relationship of the noun or pronoun that follows it to some other word in the sentence.
Pretermitted heir	One who as a child or descendant would have shared in the estate but who is not named in or provided for by the will.
Pretrial conference	Hearing among the opposing lawyers and the judge called at the discretion of the court to narrow the issues to be tried.
Prima facie case	At first sight; on the first appearance; on the face of it.
Primary authority	Constitutions, codes, statutes, ordinances, and case law.
Principal	Amount a borrower promises to pay that is written on the face of a note.
Privilege	A benefit or advantage to certain persons beyond the advantages of other persons, *e.g.*, an exemption, immunity, power, etc.
Privileged communication	Communication between a client and attorney that is protected from discovery.
Prize	Vessels or cargo of the enemy that are taken on the high seas, by the right or law of war.
Pronoun	A word used in place of a noun.
Pro se	Term used to designate a person who represents himself or herself in court.
Probable cause	Justification for believing it is more likely than not that the crime charged was committed and the suspect committed it.
Probate	Court proceeding by which a will is proved valid or invalid. Term used to mean all proceedings pertaining to the administration of an estate.
Probate assets	Those items of property owned by the decedent that must pass through the probate process.
Probate deed	An instrument by which property is acquired from an estate or guardianship, generally with-

	out warranty. Sometimes referred to as executor's, fiduciary's, or trustee's deed.
Probate proceeding	The actions and pleadings required by law to administer a person's estate.
Pro bono	Used to describe work or services (legal services) done or performed free of charge.
Probation	Sentence imposed for commission of crime whereby a convicted criminal offender is released into the community under the supervision of a probation officer in lieu of incarceration.
Procedural law	That body of laws which defines and describes the process to be followed to enforce substantive law.
Product liability	Legal responsibility of manufacturers and sellers to buyers, users, and bystanders for damages or injuries suffered because of defects in goods.
Professional Corporation	A corporation of licensed professionals rendering personal service to the public, *e.g.,* lawyers, physicians, surgeons, dentists, certified public accountants, etc.
Promissory note	A promise in writing to pay a certain sum of money at a future time.
Proof of claim	Statement under oath filed in a bankruptcy proceeding by a creditor in which the creditor sets forth the amount owed and sufficient detail to identify the basis for the claim.
Proportional spacing	Printed or displayed text where each alphanumeric character is given a weighted amount of space.
Proprietor	Owner; person who has legal right or title to anything.
Prosecutor	One who prosecutes another for a crime in the name of the government.
Protocol	A formal set of rules controlling the transmission of data.
Proving cash	Determining that the amount of cash on hand agrees with account records.
Proximate cause	The efficient cause.
Proxy	The instrument authorizing one person to represent, act, and vote for another at a shareholders' meeting of a corporation.
Prudent person	A careful, cautious, attentive person of good judgment.

Term	Definition
Public law	Law that applies to the public, such as traffic ordinances or zoning laws.
Punitive damages	An award in addition to the actual loss.
Purchase Agreement or Purchase Offer	Also, sales agreement. Agreement between buyer and seller of property which sets forth in general the consideration and terms of a proposed sale.
Putative	Alleged; supposed; reputed.
Putative father	Alleged father.
Putative spouse	A person who lives with another person of the opposite sex and believes in good faith that there is a common law marriage.

Q

Term	Definition
Qualified endorsement	Endorser assumes no legal responsibility for payment should the drawer have insufficient funds to honor a check by using the words "Without Recourse" written above the payee's signature in the endorsement.
Qualified Terminable Interest Property (Q–TIP)	A type of property which is permitted to qualify for a marital deduction under federal estate tax if the spouse has use of the property for life and other Internal Revenue Code requirements are met.
Queue	A set of documents waiting to be processed sequentially by a printer or other device.
Quitclaim Deed	A deed without warranty of title that passes whatever title the grantor has, if any, to another.
Quorum	(1) A majority of the entire body of directors or shareholders. (2) The number of members who must be present to conduct business.

R

Term	Definition
Random Access Memory (RAM)	Both software program instructions and user input, manifested by what is displayed on the screen, are stored in the internal memory storage area called Random Access Memory. Volatile, internal computer memory that temporarily stores data that can be directly accessed by the CPU.
Read Only Memory (ROM)	Nonvolatile internal computer memory that permanently stores instructions for the computer.

Reaffirmation Agreement	An agreement whereby the debtor agrees to continue payments to the creditor as before bankruptcy.
Real estate	Land and whatever is attached or affixed to it. Generally synonymous with the words "real property."
Real property	Real estate or real property.
Realty	A collective brief term used to designate real estate.
Reasonable care	Due care, or ordinary care, under all circumstances.
Rebuttal	Rebuttal occurs during the trial stage where evidence is given by one party to refute evidence introduced by the other party.
Recapture of chattels	A defense to a personal injury claim by asserting that the defendant was attempting to recover property which had been taken from the defendant.
Receiver	A person appointed by a court for the purpose of preserving property of a debtor pending an action against the debtor, or applying the property in satisfaction of a creditor's claim, whenever there is danger that, in the absence of such an appointment, the property will be lost, removed, or injured.
Reconcile	To make agree, as a bank statement and a check register.
Recordation	The act or process of recording an instrument such as a deed or mortgage in a public registry.
Rectangular survey system	System adopted in 1785 by the government for dividing tracts of land into townships and sections.
Recuse	Act of disqualifying a judge, or judge disqualifying himself, from case because of bias or personal interest.
Registered property	Real property registered upon application of the owner under the Torrens title system.
Registered Property Abstract	Abstract used in sale of registered property that summarizes information contained on the certificate of title and tax and other information.
Rehabilitative maintenance	Support paid by one spouse to the other for a physical or vocational disability.
Release and Covenant Not to Sue	An agreement by both parties to end the contract even though both parties have not fully performed the terms of the contract.

Replace	In word processing, a feature that searches for and stops at every occurrence of a specified section of text, thereby giving the operator the option to alter or accept the text.
Replacement volumes	Volumes which replace a book and its pocket parts when it becomes too bulky.
Reply to counterclaim	The answer filed by plaintiff in response to the allegations contained in defendant's claim against plaintiff.
Reporters	Books which contain published court decisions.
Reprimand	A term defined in the ABA Model Standards for Lawyer Discipline and Disability Proceedings to refer to a "form of public discipline imposed after trial or formal charges which declares the respondent's conduct to have been improper but does not limit the right to practice."
Request for Admissions	Also, requests to admit. Written statements of facts concerning a case which are submitted to an adverse party which that party must admit or deny.
Request for Production of Documents and Things	A direction or command served upon another party, witness, or other person for production of specific documents and/or things for review with respect to a suit; a discovery device.
Res judicata	The principle that states that once there has been a judicial decision the matter cannot be litigated again.
Rescission	Agreement to cancel or repeal the contract plus whatever is necessary to restore both parties to their original condition.
Residuary bequest	A gift of the remaining assets of an estate.
Residue	Pertains to what is left after the payment of specific bequests, devises, expenses, and taxes.
Res ipsa loquitur	The thing speaks for itself.
Resolution	A formal expression of the will of a public assembly, official body, or a corporation that is adopted by vote.
Respondeat superior	Let the master answer. This doctrine means that a master is liable in certain cases for the wrongful acts of a servant, and a principal for those of an agent.
Respondent	The party against whom a dissolution of marriage proceeding is initiated.
Response	Initial pleading of a respondent in a no-fault divorce proceeding.

Restatement	A publication that explains the law in a particular field.
Restitution	Act of restoring a thing to its rightful owner.
Restraining order	An order in the nature of an injunction which forbids the defendant from doing the threatened act until a hearing on the application can be had.
Restrictive covenant	Regulations of record setting forth those things that are allowed and not allowed affecting property such as minimum building lines, etc.
Restrictive endorsement	Limits the further purpose or use of the check.
Retrieval system	A system that is designed to preserve materials, such as legal research, briefs, and forms, that might be helpful to a firm in the future.
Retrieve	The ability to recall a document from the storage media.
Reversal	The annulling or setting aside by an appellate court of a decision of a lower court.
Revocable Trust	A trust in which the maker generally maintains some power over the trust as long as the maker is alive and not incapacitated; can be amended or revoked during maker's lifetime.
Revocation clause	Clause in a will revoking all former wills and codicils made by the testator.
Revocation of offer	The withdrawal by the offeree of an offer that had been valid until withdrawn.
Right of way	The right of a party to pass over the land of another.
Rules of Court	Procedures and requirements adopted by individual courts that must be followed when filing legal pleadings.

S

Sale with assumption of mortgage	A sale of real estate whereby the purchaser pays a portion of the sales price in cash and agrees to assume the seller's obligations regarding the payment of the mortgage which the seller placed on the property.
Salutation	Phrase used at beginning of letter to address person to whom letter is written.
Sanctions	The part of law which is designed to secure enforcement by imposing a penalty for its violation or offering a reward for its observance.

Scanner	Device that converts an image into a character based text file.
Screening	Process of inquiring as to who is calling and then either permitting the caller to see or talk with the lawyer or assisting the caller in some other manner.
Scrolling	A software feature that allows a system to "flip" through the pages of a document, vertically and horizontally, allowing access to all text of a multi-page document.
Seal	(1) To mark a document with a seal. (2) To authenticate or make binding by affixing a seal.
Search	An editing tool that allows the operator to quickly find a specific word, phrase, or code in a document.
Secondary authority	(1) Legal encyclopedias, treatises, legal texts, law review articles, restatements, and essays. (2) Writings which set forth the opinion of the writer as to the law.
Secret partner	A partner who takes no active part in the business and is not known to the public as a partner.
Secured debts	Debts for which the debtor has pledged something of value to guarantee payment.
Securities and Exchange Commission (SEC)	The SEC monitors the securities industry by providing disclosure to the investing public and protects the interests of investors against malpractice in the securities and financial markets.
Self-defense	The right of a person to defend one's person, property, home, or family against anyone who intends to commit a forcible felony.
Self-proved clause	A clause in a will signed by the testator and witnesses before a notary public for the purpose of allowing the will to be admitted to probate without the affidavit of the witnesses at the time of probate.
Sentence	Judgment on the verdict; usually in a criminal action.
Server	A minicomputer system on a network that stores all data for the network.
Service of process	The delivery of writs, summonses, and subpoenas by handing them to the party named in the document.
Settlor	The maker of a trust.

Share certificate	A certificate of a corporation or joint stock company that the named person is the owner of a designated number of shares of stock.
Shareholders	The persons or other entities that own shares in a corporation and therefore indirectly own the corporation.
Sheet feeder	Attachment on a printer that feeds paper into printer.
Shepardizing	Checking the subsequent history of a reported court decision to make sure it has not been overturned by a higher court.
Shortcut keys	Keys or combination of keys used to perform a task, such as Ctl + P to print.
Show cause	An order granted *ex parte* stating a date and time the opposing side must appear before the court to present evidence against the court taking certain action.
Silent partner	See, dormant partner.
Simple will	A will containing only certain required basic elements.
Slander	Damage to a person's reputation by spoken information.
Small Business Administration (SBA)	The SBA seeks to maintain and strengthen the nation's economy by aiding, counseling, assisting and protecting the interests of small businesses and by helping families and businesses recover from national disasters.
Social Security	A system of federal old-age pensions for employed persons begun in 1935. A portion of the payment is deducted from the employee's salary and the employer contributes an equal portion.
Social Security Administration	The federal agency that administers the Social Security and Medicare programs.
Social Security Number	A number obtained from the federal government. All employees must have this number so that Social Security and Medicare taxes can be deducted from earnings and applied to the employee's account.
Software	All programs needed to instruct, control, and operate the hardware of a computer system such as flowcharts, manuals, programs, routines, training, and the like.
Soldiers' or sailors' will	An oral will (noncupative) which the law allows soldiers or sailors to make disposing of personal property.

Sole proprietorship	A business owned and operated by a person who is solely responsible for its day-to-day operation.
Source paper	Any document or paper that provides information about cash received, cash disbursed, fees charged, or purchases charged.
Special endorsement	State to whom a check is to be paid.
Special exceptions	A defendant's specific exception or objection to specific allegations in a complaint whereby defendant asks the court to strike (eliminate) such allegations or require the plaintiff to replead those allegations more specifically.
Special warranty or limited warranty deed	A deed that contains a guaranty clause by which the grantor pledges that grantor has done nothing to cloud or encumber title beyond the verified encumbrances specified therein with no guarantee against any defects that occurred before the property was owned by grantor.
Specific bequest	A gift in a will of an identified asset or stated amount of money.
Speedy Trial Act	The federal act that establishes time limits for carrying out major events in the prosecution of federal criminal cases, *e.g.*, indictment, arraignment, etc.
Spousal maintenance/alimony	Allowance that a spouse pays for the support of the other spouse, usually by court order.
Spreadsheet	Electronic worksheet.
Standing	A concept requiring that the person injured is the one who must sue.
Statement of Account	A business form showing the charges, receipts and balance of a client's account.
Statute of limitations	The time period following an occurrence within which a lawsuit must be filed.
Statutory law	Law enacted by Congress, state legislatures, and local governments.
Stay	To "stay" an order or decree means to hold it in abeyance, or refrain from enforcing it.
Stepchild	The child of one of the spouses by a former marriage not adopted by the other spouse.
Stipulation	An agreement between the parties involved in a suit regulating matters incidental to the trial.
Stockbook	A continuing record of the stock ownership of a corporation.
Stock Certificate	*See* share certificate.

Term	Definition
Straight Line Depreciation	A method of depreciating building, furniture or equipment that provides for equal periodic charges to expenses over the estimated useful life of an asset.
Strict liability	Concept applied by the courts in product liability cases that when a manufacturer presents goods for public sale it represents that they are suitable for their intended use.
Styles	Collection of formatting codes that can be applied to selected text.
Subchapter S Corporation	A small business corporation taxed as if it were an individual proprietorship.
Subdivision	The division of a tract or parcel of land or lot into two or more tracts, parcels, or lots for sale or development.
Subject filing	A system where files are filed alphabetically by the subject matter involved, *e.g.*, accounting, insurance, personnel, etc.
Subject line	Phrase following salutation that states briefly the subject about which the letter is written.
Subject matter jurisdiction	The authority of a court to render a binding judgment over the matter in dispute.
Sublease	A transaction where a tenant leases to another the whole or part of the premises during the term of the tenant's lease.
Subpoena	A command to appear at a certain time and place to give testimony upon a certain matter.
Subpoena duces tecum	A command to appear at a certain time and place to give testimony and to bring items specified therein.
Subsidiary ledger	A ledger that contains a complete breakdown of a subsidiary account and which must balance with the appropriate account in the general ledger.
Substantive criminal law	(1) Law with the purpose of prevention of harm to society which prescribes punishment for specific offenses. (2) The basic law of rights and duties as opposed to "remedial law" which provides methods of enforcement.
Substantive law	The statutory or written law that governs rights and obligations of those who are subject to it.
Sub/superscript printout	The ability of the printer to print characters a fractional increment (sometimes adjustable) above and below the baseline; useful for footnotes, formulas, equations, etc.

Summary judgment	Procedural device available for prompt and expeditious disposition of controversy, without trial, when there is no dispute as to either material fact or inferences to be drawn from disputed facts, or if only questions of law are involved.
Summons	Instrument used to commence a civil action or special proceeding and is a means of acquiring jurisdiction over a party.
Surety	A person or entity who posts bond for another.
Survey	Actual ground measurement of a parcel of property giving the location of the property as well as its boundary lines.
Suspend	To interrupt; to postpone; to stay, delay or hinder; to discontinue temporarily, but with an expectation or purpose of resumption.
Syndicate	An association of individuals formed for the purpose of conducting and carrying out some particular business transaction, usually of a financial character, in which the members are mutually interested.

T

T account	A skeletal form of account showing the account title and the debit and credit sides.
Tax lien	A lien filed for nonpayment of property taxes or for nonpayment of federal, state, or local taxes such as income taxes, sales taxes, etc.
Tax sale	The sale of property that results when the property owner has failed to pay the property taxes assessed on the property.
Teleconferencing	Transmitting and receiving video and audio signals over standard communication channels.
Template	A pattern or model form which may include macro and merge features.
Temporary restraining order (TRO)	An emergency remedy of brief duration issued by a court only in exceptional circumstances, usually when immediate or irreparable damage or loss might result before the opposition could take action.
Tenancy by the Entirety	Type of ownership by which a husband and wife hold title to the entire property with the right of survivorship should one spouse die.
Tenancy in Common	The type of ownership by which each owner holds an undivided interest in the entire prop-

	erty with no right of survivorship to the parties. The owner's interest passes on to one's heirs upon one's death.
Tenant	Also, lessee. One who uses lands of another during the term of a lease.
Territorial jurisdiction	The actual geographic area over which the court has authority.
Testamentary Trust	A trust created in a will, which takes effect upon the death of the decedent.
Testate	Having died leaving a valid will.
Testator	A person who makes a will.
Testimonium clause	The clause of a deed or a legal instrument immediately preceding the signatures that reads: "In witness whereof the parties hereunto have caused this instrument to be properly executed the day and year first above written."
Third-party complaint	A complaint filed by defendant against a third party (not presently a party to the suit) which alleges that the third party is liable for all or part of the damages plaintiff may win from defendant.
Tickler system	A reminder system used in offices to supplement diaries in docket control.
Timekeeping	A system for reporting time spent by lawyers on various cases so that the lawyer can bill the clients for the time spent.
Title commitment or binder	Certificate issued by a title insurance company setting forth the status of real estate and any requirements that must be completed before title can be insured.
Title company	A business organization that searches a title to determine facts and encumbrances and sells the buyer or mortgagee an insurance policy of title.
Title examination	An investigation of the title history made for a prospective purchaser of property to determine the condition of the title and whether marketable title exists.
Title insurance	Insurance against loss or damage resulting from defects in the title to a parcel of real estate.
Title Insurance Commitment	Report issued prior to issuance of a title policy that states exceptions to a land title.
Title opinion	Written opinion of a lawyer that certifies to the validity and merchantability of title to property based on review of an abstract of title or other land records.

Title insurance policy	An insurance policy issued by a title insurance company that insures a title to land against loss resulting from defect in title.
Torrens Certificate	A Torrens Certificate is considered to be conclusive evidence of the present ownership and status of title.
Tort	A private or civil wrong or injury for which the court provides a remedy through an action for damages.
Tortfeasor	A wrong-doer; an individual or business that commits or is guilty of a tort.
Totten Trust	A trust created upon the deposit by the decedent money in decedent's name as trustee for another.
Trade name	That name which is used by manufacturers, industrialists and merchants to identify their businesses, which actually symbolizes reputation of business. In some states, synonymous with assumed name.
Trading partnership	A business whose nature is that of buying and selling.
Transcript	Usually refers to a verbatim record of a trial, deposition, hearing, or other proceeding.
Transfer or assumption fee	Money paid to mortgage company or bank as a fee for the transfer of a sale with assumption of mortgage on the mortgage company's books.
Treatise	A book or writing prepared by a legal scholar or practice expert that covers a specific area of the law.
Trespass	Illegal entry upon the land of another.
Trial	A judicial examination of issues between parties to an action.
Trial Balance	A list of all debit and credit balances prepared to check equality of accounts.
Trial brief	A written document prepared for and used by the lawyer at trial containing the issues to be tried, synopsis of evidence and witnesses to be presented, and case and statutory authority to back a legal position, and presented to the judge at trial.
Trial court	The court of original jurisdiction; the first court to consider litigation.
Tribunal	A court or forum of justice.
Trust	A fiduciary arrangement whereby property is transferred with the intention that a trustee administers it for another's benefit.

Trust account	Also, "special" account. An account held by a law firm in which clients' money is deposited and kept separate from the lawyer's account.
Trust under will	*See* testamentary trust.
Trustee	(1) An individual charged with the duty of liquidating a debtor's estate under the Bankruptcy Code. (2) A person who administers a trust.
Trustor	The maker of a trust.

U

UIFSA	Uniform Interstate Family Support Act; an act adopted by the majority of states to enforce duties of support in foreign jurisdictions.
Unauthorized practice of law (UPL)	To deprive an attorney of the right to practice law by rescinding the license to practice, as a result of illegal or unethical conduct by the attorney.
Ultra vires contract	Contract entered into by a corporation that exceeds the limitations of its power.
Undue influence	Dominance of a stronger-willed person over a weaker-willed person.
Uniform Child Custody Jurisdiction Enforcement Act (UCCJEA)	An act adopted by the majority of states to enforce child custody orders.
Uniform Commercial Code (UCC)	The uniform law governing commercial transactions. The UCC has been adopted by all states except Louisiana.
Uniform Interstate Family Support Act (UIFSA)	An act adopted by the majority of states to enforce duties of support in foreign jurisdictions.
Uniform laws	Laws in various subject areas, approved by the Commissioners on Uniform State Laws, that are often adopted, in whole or substantially, by individual states; their purpose being to make the laws on various subjects uniform throughout the states.
Uniform Probate Code (UPC)	The Code promulgated by the National Conference of Commissioners on Uniform State Laws and adopted by most states (with modifications or only in part) to make it possible for decedents' estates to be administered in the same fashion in all states and to streamline the entire probate procedure.

Unilateral contract	One where a person makes a promise conditioned on the performance of another.
Unincorporated association	An organization formed for a nonprofit purpose that has no existence apart from its members and cannot sue or be sued in its name.
Uninterruptible Power Supply	A device that maintains a constant supply of electric power despite black outs and other power fluctuations.
United States Attorney	A lawyer appointed by the President to prosecute all offenses against the United States and to defend the government in civil actions in which it is concerned in the district to which the lawyer is assigned.
United States Customs Service	The USCIS, within the Border and Transportation Security Directorate of the Department of Homeland Security, is responsible for the administration of immigration and naturalization adjudication functions and establishing immigration services policies and priorities. Immigration and Customs Enforcement include the enforcement and investigation components of the former INS, Customs, and the Federal Protective Services. U.S. Customs and Border Protection include the Border Patrol, as well as former INS, Customs, and Agricultural Quarantine Inspectors.
United States Marshals Service	The federal agency that provides protection to witnesses whose testimony endangers their lives and that of their families. It also maintains custody of prisoners after their arrest and during their transport and maintains custody and control over evidence seized.
United States Postal Service (USPS)	The Postal Service provides mail processing and delivery to individuals and businesses within the United States, and processes mail for delivery to areas outside of the United States.
United States Reports	Publication of court decisions of the United States Supreme Court.
Unjust enrichment	General principal that one person should not be permitted unjustly to enrich himself at the expense of another, but should be required to make restitution.
Unsecured debts	Debts for which the debtor has not pledged collateral to guarantee payment, such as open accounts at department stores.
USB Flash Drive	A small, mobile, rewritable memory unit that connects to a computer through a USB port.

USB Port	A rectangular connection available on most new PCs and Macintoshes. This port accommodates most types of input devices.

V

VA	Veterans Administration.
Valid contract	One which contains the four essential elements of a contract; *i.e.*, mutual consent, competent parties, lawful consideration, and lawful subject matter.
Variable	A segment of a prerecorded document that is subject to change.
Vector	The direction and distance of a line used in a metes and bounds description.
Vendee	A purchaser or buyer of property or goods.
Vendor	The person who sells property or goods.
Venue	Authority of a court to hear a matter based on geographical location.
Verb	Word or word group that tells what the subject does or is or what happens to the subject.
Verbal	A verb form (infinitive, gerund, or participle) not used as a verb.
Verdict	Finding of the jury as to the guilt or innocence of a defendant in a criminal trial.
Verification	A statement that the allegations are true and correct.
Vicarious liability	The imposition of liability on one person for the actionable conduct of another, based solely on a relationship between the two persons.
Virus	Computer code that can be copied into an existing computer program and make itself known by flashing an innocuous message on the screen or doing something as serious as destroying data or disabling the operating system.
Visa	An official endorsement on a document or passport denoting that the bearer may proceed.
Visitation	In a marriage dissolution or custody action, permission granted by court to a noncustodial parent to visit child or children. (parenting time)
Voice mail	Verbal electronic mail, similar to an answering machine, made possible by a computerized telephone system.

Voice activation	A feature of some dictation systems that stops the forward motion of the dictation media when the dictator stops speaking and activates the unit at the sound of the dictator's voice.
Voidable contract	One that is potentially defective in some respect (treated as a valid contract unless the defect is asserted).
Voir dire	The preliminary examination made in court of a witness or juror to determine his competency or interest in a matter. Literally, to speak the truth.
Volatile memory	Computer memory that loses all of its data, or has it erased, when the electricity is turned off if the data has not been saved to a permanent memory device.
Voluntary bankruptcy	A proceeding by which a debtor voluntarily asks for a discharge of his debts under the Bankruptcy Code.
Voluntary petition	One in which a debtor voluntarily asks for a discharge of their debts.

W

Wage earner's plan	A type of partial bankruptcy in which a person keeps property and pays off a court-established proportion of debt to creditors over a period of time and under court supervision.
Waive	Relinquish rights voluntarily.
Warranty	A promise that a proposition of fact is true.
Warranty Deed	A deed that guarantees that the title conveyed is good and nothing has been done to cloud or encumber title beyond the permitted encumbrances specific therein.
Web	A term used for world wide web.
Webcam	A small inexpensive camera that functions like a camera with its images being sent over the Internet.
Web Server	A computer that is responsible for storing and granting access to web pages or other internet data.
Wide Area Network (WAN)	The linking of computers that are located far apart, *i.e.*, in different cities, through cables, fiber optics, or satellites.
Will	*See* last will and testament.
Winding up or winding down	Process of settling the accounts and liquidating the assets of a partnership or corporation, for

	the purpose of making distribution of net assets to shareholders or partners and dissolving the concern.
Windows	An operating environment that uses a graphical user interface rather than a character-based command line.
With prejudice	A judgment barring the right to bring or maintain an action on the same claim or cause; a declaration which dismisses all rights.
Withholding taxes	Funds withheld by the employer from the employee's payroll check for payment of federal, state, and local income taxes and Social Security and Medicare taxes.
Without prejudice	A declaration that no rights or privileges of the party concerned are waived or lost. In a dismissal these words maintain the right to bring a subsequent suit on the same claim.
Witness	One who personally sees or perceives a thing and who testifies to what one has seen, heard, or otherwise observed.
Word processing	A method of producing written communications at top speed, with the greatest accuracy, the least effort, and the lowest possible cost through the combined use of proper procedures, automated equipment, and trained personnel.
Word-wrap	An automatic feature that moves a word to the next line when the previous line of text is full.
Workers' Compensation Commission	A state agency that handles claims of workers injured on the job.
Worksheet	Analysis document on which the financial condition of a business is summarized.
Write-off	The closing of a customer's uncollectible account.
Writ of certiorari	An order by the appellate court which is used by that court when it has discretion on whether or not to hear an appeal from a lower court.
Writ of Execution	An order of the court evidencing debt of one party to another and commanding the court officer to take property in satisfaction of the debt.
Writ of Garnishment	An order of the court whereby property, money, or credits in the possession of another person may be seized and applied to pay a debtor's debt. It is used as an incident to or auxiliary of a judgment rendered in a principal action.

Wrongful death	Type of lawsuit brought on behalf of a deceased person's beneficiaries that alleges that death was attributable to the willful or negligent act of another.
www	Abbreviation for world wide web.

Z

Zoning Commission	Local agency with jurisdiction to regulate use of properties within its geographic area.

INDEX

INDEX

INDEX

INDEX

INDEX

INDEX

INDEX

INDEX

INDEX

INDEX

INDEX

INDEX